A HISTORY OF ANCIENT GEOGRAPHY

Volume One

A HISTORY OF
ANCIENT GEOGRAPHY

AMONG THE GREEKS AND ROMANS FROM THE EARLIEST
AGES TILL THE FALL OF THE ROMAN EMPIRE

by

E.H. BUNBURY, F.R.G.S

Volume One

WIPF & STOCK · Eugene, Oregon

Wipf and Stock Publishers
199 W 8th Ave, Suite 3
Eugene, OR 97401

History of Ancient Geography, Volume 1
Among the Greeks From the Earliest Ages Till the Fall of the Roman Empire
By Burnbury, E. H.
Copyright © 1879 by Burnbury, E. H. All rights reserved.
Softcover ISBN-13: 978-1-6667-8346-9
Hardcover ISBN-13: 978-1-6667-8347-6
eBook ISBN-13: 978-1-6667-8348-3
Publication date 6/27/2023
Previously published by John Murray, 1879

This edition is a scanned facsimile of the original edition published in 1879.

A HISTORY

OF

ANCIENT GEOGRAPHY

AMONG THE GREEKS AND ROMANS
FROM THE EARLIEST AGES TILL THE FALL OF
THE ROMAN EMPIRE.

By E. H. BUNBURY, F.R.G.S.

WITH TWENTY ILLUSTRATIVE MAPS

IN TWO VOLUMES.—VOL. I.

PREFACE.

THE present work is designed to supply a deficiency, which I have reason to believe has been felt by classical scholars. While there is no want of elementary treatises on ancient geography, and the requirements of the more advanced student are fully answered by the elaborate articles in Dr. Smith's *Dictionary of Ancient Geography*, so far as relates to the details of particular places and countries, it is remarkable that there does not exist in the English language any such historical review of the subject as a whole, as is to be found in the introductions to the works of Mannert, Ukert, and Forbiger. But even these treatises, besides being confined to students who are familiar with the German language, can hardly be said to meet the demands of either the scholar or the geographer at the present day. Ukert's introductory volume was published as far back as 1816, and that of Mannert still earlier, while the more recent work of Forbiger (itself published in 1841) is so disfigured by the accumulation of cumbrous and unnecessary lists of names as to be altogether repulsive to the English reader. Since the date of the works in question, not only has there been a great advance in classical scholarship, and the critical study of the ancient authorities; but still greater progress has been made in the detailed examination of the regions and localities described by ancient geographers, many of which were very imperfectly known in modern times down to a recent period. It is not too much to say that there is scarcely a disputed question in ancient geography upon which some additional light has not been thrown by local researches and investigations within the last fifty years.

It has been my object in the following pages to present to the reader the results of these recent inquiries: and while basing my work in all cases upon a careful and critical examination of the ancient authorities, to avail myself to the fullest extent of the assistance to be derived from modern travellers and geographers. Several instances have occurred during the progress of my researches, where additional information of this kind has served to elucidate questions which were still obscure when the chapters in which they are discussed were originally written.

At the same time it must be constantly borne in mind that it is the main purpose of a historical review, such as the one I have attempted to give, of the progress and development of geography in ancient times, to record the ideas formed and the information possessed by the different authors from whom we derive our knowledge; and with a view to this I have endeavoured in every instance, so far as possible, to arrive at my conclusions from a conscientious and independent study of the ancient authorities themselves, before consulting or referring to the comments and discussions of modern writers. In pursuing this plan, I have been materially aided by the valuable editions of Strabo by

Kramer, and of Pliny by Sillig—both of them subsequent to the publication of the three German text-books above referred to—as well as by the admirable edition of the *Geographi Græci Minores* edited by Dr. C. Müller, a work which has conferred an inestimable boon upon all students of ancient geography.

In referring, as I have done above, principally to the labours of the Germans in the same field with myself, I must not be regarded as ignoring what has been done in this country and in France in connection with the same subject. The first volume of Mr. Cooley's *History of Maritime and Inland Discovery* (published in Dr. Lardner's Cyclopædia in 1833) contains a good popular sketch of the progress of geographical knowledge in ancient times; but is certainly not adapted to meet the requirements of the classical scholar. The far superior work of M. Vivien de St. Martin—the *Histoire de la Géographie et des Découvertes Géographiques*—which was not published until the present work was already far advanced—contains a sufficiently full review of the whole subject for the purposes of the general reader: but the limits within which the author was necessarily confined, in order to include in a single volume the whole history of geographical progress down to our own time, precluded his entering in detail into many questions the discussion of which formed an essential part of my own plan.

In one respect I have thought it expedient to depart from the example of my German predecessors, who have deemed it necessary to treat separately of mathematical and physical geography, apart from the descriptive and historical portions of the subject. In a work of which the historical form is an essential character, it appeared to me desirable to bring together all portions of the subject under one view; so that the reader might see at once the condition of geographical knowledge at every successive period:—say for instance in the time of Eratosthenes, Strabo, Pliny and Ptolemy—instead of having to turn to several different chapters for the information he requires. The unity and completeness thus given to the successive portions of the historical review appear to me greatly to outweigh the advantages derived from the more methodical subdivision.

The comprehensive character of such a work as the one now submitted to the reader unavoidably exposes it to one disadvantage. It must of necessity comprise many subjects which could not be fully discussed without extending it beyond all reasonable limits. The geography of Herodotus; that of the Anabasis of Xenophon; of the campaigns of Alexander; the voyages of Nearchus and Hanno—might well require a volume to each of them instead of a chapter: while several special topics, such as the passage of the Alps by Hannibal, the landing of Cæsar in Britain, or the defeat of Varus in Germany, have to be dispatched in a few pages, though each of them has formed the subject of numerous tracts and treatises amounting to a little literature of its own. In such cases I have been compelled to bring together in a brief summary the grounds of the judgement at which I have arrived in each case, without being able to enter into the discussion as fully as I could wish. If in some cases I may have in consequence appeared to pass rather slightly over the arguments on the other side, I can only beg my readers to believe that this arises from the necessity of the case rather than from any overweening confidence in my own conclusions.

In some instances, on the other hand, my readers may be disposed to complain that I have left questions unsettled, without pronouncing any opinion, where the evidence does not appear to me such as to afford reasonable grounds for a decision. To both classes of objections I can only reply in the words of Cicero—adopted by Ukert as the motto of his work—" sequimur probabilia, nec ultra quam id quod verisimile occurrerit progredi possumus, et refellere sine pertinacia, et refelli sine iracundia parati sumus."

It is only those who have devoted a considerable amount of attention to the study of ancient geography who are fully aware of the difficulties that beset the path of the inquirer at almost every step. But these difficulties have in many instances been greatly aggravated by the unwillingness of modern writers to apply to the statements of ancient authors the same rules of reasonable criticism by which they would be guided in other cases. Not only is geography in its very nature a progressive science, but the slightest attention to its history in mediæval or modern times will show that the steps of its progress are often vacillating and uncertain. Vague and fluctuating ideas concerning distant regions will be found floating as it were in a dim haze of twilight long before their outlines come to be distinctly discerned. Even the most trustworthy travellers are compelled to rely to a certain extent upon hearsay evidence, in regard to the countries or provinces that they have not themselves visited; and in the case of less qualified observers it is generally difficult to distinguish what they have really learnt from their own observation and what they have derived from other sources. Without recurring to the case of Marco Polo and other mediæval travellers, it will be sufficient to turn to the map of Central Africa as it stood before the time of Park and Hornemann, and to trace the progress of discovery in that great continent, and the various theories by which geographers sought to explain or reconcile the statements of successive travellers, in order to see what difficulties surround any such attempt in the absence of clear and definite information.

But if this is the case even in modern times, where the information of the geographer is derived from the statements of trustworthy observers and scientific travellers, far more does it apply to the position of the ancient geographer. Voyages and travels for the purpose of exploration were almost entirely unknown: and he had to pick up his information as best he could from the accounts of merchants and casual travellers. The inaccuracy of these reports, and the consequent vagueness of the statements derived from them, is frequently pointed out by ancient writers. But they had nothing else to fall back upon, and no means of correcting them by more accurate observations.

Yet, notwithstanding this obvious consideration, it has been too much the custom in modern times to treat the ancient writers on this subject as if they possessed an authority to which they are certainly not entitled. Instead of at once drawing the line, as would be done without hesitation in the case of a mediæval writer, between what was accurate and trustworthy and what was vague and inaccurate, the most fanciful suggestions have been made and ingenious theories invented to account for what was simply erroneous. Even the supposition of vast physical changes has been introduced or adopted, rather than acknowledge that Herodotus or Strabo can have made a mistake. It has been my endeavour in the following pages, as far as possible, to exercise a discriminating judgement in sifting truth from falsehood; and while doing full justice to the real merits of successive writers, to discard without scruple those statements where they have been obviously misled by imperfect information, or by adherence to a mistaken theory.

The historical form of the present work necessarily involves a certain amount of repetition. Nor have I been careful to avoid this. Many persons will, I believe, take up particular chapters of the book who will shrink from the labour of perusing the whole: and I have therefore endeavoured to make each successive portion —especially the reviews of the different leading authors on the subject, such as Strabo, Pliny, or Ptolemy—as complete in itself as possible. No English book, as far as I am aware, contains a similar analysis of these well-known authors, who are too often quoted for detached statements by writers who are wholly unacquainted with their real authority and value.

I am aware that I shall incur the censure of many of the more advanced scholars of the present day for having adhered to the old orthography of Greek names. I must confess myself one of those who fail to see the advantage of the changes recently introduced: changes that can hardly yet be said to form a permanent or established system. But, independent of my own preference for the system to which I have been accustomed from my youth, two considerations would in themselves have deterred me from introducing any such innovations in the present work. The one is that as my subject included Roman as well as Greek geography, I should have had to follow two different systems of orthography in different portions of the book, and to write the same names in two different modes, according as I was reviewing a Greek or a Latin author. To this must be added that as the book now presented to the reader is, from its nature, in some degree a supplement to the two valuable Dictionaries of Ancient Biography and Geography edited by Dr. Smith, which are at present in the hands of all scholars, I should have been unwilling to deviate from the practice which has been there adopted.

With regard to the orthography of oriental names, which are necessarily of frequent occurrence in the following pages, I have contented myself with writing them as I found them in the authority before me, or in the case of well-known names in the mode commonly received. Having no knowledge myself of any of the oriental languages, it was impossible for me to attempt to follow any uniform system in this respect.

The present work, like those of Mannert and Ukert, is confined to the geography of the ancient world as known to us through the Greeks and Romans. In the very brief introductory chapter, I have only touched upon that of other nations with reference to its bearing upon the geography of the Greeks at the earliest period when we have any information concerning it. To investigate the details of the geographical knowledge—limited as it undoubtedly was—possessed by the Egyptians or Assyrians, would be wholly foreign to my subject, and is a task for which I feel myself entirely incompetent.

It may perhaps be necessary to observe that the maps inserted in these volumes are not designed in any degree to supply the place of an Atlas of Ancient Geography, but solely to illustrate the particular subjects discussed, or to bring more distinctly before the eyes of the reader the general outline of the geographical systems formed by successive writers, so far as it is possible to extract these from their writings alone. In the preparation of these maps, I have derived the greatest assistance from the series of those contributed by Dr. C. Muller to the valuable "*Atlas of Ancient Geography edited by Dr. Smith and Mr. Grove;*" and I take this opportunity of expressing in the strongest manner my sense of the obligations that I owe him. Scarcely less valuable is the aid I have received from his admirable edition of the *Geographi Græci Minores* (already referred to), without which it would have been scarcely possible for me to have executed in a satisfactory manner the portions of my work relating to the writers in question.

CONTENTS OF VOL. I.

CHAPTER I.
INTRODUCTORY.

§ 1. Geography more or less studied by different nations according to circumstances—little cultivated by the Chaldæans or Egyptians. § 2. Or by the Jews. No influence exercised in this respect upon the Greeks. § 3. The Phœnicians; their extensive commerce and long voyages. § 4. Geographical knowledge derived from thence: its extent and limits very imperfectly known. § 5. Trade of the Phœnicians in tin: the Cassiterides, or Tin Islands. Gades, the centre of the trade. § 6. Their trade in amber, brought from the northern shores of Europe. § 7. The carrying trade of the Ægean and the Mediterranean in their hands. § 8. The Cretans the earliest Greek people devoted to navigation. Notices of them in the Odyssey. § 9. The Trojan War a proof of an advanced state of navigation .. .. .. Page 1

CHAPTER II.
VOYAGE OF THE ARGONAUTS.

§ 1. The voyage of the Argonauts a mere legendary tale—originally quite unconnected with Colchis or the Phasis. § 2. Applied by the Greek colonies to the localities on the Euxine. § 3. Various accounts of their return. § 4. That given by Apollonius Rhodius. § 5. Different accounts of earlier writers. Possible basis of truth in the legend. 19

NOTE A. Argonautica of Orpheus .. .. PAGE 28

CHAPTER III.
HOMERIC GEOGRAPHY.

SECTION 1.—*General Views.*

§ 1. Earliest notions of Greek geography derived from the Homeric Poems—these perverted by later writers and commentators. Necessity of adhering to the original. § 2. Ideas of Homer concerning the earth and heavens. His mention of Atlas. § 3. Ideas concerning the sun and stars. § 4. No names for cardinal points. Names of winds. § 5. His views of the sea and the Ocean river. § 6. No knowledge of the three continents .. .. Page 31

SECTION 2.—*Geography of the Iliad.*

§ 1. Local geography of Greece and the neighbouring seas well known to Homer: but all beyond vague or unknown. § 2. The Catalogue of the ships. § 3. Catalogue of the Trojan forces. § 4. Extent of knowledge proved by these very limited. § 5. Vague indications of more distant counties. § 6. Knowledge of Phœnicia and Egypt. § 7. Vague and fabulous ideas of Æthiopia 39

SECTION 3.—*Geography of the Odyssey.*

§ 1. The outer world in the Odyssey—the scene of poetical fictions and legends. § 2. These worked up by Homer into a poetic whole, but not into a geographical system. § 3. Attachment of legends to definite localities. § 4. Voyage of Ulysses: the Cicones, Cape Malea, the Lotophagi. § 5. The Cyclopes. § 6. The Island of Æolus. § 7. The Læstrygones. § 8. The Island of Circe—visit of Ulysses to Hades. The Cimmerians. § 9. Homeward voyage: the Sirens, Scylla and Charybdis. Thrinakia. § 10. Island of Calypso: voyage from thence to Phæacia. § 11. The Phæacians—a fabulous people, erroneously placed in Corcyra. § 12. Ithaca and the neighbouring islands: difficulties in regard to their description. § 13. Dulichium. No clear idea given of these western islands. § 14. Voyage of Menelaus. Egypt. § 15. The Ethiopians. § 16. Ignorance of Homer of the eastern nations: and of the west of Europe 49

			PAGE
NOTE	A.	Composition of the Homeric Poems ..	75
„	B	Homeric idea of the world	ib.
„	C.	The four winds in Homer ..	77
„	D.	The Læstrygones	ib.
„	E.	The Island of Circe	78
„	F	The Planctæ	79
„	G	Course from Ogygia to Scheria ..	81
„	H.	Dulichium	ib.
„	I.	Homeric Ithaca	83

CHAPTER IV.

HOMER TO HECATÆUS.

SECTION 1.—*Poetical Notices subsequent to Homer.*

§ 1. Want of materials for tracing the progress of geographical knowledge after Homer. Hesiod: his poems largely interpolated. Geographical notices contained in them. § 2. The Epic Cycle and the Homeric Hymns. § 3. Other poets before the First Olympiad. Aristeas of Proconnesus .. .. Page 85

SECTION 2.—*Colonies.*

§ 1. Great development of Greek enterprise in the 7th and 8th centuries B.C. Foundation of colonies in Sicily. § 2. In Southern Italy. § 3. At Corcyra and in the Adriatic: and in Campania. § 4. Massilia and its colonies. § 5. The extension of Greek settlements in Spain and Africa checked by the Phœnicians. § 6. Cyrene and its colonies in Libya. § 7. Commercial intercourse with Egypt. Naucratis. § 8. Exploration of the Euxine. Colonies of Miletus and Megara. § 9. Settlements on the west and south coasts § 10. On the northern shores and in the Crimea. § 11. Communications with the interior. Aristeas of Proconnesus. The Arimaspians and Hyperboreans. § 12. Destruction of Miletus, and fall of its power. § 13. The Phocæans: their voyage to Tartessus. Maritime power and trade of the Samians and Rhodians— Colonies of Rhodes. § 14. Commercial activity and naval power of Corinth. § 15. Of Megara. § 16. Of Ægina. § 17. Of Chalcis and Eretria in Eubœa. Colonies of Chalcis. Inferior position of Athens before the Persian War. § 18. Colonies and commerce limited to the inland seas—the Mediterranean and the Euxine. § 19. Relations of Greeks with the Phœnicians. § 20. And with Egypt. § 21. Individual visits to Egypt and Babylon. Increasing knowledge of Asia after the rise of the Persian monarchy 91

SECTION 3.—*Physical Philosophers.*

1. Rise of philosophical speculation in Greece. Thales of Miletus, his astronomical views. § 2. Anaximander: the inventor of maps. § 3. Anaximenes. § 4. Pythagoras and his followers: their improved system of cosmical science. § 5. How far influenced by ideas derived from the East. The spherical form of the earth not yet a recognized truth. 120

			PAGE
NOTE A.	Date of foundation of Cyrene	.. ..	127
„ B.	Dates assigned to Greek colonies in the Euxine	.. ..	128
„ C.	The "Thalassocraties" of Castor	..	130

CHAPTER V.

HECATÆUS.

SECTION 1.—*Geography of Hecatæus.*

§ 1. The work of Hecatæus of Miletus the first regular geographical treatise. His life and date. Imperfect character of existing remains. § 2. His work mostly a Periplus of the Mediterranean, but contained notices of Asia. § 3. His travels. § 4. Arrangement of his work. § 5. Extent of his information, in regard to the coasts of the Mediterranean. § 6. He had no knowledge of western and northern Europe. Imperfect acquaintance with Scythia. § 7. His knowledge of Asia in general. He gives the first notices of India. § 8. Described Egypt in detail. His notices of the rest of Africa. § 9. His general notions on geography. His map of the world. § 10. His division of the world into continents. § 11. His want of judgement .. .. Page 134

SECTION 2.—*Hecatæus to Herodotus.*

§ 1. Writers after Hecatæus. Hellanicus and Damastes. § 2. Geographical notices in Æschylus and Pindar. The wanderings of Io in the 'Prometheus Vinctus.' § 3 The 'Prometheus Solutus' and the 'Persæ.' § 4. Pindar: his geographical notions 148

                                                                                         PAGE
NOTE A. Character of extant fragments of Hecatæus 153
„ B. Intercourse of the Greeks with Etruria *ib.*

CHAPTER VI.

HERODOTUS.

SECTION 1.—*General Views—Europe.*

§ 1. Importance of the work of Herodotus in a geographical point of view. Its desultory and irregular character. Slight notice of the Carthaginians and Tyrrhenians. § 2. Brief notices of Southern Italy and Sicily. § 3. His travels: their extent. § 4. Outline of his views of the configuration of the world. Asia. The projecting Actæ. § 5. Explanation of his views. § 6. His ignorance of the west and north of Europe. He rejected the notion of the Cassiterides, and of the river Eridanus; and of a northern ocean. § 7. Imperfect knowledge of central Europe. Thrace and the Danube. The Getæ and Sigynnæ. § 8. His description of the Danube and its tributaries. The Carpis and Alpis.

§ 9. The Keltæ and Kynetes. § 10. His comparison of the Nile and the Ister: their mouths opposite to one another .. .. Page 156

SECTION 2.—*Scythia.*

§ 1. Extensive information obtained by Herodotus concerning Scythia. § 2. Derived in part from personal knowledge. He discards the fables current concerning the Hyperboreans, &c. § 3. His account of the Euxine Sea. § 4. Erroneous estimate of its length. § 5. Exaggerated notion of the Palus Mæotis. § 6. Erroneous idea of the Tauric Peninsula. § 7. Great rivers of Scythia: the Ister. § 8. Its magnitude and equable flow. § 9. The Tyras. § 10. The Borysthenes. § 11. The Tanais. § 12. Extent of his knowledge of these rivers. § 13. Other rivers: the Panticapes, the Hypacyris, and the Gerrhus, cannot be identified. § 14. The Oarus, the Lycus, &c., equally obscure. § 15. Imperfect sources of information. § 16. Valuable ethnographical notices. His Scythians a distinct people. § 17. Form and boundaries of Scythia. § 18. Division of the Scythian tribes. § 19. Nations surrounding Scythia. The Agathyrsi: the Neuri. § 20. The Androphagi: the Melanchlæni. § 21. The Budini and Geloni. § 22. The Sauromatæ. § 23. Nations towards the north-east beyond the Budini. Thyssagetæ and Iurcæ. The Argippæi. § 24. Fabulous nations to the north. The Issedones. § 25. The Arimaspians. Abundance of gold. § 26. No mention of the Volga. § 27. The Caspian regarded by Herodotus as surrounded on all sides by land 172

SECTION 3.—*Expedition of Darius into Scythia.*

§ 1. Geographical details of the expedition accord well with the other statements of Herodotus. § 2. Narrative as given by Herodotus. § 3. Its difficulties: cannot be received as historically correct; but presents few geographical difficulties 202

			PAGE
NOTE A.	The Actæ of Herodotus	.. ..	207
„ B.	The Cimmerians	.. .. ..	208
„ C.	The Greek Stadium	.. .. ..	209
„ D.	Navigation of the Borysthenes	..	211
„ E.	Rivers of Scythia	.. .. ..	212
„ F.	The river Oarus..	.. .. ..	213
„ G.	Limits of Scythia	.. .. ..	214
„ H.	Ethnographical relations of the Scythians of Herodotus	.. .. ..	215
„ I	Expedition of Darius	.. .. ..	217

VOL. I.

CHAPTER VII.

GEOGRAPHY OF HERODOTUS: ASIA.

SECTION 1.—*General Views*

§ 1. Limits of his knowledge of Asia nearly confined to the Persian Empire. § 2. Imperfect acquaintance with Arabia § 3. The Erythræan Sea and Arabian Gulf. No knowledge of the Persian Gulf. § 4. Ignorance of the countries north of the Persian Empire. § 5. Confused notions of the Araxes § 6. The Massagetæ; their abundance of gold. § 7. Account of India: his knowledge confined to the countries on the Indus. § 8. Voyage of Scylax of Caryanda. § 9. The Pactyans: their mode of procuring gold. Indian ants. § 10. Probable locality and origin of the fable. § 11. Scanty information concerning India in other respects .. .. Page 218

SECTION 2.—*Persian Empire. Satrapies.*

§ 1. His catalogue of the Satrapies derived from an authentic source. § 2. Erroneous geographical notion of Asia Minor. § 3. Imperfect ideas of the provinces of Upper Asia. No knowledge of the Taurus as a mountain system. § 4. His enumeration of the Satrapies properly ethnographical, rather than geographical. § 5. Satrapies of Asia Minor: the first, second and third, including Cappadocia. § 6. The fourth, Cilicia: the fifth, Syria: the sixth, Egypt and the Cyrenaica. § 7. The seventh Satrapy—the Gandarians, &c. § 8. The eighth, Susiana. the ninth, Babylonia and Assyria. § 9. The tenth, Media: the eleventh, the Caspians, &c. § 10. The twelfth, Bactria: the thirteenth, Armenia and adjacent tribes. § 11. The fourteenth, the Sagartians, Zarangians, &c. § 12. The fifteenth, the Sacæ and Caspians. § 13. The sixteenth, the Parthians, Chorasmians, Sogdians, and Arians. § 14. The seventeenth, the Paricanians and Ethiopians. § 15. The eighteenth, the Matienians, Saspirians, &c.: the nineteenth, the Moschi, Macrones, &c.: the twentieth, India. § 16. Character of this list: a statistical document, without any attempt at geographical arrangement. § 17. Curious account in Herodotus of a plain surrounded by mountains and sending forth five rivers. Impossible to identify.. .. 231

SECTION 3.—*Royal Road to Susa.*

§ 1. Account of the line of route from Sardis to Susa, introduced as an incidental digression. § 2. Its details and distances. § 3. Its valuable character. Difficulties in detail. § 4. Followed the upper road from Sardis to the Tigris; not that taken by Cyrus and Alexander 249

		PAGE
NOTE A.	Indian Tribute	255
„ B.	Scylax of Caryanda	256

CONTENTS OF VOL. I xix

			PAGE
NOTE C	Caspatyrus	.. ..	256
„ D	Indian ants	.. ..	257
„ E	Ecbatana	.. ..	258
„ F	Royal road to Susa	.. .. ..	259
„ G	Uncertainty of measurement	.. ..	261

CHAPTER VIII.

GEOGRAPHY OF HERODOTUS: AFRICA.

SECTION 1.—*General knowledge of the Continent.*

§ 1. Character of his acquaintance with African shores of the Mediterranean. His knowledge of the interior derived through Egypt and Cyrene. § 2. His account of the Upper Nile as far as Meroe. § 3. Meroe. The Automoli. § 4. Supposed the Nile above Meroe to flow from the west. § 5. Agreement of this view with his account of the Macrobian Ethiopians. § 6. Sources of the Nile unknown: theory of Herodotus. § 7. Narrative of the expedition of the Nasamonians into the interior. Their discovery of a great river, probably the Joliba or Quorra. § 8. The Macrobian Ethiopians: expedition of Cambyses against them. § 9. Erroneously placed on the Nile by Strabo. § 10. Division of Northern Africa into three zones. § 11. Line of inhabited spots from distance to distance in a direction from east to west. § 12. The Oasis of Ammon. § 13. Augila. The Garamantes. § 14. The Atarantes and Atlantes. § 15. Desert character of the interior. § 16. The Troglodyte Ethiopians. § 17. Libyan tribes adjoining the Cyrenaica, and along the shores of the Mediterranean. § 18. The Nasamones and Psylli. The Lotophagi: the Machlyans. the island of Cyrannis. § 19. Tales of fabulous races rejected by Herodotus. § 20. The Syrtis and the Lake Tritonis. § 21. Account of dumb commerce carried on by Carthaginian merchants on the Atlantic coast. Cape Solocis. § 22. Foundation of belief that Africa was surrounded by the Ocean.
Page 262

SECTION 2.—*Circumnavigation of Africa by Necho.*

§ 1. Narrative as reported by Herodotus. § 2. Differences of opinion concerning it in ancient and modern times. § 3. Arguments of Major Rennell in its favour. § 4. *Prima facie* improbability of the story: absence of all details. § 5. Argument from the sun being on the right hand not conclusive. Other difficulties. § 6. Subsequent neglect of the voyage and discovery paralleled by similar cases in modern times. § 7. The voyage cannot be disproved, but must be regarded as extremely improbable. § 8. Other statements of the Carthaginians. § 9. Unsuccessful attempt of Sataspes 289

CONTENTS OF VOL. I

			PAGE
NOTE	A.	Use of camels	299
„	B	Distances on the Nile	ib.
„	C.	The Dodecaschœnus	301
„	D	The Automoli	302
„	E	Distances on the Upper Nile	ib.
„	F	Course of the Nile from west to east	303
„	G.	Supposed sources of the Nile	304
„	H	Expedition of the Nasamonians	305
„	I	Difficulty of communication with interior	307
„	K.	Erroneous position of Carthage	308
„	L.	The Oases	ib.
„	M.	Symmetrical arrangement of Oases	309
„	N.	Confusion of Great Oasis with that of Ammon	ib.
„	O	The Atlantes of Herodotus	310
„	P.	The Lotophagi	311
„	Q.	The river Cinyps	312
„	R.	The Syrtis	313
„	S.	The Lake Tritonis	314
„	T.	The island of Cyraunis	316
„	V.	Circumnavigation of Africa Opinions of modern writers	317

CHAPTER IX.

VOYAGE OF HANNO.

§ 1. Narrative of the voyage transmitted to us. Its first object was colonization. Progress as far as Cerne. § 2. First voyage from Cerne to the South. § 3. Second voyage. Proceeds as far as the Southern Horn. The gorillas. § 4. Authentic character of narrative. Difference of opinion as to extent of voyage. § 5. Position of Cerne. § 6. First voyage reached the Senegal. § 7. Second voyage. Cape Verde. Theon Ochema. Southern Horn. § 8. Explanation of fires. § 9. The gorillas really apes § 10. Erroneous notions concerning the voyage of Hanno found in later writers. § 11. Difficulties in regard to earlier part of voyage. § 12. Carthaginian colonies soon abandoned.

Page 318

			PAGE
NOTE	A.	Editions of the Periplus	332
„	B.	Position of Cerne	333
„	C	Views of Heeren	334
„	D	Notice of Cerne in Scylax	ib
„	E	The river Chremetes	335

CHAPTER X.

WRITERS AFTER HERODOTUS.

SECTION 1.—*Ctesias.*

§ 1. Progress of geographical knowledge from Herodotus to Alexander imperfectly known. Its limits little extended. § 2. Thucydides. His work throws little light on geography. § 3. Antiochus of Syracuse. § 4. Ctesias: his life and works. The Persica. § 5. The Indica; full of fables and absurdities. § 6. Marvellous animals. § 7. Precious stones.
Page 336

SECTION 2.—*The Anabasis of Xenophon.*

§ 1. Historical narrative by Xenophon of the march of Cyrus and the retreat of the Ten Thousand: its charm. § 2. His estimates of distances. § 3. March of Cyrus through Phrygia to Cilicia. § 4. He crosses the Euphrates at Thapsacus. § 5. Advance from thence to Babylonia. § 6. Battle of Cunaxa and subsequent movements of the Greeks. § 7. Their retreat as far as Opis. § 8. They quit the Tigris: their march through the Carduchians into Armenia. § 9. Their line of route traced thus far. § 10. Difficulty in following it to the Euxine. Steps of the progress according to Xenophon. § 11. Cannot be identified in detail. § 12. Independent tribes on the Euxine. § 13. Interesting notices by Xenophon of the nations through which he passed.
342

			PAGE
NOTE	A.	Composition of the Anabasis	359
,,	B.	Computation of distances in Parasangs	ib.
,,	C.	Rate of marching	361
,,	D.	Route of Cyrus through Phrygia	363
,,	E.	Passes between Cilicia and Syria	364
,,	F.	March from the Gulf of Issus to the Euphrates	365
,,	G.	Thapsacus	ib.
,,	H.	Position of Pylæ	366
,,	I.	Site of Cunaxa	369
,,	K.	Sittace	370
,,	L.	The Median Wall	370
,,	M.	March along the Tigris	372
,,	N.	Ruined cities of Assyria	374
,,	O.	Sources of the Tigris	ib.
,,	P.	Descent through Armenia to Trebizond	375

CHAPTER XI.

WRITERS AFTER XENOPHON.

SECTION 1.—*Ephorus. The Periplus of Scylax.*

§ 1. Ephorus: his historical writings; contained a general geographical review. § 2. His general views. § 3. His account of Scythia. § 4. Of Asia Minor. § 5. Of Africa. § 6. Of the Nile. § 7. Theopompus: his work of comparatively little interest to geography. Mentioned the capture of Rome by the Gauls. § 8. The Periplus ascribed to Scylax: its character. § 9. Its date: erroneously ascribed to Scylax of Caryanda. § 10. Its plan and arrangement: confined to the Mediterranean Sea: imperfect knowledge of some parts. § 11. Detailed account of the Adriatic. supposed it to receive an arm of the Ister. § 12. Full account of the Greek colonies on the Euxine. § 13. The coasts of Asia Minor and Africa. § 14. Notices of the Atlantic coast of Africa: Cape Soloeis and Cerne. § 15. No account of Indian Ocean. § 16. Distances generally given in days' voyages. § 17. List of islands.
Page 379

SECTION 2.—*Aristotle.*

§ 1. Aristotle has left no regular work on geography; but notices in his works on the Heavens and the *Meteorologica*. § 2. His cosmical views: derived from Eudoxus of Cnidus. § 3. His views concerning the Habitable World. § 4. Speculations connected with physical geography. § 5. Erroneous ideas concerning the great rivers of Asia. § 6. And of the West of Europe. Imperfect knowledge of Africa. § 7. Described the Caspian Sea as isolated. § 8. The Atlantis of Plato.
395

			PAGE
NOTE A	Age of Scylax	.. ..	404
„ B	Order of islands in the Mediterranean		406

CHAPTER XII.

EXPEDITION OF ALEXANDER.

SECTION 1.—*Campaigns in Central and Western Asia.*

§ 1. Alexander's expedition into Asia forms an era in ancient geography. It first opened up to the Greeks a real knowledge of the interior of Asia. § 2. His campaign in Europe against the Triballi. He crosses the Danube. § 3. Attacks the Illyrians: recalled to Thebes. § 4. He crosses the Hellespont: battle of the Granicus. His operations in Asia Minor. § 5. Advances through Phrygia to Gordium. § 6. March by Ancyra and through the Cilician gates to Tarsus. Battle of Issus. § 7. Occupies Syria and Egypt. His expedition to the temple of Ammon. Foundation of Alexandria. § 8. His advance into Asia: crosses the Euphrates and the Tigris: battle of Arbela. § 9. Occupies Babylon and Susa: advances to Persepolis. § 10. Pursues Darius from Ecbatana through the Pylæ Caspiæ: death of Darius. § 11. Halt at Hecatompylus: descent into Hyrcania. § 12. Subsequent campaigns lay through regions previously unknown. § 13. Conditions of marches determined by nature of the country: imperfection of itineraries. § 14. He pursues Bessus, but turns off into Aria, and thence into Drangiana: advances through Arachosia to the foot of the Hindoo Koosh. Founds Alexandria ad Caucasum. § 15 Investigation of route. § 16 Site of Alexandria. § 17. Crosses the Hindoo Koosh into Bactria. § 18. Operations in Bactria and Sogdiana: advance to the Iaxartes. § 19. Impossibility of following military movements in detail. § 20. Foundation of cities: general character of the country. § 21. Improved knowledge of the rivers Oxus and Iaxartes: but the latter confused with the Tanais. § 22. Both flowed into the Caspian. § 23. Hearsay information concerning other tribes. § 24. The Scythians beyond the Iaxartes .. .. Page 407

SECTION 2.—*Military Operations in India.*

§ 1. Alexander recrosses the Hindoo Koosh: engages in the reduction of the mountain tribes: the rock Aornus. § 2. Impossibility of following his movements in detail. § 3. Or determining the position of the several tribes. § 4. He crosses the Indus and the Hydaspes: defeats Porus and advances to the Hyphasis. § 5. The point which he finally reached cannot be determined. § 6. Difficulty in following his operations in the Punjab. § 7. Returns to the Hydaspes, and descends that river and the Indus to the sea. § 8. Progress of voyage down the river. § 9. Exaggerated account of the Indus: its supposed sources. § 10. Its Delta: site of Pattala. § 11. Difficulty of identifying the tribes on the Indus: the Malli, Oxydracæ, &c. 12. Alexander designed the permanent conquest of the regions on the Indus. § 13. Accounts of the wealth and populousness of India. 438

SECTION 3.—*Return to Babylon.*

§ 1. Return of Alexander to the West through Gedrosia. § 2. Great difficulties and sufferings on the march. § 3. His progress through Carmania; rejoined by Nearchus and Craterus. § 4. Returns to Susa: visits the Persian Gulf and Ecbatana. § 5 Preparations for exploring the Caspian Sea. § 6. Returns to Babylon. receives embassies from many nations, perhaps from the Romans. § 7. Prepares a fleet for the

CONTENTS OF VOL. I.

conquest of Arabia : sends out expeditions to explore the Persian Gulf: his death. § 8. His projects. § 9 Cities founded by him Page 454

			PAGE
NOTE A	Gordium	.. ..	466
„ B	Pylæ Ciliciæ	.. ..	467
„ C.	Mountain Passes near Issus	.. ..	ib
„ D	March to the Oracle of Ammon	..	469
„ E.	The Oasis of Ammon	.. .. ..	470
„ F	Thapsacus	.. ..	471
„ G	Battle of Arbela	.. ..	472
„ H	Retreat of Darius to Ecbatana	..	475
„ I	Passes between Susa and Persepolis	..	ib
„ K.	The Pylæ Caspiæ	.. .. ..	477
„ L.	Hecatompylus	.. ..	479
„ M.	Zadracarta	.. ..	480
„ N	Estimated distances	.. .. ..	481
„ O.	Supposed measurements of Alexander's route	.. ..	ib.
„ P	Rate of travelling on dromedaries	..	483
„ Q	The Indian Caucasus	.. ..	484
„ R.	Artacoana and Alexandria in Aris	..	485
„ S.	Routes from Herat into Bactria	..	486
„ T.	Prophthasia	.. .. ..	488
„ U.	Indian tribes west of the Indus	..	ib.
„ V.	Climate of Arachosia	.. ..	489
„ X.	Site of Alexandria ad Caucasum	..	490
„ Y.	Passes of the Hindoo Koosh	.. ..	492
„ Z	Comparative value of the historians of Alexander	.. ..	493
„ A a.	Legends concerning Bacchus and Hercules	.. ..	496
„ B b	The rock Aornus	.. .. ..	ib
„ C c	Peucelaotis	.. ..	498
„ D d	Taxila	.. ..	499
„ E e	Passage of the Hydaspes	.. ..	ib
„ F f.	Geography of the Punjab	. .	500
„ G g	Altars on the Hyphasis	.. ..	503
„ H h.	Sangala and the Cathæi	.. ..	505
„ I i.	Boats on the Indus	.. . ..	506
„ K k.	Descent of the Indus	. .. .	507
„ L l	Confluence of the Hydaspes with the Acesines	. .. .	508
„ M m.	Course of the Hyphasis	.. ..	509
„ N n	The Indus identified with the Nile	..	ib
„ O o	Width of the Indus	.. .. ..	510
„ P p	Source of the Indus	.. .. ..	511
„ Q q	Delta of the Indus	.. .. ..	512
„ R r.	Site of Pattala	.. ..	513
„ S s	Cities of the Malli	. ..	514
„ T t	The Oxydracæ	.. ..	515

CONTENTS OF VOL. I. XXV

			PAGE
NOTE U u.	Changes in the course of the Indus	..	516
„ V v.	March through Gedrosia	.. ..	518
„ X x.	Route through Gedrosia and Carmania		519
„ Y y.	March of Craterus	.. .. ..	521
„ Z z.	Embassy of the Romans to Alexander		522
„ A A.	The Pallacopas ..	.. .. ..	524

CHAPTER XIII.
VOYAGE OF NEARCHUS.

§ 1. Authentic character of the narrative. Modern writers on the subject. § 2. No statement of point of departure § 3. Port of Alexander. Voyage from thence to the Arabis. § 4. Coast of the Oritæ. Cocala, Malana. § 5. Coast of the Ichthyophagi: difficulties and privations. § 6. Geographical details. § 7. More rapid progress as far as Badis. § 8. Battle with whales. § 9. Perplexing astronomical statement. § 10. Voyage along the coast of Carmania and the Persian Gulf. Meeting with Alexander. § 11. Voyage continued along the coast of Persia. § 12. Duration of voyage: its character: its importance exaggerated .. .. Page 525

			PAGE
NOTE A.	Comparison with Pliny	.. ..	542
„ B	Estimate of distances by sea Supposed difference of stadia	.. ..	544
„ C	Port of Alexander	.. .. ..	546
„ D.	The island of Ashtola ..	... .	547
„ E.	Supposed astronomical changes	..	548
„ F.	The island of Ormuz	.. ..	549
„ G	Duidotis	.. .. ..	550

CHAPTER XIV.
SUCCESSORS OF ALEXANDER.

SECTION 1.—*Megasthenes. Increased knowledge of India.*

§ 1. Establishment of Seleucus in the dominion of Upper Asia. New division of satrapies § 2. Renewed intercourse with India Sandracottus. His friendly relations with Seleucus § 3. Megasthenes. His work the chief authority of the ancients concerning India. § 4. Great Indian monarchy on the Ganges § 5. Journey of Megasthenes. the royal road § 6 His account of the Ganges. and of Palibothra § 7. Other nations of India. constitution of monarchy. § 8. Castes.

§ 9. Philosophers. § 10 Natural productions. § 11 Fabulous tales § 12 Geographical information. § 13. First accounts of Taprobane § 14. Daimachus. Notices of India by Patrocles   Page 552

SECTION 2.—*Bactrian Provinces   Patrocles.*

§ 1 Revolt of Bactria and Sogdiana: establishment of a Greek monarchy there. § 2 Very little information concerning it No extension of geographical knowledge. § 3. Wealth and power for a short time § 4. Patrocles. was governor of the provinces from India to the Caspian asserted the Caspian to be an inlet of the Ocean His authority on this point universally received   569

CHAPTER XV.

THE PTOLEMIES IN EGYPT.

SECTION 1.—*The Ptolemies in Egypt. The Red Sea. The Nile.*

§ 1. Extension of geographical knowledge arising from foundation of Alexandria, and of a Greek monarchy in Egypt. § 2. Extensive trade in the Red Sea, and foundation of cities to promote it. Arsinoë, Berenice, Myos Hormus. § 3 Settlements further south. Ptolemais Epitheras. § 4. Land of Cinnamon and the Southern Horn. § 5. Trade with India: not direct, but through the Sabæans. § 6. Account of these by Agatharchides. Arabia Felix. § 7. Progress of knowledge of the Nile. Meroe. The effluents of the Nile. § 8 The two arms: the Blue and White Nile. the Sembritæ. the Cataracts. § 9. No extension by conquests in Ethiopia or in the interior of Libya. § 10. Timosthenes: his treatise on Ports: one of the chief authorities of Eratosthenes. His division of the winds   576

SECTION 2.—*Progress of Discovery in Western Europe. Pytheas   Timæus.*

§ 1. Extension of knowledge of Western Europe: chiefly owing to Pytheas. His date. § 2 His account of Britain and Thule: received by Eratosthenes, but rejected by Polybius and Strabo. § 3. Examination of his statements with regard to Gaul and Spain. § 4. And to Britain and Thule. § 5. His supposed voyage to the Tanais. His account of the origin of amber. § 6. Other particulars concerning northern lands, founded on truth. His astronomical observations. latitude assigned to Thule § 7. No mention of Cassiterides § 8. Timæus.

his historical work. Geographical notices contained in it The island of Mictis. § 9 Theophrastus. The treatise "De Mirabilibus" ascribed to Aristotle, but belongs to third century B.C. § 10 Curious notices contained in it. First notice of the Fortunate Islands § 11. General extension of trade and intercourse .. .. .. Page 589

			PAGE
NOTE A	Myos Hormus		607
„	B	African elephants	ib
„	C.	Land of Cinnamon	608
„	D.	Monument of Adulis	609
„	E.	The winds as known to the ancients ..	610
„	F	Dimensions of Britain . ..	612
„	G.	Sir G Lewis on credibility of Pytheas	ib.
„	H	Astronomical phenomena at Thule ..	613

CHAPTER XVI.

ERATOSTHENES.

§ 1. Eratosthenes the parent of scientific geography. His date and life. § 2. Dicæarchus his predecessor: his works. § 3. His attempts to measure the elevation of mountains. § 4. State of geographical science in the time of Eratosthenes. He undertakes to reform the map of the world. § 5. His ideas of the position and figure of the earth § 6. His attempt to determine its circumference. § 7. Defects of his method, and sources of error. § 8. Result after all a near approximation. He reckoned 700 stadia to a degree. § 9. His conception of the Inhabited World. § 10. His attempts to determine its limits. § 11. Draws one main parallel from the Sacred Promontory to the Indian Ocean § 12 Points through which it passed in the Mediterranean. Its inaccuracies. § 13. Draws a meridian line through Alexandria and Rhodes at right angles with it. § 14. Errors in latitude. § 15. Still greater errors in longitude. § 16 Mode of calculation of distances. His estimate of length of Mediterranean. § 17. Other distances given in Mediterranean. § 18. His imperfect knowledge of Western Europe. Followed Pytheas in regard to Thule and Britain. Ill acquainted with Scythia and Germany. § 19. Determination of northern and southern limits of the world. § 20. Other distances along principal meridian. Excess in computation. § 21. Continuation of parallel of latitude eastward through Asia. Its coincidence with range of Mount Taurus. § 22. Distances along this parallel. Length of habitable world. § 23. His ideas of the Eastern Ocean: and of the Caspian. § 24. Of India; and Taprobane. § 25. Of Arabia § 26. Its physical character and tribes.

§ 27. Of the Red Sea. § 28. His accurate knowledge of the Nile and its tributaries. § 29. Ignorant of the rest of Africa. § 30. He gave few details of countries. § 31. His division into Sphragides. § 32. His views on Homeric geography. § 33. Imperfect ideas of physical geography. § 34. Speculations on changes in sea level. § 35. Notices of changes in surface of earth .. .. Page 615

			PAGE
NOTE A.	Observations of latitude	.. ..	661
„	B.	Gossellin's theory	662
„	C.	Southern limit of habitable world ..	664
„	D.	Distance from Alexandria to Rhodes ..	665
„	E.	Promontory of Tamarus	666

LIST OF MAPS IN VOL. I.

	PAGE
1. MAP TO ILLUSTRATE THE WANDERINGS OF ULYSSES .. *to face*	84
2. THE WORLD ACCORDING TO HECATÆUS .. .. .. ,,	142
3. THE WORLD ACCORDING TO HERODOTUS .. .. .. ,,	174
4. SKETCH OF SCYTHIA ACCORDING TO HERODOTUS .. .. ,,	206
5. MAP TO ILLUSTRATE THE VOYAGE OF HANNO .. .. ,,	330
6. MAP TO ILLUSTRATE THE MARCHES OF XENOPHON AND ALEXANDER IN LOWER ASIA .. .. ,,	350
7. MAP TO ILLUSTRATE THE OPERATIONS BEFORE AND AFTER THE BATTLE OF CUNAXA .. .. ,,	366
8. ALEXANDER'S CAMPAIGNS IN ASIA .. .. ,,	462
9. ALEXANDER'S CAMPAIGNS IN INDIA .. .. ,,	510
10. MAP OF THE WORLD ACCORDING TO ERATOSTHENES .. ,,	654

Note.—I am aware that I may appear liable to the charge of inconsistency, in presenting the reader with a map purporting to represent the voyage of Ulysses, when I have expressed in the body of my work my conviction that Homer had no such map present to his mind, and did not attempt to embody in any definite form his vague poetical conceptions of the wanderings of his hero from land to land and from one mythical island to another. But such a representation has been so generally inserted in all treatises on ancient geography, and discussions of what is termed Homeric geography, that I thought some readers would complain of its absence; and at the same time it may assist them in following the narrative in the text, and recalling to their minds the order of sequence of the localities mentioned. It will at least bring clearly before their eyes the utter absence of all relation with the *real* localities in the Mediterranean, with which those mentioned by Homer were brought in connection by local tradition and the perverse ingenuity of commentators.

With regard to the two maps attempting to represent the idea of the world as formed by Hecatæus and Herodotus, I have not deviated from the customary mode of representing the two continents of Europe and Asia, and the Mediterranean Sea, in accordance with their true position. The change in the direction of the Mediterranean introduced by Dr C. Muller does not appear to me to rest upon sufficient grounds to warrant its adoption. At the same time, it must be freely admitted that the map of the world according to Hecatæus is in great measure conjectural, for which reason I have confined myself to a rough and general outline. Even for that of Herodotus, though the historian has furnished us with many valuable materials, which have been fully discussed in the text, there remains much to be filled up by conjecture, and many difficulties that cannot be solved with any approach to certainty.

HISTORY

OF

ANCIENT GEOGRAPHY.

CHAPTER I.

INTRODUCTORY.

§ 1. THE study of Geography, like that of Astronomy, is to a certain extent a necessary concomitant of civilization, but will be found to have been pursued more or less by different nations according to the circumstances of their position. No people that have made even the first steps in the progress towards cultivation and enlightenment can have failed to direct their attention towards those heavenly bodies which so much influence the condition of all the inhabitants of this earth, which determine the changes of the seasons, and afford the only natural measures of time. Hence astronomy, in a rude and popular sense of the term, must have existed from the earliest ages among all nations that were not utterly barbarous; and there seems no doubt that it was carried to a great extent and attained a surprising degree of perfection among the earliest nations of antiquity, whose civilization we have any means of estimating. But while the natural situation and circumstances of the Egyptians, the Chaldæans, and the Assyrians—their open plains and starry cloudless skies—were eminently calculated to direct their attention to the prosecution of this study, it was otherwise with geography. In all these cases their civilization was eminently local in its character. Derived in the first instance from the peculiar local circumstances in which it grew up, it was to a great extent confined by the

VOL. I.

influence of those circumstances within the same original limits. Egypt especially retained through all the ages of its early greatness the same isolated character that China continued to hold down to a very recent period. The occasional outbreaks of ambitious monarchs, who for a time extended their dominion over the neighbouring portions of Asia, produced no permanent result: and the Egyptian monarchy, when it first came in contact with the Greeks, was still limited to the valley of the Nile, as it had been eighteen centuries before.

The same thing was the case, though to a less degree, with the monarchies of the Chaldæans and the Assyrians, which successively ruled in the valley of the Euphrates and the Tigris. The Assyrians, indeed, extended their dominion over a considerable part of Asia, and the adjoining island of Cyprus, but their peculiar civilization was confined to the district in which it arose, and a few isolated monuments alone attest their early connection with any other nations or countries.

Geography indeed may, in a certain restricted sense, be regarded as applying even to that limited knowledge of one's own country and its natural features and boundaries, which every man of cultivated intelligence must inevitably possess. But it is only in proportion as it extends beyond these narrow limits, and comprises other countries, and a more considerable portion of the earth's surface, that it approaches to the character of a science. There can be no doubt that the ancient Egyptians not only possessed what may be called an accurate geographical knowledge of Egypt; but that they had acquired at least general information concerning other countries that bordered on the Mediterranean, as well as those that adjoined them on the East. But how far they may have attained to anything like a definite geographical idea of any of those more distant lands, and their relative position, is a question that must be left to Egyptologers to determine; if indeed there exist the materials to enable us to arrive at any conclusion on the subject.

Commercial relations, which in almost all countries have been the precursors of geographical knowledge, could have produced but little effect of the kind in Egypt. Maritime commerce was indeed almost wholly wanting: for the Egyptians appear to have entertained, in all ages, a deeply rooted aversion for the sea and all maritime pursuits; and though the productions of distant lands were brought to them by their neighbours the Phœnicians, and probably also by caravans across the deserts of Syria, this mode of traffic would hardly lead to any increased information concerning the countries from which they were derived.

§ 2. The earliest nation of which the literature has survived, that of the Jews, was almost as much cut off from intercourse with other races, by the circumstances of its position, combined with its peculiar institutions, as were the Egyptians. The special character of their literature was also such as to afford little opportunity for any expositions of a scientific nature: and while the earlier books of the Old Testament contain numerous geographical details concerning Palestine and the neighbouring districts, there is nothing that affords any idea of the general notions of the Jews on the subject, or the extent of their geographical horizon. The genealogy of the sons of Noah, found in the book of Genesis, is indeed an ethnological document of the highest interest, as embodying the earliest traditions concerning the relations and affinities of the different nations and races of men known to its author; but it conveys no information as to their geographical position; nor must it be hastily assumed that the writer had any definite ideas upon this subject. There can be little doubt, for instance, that the name of Javan was the same as is found in Greek mythology in the form Iaon or Ion, as the founder of the Ionian race. But it had certainly no local connection with the people situated on the coast of the Ægean, who were designated by that appellation in the time of Herodotus: and whether it is intended to apply to the Hellenic race generally, or to the inhabitants of the peninsula now known as Asia Minor,—

in which sense it appears to have been employed at a later period,—we have no means of determining.

But whatever may have been the nature and extent of the geographical knowledge possessed by the Egyptians or the Hebrews, it may be safely asserted that it had little, if any, influence upon that of the Greeks. The latter, indeed, believed themselves to be indebted to the Egyptians for the elementary principles of geometry;[1] they probably derived from the Babylonians the invention of the gnomon, or sundial, as well as the division of the day into twelve hours.[2] But these scientific inventions were certainly not introduced into Greece until long after the period when our acquaintance with Greek literature gives us the means of judging for ourselves of their attainments in geography. The results of such an inquiry, as we shall presently see, are conclusive as to the fact that their geographical knowledge in the earliest ages was limited to the countries in their immediate neighbourhood, and to the group of nations that surrounded the Ægean Sea. All beyond was vague and indefinite: derived from hearsay reports, imperfectly understood, or mixed up with mythological fancies and fables of poetical origin.

§ 3. There was, however, one people which exercised considerable influence upon Hellenic culture and civilization, that calls for more especial notice in this place. The Phœnicians, unlike the Hebrews and the Egyptians, were essentially a commercial and seafaring people; and the earliest notices of them that we find, both in the Hebrew and Greek literature, concur in representing them as skilful and daring navigators, capable of conducting long voyages, and bringing back the productions of distant countries to exchange with their more sedentary neighbours. Unfortunately their native literature has utterly perished, and their early history is a blank.

---

[1] Herodotus, ii. 109
[2] This is expressly stated by Herodotus (*l. c*). Other writers, however, ascribed the invention of the gnomon to Anaximander, who lived in the 6th century, B C. Probably he was in reality the first to introduce it into Greece

Whether or not there be any foundation for the tradition recorded by Herodotus, that the original abode of the Phœnicians was on the Erythræan Sea, from whence they migrated to the tract on the shores of the Mediterranean which they inhabited in historical times, " and immediately betook themselves to long voyages, freighting their ships with the wares of Egypt and Assyria;"[3] it throws no light upon the origin of this peculiar tendency, which so remarkably distinguished them from all other Semitic nations. To a certain extent, indeed, its causes are not far to seek. Confined to a narrow sea-board, and excluded from all extension of their territory towards the interior by ranges of mountains, which at the same time afforded them abundant materials for shipbuilding, it was but natural that they should devote themselves to maritime pursuits: and the similar instances of Amalfi, Genoa, and Venice, in the middle ages, show how easily even a scanty population, beginning with very limited resources, but devoting all their energies to maritime commerce, may attain to a marked superiority over all their rivals.

But the extent of that commerce and the length of the distant voyages which we find them undertaking at this early period, as compared with what were customary among the Greeks and other ancient nations, even in a more advanced condition, undoubtedly present a perplexing problem, which we have no means of solving. The earliest notices which we find of them in the Hebrew literature represent them as being, as early as the time of Solomon (about B.C. 1000), already familiar with the voyage to Tarshish, by which there seems no doubt that we are to understand the region in the south of Spain known to the Greeks in the early ages as Tartessus.[4]

---

[3] Herodotus i 1. (The same statement is repeated in vii. 89.) This tradition has been adopted as authentic, or as resting upon a basis of truth by several modern writers, including Movers (*Die Phonizier*, book 1. ch. 11), while others, among whom is Mr. Kenrick (*Phœnicia*, p. 52), reject it as altogether unworthy of credit.

[4] This subject is fully investigated by Mr. Twisleton, in his article TARSHISH, in Dr Smith's *Dictionary of Biblical Antiquities*, vol. III.

It is entirely in accordance with this that one of the earliest of their colonial settlements, of which the date can be fixed with any approach to certainty, was that of Gadeira, or Gades, in the district thus designated, the foundation of which is ascribed to a period as early as B.C. 1100. It is singular that, according to the traditions preserved to us, this distant colony preceded any of those in the Mediterranean, where Utica, on the coast of Africa, was established a few years later; while Carthage, which was destined to attain to so proud a preeminence over all other Phœnician colonies, was not founded till near three hundred years later.[5]

Unfortunately the dates thus transmitted to us rest upon very doubtful authority; but the testimony of the earliest extant Greek literature, in the form of the Homeric poems, is conclusive as to the general fact that the Phœnicians were at that remote period the principal traders and navigators in the Ægean Sea and the neighbouring parts of the Mediterranean. They combined, as was generally the case with the earliest voyagers, the two objects of trade and piracy, especially for the kidnapping of slaves. But whatever may have been their evil practices in this respect, it seems clear that they possessed at this time the whole carrying trade of the seas with which the Greeks were familiar, and thus became the intermediaries through whom the arts and civilization of Egypt, Assyria, and Babylonia passed into Greece. It was through the same channel that the Greeks first became acquainted with various productions of more distant lands, such as ivory and frankincense, both of which were familiar to them in the days of Homer.

Nor were the Phœnicians engaged only in the transport of

---

[5] According to the anonymous author of the treatise *On Wonders*, falsely ascribed to Aristotle, but probably about a century later, Utica was founded 287 years before Carthage, a statement he professes to have derived from Tyrian records (*De Mirab* § 134) Unfortunately the date of Carthage itself is not known with certainty, and the conclusion adopted by Movers (*Die Phönizier*, vol. ii pt. ii pp. 150-157) and Mr Kenrick (*Phœnicia*, p. 145) of B C 813 is admitted to rest only on a balance of evidence The statement that Gadeira was settled a "few years" before Utica rests on the authority of Velleius Paterculus (i. 2).

foreign commodities. Among the productions of their own coasts was the shell-fish, from which they learnt at a very early period the art of extracting the purple dye, for which they were famous in all ages, and of which the Tyrians continued to be the chief manufacturers even under the Roman Empire. Glass also was an article extensively manufactured by them, so that its invention was by some authors ascribed to the Sidonians; and richly embroidered robes and garments are repeatedly mentioned in the Homeric poems as the work of Sidonian artists. On the other hand, we learn from the Hebrew Scriptures that Hiram, king of Tyre, was able to furnish to Solomon skilled artificers and artisans in almost every department of work requisite either for the construction or ornament of the Temple at Jerusalem.[6] In all the ornamental arts indeed the Phœnicians appear to have been at this period as much in advance of their neighbours the Jews, as they undoubtedly were of the Greeks.

§ 4. That this extensive commerce must have led to a wide expansion of the geographical horizon amongst the Phœnicians, as compared with their neighbours the Egyptians or the Hebrews, may be assumed as certain. But what were the real extent and limits of the knowledge thus acquired, and how far it was embodied in a distinct geographical form, are questions which, from the total loss of the Phœnician literature, we are wholly unable to answer. While we find in the earliest Greek records many vague and dimly-traced ideas as to the wonders of "the far west," which are in all probability derived from Phœnician sources, it is remarkable that no definite allusion is found to the countries in which that people had already established themselves, long before the date that can be plausibly assigned to the earliest remains of the Greek literature. Not only is the name of Tartessus not found in the Homeric poems, but the whole of that cycle of myths, which was in later times connected with the name of the Greek deity Herakles, but

---

[6] See 1 Kings vii., 2 Chron ii.

unquestionably belonged originally to the Tyrian god Melkarth, is conspicuously wanting. No allusion is found to the island of Erytheia and the triple-headed Geryones with his herds of cattle, or to the golden apples of the Hesperides, or the Columns of Herakles. The *name* of Atlas is indeed found, but with nothing whatever to connect him with the mountain that subsequently bore his name, or with the local habitation assigned him on the straits that led into the western ocean.[7]

Whatever ideas the Greeks may have derived from the Phœnicians concerning the western portions of the Mediterranean were of so vague and floating a character, that they can hardly be said to have assumed any geographical form; and they certainly afford us no clue to what may have been the conceptions entertained by the Phœnicians themselves. With regard to the East, on the contrary, they appear to have derived no ideas at all. Though the extent and character of the commerce carried on by the Phœnicians with the distant regions of the East is still a subject of much controversy among Oriental scholars, it may be assumed as certain that they received the commodities of India and other distant lands, either direct from the countries themselves, or more probably from an intermediate *entrepôt* in Arabia, as we shall find was the case with the Greeks at a much later period.[8] In this respect indeed they appear to have been very much in the same position as the Venetians in the middle ages, and to have constituted the only channel through which the valuable products of the East passed into the hands of the western nations. As we learn from the Hebrew writings that this was the case as early as the time of Solomon (B.C. 1000),[9] it is certainly strange that not the slightest trace or allusion in any form is

---

[7] This point will be more fully examined in the next chapter.

[8] On this subject I must refer my readers to the learned and able articles on TARSHISH and OPHIR, by Mr Twisleton, in Dr Smith's *Dict of Bibl Geogr.*, where the whole question will be found fully investigated.

[9] This appears from the well-known passage in the First Book of Kings, ch xxii. The more elaborate description of the commerce of Tyre in the 27th chapter of Ezekiel belongs of course to a much later period, about the beginning of the sixth century, B C.

to be found in the Homeric poems to those regions of the far East, which were to the Greeks in all subsequent ages preeminently the land of marvel and of mystery.

The only geographical notion—vague and floating as it was—which must have been derived by the early Greeks from this source, was that of the Æthiopians—"burnt or black men"—a nation with whom the Egyptians had long been familiar, and of whom the knowledge probably passed from them through the Phœnicians to the Greeks. Through the Egyptians also must have come the fable of a race of Pygmies, situated apparently in the South of Africa, on the Ocean stream, and engaged in constant wars with the cranes that visited their country as immigrants from the North.[1]

§ 5. It does not fall within the scope of the present work to enter into a detailed examination of the Phœnician commerce, even if there were more trustworthy materials than are really available for such an inquiry. But two of the articles which the Greeks unquestionably derived from them, and which they were supposed to import from some of the most distant regions of the known world, require a special mention in this place, from their connection with geographical questions that we shall find recurring at almost every stage of our future investigations. Tin and amber, two products of rare occurrence, and almost wholly unknown within the basin of the Mediterranean,[2] were certainly both of them well known to the Greeks; and in both cases there seems no room to doubt that they had been introduced to them by the Phœnicians. Tin, which was called by the Greeks *cassiteros*, is repeatedly mentioned in the Homeric poems,[3] and although its use as a separate metal would always be limited in extent, it was employed from a

---

[1] The passages in the Homeric poems which refer to the Æthiopians and the Pygmies will be considered in the next chapter.

[2] Amber is found, though in small quantities, near Catania in Sicily, but no notice of this is found in any ancient author, and the fact seems to have certainly been unknown in ancient times

[3] Homer, Iliad, xi 25, 34; xviii. 474, 564 Its ready fusibility is alluded to by Hesiod, *Theogon* v. 862.

very early period as an alloy of copper, its mixture with which produced the compound now known as bronze, so valuable from its superior hardness, and which on that account was extensively used by all the nations of antiquity.

But there exists much difference of opinion with regard to the quarter from whence this tin was procured by the Phœnicians in early ages. At a somewhat later period, but still long before the time of Herodotus, it is certain that the principal, if not the sole, source from which the tin used by the nations of the Mediterranean was supplied, was from certain islands in the Western Ocean, known to the Greeks by name as the Cassiterides or Tin Islands, but the situation of which was unknown to Herodotus,[4] and probably also to all his contemporaries. Later information however leaves no doubt that the islands thus designated were the Scilly Islands, together with the adjacent peninsula of Cornwall, which was erroneously supposed to be a larger island of the same group, and from which in reality all the tin was procured.[5] No allusion to these islands is however found in the Homeric poems, nor in any author earlier than Herodotus, and it is probable that for centuries the Greeks continued to receive their supplies of this important metal from the Phœnicians without any inquiry as to the locality from which it was derived. That people were also from very early ages distinguished for their skill as workers in metals, and there can be no doubt that it was from them the Greeks first learnt the art of making bronze, and probably in the first instance imported all articles composed of that metal ready manufactured.[6]

---

[4] He says distinctly that he has no *knowledge* of the islands called Cassiterides, from which tin was brought (iii. 115). But, he adds, it is certain that, as well as amber, it was brought from the extreme regions of the world

[5] No tin is found in the Scilly Islands, nor is it probable that it ever was produced there, but the occurrence of this group of islands so near the mainland naturally led to the supposition that the whole were connected together.

Tin is also found in considerable quantities in Devonshire, but from its inland position on the borders of Dartmoor, this is much less likely to have attracted the attention of traders than that of Cornwall.

[6] Homer distinguishes Sidon by the

But however conclusive is the evidence that this was the quarter from which the supply of tin was derived in historical ages, many writers have found it difficult to believe that the Phœnicians could have carried on an extensive trade with such remote islands at the very early period when tin and bronze were certainly known both to them and to the Greeks. Hence some writers have supposed that they derived their supplies in the first instance from Spain itself, where tin is also found, though in comparatively small quantities.[7] The difficulty in the way of this theory appears to be, that tin is not found in the *south* of Spain, with which alone the Phœnicians had any direct trade; but in the interior, and principally in the province of Galicia, from which it would be nearly as difficult to bring it to Gades, as from Cornwall or the adjacent islands.[8] But, moreover, it is impossible to see how on this supposition the idea could have arisen of its being brought from " the Tin Islands;" a notion which we find generally established at the earliest period when we have any geographical information on the subject at all.

---

epithet of " abounding in bronze " (πολύχαλκος, Odyss. xv 425); and the great works in that metal presented by Hiram, king of Tyre, to the temple of Solomon bear the strongest testimony to their proficiency in the art

At a later period the Tyrrhenians (Etruscans) were also renowned for their skill as workers in bronze, and objects manufactured by them were to some extent imported into Greece, but no such intercourse can be carried back to the Homeric age.

[7] Concerning the actual production of tin in Spain, see *The Cassiterides*, by Dr. G. Smith (8vo. Lond. 1863), p. 45 In ancient times Posidonius asserted that it was found in abundance among the Artabri, who occupied the north-western angle of the peninsula (the modern Galicia), and Pliny states that it was found in Lusitania and Gallæcia, which he erroneously regards as *disproving* the popular notion that it was brought from certain islands in the ocean. (Plin. H. N , xxxiv. 16, § 156; Posidonius ap Strab. iii. 2, p. 147)

[8] Tin was also found in Lusitania, and is still met with in Portugal, but only in the interior of the country, where it would be little likely to attract the attention of the Phœnicians.

The only other country in Europe where tin occurs in any quantity is Bohemia, the forests and mountains of which, as well as its inland position, rendered it one of the most inaccessible parts of Europe: so that it was unknown, till a late period, both to the Greeks and Romans, and even when they became acquainted with it they had no suspicion of its metallic wealth. The supposition that the Phœnician tin was brought from India is now generally discarded, and may be safely set aside as untenable. It is not found in any part of India nearer than the Malay peninsula.

12   HISTORY OF ANCIENT GEOGRAPHY.   Chap. I.

Whether or not their supplies were really derived in the first instance from Cornwall, or from some part of Spain, there is no doubt that Gades always continued to be the centre of the tin trade; it was from thence that the Phœnician colonists, and in later times the Carthaginians, made their adventurous voyages to the British Islands; and from this circumstance it came to be supposed that the Cassiterides were connected with Spain, a notion which became so firmly fixed in men's minds that they were described by geographers in much later times as a group of islands in the Ocean, off the coast of Spain, without any hint of their connection either with Britain or Gaul. Strange as it may appear, it is thus that they are represented not only by Strabo, but even by Ptolemy, long after Britain itself was familiar to the Romans.[9]

This fact appears in itself conclusive against the view adopted by some modern writers that the British tin was in very early times brought overland through Gaul to the neighbourhood of Narbo and Massilia, and was imported *from thence* by the Phœnicians.[1] That such was the case in later times, when the Greek republic of Massilia had gradually extended its commercial relations through Gaul to the Ocean, there can be no dispute; but to maintain that this was the route followed by the trade in the time of the Phœnicians is contrary to all the information we have on the subject. All accounts point to Gades as the mart for tin,[2] and the port from which the long voyage to the Tin Islands was undertaken; while we have no account of the Phœnicians trading with the southern coasts of

---

[9] Strabo, iii. 5,' § 11, p. 175; Ptol. ii. 6, § 76

[1] This view was especially maintained by Sir G C Lewis in his *History of Ancient Astronomy*, (pp. 450-455) The arguments on the other side are well brought together by Mr. Twisleton, in the article TARSHISH already cited, p 1439

[2] In the account of the Phœnician trade given by Ezekiel (chap xxvii)

more than 100 years before the birth of Herodotus, Tarshish is spoken of as the mart for silver, iron, lead, and tin. The authorities followed by Avienus represent "the Tartessians" as trading from an early period with the Tin Islands, where probably the Phœnician colonists of Gades are meant (Avienus *De Ora Maritima*, v. 113), but little value can be attached to the expressions of so late and inaccurate a writer.

Gaul, or having any settlement near the mouths of the Rhone, which could serve as the emporium for so important a trade as that in question.

§ 6. Another product which was certainly known to the Greeks in very early days, and the introduction of which is generally ascribed to the Phœnicians, is amber; an object that was in the earliest days much sought after as an ornament, and that continued even in later times to attract an amount of attention wholly disproportioned to its estimation at the present day. Here again, while the substance is repeatedly mentioned in the Homeric poems,[3] not the least clue is afforded to the locality from which it came. But before the time of Herodotus the tradition had come to be firmly established that it was brought from the banks of a great river called the Eridanus, which flowed into the northern ocean; and though the historian is disposed to reject this statement, as not resting upon adequate authority, he admits as an unquestionable fact that amber, like tin, was brought from the most distant regions of the earth.[4] The fact was undoubtedly true; for amber is found almost exclusively on the northern shores of Germany, and much the most extensively on those of the Baltic, though it occurs also in considerable quantities on the western coast of Sleswig and the adjacent islands.[5] But it is much more difficult to believe that the Phœnicians actually made the voyage to the Baltic, and brought amber from thence, than that they visited Cornwall in quest of tin. In later times the

---

[3] That the substance called in Homer "electrum" (ἤλεκτρον) is, in some instances at least (Odyss xv 460, xviii 296) no other than amber, appears to me certain, notwithstanding the arguments that have been urged on the other side. The recent discovery of amber beads in large quantities by Dr. Schliemann at Mycenæ lends a strong corroboration to this view, and proves beyond a doubt that amber was imported into Greece in very early ages (Schliemann's *Mycenæ and Tiryns*, pp. 203, 245.) Necklaces of gold and amber beads, almost precisely similar to those described in the Odyssey, have been found also in Etruscan tombs of early date. (Abeken, *Mittel Italien*, p 271)

[4] Herodot iii 115

[5] This was overlooked by Sir G. C. Lewis, who in his discussion of this subject assumes that amber was produced *only* on the coasts of the Baltic. (*Hist. of Ancient Astronomy*, pp. 457-466) Concerning the extent of its occurrence on the shores of the North Sea, see Redslob's *Thule*, p 26.

trade was carried on principally, if not exclusively, overland; and there seems much reason to believe that this was the case in the earliest times also. It is certain indeed that, while the original form of the tradition concerning the Eridanus appears to be that referred to by Herodotus, that it was a river flowing into the northern ocean, it had at an early period come to be associated with the river Padus of Northern Italy; with which the myth of Phaethon and his sisters, whose tears were changed into amber, gradually came to be inseparably connected.[6] It is true, as observed by Pliny, that no amber was really found there; but as he assures us that the women of that part of Italy habitually wore amber necklaces, this circumstance might have readily led to the supposition that it was a production of the country.[7] Amber was certainly in request as an ornament among the Germans of a very early period, as we learn from the contents of their tombs, and it is just such an article as may readily have passed, in the manner indicated by Pliny, from them to the inhabitants of Pannonia, and through them again to the Veneti at the head of the Adriatic, from whence it would readily find its way both into Greece and Italy.[8]

It must be observed that the connection of the Phœnicians with the trade in amber is far less clearly made out than with that of tin;[9] and with the exception of the assumption (for it

---

[6] The statement that Pherecydes, who was an earlier contemporary of Herodotus, had already identified the Eridanus with the Padus, rests only on the very dubious authority of a late scholiast. (See Pherecyd Fr 33 c, in C. Muller's *Fragmenta Historicorum Græcorum*, vol 1)

[7] Plin H N xxxvii 3, § 44 Both Pliny and Strabo justly reject as a mere fiction the supposed Amber Islands (Electrides Insulæ), placed by some poets, and geographers in the head waters of the Adriatic They were apparently invented merely by analogy with the Cassiterides or Tin Islands

[8] It is a tempting conjecture to connect the Veneti of Northern Italy with the Venedi or Wends, who in the time of Tacitus and Pliny dwelt on the shores of the Baltic, and to suppose that they brought the knowledge of amber from their original homes, and continued always to import it from thence by the same overland route which they had themselves followed in their migration

[9] It rests, indeed, solely on the fact that amber is mentioned by Homer as forming part of a necklace of Phœnician workmanship. No notice is found of amber in the passage of Ezekiel (ch. xxviii) in which he describes the commerce of Tyre, and enumerates the

really is nothing more), that they were the intermediaries through whose means it was brought from the head of the Adriatic to Greece and the adjoining countries we have no evidence of their having penetrated into the interior of the Adriatic at all. The same remark applies also to the Euxine: for though some modern writers have supposed them to have penetrated at a very early period into that inland sea, and even carried on a lucrative trade with the inhabitants of its remotest shores, there is absolutely no ancient authority for this supposition.[1]

§ 7. But whatever may have been the extent to which the Phœnicians pushed their trade in these remoter regions, it is certain that at the earliest period when we obtain any real insight into the state of society in Greece, not only was the carrying-trade of the Ægean and of the adjoining parts of the Mediterranean principally in the hands of the Phœnicians, but they had settled themselves in many of the islands and on some points of the surrounding continents.[2] Many of these foundations rest upon insufficient evidence, and were probably in many cases merely temporary establishments. But there is no reason to doubt the general fact, asserted by Thucydides, that in the earliest period of which tradition had preserved any record, the islands of the Ægean were inhabited by Phœnicians and Carians, whose piratical habits rendered the navigation of the adjoining seas insecure, and prevented that free communication between one part of Greece and another, which was essential to its progress in civilization.[3]

§ 8. According to the same testimony of tradition, the earliest

---

articles brought by her merchants from distant countries. Nor is the substance mentioned elsewhere in the Hebrew Scriptures.

[1] The alleged Phœnician colonies in the Euxine (Movers, *Die Phönizier*, tom. ii. p. 297) rest on very dubious testimony, and were, at all events, confined to the coasts near its mouth.

[2] One of the most important of these, and at the same time the most distant towards the north of the Ægean, was the island of Thasos, the gold mines of which formed a great source of attraction. Herodotus, who had himself visited them, speaks with wonder of the great scale on which the Phœnicians had carried on their mining operations (vi. 47).

[3] Thucyd. i. 4, 8.

people of Greece who asserted their own supremacy at sea, and contended successfully with the Phœnicians, were the Cretans, who, under their king Minos are said to have expelled the Phœnician and Carian pirates from the islands of the Ægean, and established themselves in the dominion of that sea.[4] Unfortunately all our information concerning them is of a very vague and dubious character. The name of Minos is so much mixed up with legends of a purely mythological character, and he himself assumes so much the aspect of a mythological personage, that we have a difficulty in accepting as historical any statement of events in which he forms a prominent figure. At the same time, as observed by Mr. Grote, there have been preserved to us two distinct sets of traditions concerning him, which have hardly anything in common except the name.[5] While the Minos of the poets and logographers is altogether an unhistorical personage and almost all that is related of him is palpably fictitious, the Minos of Thucydides and Aristotle—the founder of the first naval power in Greece, and the first who established order and security in the Greek islands—has altogether the air of a real personage; and there would be no reason to doubt the truth of the tradition concerning him, but that it is referred to a period so early that it is difficult to see how it should have been transmitted by any trustworthy authority.[6] But it is certain that, as is well remarked by Aristotle, the island itself from its position seems destined by nature for the command of the Ægean Sea and its other islands, and that when we first obtain any information concerning the Cretans, they appear as the boldest and most adventurous mariners among the Greeks, rivalling indeed in some degree the Phœnicians themselves.

Thus we find in the Odyssey, where Ulysses represents

---

[4] Thucyd. *l.c.* The same statement is confirmed by Aristotle (*Politica*, ii. 10, § 4).
[5] Grote's *History of Greece*, vol. i. p. 310.
[6] Minos was placed, according to the chronology received among the Greeks, about B C. 1300; and though this date is of course worthless, all the early traditions concurred in referring him to a period two or three generations before the Trojan War.

himself in the character of a Cretan chief, that he relates his undertaking without hesitation a voyage to Egypt, and accomplishing it successfully with a fair wind in five days.[7] The narrative referred to is indeed fictitious, but it must have represented a state of things that would appear plausible and probable, and it may certainly rank with the similar narratives in which Phœnician mariners are the agents.[8] No doubt in all these cases the expeditions partook, to a great extent, of a piratical, as well as a commercial character; and in the earliest ages piracy, and especially the kidnapping of slaves, was undoubtedly a leading stimulus to the extension of navigation. But we find Homer speaking of a Taphian chieftain undertaking, apparently as a matter of course, a voyage to Temesa in quest of bronze, and taking with him a cargo of iron.[9] If indeed we are to suppose the Temesa here mentioned to be the town of that name in the island of Cyprus, the voyage in question would be one of the longest recorded in the Homeric poems; but this view, though adopted by many of the leading commentators, both in ancient and modern times, is open to the gravest doubts.[1]

§ 9. No historical value can of course be attached to the details of the Trojan War, and we shall not at the present day pause to inquire, with Thucydides, into the size and number of the vessels that formed the Greek armament, but if it be admitted to have had any historical basis at all—and this there are probably few who would deny—the undertaking such an enterprise is in itself sufficient to show that navigation was already sufficiently advanced to afford the means of transporting large bodies of men by sea from the shores of Greece to the opposite side of the Ægean. All the traditionary information preserved to us by later writers, concerning what are called the heroic

---

[7] Odyssey, xiv. 246–257.
[8] Ibid. xiv. 288–300; xv. 415–475.
[9] Ibid. i. 180–184.
[1] The only other notices of the Taphians represent them as pirates (Odyss. xv. 427; xvi. 426); and there is no mention of them on any other occasion as a commercial people. They subsequently disappear from history.

ages, points in the same direction, and the natural circumstances of Greece would in themselves lead to an early development of maritime tendencies, which would soon come to play an important part in promoting their general civilization.

But among the legends of the heroic ages there was one which was referred by the concurrent testimony of the poets and logographers—followed in later times by the historians and chronologers—to a period anterior to the Trojan War, though not susceptible of any definite chronological determination—which will require a more particular examination in connection with our present subject.

CHAPTER II.

VOYAGE OF THE ARGONAUTS.

§ 1. It is impossible to consider the state of navigation and geographical knowledge among the Greeks in the earliest ages, without bestowing some attention on the well-known legend of the Voyage of the Argonauts: an enterprise which, if we could believe in its reality, would justly deserve to rank as the first voyage of discovery on record.[1] But it is hardly necessary to add that not only is the legendary tale, in the form with which we are all familiar, one to which it is impossible to attach any historical value, but it is equally impossible for us at the present day to arrive at any distinct idea of the original form in which it first became current among the Greeks, or the period when it was ultimately consolidated into that which has been transmitted to us by the poets of later ages.

It is certain, indeed, that the voyage of the ship Argo, under the command of Jason, and the favouring protection of Hera, was not only known to the author of the Odyssey, but is especially referred to by him as a thing familiar to all, or, as the Germans would term it, "world-famous."[2] It is equally clear that the term of the voyage was already fixed in the land of Æetes, and there can be no doubt that the quest of

---

[1] The idea that it was actually the first voyage, and that the Argo was the first ship ever built, may be safely discarded as mere poetical embellishments that had nothing to do with the original legend

[2] Οἴη δὴ κείνη γε παρέπλω ποντόπορος νηῦς,
'Αργὼ πασιμέλουσα παρ' Αἰήταο πλέουσα
καί νύ κε τὴν ἔνθ' ὦκα βάλεν μεγάλας ποτὶ πέτρας,

ἀλλ' Ἥρη παρέπεμψεν, ἐπεὶ φίλος ἦεν Ἰήσων
Odyss xii 69-72

The epithet πασιμέλουσα, literally, "an object of interest to all," is not found elsewhere, but its signification is shown beyond a doubt by the similar use of μέλω in another passage of the Odyssey, ix. 20.

the golden fleece was already designated as its object. Indeed this may probably be regarded as having formed from the first the essential nucleus of the legend. But it is a very different thing to assume—as has been done by Strabo and many other writers both in ancient and modern times—that therefore Homer was acquainted with the ordinary tradition that carried the Argonauts to Colchis and the river Phasis. Demetrius of Scepsis appears to have been the only ancient writer who ventured to doubt this conclusion: for which he is severely taken to task by Strabo, who repeatedly speaks of the voyage of the Argonauts to the Phasis as admitted by all, including Homer, though unquestionably there is no statement in the Homeric poems to that effect.[3] So far as we are dimly able to discern, the earliest form of the legend must have been that preserved to us in a fragment of Mimnermus, which represented Æetes as dwelling on the banks of the Ocean stream in the farthest East, "where the rays of the sun are stored up in a golden chamber."[4] He was, in fact, as purely mythical a being as his sister Circe, and, like her, he dwelt beside the Ocean stream, in that which was regarded by the poets as the twilight land of fable. The attempt to identify the place of his abode with Colchis and the land of the Phasis, had doubtless no more real foundation than that which sought for the land of the Phæacians in Corcyra, and the Ogygian island of Calypso in Malta.[5] But it is not difficult

---

[3] Strabo, 1 2, § 38, p 45, οἱ Ἀργοναῦται πλέοντες εἰς Φᾶσιν τὸν ὑφ' Ὁμήρου καὶ τῶν ἄλλων ὁμολογούμενον πλοῦν And again in the same section he asks how it was possible that the poet τῶν περὶ Ἰάσονα συμβάντων καὶ τὴν Ἀργὼ καὶ τοὺς Ἀργοναύτας τῶν ὁμολογουμένων παρὰ πᾶσιν ἀνήκοος ἦν, Demetrius of Scepsis denied altogether Homer's knowledge of the voyage *to the Phasis* ἀρχήν φησι μηδ' εἰδέναι τὴν εἰς Φᾶσιν ἀποδημίαν τοῦ Ἰάσονος Ὅμηρον (*l c*). He appears to have placed the abode of Æetes on the shores of the Ocean, as was done by Hesiod and Mimnermus.

[4] Αἰήταο πόλιν, τόθι τ' ὠκέος ἠελίοιο ἀκτῖνες χρυσέῳ κείαται ἐν θαλάμῳ ὠκεανοῦ παρὰ χείλεσ', ἵν' ᾤχετο θεῖος Ἰήσων
Mimnermus ap Strab 1 2, § 40, p 47

Mimnermus flourished about B C 600

[5] Concerning these legendary attributions see the next chapter. The attempt to explain the legend of the golden fleece by a practice of the barbarians in the neighbouring Caucasus to collect the gold dust in the torrent beds by placing fleeces of wool in them (Strabo, xi 2, § 19, p 499), belongs to a class of rationalizing explanations

to conceive how such a notion should have acquired currency. As soon as the Greeks began to extend their navigation into the Euxine, they would soon learn that at its eastern extremity lay the land of Colchis; and as this was the remotest region towards the east of which they had any knowledge, it would be a natural conclusion to assume that here must be that far-distant land of the rising sun, to which the celebrated voyage of the Argonauts had been directed.

§ 2. When at a later period the Milesian and other Greek colonies gradually spread themselves along the shores of the Euxine, they would continually seek to identify themselves with the interest that had gathered around so celebrated a legend, and thus we find the tale of the Argonauts mixed up with a number of local traditions, or poetic fictions, which have no more real connection with the original story, than have the settlement of Antenor and Æneas in Italy with the primitive Tale of Troy. At the same time the traditional tale adapted itself to the realities of the geography; and the voyage of the Argonauts from the Symplegades to Colchis, as we find it described in Apollonius Rhodius (in the third century B.C.), has almost the accuracy of a geographical treatise.

§ 3. But the case was very different with the return to Greece. For some reason, which it is not easy to determine, it seems to have been very early assumed that they could not, or at least did not, return by the same route which they had followed in the first instance;[6] and the ingenuity of the poets and logographers, having a wide field afforded them by the prevailing vagueness of geographical notions, was exercised in devising various routes—all equally imaginary, and equally impossible, by which the ship Argo was supposed to

---

of mythical legends of all others the most unsatisfactory, though highly popular with the Alexandrian critics and their successors. Strabo himself introduces the statement with a suspicious λέγεται.

[6] Mr. Grote suggests (*History of Greece*, vol. 1. p 344) that "it became necessary to devise another route for them on their return," in order to account for the numerous local legends connected with the visit of these maritime heroes to Libya and other places in the Mediterranean, wholly apart from the Euxine.

have effected her return to Thessaly. The original idea seems to have been that followed by Hesiod (or by one of the poets whose works were extant under his name), that the Argonauts, after attaining the object of their voyage by possessing themselves of the golden fleece, sailed *up the Phasis*, and thus passed into the Ocean stream, which was universally considered as flowing round the whole world.[7] Once embarked upon this circumfluent stream, it was not difficult to carry them wherever it was desired, and they were supposed to have followed it till they found themselves on the south coast of Libya, opposite to the Mediterranean. Here they were instructed by Medea to quit the Ocean, and they carried the Argo "over the desert surface of the land" for twelve days, until they launched it again at the mouth of the Lake Triton. This is the form in which we find the story told by the earliest extant poet who has dwelt upon it at any length, in the fourth Pythian ode of Pindar;[8] but, unfortunately, the lyric character of the composition prevents it from presenting us with anything like a continuous narrative. Another version of the story represented them as sailing up the Tanais, instead of the Phasis, and passing, by means of that river, the sources of which were still unknown, into the great northern Ocean, and thus sailing round till they re-entered the Mediterranean at its western extremity. Later writers, who were aware of the impossibility of this mode of proceeding, introduced an addition similar to that found in the other form of the legend, and described them as transporting the ship upon rollers from

---

[7] Ἡσίοδος δὲ διὰ Φάσιδος αὐτοὺς εἰσπεπλευκέναι λέγει, Schol ad Apollon Rhodium, iv. 284 In another passage (ad v. 259) the same Scholiast associates Hesiod with Pindar and Antimachus as carrying the Argonauts through the Ocean to Libya, and thence over land to the Mediterranean Ἡσίοδος δὲ καὶ Πίνδαρος ἐν Πυθιονίκαις καὶ Ἀντίμαχος ἐν Λύδῃ διὰ τοῦ Ὠκεανοῦ φασιν ἐλθεῖν αὐτοὺς εἰς Λιβύην καὶ βαστάσαντας τὴν Ἀργὼ εἰς τὸ ἡμέτερον πέλαγος γενέσθαι

[8] Pindar Pyth iv.—According to the Scholiast on Apollonius (iv 259), the historian Hecatæus introduced a variation on this version, and represented them as ascending the Phasis to the Ocean, then following the Ocean to the Nile, and descending the latter river to the Mediterranean This strange hypothesis was gravely controverted by Artemidorus and Eratosthenes

one navigable river to another, and thus reaching the outer sea.[9]

§ 4. Apparently the latest form of the legend was that with which we are in modern times most familiar, in consequence of its having been adopted by Apollonius Rhodius in his well-known poem, but which had previously found little favour with the Greeks.[1] According to this, the Argonauts, in order to elude the pursuit of the Colchians, sailed across the Euxine to the mouth of the Ister (Danube), and ascended that river as far as the point where it divided into two branches or arms, one of which flowed into the Euxine, the other into the Adriatic or Ionian Sea. This strange geographical error was, as we shall hereafter see, widely prevalent among the ancient Greeks, even at a period when such a misconception would appear impossible, and was believed even by such writers as Eratosthenes and Aristotle. It would, therefore, be readily adopted by the rationalizing critics and poets of the Alexandrian school; but it could obviously not have formed any part of the old legend, being an outgrowth, though an erroneous one, of more advanced geographical knowledge.

As if this absurdity had not been enough, Apollonius having thus brought his heroes into the Adriatic, must then conduct them up the Eridanus (which was in his time already identified with the Padus, the great river of Northern Italy), and from thence by a bifurcation similar to that assigned to the Ister, into the Rhodanus or Rhone, which they then descended to the Tyrrhenian or Sardinian Sea.[2] The object of this strange

---

[9] This was the story followed by the geographer Scymnus (ap Schol. ad Apollon iv 284), as well as by the historian Timæus (ap. Diodor. iv 56).
It is the same version, though in a very confused form, that was adopted by the author of the poem on the Argonautic expedition ascribed to Orpheus

[1] According to the Scholiast, the only writer before Apollonius who had adopted this some was one Timagetus,
the author of a work on Harbours (περὶ λιμένων); whom he cites repeatedly (Schol. ad Apollon. iv. 259, 306, 324, &c.); but his name is otherwise unknown, and we have no clue to the date at which he lived He was, however, probably a late writer. The notion of the bifurcation of the Ister was unknown to Herodotus: and does not appear until a date long subsequent.

[2] Not content with this, the poet

addition to the legend was obviously to bring them to the dwelling of Circe, whose place of abode had been long regarded as fixed on the western coast of Italy, adjoining the Tyrrhenian Sea; while her name was so inseparably associated with the legend of the Argonauts that it was thought absolutely necessary to represent them as paying her a visit. From thence they passed by the promontory of the Sirens, Scylla and Charybdis, and the Planctæ or Moving Islands, on their way home; touching also at Phæacia, as well as at Thera, Anaphe, and other points which were connected by local legends with the tale of the Argonauts.

It is natural to suppose that these Homeric localities, with their accompanying fables, were merely introduced by the poets in imitation of the Odyssey, and formed no part of the original legend. But there seems much reason to believe that there were very early legends connected with the Argonauts in the west as well as the east; and it is remarkable that the only allusion to the voyage of the far-famed ship Argo that is found in Homer is in connection with the dangers of the rocks called Planctæ, which were connected by the general consent of ancient writers with the *western* part of the Mediterranean, in common with Scylla and Charybdis, and the islands of Æolus and Circe.[3] It was precisely the conflicting character of these two sets of legends, and the necessity of attempting to reconcile them, that involved the logographers and poets in such hopeless confusion; and led to their adopting such strange geographical theories for that purpose. They had attained just sufficient geographical knowledge to see the

---

tells us that there was a third arm, leading off direct into the Ocean, which the Argonauts were on the point of following had they not been warned in time by Hera (iv. 625-642).

[3] They are distinctly placed by Homer himself (Odyss. xii 55-72) between the rocks of the Sirens and those of Scylla and Charybdis and the same view of their position is taken by Apollonius (iv. 858, 922) Strabo also tells us that Homer *invented* the Planctæ in the western sea in imitation of the Symplegades or Cyanean Rocks at the entrance of the Euxine. Later writers identified the two, and gave the name of Planctæ to the Symplegades, but this is wholly at variance with the Homeric conception. (See Nitzsch's note on the passage.)

difficulties that arose, when they attempted to combine into one narrative stories originally quite unconnected with one another, and to give a definite form to what the earliest poets and their hearers were contented to leave wholly vague and unsubstantial.

§ 5. It would be a mere waste of time to attempt to extract from these different versions of the Argonautic legend, in the form which it ultimately assumed, any indications of the primitive geographical notions with which it was associated, for we are wholly unable to distinguish these from the almost equally confused and irrational views, which were still current among the Alexandrian poets. The earliest writers, so far as we know, who treated the subject at any considerable length were Eumelus of Corinth, and the author of the poem called Naupactica; the former of whom may be assigned to a period about B.C. 761–744, while the latter may probably be referred to the same century.[4] From the very scanty fragments of them that are preserved, it is pretty clear that the general framework of the fable had already at this period assumed the form with which we are familiar; but no geographical details are cited from either poet; and the scope of their works, which was in both cases a genealogical or mytho-historical one, renders it extremely doubtful whether they troubled themselves to relate the voyage in such a manner as would have thrown any considerable light upon the subject, even if they had been preserved to us. The hypothesis of some modern writers that the poem called Argonautica, still extant under the assumed name of Orpheus, was really the production of Onomacritus, who flourished in the time of the Pisistratids, is wholly destitute of support from any ancient authority; and the work in question may safely be assigned, on its own internal evidence, to a period not earlier than the second century of the Christian era.[5]

---

[4] See Mure's *History of Greek Literature*, vol ıı p. 261, pp. 447–450; and Marckscheffel, *Hesiodı Fragmenta*, Lıps. 1840, pp. 218–223. Mr. Grote, however, assigns them to a period not less than a century later.

[5] See Note A (p. 28).

Of course it is impossible to assert that there may not have been some voyage or naval expedition at a very remote period, which attained to such a celebrity as to become the nucleus around which crystallized so many local and poetical legends; and it is difficult to explain on any other hypothesis why the original legend should assume a form so totally different from all others transmitted to us from the early ages. This is the more remarkable because the people to whom the enterprise is uniformly ascribed by the poetical traditions, in the form in which alone we possess them, is that of the Minyans, a race inhabiting Bœotia in very early ages, whose power and wealth are attested both by the Homeric poems [6] and by existing remains, but who were certainly not in historical times connected with maritime pursuits or naval enterprise. But it may be safely affirmed that, if there ever was a voyage of the Argonauts which gave rise to the traditionary tale, it was of a comparatively very limited character; and that the idea of Colchis and the Phasis was not connected with it till long afterwards. It may also be regarded as certain that it was to a great extent interwoven with legends and traditions that arose after the great extension of Greek navigation and commerce in the Euxine, which did not take place till the seventh century B.C. But to suppose the original legend to have grown up in consequence of these exploring voyages, and that the tale of the Argonauts is merely a mythical representation of the progress of Greek discovery in the Euxine,[7] not only takes no account of its inseparable connection with

---

[6] Homer, Iliad, ix. 381, where Orchomenus is cited as renowned for its wealth, in the same manner as the Egyptian Thebes He elsewhere (ii. 511) attaches to it the distinctive epithet of "Minyan"

[7] This view has been adopted by Humboldt (*Cosmos*, vol ii p. 140, Engl tians.), and by Mr Edward James in Smith's *Dictionary of Ancient Geography*, art. BOSPORUS), but to speak of the pressing forward of the Hellenic race towards the East about twelve centuries before our era appears to me a mere anachronism There is no evidence of any such tendency in this quarter until a period at least four centuries later; and the only ground for assigning it to so early a date is the wholly unsupported date affixed by the ordinary system of chronology to the Argonautic Expedition, considered as a historical fact

the Minyans, but is at variance with the fact that we know the legend of such a voyage to have been already familiar to the Greeks in the age of the Homeric poems, long before either the Milesians or Megarians had penetrated into the Euxine.

All that can be said is, that, as the legendary traditions of the Trojan War implied of necessity a state of things in which navigation had already become sufficiently familiar among the Greeks for them to transport a considerable army across the Ægean to the shores of the Hellespont, so there existed another set of traditions, unquestionably also of early date, that pointed to some enterprise of a more distinctly naval character, of sufficient importance to be connected with the names of heroes and demigods, and to become in like manner the basis upon which was accumulated a mass of mythical fictions.

NOTE A.

ARGONAUTICA OF ORPHEUS.

I SHOULD have been content to leave the consideration of the supposed antiquity of the Argonautica, as was done by K. O. Muller and Mr. Grote, as a question that had been decided beyond appeal by the successive investigations of Schneider, Hermann, and Ukert: had it not been for its having been brought forward afresh by M. Vivien de St. Martin in his recent work on the historical progress of Geography.[1] Admitting that the arguments of the German ciitics, derived from grammatical and metrical details, may be conclusive against assigning an early date to the poem in its present shape, he still maintains that it may be merely a *rifacciamento* of an earlier work, and that the poem now extant is in substance the same as that of which he ascribes the composition to Onomacritus. Two arguments appear to me conclusive against this hypothesis: the one, that, as stated in the text, this supposed *redaction* by Onomacritus of a poem on the Argonautic voyage is a pure fiction: that is to say, a mere arbitrary hypothesis, assumed without a particle of evidence. There is *some* ancient authority, though very vague and indefinite, for Onomacritus having composed hymns in the name of Orpheus, or worked up previously existing poems of a religious character into a more definite shape; and it is not improbable that the poems current under the name of Orpheus in the time of Aristophanes belonged to this class. But there is absolutely *none* for Onomacritus having handled the subject of the Argonautics, a poem of a totally different character.[2] Nor, in the

---

[1] *Histoire de la Géographie et des Découvertes Géographiques.* 8vo. Paris, 1875.

[2] Suidas, indeed, mentions a certain Orpheus *of Crotona* as having written a poem, called Argonautica (s v) And this Orpheus is evidently the same who is mentioned by another grammarian as having been associated with Onomacritus in the task of revising the poems of Homer. (Schol. ad Plaut cited by Ritschl *Die Alexandrinische Bibliothek*, p 4.) He therefore flourished in the time of the Pisistratids It is singular that more use has not been made of this statement of Suidas (*valeat quantum*), by the advocates of the early date of the poem.

second place, is there any mention of the existence of any such poem before the Alexandrian period, or indeed till long after; and the existing Scholia on Apollonius, which are of unusual fulness and value, while repeatedly referring to the different versions of the tale found in different authors, never allude to the existence of a poem on the subject under the imposing name of Orpheus. This consideration alone appears to me conclusive against its being of older date than the late Alexandrian period.

The internal evidence appears to me equally decisive. M. de St. Martin finds in it the primitive simplicity and didactic character of the earliest poets. To me it appears, in common with several distinguished critics, to have the jejune and prosaic tameness so characteristic of the declining Greek poetry of the second and third century after the Christian era. And this character is as strongly marked in the conception and mode of treatment of the subject as in the details of style and diction. For these last I must refer my readers to Hermann's elaborate dissertation, appended to his edition of the Orphica; an excellent summary of the whole subject, from the critical point of view, is given by Bernhardy in his *Grundriss der Griechischen Literatur* (2nd edition, Halle, 1856, vol. ii. pp. 347-353).

From the geographical point of view it matters little whether the poem is to be ascribed to the Alexandrian or to the Christian period. In either case it is equally worthless, and unworthy of careful examination. But the evidence that it is not (as M. de St. Martin maintains) " certainly anterior to Herodotus," appears to me overwhelming. The confusion of the writer's geography, which is regarded by M. de St. Martin as arising from his great antiquity, bears a striking resemblance to that found in several of the later geographers. It is not merely that he has erroneous ideas, even in regard to regions like the north coasts of the Ægean; that he represents the Araxes, Thermodon, Phasis, and Tanais, as all having a common origin; and that in describing the voyage from the Mæotis to the Northern Ocean, he jumbles together the names of Scythian tribes derived from all kinds of sources, and enumerates the Geloni, Sauromatæ, Getæ, and Arimaspians, among the nations dwelling around the Palus Mæotis, while he transfers the Tauri, noted for their human sacrifices, to the shores of the channel leading into the Northern Ocean. But he describes the Argonauts as passing through a narrow channel into the Ocean, " which is called by the Hyperborean tribes the Cronian Sea and the Dead Sea."

Both these names were familiar to the geographers and poets of later times;[3] but no trace of them is found before the Alexandrian period. Here they visit in succession the Macrobians, Cimmerians, and the land of Hermionia, where is the mouth of Acheron and the descent into the infernal regions : but they are especially warned to avoid the island of Ierne, in order to do which they by great exertions double the Sacred Cape, and after twelve days' voyage reach the fir-clad island, sacred to Demeter, where the poet places the fable of the Rape of Persephone. Thence in three days they come to the island of Circe, after which they pass by the Columns of Hercules into the Sardinian Sea. Here we find mentioned the customary legends of the Sirens, Charybdis, &c., but mixed up with the names of the Latins, Ausonians, and Tyrrhenians, as inhabitants of its shores. and the mention of Lilybæum in Sicily is associated with the burning Ætna, and the fable of Enceladus. It is remarkable that the "far-stretching Alps" ($\tau\alpha\nu\nu\eta\kappa\epsilon\epsilon\varsigma$ Ἄλπεις) are mentioned among the ranges of mountains—associated with the Rhipæan mountains and the Calpian ridge—that overshadowed the land of the Cimmerians, and helped to shut out from it the light of the sun. Absurd as is this statement, it shows a familiarity with the name of the Alps as a great mountain chain, though it was certainly unknown as such to the Greeks in the days of Herodotus. The mention of Ierne (or, as it is called in one passage, the Iernian Islands) is still more decisive. There is no evidence of any knowledge of the British Islands among the Greeks before the time of Pytheas, while the name of Ierne (Ireland) is not mentioned till a considerably later period.[4]

Confused and extravagant as are the geographical notions contained in the above narrative, it does not appear to me possible to pronounce upon their evidence alone, that the poem cannot belong to the Alexandrian period instead of the Roman Empire. Its assignment to the later age must rest upon considerations of style and language, as well as upon the all-important fact that no allusion to its existence is found in any ancient author, or even in any of the scholiasts or grammarians down to a very late date.

---

[3] As for instance to Dionysius Periegetes (v. 31–35), whose description of this northern ocean bears a close resemblance to that of the Orphic poet

[4] The geographical arguments against the authenticity, or supposed early date of the poem, are fully given by Ukert (*Geographie der Griechen und Römer*, vol 1 part 11), to whose elaborate dissertation on the subject I must refer my readers.

CHAPTER III.

HOMERIC GEOGRAPHY.

Section 1.—*General Views.*

§ 1. We may now proceed to consider the notions of geography entertained by the Greeks, at the earliest period when they can be regarded as possessing any real geographical notions at all. In this investigation our principal—indeed, it may be said our sole—source of information is to be found in the Homeric Poems. Whatever opinion may be entertained as to the date or mode of composition of the Iliad and Odyssey—whether we regard them as the work of one author or of several—it is certain that they represent to us the ideas and sentiments of a very early age; and we shall find as we proceed in our inquiries this character of antiquity and primitive simplicity attested not less strongly by the nature and limits of the geographical knowledge which they display, than by their evidence as to the manners, arts, and institutions of the heroic ages which they describe.[1]

In attempting to represent to ourselves, and to retrace as far as possible, the dim and vague outlines of the geographical picture that floated before the mind of the poet, and that may have been present more or less distinctly to those of his hearers, it might naturally have been thought that we should be materially assisted by the labours of the numerous commentators and interpreters who devoted themselves in ancient times to the elucidation of his ideas on this as well as on other subjects. But so far from this being the case, it will be found

---

[1] See Note A, p. 75.

that great part of the difficulties which surround the inquiry have arisen from these very commentaries, embodying, as they do, traditional interpretations of the Homeric legends, derived from a much earlier period, but of the origin or authority of which we have no knowledge whatever. There were not indeed wanting during the Alexandrian period some writers who had the boldness to assail the conclusions thus generally received, and dispute the accuracy of the traditional attributions;[2] but they appear to have found few followers, and the great authority of Strabo—a writer who in many other respects possessed a real insight into scientific geography—was unfortunately thrown into the opposite scale, and tended, to an extent that can hardly be overrated, to consolidate the fabric of the system which he found established in his time. Yet it will be found on examination that that system rests on no substantial foundation, and is in many instances opposed to the most simple and natural interpretation of the poet's meaning.

It is only quite in recent times that modern writers have shaken themselves clear of that blind reverence for the opinions of the ancients which led men to accept without hesitation the conclusions of Strabo or Pliny, and receive as established truths the interpretations that had been put upon the ideas of the poet by traditions of much later date, or by the attempts of rationalizing critics to bring them into accordance with the known facts of geography. The simple and vague ideas of Homer have been disfigured and disguised by the desire to reconcile them with the scientific knowledge of after ages, and to adapt them to a system of which neither the poet nor his contemporaries had the slightest conception.[3]

---

[2] The most prominent among these was Eratosthenes, to whose opinions on the subject we shall repeatedly have to refer. His views were also adopted by Apollodorus, and to some extent at least by Demetrius of Scepsis

[3] Crates, the celebrated grammarian and Homeric commentator, who was a contemporary of Aristarchus, was conspicuous by his attempts at this kind of interpretation (see Strabo, I. pp. 3, 5, 32, &c ' for which he is justly reproved by Geminus. (*Elem Astron.* c. 13.)

Hence in all inquiries into the Homeric geography, it is above all things necessary to divest ourselves of all these subsequent additions, and to confine our attention as entirely as possible to the words of the poet himself, and the conclusions that may be legitimately drawn from his own language.[4]

§ 2. There can be no doubt that Homer, in common with all his successors down to the time of Hecatæus, believed the earth to be a plane, of circular form, surrounded on all sides by the Ocean, which they conceived, not as a sea, but as a vast continuous stream, for ever flowing round and round the earth.[5] The vault of heaven, which he terms "brazen" or "of iron," epithets used to denote its solidity, he conceived as a solid concave surface, like the "firmament" of the Jews, of equal extent with the earth so as to rest on it on all sides.[6] But at the same time he seems to have supposed it to stand in need of some additional support, and therefore to rest upon tall pillars "which keep the heaven and the earth asunder."[7] These pillars are in the charge of Atlas, but it is not stated that Atlas himself supported the heavens, according to the notion prevalent in later times, and adopted by almost all subsequent poets. Nor is there the slightest indication of the situation of these mighty pillars; or anything whatever to

---

[4] It is one of the great merits of two of the leading writers on this subject, Volcker and Ukert, that they have adhered steadfastly to this system. Mr Gladstone has adopted the same line. and I cordially assent to his remarks upon the course to be pursued in the investigation (*Homer and the Homeric Age*, vol. iii. pp. 262–265), widely as I differ from him in respect to the results.

[5] See Note B, p. 75.

[6] This is distinctly stated by Hesiod (*Theogon* vv. 126–7).

Γαῖα δέ τοι πρῶτον μὲν ἐγείνατο ἶσον ἑαυτῇ,
Οὐρανὸν ἀστερόενθ', ἵνα μιν περὶ πάντα καλύπτοι.

There is no passage in Homer where the conception is stated with equal distinctness, but his expressions all agree with it, and it was undoubtedly the idea entertained by the Greeks down to a much later period.

[7] . ἔχει δέ τε κίονας αὐτὸς
μακρὰς, αἳ γαῖάν τε καὶ οὐρανὸν ἀμφὶς
ἔχουσιν.
Odyss. i 54

That the sense given in the text is the true meaning of ἀμφὶς ἔχουσιν, I feel no doubt, notwithstanding the different interpretation proposed by some of the commentators: and it seems most natural to translate ἔχει in the first line as "keeps" or "guards." The idea that Atlas himself held and *supported* the columns seems to have arisen from a desire to explain the passage in accordance with the myth as generally received in later times

VOL. I.

connect them with the mountain chain in the distant regions of the west, to which the name was applied by the Greeks of later ages. The statement appears, so far as Homer is concerned, as a purely mythological fiction, which has nothing to do with geography.

§ 3. It is repeatedly stated in the Homeric poems that the sun rose out of the Ocean stream, and again sank into the same at its setting.[8] How it was carried back to the point from which it was to start afresh on its course it is probable that no one in his day ever troubled himself to inquire. It is certain that no trace is found of the absurd inventions by which later poets and meteorologers endeavoured to overcome this difficulty.[9] The stars also are represented as following the same course and bathing every day in the waters of the Ocean. There was however one exception. Even the rudest observers could hardly gaze on the beautiful starry skies of Greece without noticing that there was one conspicuous group of stars—the constellation of the Great Bear—which never set, but, in the words of Homer, "keeps turning round in the same place, and alone has no share in the baths of Ocean."[1] Besides the Great Bear—which was already known by the two names of "the Bear" and "the Waggon"—Homer mentions other con-

---

[8] Iliad, vii. 421-423; viii. 485; xviii. 240; Odyssey, xix 433, &c.

It was preceded by the Dawn ('Hώs), which in like manner "arose from the streams of Ocean, to give light to immortals and to men." — Iliad, xix. 1.

[9] It is difficult to believe that the story of the Sun being carried back along the Ocean stream, reclining in a golden bowl, which is found not only in Mimnermus, but even in Stesichorus, and the logographer Pherecydes (ap. Athenæum, xi. p 469-70), could ever have been regarded as anything more than a mythological fiction. But the earlier meteorologers, according to Aristotle, got over the difficulty by supposing that the sun travelled round in the night by the north to the east, but that its course was not visible, on account of the elevation of the northern parts of the earth. (Arist. *Meteorol.* ii. 1, § 16)

[1] Ἄρκτον θ', ἥν καὶ ἄμαξαν ἐπίκλησιν καλέουσιν,
ἥτ' αὐτοῦ στρέφεται, καὶ τ' Ὠρίωνα δοκεύει,
οἴη δ' ἄμμορός ἐστι λοετρῶν Ὠκεανοῖο.
Odyss v. 273-275.

The same three lines occur also in the Iliad (xviii. 487-489). It is to be observed that in the Odyssey (*l.c.*) Ulysses is represented as steering by watching the Bear (*i.e.* the Great Bear). It would appear, therefore, that the refinement of steering by the Little Bear, or Pole Star, which is ascribed to the Phœnicians, was not yet familiar to the Greeks in the days of Homer, or at least was not yet known to the poet.

stellations; "the late-setting Bootes," and "the Pleiades, and the Hyades and the mighty Orion;"[2] but it would be absurd to suppose that because these are all that he notices by name, they were the only ones with which he was acquainted. Indeed the mention of so obscure a group as the Hyades sufficiently shows that the nomenclature of the stars was in his time pretty well advanced. The only single star that he notices is the dog-star, with the baleful influence of which he was familiar, as well as with its peculiar brightness.[3]

§ 4. We do not find in the Homeric poems any distinctive terms for the cardinal points, or four quarters of the heavens, *as such*: that is to say, he has no words answering to the simple terms, North, South, East, and West. He indeed repeatedly contrasts the two latter—which must always have been clearly marked by the course of the sun—designating the one as "towards the dawn and the Sun;" the other as "Darkness"—on account of the setting sun being immediately followed by darkness.[4] But his use of the terms is, as might be expected of a poet, especially in a rude age, somewhat vague and general, and this has actually led several writers, both in ancient and modern times, to dispute the signification of the terms, and to maintain that by the quarter or region of darkness Homer meant the north; and the south by that of the sun; a theory which is at once met by the unanswerable objection that it takes no account of the mention of the Dawn, which is in these phrases invariably associated with that of the Sun.[5] The

---

[2] Πληιάδας θ' Ὑάδας τε, τό τε σθένος Ὠρίωνος. Iliad, xviii 486. Compare Odyssey, v. 272.

[3] He calls it "the dog of Orion" (Iliad, xxii. 29) It had apparently not yet acquired the distinctive appellation of Sirius, *i e.* "the burning," which is already found in Hesiod (*Op. et Di* v. 607). The ἀστὴρ ὀπωρινὸς mentioned in v. 5 is supposed by some commentators to be Arcturus, but it is more probable that here also Sirius is meant.

[4] The one is always πρὸς ἠῶ τ' ἠέλιόν τε: the other, as opposed to it, πρὸς ζόφον, or ποτὶ ζόφον ἠερόεντα (Iliad, xii. 239, Odyssey, xiii. 240, &c)

[5] This paradox was put forward in ancient times by Strabo (x. p. 455), and apparently before him by Ephorus (ap Strab. i. p. 84). It has in modern times been adopted by Voss, who made it the foundation of his whole system of Homeric geography; but is, in my opinion, fully refuted by Volcker (*Homerische Geographie*, pp. 42–46), and has been generally rejected by the most recent inquirers (Ukert, Nitzsch,

question could not have arisen, but for the absence of any corresponding terms to designate the North and South.

The expressions employed by Homer to distinguish what we should term the quarters of the heavens, are almost always derived from the winds, the names of which must have been from the earliest ages familiar to the Greeks as a seafaring people. Of these he knew only four, which he describes as opposed to one another in pairs, and which may fairly be taken as representing in a general way the four cardinal points of the compass.[6] Boreas, the north wind, blowing from Thrace, assumes in Homer the same prominent position that it does at the present day to all navigators of the Ægean. It was the bringer of fine weather and a clear sky, but nevertheless a strong and violent wind "that rolled mighty waves."[7] Notus, the south wind, which was directly opposed to it, was a stormy wind, bringing sudden squalls dangerous to navigators. Zephyrus, the west wind, was dreaded on the same account, and is repeatedly represented as a stormy wind;[8] while Eurus, the east wind, is but seldom mentioned, and bears a subordinate part: very different from what it would have done, had the poet lived in England.

§ 5. Homer abounds in descriptions and descriptive epithets of the sea, from which a large part of his similes are taken. No

---

Buchholz, &c). Mr Gladstone, after pointing out the true meaning of the phrases, and justly adding that they must at the same time be received with a certain amount of vagueness, proceeds to argue as if they are to be taken *definitely* as corresponding to *north-west* and *south-east* (vol. III p 266), a proposition for which I cannot see the slightest foundation, though he thenceforth relies on it as an established fact The deviation from the ecliptic, to which he appeals (even if its influence be admitted), would of course give an equal amount of variation in each direction, to the south as well as to the north, of the equinoctial line of sunset and sunrise

[6] Note C, p. 77

[7] καὶ Βορέης αἰθρηγενέτης, μέγα κῦμα κυλίν-δων
Odyssey, v 296
But it was generally associated with fine weather and a clear sky (whence the epithets αἰθρηγενὴς and αἰθρηγενέτης), and is described in a remarkable passage in the Odyssey as "breaking down before it" the waves that had been raised by the other winds—
ὦρσε δ' ἐπὶ κραιπνὸν Βορέην, πρὸ δὲ κύματ' ἔαξεν
v 385
a fact familiar to all who have had much experience either of the Ægean or Mediterranean But as coming from the north it was naturally the wind that brought frost and snow (Iliad, xix 358, Odyssey, xiv. 475).

[8] See especially the passage in the

poet has ever equalled him in the knowledge he shows of its varied moods and aspects, with which every Greek was necessarily familiar. But he affords us scarcely any geographical statements concerning it. He never applies the name of Ægean, so well known to the later Greeks, to the sea between Greece and Asia: for which he had no distinctive appellation, for the same reason that the Greeks in later ages had none for the Mediterranean: it was "*the* sea," the sea which everybody knew, and had he wanted to distinguish it, he would doubtless have called it in like manner "*our* sea." But in two passages he designates smaller portions of it by the local names of the Thracian Sea and the Icarian Sea: and other such appellations were doubtless in use in his time. Hence he speaks of "every sea," as if there were many such, and tells us that all seas, as well as all rivers, were the offspring of Ocean, which was indeed the source of all the waters on the earth, even fountains and wells.[9] But the distinction between the mighty river of Ocean, and the sea which was enclosed within it, is throughout clearly maintained. The idea of the Ocean as an outer sea, separated from, but communicating with, the inner sea, was wholly foreign to the mind of Homer, and many of the difficulties and errors of his commentators have arisen from their attempting to introduce into the Homeric geography this conception of the Ocean, as it was familiar to their own minds.[1]

It must be added that no indication is found in Homer of any knowledge of the Euxine as a separate sea. He was of course familiar with the Hellespont, from its proximity to Troy, and must have known that beyond that narrow strait

---

Odyssey (xii 288-290) where the Notus and Zephyrus are spoken of as raising sudden squalls and gales such as were the cause of shipwrecks Again in the same book (v 408) there comes on suddenly "a shrilly west wind with a violent squall," κεκληγὼς Ζέφυρος. μεγάλῃ σὺν λαίλαπι θύων It is only in describing the Elysian Fields

that the Zephyrus blowing from the Ocean is represented as a gentle cooling breeze (Odyssey, iv 568):

[9] βαθυρρείταο μέγα σθένος 'Ωκεανοῖο,
ἐξ οὗ περ πάντες ποταμοὶ, καὶ πᾶσα θάλασσα,
καὶ πᾶσαι κρῆναι, καὶ φρείατα μακρὰ
ναουσιν.
Iliad, xxi 195-197

[1] This difficulty was apparently en-

there was again a broad open sea—the Propontis or Sea of Marmora—but there is nothing to show that he had any knowledge of the Bosphorus, or of the far more extensive sea beyond.[2] He supposed the Achelous to be the greatest of rivers, which sufficiently shows that not even any obscure rumour had reached him of such mighty streams as the Ister and Borysthenes.

§ 6. It is hardly necessary to mention that the primitive geography of the Homeric times knew nothing of a division of the world into three continents: and that the names of Europe, Asia and Africa, in this sense, were wholly unknown to the poet. He indeed mentions the name of Libya (as Africa was always called by the Greeks) as that of a particular region of great fertility, doubtless referring to the country west of Egypt which always continued to be known by this special designation. But he never mentions the name of Asia, even as that of a country: and though he speaks of the Asian meadows on the banks of the Cayster, this was evidently a mere local appellation.[3] The name of Europe does not occur in the poems at all.[4]

---

counted by the Alexandrian critics who, like Eratosthenes, transferred the wanderings of Ulysses to the outer Ocean, while they still retained the idea of the Ocean, such as it was known to them, instead of the deep, gently flowing, stream that Homer describes, encircling the whole world, earth, and sea alike.

[2] He was, indeed, acquainted with the river Sangarius which flows into the Euxine (Iliad, iii 187, xvi. 719), but only as a river of Phrygia, and there is no reason to suppose that he knew anything of its real outflow, or of any distinction between the Propontis and the Euxine. He knew generally that there was sea somewhere to the north, and that was all.

[3] Ἀσίῳ ἐν λειμῶνι, Καυστρίου ἀμφὶ ῥέεθρα
Iliad, ii 461

[4] It is first found in the Homeric Hymn to the Pythian Apollo (v 73, 112), which is probably at least two centuries later than the Iliad or Odyssey. But even there the name of Εὐρώπη is used only to designate continental Greece, in contradistinction to the Peloponnese and the Islands. Its extension to the continent generally was probably of much later date, though it was, as we know, already well established in the time of Hecataeus.

Section 2.—*Geography of the Iliad.*

§ 1. In proceeding to investigate the *local* geography of the Homeric Poems, and to point out the extent and character of the knowledge which they really display of different seas and lands, we may safely start from the principle which was long ago laid down by Eratosthenes, that the poet was well acquainted with the regions near at hand, but ignorant of those afar off.[5] This conclusion indeed appears at first so obvious, or rather so self-evident, that it is difficult to suppose it could ever have been contested: and it is strange to find it rejected with scorn by such writers as Strabo and Polybius. But the reverence for the supposed authority of Homer, which had arisen into a kind of blind superstition among the later Greeks, led them to regard with indignation any attempt to curtail the domain of knowledge attributed to him. He was the father of geography as well as of history, and it was held to be equally heretical to dispute his statement as to a supposed geographical fact, as to deny the reality of the Trojan War, or to doubt the personal existence of Ajax or Patroclus.

At the same time, strangely enough, this unquestioning belief in the accuracy of the poet was coupled with an equally ready admission of the popular legends which identified the localities described in the Odyssey with certain definite spots that had become familiar to Greek colonists and navigators in later times. How these attributions had at first arisen, we are in most cases utterly unable to divine; but, once established, they maintained their ground with a singular tenacity, even where they were in palpable contradiction with the statements of the poet himself. Thus the abode of Æolus was considered as fixed beyond dispute in one of the Lipari, or, as they were called by the ancients, the Æolian Islands, though Ulysses is

---

[5] Eratosthenes ap. Strab i. p. 18, vii p 298. ἐπαινεῖ γὰρ ’Ερατοσθένους ἀπόφασιν, ὅτι φησὶν ἐκεῖνος καὶ "Ομηρον καὶ τοὺς ἄλλους τοὺς παλαιοὺς τὰ μὲν Ἑλληνικὰ εἰδέναι, τῶν δὲ πόρρω πολλὴν ἔχειν ἀπειρίαν This principle was adopted by Apollodorus, which excites the indignation of Strabo.

described as sailing from thence with a west wind in a direct course to Ithaca.[6] Such a course was obviously impossible, unless we suppose him to have sailed right across the mountains of Calabria, or frankly admit that Homer was unaware of the existence of any such obstacle.

We are met by no such difficulties nearer home; and as long as our attention is confined to the shores of the Ægean Sea, and the countries that immediately adjoin it, we find the poet generally well informed, and we have sometimes clear evidence of accurate personal observation. It is only when we wander beyond this limited range, that we begin to meet with contradictions and absurdities, and statements bearing the stamp either of vague ignorance, or of palpable poetic fiction. The distinction thus established between what have been well called the Inner and the Outer Geography of Homer, coincides nearly, though not entirely, with that of the two poems. As the action of the Iliad is confined within the limits of the inner circle, and the nations represented as engaging in conflicts on the plains of Troy are the inhabitants only of the regions bordering on the Ægean, the allusions to anything beyond those limits are few and incidental, and it will be found convenient to take the geography of the Iliad in the first instance by itself, as representing the more definite portion of what was known to the Greeks in these early days, before entering on the wider field of the unknown regions opened out to us in the Odyssey. But in adopting this division of the subject, I desire not to be understood as resting it upon any other basis than convenience, or adopting the opinion of those who would assign the Iliad and Odyssey to different authors, and even consider them as separated by a considerable interval of time. So far as geographical evidence goes, I can see nothing to necessitate or to warrant such a separation.[7]

---

[6] Odyssey, x. 25–30.
[7] The treatises that have been written in modern times on the geography of Homer, especially that of the Odyssey, are so numerous as to form almost a literature in themselves.

§ 2. The most prominent place in the geography of the Iliad must undoubtedly be assigned to the Catalogue of the Ships, as it is commonly called, though it would certainly be more accurately termed the Catalogue of the Forces, with the names of the leaders under whom the several contingents were arrayed. Such an enumeration naturally gave occasion to the poet to show his accurate and minute acquaintance with the divisions of the population, such as they existed, or as he supposed them to exist, at the time of the Trojan War, as well as with the names of the cities and towns that they possessed; and as the reverence for the name of Homer continually increased, this Catalogue gradually came to be invested with a kind of official authority. At the same time this very cause afforded great inducement to interpolation, for which the peculiar character of this part of the poem presented the greatest facilities.[8] But while it cannot be denied that such interpolations may have been introduced—perhaps even to a considerable extent—two considerations appear to prove that the Catalogue in its present state is substantially the work of a very early period. The one of these is the close agreement of the names and attributes of the leaders and chiefs enume-

---

It may suffice to refer to those of Ukert (*Bemerkungen uber Homer's Geographie*, 8vo. Weimar, 1814, and in his *Geographie der Griechen u Romer*, vol 1 pp. 13–33), Volcker (*uber Homerische Geographie und Weltkunde*, Hanover, 1830), and to the valuable notes of Nitzsch on the Odyssey (*Anmerkungen zu Homer's Odyssee*, 3 vols 8vo Hanover, 1826–40) as well as the more recent investigations of Dr Buchholz (*Die Homerischen Realien*, 8vo Leipzig, 1871, vol 1.) The subject has been reopened in this country by Mr. Gladstone (in his *Homer and the Homeric Times*, vol III pp 249–365), whose views differ more widely from those of all previous inquirers than any other. Their untenable character has in my opinion been fully shown in an able article in the *Edinburgh Review* (for October, 1858), which I have reason to know to have been written by the late Mr Herman Merivale The reviewer, however, while successfully combating the novel theories of Mr Gladstone, has gone much further than I am disposed to follow him in support of the traditionary system, as handed down to us from the commentators and geographers of antiquity

[8] A well-known instance of this is mentioned by Strabo (ix 1, p 394), in regard to the two lines describing the contingent of Ajax

Αἴας δ' ἐκ Σαλαμῖνος ἄγεν δυοκαίδεκα νῆας,
στῆσε δ' ἄγων, ἵν' Ἀθηναίων ἵσταντο φάλαγγες

where the second line was asserted by the Megarians to have been fabricated by the Athenians in support of their pretensions to the island of Salamis.

rated, with the subsequent notices of them scattered through the Iliad: the other is the fact that in the enumeration of the towns from which they came, we find the names of obscure places which had dwindled into insignificance, or whose very sites were unknown in later days, freely intermingled with those of illustrious cities, whose names were familiar to all.[9] A considerable portion of Strabo's geographical description of Greece is taken up with investigating cases such as these, or explaining topographical difficulties, which could not have arisen unless the state of things described by the poet had been separated by a considerable interval from the historical period of Greece.

As might well have been expected, the Catalogue contains very little geographical information, properly so called: it is a mere enumeration of names and places, with but rarely any reference to their geographical position, beyond what is implied by their being included in a given nationality.[1] But that by which it is especially characterized is the number and variety of the epithets applied to the different towns enumerated: epithets sometimes of an ordinary character, and frequently repeated; in others singularly distinctive and appropriate. Such are the terms of "well-walled" (or more literally "wally"), applied to Tiryns;[2] of "abounding in doves," to Thisbe, in Bœotia;[3] and the "hollow Lacedæmon cleft with

---

[9] Thus Strabo himself says in regard to Laconia: τῶν δ' ἄλλων τῶν ὑπὸ τοῦ ποιητοῦ κατωνομασμένων τὰ μὲν ἀνῄρηνται, τῶν δ' ἴχνη λείπεται, τὰ δὲ μετωνόμασται while he admits that some could not be pointed out at all (οὐδαμοῦ δείκνυσθαί φασι), viii 5, p. 364.

[1] Sometimes, however, the poet adds a few words indicating the position of a town with reference to a mountain or river. Thus he describes Lilæa as situated at the sources of the Cephissus (ii 523), Tarphe and Cronium on the banks of the Boagrius (ib. 533), Pheiæ by the lake Bœbeis (ib 711), and the Magnesians as dwelling around the Peneus and the wooded Pelion (ib. 757).

[2] Τίρυνθά τε τειχιόεσσαν
Iliad, ii 559.
The only other city to which the same epithet is applied, is Gortyna in Crete (ib 646), where, however, there are no remains of Cyclopean walls.

[3] πολυτρήρωνά τε Θίσβην
Iliad, ii 502
The abundance of wild pigeons in the rocks of this locality is attested both by Colonel Leake (*Northern Greece*, vol. ii. p 507) and Sir Thomas Wyse (*Impressions of Greece*, p. 85), as well as by Strabo. The same epithet is applied to Messe in Laconia (v 582), but the exact locality is in this instance uncertain.

glens;"[4] a description which, from its recurrence in the Odyssey, was probably become one in general use. Indeed it may always be doubtful whether the distinguishing epithets that we find in Homer were selected by himself, or had already become traditional from their employment by earlier poets.[5] Be this as it may, we must take the case as it stands. It is impossible for us now to determine how far the Homeric Catalogue was based upon previously existing materials, as well as to what extent it may have been interpolated in later ages. If we cannot accept its authority with the blind deference shown by the later Greeks, we must receive it as a document of the highest interest from its antiquity, but which it is impossible for us to criticize or dissect, from the total absence of the requisite materials.

§ 3. Of a very different character from the Catalogue of the Greek forces, is that of the Trojans which follows it, and which has very much the appearance of being a subsequent addition to the poem. Its meagre and jejune treatment of the subject presents a striking contrast to the fulness and richness of the Greek Catalogue, and it is as inferior to the latter in geographical interest as in poetic merit. But it was universally admitted in ancient times as an integral part of the Iliad; so much so, indeed, as to be made the subject of an elaborate commentary by Demetrius of Scepsis, a work extending to not less than thirty books.[6] We must, therefore,

---

[4] κοίλην Λακεδαίμονα κητώεσσαν
Iliad, ii 581
The signification of this last epithet, which occurs both in the Iliad and Odyssey (iv 1), but only as applied to Lacedæmon, would be uncertain, but for the very peculiar character of the scenery there, which (as Mr. W. G. Clark justly observes, *Peloponnesus*, p 156) at once helps one to the meaning of the word.
[5] This is suggested by Mr. Clark (Ibid. p 210), and appears to me almost certain. Such an habitual application of distinguishing epithets is characteristic of all early ballad poetry,

such as must have preceded the Iliad or the Odyssey
[6] Strabo not unnaturally expresses his wonder at the diffuseness of a writer who devoted thirty books to a commentary on little more than sixty lines of Homer (xiii 1, p 603). But from the quotations preserved to us it is evident that it comprised much valuable matter, and Demetrius appears to have been one of the writers who shared in those more sceptical views regarding the Homeric geography, which were viewed with so much disfavour by Strabo himself.

be content to include this also in our estimate of the Homeric geography, though not without a passing protest.[7]

§ 4. The most interesting question, in a geographical point of view, that arises from the two Catalogues is, the extent of the knowledge which they evince of the countries adjoining the Ægean, for all that is comprised within their limits may be assumed to have been well known to the poet. It cannot, on the other hand, be affirmed that all beyond these limits was unknown, or at least imperfectly known, though we shall find reason to believe that his real knowledge extended but little farther. The description in the Catalogue extends over all continental Greece, including the Peloponnese and Thessaly, but excluding Epirus and Acarnania. It comprises, moreover, the islands on the west, opposite to Elis, Cephallenia, Ithaca, and Zacynthus, as well as Dulichium and the Echinades nearer to the mainland; and all the islands in the south of the Ægean—not only the important islands of Crete and Rhodes, but Carpathus, Cos, and even such insignificant islets as Casos, Syme, Nisyros, and the Calydnæ—being distinctly mentioned by name. On the other hand, none of those which might be thought especially the Greek islands, viz. the Cyclades, and those connected with them, are mentioned as sending a contingent to the Greek forces, though it cannot be doubted that Homer was well acquainted with them.[8] In like manner we know that he was familiar with those near the coast of Thrace, Lemnos, Imbros, and Samothrace,[9] as well as

---

[7] It is a strong argument against the authenticity of this portion of the poem, that the *Cypria* of Stasinus, a work which seems to have been composed with especial reference to the Iliad, contained also a catalogue of the Trojan forces, a strangely inappropriate addition, if the one now extant was then found in the Iliad (Welcker, *Der Epische Cyclus*, vol ii p 508, Mure's *History of Greek Literature*, vol ii p. 281)

[8] No allusion is found in the Iliad to the island of Delos and its celebrated sanctuary. But it is incidentally referred to in the Odyssey (vi 162), and its non-occurrence in the Iliad may well be accidental

[9] It is scarcely necessary to refer to the well-known passage in Mr Kinglake's *Eothen*, in which he points out the accurate local knowledge displayed by Homer in selecting Samothrace as the point from whence Neptune looked down upon the plains of Troy; an idea wholly at variance with the natural presumption from its position on a map.

SECT. 2.   HOMERIC GEOGRAPHY.   45

with the great mountain promontory of Athos. If we now take up the Trojan Catalogue we shall find it describing in detail only the Troad and its immediate neighbourhood, but enumerating also contingents from the opposite coasts of Thrace, including the Pæonians from the banks of the Axius, a stream which the poet describes as "the fairest that flows upon the earth."[1] The auxiliary forces from the Asiatic side were naturally more numerous: these were the Mysians, Phrygians, Mæonians—whose site in Lydia is marked by the Gygæan Lake and Mount Tmolus—the Carians, with whom are associated "the streams of Mæander and the lofty summits of Mycale" and the Lycians, who came "from the far Lycia and the banks of the eddying Xanthus." These were the farthest people to the south. To the north we find mention of the Paphlagonians, occupying apparently the same region as in historical times; and beyond these the Halizones "from Alybe afar, where is the birthplace of silver."[2] Whether these were the same people subsequently known as the Chalybes, was a point much disputed among ancient authors: at all events we must clearly place them to the east of the Paphlagonians, and may therefore safely assume that Homer (or, at least, the author of the Trojan Catalogue) was acquainted by name with the nations on the south coast of the Euxine as far as the Halys, though the name of that river does not occur in the poems.

§ 5. But if the limited area thus circumscribed may be taken as including all, or nearly all, of which the poet of the Iliad can be shown to have any definite knowledge, there are not wanting indications that point to an acquaintance, however vague, with far more distant regions. And the very fact that these notices are for the most part merely incidental,

---

[1] Ἀξιοῦ, οὗ κάλλιστον ὕδωρ ἐπικίδναται αἶαν
   Iliad, ii 850
[2] τηλόθεν ἐξ Ἀλύβης, ὅθεν ἀργύρου ἐστὶ γενέθλη
   Ibid 857
For the discussions raised concerning it, see Strabo, xii. pp. 549-553 The name of the Halizones had disappeared in later times, but it is found in another passage in the Iliad (v. 39), so that it does not rest only on the dubious authority of the Trojan Catalogue.

points the more strongly to their being notions already familiar to the poet himself, and which he might conceive to be equally well known to his hearers. One of the most remarkable of these passages is that in which he describes Zeus as turning away his eyes from the battles before Troy to gaze on "the land of the horse-loving Thracians and the close-fighting Mysians, and the noble Hippemolgi, who live on milk alone, and the Abii, the most virtuous of mankind."[3] It is a question that has been much disputed, and that cannot be decided, whether the terms Hippemolgi, "milkers of mares;" Glactophagi, "feeders on milk;" and Abii, "men without property,"[4] are used by the poet as proper names, or only as descriptive adjectives,[5] but in any case it is clear that the poet was vaguely acquainted by hearsay with the fact that beyond the mountains of Thrace were to be found extensive plains, over which roamed wandering tribes, having the peculiarity that they subsisted mainly on the milk of their mares, instead of that of cows or sheep. This characteristic has in all ages distinguished the Scythian tribes, that is, the nomad races of Central Asia, or who have passed over from thence into Europe, and was familiar to the Greeks in later times. But neither the name of Scythians, nor that of any of the

---

[3] νόσφιν ἐφ' ἱπποπόλων Θρηκῶν καθορώμενος αἶαν
Μυσῶν τ' ἀγχεμάχων καὶ ἀγαυῶν Ἱππημολγῶν
γλακτοφάγων, Ἀβίων τε, δικαιοτάτων ἀνθρώπων.
Iliad, xiii 4–6.
The Mysians here mentioned are evidently the European people of the name, the same afterwards known to the Romans as the Moesians, from whom, according to the belief universally prevalent among Greek writers, the Mysians of Asia Minor derived their origin.

[4] Ἄβιοι, literally, "men without the means of life," i.e. with poor and scanty means" ὀλιγόβιοι, εὐτελεῖς γάρ εἰσι καὶ ἁπλοῖ τὴν δίαιταν, Eustath ad loc The idea of their justice and virtue was evidently derived from their simple and frugal habits of life; and continued to prevail among the Greeks through all ages, though applied sometimes to one nomad tribe, sometimes to another (see Æschylus, Prometh. Solut Fr 184, Arrian, Anabasis, iv. 1).

[5] See the subject fully discussed by Strabo, vii 3, §§ 2-10, and by Eustathius, ad Iliad l c. The analogy of such names as Ichthyophagi, Troglodytæ, Macrobii, &c, which were certainly used by the Greeks as Gentile appellations, is in favour of their being so in this case also; and accordingly we find that the Hippemolgi and Abii were generally regarded as such. But little or no value can be attached to the usage of later writers in this respect, in interpreting the language of Homer.

subordinate divisions of that great people which we meet with in Herodotus and Ephorus, is to be found in Homer.

§ 6. In regard to the countries lying to the south and east, there are many more indications of knowledge, and even in a certain sense of familiar intercourse with the civilized nations at the south-eastern angle of the Mediterranean—the Phœnicians and Egyptians. To the former people, indeed, as has been already shown, the Greeks were indebted for almost all their foreign trade; and they must have been therefore quite familiar with the name, as well as with the articles exported from thence.[6] But not only does Homer represent Paris as possessing many valuable things of Phœnician manufacture, but he distinctly describes him as having brought them himself from Sidon, "after having sailed over the broad sea."[7] He was apparently regarded as having been driven there by a violent storm, in the same manner as Menelaus was in the Odyssey; but in both cases it is clear that the poet looked on such an adventure as not improbable. In the case of Egypt again, though accidentally the name of the *country* does not occur in the Iliad, we find an incidental reference to the Egyptian Thebes, which shows that exaggerated rumours of its wealth and grandeur were already familiar to the poet. In the ninth book Achilles alludes, as the acme of all imaginable wealth, to that which was stored up within the houses of the Egyptian Thebes, "a city that had an hundred gates, through each of which there passed every day two hundred men with

---

[6] It is remarkable, as has been frequently pointed out, that the name of "Phœnician," though of frequent occurrence in the Odyssey, is only once found in the Iliad; the manufactured articles are always called "Sidonian," and Paris is described as bringing them from Sidon. But this is easily accounted for by the preponderance of the capital. The name of Tyre is not found in either poem.

[7] ἔνθ᾽ ἔσαν οἱ πέπλοι παμποίκιλοι, ἔργα γυναικῶν
Σιδονίων, τὰς αὐτὸς Ἀλέξανδρος θεοειδὴς
ἤγαγε Σιδονίηθεν, ἐπιπλὼς εὐρέα πόντον.
Iliad, VI 288-291

As the poet places this visit on his return voyage from Sparta, after having carried off Helen (*ib.* 292), it has been sought to connect it with the story, adopted by Euripides and Herodotus, of Paris having touched in Egypt also on his return; but there is nothing to warrant this assumption, except that it is more probable he should have been driven, like Menelaus, to Egypt, than direct to the Phœnician coast.

their horses and chariots."[8] Even these fabulous tales are sufficient proof that the Greeks in the time of Homer had intercourse, more or less direct, with Egypt, as we shall find more clearly shown in the Odyssey.

§ 7. Through Egypt also was unquestionably derived the notion of the Æthiopians (burnt or black-faced men), who must have been regarded as dwelling beyond the Egyptians to the south, on the borders of the Ocean stream. The utterly vague and fabulous character of all that was known concerning them is sufficiently shown by the fact that they are never mentioned except in connection with the gods, who were supposed to repair to the banks of the Ocean to feast on the sacrifices offered by them.[9] Equally vague is the indication of another people, the Pygmies, who were also supposed to dwell by the shores of the Ocean stream, where they were engaged in continual wars with the cranes, who migrated thither to fly from the winter and the storms of Greece.[1] The notion of the existence of such a race of dwarfs in the interior of Africa, which was long prevalent among the Greeks, and has recently been shown to be not altogether without foundation,[2] could only have reached the Greeks of Homer's time through an Egyptian channel.

---

[8] οὐδ' ὅσ' ἐς Ὀρχόμενον ποτινίσσεται, οὐδ' ὅσα Θήβας
Αἰγυπτίας, ὅθι πλεῖστα δόμοις ἐν κτήματα κεῖται,
αἵ θ' ἑκατόμπυλοί εἰσι, διηκόσιοι δ' ἀν' ἑκάστας
ἀνέρες εἰσοιχνεῦσι σὺν ἵπποισιν καὶ ὄχεσφιν.
Iliad, ix. 381–384.

Diodorus (i. 45) asserts, as if he had undoubted authority for the fact, that Thebes, in the days of its greatness, *really did* possess 20,000 war chariots.

[9] Iliad, i. 428; xxiii 206. Precisely the same notion is found in the Odyssey also (i. 22–25, v. 282).

[1] ἠύτε περ κλαγγὴ γεράνων πέλει οὐρανόθι πρό,
αἵ τ' ἐπεὶ οὖν χειμῶνα φύγον καὶ ἀθέσφατον ὄμβρον,
κλαγγῇ ταί γε πέτονται ἐπ' Ὠκεανοῖο ῥοάων,
ἀνδράσι Πυγμαίοισι φόνον καὶ κῆρα φέρουσαι
Iliad, iii 3–6

It is evident that the tradition here alluded to is one that the poet assumes to be familiar to all.

[2] Rumours of the existence of a race of dwarfs in the interior of Africa have from time to time reached the ears of modern travellers, as they penetrated farther and farther into the continent. Quite recently (1870) M. Schweinfurth has established beyond a doubt the fact that such a race is really found adjoining the tribe of Nyamnyam in Central Africa They are known by the name of Akka, and have many points of resemblance with the Bushmen of Southern Africa. It is not improbable that such tribes were once more widely diffused, and may well have come within the cognisance of the Egyptians. (See Schweinfurth's *Travels in the Heart of Africa*, vol ii. ch. xvi., and Keith Johnston's *Africa*, p. 241.)

SECTION 3.—*Geography of the Odyssey.*

§ 1. Few and scanty as are the allusions in the Iliad to distant regions and countries, they are still sufficient to show that the author of that poem was well aware of the existence of an outer world, beyond the limits of that to which the view of the Greeks was in his day habitually confined. This outer world is far more fully opened to our view, though still enveloped in the dim haze of uncertain distance, in the Odyssey, and especially in that part of the poem which has always been the most attractive and the best known. The wanderings of Ulysses, as related by himself to the Phæacians, have had a charm for all readers of all ages from the times of Homer to our own: and few, very few comparatively, have been those who have paused to enquire what slender foundation of truth might underlie these delightful fictions, and whether the scenes of his adventures were real localities disguised under a thin veil of poetic ornament, or were mere creations of fancy, as shadowy and unreal as the Elysian Fields or the gloomy realms of Hades. One point, indeed, may be taken as universally admitted. The legendary and mythical tales, which received their definite embodiment in the Odyssey, were not the creation of the poet. The names of the Sirens and Circe, of Scylla and Charybdis, of the Lotus-eaters and the Læstrygones, were already familiar to the Greeks before they were wedded to immortal verse by Homer: and there can be no doubt that the Wanderings of Ulysses, like the Voyage of the ship Argo, had formed the subject of many a rude ballad, before they were worked up into a polished and coherent narrative by the author of the Odyssey. It is especially necessary to bear this in mind, in attempting to investigate the questions concerning the geographical foundation of the story as we find it there related: or rather to enquire how far there existed any such foundation at all. We must represent to ourselves the poet as having to deal with a mass of heterogeneous materials: sometimes obscure reports gathered from

Phœnician mariners of the marvels of the "far west;" others purely mythological fables of unknown origin; others again traditional tales belonging to that border-land of truth and fiction, in which it has become impossible for after ages to discern the boundary.

All this he had to work up into one poetic whole, and no one can dispute his success; but when it has been maintained, both in ancient and modern times, that he undertook also to work it up into one geographical system, it may well be asked whether he had any geographical system at all? The ancient writers, indeed, for the most part believed that in this respect, as in all others, Homer was the master-spirit and guide to all learning,[3] and Strabo expressly describes him as the founder of scientific geography and the precursor in this department of Anaximander and Hecatæus.[4] But it is strange that the same erroneous estimate of the scope and character of such a poem as the Odyssey should prevail even in our own day, and that one of the latest attempts to investigate its geography should be based upon the assumption that Homer had present to his mind an elaborate and complicated map of the wanderings of Ulysses, utterly without foundation in fact, but as distinct and definite as a chart of the voyage of Magellan or Vasco de Gama.[5]

---

[3] "Il maestro di color che sanno"
Dante, *Inferno*, canto iv v 131
The expression is, however, applied by the Italian poet with better judgment to Aristotle.

[4] Strabo, i. 1, where he distinctly asserts that geography is a branch of philosophy, and that all those who had taken it up—among whom he gives the first place to Homer—were τοιοῦτοί τινες, *i.e.*, men of a philosophical turn of mind.

[5] This appears to me to be the fundamental fallacy, pervading all Mr. Gladstone's system of Homeric geography. According to his own statement: "The question before us is what map of the earth did Homer shape in his own mind, that he might adjust to it the voyages of his heroes, Menelaus and Ulysses" (vol. iii. p. 250) But what right have we to assume that he shaped any such map at all? The use of maps was not introduced into Greece till centuries after the time of Homer; and all experience shows that it is only by the habitual use of maps that men come to form clear conceptions of the geographical relations and relative positions of different countries. Without this training I believe it to be impossible for any one to frame in his own mind any system of such geographical relations, as between distant countries; though he may clearly picture to himself those of neighbouring lands and islands, such as the shores of the

§ 2. We have already seen how deeply rooted among the ancients, both Greeks and Romans, was the belief that attached the names of the Homeric localities to particular places, well known in later times. How these attributions had grown up in the first instance, we are in most cases utterly unable to conjecture. In some they were probably local legends or myths that had some kind of resemblance to those that were found in the Odyssey, and they were in consequence eagerly laid hold of in order to connect the particular localities with names that were celebrated throughout the Greek world. It is certain that they rarely, if ever, arose from any geographical attempt to explain or account for, the wanderings of the hero, in accordance with the statements of the poet.[6] On the contrary, it has been already observed that these popular attributions were in many cases in direct contradiction with the text; and later writers in vain struggled to reconcile the two. The only safe course that can be pursued in this enquiry is to discard in the first instance all those commonly received identifications, and simply follow the statements of Homer, pointing out where they really afford some clue to their own interpretation, and where they are clearly at variance with the ideas that have been commonly attached to them.

§ 3. The voyage of Ulysses, on his return from Troy, began of course in the well-known waters of the Ægean, and here the account is, as might be expected, clear and consistent. He was driven in the first instance, by unfavourable winds, to the land of the Cicones on the coast of Thrace:[7] a people who appear in the Iliad among the Trojan allies,[8] and with whom

---

Ægean, which he within the range of his own experience and observation.

[6] The only exception would be the fixing on Gaudos (Gozo) as the island of Calypso, if we are to understand Strabo's words (vii. 3. p 299) as implying that Callimachus was the first to make this attribution, but it appears probable that in this case, as in that of Scheria, he merely adopted the popular tradition.

[7] Ἰλιόθεν με φέρων ἄνεμος Κικόνεσσι πέλασσεν
Odyss ix 39

[8] Iliad, ii 846 According to Herodotus (vii 59), the Cicones inhabited the coast land about Doriscus and the mouth of the Hebrus, but they were extinct as a people in the time of the historian

Ulysses engaged in hostilities. Sailing again from thence, he had a north wind (Boreas) which would have been favourable for his course, but its increasing violence drove him to seek shelter on the land, *where* we are not told : nor have we any hint as to his course from thence, except that it was a direct course with a fair wind (evidently, therefore, still a north wind), as far as Cape Malea, where the violence of the wind, and of the waves and current, drove him out to sea, and prevented his seeking shelter under Cythera.[9] Here we have a very characteristic trait, Cape Malea having been renowned in all ages for sudden and violent storms, so that its circumnavigation has been always regarded with dread both by Greek and other mariners. In the Odyssey itself it is twice again mentioned as having caused similar disasters.[1]

From thence they were driven "by wicked winds" for nine days over the open sea.[2] A voyage of that length would undoubtedly carry a Greek navigator of those days altogether out of the sphere of his knowledge, and accordingly when on the tenth day they arrived in the land of the Lotophagi, we find ourselves at once within the limits of that outer world, all statements concerning which were more or less mixed with fable. But in this case the existence on the north coast of Africa of a people who subsisted mainly on the fruit of the lotus-tree, was found in later times to be a well-established fact ; and the sweetness of the fruit was supposed to have given rise to the fable of its making people forget their country.[3] Some notion of this might easily have been gained from Phœnician navigators, nor is it impossible that even a Greek ship might have been really driven there, as Ulysses

---

[9] ἀλλά με κῦμα ῥόος τε περιγνάμπτοντα Μάλειαν
καὶ Βορέης ἀπέωσε, παρέπλαγξεν δὲ Κυθήρων
Odyss ix. 80-81

[1] First Menelaus, then Agamemnon, is described as being driven out of his course by violent squalls while doubling Cape Malea (iii. 287, iv. 514). The same incident is introduced in the fictitious narrative of Ulysses (xix.

187) Its evil repute in ancient times is attested by numerous passages, and in modern days will be familiar to all who have ever navigated the Ægean.

[2] ἔνθεν δ᾽ ἐννῆμαρ φερόμην ὀλοοῖς ἀνέμοισιν,
πόντον ἐπ᾽ ἰχθυόεντ᾽ αὐτὰρ δεκάτῃ ἐπέβημεν,
γαίης Λωτοφάγων, οἵ τ᾽ ἄνθινον εἶδαρ ἔδουσιν
Ibid ix. 82-84

[3] See Polybius (xii. 2), who describes it from personal observation

was supposed to be. And as he was driven off in the first instance from Cape Malea by a north wind, the natural inference would be that the land of the Lotus-eaters was somewhere away to the south. Hence there is nothing improbable in the supposition, which has been adopted by almost all commentators and geographers, that in this instance the fable had a foundation in fact, and that the Lotophagi were really situated somewhere on the north coast of Africa.

But we are not entitled to go farther, and assume that Homer had a definite idea of the position of the Lotus-eating people. Later writers either placed the Lotophagi on the coast between the Lesser and the Greater Syrtis,[4] or restricted them more specially to the island of Meninx,[5] the beauty and fertility of which would appear to correspond to the poetical idea of the country of the Lotus-eaters, and where the Lotus shrub actually grows in great abundance.[6] But it is most unlikely that the poet had anything more than a vague and general idea that the Lotophagi dwelt to the west of Libya, with the name of which, as we have seen, he was also acquainted.

§ 4. With the next step we plunge into complete uncertainty. We are told only: "From thence they sailed on, grieving in their hearts, and came to the land of the Cyclopes;"[7] whom the poet proceeds to describe as a lawless, cruel race, ignorant of agriculture and of all the other arts of life, dwelling in caves, but inhabiting a fertile land, which produced all kinds of grain without the need of cultivation. They were wholly unacquainted also with navigation, so that when Ulysses and his companions landed on a small island, opposite to the mainland, they found it full of wild goats which lived there

---

[4] Scylax, § 110.
[5] Strabo, 1 2, § 17
[6] See Barth, *Wanderungen durch die Kustenlander des Mittelmeeres*, vol 1 pp 259-265, Guérin, *Voyage Archéologique dans la Régence de Tunis*, vol 1. pp. 203-207.
[7] ἔνθεν δὲ προτέρω πλέομεν, ἀκαχήμενοι ἦτορ κυκλώπων δ' ἐς γαῖαν ὑπερφιάλων, ἀθεμίστων,
ἱκόμεθ' Odyss ιx 105-107

The assumption of Volcker that it was only one day's voyage from the land of the Lotophagi is certainly not justified. The poet indeed tells us that they arrived at the Island of Goats *in the night* (v. 143); but there is nothing to show that this was the *first* night after they left the Lotophagi.

unmolested. Here also the greater part of his ships remained in safety, while Ulysses, with the crew of one vessel, went through his memorable adventures in the cave of Polyphemus.

That the land of the Cyclopes was Sicily, and that they dwelt on the slopes of Mount Ætna facing the sea, has so generally been believed, both in ancient and modern times, that it had become, as we know from the Cyclops of Euripides, as fixed an article of popular faith in his day, as it was in that of Virgil.[8] Yet it is certain that there is nothing in the Odyssey to lead to that conclusion. There is no indication either of the distance or the direction of the voyage from the land of the Lotus-eaters thither: and it is scarcely necessary to add that neither the name of Sicily, nor that of Ætna, is found in Homer. Nor is there any island adjoining this coast at all correspondiug to that described as abounding in wild goats. To this it must be added, that Homer elsewhere (as we shall see) speaks of an island ealled Thrinakia, which has been almost universally identified with Sicily: and not only is there nothing to connect this with the land of the Cyclopes, but the two appear in the mind of the poet to have been wholly separate. These difficulties have led some writers in modern times to reject the view, which seems to have been universally adopted in antiquity, placing the Cyclopes on the east coast of Sicily, and to transfer them to the south-west coast of that island, or else to the opposite mainland, the southern extremity or *toe* of Italy.[9] Both hypotheses are equally devoid of any adequate support. All we can say is, that Homer conceived the Cyclopes as dwelling in a mountainous land of considerable extent,[1] somewhere to the west

---

[8] The Cyclops of Euripides is full of allusions to the site of his cave among the rocks of Ætna (see vv 20, 56, 82, 101, &c). In the Æneid its proximity is noticed at the very outset of the narrative

"Portus ab accessu ventorum immotus, et ingens
Ipse, sed horrificis juxta tonat Ætna ruinis"
iii 570

[9] Volcker (*Homerische Geographie*,

pp 110–113) maintains the former theory, Ukert (*Geographie*, 1 p 23) the latter, though with a reasonable expression of doubt Forbiger and Buchholz follow Volcker.

[1] Not only does Homer expressly call it "The *land* of the Cyclopes," like ' the *land* of the Lotophagi,' not the "island", as he terms the abodes of Æolus, Circe, and Calypso, but he elsewhere tells us that the Phæacians,

of Greece, and apparently to the north of the land of the Lotophagi.²

§ 5. The next stage in the progress is equally obscure and indefinite. Again "they sailed on, grieving in their hearts;" grieving for the loss of their companions, though rejoicing to have themselves escaped from death.³ But not a word as to the direction or duration of the voyage. We are only told that they arrived at the island of Æolus, where that hero dwelt in patriarchal state with his six sons and six daughters, in a floating island, which was girt all around with an impenetrable wall of brass, and with smooth rock rising up on high.⁴ He was appointed by Zeus to be the guardian of the winds: and being favourably disposed to Ulysses, after entertaining him hospitably for a month, he sent him forth on his voyage again, having tied up all the winds in a bag, which he committed to his charge; except only the west wind, Zephyrus, which was to send him on his way. With this favouring wind they sailed for nine days and nine nights, and on the tenth day they were already within sight of their native land, when Ulysses fell asleep, his companions opened the bag, and all the winds rushing forth produced a storm, which drove the ships back all the way to the island of Æolus.⁵

There is perhaps no incident in the whole poem more glaringly fabulous than that just related. Yet several modern inquirers have attached importance to the statement that the voyage from the island to Ithaca was one of ten days' duration with a west wind: and it must be admitted at least that it shows the marvellous island to have been situated in the poet's mind at a considerable distance to the west of Ithaca.⁶ It was

---

before migrating to Scheria, had dwelt in the open country of Hypereia, near to the Cyclopes, whose violence had compelled them to remove. (Odyssey, vii 4-8.)
² This last inference rests upon the assumption that the navigators, having been driven out of their course to the south, would try to rectify their position by steering towards the north; a legitimate inference in the case of a real voyage; but of very questionable application in regard to a fictitious one
³ Odyss. ix. vv 565-6.
⁴ Αἰολίην δ' ἐς νῆσον ἀφικόμεθ' ἔνθα δ' ἔναιεν
Αἴολος Ἱπποτάδης, φίλος ἀθανάτοισι θεοῖσιν,
πλωτῇ ἐνὶ νήσῳ · πᾶσαν δέ τέ μιν περὶ τεῖχος
χάλκεον, ἄρρηκτον λισσὴ δ' ἀναδέδρομε πέτρη
Ibid. x 1-4
⁵ Ibid x 14-55
⁶ Those who consider that every

almost as settled a conclusion among the ancients that the island of Æolus was one of the remarkable group of volcanic islands to the north of Sicily, to which they in consequence gave the name of the Æolian Islands, as that the Cyclopes dwelt at the foot of Ætna; though the two assumptions were in fact incompatible:[7] and it was equally impossible to reconcile the position thus assigned to the magic isle of Æolus with the account of the voyage from thence to Ithaca, as given by the poet himself.[8] It cannot indeed be denied that some of the Lipari Islands—especially Stromboli, the one selected by popular tradition in the time of Strabo and Pliny as the abode of the ruler of the winds[9]—have something in their form, and in the steepness with which they rise out of the middle of the sea, that may serve to recall, if not to suggest, the idea of the island girt with a wall of brass and a smooth precipice of rock all round. But even if it be admitted that some exaggerated account of this appearance, as transmitted through Phœnician traders, may have given rise to one part of the fable; there can be no doubt that Homer had no real idea of its situation, and simply conceived it as lying a long way off, in the middle of the sea, to the west of Ithaca. Of its position with respect to Sicily or to the land of the Cyclopes, he had apparently no idea whatever.

§ 6. With the ill-fated return of the hero to the island of Æolus begins a new series of adventures. That personage having refused to furnish any further assistance to one who was

---

statement of the poet is to be construed literally and strictly, naturally point out that the duration of the voyage from the island of Æolus to Ithaca is the same as that from Cape Malea to the land of the Lotophagi, so that Ulysses would have exactly "made up his lee way." I cannot believe that the "nine days and nine nights" is in either case anything more than a vague and general expression.

[7] It is evident that had the Cyclopes dwelt at the foot of Ætna, Ulysses could not have passed from thence to the Æolian Islands, without either passing through the strait between Scylla and Charybdis—which he did not do until a much later period—or circumnavigating the whole of Sicily, a most improbable assumption. But this difficulty, like all others connected with the vulgar attributions generally adopted was overlooked by almost all ancient writers.

[8] See above, p 39

[9] Strabo, vi 2, § 6, 11, p 276, Plin N. H iii 9, § 94

evidently hated by the gods, the winds were unfavourable, and it was only after six days and nights of laborious rowing that Ulysses and his companions reached the city of Lamus, the king of the Læstrygones, which had a land-locked port, guarded at the entrance by two projecting rocks.[1] Here again nothing is told us of the direction of the voyage: and the utter vagueness of the *data* for determining the place of abode of the Læstrygones—a people of giants and cannibals, as obviously fabulous as the Cyclopes—is sufficiently proved by the fact that the prevalent opinion among the Greeks assigned them to Sicily,[2] while the Romans transferred them to Formiæ on the coast of Campania.[3] Both suggestions may be safely dismissed as utterly without foundation. Nor is there any clue to afford grounds for a more plausible conjecture.[4]

§ 7. After the destruction of the greater part of his ships by the giant Læstrygones, Ulysses with one vessel only "sailed on"—as usual without affording us any indication of the direction of his course, or the length of his voyage—till he came to the island of Æa, the abode of the goddess Circe, the sister of "the wicked-minded Æetes."[5] The purely mythical character of everything connected with Circe and her island, is evident, not only from the adventures encountered by Ulysses and his companions, but from her being styled a goddess, like Calypso, and from her connection with Æetes, a being as clearly mytho-

---

[1] Odyssey, x vv 80-90 Nothing can be more distinct or graphic than the description of this haven, which is evidently the original copied by Virgil in the first book of the Æneid (vv. 159-169) Yet the one is in all probability as purely a creation of the poet's fancy as the other

[2] What is still more extraordinary, the current tradition placed them near Leontini, in the interior of the island. (Strabo, 1. p 20, Plin. *N H.* iii 8, § 89)

[3] Plin. iii 5, § 59 The same tradition is frequently alluded to by the Roman poets Yet the beautiful bay of Formiæ (the Gulf of Gaeta) is as unlike as can well be to the description in the Odyssey On the other hand, I was told by Colonel Mure that the little bay of Sapri, on the coast of Calabria, not far from Policastro, was the very image of the port of the Læstrygones as described by Homer Others have found a striking similarity in that of Balaklava !

[4] Note D, p 77

[5] αὐτοκασιγνήτη ὀλοόφρονος Αἰήταο
                      Odyss x 137.

The epithet ὀλοόφρων is applied also to Atlas, as the father of Calypso (Odyss i 52), in both cases it appears to indicate a being of supernatural powers, to be dreaded as such

logical as Atlas. And of all the attempts to give a "local habitation" to the legends related in the Odyssey, none is more absurd than that which attached the name to the Circeian promontory, on the coast of Italy, which is not an island at all.[6] Whether the idea arose from the identification of the magician goddess with some local divinity of similar attributes, or from a mere casual resemblance of name, we are wholly unable to decide.[7] Equally impossible is it to attempt any other determination of an island of which nothing is told us that is not on the face of it purely fabulous. We can only assume that, as the poet represents the abode of Circe as the place from whence Ulysses took his departure for the gloomy realms of Hades, he must have conceived it as situated *towards* "the region of darkness;" that is, the west or north-west.[8]

It is certainly not worth while to enquire what geographical idea the poet formed in his own mind of this visit to the regions of Hades, or to attempt to define the locality of the Cimmerians, whom he describes as wrapped up in mist and cloud, and overshadowed by perpetual night, never beholding the sun either as he ascends the heavens, or as he declines towards his setting.[9] They dwelt *upon the Ocean*

---

[6] Yet we find Pliny seriously writing "Circeii quondam insula immenso quidem mari circumdata (ut creditur Homero), at nunc planitie" (*H N* iii. 5, § 57) The same statement was already made at a much earlier period by Theophrastus (*Hist Plant* v 8, § 3), but he judiciously reports it only as the tradition of the natives, while Pliny gravely infers that all the intermediate and surrounding land was a recent addition.

[7] It is certain, however, that traditions connected with Circe had attached themselves to Latium at a very early period, as we find her introduced as the mother of Agrius and *Latinus* in a passage of Hesiod (*Theogon* v 1011–1013), which, though it is almost certainly a subsequent addition to the poem, cannot be referred to a late date.

[8] See Note E, p 78 The only thing we are told of it is that it was surrounded by a boundless sea —
νῆσον, τὴν περὶ πόντος ἀπείριτος ἐστεφάνωται
Odyss x 195

[9] ἣ δ' ἐς πείραθ' ἵκανε βαθυρρόου Ὠκεανοῖο
ἔνθα δὲ Κιμμερίων ἀνδρῶν δῆμός τε πόλις τε,
ἠέρι καὶ νεφέλῃ κεκαλυμμένοι· οὐδέ ποτ' αὐτοὺς
ἠέλιος φαέθων καταδέρκεται ἀκτίνεσσιν,
οὔθ' ὁπότ' ἂν στείχῃσι πρὸς οὐρανὸν ἀστερόεντα,
οὔθ' ὅτ' ἂν ἂψ ἐπὶ γαῖαν ἀπ' οὐρανόθεν προτράπηται,
ἀλλ' ἐπὶ νὺξ ὀλοὴ τέταται δειλοῖσι βροτοῖσιν
Ibid xi 13–19

It is remarkable that Circe, when she was indicating to Ulysses his route to the abode of Hades (x 506–510) says nothing of the Cimmerians, with whom also the hero and his companions have no intercourse, they are only mentioned in passing, in the lines above cited.

stream, but whether on the nearer side, or beyond its waters, is a point upon which the ancient interpreters were divided, and the language of the poet appears ambiguous. One thing only is clear; the voyagers had to navigate the Ocean stream itself, into which they passed, and from which again they passed into "the sea," on their return, without any difficulty, or any explanation.¹ The supposition that they must have passed through a strait, like that which really leads from the Ocean into the Mediterranean, rests upon no foundation at all, and belongs to an order of ideas wholly different from that which was present to the mind of the poet.²

§ 8. From the island of Circe, Ulysses set out on his homeward voyage, after having been duly instructed by the goddess with regard to the dangers that awaited him, and beset his course. The first of these was that of the Sirens, who seduced all passers-by with the sweetness of their songs. After this came the choice between two routes; the one passing by the Planctæ, rocks of the most formidable character, from the terrific surf that broke at their foot, with which is associated, though in a very obscure manner, the mention of fire and smoke.³ Their aspect was indeed so alarming, that Ulysses and his companions preferred passing wide of them, and following the other route, although this involved the necessity of passing between Scylla and Charybdis, of the perils of which the hero had been sufficiently warned by Circe. They however succeeded in accomplishing the passage with the loss

---

¹ xi 9-13, 639-640; xii. 1-2 The passage *into* the Ocean is very obscurely indicated in the first of these passages, as well as in the preliminary directions given by Circe (*l c*), but the contrast at their *exit* is more clearly marked:

αὐτὰρ ἐπεὶ ποταμοῖο λίπεν ῥόον Ὠκεανοῖο
νηῦς, ἀπὸ δ' ἵκετο κῦμα θαλάσσης εὐρυπόροιο
Odyss xii 1, 2

² This appears to be the error in which Eratosthenes and other ancient investigators found themselves, who transferred the wanderings of Ulysses into the Ocean, that they could not divest themselves of their more scientific ideas on the subject, and were consequently obliged to explain how he *got back again* into the Mediterranean, a difficulty that evidently never presented itself to the mind of the poet. The same fallacy pervades still more strongly the views of Mr Gladstone and the marvellous map in which he has embodied his conception of this part of the Odyssey.

³ See Note F, p. 79.

of only six of their number, and arrived without further obstacle at the sacred island of Thrinakia, which was occupied by the consecrated herds of the Sun (Hyperion), under the guardianship of two nymphs, his daughters. These herds Ulysses had been especially warned not to touch, but being detained in the island a whole month by contrary winds,[4] his companions yielded to the pressure of hunger, and slaughtered and ate some of the sacred cattle: an act of impiety, which was soon punished when they again set out on their voyage, their ship being caught in a violent storm, and shivered to pieces by a thunderbolt. Ulysses alone contrived to float upon a portion of the wreck, and was again driven through the strait, where he narrowly escaped the dangers of Charybdis; after which he was carried along for nine days and nights, till he arrived at the island of Calypso.

No portion of the wanderings of Ulysses is more familiar to all readers than that just related. The dangers of Scylla and Charybdis are become as proverbial as the cup of Circe and the songs of the Sirens. The locality assigned to them by tradition was as definitely established as in most other cases; but in this instance alone could it be shown to be based upon physical phenomena, which had a real existence, and which might easily have given rise to exaggerated fables such as those related by the poet. The navigation of the Straits of Messina must really have presented considerable difficulties and dangers to the mariners of early days: and these dangers were in part of a character wholly unknown elsewhere, arising from the complicated action of the tides and currents produced by the meeting of the waters of two great seas in a narrow and crooked

---

[4] In this instance the winds are specified with unusual definiteness. the south wind (Notus) blew for a whole month without ceasing, nor was there ever any wind, except from the east or south (Eurus or Notus) (xii 325–326) But it appears from verse 400 that it was the violence of these winds as much as their direction, if not more, that prevented them from sailing. When they at last set out with fair weather, and are out of sight of land, they are caught by a sudden gale from the west (Zephyrus, ib 408), and, after that abates, there arises a south wind (Notus), by which Ulysses is driven back to Charybdis (ib. 427).

channel.⁵ Nothing like the eddies resulting from these causes is to be found elsewhere in the Mediterranean, as the Straits are the only place where the tides are felt with such strength and regularity: a phenomenon frequently noticed by the ancients, and which they correctly sought to bring into connection with the Homeric accounts of Charybdis.⁶ It may be added that anything in the nature of a whirlpool appears in all ages to have been peculiarly subject to exaggeration, and the fables related of the Maelstrom in Norway, and even of Corrievrechan in the Hebrides, are scarcely inferior to those current among the Greeks concerning Charybdis.⁷ We may, therefore, safely assume that in this case the descriptions of the poet—exaggerated and extravagant as they undoubtedly are—rested upon a certain basis of fact: and that in associating the dangers of Scylla and Charybdis with the Straits of Messina, the tradition of later days was not a mere random attribution, like that of the islands of Circe and Calypso, but was derived, like that of the Lotophagi, from real information, however vague, and disfigured by fabulous additions.

But it would be wholly unwarranted to assume that because Homer had really heard some vague account of Scylla and Charybdis, he had therefore any definite idea of their situation, and knew that the strait between them was that which separated Italy and Sicily. He appears to have placed them

---

⁵ The real nature of these dangers is stated with great clearness by Thucydides (iv 24) ἔστι δὲ ὁ πορθμὸς ἡ μεταξὺ ʽΡηγίου θάλασσα καὶ Μεσσήνης, ᾗπερ βραχύτατον Σικελία τῆς ἠπείρου ἀπέχει, καὶ ἔστιν ἡ Χάρυβδις κληθεῖσα τοῦτο, ᾗ ʼΟδυσσεὺς λέγεται διαπλεῦσαι· διὰ στενότητα δὲ καὶ ἐκ μεγάλων πελαγῶν, τοῦ τε Τυρσηνικοῦ καὶ τοῦ Σικελικοῦ, ἐσπίπτουσα ἡ θάλασσα ἐς αὐτὸ, καὶ ῥοώδης οὖσα, εἰκότως χαλεπὴ ἐνομίσθη.

The present phenomena of the Strait, and the action of the tides and currents within them, are fully described by Admiral Smyth (*The Mediterranean*, pp. 178–182), who admits that the difficulties of the navigation are such as might reasonably have given rise to the reputation of its dangerous character.

⁶ Strabo, 1 2, § 36, pp 43–44.

⁷ In both these cases the danger is, however, a reality, though, as in the case of Charybdis, varying much with the circumstances of wind and tide See the description of Corrievrechan in Anderson's *Guide to the Highlands of Scotland*, p 76, 3rd edit, and an excellent account of the Maelstrom, by Dr. Charlton, cited in Murray's *Handbook for Norway*, 3rd edit. 1871.

somewhere in the "far west," like the islands of Æolus and Circe; to enter into any more precise examination of the locality was as foreign to the mind of the poet as to that of his hearers. Hence it would be idle to take this identification as a fixed point from which to attempt to determine the others that are more or less connected with it. All these must indeed be left in a state of utter uncertainty. The name of Thrinakia —the sacred island of the Sun—was generally regarded by the ancients as identical with that of Trinacria, which, according to a tradition generally received, had been the ancient appellation of Sicily;[8] and they therefore did not hesitate to suppose that the island meant by the poet was Sicily itself. But to say that the voyagers, after passing through the Straits between Scylla and Charybdis, came to the island of Thrinakia, would on this supposition be as strange a mode of expression as to say that a modern captain, after sailing through the Straits of Dover arrived at the island of England! And, what is more conclusive, Thrinakia is distinctly described as a small island, devoid of inhabitants, and having no natural resources, except the sacred flocks and herds, so that the companions of Ulysses were in actual danger of starvation, when they had recourse to the sacrilege.[9] Hence it seems clear that, whatever may be the explanation of the name, the island of Thrinakia had no connection with the large and fertile island of Sicily.

§.9. Of the island of Calypso, to which the poet gives the name of Ogygia, it may safely be asserted that it is altogether as

---

[8] This tradition is referred to as an established fact by Thucydides (vi 2), and was followed by Strabo and all later writers Yet it may well be doubted whether the name of Trinacria was ever in use, except among the Greek poets and logographers. It could certainly never have been a national appellation, and it is most unlikely that such a name as "the three-cornered" was ever in use, even among mariners, for so large an island as Sicily, the triangular shape of which could only have been known when it came to be much visited, and its coasts fully explored. Timæus, it appears, maintained that its original name was Thrinakia (ap. Schol Apollon iv. 965), and it seems very probable that both names were in reality mere inventions, in order to connect it with the Homeric Thrinakia The name of Sicania for Sicily is found elsewhere in the Odyssey, but only in the last book (xxiv. 307), which is generally regarded as of later date than the rest of the poem

[9] Odyss xii. 325–373.

vague and visionary as that of Circe. It was situated "in the centre of the sea;"[1] far out of the way of all resort, and unvisited alike by deities and mortal men.[2] Ulysses is represented as arriving there after drifting for nine days and nine nights (the ever recurring number) on a fragment of wreck from Charybdis.[3] On the other hand, it is apparently more than twice that distance from Phæacia; for on his departure he is represented as sailing for seventeen days with a favourable breeze, and on the eighteenth coming in sight of "the shadowy mountains of the Phæacian land."[4] This much only may be affirmed with certainty, that the poet conceived the island of Calypso as situated a long way off *to the west of the Phæacians*. For he distinctly tells us that the nymph had warned the hero, in steering his course across the vast expanse of open sea that he had to traverse, " to keep the constellation of the Great Bear steadily on his left hand;"[5] that is to say, to steer from west to east. This is the only allusion in either poem to steering by the stars; and it is the most definite indication to be found in the Odyssey of the course pursued, or supposed to be pursued, by the wandering hero. Yet, strange to say, it has hardly been accepted in its plain and obvious

---

[1] νήσῳ ἐν ἀμφιρύτῃ, ὅθι τ' ὀμφαλός ἐστι θαλάσσης
Odyss 1 50
The use of ὀμφαλός in this sense as the centre or middle point of the sea, is obviously derived from its application as the boss in the centre of a round shield. In like manner in later times Delphi was called "the navel of the earth" (ὀμφαλὸς τῆς γῆς, Strabo, ix. p. 419)
[2] Ibid. v. 101, 176
[3] He was driven by a south wind (Notus) to Charybdis. If we are entitled to assume that he afterwards continued the same course, we must place the island of Calypso to the north of the Strait; and this has been generally done by the modern writers who have attempted to arrange the localities of the Odyssey (see Volcker, p. 121), though wholly opposed to the popular tradition which identified it with Gaulos, or Malta.

[4] ὀκτωκαιδεκάτῃ δ' ἐφάνη ὄρεα σκιόεντα, γαίης Φαιήκων.
Ibid. v 280.
It may be observed that Homer always uses the expression "the *land* of the Phæacians" He never calls it an island, like those of Æolus, or Circe, or Calypso, which shows that he considered it as a tract of considerable extent This does not, however, exclude the idea of its being a large island like Sicily or Crete.
[5] τὴν γὰρ δή μιν ἄνωγε Καλυψώ, δῖα θεάων, ποντοπορευέμεναι ἐπ' ἀριστερὰ χειρὸς ἔχοντα
Ibid v 277
The lines immediately preceding contain the description of the constellation of the Great Bear, which has been already quoted (note to p. 34).

sense by any of the geographical commentators on the poem; one has understood it as indicating a course to the *north-east*, another to the *south-east*, in order to accord with their preconceived hypotheses concerning the relative positions of Ogygia and Scheria.[6] It seems much more simple to understand the words as pointing only to the broad fact that Ulysses was returning from the far west, and that his voyage must therefore have had a general direction from west to east.[7] The unusual length of the voyage across the open sea would render it especially necessary to steer by watching the stars, and this may account for the practice being mentioned in this instance only.

§ 10. We are now arrived at the last stage of the protracted wanderings of Ulysses. It was a predetermined arrangement of the gods (as the poet tells us), that he should not be conducted to his native home either by gods or men, but by the Phæacians, a semi-divine people, who partook of the qualities of both.[8] Hence, when he was at length permitted by Calypso to quit her enchanted island, his voyage was directed, not straight to Ithaca, but to Scheria, the land of the Phæacians, where he ultimately landed in safety, notwithstanding the storm raised by Poseidon. Here, therefore, the difficulties of the hero's voyage were at an end: and here also, if we adopt the popular view, there is an end of all geographical difficulties in connection with it. That the island of Scheria was the same that was afterwards known as Corcyra was the established belief in ancient times;[9] and has continued to be as generally received in modern days: and though it is admitted that the

---

[6] See Note G, p. 81.

[7] I say a *general* direction, because there is no ground to believe that in this, any more than in other passages in the Odyssey, did the poet mean to designate any precise quarter of the heavens, or quadrant of the circle, with the accuracy of a modern manual of sailing directions, as has been too often assumed by the commentators.

[8] Φαιήκων ἐς γαῖαν, οἱ ἀγχίθεοι γεγάασιν
Odyss v. 35.

In the same manner Alcinous speaks of the Phæacians as favoured by the gods:—

. . ἐπεί σφισιν ἐγγύθεν εἰμέν,
ὥσπερ Κύκλωπές τε καὶ ἄγρια φῦλα Γιγάντων
Ibid. vii. 206

[9] We find it already referred to as such by Thucydides (i. 25).

people of the Phæacians had disappeared before historical times—a conclusion, indeed, not obscurely intimated by the poet himself—it is still supposed that the place of their abode can be determined without a doubt, and that local peculiarities which occur in the poet's description may be still traced in the island of Corfu.[1]

Even in ancient times, however, there were to be found a few critics who raised the voice of scepticism with regard to this popular attribution, as well as to most similar identifications;[2] and attention has been repeatedly drawn by modern scholars to the strong tinge of mythical colouring which is cast around everything connected with the Phæacians.[3] Not only were they closely connected with the gods, but they were in the habit of receiving frequent visits from them, and associating with them on equal terms.[4] On the other hand, they dwelt afar off, out of the way of all mortal visitors;[5] their skill in navigation was of a distinctly supernatural character;[6] and the circumstances of the voyage when they conduct

---

[1] This is stated particularly strongly by the Edinburgh Reviewer (p. 522), but very few of the visitors to Corfu share his enthusiasm on the subject. Colonel Mure is sceptical. Dr. Schliemann, with his usual enthusiasm, finds everything in precise accordance with Homer. The result of my own observation is entirely in accordance with that of Colonel Mure. Without denying that some resemblance may be traced to the Homeric description, if we *assume* the identity, I certainly can see nothing of a character that would in itself lead one to such a conclusion.

[2] Eratosthenes appears to have led the way, and was followed by Apollodorus, who reproached Callimachus with having identified the island of Gaudos with that of Calypso, and *Corcyra with Scheria*; a thing excusable, as he considered, in the vulgar, but not in a writer like Callimachus, who claimed to be a man of learning (καὶ τοῖς μὲν ἄλλοις συγγνώμην εἶναι, Καλλιμάχῳ δὲ μὴ πάνυ, μεταποιουμένῳ γε γραμματικῆς ὃς τὴν μὲν Γαῦδον Καλυψοῦς νῆσόν φησι, τὴν δὲ Κόρκυραν Σχερίαν—Strabo, vii 3, § 6, p 299

[3] This has been most ably and fully worked out by Welcker in his memoir, *Die Homerischen Phaaken und die Inseln der Seligen* (reprinted in his Kleine Schriften, vol ii), but the same view has been adopted by several other writers in recent times, Nitzsch, Bursian, &c. The Phæacians are, indeed, placed by Homer himself on the same level with the Cyclopes and the Giants (Odyssey, vii. 206), and all three races must be regarded as equally mythical. (See Preller, *Griechische Mythologie*, vol i pp 387-395)

[4] Odyssey, vii. 201-206.

[5] Ibid. vi. 204-205.

[6] Ibid. viii. 556-564. Their ships had no need of steersmen or rudders, but knew of their own accord where they were to go, and held their way wrapped in mist and darkness, performing even the longest voyages within a single day.

Ulysses to his native land—the nocturnal voyage and the landing him while fast asleep—seem as if expressly designed to mask the transition from the land of fable in Phæacia to the realities of Ithaca. In the same manner the prophecy as to their future extermination and the destruction of their city,[7] is calculated to transport them into the realm of the ideal, and to show that they were to be regarded as a mere poetical creation, not a really existing people. As usual, we are wholly at a loss to explain the reasons that led the Greeks in early times, notwithstanding all these peculiar characteristics, to treat the Phæacians as a historical people, and to identify the Homeric Scheria with the island of Corcyra, which was situated within less than 100 miles of Ithaca, and directly opposite to the coast of Thesprotia, which is repeatedly mentioned in the Odyssey, but never in connection with the Phæacians. But whatever may have been the origin of this tradition, it was strongly encouraged and perpetuated by the Corcyræans themselves, after the establishment of the Corinthian colony in that island (about B.C. 735). Having speedily risen to a prominent position as daring and successful navigators, they asserted their claim to be recognized as the representatives, if not the lineal descendants of the Phæacians of Homer.[8]

No clue is afforded us in the Odyssey to the position of Scheria with respect to Ithaca: indeed, the passage between the two appears (as already pointed out) to be intentionally veiled in mystery. The only statement that brings the island of the Phæacians into connection with any known point in geography, is that of Eubœa being the most distant land to which they had ever had occasion to convey a wandering guest:[9] an expression which certainly appears to point to their being situated on the *western* side of Greece.

We must, therefore, be content to banish the kindly and hospitable Phæacians, as well as the barbarous Cyclopes and

---

[7] Odyssey, xiii. 172–184.
[8] This is expressly stated by Thucydides in the passage already cited (i. 25). [9] Ibid. vii. 322.

Læstrygones, to that outer zone of the Homeric world, in which everything was still shrouded in a veil of marvel and mystery. We can as little explain in the one case as in the other, what gave rise to the original legend that has been amplified by the creative genius of the poet into the form with which we are all familiar. The attempt to find a substantial basis of reality, either for these, or for the other legendary tales introduced into the Odyssey, is in almost all instances utterly futile, and it is still more idle to endeavour to arrange them in accordance with any preconceived geographical system, or assign a definite and rigorous meaning to expressions which were doubtless employed by the poet in a mere vague and general—that is to say, in a *poetical* sense. In the very few cases in which it is probable that some slender basis of fact did really underlie the fictions that he presents to us—the Lotophagi and the Strait of Scylla and Charybdis are the only instances in which its existence can be plausibly traced—it is clear that any such notices were accompanied by no definite indications of locality, and there is no reason to suppose that Homer attached any more correct geographical notions to the one set of legends than to the other.

§ 11. In passing from the land of the Phæacians to Ithaca, we might fairly presume that we were passing also from the ideal to the real—from the unknown to the known. It might, indeed, be naturally supposed that the poet of the Odyssey would be as familiar with the island home of his hero and the geography of the group of islands that surround it, as the poet of the Iliad undoubtedly was with that of the Troad and the adjacent islands. It is strange, therefore, to find, that instead of his notices of them being marked by the same clear and definite conception of their position and geographical relations, which is displayed in many other instances, we are met by difficulties which have been a stumbling-block to the commentators in all ages, and have never yet received a satisfactory solution. Ithaca itself, is, indeed, correctly described as pre-eminently rugged and rocky, abounding in goats, but altogether unsuited for rearing or keeping horses.¹ In it was a mountain, called Neriton, " waving with foliage;" an epithet wholly inappropriate at the present day, but which may probably have been applicable in early times. But in the only passage in which the poet undertakes to describe its position with respect to the surrounding islands, " Dulichium and Same and the wooded Zacynthus," which lie, as he tells us, all round it, very close together, he adds: " Ithaca itself lies low, the farthest off of all, in the sea, towards the west, and the others away towards the dawn and the rising of the sun."² This certainly appears to be the obvious sense of the words, though, as usual, they have been distorted by the grammarians and commentators both in ancient and modern times; in the vain hope to reconcile them with the real circumstances of the case. Ithaca certainly is not a low island; as the poet himself tells us, it contains a conspicuous mountain, or rather two,³ and instead of lying to the west of the others of the same group and afar off, it is situated to the north-east of Cephallenia, between the larger island and the mainland, but almost close to the former, from which it is separated only by a narrow strait. The only real solution of the difficulty appears to be, to admit that Homer was not personally acquainted with the group of islands in question, and that, though familiar with their names, and with some of their leading natural characteristics, he had an indistinct and

---

¹ Hence Telemachus declines the offered present of Menelaus of horses and a chariot, as wholly useless to him
ἐν δ' Ἰθάκῃ οὔτ' ἄρ' δρόμοι εὐρέες, οὔτε τι λειμών,
αἰγίβοτος, καὶ μᾶλλον ἐπήρατος ἱπποβότοιο,
οὐ γάρ τις νήσων ἱππήλατος οὐδ' εὐλείμων,
αἳ θ' ἁλὶ κεκλίαται· Ἰθάκη δέ τε καὶ περὶ πάσεων.
Odyss iv 605–608
² ναιετάω δ' Ἰθάκην εὐδείελον ἐν δ' ὄρος αὐτῇ
Νήριτον, εἰνοσίφυλλον, ἀριπρεπές ἀμφὶ δὲ νῆσοι
πολλαὶ ναιετάουσι, μάλα σχεδὸν ἀλλήλῃσιν,
Δουλίχιόν τε, Σάμη τε, καὶ ὑλήεσσα Ζάκυνθός·
αὐτὴ δὲ χθαμαλὴ πανυπερτάτη εἰν ἁλὶ κεῖται
πρὸς ζόφον, αἱ δε τ' ἄνευθε πρὸς Ἠῶ τ'
Ἠέλιόν τε   Odyss ix 21–26
The sense of πανυπερτάτη as meaning " the farthest out to sea," is clearly established by such passages as Odyss. III 170   Eustathius explains it as ἐσχάτη
³ Colonel Leake, who was unprised pared for it, remarked with surprise on entering the Gulf of Molo " To the right rises with extreme steepness the great mountain of Anoi, which, being the highest and greatest in the island, we can have no difficulty in identifying with the Neritum of the poet" (Northern Greece, vol III p 24) It attains to a height of 2625 feet, while that called Merovughi or S Stephanos in the southern portion of the island rises to 2200 feet

erroneous conception of their geographical position. As a confirmation of this may be mentioned his description of the little island of Asteris, between Ithaca and Cephallenia, which is certainly as unlike as possible to the rock of Daskalio, the only islet to which it can possibly refer.[4]

§ 12. A still graver difficulty in connection with the same group of islands, is the repeated mention of one called Dulichium, for which no representative can be found. And in this case the difficulty is enormously increased by the circumstance that Dulichium appears in the Iliad also, in the catalogue of the ships,[5] where it figures as a district of sufficient importance to send forty ships to the war, while Ithaca, Cephallenia and Zacynthus together furnished only twelve. It must, therefore, have been a large island, and is elsewhere described as fertile, abounding in wheat, and affording good pasturage.[6] Yet the name had totally disappeared in the historical times of Greece, and as early as the time of Hellanicus it was a question what was the island designated. Strabo supposed it was one of the group of islets or rocks, called the Echinades, lying close to the mainland off the mouth of the Achelous;[7] and most modern writers have acquiesced in the same conclusion, assuming at the same time, that it extended its dominion over the neighbouring tract of the mainland, which would be justly designated as abounding in wheat and grass.[8] It must be

---

[4] See the remarks of Leake (*l c* p 46), Col. Mure (*Tour in Greece*, vol 1 p 62), and Sir G Bowen (in Murray's *Handbook for Greece*, p 89), as well as of Sir W. Gell (*Ithaca*, p 78) The point is one of little importance in itself, except as serving to confirm the other evidence of the poet's imperfect acquaintance with the group of islands in general. The case is very much the same as if some one who had heard of the Needles in connection with the Isle of Wight, transformed them into islands such as Sark and Herm

[5] Iliad, ii. 625. It is here associated with "the sacred islands of the Echinæ, which are situated across the sea, opposite to Elis:" obviously the same more commonly known as the Echinades; but the name of the latter does not occur in the Odyssey.

[6] πολυπύρου, ποιήεντος.
Odyss xiv. 335; xvi 396

[7] Strabo, x. p. 458.

[8] This is the view adopted by Colonel Leake (*Northern Greece*, vol. iii p 51), but he strangely adds that "there is no proof in the Iliad or Odyssey that Dulichium, although at the head of an insular confederacy was itself an island." This is true of

admitted that the explanation is a forced one, and it seems far more simple to suppose that the island intended was that of Santa Maura, the only other large island in the group, which was known in the historical ages of Greece as Leucadia, but is never mentioned by that name in Homer. On that supposition, the poet would in this instance be free from geographical inaccuracy, and would enumerate the three principal islands in the natural order of their occurrence.[9]

§ 13. It is certain that there is no passage in the Odyssey which shows that sort of clear and distinct conception of the geography of Western Greece and the adjoining islands, which we find displayed in regard to the Eastern (or Asiatic) shores of the Ægean. When Nestor described himself and the other Greek chiefs as halting at Lesbos, and pondering on the long voyage before them "whether they should sail outside of Chios, direct to the island of Psyria, keeping it on their left hand, or within Chios, by the lofty Mimas," and ultimately running with a strong wind straight across to Geræstus in Euboea—we feel that the poet is describing a voyage with which he was himself familiar, and his expressions are as precise as they are correct when applied to the real geography.[1] Nothing like this is to be found in regard to the western sea. The Thesprotians are frequently mentioned, as are also the Taphians, but there is no distinct indication of their locality,[2] any more than of that of Temesa, to which the

---

the passage in the Catalogue of the Ships, but in the Odyssey the enumeration of the three islands

Δουλίχιόν τε Σάμη τε καὶ ὑλήεσσα Ζάκυνθος,

which occurs *three times* in the course of the poem, is *in every instance* preceded by a statement terming them all alike islands. (Odyss 1 246; ix. 24, xvi. 123) Yet Mr Gladstone is content to accept an explanation, suggested by some ancient writers, that the *three* islands were in fact *two*, and that Dulichium and Same were only two names for different portions of Cephallenia

[9] See Note H, p. 81.
[1] ἐν Λέσβῳ δ' ἔκιχεν δολιχὸν πλόον ὁρμαίνοντας,
ἢ καθύπερθε Χίοιο νεοίμεθα παιπαλοέσσης,
νήσου ἐπὶ Ψυρίης, αὐτὴν ἐπ' ἀρίστερ' ἔχοντες,
ἢ ὑπένερθε Χίοιο, παρ' ἠνεμόεντα Μίμαντα.
Odyss iii 169-172

The occurrence of this passage *in the Odyssey* is especially worthy of notice, as showing that the author of that poem was as well acquainted with the west coast of Asia Minor as the author of the Iliad, and therefore tending *pro tanto* to confirm the common authorship of the two poems.
[2] The Thesprotians always retained

Taphian chief was bound in quest of brass.³ Everything is vague and indefinite, with the exception of the island of Ithaca itself, the localities of which are described with a minuteness essential to the conduct of the poem. Here, indeed, many modern writers have found, as they considered, unmistakable evidence of the poet's accuracy, and of his personal acquaintance with the scenes which he describes; but it may well be doubted whether these topographical details are of a character to warrant such an inference, or to outweigh the argument to be drawn from the geographical difficulties just pointed out.⁴

§ 14. Besides the far-famed voyage of Ulysses, there is a brief notice in the Odyssey of the wanderings of another Greek hero, which cannot be passed by without mention, though they have attracted, particularly in ancient times, considerably more attention than they deserved. We are told that Menelaus, like Ulysses, was driven out to sea in attempting to double Cape Malea, and a part of his ships were carried to Crete, while the remainder, with Menelaus himself, were driven as far as Egypt. Here he remained a considerable time, and entered into friendly relations with the kings of the country,⁵ but he made also excursions (apparently of a predatory kind) to the neighbouring lands, and visited all the countries that surround the eastern head of the Mediterranean. He himself tells Telemachus that he had wandered to Cyprus, Phœnicia, and Egypt, and had visited the Æthiopians, the

---

their name, and continued to inhabit the southern part of Epirus, and there is no reason to doubt that they did so in the days of Homer. Nor is there any ground for rejecting the tradition, generally adopted in later times, that the Taphians, who appear repeatedly in the Odyssey as a trading or piratical people (Odyss. i. 181; xiv 452; xv. 427; xvi. 426), were the inhabitants of the three small islands between Leucadia and the mainland, now known as Meganisi, Kalamo, and Kastus; though the name had disappeared in historical times, and the islands had sunk into insignificance. (Strabo, x. p. 459.) But there is no geographical statement in the poem from which this can be clearly inferred: and no mention is found of the Taphians in the Catalogue of Ships.

³ Odyss. i. 184. The supposition that the Temesa here mentioned was situated in the island of Cyprus seems to me utterly improbable.

⁴ See Note I. p. 83.

⁵ Ibid. iv. 125–130, 226–230.

Sidonians, and the Erembi, as well as Libya, "where the lambs acquire horns directly after birth, and sheep bring forth young three times in the year."[6] The country here meant was evidently the Cyrenaica, the fertility of which was celebrated in ancient times, and which always continued to be specially known to the Greeks as Libya. Cyprus, Phœnicia, and Egypt, of course, occasion no difficulty. But it is otherwise with the Æthiopians and the Erembi. The Æthiopians, as the commentators well know, dwelt far in the interior, above Egypt, and could not have been visited by sea; while the Erembi were otherwise wholly unknown. But Menelaus may well be supposed to have seen some race of black men, whom he took for Æthiopians; and though the name of the Erembi was not found in later times, it may probably have been used to designate some of the wild Arab tribes dwelling on the borders of Egypt and Syria.[7]

But though the poet here treats of Egypt as a land comparatively familiar, and we elsewhere find him representing a voyage from Crete to Egypt as an ordinary undertaking,[8] it is clear that his knowledge of the country was very imperfect. He was unacquainted with the name of the Nile, which he calls only the river Ægyptus;[9] and, though he had heard of the isle of Pharos, he placed it in the open sea, a full day's voyage from the land.[1]

§ 15. With the exception of the passage just cited, the Æthiopians appear, in the Odyssey as in the Iliad, only as a semi-fabulous people, to whom the gods of Olympus resorted

---

[6] Odyssey, iv 81-86
[7] See the discussion of these names and the difficulties connected with them in Strabo (i 2, §§ 31-35) The prevalent conclusion, to which Strabo himself inclines, was that the name of the Erembi was only distorted from that of the Arabes The latter form was apparently known to Hesiod.
[8] See the account given by Ulysses in his assumed character of a Cretan, of the voyage which he undertook to Egypt (Odyss xiv. 246, &c.); for though the narrative is a fiction, it is obviously intended to be in accordance with ordinary experience. In the same narrative we find a voyage from Phœnicia to Libya alluded to as an ordinary occurrence. (Ibid. v. 293)
[9] Ibid iv 581 , xiv. 257.
[1] This is unquestionably the natural meaning of the words in which it is described by the poet (iv 353-357), though, as usual, the commentators have tried to explain it away, because it was at variance with the real state of the case.

from time to time to feast on hecatombs of slaughtered bulls and lambs.² In one passage, however, we find the remarkable addition to this notice, that they were divided into two portions, or nations, both of them dwelling at the extreme limits of the inhabited world, the one towards the setting, the other towards the rising sun.³ This would appear to show that some obscure notion of the existence of black races, both in the east and west of Africa, had already reached the ears of the poet. We shall find this notion of the two races of eastern and western Æthiopians — based originally upon this very passage of Homer—pervading the geography of the Greeks down to a late period.⁴

One other passage in connection with the Æthiopians deserves a passing notice. It is that where Poseidon, returning from his feast among them, espies Ulysses on his raft afar off, "from the mountains of the Solymi."⁵ Now, the Solymi are mentioned in the Iliad⁶ as a people inhabiting Lycia; and the mountains of that country, which rise to a height of more than 10,000 feet, towering immediately above the sea, would afford a splendid outlook—just such a station as the poet would choose for his purpose. It is strange that the perverse ingenuity of some commentators has endeavoured to mar the effect of this striking picture by transferring the Solymi to other regions.

§ 16. In reviewing the domain of geographical knowledge, over which we find the poet ranging, with more or less certain information, it is impossible not to be struck with one *negative* fact, common alike to the Iliad and the Odyssey, that the Phœnicians and Egyptians are the only civilized nations beyond the immediate neighbourhood of the Ægean, with whom the poet shows the slightest acquaintance. Not a trace is found that even the faintest rumour had reached his ears of the great Oriental monarchies that had so long been esta-

---

² Odyss. 1. 22-25; v. 282.
³ Αἰθίοπας, τοὶ διχθὰ δεδαίαται, ἔσχατοι ἀνδρῶν,
οἱ μὲν δυσομένου Ὑπερίονος, οἱ δ' ἀνιόντος
  Odyss 1 23, 24

⁴ See Strabo, i. pp 30-35, 38-40, &c.
⁵ τὸν δ' ἐξ Αἰθιόπων ἀνιὼν κρείων Ἐνοσίχθων τηλόθεν ἐκ Σολύμων ὀρέων ἴδεν
  Odyss. v. 282, 283
⁶ Iliad, vi. 184, 204.

blished on the banks of the Euphrates and the Tigris. The names of the Assyrians and Babylonians were apparently as unknown to him as those of the Medes and Persians. The Mæonians and Phrygians are the only nations of the interior of Asia Minor that find mention in the poems, and this, apparently, as the remotest people with which he was acquainted in that direction.[7] Whatever influence the Assyrians and Chaldæans may have exercised on the arts or civilization of Greece, must, according to all appearance, have belonged to a period subsequent to the Homeric poems.

But even with regard to the West, though we have seen that Homer had apparently some vague ideas, derived, in all probability, through Phœnician navigators, these are very far from indicating such a range of knowledge in that direction as might reasonably have been supposed. It is, at least, highly probable (as we have already seen) that the Phœnicians had before his time really extended their voyages as far as Tartessus and the Straits of Gibraltar; and we find not long afterwards that not only was the name of Tartessus familiar to the Greeks, but a whole string of legends had grown up in connection with this part of Spain, all connected with the mythical adventures of Hercules, which there is every reason to believe were originally derived from a Phœnician source.[8] But no trace is found in the Homeric poems of any of these legends—the columns of Hercules, the island of Erythea, the herds of Geryones, or the islands of the Hesperides—and it has been already pointed out that in the only passage in which Atlas is mentioned, there is nothing whatever to connect him with the mountain in the far west to which his name became afterwards inseparably attached. The Homeric conception of the Ocean stream had in reality no more connection with the really existing Atlantic Ocean beyond the outlet of the Mediterranean, than it had with the Erythræan Sea or the Southern Ocean beyond the continent of Africa.

---

[7] Iliad, iii 401; xviii. 291.
[8] All these legends were known to Hesiod, or at least are found in the poems extant under his name.

NOTE A, p. 31.

COMPOSITION OF THE HOMERIC POEMS.

It would be impossible within the limits of a note, as well as unsuited to the character of the present work, to enter into an elaborate investigation of the complicated questions connected with the authorship and composition of the Homeric poems. But in order that my readers may understand the point of view from which I have regarded them in the present chapter, with respect to the geographical statements found in them, it is perhaps necessary that I should state briefly my own views on the subject. For this purpose it will be sufficient to say, that I look upon the Iliad and the Odyssey as each of them forming an organic whole, worked up to a great extent out of previously existing materials, but in its present form the production of one master mind; and preserved to us substantially as originally composed. The few instances in which there seems good reason to suspect considerable interpolation have, with one exception, no bearing on my present subject. Nor am I able to find any conclusive proof from internal evidence that the two poems are not the work of the same author, or that they do not belong to the same age: by far the more important question of the two in regard to the inquiry before us. I have stated in the present chapter several instances which seem to me to show that there was no real difference in the amount of geographical knowledge possessed by the authors of the Iliad and the Odyssey, notwithstanding the much wider field embraced in the latter poem.

NOTE B, p. 33.

HOMER'S CONCEPTION OF THE EARTH.

This was, as we know, the popular conception of the earth, even in the days of Herodotus, who ridicules the maps that were based upon it, including probably those of Anaximander and Hecatæus:
γελῶ δὲ ὁρέων γῆς περιόδους γράψαντας πολλοὺς ἤδη, καὶ οὐδένα νόον ἔχοντας

ἐξηγησάμενον· οἳ ὠκεανόν τε ῥέοντα γράφουσι πέριξ τὴν γῆν ἐοῦσαν κυκλοτερέα ὡς ἀπὸ τόρνου (iv. 36). And the same notion still continued to retain its hold on the popular maps even in the days of Aristotle. διὸ καὶ γελοίως γράφουσι νῦν τὰς περιόδους τῆς γῆς· γράφουσι γὰρ κυκλοτερῆ τὴν οἰκουμένην. (Arist. *Meteor.* ii. 5, § 13.)

Geminus, a Greek writer on astronomy, correctly describes the notions of Homer and his successors on this subject: " Homer (he says) and nearly all the ancient poets conceived the earth to be a plane: they likewise supposed the Ocean to encircle it as a horizon, and the stars to arise from and set in the Ocean. Hence they believed the Æthiopians, who dwelt in the remote east and west, to be scorched by the vicinity of the sun." (*Elem. Astron.* c. 13.)

The belief in the circular form of the earth was probably derived (as suggested by Sir G. Lewis, *History of Astronomy,* p. 3) from observation of the circular appearance of the horizon, when viewed from a height, especially one commanding an extensive prospect of the sea, such as were familiar to all Greeks.

It is much more difficult to imagine what could have given rise to the notion of the earth being surrounded by the circumfluent stream of Ocean. It was probably in the first instance a mere mythological fiction, which found support in later times, when it was found that there was really *water* at the farthest limits of the known world, in so many directions that it was easy to jump to the conclusion that it would be found in all. But the supposition, adopted by Strabo, as well as by many modern writers, that the idea was originally derived from obscure traditions of this geographical fact, fails to account for the peculiar characteristic of the Ocean as conceived by Homer—that it was *not a sea*, surrounding the earth, as it became in later works on geography, but a mighty *river, flowing* all round the earth. This is repeated again and again . the expression of the stream of Ocean (ῥόος Ὠκεανοῖο) and the streams of Ocean (Ὠκεανοῖο ῥοαί) are of perpetual recurrence, and it is more than once distinctly termed the *river* Ocean (ποταμοῖο ῥέεθρα Ὠκεανοῦ, Iliad, xiv. 246, xviii. 607), and is described as the greatest of all rivers, exceeding even the Achelous (xxi. 194). It is termed also "gently flowing" (ἀκαλαρρείτης) "deep flowing" (βαθύρροος, and βαθυρρείτης), and " back flowing" (ἀψόρροος), *i.e.* flowing back upon itself, in allusion to its circular course; though this last epithet was absurdly interpreted by some ancient writers as having reference to the *tides* of Ocean! (Strabo, i. 1, p. 4.)

NOTE C, p. 36.

THE FOUR WINDS IN HOMER.

That the four winds which alone were known to Homer corresponded to the four quarters of the heavens, is taken for granted by Ukert and Volcker, and has been admitted, I believe, by all writers on the subject, except Mr. Gladstone. Of course it is not therefore assumed that they blew *direct* from the four cardinal points. The terms would be used with considerable latitude and vagueness, as expressing generally the quarters from which they blew. Even at the present day, when every one is familiar with eight, if not sixteen, points of the compass, we habitually speak of " the east winds of March," although in point of fact the wind at that season most frequently blows from the north-east. To attempt, as Mr. Gladstone has done, to define within particular limits, the precise " quadrant " of the heavens from which each wind blew, and to assume that Homer always used the names of the several winds with distinct reference to these limits, appears to me to involve a total misconception both of the character of the Homeric poetry, and of the state of science, or rather total absence of science, in the Homeric age. When Homer, writing of the Troad, speaks of the two winds, Boreas and Zephyrus, which blow from Thrace (Βορέης καὶ Ζέφυρος, τώ τε Θρήκηθεν ἄητον, Iliad, ix. 5), he had doubtless present to his mind the fact that Thrace was situated to the northwest of Troy—and when again he selects the Eurus and Notus as the two winds that swept the Icarian Sea and lashed it into huge waves (ii 145), he represents correctly the fact that that portion of the Ægean would be peculiarly exposed to winds from the south and south-east. In both these cases he would be speaking from his own observation : but it is quite another thing to assume that whenever he mentions these winds, in reference to imaginary or unknown localities, he meant to attach to them a precise and definite meaning, as if he had composed the Odyssey with a mariner's chart perpetually before him.

NOTE D, p. 57.

THE LÆSTRYGONES.

A very strange theory has been started by Nitzsch in his notes on the Odyssey (x. 83), that the obscure passage in which Homer describes the relations between day and night among the Læstrygones, indicates an acquaintance, though of course vague and imperfect, with the fact of the prolonged days and short nights of the northern regions of Europe: an idea which is also suggested, though very vaguely, by Ukert, and has been partially adopted by Mr. Gladstone. The same notion had been already put forward by Crates of Pergamus, who was always trying to adapt the expressions of Homer to the more advanced scientific views of his own time. See Eustath. *ad loc.*

Without a strong predisposition of this kind, it seems difficult to see how the enigmatical expression of Homer "for the ways of night and day are near together," can suggest such an interpretation: especially as the lines immediately preceding refer distinctly to the proceedings of herdsmen and shepherds. But even if it be admitted that some strangely misconceived notion of the kind lay at the bottom of the story, it affords no foundation for assigning the Læstrygones to a remote northerly position. Homer's astronomical ideas were much too vague to lead him to understand that this was requisite for the supposed phenomenon: and just as he applied to the Cimmerians in the west a description which, if really based upon any foundation of fact, could only have referred to a people in a northern climate, so there is nothing to prevent his transferring in like manner the Læstrygones to the western sea. It is clear that he did not conceive them as very remote from the island of Æolus, since six days and nights of toilsome rowing (εἰρεσίης ἀλεγεινῆς, x. 78) were sufficient to bring him from the one to the other.

NOTE E, p. 58.

THE ISLAND OF CIRCE.

There is indeed one passage that appears to militate against this view, and which has been strongly pressed by Mr. Gladstone, as favouring his theory which transfers all these localities from the west to the east.

After quitting the Ocean stream, the ship (as the poet tells us) reached the wavy expanse of the broad sea, and arrived at the island of Æa, "where are the house and the dancing-places of the Dawn, and the rising of the sun" (xii. 1-4). It must be admitted that the first impression of these lines is that the island was situated *in the east*, and the difficulty was felt by the early commentators. It is remarkable that this description of the island of Circe occurs only on the return from Hades, and appears directly at variance with a previous passage (x. 190-192), in which Ulysses, after their first arrival in the island, observes that they do not know where is the west, or where is the east; where the sun rises or where it sets. It seems impossible to reconcile the two passages. Most of the commentators overlook this point, and content themselves with explaining the statement at the beginning of the twelfth book, as referring to the contrast presented by the bright and sunny island of Circe with the gloomy land of the Cimmerians where the sun was never visible. This is not satisfactory: though it is far better than the alternative adopted by Mr. Gladstone of transferring the gloomy land of darkness with its associated infernal regions, to the far east, the land of the sun and the bright dawn! The island of Circe is represented as not far distant from that of the Cimmerians—this is undoubtedly the impression conveyed by the description of the voyage, though there is no definite statement to that effect. But Circe was the daughter of the Sun (x. 138), and hence her island would naturally be associated in the mind of the poet with bright and sunny images, which he might well introduce in a passing notice without considering how far they were geographically appropriate.

NOTE F, p. 59.

THE PLANCTÆ.

From the circumstance that Ulysses avoided the dangers of the Planctæ by keeping as far away from them as possible, they have generally attracted less attention than most of the other localities mentioned in his voyage. But they are of interest, both as being the occasion of the only mention of the ship *Argo* which occurs in Homer,[9] and on account of the confusion that arose in later days between them and the Symplegades. It is certain that Greek writers at a subsequent time confounded the two, or rather transferred the name of the Planctæ to the well-known rocks at the entrance of the Euxine, while they disappeared from the list of the

---

[9] See Note, p. 19.

Homeric localities that obtained a recognized position in the neighbourhood of Italy and Sicily. Strabo even supposes that Homer *invented* them, in imitation of what he had heard of the Symplegades. Apollonius Rhodius, however, fully recognized their existence in connection with the voyage of the Argonauts, and placed them among the dangers encountered by the latter on their way from the island of Circe to Scheria (iv. 922-927). He brings them also into very close proximity with Scylla and Charybdis; and this certainly appears to be a correct interpretation of the Homeric view. In the Odyssey they figure as the alternative danger, and the more formidable of the two; but the nature of this danger is very obscurely indicated. There is nothing in the description (if it be read without a preconceived impression) to indicate such a phenomenon as the clashing together of the rocks, from whence the Symplegades derived their name. The name of Planctæ "the wandering," is the only thing from which we can infer that they were moveable. The Homeric description, both in Circe's preliminary warning (xii. 59-68), and in the account of their appearance when Ulysses came in sight of them (Ib. 201-5), is rather that of rocks of vast altitude, and overhanging (ἐπηρεφέες), towards which ships were driven by a violent current and dashed to pieces at their foot. The mention of fire (v. 68) and smoke (v. 202) is probably merely a poetical embellishment to express the tumult of the elements. It seems very hazardous to interpret it, as Volcker and Buchholz have done, of volcanic action.[1]

It seems probable that the application of the name to the Symplegades, or Cyanean rocks, at the entrance of the Euxine, began at an early period. Herodotus already applies it to them, though only as an adjective (ἔπλεε ἐπὶ τὰς Κυανέας καλευμένας, τὰς πρότερον πλαγκτὰς Ἕλληνές φασι εἶναι, iv. 85); but it would soon pass into use as a proper name. But it is impossible to say which was the original form of the legend, or to which locality it was first applied.

---

[1] Apollonius, however, certainly took the same view, and his description (*l. c.*) which has very little resemblance to that of Homer, would apply very fairly to one of the Æolian or Lipari islands.

NOTE G, p. 64.

COURSE FROM OGYGIA TO SCHERIA.

Thus Nitzsch and Volcker, who place Ogygia in the north-west, understand the passage as meaning that Ulysses steered to the *south-east*. Mr. Merivale, who believes in the identification of Calypso's isle with Malta, says "he was to hold an easterly, *or rather north-easterly*, course,"—the last qualification being introduced solely with a view of making the direction suit his theory.

The most extreme course has been taken by Mr. Gladstone, who fully appreciates the importance of the passage, and, candidly admitting that, if taken in its obvious and natural sense, it is destructive of the whole fabric of his ingenious and elaborate system, actually attempts to prove that Homer meant just the contrary of what he has been generally understood to mean, and that ἐπ' ἀρίστερα χειρὸς does not mean " on his left hand," but *on his right*. Among all the subtle attempts that have been made from the days of the Alexandrian critics to our own, to explain away the poet's meaning, where it did not suit their purpose, it would be difficult to find a more ingenious piece of special pleading than the elaborate *excursus* in which Mr. Gladstone attempts to support this strange paradox (*Homer and the Homeric Age*, vol. iii. p. 349-365). The precise phrase does not indeed occur elsewhere in the poems, though it is found in Apollonius Rhodius (ii. 1266), who unquestionably understood it in its usual and natural sense. It is difficult to believe that any one so familiar as Mr. Gladstone with the language of Homer can refuse to see that ἐπ' ἀρίστερα χειρὸς is simply accommodated to the exigencies of epic verse, just as the phrase he himself quotes from Euripides (χειρὸς ἐξ ἀριστέρας) is to the iambic verse of tragedy.

NOTE H, p. 70.

DULICHIUM.

This view of the Homeric Dulichium has found little favour either in ancient or modern times, though a glance at the map would certainly seem to suggest it as the most obvious and natural solution of the difficulty. The three large islands of the group— Santa Maura, Cephalonia, and Zante—present themselves in the order in which the three—Dulichium, Same, and Zacynthus—are enumerated by the poet; and if we refuse to identify the two, we find no mention of Santa Maura (Leucadia) in any of the passages concerning the islands, though it is one of the largest and most important of the group, ranking, in fact, next to Cephalonia. The ancients were indeed led to explain this by identifying Leucadia with the ἀκτὴ ἠπείροιο, mentioned in a single passage in the Odyssey (xxiv. 378), though certainly there is nothing in the manner in which it is there alluded to, to lead to such an inference; and the notion that Leucadia was originally a peninsula was a tradition resting apparently on this very assumption (see Strabo, x. p. 451). Colonel Leake is clearly of opinion that it was naturally an island, and was subsequently joined by an artificial mound to the mainland (*Northern Greece*, vol. iii. p. 19), and all geological analogies would be in favour of this view. But at all events it was so nearly insulated, that it would be generally regarded as such; and there is no other instance in the Homeric poems in which ἀκτὴ is used in the sense of a projecting peninsula. It must be added that the expression is here applied in immediate connection with the city of Nericum or Neritum (also mentioned in this passage only), in a manner that makes it very difficult to suppose it intended to designate a great peninsular tract like Leucadia.[2]

Mr. Clark (*Peloponnesus*, p. 206), who mentions Santa Maura only to reject it, objects that it is not large enough, and that Dulichium lay in the poet's mind to the south of Ithaca. But the passage on which he relies to prove this (xiv. 334) is by no means conclusive; and Santa Maura is four times as large as Ithaca, and much more fertile. It may be admitted that the suggestion does not solve all difficulties, but it appears to me to be attended with fewer than any other that has been proposed. I cannot at all bring myself to believe that Dulichium is (as suggested by Mr. Clark) "altogether a fiction of the poet's brain," though I can well believe that he had erroneous ideas of its magnitude and position.

---

[2] οἷος Νήρικον εἷλον ἐϋκτίμενον πτολίεθρον,
ἀκτὴν ἠπείροιο, Κεφαλλήνεσσιν ἀνάσσων.
xxiv 377-378.

One of the principal objections urged against Santa Maura is that it is too rugged and mountainous to deserve the epithet of πολύπυρος (abounding in wheat) applied to it by Homer; but it is remarkable that the two small islands of Meganisi and Kalamo, almost immediately adjoining it, and at present mere dependencies of the larger island, are noted even in modern times for the excellence of their wheat, which is the finest found in the Ionian Islands. (Gell's *Ithaca*, p. 92.)

NOTE I　　　HOMERIC GEOGRAPHY.　　　83

The passage in the Catalogue (Iliad, ii. 625-6) on which Völcker especially relies as proving that Dulichium lay opposite to Elis, and therefore to the south of Ithaca, fails to prove his point, as the expression

αἳ ναίουσι πέρην ἁλός, Ἤλιδος ἄντα

may equally well be understood as referring to the Echinades only, to which it is perfectly applicable.

NOTE I, p. 71.

HOMERIC ITHACA.

It would be unsuited to the purpose of the present work to enter into any detailed examination of the topography of Ithaca. Since the island was first explored—we might almost say rediscovered—by Sir W. Gell in 1806 it has been visited and examined with the greatest care by numerous scholars and travellers (Colonel Leake, Colonel Mure, Sir G. Bowen, Dr. Schliemann, &c.), who have for the most part acquiesced, more or less completely, in the conclusions of Sir W. Gell. Colonel Leake, however, dissents from the view generally adopted, which places the site of the palace of Ulysses on the hill called Aeto, on the rocky isthmus that unites the two portions of the island, a commanding situation, which seems marked by nature (as Colonel Mure observes) for the residence of the chief of the island. It is certainly remarkable that no allusion is found in the poem to any of the marked peculiarities of this site; and it is difficult to understand how the town or city could have stood there. Yet it seems impossible to suppose that the palace of Ulysses was separated by any considerable distance from the city. There is very little doubt that the chief town on the island in later times, which bore the same name with the island (Scylax, § 34; Ptolem. iii. 14, § 13) was in the northern portion of it, on the site still called Polis; and both Colonel Leake and M. Gandar are of opinion that this was also the city of Ulysses. But the very fact that there exists a difference of opinion as to this capital point in the topography of the island, and that "the northern faction," as Colonel Mure terms them, are able to make out a complete set of localities, and show *their* rock Korax, *their* fountain of Arethusa, and *their* cave of the nymphs, as well as those who place all these localities in the southern portion of the island, would seem sufficient proof that these topographical details are not marked with such clearness as to afford irrefragable proof of the poet's description being derived from personal knowledge.

(See on this subject, Gell's *Geography and Antiquities of Ithaca,* 4to, 1807; Leake's *Northern Greece,* vol. iii. pp. 24-54; Mure's *Tour in Greece,* vol. i. chap. vi.; Sir G. Bowen's art. *Ithaca,* in Smith's Dictionary of Geography; Ansted's *Ionian Islands,* pp. 229-289; Gandar, *de Ulyssis Ithaca,* Paris, 1854; Schliemann's *Ithaka, der Peloponnesus u. Troja,* pp. 14-78 , and compare the views of Volcker in his *Homerische Geographie,* pp. 63-74.) [3]

The most recent investigation is that by Mr. Gladstone in an article in *Macmillan's Magazine* for October, 1877, who has adopted the same view with Colonel Leake, but I cannot say that his arguments carry any more conviction to my mind than those of his predecessors. His *negative* arguments against Sir W. Gell and his followers appear to me very strong; but he equally fails in establishing his counter theory.

Since the above note was written, the researches of Dr. Schliemann (an account of which is given in the *Times* newspaper for September 26, 1878) have thrown an unexpected light upon the matter, and have established, in my opinion, beyond a doubt that the ancient capital of Ithaca, the royal city of Ulysses—if Ulysses is to be admitted as an historical personage at all—was situated on the hill of Aeto, where Colonel Leake had long ago noticed the occurrence of very ancient walls and foundations. But if this interesting discovery may be considered as settling the question of the true topography of Ithaca, it leaves the still more interesting inquiry, how far the real topography can be reconciled with the Homeric descriptions, to be solved by some competent scholar who may examine the localities in a less enthusiastic spirit than Dr. Schliemann.

---

[3] A full review of the German literature of the subject will be found in Buchholz, *Die Homerische Realien,* vol 1 pp 120-146.

CHAPTER IV.

HOMER TO HECATÆUS.

SECTION 1.—*Poetical Notices subsequent to Homer.*

§ 1. It would be of the highest interest if we were able to trace the successive steps by which the geographical knowledge of the Greeks advanced from the days of Homer to those of Herodotus; and especially to mark how their ideas of the western regions of Europe, and the remoter parts of the Mediterranean, which were to the earlier poet nothing but a vague region of marvel and mystery, gradually assumed form and consistence, as the Greeks extended their colonies and commerce in that direction. Unfortunately the materials for such a connected review are in great measure wanting. Contemporary evidence there is none. During almost the whole of the period in question prose writing was unknown; there were consequently no professed writers on geography or history, to supply us with definite and trustworthy information. Even the works of the poets, upon which we should be compelled to fall back in the absence of more authentic guidance, are for the most part lost to us, and we are reduced to glean what few hints we can gather from incidental notices in the fragments that remain, or from the citations of later writers, the accuracy of which we have no means of testing.

The extant poems of Hesiod are not of a nature to give occasion for many notices of a geographical kind. They nevertheless contain sufficient evidence that the horizon of the Greek world had already expanded considerably beyond the limits which bounded it in the days of Homer. Unfortunately the attempt to compare the two is hampered by almost insuperable difficulties, in consequence of the condition in which these poems have come down to us, and the probability, or rather certainty, that they have been largely interpolated at a period subsequent to their original composition. This is especially the case in regard to the Theogony, the only one of the three poems which can be said to contribute anything to the purpose of our present enquiry. Here we find a catalogue of rivers, enumerated as the offspring of Oceanus and Tethys, in which occur the names of the Nile, the Eridanus, the Phasis, and the Ister,[1] all of which, as we have seen, were unknown to Homer. Atlas had already assumed the mythical character, which he retained in all later writers, as well as the "local habitation" in the far west. He is described as "supporting the heavens with his head and unwearied hands, under the pressure of stern necessity, standing at the farthest limits of the earth, in front of the clear-voiced Hesperides."[2] In another passage the Hesperides are spoken of as guarding their beautiful golden apples and the trees that bore the precious fruit "beyond the waters of Ocean."[3] Geryones also, the three-headed giant, dwelt in the sea-girt island of Erythea, across the stream of Ocean, from whence Hercules drove away his herd of oxen.[4] Here therefore we find this cluster of legends—almost certainly of Phœnician origin—already gathered around the same locality. The name of Tartessus is not, however, found in the poems of Hesiod, nor is there any allusion to the Columns of Hercules. All was yet vague and mythical in those remote regions on the borders of the earth.

---

[1] Hesiod, Theogon. vv. 337–345.
[2] Ibid. vv. 517–519.

'Ατλας δ' οὐρανὸν εὐρὺν ἔχει κρατερῆς ὑπ' ἀνάγκης,
πείρασιν ἐν γαίης, πρόπαρ Ἑσπερίδων λιγυφώνων,
ἑστηώς, κεφαλῇ τε καὶ ἀκαμάτῃσι χέρεσσι

The entirely different conception of this myth entertained by Homer has been already pointed out

[3] 'Εσπερίδας θ' αἷς μῆλα πέρην κλυτοῦ Ὠκεανοῖο
χρύσεα καλὰ μέλουσι φέροντά τε δένδρεα καρπόν
    Hesiod, Theogon. vv 215, 216.

The same expression of their dwelling "beyond the famous Ocean" is found also in v. 274, where they are associated with the Gorgons.

[4] Ibid. vv 287–294. He dwelt περιρρύτῳ εἰν Ἐρυθείῃ. but in v. 294 his herds are described as dwelling πέρην κλυτοῦ Ὠκεανοῖο : and Hercules had to cross the stream of Ocean to get at them (διαβὰς πόρον Ὠκεανοῖο, v 292). The Hesperides were probably in like manner considered as dwelling in an island.

Oceanus, the father of all rivers, is still, in the mind of Hesiod, itself a mighty river, "the Ocean stream," or, as he elsewhere calls it, "the perfect river"—an expression apparently referring to its complete circular course, flowing round and encompassing all things.[5] But in the passages just cited we see the notion that there was something still beyond the stream of Ocean, or at least surrounded by its arms. In like manner we find mention elsewhere of "the islands of the blest," by the deep eddies of Ocean [6]—an idea which took firm possession of the Greek mind, so that we shall find it recurring, in one form or another, throughout the history of their geographical views.

No mention is found in Hesiod of either Italy or Sicily by name, but there is one passage in which he speaks of Latinus and Telegonus, the sons of Ulysses and Circe, as "reigning over the far-famed Tyrrhenians in the distant recesses of the sacred islands"[7]—a notice that undoubtedly proves the name of the Tyrrhenians to be already familiar to the writer, and even shows some acquaintance with that of the Latins,[8] though his ideas concerning their position were extremely vague. But these lines are found in a part of the poem which is almost certainly a subsequent addition, and is in all probability connected with the long poem, now lost, but long extant under the name of Hesiod, called the Catalogue of Women. It is still more difficult in this case than in that of the extant poems, to determine how far it can be considered as belonging

---

[5] This appears to be certainly the most probable translation of the epithet *τελήεντος ποταμοῖο*, which is twice applied by Hesiod to the stream of Ocean (Theogon vv. 242, 959 See Van Lennep's note). Once only is the Homeric epithet of ἀψόρροος employed by Hesiod (Ibid v. 776).

[6] ἐν μακάρων νήσοισι παρ' Ὠκεανὸν βαθυδίνην
Op et Di. 171
Here was the dwelling-place of the heroes who had fought at Thebes and before Troy It is evident that this is only an expansion of the idea, already found in the Odyssey (iv 563), that Menelaus was destined to a separate existence, apart from the other dead, 'in the Elysian plain, at the farthest limit of the earth·'" but in Hesiod we already find these regions designated as "the *islands* of the blest."

[7] οἱ δ' ἤτοι μάλα τῆλε μυχῷ νήσων ἱεράων πᾶσιν Τυρσηνοῖσιν ἀγακλειτοῖσιν ἀνασσον
Theogon. vv 1015, 1016

[8] It can hardly be doubted that Latinus was introduced in this passage in connection with the Latins, though they are not named as a people.

to the age of Hesiod, and to what extent it may have been interpolated at a later period. Nor, if we consider it as belonging altogether to a later age, have we any evidence as to the date of its composition. The same remark applies to other poems attributed to Hesiod, and hence it is impossible to rely with any confidence upon the citations of later geographers and grammarians, many of which refer only to the name of Hesiod, without any indication of the particular work. It is only in this vague manner that we are told that he was acquainted with the name of Ætna, and with the little island of Ortygia, off the coast of Sicily, which was subsequently occupied by the Syracusans.[9] He was also the first to mention the Ligyes or Ligurians, as well as the Scythians, both of which names he associates with that of the Æthiopians, in a manner that seems clearly to indicate the three as forming the limits of the poet's knowledge.[1] To Hesiod also is ascribed the first mention of many of the fables which ever after retained a place among the Greeks, while later geographers struggled in vain to assign them a definite habitation and locality. Among these were the Hyperboreans, who dwelt beyond the north wind, and consequently enjoyed a perfect climate;[2] the Griffins, with their "guarded gold;"[3] and the races of men with dogs' heads (Hemicynes or Cynocephali), and others with heads of monstrous size (Macrocephali). These last he associated with the Pygmies,[4] and probably therefore supposed them to be situated in the extreme south, where the deserts of Africa continued long after to be peopled with these and other fabulous creations.

---

[9] Strabo, i. 2, p. 23. Ἐρατοσθένης δὲ Ἡσίοδον μὲν εἰκάζει πεπυσμένον περὶ τῆς Ὀδυσσέως πλάνης, ὅτι κατὰ Σικελίαν καὶ Ἰταλίαν γεγένηται, πιστεύσαντα τῇ δόξῃ μὴ μόνον τῶν ὑφ' Ὁμήρου λεγομένων μεμνῆσθαι, ἀλλὰ καὶ Αἴτνης καὶ Ὀρτυγίας τοῦ πρὸς Συρακούσας νησίου καὶ Τυρρηνῶν.

[1] Αἰθίοπας Λίγυάς τε ἰδὲ Σκύθας ἱππημολγούς.—Cited by Eratosthenes, ap. Strab. vii. 3, p. 300.

[2] ἀλλ' Ἡσιόδῳ μέν ἐστι περὶ Ὑπερβορέων εἰρημένα.—Herodotus, iv. 32. The full development of the myth is first found in Pindar.

[3] περὶ γρυπῶν Ἡσίοδος πρῶτος ἐτερατεύσατο—Schol. ad Æschyl. Prometh. v. 793. (Hesiodi Fragment. 123, Goettling.)

[4] Strabo, i. p. 43. Ἡσιόδου δ' οὐκ ἄν τις αἰτιάσαιτο ἄγνοιαν, Ἡμίκυνας λέγοντος καὶ Μακροκεφάλους καὶ Πυγμαίους.

§ 2. Of the voluminous series of poems extant in ancient times under the title of the Epic Cycle, the fragments which have been preserved to us are so few and scanty that we cannot expect them to contribute anything to our geographical knowledge. In the Homeric hymns, on the contrary, there occur a few incidental notices that deserve a passing mention. Thus we not only find in the hymn to the Delian Apollo a very full enumeration of the islands in the Ægean Sea, to which the subject naturally led;[5] but in that to the Pythian Apollo there occurs repeatedly the name of the Peloponnesus, a distinctive appellation unknown to Homer; while, singularly enough, the term used in contrast to it to signify the mainland or continental Greece, as opposed to the peninsula and islands, is that of Europe, which evidently had not yet acquired the more general signification.[6] These two hymns are generally regarded as among the most ancient of the series. That to Dionysus, in which we find Tyrrhenian pirates introduced as a familiar notion, is probably of a much later date.[7]

§ 3. The great uncertainty which prevails with regard to the age of all these poems renders their testimony of little value in tracing the extension of geographical knowledge, while of the poets that may be considered as unquestionably belonging to a later period—after the beginning of the Olympiads—Pisander, Eumelus of Corinth, and the author of the Naupactica, scarcely any fragments remain. The two last writers, as has been already mentioned, were among the first to dilate upon the history of the Argonautic voyage, which had already assumed the same general form that it ever after retained.[8] Epimenides of Crete, who may probably be assigned to the

---

[5] Hymn ad Apoll. Del. vv. 29-44.
[6] ἠμὲν ὅσοι Πελοπόννησον πίειραν ἔχουσιν,
ἠδ' ὅσοι Εὐρωπήν τε καὶ ἀμφιρύτας κατὰ νήσους.
Hymn ad Apoll. Pyth vv 72, 73
The same two verses are repeated (vv. 112, 113); but the name of the Peloponnesus occurs again also (v. 241), in describing the voyage of the Cretan ship to Delphi.
[7] In the same hymn (v. 29) the Hyperboreans are incidentally mentioned as an idea familiar to all.
[8] See above, Chap. II. p. 25.

seventh century B.C., is said to have composed an entire poem upon the same subject; but the statement rests upon very doubtful authority.[9] Another poet, whose age is very uncertain, but who probably flourished in the succeeding century, Aristeas of Proconnesus, was the author of a work of a more decidedly geographical character. His Arimaspea, which is cited by Herodotus, and was still extant at a much later period,[1] contained an account of the Scythian tribes to the north of the Euxine, derived to a considerable extent from personal observation, and which appears to have contained geographical information of real value, though mixed with absurd fables, treated with the exaggeration natural to a poet.[2]

But long before the period to which the poets in question must probably be assigned, we have more trustworthy evidence of a wholly different character, as to the extent to which the Greeks had increased their navigation and commerce, both in the Mediterranean and the Euxine. No contemporary evidence is indeed available with respect to their actual voyages, or even in most cases to their commercial relations; but the fact that we find them founding in distant countries, both to the east and west, numerous colonies, which continued to subsist and flourish for many centuries afterwards, is a sufficient proof of the greatly extended horizon which had opened to their view, and of the greatly increased zeal, as well as knowledge

---

[9] All the works ascribed to the Cretan sage by Diogenes Laertius (i 10) may be considered as of very doubtful authenticity, if not altogether apocryphal. Among these he mentions, "The building of the Ship Argo, and the voyage of Jason to Colchis. a poem in 6500 verses" But no reference is found to it in any other author.

[1] Herodot iv 13. It is certain that a poem called Arimaspea was extant long afterwards, and is cited both by Strabo and Pausanias, as well as by other writers under the Roman Empire (Strabo, 1 2, p 21, xiii. 1, p 589, Pausan. i 24, § 6, v. 7, § 9), but its authenticity was denied by some critics Whether this was the same work which was known to Herodotus we have no means of judging, but there seems to be no good reason to doubt it.

[2] According to Suidas (s. v) Aristeas flourished in the time of Crœsus and Cyrus and it seems probable that he may be assigned to about the middle of the sixth century (B c. 560–540). The accounts which refer him to a much earlier period are probably connected with the fables concerning his previous life and reappearance See Herodotus, iv. 14, 15, and Suidas, l. c.

and skill, with which the Greeks had begun to devote themselves to maritime pursuits. It may be reasonably assumed that, in most, if not all, cases, the foundation of colonies, which affords us the only chronological evidence of the extension of Greek power and civilization, must have been preceded by some degree of acquaintance and intercourse with the regions that they selected for their distant settlements.

SECTION 2.—*Colonies.*

§ 1. The very imperfect knowledge which we possess of the history of Greece before the Persian war, does not enable us to trace the causes of the remarkable movement of the Hellenic mind, which characterizes the seventh and eighth centuries before the Christian era. But we may observe the results of this early development of the national energies, displaying itself at once in almost every direction during the period in question. Nowhere is this more strikingly shown than in the rapid extension of their colonies around the shores of the Mediterranean and the Euxine, until they had laid the foundations of a colonial empire, which bore much the same relation to the narrow and limited area of the parent country, as does the British Empire at the present day to the British Islands.

Their enterprising spirit was directed in the first instance towards the west, where the fair and fertile regions of Italy and Sicily were eminently calculated to attract their attention and excite their cupidity. These countries were probably thinly peopled, and the native races that occupied them appear to have been more or less closely connected by ethnical affinities with the Hellenes themselves. At all events, they seem to have offered but little resistance to the establishment of the Greek colonists. As early as the middle of the eighth century B.C., the eastern coast of Sicily was occupied by two successive bodies of emigrants, proceeding from two different cities, and representing the two great branches of the Hellenic race. The foundation of Naxos, at the foot of Mount Ætna by a body of Ionic colonists from Chalcis in Euboea, took place in B.C. 735, and was followed the very next year by that of Syracuse, a Dorian colony from Corinth.[3] Both settlements were originally established on sites such as those habitually selected by the Phœnician colonies; Naxos stood on a projecting peninsular headland, capable of easy defence on the land side, and the original city of Syracuse was confined to the small island of Ortygia, which was separated from the mainland by a narrow strait. But the same impulse that led to the original establishment of these colonies, seems to have quickly attracted other emigrants to follow in the same track, so that the Naxians were able, within a few years after their own foundation (B.C. 730), to establish in their turn the two colonies of Leontini and Catana, both of which eventually became much more powerful and important than the parent city. Nearly about the same time, the Hyblæan Megara (as it was called for distinction's sake) was founded by an independent colony from the city of the same name in Greece (B.C. 728).[4] From this period a considerable interval elapsed before we hear of any fresh colonies in Sicily. Even Syracuse itself seems to have at first risen but slowly to power. It was not till seventy years after its foundation that it established its first colony at Acræ in the interior of the island, and this was followed twenty years later by that of Casmenæ. But neither of these ever rose to be places of consideration; the more flourishing colony of Camarina was not settled till 135 years after the foundation of Syracuse (B.C. 599).[5]

§ 2. Meanwhile, the tide of emigration had been directed to the shores of Southern Italy. The earliest settlements here were all of Achæan origin. Sybaris, founded in B.C. 720, Crotona,

---

[3] Thucyd. vi. 3; Strabo, vi. 2, pp 267, 269. See Clinton, *Fast. Hell* vol. i. p 164.

[4] Thucyd. vi. 4. Concerning the date, see Clinton, *F. H.* vol. i. p. 166.
[5] Thucyd. vi. 5.

about ten years later, and Metapontum, not later than B.C. 700,[6] all rose in succession to be opulent and flourishing cities, and became in turn the parents of many minor colonies. The powerful city of Tarentum, on the northern shore of the same gulf, having the advantage of a situation inferior only to that of Syracuse, was a Lacedæmonian colony—one of the few planted by that people, and this exception was due, not to any commercial enterprise on their part, but to the exceptional political circumstances arising out of the first Messenian war. Its foundation appears to have taken place about B.C. 708.[7]

§ 3. Nearly contemporary with the earliest colonies in Sicily and the south of Italy, was the settlement of the Corinthians in the important island of Corcyra (about B.C. 734)[8] which rapidly rose to such power as to be able, within less than a century after its foundation, to contend at sea with the mother city. Its position at the entrance of the Adriatic naturally secured to it in great measure the command of that sea, and, in order still further to establish their power in this quarter, the Corcyræans at a somewhat later period, founded in their turn the two colonies of Apollonia and Dyrrhachium, both on the eastern shore of the Adriatic.[9]

The naval power of the Tyrrhenians in the western part of the Mediterranean, must have presented a formidable obstacle

---

[6] Metapontum was founded according to the testimony of Strabo, by Crotona and Sybaris in common, and *after* the foundation of Tarentum (Strabo, VI. 1, pp. 264, 265.) Hence the date assigned by Eusebius, who would carry it back as far as B C. 774, is certainly erroneous See the article METAPONTUM in Smith's *Dict of Ancient Geography* vol. II. p. 346

[7] Clinton, *F. H* vol. I. p 174. For the circumstances which led to its foundation see the narratives of Antiochus and Ephorus, cited by Strabo (VI 3, pp. 278, 279)

[8] According to Strabo (VI 2, p 269), Corcyra was colonized by a portion of the same body of emigrants who founded Syracuse Its foundation may therefore be assigned to the same date. Hieronymus, indeed, places it twenty-six years later (B C. 708), but the authority of Strabo is certainly preferable, and is confirmed by collateral circumstances (See Clinton, *F. H* vol I p 164)

[9] Dyrrhachium, or Epidamnus, as it was more commonly called by the Greeks, was founded in B C 625 (Euseb. *Chron ad ann*), Apollonia somewhat later, during the reign of Periander at Corinth Both cities attained to great power and prosperity, and carried on an extensive trade with the Illyrian tribes of the interior

to the development of the Greek commerce, as well as of their colonial system, in that direction: yet it is certain that the Greeks had at an early period, though the exact date cannot be ascertained, established themselves on the coast of Campania, where they founded, in the first instance, the isolated colony of Cumæ;[1] a city that became the nucleus of a remarkable local development of Greek influence and civilization, which not only maintained itself through three centuries against all the efforts of the neighbouring nations, but long continued even under the Roman domination to retain its distinctive Hellenic character. Neapolis, a younger offshoot of Cumæ, was even in the days of Strabo a distinctly Greek city.[2]

§ 4. Still more important and influential was the more distant settlement of Massilia, a colony from Phocæa in Asia Minor, which was founded in B.C. 600, upon the southern coast of Gaul, as the country would be described by later geographers, but in a region which was then occupied by tribes of Ligurian origin.[3] The excellence of its capacious and land-locked harbour, as well as the ready communications with the interior afforded by the valley of the Rhone, caused Massilia to rise quickly to great prosperity, and while the remoteness of its situation naturally kept it aloof from all participation in the wars and revolutions that affected other portions of the Greek world, its wise and vigorous government, which presents strong features of similarity to that of Venice, secured it an un-

---

[1] It is singular that, according to the distinct statement of Strabo (v. 4, p 243), Cumæ, notwithstanding its more remote situation, was the earliest of all the Greek settlements in Italy or Sicily and the particulars given by him concerning its foundation have every appearance of being historical On the other hand, the date given by the later chronologers (Eusebius and Hieronymus), who would carry it back as far as B C 1050, may be safely rejected, as belonging to the period of mythical traditions, before the establishment of anything like historical chronology (See the subject more fully discussed in Dr. Smith's *Dict. of Ancient Geography*, art. CUMAE, vol. 1. p. 716.)

[2] Strabo, vi. 1, p. 253.

[3] The date rests upon the authority of Timæus (cited by Scymnus Chius, v. 214), who placed it 120 years before the battle of Salamis. For the other authorities, see Clinton, *F. H.* vol. 1. p 220.

exampled amount of internal tranquillity. Like all the other principal colonies of the Greeks in outlying situations, the Massilians by degrees established smaller settlements along the coast on both sides of them—Olbia, Antipolis, and Nicæa to the eastward; Agathe, Rhoda, and Emporiæ to the west; and though none of those towns rose to any great importance, they doubtless all contributed to maintain and extend the influence of Greek civilization among the barbarous native tribes.[4] The parent city, meanwhile, extended its commercial relations far into the interior, and the geographical knowledge which the Greeks gradually attained of these western regions of Europe, was due in great measure to the enterprising traders of Massilia.

§ 5. The eastern and south-eastern coasts of Spain would seem to have offered a still fairer field for Greek colonization, but here they were met and opposed by the influences of the Phœnician and Carthaginian colonists, who had established themselves at an early period in the possession of the Spanish trade. Notwithstanding the favourable reception afforded by the native king to a body of Phocæan navigators who were accidentally carried to the south of Spain,[5] we hear of only a few isolated attempts at colonization in that quarter, and those few produced little result. The town of Mænaca, situated on the coast of Bætica, somewhere to the east of Malaca, was a colony of Massilia, the farthest in this direction, but it never became a place of consequence,[6] and neither the period of its foundation nor its exact situation can be determined with any certainty.

The same causes would naturally operate to prevent the establishment of Greek colonies along the northern shores of

---

[4] Rhoda and Emporiæ both retained a decidedly Hellenic character down to the time of the Roman conquest: and struck coins bearing Greek legends and showing the manifest impress of Greek art

[5] Herodotus, 1. 163.

[6] Strabo, iii 4, p. 157. Saguntum also, according to the same author, was originally a Greek colony from Zacynthus (ib. p. 159), but it appears to have lost all Greek character, and become a mere Spanish town before it figures in history

Africa where the power of the Carthaginians had been established from an early period. Even in Sicily it was long before they pushed on their settlements towards the western half of the island; but here the Phœnicians gradually gave way before them, and withdrew to the north-western corner of Sicily, from whence they could easily keep up uninterrupted communication with Carthage.[7] In Sardinia, on the contrary, Phœnician and Carthaginian influence always continued paramount, and nothing but very few and faint indications are preserved of any attempts at Greek colonization in that large and fertile island. A vigorous endeavour was, indeed, made to establish a Greek colony in the neighbouring island of Corsica, the proximity of which to Massilia would have rendered it an important acquisition to that city; but the efforts of the Phocæans were foiled by the united arms of the Tyrrhenians and Carthaginians, and the island was allowed to lapse again under the yoke of the former people.[8]

§ 6. The Carthaginians, as has been already observed, held undisputed supremacy over the southern shores of the Mediterranean, from the Straits of Gibraltar to the Syrtes; but in the interval between those much-dreaded gulfs and the Egyptian frontier, there lay a region of great natural fertility which was unoccupied by any power more formidable than the wandering native tribes; and here arose another group of Greek cities, which preserved through many centuries all the essential characteristics of Hellenic culture, and formed for a long period a flourishing oasis of civilization in the midst of surrounding barbarism. Cyrene, founded in B.C. 631, by a colony of Dorians from the island of Thera,[9] became the metropolis of the district, and around it were grouped the four minor cities of Barce, Teucheira, Hesperides, and Apollonia, all of them colonies or offshoots of Cyrene itself.

§ 7. In Egypt the existence of a long-established native civili-

---

[7] Thucyd vi 2
[8] Herodotus, 1 165-167.; Diodor. v 13
[9] Herodot. iv 150-158. Concerning the date, see Note A, p. 127.

zation precluded the settlement of Greek colonies; but here also the Greeks had succeeded in establishing commercial relations: the jealousy of all intercourse with foreigners, which had prevailed under the earlier dynasties, having given way about the middle of the seventh century B.C., when Psammetichus, who had been assisted by some Ionian Greek mercenaries in establishing himself on the throne of Egypt, requited their services by opening his ports to their countrymen. The city of Naucratis, on the Canopic or western branch of the Nile, became an important emporium of Greek commerce, and traders of that nation settled there in such numbers that it is termed by some writers a Greek colony.[1]

From the above brief review of the progress of Greek colonization during this early period, it will be seen that before the middle of the sixth century B.C. their settlements had spread around almost the whole extent of the Mediterranean, and although it cannot be assumed that the colonies in all cases maintained much continuous intercourse with the parent cities, it is clear that they were never cut off from the rest of the Hellenic world, and, hence, they not only serve to prove the extent to which Greek commerce and navigation had already attained in these remote regions; but they became in their turn the centres from which Greek arts and civilization were able to penetrate into the surrounding countries.

§ 8. During the same period, the adventurous Greek navigators had not only explored the long-dreaded shores of the Euxine, but had rendered them so familiar that they had almost lost their terrors, and here also numerous and flourishing colonies had arisen, not only on the southern and western shores of this inland sea, but even on its northern coast, among the wild nomad tribes that occupied the vast solitudes of Scythia, from the mouth of the Danube to the shores of the Cimmerian Bosporus. When we first obtain authentic information concerning the Greek colonies in these quarters, we find them in

---

[1] Herodot. ii. 154, 178; Strabo, xvii p. 801.

a state of great prosperity, exercising important influence over the neighbouring tribes—in some cases apparently direct dominion—while they maintained regular commercial relations with the more distant nations of the interior.

We have no authentic information as to the period when Greek navigators first penetrated into the recesses of the Euxine. The statement repeated by many ancient writers [2] that the original name given to it was Axenos or Axeinos—" the inhospitable "—on account of its stormy and dangerous character, as well as the barbarous habits of the tribes that surrounded it, and that this was afterwards changed into Euxeinos—" the hospitable "—when it had been thrown open to Greek navigation and commerce—may very probably be nothing more than an etymological fancy; but the change of relations upon which it was based was undoubtedly a fact. The establishment of Greek colonies in this quarter, however, did not commence till a later period than in Italy and Sicily. None of those concerning which we have any trustworthy chronology can be assigned to the eighth century B.C., and even as late as the middle of the seventh, we find the rival cities of Miletus and Megara vying with one another in founding colonies on the shores of the Propontis and Bosphorus, while neither of them as yet attempted to extend their settlements within the Euxine itself.

The rivalry between these two cities—both of them at this time among the leading states of Greece for commercial and maritime enterprise—may remind one, on a much smaller scale, of that between Spain and Portugal in the fifteenth and sixteenth centuries. Thus, while Megara had founded during the first half of the seventh century B.C., the important colonies of Chalcedon and Byzantium at the entrance of the

---

[2] Strabo, vii. pp 298, 300, who cites Apollodorus and other earlier writers (Scymn Ch v. 785) No allusion to such a change is found in Herodotus, but Pindar uses the expression Ἄξεινος where he is describing the voyage of the Argonauts (*Pyth.* iv. 203), though he elsewhere employs the usual term Εὔξεινος. (*Nem.* iv. 49)

Bosphorus, as well as the less considerable towns of Selymbria and Astacus on the Propontis,³ Miletus had occupied the southern shore of the same land-locked sea by its settlements at Abydus, Cyzicus, and on the little island of Proconnesus.⁴ The possession of two such important positions as Byzantium and Chalcedon, commanding the very entrance of the Euxine, would seem calculated to secure to the Megarians the exclusive control of that sea; and it is strange to find that it was not till near a century later (B.C. 559) that they pushed forward their settlements within the Bosphorus, and founded the city of Heraclea on the coast of Bithynia, a place which continued until a late period to be one of the most important of the Greek colonies on the Euxine.⁵ This new city rapidly rose to power, and was soon able to send out colonies in its turn; of which the most important were Callatis or Callatia, on the western shore of the Euxine, between the Bosphorus and the Danube, and the more celebrated city of Chersonesus—called for distinction's sake Chersonesus Heraclea—near the south-western extremity of the Tauric peninsula, occupying very nearly the same site with the now famous city of Sevastopol.⁶

§ 9. Meanwhile their rivals, the Milesians, had already established themselves on both sides of the Euxine, and extended their settlements along its shores both to the right and left of the Bosphorus. Their earliest colonies within that strait seem to have been on the western coast of the Euxine, where they founded Istrus or Istropolis as early as B.C. 633, and Tomi apparently soon after.⁷ The object of these two settlements

---

³ Chalcedon was founded in B C 674; Byzantium not till B C 657. Selymbria was founded before Byzantium. (Scymn. Ch. v. 716.) Concerning the date of the latter and of Chalcedon, see Clinton, *F. H.*, vol. i. pp 186, 194.

⁴ Cyzicus, which became by far the most important of these settlements, was founded, according to the best authorities in B.C. 675. (See Note B, p. 128.)

⁵ The date is fixed by Scymnus Chius (v. 975) as contemporary with the overthrow of the Median monarchy by Cyrus.

⁶ The date of the foundation of the city of Chersonesus is wholly unknown. Neumann assigns it to the first half of the fifth century B.C (*Die Hellenen im Skythenlande*, p 383) but his grounds are merely conjectural.

⁷ The foundation of Istrus is fixed by Scymnus Chius (v. 770) as con-

was evidently to secure the shortest communication by land with the Danube, and thus to command the commerce of that great river, the actual mouths of which, from their marshy and unsettled character, have never been occupied by any town either in ancient or modern times. The subsequent foundation of Apollonia and Odessus, on the same line of coast, but nearer to the Bosphorus,[8] was probably designed chiefly to maintain the communication with these outlying settlements: but the former city rose at a later period to be one of the most considerable in this part of the Euxine.

A far more important colony was Sinope, on the southern coast of the Euxine, which was founded, according to what seems the most probable chronology, about B.C. 630.[9] It soon rose to be a flourishing city, and sent out colonies in its turn, the most important of which was Trapezus—the modern Trebizond—which has continued down to our own times to be one of the principal emporiums of trade with the East. Cerasus and Cotyora, on the same line of coast, were also colonies of Sinope.[1] Amisus on the other hand, which soon rose to be a place of consideration, was apparently a settlement direct from the parent city of Miletus.[2] The remoter colonies of Phasis, at the mouth of the river of the same name, and Dioscurias, nearer to the foot of the Caucasus, though carrying on an

---

temporary with the irruption of the Scythians into Asia in pursuit of the Cimmerians, and that of Odessus with the accession of Astyages to the throne of Media (v 749) This mode of marking dates, by reference to some contemporary event, bears with it a much greater stamp of probability than the arbitrary dates assigned by later chronologers The anonymous author of the little work extant under the name of Scymnus Chius had very good information concerning these Greek colonies on the Euxine, which he apparently derived principally from Demetrius of Callatia (see v 720)

[8] Apollonia was founded about fifty years before the accession of Cyrus (Scymn Ch v 731), or about B C 609. Odessus shortly after 694. See preceding n.te

[9] Concerning the date of Sinope, and its colony Trapezus, see Note B, p 128

[1] Xenophon, *Anabasis*, v 3, § 2, 5, § 3.
[2] Theopomp. ap Strab xii p 547 Scymnus Chius, on the contrary, calls it a colony of the Phocæans (v 919) According to the same author Phanagoria, on the Cimmerian Bosporus, was a colony from Teos (v 892) It is probable that in both cases there may have been a body of colonists from those Ionian cities, but under the guidance and command of the Milesians

§ 10. Far different was the case with the cities founded on the northern shores of the Euxine. It is evident that the Milesians early became alive to the importance of the great rivers that flow into the Euxine on this side, as channels of commercial intercourse and communication with the interior: and accordingly we find them securing to themselves the possession of this trade by the establishment of colonies at the entrances of all these great streams. Tyras, at the mouth of the river of the same name, now the Dniester, never attained to any great importance: but the wealth and prosperity of Olbia, situated at the mouth of the Borysthenes, were such as fully to justify the name given to it by the inhabitants: while Panticapæum, on the site of the modern Kertch, commanding the entrance to the Palus Mæotis and the Tanais, rose to a still higher degree of power and opulence, and became for centuries the capital of the surrounding countries. It was not till a much later period—apparently after the time of Herodotus—that a colony was established at the mouth of the Tanais itself, in the farthest recesses of the Palus Mæotis.[3] But Theodosia, on the southern coast of the Crimea, almost exactly on the same site as was occupied in the middle ages by the flourishing Genoese colony of Caffa—and Phanagoria, on the Asiatic side of the Cimmerian Bosporus, though in some degree eclipsed by the superior greatness of Panticapæum, both of them became, and continued down to the time of Strabo, to be flourishing towns and important places of trade.[4]

---

[3] No mention of it is found in Herodotus. Nor does its name occur in Scymnus Chius, but the fragmentary nature of this portion of his work prevents us from drawing any secure conclusion from its absence. Strabo says that it was founded by the Greek settlers on the Bosporus (κτίσμα τῶν τὸν Βόσπορον ἐχόντων Ἑλλήνων, xi. 2, p. 493): it was probably not founded till after the establishment of the Greek *monarchy* in the fifth century, B C

[4] Strabo, vii. 4, p. 309, xi 2, p. 495.

§ 11. All these colonies on the north of the Euxine—with the single exception of Heraclea or Chersonesus, already noticed—were of Milesian origin;[5] and they doubtless continued to keep up permanent intercourse with the parent city, and thus contributed to the extension of geographical knowledge in Greece. Of the successive steps by which they developed their commercial relations with the interior we have no information, and we are only able to judge of the extent to which they ultimately carried their trade, by the accounts that we receive concerning it at a later period. But it is certain that the name of the Issedones, who were still in the time of Herodotus the remotest people with whom the Greeks had any communication, was known to writers of a much earlier date:[6] and before the middle of the sixth century B.C., Aristeas of Proconnesus, whose poem of the Arimaspea has been already mentioned, is said to have himself penetrated into the interior as far as the country which they inhabited, and to have there collected the information which he embodied in his poem, concerning the one-eyed Arimaspians, the gold-guarding griffins, and the Hyperboreans.[7] Whether he had really derived these legends from the Scythian tribes of the interior, or whether—as appears more probable—they were fables already current among the Greeks,[8] to which he sought thus to lend consistence and authority, it is certain

---

[5] The date of the foundation of these northern colonies is very uncertain. That of Borysthenes (Olbia) is placed by Hieronymus as early as B C 654, but this is extremely improbable, and at variance with all we know from other sources of the progress of the Milesian colonization. Scymnus Chius says only that it was founded during the time of the Median monarchy (κατὰ τὴν Μηδικὴν ἐπαρχίαν, v 836), which would allow of any date between 711 and 559 B C. But the latter half of this period is certainly the most probable. Concerning Panticapæum we have no definite statement, but it seems probable that it was not founded till the 6th century. Boeckh places it about B C. 540 (*Corpus Inscr* vol II

p 91)

[6] If we can trust to Stephanus of Byzantium (*s v*), they were mentioned by the poet Alcman, who flourished as early as B C 671-631, at which period the Milesian colonies in this quarter were certainly not yet founded. But some vague notion of the name and people may have reached the ears of the Greeks long before.

[7] Herodotus, iv 13

[8] We have seen that, if we can trust to the citations of later writers, both the griffins and the Hyperboreans were already known to Hesiod, or were at least mentioned in the poems extant under his name, which could hardly be later than the seventh century B C

that from this time forth they not only took a firm hold on the popular belief in Greece, but assumed a definite geographical place in the regions in question. Even Damastes, a contemporary of Herodotus, in a professed geographical work, stated as a matter of fact that "beyond the Scythians dwelt the Issedones: beyond these again the Arimaspians, and beyond the Arimaspians were the Rhipæan Mountains, from which the north wind blew, and which were never free from snow. On the other side of these mountains were the Hyperboreans, extending down to the sea."[9] It is singular that no mention was apparently made by Aristeas of the Rhipæan Mountains, though without them the fable of the Hyperboreans had no meaning:[1] but he distinctly spoke of the Hyperboreans themselves as extending down to the sea;[2] a circumstance which clearly shows that the notion of a northern ocean, beyond the wild tracts of Scythia, was already become familiar in his time.

§ 12. The completion of this girdle of colonies, with which the Milesians had thus encircled the Euxine—except only the rugged and mountainous tract extending along its eastern coast from Dioscurias to the Cimmerian Bosporus—was probably not fully accomplished till the middle of the sixth century B.C.: and within about half a century afterwards the capture and destruction of Miletus by the Persians (B.C. 494) inflicted a blow upon the parent city from which it never recovered. For two centuries previous to that event Miletus had enjoyed an amount of wealth and prosperity surpassing in all probability that of any other Greek city, certainly far exceeding that of any city of Greece itself at this early period.[3] The luxury with which the Milesians are reproached by later writers is in itself a proof of their opulence, and besides their

---

[9] Damastes ap. Steph. Byzant v Ὑπερβόρεοι The passage is cited from Damastes ἐν τῷ περὶ ἐθνῶν

[1] The essential character of this "meteorological myth," as it has been aptly called by Humboldt, is that they dwelt beyond the region from which the north wind blew. This was doubtless originally placed in Thrace, from whence the cold north winds that prevailed in Greece appeared to proceed. It was afterwards found necessary to transfer it much farther to the north

[2] τούτων δὲ τοὺς Ὑπερβορέους καθήκοντας ἐπὶ θάλασσαν. Herodot. l c.

[3] Athenæus, xii. c. 26.

trade with the Euxine, they were renowned for their woollen manufactures, especially for their carpets and hangings, which were made of the fine wool brought from the interior of Asia Minor, and enjoyed a reputation similar to that of Turkey carpets in modern times.[4] The close and friendly relations which they maintained with Sybaris in Italy, down to the date of its destruction in B.C. 510, are a sufficient evidence of the extent of the commercial intercourse between the two cities.[5] Miletus also had a separate factory, or commercial establishment, at Naucratis in Egypt, apart from the other Greeks who traded there, which is sometimes erroneously termed a Milesian colony.[6] But we hear of no colonies of Miletus properly so called, on the shores of the Mediterranean, beyond the limits of the Ægean.

§ 13. While the energies of the Milesians were thus directed principally to their settlements in the Black Sea, those of their neighbours the Phocæans had continued to be turned towards the western shores of the Mediterranean. That people had indeed, according to Herodotus, been the first of all the Greeks who undertook long voyages, and who made known to their countrymen the Adriatic and Tyrrhenian seas.[7] We have already seen that they founded, in B.C. 600, the important colony of Massilia on the north shore of the Mediterranean. It was probably about the same time that they pushed their enterprising voyages as far as the south of Spain, and visited

---

[4] Id. xii p 553, xv. p. 691.
[5] Herodot. vi. 21. Timæus (ap. Athenæum xii. c. 17, p 519) expressly attributes the intimate relations between the two cities to the predilection of the luxurious Sybarites for the woollen garments of Miletus
[6] Strabo, xvii p 801. The real relations between the Greeks in Egypt and the native rulers are clearly described by Herodotus (ii. 178) But it appears that the Milesians had at one time certainly established a fortified post on the sea coast, which retained long after the name of τὸ Μιλησίων

τεῖχος (Strab l c).
[7] Herodot. i 163. οἱ δὲ Φωκαιεες οὗτοι ναυτιλίῃσι μακρῇσι πρῶτοι Ἑλλήνων ἐχρήσαντο, καὶ τόν τε Ἀδρίην καὶ τὴν Τυρσηνίην καὶ τὸν Ταρτησσὸν οὗτοί εἰσι οἱ καταδέξαντας

On these voyages of discovery he tells us that the Phocæans employed pentecontors, instead of "round ships," as ordinary merchant vessels were called Probably this was done with a view to the probability of hostile collisions with the Phœnicians or Carthaginians

Tartessus, where they established relations of such a friendly character with Arganthonius, king of the country, that we are assured by the historian they would have emigrated thither in a body, on the capture of their city by Cyrus, had not the friendly monarch been already deceased.[8] They in consequence turned their attention to Corsica, but being frustrated in their endeavours to establish themselves permanently in that island, they ultimately founded the colony of Velia or Elea on the coast of Italy.[9]

Other cities of Asia Minor shared in this general movement, of which Miletus and Phocæa were the leading representatives. Among these the two islands of Samos and Rhodes bore a conspicuous part, and were early distinguished by the zeal with which they devoted themselves to maritime pursuits. It was a ship of Samos, under a commander named Colæus, that was the first to visit Tartessus, and bring home from thence a cargo of incalculable value:[1] and although this was the result of an accident, yet it is evident from the narrative of Herodotus that Samian ships were at this time carrying on an extensive trade in different parts of the Mediterranean. This voyage of Colæus was contemporary with the foundation of Cyrene (about B.C. 631): but more than half a century earlier they had already attained to a prominent position among the naval powers of Greece. The Samians are mentioned by Thucydides as among the first to adopt the use of triremes, which they learnt from the Corinthians as early as B.C. 700.[2] But it was not till a later period, under the government of Polycrates (about B.C. 532-522) that Samos attained its greatest power. That ruler is said to have possessed a fleet of a hundred ships of war:[3] and the island for a time enjoyed unexampled pro-

---

[8] Id. ib. 163, 165 As Arganthonius, according to Herodotus, lived to the age of 120 years, of which he reigned 80, this does not give us much clue to the date of the first intercourse with that monarch.
[9] Id ib. 167, Strabo, vi. 1, p. 252.
[1] Herodot. iv. 152. His statement that Tartessus was at this time wholly unvisited by the Greeks (τὸ δὲ ἐμπόριον τοῦτο ἦν ἀκήρατον τοῦτον τὸν χρόνον) seems at variance with what he tells us of the Phocæans in the passage already cited
[2] Thucyd i 13.
[3] Herodot iii. 39. See also Thucy-

sperity under his authority. The Samians had at this time a separate establishment at Naucratis in Egypt, and Polycrates maintained intimate relations with Amasis, the king of that country.[4]

The accounts of the maritime power of Rhodes are less satisfactory. It is stated indeed that from a very early period—many years before the first Olympiad[5]—they devoted their attention to maritime enterprises, and undertook long voyages to Spain and Italy, where the foundation of several colonies was ascribed to them. But these accounts, which are transmitted to us in a very vague form, seem directly at variance with the statement of Herodotus that the Phocæans were the first to open out these western regions to the Greeks: and of the three colonies assigned to the Rhodians by Strabo—Rhoda in Spain, Parthenope in Campania, and Salapia on the Adriatic coast of Italy—the two last at least rest on very questionable authority.[6] On the other hand the settlement of Gela in Sicily, forty-five years after the foundation of Syracuse (B.C. 690) by a joint colony from Rhodes and Crete, is well attested.[7] Phaselis also, on the east coast of Lycia, facing the Pamphylian Gulf, which rose to be a flourishing commercial city, was a colony of Rhodes, founded about the same time with Gela.[8] There can indeed be no doubt that Rhodes itself was, as early as the seventh century B.C., an important trading community, for which the opportune situation of the island gave it extraordinary advantages. In the following century we find the Rhodians, as might be expected, taking advantage of the opening of the

---

dides, 1. 13. His ships, however, were, according to Herodotus, only pentecontei s.

[4] Herodot ii. 178, iii. 39. 40

[5] πρὸ τῆς 'Ολυμπικῆς θέσεως συχνοῖς ἔτεσιν. Strabo, xiv. 2, § 10, p 654
This tradition of the early maritime greatness of Rhodes was probably connected with the strange statement of Diodorus (derived apparently from Castor), that the Rhodians held the "dominion of the sea" for a period of 23 years, beginning as early as B C. 918 (Diodor. ap. Euseb. *Chron Arm.* 11. p 91)

[6] Strabo, *l c.* The settlements in Italy in all probability belong to mythical times, and are not mentioned by Strabo himself in treating of the places to which they relate.

[7] Thucyd vi 4; Schol ad Pind. *Olymp.* ii 16

[8] Athenæus, vii. p. 298 ; Steph. Byzant. v Γέλα.

trade with Egypt, and joining in the establishment of the Greek factory at Naucratis.⁹ But it was not till a much later period, after the foundation of the *city* of the same name (B.C. 408) that Rhodes attained to the position which it so long enjoyed, of one of the leading commercial and naval powers of the Greek world.

§ 14. While the Greek cities of Asia Minor were devoting themselves with so much zeal and energy to the pursuit of navigation and commerce, the same spirit was developing itself with equal activity among some of the older commonwealths of European Greece. The foremost place among these was undoubtedly taken by Corinth, a city which, from its peculiar position, enjoyed advantages such as no other could compete with. As Thucydides observes, it was situated equally favourably for traffic by land and sea; and as navigation became more general, its two ports, Lechæum and Cenchreæ, gave it the command of the Corinthian and Saronic Gulfs.¹ On the side of the Ægean, however, the Corinthians had many competitors; hence it was principally towards the west that their efforts were directed, and it is in this quarter only that we find them extending their colonial empire. The foundation of the two important colonies of Syracuse and Corcyra, as early as the middle of the eighth century, has been already mentioned. Both of these belong to the period while Corinth was still under the government of the oligarchy known as the Bacchiadæ, a period during which the city undoubtedly rose to a high state of power and prosperity.² It was, according to Thucydides, the first state to organize a regular naval force, with ships built in the same manner as those used by the Greeks in later times. The invention of the trireme is expressly ascribed by him to the Corinthians; and it was a Corinthian named Ameinocles who first taught the art of

---

⁹ Herodot. ii 178.
¹ Thucyd 1 13 Corinth was already celebrated for its wealth in the days of Homer (Iliad, ii. 570).
² The oligarchy of the Bacchiadæ held possession of the government at Corinth for about 90 years, until it was overthrown by Cypselus about B C 655.

constructing ships on the new model to the Samians, who appear to have been the first to follow their example.³

In the following century Corinth passed under the despotic rule of Cypselus and his son Periander (B.C. 655-585); but it continued to enjoy a great amount of wealth and prosperity, and extended its power by the foundation of numerous additional colonies. None of these, however, were planted in distant regions; and the establishment of such settlements as Leucas or Leucadia on the coast of Acarnania, and that of Anactorium and Ambracia in the same district, must have been designed as much to secure political power in Greece as to extend their commercial relations, or open an intercourse with distant countries. All these colonies were in the first instance mere dependencies of Corinth, with which they continued long after to maintain friendly relations. Corcyra alone was an exception, having early risen to such power as to be able to compete with the parent city, which led to constant disputes, and a permanent feeling of enmity between the two.⁴ Thucydides tells us that the first naval battle on record was one between the Corinthians and Corcyræans, which was fought in the year B.C. 664, only seventy years after the foundation of the colony.⁵ The result is not mentioned;⁶ but we know that

---

³ Thucyd. i 13. This took place, according to Thucydides, about 300 years before the end of the Peloponnesian war, or B C. 704. He does not mention the date of the first invention of triremes by the Corinthians, but it was probably not long before The date given by Hieronymus in his version of the chronicle of Eusebius, who places it ten years before the first Olympiad, or B C 786 (Trieres primum navigat in Corinthum; Hieronym Chron ad ann. 1230), is almost certainly too early. The same author has at the 3rd year of the 4th Olympiad (B C. 762) the notice "Athenis primum trieies navigavit, Ameinocleo cuisum dirigente," which in all probability refers to the same event as that mentioned by Thucydides, though it is transferred to the Athenians instead of the Samians, and placed 58 years too early. This sufficiently shows how little dependence can be placed upon the other date.

Pliny erroneously understands Thucydides as representing Ameinocles as the first inventor of triremes (Triremem Thucydides Ameinoclem Corinthium [primum fecisse] Plin. H. N. vii. c. 56, § 207)

⁴ Herodot. iii 49; Thucyd. i. 38.
⁵ Thucyd i 13.
⁶ Chevr. Bunsen assumes that the Corinthians were defeated, and that this was the event which put a stop to their "dominion of the sea" But everything connected with these "tha-

Corcyra, though for a time reduced to subjection by the despot Periander, soon recovered its liberty, and ever afterwards continued independent of the mother-country. But though Corinth, as was usual with Greek cities, soon lost all political control over her more distant colonies, she continued to be one of the most opulent commercial cities in Greece; and even at a later period her naval power was second only to that of Athens.

§ 15. Contemporary with the early greatness of Corinth was that of the neighbouring city of Megara, which, though in the later periods of Greek history a place of comparatively little importance, and altogether subordinate to its more powerful neighbours, Corinth and Athens, developed in the early ages an amount of commercial energy and enterprise which is sufficiently attested by its numerous and flourishing colonies. Of these the Hyblæan Megara, in Sicily, already mentioned,[7] appears to have been an isolated effort in that direction; with this exception, it was towards the north-east that the attention of the Megarians seems to have been principally directed; and here, as we have already seen, their colonies on the shores of the Propontis and the Euxine for a time rivalled those of the Milesians. By far the most important of these were the two cities of Byzantium and Chalcedon, at the entrance of the strait of the Bosphorus, the first of which was not long in attaining to that high degree of wealth and prosperity for which its unrivalled advantages of situation have marked it out in all ages. It is strange that the Megarians were so slow to perceive the superiority of its position over that of its opposite neighbour, that it was not till seventeen years after the foundation of Chalcedon that they established their settlement on the European side of the strait—an oversight for

---

Iassocrates" is in the highest degree uncertain and untrustworthy. (See note C, p. 130.)

[7] Thucyd vi 4 The far more important colony of Selinus, on the south-west coast of Sicily, was founded by a colony from the Sicilian Megara, about 100 years after its own establishment (B.C. 628) On this occasion a fresh body of colonists from the parent city joined in the settlement of the new colony (Thucyd *l c*).

which they were justly reproached with blindness by the Persian Megabazus.[8]

The power and prosperity of Megara itself, at the time that it was sending forth these successive colonies, are confirmed by the little we know of its history in other respects. The contest which it was so long able to carry on single-handed with Athens for the possession of Salamis,[9] is a sufficient proof of the position it then occupied in the Hellenic world. But the final loss of that important island must have been a great blow to its prosperity; and it probably continued to decline, as its more fortunate rival advanced in power. As late as the Persian War, however, Megara was still able to furnish a contingent of twenty ships to the fleet that fought at Artemisium and Salamis.[1]

§ 16. Besides the rising power of Athens, the commercial prosperity of Megara must have been materially interfered with by that of the neighbouring island of Ægina, which, before the end of the period we are now considering, had risen to be an important maritime power. Its early history is indeed very obscure. But it seems certain that the Æginetans were celebrated in very early times for their skill in navigation; and they even enjoyed the reputation of being the first to introduce the use of ships with sails and banks of oars [2]—a tradition worthless in itself, but a proof how early they were supposed to have attained to excellence as a maritime people.

Ephorus also tells us that the island became an important commercial emporium, on account of the ruggedness of the soil compelling the inhabitants to betake themselves to maritime pursuits [3]—a cause which undoubtedly contributed to produce the result, but which was in a great degree common

---

[8] Herodot. iv 144.
[9] Plutarch, *Solon*, c. 8; Strabo, ix. p 394; Pausan. 1. 40, § 5.
The date of this protracted contest appears to have been from about 620 to 600 B.C.
[1] Herodot. viii. 1, 45.

[2] This is stated in a fragment of one of the lost poems of Hesiod, preserved to us by the Scholiast on Pindar (*ad Olymp* viii. 26, *ad Nem.* iii. 21). See Marksscheffel, *Fragm. Hesiod.* 92.
[3] Ephorus ap. Strab. viii. 6, p. 376.

to all the smaller Greek islands. Its commanding position, in the centre of the Saronic Gulf, and its good port, were more special advantages; but still we are at a loss to determine the circumstances that marked it out for a career of prosperity, and enabled it to play a part so disproportioned to its size and natural resources.[4] The fact, however, is unquestionable. The general statements of Ephorus and other writers might indeed have referred to a later period, but the circumstance that it was to Ægina that the Greeks were indebted for the first coinage of money,[5] and that the standard introduced by them continued ever after to bear the name of Æginetan, is a sufficient testimony to the early power and influence of this little island. The date of the first coinage of silver in Ægina by the tyrant Pheidon of Argos, is determined approximately by the connection of that despot with the Olympic games, and may be assigned to about the eighth Olympiad, or B.C. 748.[6] It seems, therefore, impossible to doubt that as early as the middle of the eighth century B.C. the Æginetans had already attained a commanding position among the commercial states of Greece.

But the epoch of their greatest maritime power belongs to a considerably later period—to the century immediately preceding the Persian War. The Æginetans were undoubtedly at this time one of the leading commercial states of Greece, and their naval power was more than a match for that of Athens, which was indeed still in its infancy. In B.C. 563,

---

[4] Events that have taken place in our own day tend to illustrate and explain the importance thus early assumed by the "Æginetan rock," as it is contemptuously termed by Mitford. The little island of Hydra, off the coast of Argolis, which is of less extent than Ægina, and much more barren, rose under the pressure of circumstances, just before the war of the Greek revolution, to be one of the most important places in the Archipelago. The population was estimated at 40,000, and the commercial navy amounted to 150 vessels, some of them of considerable size, which carried their voyages beyond the limits of the Mediterranean See Gordon's *Hist. of the Greek Revolution;* Waddington's *Visit to Greece*, 1823-24, pp. 101-113. Since the war the island of Syra has risen with almost equal rapidity.

[5] Ephorus, *l. c.*

[6] Concerning the date, see Clinton, *F. H* vol. 1. pp. 247-250; Grote's *Hist. of Greece*, vol. ii. pp. 419-433.

during the reign of Amasis in Egypt, the Æginetans carried on an extensive trade with that country, and had a separate settlement at Naucratis, where they are the only European Greeks who are mentioned as taking part in the Egyptian trade, all the others being Asiatic Greeks from the coast-cities of Asia Minor.[7] But it is remarkable that we hear of no colonies of Ægina: a circumstance the more singular, as the extremely restricted size of the island must have rendered it incapable of long supporting an extensive population.[8]

§ 17. Among the cities which in the early ages of Greece occupy a prominent place, from their commercial wealth and activity, are two others, which, like Megara and Ægina, had sunk into a subordinate position during the period when we are most familiar with Greek history. Chalcis and Eretria in Eubœa, both of them cities of Ionian origin, were at one period among the foremost states of the Ionic name; and they not only carried on an extensive trade, but founded numerous colonies in different parts of the Greek world. One important group of these occupied the singular peninsula on the Macedonian coast, which derived from the first of them the appellation of Chalcidice, though Eretria also appears to have borne its full share in the settlement of the numerous towns, with which the coasts of the peninsula and its three projecting promontories were gradually studded. Methone, the most ancient of these, is assigned to a date as early as B.C. 720; the rest appear to have followed at uncertain intervals till about B.C. 600 The power and opulence of the Eretrians in early days were attested by an inscription still extant in the time of Strabo, according to which the inhabitants were at one time able to display in their sacred processions not less than 3000 hoplites, 600 horsemen, and 60 chariots.[9] They were at the same

---

[7] Herodot ii. 178.
[8] Strabo indeed asserts that the Æginetans sent out two colonies: one to Cydonia in Crete, the other to Umbria (viii. p 376). But the former statement probably refers to the transaction related by Herodotus (iii. 59), which certainly does not point to the establishment of a colony properly so called; and of the second nothing is known.
[9] Strabo, x. 1, p. 448.

period masters of Andros, Tenos, Ceos, and other neighbouring islands.[1]

But the Chalcidians were far from confining their attention to the coasts of Thrace and Macedonia. At an early period (as we have already seen) they extended their voyages to the coasts of Italy and Sicily, where they founded the colony of Cumæ, on the coast of Campania, as well as the important towns of Zancle (afterwards better known as Messana) and Rhegium, on the opposite sides of the Sicilian Straits.[2] Naxos also—the earliest of all the Greek colonies in Sicily—was of Chalcidic origin; and this, together with its more important offspring, Catana and Leontini, continued to be always distinguished as "the Chalcidic cities" of the island, as opposed to the more flourishing and powerful Dorian cities.

It is a sufficient proof of the important position held by these two cities of Eubœa, that a war which broke out between them assumed such grave proportions as to induce many of the other states of Greece to take part in the quarrel. Even some of the Asiatic cities sent forces to the assistance of the two rivals; the Samians supporting the Chalcidians, while the Milesians lent their aid to the Eretrians.[3] It was in return for this that at a later period the Eretrians, though already much fallen in power, sent a small squadron to the assistance of Miletus at the time of the Ionic revolt, B.C. 499.[4] A still more decisive evidence of the commercial importance of these two cities in early days is to be found in the fact, that after the general introduction of coined money into Greece, the standard in most general use, after the Æginetan, was known by the name of the Euboic—a designation which subsequently

---

[1] Strabo, *l. c.* Herodotus mentions, among the suitors for the hand of Agarista, the daughter of Cleisthenes, Lysanias, from Eretria, "which was at that time a flourishing city" (ἀπὸ 'Ερετρίης ἀνθεύσης τοῦτον τὸν χρόνον. Herodot. vi. 127). This was about B.C. 590.

[2] Thucyd. vi. 4; Strabo, vi. p. 257.

Himera also, on the north coast of Sicily, was a joint colony from Zancle, and the parent city of Chalcis (Thucyd. vi. 5).

[3] Thucyd. i. 15; Herodot v. 99. The date of this war, as well as all further details concerning it, are unknown; but it may probably be assigned to the sixth century B C.

[4] Herodot. *l c.*

fell into disuse as the commercial greatness of Chalcis and Eretria became a thing of the past.[5]

§ 17. While several of the smaller states of Greece, at this time, occupied so prominent a position, it is remarkable that Athens, which was destined, at a later period, to eclipse all rivals by its commercial and maritime supremacy, held as yet but a very subordinate place. We have seen how long the Athenians had to contend with the neighbouring state of Megara for the possession of Salamis: and at a considerably later period they were still unable to cope at sea with the Æginetans, and were compelled to have recourse to the aid of the Corinthians, who furnished them with twenty ships, in order to raise their fleet to an equality with that of their rivals.[6] It was Themistocles who first raised the Athenian fleet to the position of supremacy which it subsequently enjoyed; and the result of his efforts, which were made with a view to the war with Ægina, was fortunately accomplished just in time for the great struggle with Persia.[7] But though the sudden development of energy and power on the part of the Athenians, which followed the expulsion of the Pisistratids, doubtless gave increased vigour to their commercial activity, they were still far from occupying a foremost place among Greek cities in this respect. Even after the Persian War, we find Æschylus referring to the silver mines of Laurium as the principal source of the wealth and power of Athens, without any allusion to its trade or shipping.[8]

§ 18. From the above brief review of the colonies and com-

---

[5] The relations between the three standards of money used in Greece are still very obscure. But it is certain that, as stated in the text, the Æginetan and Euboic were the two most prevalent in early times, while the Attic did not come into general use till a later time. Its adoption was probably owing at least as much to the care bestowed by the Athenians upon their coinage, and the large amount of silver furnished them by the mines of Laurium as to the extension of their commercial relations. (See the passage in Aristophanes, *Ranæ*, v 720-5, where the writer dwells upon the estimation in which the Athenian coinage was held "among the Greeks and barbarians everywhere")

[6] Herodotus, vi. 89-93.
[7] Id vii. 144.
[8] ἀργύρου πηγή τις αὐτοῖς ἐστι, θησαυρὸς χθονός.
Æschyl. *Persæ*, v 238

mercial relations of the Greeks, during the three centuries that preceded the Persian War, it will sufficiently appear that before the year B.C. 500, they had not only become well acquainted with the whole of the Mediterranean Sea, as well as the more inland waters of the Euxine, but had established colonies on a large portion of its shores and islands, all of which became the means of diffusing, within a circle more or less extensive, Hellenic ideas and Hellenic cultivation. But as yet everything beyond the basin of these inland seas was either wholly unknown to the Greeks or known to them only from the reports of other nations. No Greek navigator had ever ventured on the waters of the Western Ocean beyond the Pillars of Hercules, or on those of the Erythræan Sea, that bathed the southern shores of Asia. No adventurous traveller had sought to penetrate to the recesses of Æthiopia or India. What faint rumours might have reached the Greeks concerning these distant lands were derived only from the Egyptians, the Phœnicians, and in later times from the Persians.

§ 19. There are few subjects upon which full information would be more interesting than that of the early relations of the Greeks with their more civilized neighbours of the East; but, unfortunately, there are few in regard to which we are more totally devoid of any trustworthy records. The unquestionable fact of the derivation of their alphabetical writing from the Phœnicians; the numerous allusions in the Homeric poems to Phœnician arts and manufactures; as well as the strong internal evidence of the resemblance of early Greek works of art with those of Asia,—all conspire to prove how strong must have been the influence of the Asiatic civilization upon their then ruder neighbours, and this in itself shows that there must have been frequent and long-continued intercourse between them from a very early period.[9] The colonies in Asia Minor

---

[9] Recent researches have also shown that the Greek system of weights, which was applied also to the computation of their money—the talent, the mina, and the drachm—was almost certainly derived from that of Babylon (See

were undoubtedly the main stepping-stones of such an intercourse, and the great and rapid development of those colonies, though owing in great measure to the natural resources of their fertile and luxuriant territories, was doubtless materially aided by their early intercourse with the East, through means of their Lydian neighbours. At the same time, we cannot doubt that the Greeks continued to carry on extensive commercial intercourse with the Phœnicians themselves;[1] and notwithstanding the jealousy that may have very naturally existed between the two nations, it is remarkable that we do not hear of a single hostile collision between them. We know that there existed at one time Phœnician settlements in Thasos, Rhodes, Thera, and other islands of the Ægean, which were subsequently occupied by Greek colonists, so far as we learn, without opposition.[2] It is still more remarkable that the Phœnicians should apparently have opposed no obstacle to the establishment of Greek colonies in the large and fertile island of Cyprus, which was situated in their own immediate neighbourhood, and had been in the first instance occupied almost entirely by Phœnician colonists.[3] As we find them in Sicily, gradually, but peaceably, giving way before the increasing power and influence of the Greek colonists[4]—so they appear to have elsewhere quietly retired before the encroachments of

---

(See Brandis, *Das Munz- Mass- und Gewichtswesen in Vorder Asien*, 8vo, Berlin, 1866.) It is impossible to determine the period at which this system passed into use among the Greeks, but it may probably have accompanied the introduction of coined money, the invention of which is distinctly ascribed by Herodotus to the Lydians (i. 94); a statement there is no reason to dispute.

[1] Thus we find Xenophon, less than three centuries B.C., referring to a Phœnician ship of great size, which he had seen evidently in one of the Athenian ports (*Œconomica*, c. 8, § 11).

[2] In the case of Thasos, which had been one of the principal Phœnician colonies in the Ægean, we know that it was occupied by Greek settlers from Paros in the seventh century B.C. (Movers, *Die Phonizier*, vol. ii. p. 277; Grote's *Greece*, vol. iv. p. 34), one of whom was the poet Archilochus.

[3] The whole subject of the Greek colonies in Cyprus, and their relations with the Phœnicians, is extremely obscure. The only cities that seem to have been unquestionably of Greek origin are Salamis, Soli, and Marium (Scylax), and the dates of the foundation of these are wholly uncertain. The traditions connecting them with Athens and Attica are almost certainly fictitious, but the fact of their Attic origin may be true, though the legends themselves are inventions.

[4] Thucyd. vi. 2.

their more enterprising rivals. But of the nature and extent of the commercial relations which must have continued to subsist between the two nations, we are wholly ignorant.

§ 20. Somewhat more information has been preserved to us concerning the early relations of the Greeks with Egypt. Here the traditionary policy of the Egyptians, which had maintained the exclusion of all foreigners, as rigidly as was the case in China and Japan down to a recent period, was broken through by Psammetichus, who (as we have already seen) established himself on the throne by the aid of Ionian and Carian mercenaries (about B.C. 660), and in gratitude for this assistance opened the trade with Egypt to their countrymen.[5] As in the similar cases already alluded to, this permission was, in the first instance, restricted to a single port; all trade was confined to the Canopic or western mouth of the Nile, where the city of Naucratis became the emporium of Greek commerce, in which a large number of Greek merchants and others permanently settled. It never was a Greek colony, properly so called, as it is erroneously termed by Strabo and later writers;[6] but the Greek merchants who settled there obtained considerable privileges, which were afterwards extended by Amasis (B.C. 570–526), and they seem to have formed a regular community or corporation under the direction and control of officers elected by themselves. They were allowed also the exercise of their own religious rites, and they erected there a temple called the Hellenium, which was built conjointly by the Ionian, Dorian, and Æolian cities that participated in the trade, with the exception of Miletus and Samos, each of which had its own peculiar sanctuary.[7] Ægina also, the only city of European Greece that is mentioned in connection with this account, had its separate temple of Zeus.[8] Of the trade

---

[5] Herodotus, 11. 152-154.
[6] Strabo, xvii. 1, § 18, p. 801.
[7] The cities that united in the foundation of the common temple were: Chios, Teos, Phocæa, and Clazomenæ, of Ionic origin; Rhodes, Cnidus, Halicarnassus, and Phaselis, of Dorian; and Mytilene alone of Æolian race (Herodot. 11. 178).
[8] The above account of the Greek factory—to use a modern term, which is almost exactly applicable—at Nau-

carried on by the Greeks we only learn incidentally that wine formed an important article—as we are told, that Charanus, the brother of the poetess Sappho, had gone to Naucratis with a cargo of Lesbian wine, when he fell in love with the celebrated courtezan Rhodopis.[9]

After the opening of Egypt to the Greeks, it appears to have been not unfrequently visited by travellers, not for commercial purposes, but either simply to view its wonders, of which it was reputed to contain more than any other land,[1] or for the purpose of obtaining instruction in that recondite wisdom which the Egyptian priests were supposed to possess. The visit of Pythagoras, with this latter object, appears to be well authenticated, and may be placed between B.C. 560 and 540; during the reign of Amasis, who, as we learn from Herodotus, especially favoured the intercourse with foreigners. The poet Alcæus had also been in Egypt at a somewhat earlier period;[2] the visit of the historian Hecatæus probably took place before the end of the same century.

§ 21. Pythagoras is reported to have in like manner visited Babylon, in order to learn from the Chaldæan priests; but this statement rests on more doubtful authority, and we have no account of any other Greek traveller visiting that city before the time of Herodotus. But the Phœnicians undoubtedly maintained active commercial intercourse with the Assyrian and Babylonian capitals, long before the rise of the Persian empire: and there could be nothing to prevent a Greek from joining one of these caravans from Tyre or Sidon. We know also that Antimenidas, the brother of the poet Alcæus, actually served in the army of the king of Babylon, to whom he is said to have rendered important assistance.[3] Such an occurrence could hardly be an isolated case, and it

---

cratis is derived wholly from Herodotus (ii. 178), who speaks from personal knowledge as to the state of things existing when he visited Egypt, and could readily obtain authentic information at least as far back as the reign of Amasis.
[9] Strabo, xvii. p. 808.
[1] Herodot ii. 35.
[2] Strabo, i. p. 37.
[3] Strabo, xiii. p. 617; Alcæi Fragm 33, ed. Bergk.

therefore serves to show that there must have existed at this early period (about B.C. 590–580) more intercourse with the great cities of the interior of Asia than we are generally led to suppose.

The rise of the Persian monarchy, and especially the conquest of the Greek cities of Asia Minor by the Persian general Harpagus, must have excited a greatly increased amount of interest concerning the interior of Asia, and when the inhabitants of Miletus or Samos found themselves the subjects of the Great King, who had his abode by the distant waters of the Euphrates or Choaspes, they would naturally become curious to learn all they could concerning the remoter provinces of the empire. The continuous official intercourse that must have been maintained between the capital and the satrapies of Asia Minor, would afford them increased facilities for obtaining such information, and though the case of the Greek physician Democedes, who was carried a captive to Susa, where he rose to great distinction at the court of Darius, may have been an isolated one,[4] it is scarcely possible but that somewhat similar occurrences must have from time to time led to direct communication with the royal cities. Again, the expedition of Darius into Scythia, when the fleets of the Ionian and Æolian Greeks found themselves associated with the lévies of the Persian monarch from the most distant provinces of his dominions, would at once have stimulated their curiosity and afforded them increased opportunities of gratifying it. But it was probably not till after the Persian War and the expedition of Xerxes, that it was possible for a Greek to obtain that full and complete knowledge of all the provinces of the Persian Empire, the extent and accuracy of which surprise us in the pages of Herodotus.

[4] Herodot. III. 129–138.

Section 3.—*Physical Philosophers.*

§ 1. The same period which witnessed this great extension of the practical knowledge of the inhabited world possessed by the Greeks, beheld also the first imperfect attempts among them at what may be called scientific geography. The sixth century before the Christian era was an age of remarkable intellectual activity among the Greeks, and was marked at once by the first rise of prose writing and by the earliest recorded essays of philosophical speculation. THALES of MILETUS, the founder of the Ionic school of philosophy, is generally recognized also as the founder of physical science among the Greeks.[5] But it is extremely difficult to ascertain what were really the views that he entertained or the doctrines that he taught. It is admitted that he left nothing in writing: and the statements of later authors concerning his philosophical tenets are frequently at variance with one another, and have every appearance of being adapted to a more advanced condition of scientific speculation. Thus we are told by Herodotus, that he predicted the eclipse of the sun which separated the Median and Lydian armies under Cyaxares and Alyattes,[6] and according to later authorities, he correctly explained the causes of eclipses both of the sun and moon, attributing the latter to the interposition of the earth between the sun and moon, and the former to the interposition of the moon between the sun and the earth.[7] We are even told that he first instituted the division of the heavens into five zones, with a meridian cutting

---

[5] There is much discrepancy in the statements of ancient authors concerning the date of Thales and the period at which he flourished. The subject is fully investigated by Sir G. Lewis, who arrives at the conclusion that "the active part of the life of Thales may be referred with confidence to the first half of the sixth century B C." (*Astronomy of the Ancients*, p. 80.)

[6] The date of this eclipse has also been the subject of much controversy, but it appears to have been satisfactorily fixed by the investigations of the Astronomer Royal at B C. 585, which agrees with the date given by Pliny (ii. 12, § 53), of 170 U.C." (See Sir G Lewis, *l. c* p 87.)

[7] Plutarch *de Placit Philosoph* ii 24.
He was also clearly of opinion that the moon derived its light from the sun, an opinion which was strangely abandoned by Anaximander and others of his successors (Ibid. 27).

through them from north to south, and an oblique line called the zodiac passing through the three inner zones, and corresponding to the course of the sun.[8] It is difficult to believe that so much astronomical knowledge was coupled with the vulgar notion of the earth being a plane surface; and later philosophers undoubtedly supposed Thales to have been acquainted with the spherical form of the earth, and to have placed it in the centre of the universe, according to the system generally received in later times.[9] But other accounts, which appear to be sanctioned by Aristotle, represent him as stating that the earth was supported by water, upon which it floated, like a log, or a ship;[1] a strange idea, which certainly seems to imply that he regarded the earth, or at least the known world, as a plane surface.

Thales is also said to have speculated upon the causes of the annual inundation of the Nile,[2] a phenomenon which must have attracted the attention of the Greeks as soon as they began habitually to frequent the ports of Egypt. But the statement that he had himself visited that country, and derived from the Egyptian priests the foundation of his philosophical speculations, is in all probability apocryphal.

§ 2. It is unnecessary to follow the crude speculations of the philosophers that succeeded Thales in regard to the nature and movements of the heavenly bodies, and their relations

---

[8] Plutarch *de Placit Philosoph.* ii. 12. But this statement is ushered in with the expression: . "Thales, Pythagoras, and his disciples, divide the heavens," &c. There can be little doubt that the conclusions in question really belonged to Pythagoras and his disciples and Plutarch himself says that Pythagoras was the first to discover the obliquity of the zodiac (*l c*).

[9] This is distinctly asserted by Plutarch. Θαλῆς, καὶ οἱ Στωικοὶ, καὶ οἱ ἀπ' αὐτῶν, σφαιροειδῆ τὴν γῆν, *de Plac Phil.* iii. 10; οἱ ἀπὸ Θάλεω τὴν γῆν μέσην, ibid 11. But the same remark as in the preceding note applies in this case also.

[1] Aristot. *de Cœlo* ii. 13, § 7. οἱ δὲ ἐφ' ὕδατος κεῖσθαι (τὴν γῆν)· τοῦτον γὰρ ἀρχαιότατον παρειλήφαμεν τὸν λόγον, ὅν φασιν εἰπεῖν τὸν Θαλῆν τὸν Μιλήσιον, ὡς διὰ τὸ πλωτὴν εἶναι μένουσαν ὥσπερ ξύλον, ἤ τι τοιοῦτον ἕτερον He is said to have accounted for earthquakes by the fluctuations of this water, on which the earth rested Seneca, *Nat Quæst* iii 13, Plut *de Plac Phil* iii 15

[2] Plut *op cit* iv 1; Diodor i 38 He was apparently the first author of the theory which ascribed the swelling of the Nile to the opposition of the Etesian winds, one of the views combated by Herodotus (ii. 20)

with the earth: theories in some instances so fanciful that they seem dictated solely by the desire to invent something different from the views of preceding writers. Even in regard to the earth itself they seem to have adopted views of which it is difficult to conceive the origin. Thus, ANAXIMANDER is said to have held that the earth was of cylindrical form, like a stone pillar; the inhabited part being apparently the circular upper surface.³ Some of his astronomical speculations were equally fanciful and unfounded. But notwithstanding these absurdities, Anaximander was the author of one of the most important steps in geographical science by being the first to publish a map of the earth's surface: an invention ascribed to him by all ancient writers on the subject.⁴ There can be little doubt that the bronze tablet, which was brought by the Milesian Aristagoras to Sparta in B.C. 500, on which, according to Herodotus, there was engraved "the whole circuit of the earth, and every sea and all rivers" was in substance a reproduction of this original map of Anaximander.⁵ It probably differed but little from that subsequently drawn up by Hecatæus.

To Anaximander is also generally attributed the invention of the gnomon, or primitive sun-dial; an instrument of great importance in the progress of geographical, as well as astronomical science.⁶ It continued for ages to supply the only means practically known to the Greeks for the direct determination of terrestrial latitudes.

---

³ Plut *Plac Phil* ii 10; Origen (Hippolytus) *Philosoph* 1 p 11
Anaximander was the disciple and successor of Thales His birth is fixed in 610, and his death in 547 B C
⁴ Eratosthenes ap Strab 1 1, § 11, p 7; Diog Laert ii 1, § 2; Agathemer *Geograph* 1 1
⁵ Herod v 49 τῷ δὴ ἐς λόγους ἤιε, ὡς Λακεδαιμόνιοι λέγουσι, ἔχων χάλκεον πίνακα ἐν τῷ γῆς ἁπάσης περίοδος ἐνετέτμητο, καὶ θάλασσά τε πᾶσα καὶ ποταμοὶ πάντες It appears from the expressions of the historian as if this was the first map of the kind that had been seen *at Sparta*, which is in accordance with the statement that it was an Ionic invention

⁶ Diog. Laert. ii. 1. Suidas, v. Ἀναξίμανδρος, γνώμων, and ἡλιοτρόπιον. According to Herodotus, however, who lived little more than a century after Anaximander, the use of the gnomon and the *polus* (another instrument resembling a dial) was derived by the Greeks from the Babylonians (Herodot. ii 109) It is highly probable that they were in fact only *introduced* by Anaximander, not invented by him

§ 3. ANAXIMENES, the successor of Anaximander, and the third in the series of Ionic philosophers, is said to have held that the earth was of irregular quadrangular form, a flat trapezium, which was supported by the air beneath it, in consequence of its pressing it down like the lid of a vessel.[7] He maintained also that the sun and stars did not descend beneath the earth, and rise again at its other extremity, which appears to have been the prevalent doctrine in his day, but that they were carried round the earth, at a great distance, and that the light of the sun was intercepted during the night by high mountains.[8]

§ 4. PYTHAGORAS and his immediate followers were the first to introduce among the Greeks a cosmical philosophy somewhat more approaching to the truth. As that celebrated philosopher left nothing in writing, it is in many cases impossible to distinguish what was really taught by the master, and what was added by his disciples. But there is no reason to doubt that the leading physical doctrines ascribed to him were really held by Pythagoras himself, and they have been transmitted to us with unusual clearness. According to this system, as explained by Aristotle,[9] the earth was a sphere, which was not situated in the centre of the universe, but in common with the sun, moon, the planets, and the fixed stars, revolved around a central fire, which occupied the middle point of the whole system. Besides these, there was another body, named *anti-*

---

[7] Aristot. *de Cœlo*, ii. 13, § 10; Plut *Plac Phil*. iii. 10.
The age of Anaximenes is not determined with certainty, but he was certainly intermediate between Anaximander and Anaxagoras, and may be regarded as having flourished in the last half of the sixth century B.C (See Sir G. Lewis, *Hist. of Anc. Astron.* p. 95)
[8] Plut. *Plac Phil* ii 13, 19; Origen. *Philosophumena*, p 12
It is evidently this last opinion which is referred to by Aristotle as held by "many of the ancient meteorologists," without naming Anaximenes (*Meteorol*

ii. 1, § 16)
[9] Aristot. *de Cœlo*, ii 13 The doctrine is attributed by Aristotle to "the Pythagoreans," not to the master himself. but as Pythagoras himself left nothing in writing, the only definite information as to his opinions was necessarily derived from the writings of his disciples The earliest of these, whose works were extant in later times, was Philolaus (a contemporary of Socrates), to whom the system described by Aristotle is expressly ascribed by Stobæus (*Eclog. Phys.* 1 22), and by Plutarch (*Plac Phil* iii. 13)

chthon, as the opposite or counterpoise of the world, which in like manner revolved round the central fire, but was never visible from the earth. The nature and purpose of this last body it is not easy to determine:[1] but it is unnecessary for our present object to enter into any detailed examination of this curious and complicated system, which was founded almost entirely upon abstract theoretical speculations.[2] Even the important conclusion that the earth was of spherical form, seems to have not been derived from mathematical observations, but to have been an arbitrary assumption based upon the idea that a sphere was the most perfect of all forms. Be this as it may, it is certain that the Pythagoreans continued steadily to maintain the globular form of the earth, which may be considered as the fundamental principle of scientific geography. The same doctrine was held also by Parmenides and his followers of the Eleatic school:[3] while among the Ionic philosophers the primitive belief in the flatness of the earth continued to maintain its ground down to a comparatively late period. Thus, we are distinctly told that Anaxagoras, who was fully a generation later than Hecatæus, and not many years older than Herodotus, still adhered to the doctrine of Anaximenes, that the earth was a plane surface, which on account of its flatness was buoyed up and sustained by the air beneath it.[4] We cannot, therefore, wonder that the

---

[1] It must not be supposed that it had anything in common with the Antichthon of Pomponius Mela, which was merely a fictitious continent in the southern hemisphere, devised for the purpose of *balancing* the land in the northern hemisphere

[2] It is fully investigated by Sir G Lewis (*Astronomy of the Ancients*, pp 124-128), who justly points out that it has nothing in common with the Copernican system, with which it has been erroneously identified by some modern writers In the scheme of Pythagoras (or Philolaus), the sun, like the earth, moved round the central fire, instead of being itself fixed in the centre of the universe.

[3] According to Diogenes of Laertius, Parmenides was the first to maintain that the earth was spherical, and was situated in the centre of the universe (ix 3, § 21) His claim to priority is doubtful, but it seems certain that he held the doctrines in question, and perhaps was the first to put them forth clearly.

[4] Origen (Hippolytus), *Philosoph* p. 14 The same view appears to have been entertained by Democritus also, who belonged to the next generation after Anaxagoras, and was a contemporary of Socrates (Aristot *de Cœlo*, ii 13, § 10).

popular belief on this subject continued unshaken, and was shared by the two eminent writers to whom we have just adverted.

To Pythagoras is also distinctly ascribed the application of the division already adopted of the heavens into zones, to the terrestrial globe also. Of these the central or equatorial zone was supposed to be uninhabitable on account of heat: between this and the two polar zones, the arctic and antarctic, lay the temperate, or as he called them the summer and winter zones, which alone were habitable.[5] Other writers, however, assign the merit of first introducing this division to Parmenides, who was about a generation later than Pythagoras.[6] It would certainly seem as if such a relation between the circles of the heavens and the corresponding circles on the earth naturally involved the supposition that the earth was situated in the centre of the universe: a doctrine which was certainly held by the later Pythagoreans, but not, as has been just pointed out, by the great philosopher himself, or his immediate disciples.

§ 5. How far the speculations of these early Greek philosophers may have been influenced by ideas derived from the East or from Egypt, is a question which we have no means of determining. The statements of the later Greek authors on the subject are vague and contradictory, and it is remarkable, that in the case of Pythagoras—the only one in which the evidence of his intercourse with Egypt is of any value—the system ascribed to him by Aristotle (a really trustworthy witness) is wholly at variance with the astronomical views of the Egyptians. The question, however, is fortunately one that has little importance in regard to the subject of the present work. The descriptive and physical geography of the Greeks certainly developed themselves independently, with little or no influence from without, and the cosmographical or astronomical

---

[5] The statement of Plutarch (*de Plac Philos* iii 14), who ascribes this division to Pythagoras, is confused and unintelligible as to the details, but it seems probable that the statement in the text represents correctly the idea which he intended to convey

[6] Posidonius ap Strab ii 2 p 94

theories of the earlier philosophers appear to have produced little impression. There seems to be no doubt (as has been already pointed out) that the spherical form of the earth was known to several of these philosophers,—whether derived from their own mathematical observations, or from communication with the learned men of other nations: but an idea so contrary to the ordinary impressions of mankind [7] would win its way but slowly, and, accordingly, it is not till a much later period that we find it assuming the position of a recognized truth.

---

[7] Dr Whewell justly remarks in his *History of the Inductive Sciences,* vol i. p 115, 3rd edit that "the establishment of the globular form of the earth is an important step in astronomy, for it is the first of those conditions, directly opposed to the apparent evidence of the senses, which astronomy irresistibly proves" The proof is indeed easy to a mind that has received a mathematical training; but these will in all ages be comparatively few Even at the present day, of the thousands of half-educated persons who believe the world to be round, a very large part would be able to give no other reason for their belief, than that people are in the habit of sailing round it. a conclusive proof indeed, but one that was never known to the Greeks.

NOTE A, p. 96.

DATE OF FOUNDATION OF CYRENE.

THE history of the foundation of Cyrene by a colony from Thera is related in full by Herodotus, but he gives us no clue to the date. This is, however, assigned by Eusebius to the year B.C. 631, a date which, as pointed out by Mr. Clinton, is consistent with a statement of Theophrastus (*Hist. Plant.* vi. 3), that Cyrene was founded *about* 300 years before the archonship of Simonides (B.C. 311), and is further confirmed by the statement of Herodotus that Cyrene was governed in succession by four kings of the name of Battus, and four of that of Arcesilaus (Herodot. iv. 163). It was the last of these Arcesilai, the eighth in descent from Battus, whose victory at the Pythian games, in B.C. 466, was celebrated by Pindar (*Pyth.* iv. v. 65; Schol. ad Pind. iv. 1). The date may therefore be considered as well established, at least within a few years.[8] But Eusebius himself in another passage represents Cyrene as founded by the Thebans (obviously a mistake for Theræans), under the command of Battus, 128 years before, in the second year of the fifth Olympiad, or B.C. 759 (Euseb. *Chron.* ad ann. 1257). And as this notice is confirmed by Hieronymus and Syncellus, as well as by the Armenian version of Eusebius, there is no doubt that the error proceeds from Eusebius himself.

The origin of this double version of the date is in this instance wholly unaccountable, for the colony in *both* cases is distinctly referred to as that led by Battus; and the circumstantial account given by Herodotus, from the traditions of the Cyrenæans themselves (iv. 154, init.), excludes the supposition of any former settlement. The point is important, as showing the probable worthlessness of the earlier dates in other similar cases, not a few instances of which are found in the chronicles of Eusebius and Hieronymus.

---

[8] See Clinton's *Fasti Hellen.* vol 1 p 204

NOTE B, p. 99.

DATES ASSIGNED BY THE GREEK CHRONOLOGERS TO THE COLONIES IN THE EUXINE.

There is considerable uncertainty with respect to the dates of the foundation of many of these colonies in the Euxine. Those given by the author generally known as Scymnus Chius are apparently trustworthy, and consistent with one another, as well as with the probable progress of colonization under the circumstances. He appears, indeed, as we shall hereafter see, to have had good authorities for his description of the Euxine. But the case is quite otherwise with the dates given by the later chronologers, Eusebius and his followers Hieronymus and Syncellus. Here, indeed, we not unfrequently find a double set of dates, inconsistent with each other, just as in the case already examined of Thera. Thus, within a few years after the alleged foundation of Cyrene, we find in Eusebius, under the first year of the sixth Olympiad (B.C. 756), the notice, "In Ponto Trapezus conditur," and the same statement is copied from him by Syncellus. Hieronymus, on the contrary, omits Trapezus at this date, but inserts at Ol. 7. 3 (B.C. 750), "Aradus insula condita. Cyzicus condita," a notice which is not found either in Eusebius or Syncellus. Now we know from good authority that Trapezus, as well as the neighbouring cities of Cotyora and Cerasus, was a colony from Sinope,[9] not direct from Miletus; and the foundation of Sinope is assigned by Eusebius himself to the year B.C. 629, or 127 years *after* that of its offspring![1] There is, indeed, an obscure tradition, preserved by Scymnus Chius (v. 947), that there was an earlier Milesian settlement at Sinope, which was destroyed by the Cimmerian invasion; and Mr. Clinton supposes that this may have subsisted long enough to have become the parent of Trapezus. But this is a gratuitous assumption, in order to vindicate the credit of Eusebius, who does not himself make any allusion to such an earlier colony.

Again, in the case of Cyzicus, its foundation is first mentioned by Eusebius himself, at Ol. 26. 2 (B.C. 675);[1] while his copyist

---

[9] Xenoph. *Anab* iv. 8, § 22; Steph. Byz. *s v.* Τραπεζοῦς; Arrian, *Peripl. Eux.* c. 1.

[1] He has, indeed, a notice at a *much* earlier period, according to which Cyzicus was originally founded in the year B C 1276, just three years before the Expedition of the Argonauts (!); but this mythical legend has of course no connection with the question we are now considering

NOTE B. HOMER TO HECATÆUS. 129

Hieronymus, who had previously noticed its foundation in 750, inserts it again at Ol. 24. 2 (B.C. 682), seven years before the date of Eusebius (Cyzicus condita est et Locri in Italia). Cyzicus was, according to the concurrent testimony of all the best authorities,[2] a Milesian colony; Joannes Lydus alone (a very late writer) represents it as a Megarian one. In order to reconcile the two accounts, as well as the two dates of Hieronymus, Mr. Clinton supposes that it was first founded by the Milesians, in B.C. 750, and that this settlement having decayed, it received a second colony from Megara. But it was certainly recognized in after times as a Milesian colony, so that this supposition is clearly untenable, and the authority of Joannes Lydus is worth very little. The later date for its foundation is certainly by far the more probable in itself, and the authority of Eusebius is at least preferable to that of Hieronymus.

Mr. Clinton has recourse to a similar expedient in several other cases where different, and often widely diverging, dates are given for the foundation of the same colony; and it is no doubt a plausible mode of reconciling such differences in all cases where there is reason to believe that both dates rest upon adequate authority. But it may well be questioned whether this is the case with the chronology of Eusebius, or still more of Hieronymus, for the seventh and eighth centuries B.C. We are in almost all cases ignorant of the sources from which they derived the notices appended to their chronological tables, but it is sufficiently clear that these were taken from very multifarious authorities, and it seems probable that they in many instances wrote down without hesitation whatever they found immediately to their hand, without troubling themselves about having elsewhere recorded a different date for the same event. In regard to the more important dates, such as the Trojan War, the foundation of Carthage, and the age of Homer and Hesiod, the chronographers themselves notice the discrepancy of their authorities. In regard to less considerable events they have not thought fit to do so, but it is not the less probable that the same cause was in operation, and that their different chronological statements were simply derived from different authorities, which they did not attempt to reconcile.

---

[2] Strab xiv p 635, Plin. *H N* v. 32, § 142; Schol ad Apollon Rhod 1. v. 1075 Apollonius himself calls it an Ionian colony, which probably means a Milesian one.

There were doubtless current in most of the Greek colonies that rose to be considerable cities many floating traditions as to their foundation—about as trustworthy as those which ascribe the foundation of the Tower of London to Julius Cæsar, and the University of Oxford to Alfred; and these would be naturally taken up by the local historians, and reduced to that definite chronological form with which writers of the Alexandrian school sought to disguise the imperfection of their materials. A careful examination of the chronological notices given by Eusebius and Hieronymus for the four centuries from the Trojan War to the First Olympiad, will sufficiently show the utterly uncritical character of the compilation; and although there were undoubtedly somewhat better materials at their command for the two centuries that followed, they were not likely to apply more skill and care to the employment of them. It may, indeed, surprise us to find that there was often so much uncertainty as to the date of the settlement of important colonies at so late a period as the seventh and eighth centuries B.C., but the fact is indisputable, explain it how we may. Allowance must always be made for the tendency of all local writers—and every city of Greek origin had its local historian—to exaggerate the antiquity of their native city; and it is probably from such sources that many of the notices in Eusebius and Hieronymus have, directly or indirectly, proceeded. In almost every case where there is good *independent* testimony, this is found to be in favour of the later date.

NOTE C, p. 109.

THE " THALASSOCRATIES " OF CASTOR.

I cannot bring myself to attach any historical value to the list of "Thalassocraties," or "Empires of the Sea," which has been preserved to us by Eusebius in his Chronicle. In the first book, where he gives the list in a connected form (though much mutilated in our MSS.), he distinctly cites it on the authority of Diodorus; but it is generally supposed that that author must have derived it from the work of one Castor, a Rhodian, who wrote in the time of Julius Cæsar, and was the author of a special work, entitled Ἀναγραφὴ τῶν·θαλασσοκρατησάντων (Suidas, *s. v.* Κάστωρ). The catalogue in question has been recently made the subject of a careful investigation by the Chevalier Bunsen (*Egypt's Place in Universal History*, vol. iii. pp. 612-639), who ascribes to it an importance and authority far beyond what I can see anything to justify.

An obvious difficulty presents itself in the first instance in regard to the precise meaning of the phrase "Dominion of the Sea," or how its exact duration was to be determined. Thus, when we are told that the Milesians or the Phocæans held the dominion of the sea ("mare obtinuerunt")[3] for a certain number of years, it is difficult to understand by what rule that particular interval was selected out of the long period during which those two cities carried on extensive commerce, and must have possessed considerable maritime power. In modern times, when at least our historical information is complete, how could we define the period during which the Dutch or the Spaniards were rulers of the seas, though there undoubtedly was a time when those nations were among the most formidable naval powers in Europe? In the middle ages, again, the Pisans, Genoese, and Venetians were for a long period the chief maritime powers in the Mediterranean, but it would be very difficult to define the exact date at which the "naval empire" of each began and ended.

But apart from this difficulty—which might, perhaps, be partly solved if we possessed the original work of Castor—it must be observed that all the statements transmitted to us refer to the period previous to the Persian War, and by far the greater part of them to a time concerning which we possess no connected history: and we are almost certain that the contemporaries of Castor could possess none. Strabo, who wrote not long after him, and must have had access to any sources of information as to the early history of the Greek cities and colonies which were available to Castor, had evidently no knowledge of any such definite character concerning the cities in question. He notices, in vague and general terms, the early commercial activity, and the resulting wealth and prosperity, of such cities as Miletus, Rhodes, Samos, &c., but he has no hint of the exact period during which such prosperity and power was in each case at its acme, or that there was any reason for limiting it to any such definite period. The notices given by Thucydides and Herodotus in respect to these

---

[3] ἐθαλασσοκράτησαν, as the phrase is rendered by Syncellus

early ages are equally vague and general. The former writer has, indeed, given us two positive dates—the one, of the first sea fight between the Corinthians and Corcyræans, which he places in B.C. 664; and the other, the construction of the first triremes for the Samians, in B.C. 704. But both of these were definite events, the dates of which were easily fixed and recorded. If there were any similarly definite events that might fairly be taken as marking the commencement and duration of each period of naval supremacy, it is strange that no indication of them should appear in either of the writers just referred to, or in the valuable and elaborate work of Strabo. So far from this being the case, it will be found that the notices given by the latter author, as well as those to be gathered from Herodotus and Thucydides, accord very imperfectly with the chronological summary of Castor.[4]

Had the original work of Castor been preserved to us we should have been better able to judge of the authorities on which he relied, and should perhaps have been able to glean from him some scraps of valuable information. But from the other extracts and notices from his works preserved to us by Eusebius, it seems clear that he was one of those Alexandrian chronographers who occupied themselves with arranging the early Greek history in a definite chronological form, and giving positive statements concerning periods for which he unquestionably could not possess any authentic data. Thus we find him cited as an authority concerning the early kings of Sicyon, beginning with Ægialeus, those of Argos, from Inachus downwards, and of Athens, from Cecrops to Theseus. In every case he gives the exact number of years in each reign, as well as the succession of the kings, as definitely as if he were treating of the Ptolemies in Egypt, or the Seleucidans in Syria. But the utter worthlessness of such chronological schemes applied to the floating legends of antiquity is now generally admitted. The equally definite and positive catalogue of the Thalassocraties appears to me equally worthless. For the earlier period it is difficult to believe that it rested on any substantial basis at all; while even for the later, and historical period, it is found so much at variance with the more authentic statements

---

[4] Herodotus, indeed, distinctly tells us (III 122) that Polycrates of Samos, who was a contemporary of Cambyses (about B C 532–522) *was the first after Minos* who attempted to acquire the dominion of the sea (θαλασσοκρατέειν).

transmitted to us by Herodotus and Thucydides, and involves such historical as well as chronological difficulties, that it is utterly impossible to rely upon it as an authority.

How little dependence can be placed upon the brief notices appended to the chronological tables of Eusebius and Hieronymus in regard to these earlier ages, is shown by numerous instances, some of which have been already examined. See Note B, p. 128.

CHAPTER V.

HECATÆUS.

SECTION 1.—*Geography of Hecatæus.*

§ 1. WHILE the early philosophers were thus speculating on the general constitution of the universe, and establishing first principles in regard to the form and position of the earth, and its cosmical relations with the heavenly bodies, there were not wanting those who occupied themselves with the more practical task of registering the knowledge actually attained concerning the inhabited world. The introduction of prose writing, as applied to literary composition, did not date farther back among the Greeks than the sixth century before the Christian era (B.C. 600–500), but one of its earliest applications was to the record of geographical, as well as historical, facts. The first regular treatise of this kind of which we have any distinct account is that of HECATÆUS of Miletus, which was probably published before the end of the sixth century, and is generally referred to by later writers as the first systematic description of the world as it was then known to the Greeks.[1]

Its author was a citizen of distinction in his native city, and is repeatedly mentioned by Herodotus as taking a leading part in the deliberations of the Ionic cities, especially on the occasion of their ill-fated revolt from Persia in B.C. 500.[2] He must therefore have been at that time a man of mature age

---

[1] Eratosthenes ap Strab. i 1, § 11, p 7; Agathemerus, i 1.
[2] Herodot. v 36, 125; Diodor. x. 25 (*Exc Vat* p 38) Herodotus designates him on both these occasions as λογοποιὸς, an expression evidently used with reference to his historical work, which appears to have been quite of the same character with those of Acusilaus and other writers known in later times as the "logographers"

and experience; and these notices accord well with the statement of Suidas, which represents him as flourishing in the 56th Olympiad (B.C. 520).³ We may therefore probably assume that his works were composed during the period between B.C. 520 and 500. One of these, his "Genealogies," was of a historical character, though principally occupied with the mythical legends of the heroic ages; the other, with which alone we are here concerned, was entitled a "Periodus," or Description of the Earth, and contained not merely a description of the coasts and islands of the Mediterranean and its tributary seas, but apparently a general outline of all the countries of the world, so far as they were then known, or supposed to be known, to the Greeks.⁴ Such a comprehensive treatise would have been the more valuable to us had it been preserved to us in its entirety, as the great work of Herodotus, though containing a vast mass of geographical information, was not primarily designed for geographical purposes, and is therefore far from affording us a regular and systematic review of the subject.

Unfortunately the scanty fragments that have been preserved to us of the work of Hecatæus are wholly inadequate to enable us to estimate the real extent of the geographical information possessed by its author.⁵ The number of citations from his treatise is indeed large, but by far the greater proportion of these are mere names, quoted by late grammarians, especially by Stephanus of Byzantium, and convey to

---

³ Suidas, s v Ἑκαταῖος
⁴ It appears that doubts were entertained by some of the Alexandrian critics as to the authenticity of the Periodus extant under the name of Hecatæus But Eratosthenes pronounced in its favour, on account of the resemblance of style to his other work (πιστούμενον ἐκείνου εἶναι ἐκ τῆς ἄλλης αὐτοῦ γραφῆς Strab 1 p 7) The same doubt is alluded to also by Athenæus (ii 82, p 70), but the work appears to have been generally recognized

⁵ The fragments of Hecatæus have been collected and published, with copious notes and a life of the author by Klausen (8vo Berolin 1831), and his collection has been republished, almost without alteration, by C Muller in his *Fragmenta Historicorum Græcorum*, vol 1 Didot, Paris, 1841) A full account of his life and writings will be found in Colonel Mure's *History of Greek Literature*, vol iv (London 1853)

us no other information than that the places or tribes were mentioned by him, and therefore included within the range of his knowledge. Moreover the quotations by Stephanus, which are much the most numerous,[6] have the further disadvantage that, being arranged in alphabetical, instead of geographical, order, they have lost all trace of the geographical sequence in which they occurred in the original, and which would often have constituted their chief value.

§ 2. It is certain indeed, even from the existing remains, that the work was very much in the nature of what was termed by the Greeks a Periplus, or description of the coasts of the Mediterranean and adjoining seas, analogous to that found in the treatise extant in later times under the name of Scylax. The whole range of the countries familiar to the Greeks at this period grouped itself so naturally around this great internal basin, that such an arrangement presented itself almost as a matter of course to the geographer. But we learn also with certainty that Hecatæus included in his work notices, however brief and meagre, of many inland tribes in the countries bordering on these seas, and even of some quite in the interior of the continents. It seems clear also that he appended to the Asiatic part of his treatise an enumeration at least, if not a description, of all the nations and provinces of the Persian Empire, even to the frontiers of India. The materials for such a summary could hardly be wanting in his day, and there appears no doubt that his work was intended to comprise, in one way or another, a general but complete review of all the countries known to the Greeks.

§ 3. Hecatæus is reported to have travelled extensively; but, with the exception of Egypt, we have no definite information as to any of the countries that he visited. The existing fragments of his work throw no light upon the subject; and it is idle to assume, as has been done by some of his late editors,

---

[6] According to Colonel Mure they amount to not less than 300 out of the 330 fragments collected by Klausen.

that he must have visited in person all the countries concerning which he appears to have possessed trustworthy information.[7] Such information could undoubtedly be procured in his time, as it was in that of Herodotus, by consulting merchants and other travellers who had themselves visited these more remote regions, and the extensive commercial relations of his native city of Miletus would afford him most favourable opportunities in this respect. Thus he would easily obtain information concerning the shores of the Euxine, which were surrounded with a girdle of Milesian colonies, and even concerning the barbarian tribes of the interior with which these cities traded, without it being necessary to suppose that he had himself visited the distant ports of Colchis or the Cimmerian Bosporus. In like manner he could doubtless learn from the Phocæans the names of places connected with their distant colony of Massilia; and the ports on the Spanish coast which their traders were in the habit of frequenting, without having himself made a voyage to these remote regions.

§ 4. The work of Hecatæus, as we learn from the citations of late grammarians, was divided into two books, the one containing Europe, the other Asia, under which latter head not only Egypt, but Ethiopia and the rest of Africa, appear to have been included. His method of arrangement was different from that adopted by most subsequent geographers.[8] Instead

---

[7] This is the assumption made by Klausen in the life of Hecatæus prefixed to his edition of the Fragments (pp 6-12), and very much the same conclusion is adopted by Colonel Mure (*Hist of Gr Lit* vol iv pp 145, 155), though, as it appears to me, without any proof The only authority for the extent of his travels is the vague expression of Agathemerus, a geographer of very late date, who calls him ἀνὴρ πολυπλανὴς (Geogr 1. c. 1); and it seems highly improbable that Herodotus, who has so repeatedly referred to his remarks on Egypt, should have taken no notice of his observations on other countries had he professed to have in like manner visited them in person

[8] In regard to this point I have followed the view of Klausen (*Vita Hecatæi*, pp. 14-17), which has been also adopted by C Muller in Didot's edition (*Fragm Histor Græcor* vol 1 p xii), as well as by Colonel Mure, though I confess the evidence on the subject does not appear to me conclusive. But the point is not one of much importance

of beginning with the Pillars of Hercules as the farthest limit of the known world, he started from home, and beginning apparently at the Hellespont, described first in detail the shores of Greece and the European coast of the Ægean; thence proceeding westwards by the Adriatic, Italy, and Liguria, to Spain and Tartessus; then returning again to his starting-point in order to describe Thrace, Scythia, and the north coast of the Euxine, as far as the Caucasus. In like manner in his second book he appears to have begun the description of Asia from the Hellespont, and proceeded along the south coast of the Euxine to the Caucasus; then returning to the Hellespont again, and following the shores of the Ægean and the Mediterranean to Syria, Egypt, and Libya. The notices of the Medes, Parthians, Persians, and Indians, were perhaps annexed to those of the Colchians and other nations adjoining the Euxine. But this is very uncertain.

§ 5. So far as we can gather from the imperfect remains that have been transmitted [9] to us, the geographical knowledge of Hecatæus was very much what might have been anticipated from the extent and distribution of the Greek colonies and settlements. He was well acquainted not only with the shores of the Ægean and Ionian Seas, and with those of Southern Italy and Sicily, but with the eastern coast of the Adriatic, where he enumerates various obscure tribes of the Illyrians and Liburnians, with which the Greek colonies of Epidamnus and Apollonia had probably brought them in connection.[1] Near the head of that sea he placed the Istri, "a people on the Ionian Gulf"—but without any allusion to their generally-received connection with the river Ister—and the city of Adria, with a river of the same name, which he describes as situated in a region of surpassing fertility.[2] In Southern Italy, or Magna Græcia as it was called in later times, he enumerates a crowd of names, including not only Greek settlements, but many towns of the Œnotrians, or native

---

[9] Note A, p 153   [1] Fr. 60-69   [2] F_1 58

tribes in the interior [3]—for the most part otherwise unknown, having probably disappeared during the revolutions that those countries subsequently underwent, which brought about a complete change in the population.

In the Tyrrhenian Sea he was not only familiar with Corsica and Sardinia, but mentioned Elba under the name of Æthale, an island of the Tyrrhenians, already celebrated for its mines of iron,[4] as well as the less important island of Capreæ. Of the towns in the interior he mentioned Capua and Nola, both of which were in the immediate neighbourhood of the Greek colonies in Campania, and were doubtless in constant communication with them. But no reference is found in the existing fragments to any of the cities on the mainland of Italy north of this; and the whole coast of Western Italy, occupied 'by the Latins and Campanians, is a blank.[5] It may be considered certain that he did not mention the name of Rome, otherwise so important a testimony could not have been omitted by Dionysius of Halicarnassus.

The existence of so considerable a gap in this part of his geography is the more remarkable, as the next place we find mentioned is the insignificant seaport of Monœcus (Monaco), on the coast of Liguria.[6] It was probably frequented, if not already occupied, by the Massilians; and it was doubtless through the same channel that Hecatæus had derived his knowledge of Narbo, which he terms a Gaulish city and emporium, thus indicating that it was already known as a centre of trade with the interior.[7] The adjoining coast was apparently occupied by the Helisycians, who were noticed by Hecatæus as a Ligurian tribe.[8]

A number of names, many of them obscure or otherwise unknown, are mentioned by him on the east coast of Spain, and in the neighbourhood of Tartessus and the Pillars of Hercules: a circumstance which appears to indicate that the

---

[3] Fr. 30–40 [4] Fr. 25. [5] See Note B, p. 153.
[6] Fr. 23. [7] Fr. 19. [8] Fr. 20.

Massilians carried on more trade, and held more intercourse with these countries, than was the case in later times, when they were almost entirely driven out by the Carthaginians.⁹ But no trace appears of any knowledge of the Atlantic shores of Spain. Even the name of Gadeira, or Gades, does not seem to have been mentioned by him. It was, perhaps, confounded by the Greeks with the city of Tartessus, a name which was in these early days employed very vaguely.¹

§ 6. It is almost certain that Hecatæus had no knowledge whatever of the western and northern shores of Europe; and if, as appears probable, he assumed the existence of a continuous ocean in that direction, this was merely an inference from the established notion, so deeply implanted in the Greek mind, that the whole world was surrounded by a circumfluent ocean.² Of the countries north and west of the Euxine, on the other hand, he had certainly considerable means of acquiring information through the Milesian colonies that were scattered all around its shores. But we have hardly the means of judging how far this information was actually embodied in his work. The citations from this part of it are few and scanty, and for the most part contain only the names of obscure or unknown Scythian tribes; but it seems impossible that he should have omitted to mention the numerous and flourishing cities on the shores of the Euxine,³ more particularly as he is cited as an

---

⁹ Several of these are placed among the Mastieni, whom he described as a nation adjoining the Pillars of Hercules (Fr 6) their name is again incidentally mentioned by Polybius (iii 33), but appears to have been lost, as an ethnic appellation, after the Roman conquest, and is not found in any of the later geographers. Its occurrence in Polybius is, however, a strong confirmation of the accuracy of Hecatæus

¹ Gadeira is, however, mentioned by Herodotus (iv 8), who terms it a city on the Ocean beyond the Pillars of Hercules But it appears that Hecatæus rejected altogether the ordinarily received account of the labour of Hercules in this quarter, and denied that Geryones and the island of Erythea had anything to do with Spain (Arrian, Anab ii 16)

² The statement of Pliny (Hist Nat iv 13, § 94), that the northern ocean was called "Amalchian" by Hecatæus, probably refers to Hecatæus of Abdera, not to our author See Note 7, p 148.

³ The omission of all such names in the existing fragments is a strong instance how little we can rely upon any negative evidence derived from such imperfect sources of information as we possess Even on the south coast of the Euxine, which Klausen and Colonel Mure suppose him to have

authority for the small town of Carcinitis, at the head of the gulf of the same name,[4] which is mentioned also by Herodotus,[5] but not noticed by any later geographer. Of the Scythian tribes of the interior he mentioned the Melanchlæni,[6] who are noticed also by Herodotus; the Dandarii,[7] a tribe adjoining the Caucasus, whose name is still found in Strabo; and the Issedones, a name that, as we have seen, had been already rendered familiar to the Greeks by Aristeas of Proconnesus.[8] Even these few names are sufficient to show that his knowledge was not confined to the nations bordering on the coast, but that he had collected at least a certain amount of information concerning the remoter tribes of the interior.

§ 7. In Asia also he was not only well acquainted with the Colchians, the Chalybes, the Moschi, and other barbarian tribes in the neighbourhood of the Euxine, but was familiar also with the name of the Matieni, a people of the interior, adjoining the Armenians;[9] as well as with that of the river Araxes, which flows into the Caspian Sea.[1] This sea itself he described, under the name of the Hyrcanian Sea, as surrounded by lofty mountains, which were covered by dense forests,[2] a statement which is true only of a part of its shores. In its neighbourhood he placed the Parthians, and to the east of them the Chorasmians,[3] two well-known names, which here appear for the first time. But it must not be assumed that he was acquainted with the true position of the latter people, beyond the Caspian towards the east, or that he had any true idea of the configuration of that inland sea.

---

visited in person, the citations refer principally to obscure barbarian tribes, while all the more important Greek colonies are omitted
[4] Fr 153
[5] Herodot iv 99
[6] Fr 154   [7] Fr 161
[8] Fr 168 It is to be observed that Hecatæus placed the Issedones in Asia, while Herodotus (iv 13, 25) included them in Europe But this discrepancy evidently arose from the difference between the two writers in regard to the limits assumed for the two continents See p 147
[9] Fr 189 These Matieni were separated from the Phrygians by the river Halys in the upper part of its course (Herodot i 72) They must not be confounded with the more powerful nation of the same name that dwelt east of the Tigris
[1] Fr 170   [2] Fr 172
[3] Fr 173

It is more remarkable that he appears to have collected some information, not altogether untrustworthy, concerning India—the name of which, as well as that of the river Indus, is for the first time found in the extant fragments of his work.[4] He mentions, indeed, several names of tribes and cities in that country, among which the Gandarii are known to us also from Herodotus, and appear to have occupied the country about the upper Indus and the valley of Cabul.[5] Caspapyrus, or Caspatyrus, their capital city, the name of which was also known to Hecatæus, was situated on the river itself; and it was from thence that, according to Herodotus, Scylax of Caryanda embarked on his expedition to descend the Indus.[6] It is not improbable that some account of that voyage—conducted as it was by a Greek of Asia Minor—might have already reached Hecatæus, and been one of his sources of information concerning these remote countries. Of the other tribes mentioned by him the Calatians are also noticed by Herodotus, but we have no clue to their position. The Opians, as he tells us, dwelt on the river Indus;[7] their name is otherwise unknown, but is perhaps preserved in that of Alexandria Opiane, the city founded by Alexander at the foot of the Indian Caucasus.[8] Argante, "an Indian city," the name of which is also cited from our author,[9] is wholly unknown. Meagre and scanty as are these earliest notices of India, we are almost surprised to find that so much was known to Hecatæus, when we remember that the Indian provinces were first annexed to the Persian Empire by his immediate contemporary Darius. But the India of Hecatæus, like the Persian dominion, was doubtless confined exclusively to the provinces west of the Indus, and did not extend beyond that river.

---

[4] Fr. 174–178
[5] Fr 178. Herodot iii 91, vii 66 Herodotus, however, did not consider them as being properly an Indian nation
[6] Herodot iv 44. See Chap VI § 1
[7] Fr 175

[8] See Chap XII
[9] Fr 176. 'Αργάντη, πόλις 'Ινδίας, ὡς 'Εκαταῖος Steph Byzant s v This is a specimen of the class of notices, out of which we are to attempt to reproduce the lost work of Hecatæus!

Of his general knowledge of the interior of Asia we have hardly the means of judging, very few citations having been preserved to us from this part of his work. But there can be no doubt that he had a general acquaintance, by name at least, with all the provinces of the Persian Empire. Herodotus represents him as enumerating to the assembled Ionians (in order to dissuade them from their intended revolt) "all the nations that were subject to the Persian king;"[1] and it is certain that such knowledge must have been readily attainable in his day. But what amount of information he possessed concerning them, or what ideas he had formed of their relative geographical position, we are unable to judge. He appears, however, to have had at least a vague notion of the existence of the Persian Gulf;[2] and he mentioned the name of the Myci, or Mycians,[3] a people noticed also by Herodotus, and who probably dwelt in the neighbourhood of the Erythræan Sea.

It is remarkable that no reference is made to any mention by him of Babylon, or of any of the great cities in the valley of the Euphrates and Tigris (except Sitace, the capital of the district afterwards called Sittacene[4]), a circumstance which certainly tends strongly to negative the possibility of his having himself extended his travels into those countries, so full of interest to the Greeks, and which had been rendered comparatively easy of access in his day, from the union of all Western Asia under the Great King.

§ 8. Egypt appears to have occupied a considerable place in his work, and to have been described in unusual detail. We know with certainty that Hecatæus had not only himself visited the country, but had ascended the Nile as far as Thebes, and there conversed with the priests of Ammon, as did his successor, Herodotus, after him.[5] We are told, indeed,

---

[1] Herodot v 36 'Εκαταῖος δ' ὁ λογοποιὸς . . . πρῶτα μὲν οὐκ ἔα πόλεμον Βασιλέι τῶν Περσέων ἀναιρέεσθαι, καταλέγων τά τε ἔθνεα πάντα τῶν ἦρχε Δαρεῖος καὶ τὴν δύναμιν αὐτοῦ
[2] Fr. 182, with Klausen's note.
[3] Fr. 170.   [4] Fr 184.
[5] Herodot ii 143

that the later writer copied many things from his predecessor literally—among others the history of the phœnix, the description of the hippopotamus, and the account of the manner in which the natives caught crocodiles.[6] It appears therefore that, in this part of his work at least, Hecatæus was far from confining himself to a dry geographical description of the country, but dilated at considerable length upon its natural curiosities, and the manners and customs of the inhabitants. He, however, certainly added a number of mere geographical details, such as are not found in Herodotus, as we find the names of not less than fifteen cities of Egypt cited from him by Stephanus.[7]

The remaining part of his work, comprising the coast of Libya from the confines of Egypt to the Straits of Hercules,[8] was a mere Periplus, or coast-description, noticing many ports and small islands; while the only tribes of the interior he is known to have mentioned are the Mazyes and Zygantes— obviously the same with the Maxyes and Gyzantes of Herodotus, both of which lived within a short distance of the sea, near the Tritonian Lake.[9] The most distant places that he enumerates towards the west are Metagonium, a name which we find in later times applied to a promontory and people not far from the Pillars of Hercules;[1] and Thinga, evidently the same place that was subsequently called Tinga, or Tingis (the modern Tangier), just without the Straits.[2] It is probable also that his river Liza was the same with the Lixus of later geographers, on the Atlantic coast of Mauritania, but this is far from certain.

§ 9. In regard to the general notions of geography entertained by Hecatæus we are, unfortunately, very much in the dark. It is certainly probable that he was one of those writers whom Herodotus had in view when he censures "those who repre-

---

[6] Porphyrius ap. Euseb *Præp Evangel* x 3, p 166, cited by Klausen, on Fr 292
[7] Fr 269-288.   [8] Fi. 299-328

[9] Herodot iv 191, 194
[1] Fr 324   The name is again found in Scylax (§ 110), and in Polybius (iii. 33)   [2] Fr. 326.

SECT 1   HECATÆUS.   145

sented the earth as "exactly round, as if drawn with a pair of compasses, and the Ocean flowing all around it."[3] This was clearly the popular idea, derived originally from the Homeric poems; and, from all we know of the progress of the Greek mind, there can be no doubt that they would be very slow to emancipate themselves from the influence of an error once established upon such authority. Anaximander of Miletus, the countryman of Hecatæus, as we have seen, was the first that drew up a map of the world, and there can be little doubt that this formed the foundation of that of Hecatæus.[4] But though the latter is said to have introduced material improvements on the work of his predecessor, there can be no doubt that both would be still very rude and imperfect attempts, which might well excite the ridicule of Herodotus. In this case, as in so many others, it is probable that the scientific tendency of the Greek mind came into play, and that they *assumed* the round form of the earth and the circumfluent Ocean as first principles, without any actual knowledge of the facts. We are told also that they placed Greece in the centre of the world, and Delphi as the central point of Greece.[5] This last notion appears to have obtained a fixed hold on the Greek mind, and is frequently alluded to by the poets of the fifth century B.C., as a received article of popular faith.[6] Just in the same manner the geographers of the middle ages assumed that Jerusalem was the centre of the world, and arranged other countries accordingly.

§ 10. It was evidently the same symmetrical turn of mind that led Hecatæus to divide the world into two great continents or primary divisions of equal extent. But this question of the division of the continents is not free from difficulty. Herodotus, in the passage already referred to, ridicules those who made Asia of equal size with Europe, in terms which seem to

---

[3] Herodot iv 36   See Chap VI § 1, p 160
[4] Agathemer Geogr i c 1, Strab i p 7
[5] Agathemerus, l c 1
[6] Æschyl *Choeph* v 1036. Eurip *Ion* v 462; Pind *Pyth* iv 74 (183), vi 3   See also Strabo, ix p 419

exclude all consideration of a third continent; and Hecatæus, by including all Libya, as well as Egypt, under the head of Asia,[7] appears to have sanctioned this arrangement. On the other hand, it is clear that the division into three continents was well established in the time of Herodotus, so that he himself tells us that he continues to use the divisions and the names "because they are sanctioned by custom," though he thinks them unreasonable, and without good foundation. And in another place he censures "the Ionians," who divided the world into the three portions of Europe, Asia, and Africa, but considered the two last as separated by the Nile; thus, as he points out, leaving the Delta unaccounted for.[8] It is difficult to suppose that among these "Ionians" Herodotus did not mean to include Hecatæus—the most recent as well as the most eminent of Ionic writers on geography—or that, if Hecatæus had departed from the generally received doctrine on so important a subject, this would not have been noticed by Herodotus. It seems therefore probable that, although Hecatæus undoubtedly divided his work into only two books or parts, the second of which included the description of Libya as well as that of Asia, he nevertheless recognized the established division of the three continents, regarding Asia and Africa together as equal in size to Europe.

At the present day we are so accustomed to our modern maps, and to the small size of Europe, as compared to the other two great continents, that we find it difficult to represent to ourselves the opposite view. But Herodotus undoubtedly regarded Europe *as greatly exceeding in size both Asia and*

---

[7] This appears to be clearly established by the numerous citations of names of places in Libya from "Hecatæus in his description of Asia" There are, however, many others in which the "Periegesis of Libya" is cited as if it were a distinct work, but the same thing applies to his description of Egypt It is probable, therefore, that these were separate subdivisions or portions of the work, included under the main head of Asia A regular division into *books*, as usual with later writers, is not to be thought of at so early a period

[8] Herodot ii 16

Africa together,[9] and therefore treats it as a gross blunder on the part of Hecatæus to have considered it as *only* equal to Asia. One point that doubtless affected the comparison was, that Hecatæus regarded the Cimmerian Bosporus and the Tanais as the limit between Europe and Asia [1]—a view generally adopted in later times—while Herodotus extended the confines of Europe to the river Phasis. Both systems were current in their time, as we learn from the poet Æschylus, who in one passage adopts one view, in another follows the other.[2]

§ 11. A traveller who had visited Egypt could hardly fail to have formed or adopted some theory concerning the much controverted questions respecting the Nile and its annual inundations, a subject which, as we have seen, had already exercised the ingenuity of several of the Ionic philosophers. But on this point Hecatæus appears to have acquiesced in the view which, if we may trust to Diodorus, was that of the Egyptian priests:[3] that the Nile derived its waters from those of the circumfluent stream of Ocean—a theory which Herodotus justly sets aside as unworthy of refutation.[4]

A similar want of judgement was displayed by him in accepting, as he appears to have done without scruple, the fabulous tales that were current in his day concerning the Pygmies and the Sciapodes,[5] both which nations he placed in Ethiopia, in accordance with the opinion prevalent among the

---

[9] Id See the next chapter
[1] This is clearly established with regard to the Cimmerian Bosporus by the fact that Hecatæus placed Phanagoria, which was just to the east of the Strait, *in Asia* (Fr. 164, 165) The Tanais is not mentioned in the extant fragments, but, besides that the two were generally combined by all later writers who followed Hecatæus, the fact that he placed the Issedones in Asia (Fr 168) is a strong presumption that he also adopted the Tanais as the boundary
[2] Æschyl *Prom. Vinct.* vv 729-735;

Prom. Sol Fr 1. See § 2, p 150
[3] Diodor 1 37, § 7
[4] Herodot 11 28 He there includes this among the theories set up by Greeks "who wished to be thought wiser than their neighbours" (11 20); and there can be little doubt that he had Hecatæus in view, as he certainly had Thales in the first theory which he refutes. See Klausen on Fr. 278. But this seems directly contrary to the statement of Diodorus just cited, according to which the same view was entertained by the Egyptian priests
[5] Fr 265, 266

Greeks. It would be interesting to know whether he had really heard these fables in Egypt.

On the other hand, the detailed account of the Hyperboreans, generally ascribed to Hecatæus of Miletus, undoubtedly belongs to a later writer of the same name, Hecatæus of Abdera, who lived in the time of the first Ptolemy, and composed a book expressly on the subject.[6] Whether the older writer made any mention of such a people we have no definite information, but the existence of a northern ocean was certainly consistent with his geographical system, as well as with the current belief of his day;[7] and with this belief, as we have seen, the tales of the Rhipæan Mountains and the Hyperboreans were almost inseparably connected.

SECTION 2.—*Hecatæus to Herodotus.*

§ 1. Of the progress of geographical knowledge from the time of Hecatæus to that of Herodotus, we have hardly any information. The work of HELLANICUS appears to have been purely historical, and we are told that he did not occupy himself much with geographical questions.[8] DAMASTES of Sigeum, on the contrary, who was nearly contemporary with Herodotus,[9] is mentioned as having left a Periplus, and perhaps another work of a specially geographical character.[1] Both

---

[6] This work is cited by the Scholiast on Apollonius Rhodius (ii v 675), as well as by Ælian (*Hist Anim* xi 1) See Wesseling's note on Diodorus (ii 47), and Klausen on Hecatæus (Fr 373).

[7] The statement of Pliny that he distinctly mentioned the northern ocean under the name of the Amalchian Sea (Plin. *H N.* iv. 13, § 94), in all probability refers to Hecatæus of Abdera, though the name has been inserted in the maps of the world according to Hecatæus both by Klausen and Colonel Mure

[8] Agathemer *Geogr* § 1 At the same time Strabo repeatedly mentions him with contempt as a collector of fables, and unworthy of serious attention (Strabo, 1. p 43 ; xi p 508).

[9] Suidas (*s v*) calls him σύγχρονος 'Ηροδότῳ; and both he and Dionysius of Halicarnassus (*Jud de Thucyd.* c 5) place him before the Peloponnesian War His date cannot be more accurately determined See Clinton (*F H* vol ii p 371) and C Muller (*Fragm Hist Græc* vol ii p 64)

[1] It is not clear whether the work referred to as περὶ ἐθνῶν was distinct from the Periplus or not

works are entirely lost; but as we are told that their author copied for the most part from Hecatæus,[2] and he is censured by Strabo as a careless and inaccurate writer,[3] there is, perhaps, little reason to regret their loss.[4]

§ 2. But before proceeding to investigate the ample materials furnished by Herodotus for estimating the extent of geographical knowledge to which the Greeks had attained in his time, it will be well to advert briefly to the works of two poets, ÆSCHYLUS and PINDAR, both of whom may be considered as intermediate in age between Hecatæus and Herodotus.[5] We cannot, indeed, receive their statements as indicating in all cases the same simple belief in the legends which they related, as may fairly be ascribed to the poets of an earlier age; nor are we entitled to assume them as representing the limits of geographical science in their day. They wrote as poets, not as geographers, and must be criticized as such. But several passages, as well as incidental notices in their works, are interesting as showing the popular notions on the subject, as compared with the more definite and elaborate information of writers like Hecatæus and Herodotus.

Of all the passages in the extant plays of Æschylus that may be regarded as showing his geographical knowledge, the one that has most exercised the ingenuity of critics and commentators is unquestionably that which relates to the wanderings of Io in the Prometheus Vinctus. Much laborious subtlety has been wasted on the vain attempt to explain these in a manner to accord with some definite geographical system; while the probability is that the poet had no such system present to his mind. He was dealing with a wholly mythical

---

[2] Agathemerus, 1 1 εἶτα Δαμάστης ὁ Κιττιεὺς (scr Σιγειεὺς) τὰ πλεῖστα ἐκ τοῦ Ἑκαταίου μεταγράψας Περίπλουν ἔγραψε
[3] Strabo, 1 p 47.
[4] The most interesting of the few notices that have been preserved to us from his work, is that he was the first Greek author who mentioned the name of Rome (Dionys Halicarn 1 72)
[5] Æschylus obtained his first prize in B C 484, and died in 456 The extant odes of Pindar belong to a period extending from B C 502 to 452 (See Clinton, F. H vol ii)

subject, and by far the greater part of the names that he introduces were of a mythical or fabulous character; hence it probably never occurred to him to consider their geographical position, or arrange them in geographical sequence. Even the few statements that have an apparently definite character will be found as difficult to arrange in any systematic order, as those of a more vague and fabulous description. Thus we are distinctly told that Io, when crossing the Cimmerian Bosporus would "leave the plains of Europe, and enter on the continent of Asia."[6] Yet we find Æschylus himself in another passage as distinctly terming the river Phasis the boundary between Europe and Asia.[7] Both views, as we have already seen, were currently entertained in his day, and the poet obviously did not trouble himself to reconcile the two. Again, the iron-working Chalybes, who are represented as "a savage people, not to be approached by strangers,"[8] are placed in the north, adjoining the "wandering Scythians who dwelt in wattled huts, elevated on wheeled cars;" and both these nations are described as situated on the northern side of "the star-neighbouring summits" of Caucasus.[9] Even the dreaded bay of Salmydessus, the terror of navigators in the Euxine — "the step-mother of ships," as it is termed by the poet[1]—is transferred by him from the coast of Thrace to the southern shore of the Euxine, adjoining the river Thermodon, and the abode of the Amazons.

The course of Io's wanderings after crossing the Cimmerian Bosporus is, if possible, still more extraordinary. The first people to whom she comes are the Phorcides and Gorgons— mythical beings whom the tradition generally current placed

---

[6] *Prom* V v 729-735
[7] *Prom Sol* Fr 1.
[8] *Prom.* V v 715
[9] Ibid vv 709-722 The river 'Υβριστής, which he describes as pouring down its waters from the highest summits of the Caucasus, cannot be identified. the name is not found in any other writer, whether poet or geographer The name of the Caucasus here appears for the first time, though it must have been known to the Greeks long before It is termed by the poet "the most lofty of mountains" (ὁρῶν ὕψιστον), a statement, as we shall see, confirmed by Herodotus

[1] τραχεῖα πόντου Σαλμυδησία γνάθος
ἐχθρόξενος ναύταισι, μητρυιὰ νεῶν.
Ibid v. 727.

in Africa; next to these come the Griffins and the Arimaspians, whom she is especially told to avoid, and after doing so she will come to "a race of black men, who dwelt at the sources of the sun, where is the river Æthiops," the banks of which she is directed to follow till she arrives at "the descent where the river Nile pours its grateful waters down from the Bybline Mountains."[2] It is impossible to believe that in this confused and unintelligible jumble of names and ideas Æschylus had the map of Hecatæus, or any other, present to his mind. He was evidently familiar with certain geographical names, such as the Caucasus and the Cimmerian Bosporus, and introduced them in the midst of such as were purely mythical and fabulous, without any attempt to combine the whole into any intelligible form, or any idea that his hearers would trouble themselves to do so.

The place of punishment of Prometheus is itself very obscurely indicated, but it is clear that the poet did not conceive him, according to the tradition current in later times, to have been affixed to a rock on Mount Caucasus, but somewhere on the far borders of Scythia, perhaps to the Rhipæan Mountains.[3]

§ 3. From the fragments of the Prometheus Solutus that have been preserved to us, it is evident that that play contained a prophetic narrative of the journey of Hercules from the Caucasus to the land of the Hesperides, of a somewhat similar character to that of Io in the sister play. Such an episode could hardly have failed to contain some notices of interest in connexion with those distant regions of the West, which were still so imperfectly known to the Greeks.[4] But it was probably of as mythical a character as the corresponding episode in the extant play, and with as little pretension to

---

[2] καταβασμὸν, ἔνθα Βυβλίνων ὀρῶν ἄπο ἵησι σεπτὸν Νεῖλος εὔποτον ῥέος
Ibid v 812

[3] This is evident both from the opening lines of the play and from the fact that it was not till after long wanderings that Io was to come to the Caucasus (See the passage already cited)

[4] Among the few such notices preserved to us is that of the curious legend invented to account for the stone-covered plain of the Crau near Marseilles, which is placed by the poet among the Ligurians (*Prom Sol* Fr. 6).

anything like geographical accuracy. Among the few statements cited from it is that the Ister took its rise in the land of the Hyperboreans and the Rhipæan Mountains,[5] an idea obviously founded upon a mere assumption, like that of the Nile descending from the Bybline Mountains in the south.

The notices of geographical names that occur in the Persæ —a play of a purely historical character—are of a very different description, and are interesting as showing that the Greeks, as might have been expected, after the expedition of Xerxes, were familiar not only with the names of the great cities of the Persian Empire—Susa, Ecbatana, and Babylon— but with those of remoter tribes and nations that were subject to the Great King, such as the Parthians, Mardians, and Bactrians. But unfortunately these are nothing but mere names. From the nature of the subject, the play could hardly contain any indications of the real extent or character of the poet's geographical knowledge.

§ 4. The same remark applies with still greater force to the poems of PINDAR, the lyric character of which precludes the possibility of anything more than merely incidental allusions to geographical names or facts. The only passages that can be referred to as of any interest in this respect are his narrative—if such it can be called—of the voyage of the Argonauts, from the Phasis to the Lake Triton,[6] which has been already noticed; and the striking description of the land of the Hyperboreans, "behind the breath of the cold north wind," from whence Hercules was supposed to have transplanted the olive to Olympia.[7] But he himself adds in another passage that no mortal can find the wondrous way to this blessed people either by land or sea.[8] It may be added that he elsewhere alludes to the Columns of Hercules,[9] to the Phasis and the Nile, as figurative expressions for the extremities of the known world.

---

[5] Schol. ad Apollon. Rhod iv 284
[6] Pind *Pyth.* iv vv. 20-43
[7] *Olymp* iii vv 14-31, *Pyth* x vv 31-44

[8] ναυσὶ δ' οὔτε πεζὸς ἰὼν ἂν εὕροις ἐς Ὑπερβορέων ἀγῶνα θαυματὰν ὁδόν
Pyth x 30
[9] *Olymp* iii 44

NOTE A, p. 138.

CHARACTER OF EXTANT FRAGMENTS OF HECATÆUS.

THE extent and importance of these appears to me to be greatly overrated by Colonel Mure (*Hist. of Gr. Lit.* vol. iv. p. 151), who says. "The fragments of the Periodus are so numerous as to warrant the belief that they represent a large portion of the substance of the original text, and might perhaps admit of being fashioned into a skeleton of what was, even when entire, a meagre and fleshless body." But the extant fragments, though numerous, are, as has been already pointed out, with few exceptions, *mere names*, which, not being arranged in geographical order, afford us no clue to what may have been omitted. There can, indeed, be little doubt that the work was meagre and jejune enough, as is the case with the Periplus of Scylax, to which it has been already compared; but the extracts found in Stephanus of Byzantium— or rather in the miserable epitome that is now extant of his treatise—certainly cannot be taken as representing the original; and there are not wanting indications that Hecatæus in some parts of his work introduced notices of the character and productions of the lands he described. (See Fragments 58, 72, 172, 173.)

NOTE B, p. 139.

INTERCOURSE OF THE GREEKS WITH ETRURIA.

Colonel Mure, in commenting upon the omission in Hecatæus (to judge from the existing fragments) of all notice of the flourishing Pelasgian or Etruscan cities on the west coast of Italy, as well as of the rising State of Rome, adverts to the similar absence of "all special notice of central Italy" in the "copious historical miscellany" of Herodotus, and infers from this coincidence that there was no commercial intercourse between the two nations. The conclusion seems to me quite untenable. It is true that we find the Greeks and Tyrrhenians on several occasions on terms of hostility with one another, as in the case of the league formed by the Tyrrhenians and Carthaginians to prevent the Phocæans from forming a settlement in Corsica (Herodot. i. 166); and again, in B.C. 474, when the same two powers combined to attack the Greek city of Cumæ, which was saved by the intervention of Hieron of Syracuse. But such occasional hostilities at long intervals can certainly not be held to imply the absence of peaceful commercial relations in the intervals. The piratical depredations of the Tyrrhenians would undoubtedly be liable to give rise to frequent disputes and minor quarrels; nor can it be denied that the jealousy evinced by the commercial states of ancient times frequently operated as a check upon their free intercourse. But there must always have been a limit to the restraint thus imposed. And that there existed at an early period—certainly as early as the sixth century B.C.—frequent communication between the two nations, is clearly shown by the exceedingly close resemblance of their works of art—a resemblance which no one can suppose to be fortuitous or occasional. Whatever theory may be adopted to account for the existence in Etruscan sepulchres of countless works of art—especially of painted vases in almost incredible numbers— not only stamped with the unquestionable impress of Greek art, but bearing Greek inscriptions, and even the names of Greek artists, it is impossible to deny that they are a clear evidence of frequent and long continued intercourse between the two countries. Even if it be supposed that these works were actually manufactured in Etruria by a colony of Greek artists, this hypothesis would still require that such a colony should have continued to maintain constant intercourse with the mother-country, for not only are the vases found in Etruscan tombs in many cases absolutely undistinguishable from those found in Greece proper and the islands of the Ægean, as well as in the Greek colonies in Campania and Sicily, but this similarity is found to prevail in works of every different age and style—the most ancient as well as the later and more perfect compositions. A very large proportion of those discovered in the Etruscan sepulchres certainly belong to a period of art earlier than the time of Herodotus, or even of Hecatæus, the period during which Colonel Mure would lead us to believe that there was almost no intercourse between Greece and Etruria.

The Etruscans were celebrated, from a very early period, for their skill in working in metals, especially bronze. The Tyrrhenian trumpets were celebrated in the days of Æschylus and Sophocles (Æschyl. *Eumen.* v. 567 ; Sophocl. *Ajax*, v. 17); and their candelabra, lamps, and all kinds of ornamental works in bronze enjoyed a high reputation among the Greeks (Critias ap. Athenæum, i. p. 28 b). Their embossed gold drinking-cups are also mentioned with especial praise (Ibid.).

We learn, moreover, that the opulent and luxurious republic of Sybaris maintained relations of peculiar amity with the Tyrrhenians (Athenæus, xii. p. 519), which must in all probability have been founded—like those with the Milesians—upon commercial relations, and the mutual interchange of works of art and objects of luxury.

CHAPTER VI.

HERODOTUS.

SECTION 1.—*General Views. Europe.*

§ 1. THE great work of Herodotus constitutes almost as important an epoch in the progress of geography, as in that of history.[1] But in attempting to collect and arrange the vast mass of geographical information which it contains, and to derive from it a correct estimate of the geographical knowledge really possessed by its author, it is necessary to bear in mind the desultory and irregular manner in which this information is communicated to us. His history, as he himself remarks, is full of digressions and episodes incidentally introduced;[2] and not only does this apply with equal force to the geographical portions of the work, but the whole of these portions is introduced in this parenthetical manner. There is nothing like an attempt to begin with a general outline of a systematic cha-

---

[1] The commentaries on the geographical information embodied in the history of Herodotus are so numerous that it is unnecessary to attempt to refer to them all. The work of Major Rennell (*The Geographical System of Herodotus examined and explained*, 1st edit 4to, Lond 1800, 2nd edit 2 vols 8vo, 1830) is still of the greatest value, notwithstanding the imperfect character of the materials at his command for the actual geography of many of the regions in question. Niebuhr's able essay, of which an English translation was published at Oxford in 1830, was the first that pointed out the true character of the map that Herodotus had present to his mind and the necessity of adapting all inquiries to this supposed scheme, rather than to the actual geography, such as we find it in modern maps. A mass of valuable information, in illustration of his author, from modern sources and recent investigations, will be found in the notes and appendices to Mr Rawlinson's translation (4 vols 8vo Lond 1858) As I find myself frequently compelled to differ from his conclusions, I take this opportunity of expressing the obligations I feel for the industry and diligence with which he has brought together the materials for a full investigation of many disputed points

[2] προσθήκας γὰρ δή μοι ὁ λόγος ἐξ ἀρχῆς ἐδίζητο, iv 30 See also vii 171

racter, and to fill up the different parts from time to time; but some countries which he had himself visited are described with a disproportionate amount of detail, while others are slurred over or neglected; in some instances, no doubt, because he had really no information concerning them, but in others only because no opportunity occurred of introducing them into his history. The influence of both causes may be distinctly traced; and it would be a great mistake to suppose that we are entitled to infer his ignorance of any particular region or country merely from the fact that he gives us no detailed information concerning it.

A single instance abundantly suffices to prove this. The great republic of Carthage was at this time almost at the height of its power and prosperity, yet it occupies but a very subordinate place in the history of Herodotus. The Carthaginians are indeed repeatedly mentioned incidentally, and they are even cited as authorities for specific facts, in connection with other countries;[3] but there is no attempt at any geographical account of their dominions in Africa, nor any hint of the extent of their colonial empire. Even when the author has occasion to mention the invasion of Sicily by Hamilcar, at the time of the expedition of Xerxes against Greece, which prevented the Sicilian Greeks from furnishing assistance to their fellow-countrymen, he contents himself with telling us that the Carthaginian general was at the head of an army of 300,000 men, composed not only of Carthaginians and Libyans, but of Iberians, Ligurians, Helisycians, Sardinians and Corsicans.[4] This list of names—especially the mention of the Helisycians, an obscure Ligurian tribe, whose name is cited also from Hecatæus,[5] but disappears in later times—suffices to show that Herodotus must have had accurate information on the subject, and could doubtless have told us much

---

[3] Herodot iv. 43, 195, vii 167
[4] vii 165
[5] See Chap V p. 139. The conjecture of Niebuhr, who attempts to identify them with the Volscians, appears to me to be utterly untenable

more about the invading power, had he considered it as coming within the scope of his work.

In like manner there occur none but incidental notices of the Tyrrhenians, though these are sufficient to prove that Herodotus was well acquainted with that people as a formidable naval power.[6] He, moreover, mentions details concerning the Agyllæans in particular, which certainly imply that they at least maintained habitual intercourse with the Greeks.[7] There could therefore have been no difficulty in obtaining further information concerning them, had it suited his purpose. Nor are we entitled to assume from his silence concerning Rome, that the name of that city had never reached his ears. It appears to have been certainly known to his contemporary Damastes,[8] as well as to Antiochus of Syracuse, who was not many years his junior. We must therefore be careful how we admit mere negative evidence, as proving the limits of his knowledge, except where the nature of the case is such as to render his silence in itself significant.

§ 2. There seems no doubt that the history of Herodotus, in the form transmitted to us, was not completed till after his emigration to Thurii (B.C. 443), or must at least have received additions and finishing touches subsequently to that period.[9] But notwithstanding the increased interest that his removal to that colony would naturally excite in his mind with regard to Italy and the adjoining lands, we find very few traces of this in his work; and there is nothing like a connected or syste-

---

[6] The contest in which they had engaged, in alliance with the Carthaginians, against the Greeks of Cumæ, supported by Hieron, king of Syracuse, was in itself calculated to impress this fact upon the mind of every Greek The victory of Hieron, celebrated by Pindar in a well-known passage (*Pyth.* i vv 136–146), took place in B C 474.

[7] Herodot 1 166, 167

[8] Dionys Halicain 1 72

[9] Concerning the life of Herodotus, and the period of the composition of his work, I must be content to refer my readers to the Introduction to the translation of his history by Mr. Rawlinson (chap. i), who has in my opinion successfully refuted the paradoxes of some modern writers (especially Dahlmann, in his *Life of Herodotus*), who would bring down the date of its publication to so late a period as B C 407, when the historian would have been in his seventy-seventh year! M Stein, in his edition of Herodotus (8vo, Berlin, 1856), adopts substantially the same views as Mr. Rawlinson (*Einleitung*, pp 23, 44)

matic review of the Greek colonies in Magna Græcia, similar to that which Thucydides has given of their settlements in Sicily. Probably Herodotus assumed his readers to be as familiar with the shores of Southern Italy and Sicily, which were in his days studded with Greek colonies, as they were with those of Greece itself and the opposite coasts of the Ægean. But the omission does not the less serve to show how little he aimed at any systematic geographical description of the countries that were known to him.

§ 3. It is certain that Herodotus had travelled extensively, and that many of the geographical details with which he has furnished us were the result of personal observation. But it is not easy to determine the extent and limits of his travels, and modern commentators and geographers have differed considerably in the conclusions they have arrived at on this subject.[1] It may, however, be taken as certain that he visited Egypt—where he ascended the Nile as far as the first Cataract—Babylon, and the adjoining country, and perhaps Susa. He also unquestionably describes Cyrene from personal observation; and the same remark applies to the northern shores of the Euxine as far as Olbia, on the Borysthenes. His observations also on the Colchians and their personal characteristics,[2] certainly seem to imply that he had himself visited their country. Towards the west we have no evidence of his having extended his personal researches beyond the south of Italy,[3] where he spent the latter part of his life. But we learn from incidental notices that he visited the island of Zacynthus and the oracle of Dodona, in Epirus; in both cases evincing that zealous curiosity and diligent spirit of inquiry that were so characteristic of his mind.

---

[1] See Mr. Rawlinson's Introduction, already cited, pp 8-12, and Stein's *Einleitung*, pp 13-21, and compare them with Col Mure's *History of Greek Literature* (vol iv pp. 245-248), who has in my opinion greatly exaggerated the extent of his travels.

[2] Herodot ii 104

[3] As Mr Rawlinson observes (*Herodotus*, vol 1. p 12), the only places that he can *be proved* to have visited, even in the south of Italy, are Thurii, Crotona, and Metapontum. and there is no evidence of his having ever been in Sicily

§ 4. It is fortunate that Herodotus was led, in one of the many digressions to which we have already adverted, to give a brief general outline of his ideas concerning the magnitude and position of the chief portions of the earth's surface with which he was acquainted; and though it is extremely difficult to gather from his description a distinct notion of the configuration of these countries as he represented them to his own mind, we at least derive from it certain information concerning the extent and limits of his knowledge.

After expressing his disbelief in the tales concerning the Hyperboreans, which he justly treats as a Greek fable, and not one of indigenous origin,[4] he proceeds to ridicule the pretensions of those who drew maps of the world, "without any sense to guide them," in which they made the whole earth round, as if drawn with a pair of compasses, with the Ocean stream flowing round it, and represented Asia and Europe as of equal size.[5] He then adds that he will describe in a few words the size and configuration of the two continents.[6] Beginning with Asia, he tells us that there were four nations which occupied the whole breadth of the continent from south to north, extending from one sea to the other. First, the Persians, who extended down to the southern or Erythræan Sea; next beyond them to the north, the Medians; then the Saspirians,[7] and beyond them the Colchians, who

---

[4] Herodot. iv 32.

[5] Though it is probable enough, as already suggested, that in these words he refers to Hecatæus, his structures are certainly not directed only against that author as he expressly speaks of *many* such representations—γελέω δὲ ὁρέων γῆς περιόδους γράψαντας πολλοὺς ἤδη, καὶ οὐδένα νόον ἔχοντας ἐξηγησάμενον οἳ Ὠκεανόν τε ῥέοντα γράφουσι πέριξ τὴν γῆν ἐοῦσαν κυκλοτερέα ὡς ἀπὸ τόρνου, καὶ τὴν Ἀσίην τῇ Εὐρώπῃ ποιεύντων ἴσην (iv. 36) It appears, therefore, that such maps were not uncommon in his time

[6] ἐν ὀλίγοισι γὰρ ἐγὼ δηλώσω μέγαθός τε ἑκάστης αὐτέων καὶ οἵη τίς ἐστι ἐς γραφὴν ἑκάστη (iv. 36)

[7] The Saspirians or Saspeires (Σάσπειρες) are also mentioned in the first book (c 104), as situated between the Colchians and Medians They were included, with the Matienians, in the 18th satrapy of the Persian Empire (iii 94), and would seem to have occupied the eastern part of Armenia But the name is not found in any of the later geographers, though cited by Stephanus, who writes it Σάπειρες as does also Apollonius Rhodius (ii vv 397, 1246), perhaps only for the sake of the metre This last author places them

extend to the northern sea (the Euxine), into which the Phasis pours itself.[8]

From the broad central tract of Asia thus defined there extended two projecting tracts,[9] or Actæ, as he terms them, thrown out towards the west, and both of them reaching to the sea. The one of these (nearly corresponding with what is now known as Asia Minor) extended from the mouth of the Phasis to the Gulf of Myriandrus, and stretched towards the west as far as the Hellespont and the Triopian Promontory; the other included the countries between the Erythræan Sea and the Mediterranean, west of Persia, viz. the Assyrians, Syrians, Phœnicians, and Arabians, and ended at the Arabian Gulf. But he adds that this was no real limit, for that Egypt was connected with the tract in question by a narrow neck of land about 1000 stadia (100 G. miles) across. And he proceeds, still more strangely, to include the whole of Libya (meaning the continent of Africa) in this second Actè or projecting tract, although, as he justly remarks, beyond the narrow neck just described Libya spreads out again to a very great breadth.[1]

The eastern portion of Asia—that is to say, east of the line above drawn from the Persian Gulf· to the Euxine—was bounded on the south by the Erythræan Sea, and on the north by the Caspian Sea and the river Araxes, which flowed from west to east. It was known and inhabited as far as India, but beyond this the country was uninhabited, and altogether unknown.[2] The same was the case with regard to the north and east of Europe, concerning which no one was able to say whether they were bounded by the sea or not.[3] But even what was known of Europe greatly exceeded in size both Asia and Libya, being equal in length to them both together, and beyond all comparison of greater breadth.[4]

---

on the *coast* of the Euxine, but this is clearly opposed to the view of Herodotus, and the geographical authority of Apollonius is of very little value.
[8] iv 37

[9] See Note A, p. 207.
[1] iv 38, 39
[2] iv. 40. [3] iii. 115.
[4] μήκει μὲν γὰρ παρ' ἀμφοτέρας παρήκει ἡ Εὐρώπη, εὖρεος δὲ περὶ οὐδὲ συμ-

Libya (Herodotus adds) was known to be surrounded by the sea; for it had been circumnavigated by the Phœnicians in the time of Necho, king of Egypt;[5] and the greater part of Asia had been discovered in the time of Darius, by whose orders Scylax of Caryanda had sailed down the river Indus to the sea, and then turning westward, had followed the shores of the Erythræan Sea till he arrived at the head of the Arabian Gulf.[6] But the limits of Europe were quite unknown.[7]

§ 5. The *general* idea which Herodotus wishes to express in the above description is not difficult to seize, though it is difficult to follow it out in detail, or to represent it on a map. The main point of all is the line of separation between Europe and Asia, which he undoubtedly conceived as running—not from south to north, as we naturally assume it—but *from west to east*—beginning with the river Phasis, which flowed into the Euxine, and prolonged from thence to the Caspian Sea; and eastward from that again by the river Araxes [8] for an indefinite distance, ending in the unknown regions to the eastward. Europe thus extended from the Pillars of Hercules in the west, lying opposite to Africa in the first instance, from which it was separated by the Mediterranean; and subsequently to Asia, from the Hellespont to the land of the Issedones and the Massagetæ, who appear to have been the remotest nations known to Herodotus towards the east. This explains his expression (twice repeated) that Europe extends along by the side of the other two continents, so as to be equal to them both in length.[9]

βαλέειν ἀξίη φαίνεταί μοι εἶναι, iv 42 The last words are susceptible of two different meanings, but the reasoning of the whole passage leaves no doubt of the sense in which they are used by the author The ambiguity, however, was the means of misleading Major Rennell, who trusted to Beloe's translation, and thus led him to entertain a wholly erroneous idea of the views of Herodotus (*Geogr of Herodot* p 412)
[6] iv. 44
[5] Herodot. iv 42.
[7] iv. 45
[8] The difficulties connected with the meaning of this name in the Herodotean geography will be considered hereafter But there can be little doubt that *in this passage* he means the river Iaxartes, though he erroneously conceived it as flowing *from west to east* (iv. 40)
[9] iv 42, 45

On the other hand he greatly underrated the size both of Asia, even as then known to the Greeks, and of Africa. With regard to the latter especially he seems to have been led to a very erroneous estimate of its dimensions by the fact that it had been circumnavigated, though, according to his own account, the voyage had occupied between two and three years.[1] In common with most ancient geographers, he supposed its greatest length to extend from the Pillars of Hercules to the Isthmus of Suez; and its breadth from the mouth of the Nile to the southern confines of Ethiopia. But it is difficult to understand how, even on this supposition, he could have so greatly underestimated its extension towards the south. In another passage he distinctly speaks of Arabia as the most southern of all inhabited countries,[2] and Ethiopia as the one extending farthest *to the west*. He therefore appears to have regarded the form of Africa as trending away abruptly towards the west, from near the entrance of the Arabian Gulf; and it is in conformity with this view that he describes the Nile, above the Egyptian frontier at Elephantine, as flowing *from west to east*.[3] These erroneous notions, on points of fundamental importance, must be carefully borne in mind in endeavouring to represent to ourselves the map of the world, as it was conceived by Herodotus.

It is not clear whether he regarded the African continent as projecting far to the west beyond the Pillars of Hercules. He mentions indeed the promontory of Soloeis, on the western coast, as the extreme western limit of Africa, and he cites the name as one with which he was familiar;[4] it was doubtless well known to the Carthaginians in his day. But this is far from implying that he was really acquainted with its geographical position.[5]

---

[1] The much controverted question as to the reality of this circumnavigation will be considered in a future chapter. For our present purpose it is sufficient that Herodotus undoubtedly believed it, and founded his geographical views upon it

[2] Herodot. iii. 107.

[3] ii. 31. See Chapter VIII

[4] ii 34, iv 43

[5] The Soloeis of Hanno and Scylax is certainly Cape Cantin, on the western coast, but the expressions of Herodotus

§ 6. With the extreme west and north of Europe on the other hand he was, as he himself tells us, altogether unacquainted. He was indeed familiar with the *name* of Tartessus, as a country of considerable extent in the south of Spain, which as late as the middle of the preceding century had been under the government of a king of its own, who had entered into friendly and commercial relations with the Phocæans.[6] The region thus designated was probably the part of Spain adjoining the mouth of the Bætis, or Guadalquivir, though it may also have been applied to the southernmost tract of Spain immediately within the Straits. At all events Herodotus was certainly acquainted with the name of Gadeira or Gades, at that time a flourishing Phœnician colony, and which he distinctly describes as situated " without the Pillars of Hercules, upon the Ocean."[7] But this was probably the limit of his knowledge towards the west. How far the European continent extended in that direction he had no knowledge. He had indeed heard of the Cassiterides, " the islands from whence tin was brought," but had no definite information concerning them, and appears to have disbelieved in their existence.[8] In like manner he rejected the notion (generally received in his time) of a river called the Eridanus, flowing into the northern sea, from which amber was brought;[9] and he distinctly adds that, " though he had taken

---

have been thought to point rather to Cape Spartel, the first promontory after passing through the straits It seems to me more probable that he had confounded the two, or rather that in fact he had no distinct idea on the subject at all He had heard, *from Carthaginian sources* (see iv. 43), of the name of the promontory of Soloeis, as the western extremity of Libya, and knew that it was *beyond* the Pillars of Hercules, but that was all.

[6] Herodot 1 163.

[7] iv 8. He here speaks of the fabulous Geryones as κατοικημένον τὴν "Ελληνες λέγουσι 'Ερύθειαν νῆσον τὴν πρὸς Γηδείροισι τοῖσι ἔξω 'Ηρακλέων στηλέων ἐπὶ τῷ 'Ωκεανῷ.

[8] iii 115. 'οὔτε νήσους οἶδα Κασσιτερίδας ἐούσας, ἐκ τῶν ὁ κασσίτερος ἡμῖν φοιτᾷ.

[9] It would seem clear that the identification so strangely made in later times of the Eridanus with the Padus, the great river of Northern Italy, had not yet come to be adopted Herodotus had only heard of it in connection with the northern sea, and the amber trade, and certainly did not connect it in any way with the Adriatic. The *name* Eridanus, as he justly observes, was clearly Greek, and he conceives it to have been invented by some poet. It was more probably merely a Greek modification of some barbarian name; and appears to contain the same root as

much pains to inquire," he had been unable to meet with any one who could state *from personal observation* that there was sea to the north of Europe.¹

The passage is a curious one, both as showing the pains that Herodotus took to obtain trustworthy information upon any subject that appeared to him of real interest; and as an instance (not uncommon in the history of science) where the more philosophic mind is practically led into error by an excess of caution, fully justifiable in itself. The popular notion, which had been followed by Hecatæus, *assumed* the existence of an Ocean on all sides of the earth, though the Greeks at this time had certainly no sufficient evidence of the fact.² Herodotus, on the contrary, required such information as would satisfy his mind, before he gave credence to this article of general belief; and, failing this, he rejected the fact. We now know that he was wrong, and that the fact is true—though in a very different sense from that supposed by Hecatæus and his contemporaries—but it cannot be denied that the course taken by Herodotus was the more philosophical of the two.

Towards the north, then, the world as known to our author had no definite limits. Beyond the Scythians, who occupied the broad steppes to the north of the Euxine, dwelt various other barbarian nations whose names, as well as many other particulars concerning them, are recounted to us in detail by Herodotus, from information furnished him by the Greek colonists on the Euxine. But beyond these tribes, who formed a kind of belt around Scythia proper—extending from

---

Rhodanus and Rhenus: though it is impossible to identify it with either of these two rivers. (See Latham's *Germania*, p 13, and the article *Eridanus* in Dr Smith's *Dict. of Ancient Geography*.)

¹ τοῦτο δὲ οὐδένος αὐτόπτεω γενομένου δύναμαι ἀκοῦσαι τοῦτο μελετέων ὅκως θάλασσά ἐστι τὰ ἐπέκεινα τῆς Εὐρώπης, iii. 115 It is certain, however, he adds,

that both tin and amber were brought from the farthest parts of the continent. ἐξ ἐσχατῆς δ' ἂν ὅ τε κασσίτερος ἡμῖν φοιτᾶ καὶ τὸ ἤλεκτρον.

² This is again pointed out by Herodotus in another passage (iv. 8): τὸν δὲ Ὠκεανὸν λόγῳ μὲν λέγουσι (οἱ Ἕλληνες sc) ἀπ' ἡλίου ἀνατολέων ἀρξάμενον γῆν περὶ πᾶσαν ῥέειν, ἔργῳ δὲ οὐκ ἀποδεικνῦσι.

the Carpathians to the Ural Mountains—nothing was known, and it was generally supposed that these regions were uninhabitable from cold. It is an additional proof of the good sense of Herodotus that he has no mention of the Rhipæan Mountains, which, fictitious as they were, so persistently maintained their place in the geography of the Greeks down to a late period.

§ 7. It is more surprising to our minds to see how very imperfect and limited was the knowledge possessed by Herodotus of the central and western portions of Europe. With Thrace indeed he was pretty well acquainted. But he gave to the country designated under that name a much wider extension than later geographers, so as to include the land of the Getæ, and the whole region from Mount Hæmus (the Balkan) to the Danube. Hence he speaks of the Thracians as, next to the Indians, the most numerous people in the world.[3] They were divided into many tribes, among which he particularly specifies the Getæ, the Trausi, and the Odrysæ. The Getæ dwelt near the Danube, extending to the south bank of that river, and hence they were traversed and subdued by Darius on his march to the Danube, when he was on his way to attack the Scythians.[4] In the lower part of its course that river formed the boundary between the Thracians and Scythians; but the country due north of the Danube was for the most part unknown, and was believed to be uninhabited. The only people on the other side of the river whose name had reached the ears of Herodotus were the Sigynnæ, a tribe who had a race of small horses—ponies in fact—with long, shaggy hair,

---

[3] Herodot. v. 3
[4] iv. 93, v 3   The ethnological relations of the Getæ have been the subject of so much controversy that it is important to bear in mind that Herodotus, the earliest author by whom they are mentioned, distinctly regarded them as a Thracian tribe, and calls them the most warlike, as well as the most just, of all the Thracians (οἱ δὲ Γέται . . . αὐτίκα ἐδουλώθησαν, Θρηίκων ἐόντες ἀνδρηιώτατοι καὶ δικαιότατοι, iv. 93).

The Odrysæ, who, under Sitalces, assumed so prominent a position, and became for a time the dominant power among the Thracians (Thucyd ii 96, 97), appear in Herodotus only in a very subordinate character.

SECT. 1.   HERODOTUS.   167

which were well adapted for chariots.⁵ According to our author's view the country inhabited by them extended to the borders of the Eneti, or Veneti, who dwelt near the head of the Adriatic.⁶ From this incidental mention of the Veneti, it is clear that not only was their name familiar to Herodotus, but he was acquainted, in a general way, with their true geographical position. He elsewhere terms them an Illyrian tribe.⁷

§ 8. As might have been expected Herodotus was evidently familiar with the name of Mount Hæmus (the Balkan), though he gives us no geographical particulars concerning it, and only mentions it incidentally, as the source from whence several considerable tributaries flow into the Danube.⁸ With that great river itself he was in a certain sense well acquainted, though his knowledge of it will be found on examination to be neither extensive nor accurate. Its mouths indeed were well known to the Greeks, who had founded a colony almost at their entrance,⁹ and probably traded up the river for a considerable distance. Hence Herodotus had learnt the names of several of the minor streams that flow into it from both sides, and there is no reason to doubt the accuracy of his information in this respect, though many of these names cannot now be identified. But the navigation up the river was probably checked by the rapids at the point now known as the Iron Gates; and the accounts that had reached the Greeks of the upper part of its course were of the vaguest kind. After describing in detail the streams that descended from the

---

⁵ Id v 9 No other mention is found of these Sigynnæ as an European people in any ancient author, except Apollonius Rhodius, who appears to have regarded them as dwelling *on the Euxine* (iv 320) Strabo, on the contrary, describes a people called Siginni, with their long-haired ponies, in almost the same terms as Herodotus, but places them in the neighbourhood of the Caspian and the Caucasus! (xi. 11, § 8, p. 520)

⁶ κατήκειν δὲ τούτων τοὺς οὔρους ἀγχοῦ

'Ενετῶν τῶν ἐν τῷ 'Αδρίῃ (v 3).
⁷ i 196.   ⁸ iv 49.
⁹ The Greek colony of Istrus or Istropolis was situated on the Euxine between Tomi (the site of which is clearly fixed at Kustendje) and the mouths of the Danube, but its precise position has not been determined It appears to have been a place of considerable trade, and continued to subsist down to the Roman Empire (Ammian. Marcell. ii. 8, § 43).

Illyrian Mountains through the plains occupied by the Triballians, Herodotus adds: "Two other streams also fall into it (the Ister) that have a northerly course, proceeding from the country above the Umbrians—the river Carpis and the Alpis. For the Ister flows through the whole length of Europe, rising in the land of the Keltæ, who, next to the Kynetes, dwell the furthest towards the west of all European nations. And after thus flowing through the whole of Europe, it issues forth upon the flanks of Scythia."[1]

It would be difficult to find a more curious instance of the sort of geographical confusion to which the first hearsay accounts of unexplored regions are liable. The "country above the Umbrians" must undoubtedly mean the north of Italy, for Herodotus elsewhere[2] speaks of the Tyrrhenians (Etruscans) as settling "in the land of the Umbrians;" but so little did he know of these regions that he was evidently unacquainted with the existence of the great mountain chain of the Alps, and erroneously supposed the name to be that of a river. The Carpis in like manner is in all probability due to some confused account of the Carpathian Mountains, though in this case the *direction* of the river would also be erroneous. As if to complete the confusion, Herodotus elsewhere describes the Ister as flowing from the land of the Keltæ and the city of Pyrēne,[3] where we have no doubt a mention of the Pyrenees, the third great mountain-chain of central Europe, though applied in an equally distorted manner.[4]

§ 9. In the passage above quoted[5] Herodotus speaks of the Keltæ as the most westerly people of Europe, with the exception of the Kynetes or Kynesians. The same statement is repeated in the somewhat parallel passage,[6] where he com-

---

[1] Herodot. iv. 49. [2] i. 94
[3] ii 33
[4] Even Aristotle supposed the Danube to have its source in "Pyrene in the land of the Kelts" (*Meteorol* i 13, § 19); but he was aware that Pyrene was a mountain, which he placed in the far west of Gaul: and thus describes the Ister, in almost the same words as Herodotus, as traversing the whole of Europe to the Euxine Sea.
[5] iv 49. [6] ii. 33.

pares the course of the Danube with that of the Nile. But he here adds that the Kelts are situated beyond the Pillars of Hercules, so that he seems to have considered their country as stretching out towards the west, far beyond its real position. Yet in this second passage he again speaks of the Kynesians as dwelling the farthest to the west of all European nations, and *beyond* the Kelts. The name is unknown to later geographers,[7] but it is cited from Herodorus of Heraclea, a contemporary of Socrates, as that of a region of Spain, adjoining the Ocean.[8] What idea Herodotus had formed to himself of their geographical position and that of the Keltæ, it is impossible to say; but it is clear that he had no knowledge whatever of the western, or Atlantic, coasts, either of Spain or Gaul. The name of Iberia is used by him only in reference to the *eastern*, or Mediterranean side of Spain;[9] and that of the Kelts occurs only in the two passages already referred to. Yet he could hardly have been ignorant of the Kelts who adjoined the sea between the Rhone and the Pyrenees, whose city of Narbo was already mentioned by Hecatæus as an important emporium of trade.[1]

§ 10. Another passage that affords us important assistance in the attempt to comprehend the general idea that Herodotus had formed to himself of the geography of the earth's surface, is that in which he institutes a comparison between the two greatest rivers known to him, the Nile and the Ister.[2] After showing that there was reason to believe that the Nile had its sources far away in the west of Africa, and that it flowed for the greater part of its course *from west to east*—a subject to

---

[7] It is not found in Strabo, Pliny, or Ptolemy, but reappears in Avienus (*de Ora Maritima*, v. 566), much of whose information is derived from very early authorities.

[8] Steph Byzant. s. v. Κυνητικόν.

[9] Thus he speaks of the Phocæans as being the first to make long voyages, and who showed the Greeks the way to Tyrrhenia, Iberia, and Tartessus (1. 163). It was from thence that the Carthaginians drew a portion of their mercenary troops, with which they invaded Sicily, under Hamilcar, the son of Hanno (vii. 165)

[1] Niebuhr must have overlooked this passage of Hecatæus (Fr. 19) when he says that the Celts, in the time of Herodotus, had not yet extended to any part of the coast of the Mediterranean (*Geogr of Herodot*. p. 12, Eng. transl.).

[2] ii. 33, 34.

which we shall hereafter have to revert—he proceeds to say that he conceives the Nile and the Ister to have somewhat parallel courses, the one dividing Europe through the middle, and the other flowing in like manner through the midst of Africa; and that they both had their origin at about equal distances from their mouths,[3] the Ister rising in the far west of Europe, and the Nile (as he conjectured) in the western regions of Libya. He then adds that their mouths were in fact *opposite to* one another, for that Egypt lay just about opposite to the mountainous parts of Cilicia, from whence it was a direct journey, in a straight line, of only five days to Sinope, and that city was situated opposite to the mouth of the Ister.

He here appears to be, as it were, in a rude manner, drawing a meridian line from the mouth of the Nile to that of the Danube; and infers that, as these were in this sense opposite to one another, and their sources were so likewise (according to his own views concerning the origin of the Nile), the length of both rivers would be about equal. It is scarcely necessary to point out how erroneous was his reasoning concerning the Nile, the upper course and sources of which were, as he himself tells us, utterly unknown; and we have already seen how extremely imperfect was his information concerning the upper course of the Danube, though this he supposed to be well ascertained, for (he tells us) "the Ister flows through an inhabited region, and is therefore known to many."[4] It is more curious that, while his inference concerning the relative position of the mouths of the two rivers is approximately correct—the Canopic, or western

---

[3] This appears to me to be certainly the sense of the somewhat obscure expression that the Nile τῷ Ἴστρῳ ἐκ τῶν ἴσων μέτρων ὁρμᾶται. The two rivers had a general analogy in all respects; they both flowed from west to east, they had their mouths opposite to one another, and so were their sources. The sense is very much the same as we should express in modern geographical phrase by saying that they flowed through the same number of degrees of longitude: though of course no such idea, in a distinct form, was present to the mind of Herodotus.

[4] ὁ μὲν δὴ Ἴστρος ῥέει μὲν γὰρ δι' οἰκευμένης, πρὸς πολλῶν γινώσκεται, ii. 34.

mouth of the Nile, differing in fact only a few miles in longitude from those of the Danube—the data upon which it is founded are glaringly erroneous. Cilicia Trachea, as the mountainous part of Cilicia was called, lies considerably to the east of the whole Delta of Egypt, and Sinope still more so; so that that city is in fact more than five degrees of longitude to the eastward of the Canopic mouth of the Nile. But on the other hand, it is in fact by about as much further east than the mouths of the Danube, to which Herodotus considered it as directly opposite. Thus, in this case, it accidentally happens that the two errors committed by him just about neutralize one another. Had he not mentioned the steps of the process, we might have wondered at the accuracy of the result, and given him credit for an amount of geographical knowledge which he certainly did not possess.

There can be little doubt that Herodotus was led to institute this parallel between the two rivers by something of that feeling of symmetry so congenial to the Greek mind. But we must not press the comparison too far. It is hardly to be inferred from the passage in question that the historian considered the Ister as making a great bend analogous to that of the Nile where it entered Egypt. Yet it appears certain from other passages that he did consider it as turning *southwards* in order to reach the sea, and he distinctly tells us that where it entered the Euxine its mouth was turned towards the south-east.[5] This would in fact be the direction of one of the mouths that formed the delta of the river, and

---

[5] ὁ Ἴστρος ἐκδιδοῖ ἐς αὐτὴν (τὴν θάλασσαν sc) πρὸς εὖρον ἄνεμον τὸ στόμα τετραμμένος, iv. 99. This passage is, in my opinion, mistranslated by Mr. Rawlinson, who renders it " the Ister falling into the sea at this point, with its mouth facing *the east.*" But the Εὖρος ἄνεμος of Herodotus is certainly meant to designate *the south-east*, in accordance with the usage which we find established in the time of Aristotle. Only a few lines further on, he distinctly uses the expression πρὸς ἀπηλιώτην ἄνεμον in the sense of "towards the east," and he elsewhere repeatedly uses the same term for the *east* wind (iv. 152, vii. 188). M. Kiepert, in his map annexed to Stein's edition of Herodotus, has correctly represented the Danube, in accordance with the views of the author; as has also Dr. C. Müller in Smith's *Historical Atlas of Ancient Geography.*

this perhaps gave rise to the misconception that it was that of the main stream. But it will be found impossible, as we shall hereafter see, to understand the view taken by Herodotus of the geography of Scythia, without bearing in mind this fundamental error concerning the course of the Danube.

SECTION 2.—*Scythia*.

§ 1. The very scanty and imperfect knowledge which Herodotus displays of so large a portion of Europe contrasts strangely, to the modern reader, with the large amount of information which he has furnished us in regard to the countries north of the Euxine, and the vast tract of country that was commonly included by the Greeks under the vague and general appellation of Scythia.

Several circumstances had indeed combined from a very early period to direct the especial attention of the Greeks to the countries in question. The first of these was the great migratory movement of the people called by the Greeks Cimmerians, who, according to the tradition universally received, and adopted by Herodotus, had originally occupied the tract of country north of the Euxine, between the Ister and the Tanais; but having been expelled from thence by the Scythians, had poured themselves in a vast horde down upon Asia Minor, where they had carried devastation and terror to the gates of the Greek cities of Ionia. This invasion is undoubtedly entitled to be received as an historical fact;[6] nor is there any reason to doubt the traditionary belief that the people in question came from the regions north of the Euxine, in which the Scythians were found in the time of Herodotus. Such a displacement of one of these nomad nations by another,

---

[6] The invasion of Asia by the Cimmerians is alluded to by the earliest Greek elegiac poets, Archilochus and Callinus, who were contemporary with it (Callinus, Fr. 2, 3, ed. Bergk; Strabo, xiii. p 627) It was doubtless from these early authorities that Callimachus derived the picture he drew of them as "dwelling in waggons" and "milkers of mares" (*H. ad Dian.* v. 252-260)

is entirely in accordance with what we know to have taken place at subsequent periods; and is of great interest as the first authentic record of those great movements of nations that have taken place in all ages on the frontiers of Europe and Asia.[7]

The gradual extension of the Greek colonies along the northern shores of the Euxine, and the settlement of such powerful cities and commercial centres as Olbia and Panticapæum, would naturally add to the general interest felt by the Greeks in these countries; and the expedition of Darius into Scythia, before the close of the sixth century B.C., must have given a fresh stimulus to their curiosity as to the vast regions that lay beyond the Danube. The grossly exaggerated rumours that reached their ears with regard to the extent and circumstances of that expedition would only tend to increase this feeling. It was doubtless the same cause that led Herodotus himself to visit the remote Greek settlements in this quarter, and to collect there by personal inquiry and observation the valuable mass of information which he has embodied in the fourth book of his history.[8]

§ 2. There are indeed few parts of that great work that display in a more striking manner at once the merits and defects of the writer. It is difficult to determine the extent of his personal knowledge of the regions that lay to the north of the Euxine, but it is certain that he spent some time at Olbia on the Borysthenes, where he evidently occupied himself diligently in collecting information from the traders and others that were accustomed to penetrate into the interior. He mentions having himself seen a remarkable monument at a place called Exampæus, or "the Sacred Ways," four days' voyage up the river Hypanis,[9] but we have no proof that his personal

---

[7] See Note B, p. 208.

[8] In regard to this portion of the geography of Herodotus, every student of that author must consult the valuable work of M Neumann (*Die Hellenen im Skythenlande*, 8vo, Berlin, 1855).

[9] Herodot IV. 81. He appears also to have been on shore at the mouth of the Tyras, where there was a Greek colony of the name, as he mentions two things to be seen there in a manner that cer-

observation extended farther inland. The lively picture that he has drawn of the mode of life and customs of the nomadic Scythian tribes would readily lead us to suppose that he had himself seen them in their native wilds; but it is difficult to reconcile this with the geographical inaccuracies which we shall hereafter have to point out; and it seems more probable that his personal acquaintance with them was limited to those he might have seen at the fairs and markets of Olbia or other Greek towns, while he had gathered fuller particulars from careful inquiry. In proportion indeed as he recedes from the shores of the Euxine, his information becomes more vague and untrustworthy; for his geographical *data* had to be derived from the statements of traders who had travelled only with a view to their own commercial objects, and who had doubtless never seen a map, or attempted to form in their own minds any definite geographical idea of the countries they had visited.

Still, the amount and extent of his information concerning the various tribes and nations of the interior is in every way remarkable; and leads us to the unquestionable inference that the Greeks of his day had carried their commercial relations, either by land or water (probably the former), to an extent that remained unsurpassed until a much later period. Even in the days of Augustus, Strabo was able to add little or nothing to the extent of our knowledge of the countries in question, while Pliny and Mela mix up the statements of Herodotus with those of later writers, referring to a wholly altered state of things, in a manner which throws the whole subject into inextricable confusion.

In another respect Herodotus stands conspicuously distinguished from his predecessors. All previous writers—so

---

tainly seems to point to personal observation (iv. 11, 82) But there is no other point on the coast of the Euxine where he can be proved to have touched on his way to Olbia, after leaving the Thracian Bosphorus, where he refers to the brazen bowl set up by Pausanias in a manner that clearly shows that he had himself seen it (iv. 81).

far as we can judge from the fragments that remain to us—had concurred in making the Scythian deserts the abode of mythical races, and the scene of poetical fables. Herodotus, on the contrary, is careful to distinguish what he received on credible testimony from all such fabulous accounts; and though he does not refuse to mention the Arimaspians, he expresses his doubts of their existence, and distinctly tells us that the fact rested only on the authority of the Issedones, from whom the Scythians had learnt the tale, which had passed through them to the Greeks.[1] Of the Hyperboreans on the contrary, as we have already seen, he altogether disbelieved the existence.[2] Nor is any mention found in his work of the Rhipæan Mountains, and his silence may be considered in this instance conclusive, as he could not have failed to notice them in connection with the great rivers of Scythia, had he believed in their existence.

§ 3. Before attempting to examine the account given by Herodotus of the Scythians and the adjoining tribes, it is necessary to advert briefly to his ideas on the subject of the Euxine itself, and its subordinate or tributary sea, the Palus Mæotis. His misconceptions concerning the extent and configuration of these two great basins of water will be found to have an important bearing on the geographical arrangement of the numerous tribes that adjoined their shores; and it is impossible to represent to ourselves the idea that he had formed of the Scythian territories, and the succession of the different tribes, without clearly comprehending the wide divergence of his notions on this subject from the reality.

Herodotus had himself navigated the Euxine, and its waters were in his days frequently traversed by Greek traders in all

---

[1] iii. 116, iv. 27. He speaks with equal caution of the strange races reported by the Argippeans to dwell beyond them to the north (iv. 25).

[2] See above, p 160

It is an important lesson to us, of the caution necessary in making use of the statements quoted by late grammarians from earlier writers, that Eustathius (ad Dionys Perieg. v. 31) cites Herodotus as affirming the very fact that he combats: viz the existence of the Hyperboreans, beyond the Arimaspians and the griffins, extending to the sea: the account quoted indeed by Herodotus from Aristeas (iv. 13), but of which he repeatedly expresses his disbelief (Ibid. 16, 32)

directions. But we must not hastily conclude that he had therefore correct ideas as to its form and magnitude, or that he was acquainted with its true geography, in the modern sense of the term. He had indeed arrived at definite conclusions on the subject, which prove the pains he had taken to inform himself; while their erroneous character shows the difficulty that existed in his time in arriving at a correct result. He tells us that the Euxine, which he terms "the most wonderful of all seas" is eleven thousand one hundred stadia in length, and its breadth, at the widest part, is three thousand three hundred stadia. The greatest length he considers to be from the mouth of the Pontus (i. e. the Thracian Bosphorus) to the Phasis; and its greatest breadth to be between Themiscyra at the mouth of the river Thermodon, and Sindica (the peninsula of Taman) at the entrance of the Cimmerian Bosphorus. The last supposition involves a considerable error. The broadest part of the Black Sea is in reality between Heraclea on the coast of Bithynia, and the mouth of the estuary of the Borysthenes, where its breadth is not less than 325 geographical miles, or 3250 stadia—very nearly agreeing with the estimate of Herodotus—while the actual distance between the points selected by him does not exceed 235 G. miles or 2350 stadia. The length on the other hand is enormously exaggerated; the distance from the mouth of the Thracian Bosphorus to that of the Phasis being in a direct course not more than about 5500 stades, or just about *half* that stated by Herodotus.

§ 4. The source of his error is not far to seek; for he has himself told us in this instance the process of computation by which he arrived at his result. "In a long day (he tells us) a ship usually accomplishes about 70,000 fathoms, and about 60,000 fathoms in the night."[3] Now from the Phasis to the mouth

---

[3] The mention of fathoms in this calculation seems to show that this was the customary *nautical* mode of measurement It is Herodotus himself who converts these fathoms into stadia—the common measure of *land* distances.

It would be very curious to know what was the mode employed by the

of the Bosphorus was a voyage of nine days and eight nights; and from Sindica to Themiscyra was a voyage of three days and two nights. Hence he computed the distances by a simple process of multiplication; reckoning, as the Greeks always did, 100 fathoms, or 600 feet, to the stade.[4]

Here it is evident that the error arose simply from an over-estimate of the average rate of sailing. It was no doubt possible that a Greek merchant vessel should, *under favourable circumstances*, accomplish as much as 700 stadia (70 G. miles) in a day, and 600 in the night; but it was a great mistake to take this as the distance performed *on the average*. The ordinary estimate of later geographers is 500 stadia a day, and the same for a night.[5] But even this would make the estimate of Herodotus greatly exceed the truth, and it is evident that we must allow for considerable loss of time, in consequence of the windings of the coast, baffling winds, caused by projecting headlands, and other causes of delay, of which Herodotus took no account. On the other hand his estimate of the width is comparatively so little in excess, that it shows clearly that the Greek sailors of those days were in the habit of taking advantage of the prevalence of north winds, and stretching directly across from the mouth of the Cimmerian Bosporus to the Greek settlements on the southern shores of the Euxine.

§ 5. But if his ideas of the dimensions and form of the Euxine, or Pontus, as he generally calls it, were thus disfigured by grave errors, his conception of the Palus Mæotis—" the mother of the Euxine," as it was commonly termed by the Greeks— was still more erroneous. "The Pontus (he tells us, after describing its dimensions in the above passage) has also a lake belonging to it, *not very much inferior to itself in size;* the waters of which flow into it. It is called Mæotis, and the mother of the Pontus." This is indeed a startling misstatement. At the present day the Sea of Azov covers an

---

shipmasters of the Euxine in order to calculate the distance run in a day, but to this we have unfortunately no clue [4] See Note C, p 209
[5] Scylax, *Periplus*, § 69.

area of about 14,000 square miles, which is little more than *one-twelfth* of that of the Black Sea. Hence many geographers and commentators on Herodotus (including even his most recent translator) have thought it necessary to suppose that some great physical changes have taken place since his time, and that the Palus Mæotis was really much more extensive in ancient times than at the present day.[6] It is certain indeed that the Sea of Azov, which is throughout its extent very shallow, is gradually filling up, and becoming perceptibly shallower; while the continual deposit of silt and mud by the river Don is necessarily pushing forward its delta into the sea, and a similar deposit is taking place at the mouth of the Kuban also, on the southern shore of the sea.[7] It is true also that there are geological reasons which have led Pallas and other writers to speculate on the probability that the whole tract between the Caspian and the Sea of Azov was submerged, and the two seas consequently united, at no very remote period, *geologically speaking*. But it would be very hasty to assume from this that any material change has taken place within the historical period, or since the time of Herodotus, and it is to be remarked that Scylax (or the author of the Periplus that bears his name), writing little more than a century after Herodotus, estimates the Mæotis at only *half* the size of the Euxine.[8] This is, of course, still a great exaggeration; but the idea of its great size seems to have continued fixed in the minds of the Greeks for ages afterwards, and even Ptolemy still represented it as enormously larger than it really is.[9]

[6] See Mr Rawlinson's note to his translation of Herodotus, vol iii p 79

[7] All these causes were in full operation in the time of Polybius, who enters into some interesting speculations on the subject anticipating the time when not only the Palus Mæotis, but even the Euxine itself, might be filled up by these deposits (iv 40) These views are perfectly sound, as a matter of geological theory; but the rate of progress has been very much slower than he supposed, and the amount of actual change that has taken place within 2000 years is comparatively trifling (See Chapter XVII)

[8] Scylax, *Peripl* § 69

[9] Ptolemy supposed the Palus Mæotis to extend through nearly *six* degrees of latitude from S to N, with a breadth more than equal, if we include the

The truth appears to be, that the Palus Mæotis was generally regarded by the Greeks as *a lake*, not as an inland sea; considered *as such*, it was enormously larger than any other lake with which they were acquainted; and the idea thus formed of its vast size led readily to an exaggerated estimate of its real dimensions. It seems much more natural to believe that Herodotus was misled by erroneous information than to have recourse to the supposition of physical changes having taken place with unexampled rapidity.

§ 6. No allusion is found in Herodotus to the fancied resemblance of the general form of the Euxine to a Scythian bow, so familiar to the later Greek geographers. This comparison indeed implies a much more accurate conception of its general configuration than was possessed by the historian, and especially of the true size and position of the Tauric peninsula, concerning which he entertained strangely erroneous notions, for one who had himself navigated the Euxine, of which it forms so prominent a feature. He indeed correctly describes the Tauric territory as a mountainous district projecting into the Pontus, and forming the advanced point of Scythia between the seas that bounded it on the south and east; but in order to convey to his readers an idea of its form, he compares it successively with the projecting portion of Attica, and with that of Iapygia in Italy, beyond the line from Brundusium to Tarentum.[1] Both comparisons show clearly that he conceived it only as an Actè, or projecting tract of land, and that he was unaware of its being a peninsula in the strictest sense of the term, joined to the mainland only by a narrow neck or isthmus: otherwise the Peloponnese must have offered itself as a much apter comparison, and one familiar to all Greeks. The two peninsulas are indeed very nearly about the same size, and the Isthmus of Perekop, which unites the Crimea to the continent, is little broader than that of Corinth.[2]

---

inlet, which he calls Byce Lacus, and which must represent the Putrid Sea of Strabo, of which Ptolemy had appa- rently a very imperfect notion (See Chapter XXVII) [1] Herodot iv 99 [2] The resemblance between the two

Here again it has been suggested that some physical change may have taken place, and that the shallow inlet now called the Putrid Sea, which alone gives this strictly peninsular form to the Crimea, may not have existed in the time of Herodotus. It must be admitted that a very slight alteration of levels would effect this, and would transform what is now a shallow inland sea into a mere salt-marsh, or even into dry land. But even then the description of Herodotus would be far from characteristic, and it seems much safer in this instance also to acquiesce in the conclusion that he was simply misled by imperfect information.[3]

§ 7. But however imperfect were the geographical notions of the Greek settlers as to the extent and configuration of the Euxine, and its tributary the Mæotis, they had long been familiar with the great rivers which flow into those seas, and constitute the leading characteristic of Eastern Europe. The Ister or Danube, the Tyras (now the Dniester), the Hypanis (Bug), the Borysthenes, or Dnieper, and the Tanais or Don, are not only all mentioned by Herodotus, and enumerated in their correct order, but they are described more or less fully. Of the Ister (as we have already seen) he speaks in considerable detail,[4] and seems to have had pretty accurate information concerning the lower part of its course, where it formed, according to his view, the frontier between Scythia and Thrace.[5] But as he makes no mention of the cataracts or rapids at the Iron Gates, which have in all ages opposed so serious an obstacle to the navigation of the river, it is clear

---

is well pointed out by Strabo (vii 4, § 5) ἡ δὲ μεγάλη χερρόνησος τῇ Πελοποννήσῳ προσέοικε καὶ τὸ σχῆμα καὶ τὸ μέγεθος

[3] The improbability of any such change having occurred within the historical period is greatly augmented by the circumstance that Strabo describes the Tauric peninsula, and the Putrid Sea in particular, with great accuracy, and precisely in accordance with their present condition (Strabo, vii 4). But if any great physical change had taken place in the interval between Herodotus and Strabo, in the immediate neighbourhood of the flourishing Greek settlements on the Bosporus, which were during this period at the very height of their prosperity, some tradition of it would surely have been preserved, and have become known to the later geographer

[4] Herodot iv 48-50
[5] iv 99

that he had no full or complete knowledge of its course, as high as that point (about 450 miles from its mouth), and we have already seen how extremely vague and imperfect were his notions concerning the upper part of its course, and the affluents it there received. Even in the lower portion, though he enumerates the tributaries that fall into it on the one side or the other, as if he had accurate knowledge on the subject, it is impossible to identify with any certainty the streams really meant, with the exception of the Porata, or Pruth, which, as it joins the Danube but a short distance above its delta, and has a course nearly parallel with that of the Tyras, would naturally be well known to the Greek colonists of the Euxine.[6]

Farther inland indeed he mentions the Maris, as flowing from the land of the Agathyrsi, which may in all probability be identified with the Marosch, the principal river of Transylvania:[7] but the other names enumerated by him, are not mentioned by any later writer, and can for the most part only be identified by arbitrary selection among the numerous streams that pour their waters into the Danube on the one bank or the other.

§ 8. Herodotus expressly calls the Ister the greatest of all known rivers,[8] though he elsewhere remarks that it owes its predominance to its numerous tributaries: for that, taking the main streams separately, the Nile was far superior to it in the volume of its waters.[9] Besides its magnitude, another circumstance that particularly attracted his attention in this mighty stream was its equable flow, which presented no difference in

---

[6] Herodotus himself tells us (iv 48) that it was called Porata by the Scythians, but Puretos by the Greeks, a statement that clearly shows the name to have been one familiar to Greek ears.

[7] It is true that the Marosch does not fall directly into the Danube, but into the Theiss, which is itself a tributary of the Danube But this is a point of little importance. Even at a much later period geographers do not seem to have appreciated the superior importance of the Theiss Strabo speaks of the Marisus as flowing into the Danube, and serving as the channel by which the Romans sent up their supplies for the Dacian war (vii. 3, § 13), while the name of the Tibiscus, or Theiss, is first found in Ptolemy

[8] Ἴστρος μὲν ἐὼν μέγιστος ποταμῶν πάντων τῶν ἡμεῖς ἴδμεν (iv. 48).

[9] Ibid. 50

winter or summer: affording in this respect a marked contrast, not only to the Nile, but to all those rivers with which Herodotus was likely to be most familiar, either in European Greece or Asia Minor. This peculiarity he justly attributes to the melting of the accumulated snows by the summer heat compensating for the increased evaporation at that season.[1] But he was not aware that this great accumulation of snow was owing to the chains of high mountains that supply the main tributaries of the Danube, and he ascribed it to the ordinary severity of the winter, in the lands from which they flowed;—the climate of which he supposed, naturally enough, to resemble that of Scythia.

§ 9. As has been already pointed out, he describes the Ister as flowing into the Euxine with its mouth facing the southeast: the next of the great rivers, the Tyras, flowed from north to south, having its sources in a large lake on the outer confines of Scythia, where it adjoined the land of the Neuri.[2] The Hypanis, which came next, also rose in a large lake, which was thence called "the mother of the Hypanis:" its waters were at first quite fresh, but in the lower part of its course they were rendered bitter or salt by the admixture of those of a source of extremely salt water, at the distance of four days' voyage from the sea.[3] It is singular that Herodotus describes the Hypanis, though he calls it a river with which few could compare in size,[4] as if its whole course was only nine days' voyage from its sources to the sea, and though these are obviously intended to be reckoned *descending* the stream, the statement is nevertheless difficult to understand.[5]

§ 10. The Borysthenes, which he justly accounted the largest

---

[1] Ibid [2] iv 51 [3] Ibid 52
[4] τὸν Ὕπανιν ἐόντα ποταμὸν ἐν ὀλίγοισι μέγαν (iv 52) It is strange that Mr Rawlinson should translate these words as "a large stream among those of the second order." They are correctly rendered by Valckenaer (*ad loc*) "flumen in paucis magnum"
[5] The Bug is in reality about 480 miles in length, and not less than 300 miles in a direct line from its source to its mouth It is probable that there is some confusion in our existing text, and that Herodotus did not mean the five days' voyage mentioned in the first instance to comprise the whole distance from the lake to the salt fountain.

of the Scythian rivers, after the Danube, was, he adds, the most productive of all rivers, not only in Scythia, but in the world, with the single exception of the Nile. The vast quantity and variety of fish that it produced, some of them of the largest size; the richness and extent of the pastures on its banks; the fertility of the soil for cultivation; and the sweetness of its clear waters,—at the same time that salt was produced in abundance at its mouth—gave it the palm over all its competitors.[6] Nor are these praises exaggerated. The Greek colony founded near its mouth, and from thence generally known among the Greeks as Borysthenes, but called by its inhabitants Olbia or Olbiopolis ("the prosperous city") owed its wealth and prosperity mainly to its position at the entrance of this great stream, which opened out the access to the richest and most fertile provinces of Southern Russia.

Yet even of the Borysthenes itself his geographical knowledge was very imperfect. He himself tells us that no one was acquainted with its source, but that it was known for a distance of forty days' voyage, as far as a place called Gerrhus, and that its course was from north to south.[7] He therefore evidently considered it as flowing parallel with the Hypanis, and had no conception of the vast bend by which the Dnieper sweeps round from below Kiev by Ekaterinoslav to Kherson. It is more remarkable that he seems to be unacquainted with the cataracts or rapids, which interrupt the navigation of the river during this part of its course, for a distance of more than forty miles, and must in all ages have opposed a barrier to communication with the regions beyond. But he himself tells us that it flowed through the land of the Georgi, or agricultural Scythians, for the lowest ten days' voyage, and above that its course lay through uninhabited

---

[6] Herodot. iv 53. This character of the Borysthenes seems to have become traditional. Scymnus Chius, who probably copied *directly* from Ephorus, says of it in like manner.

οὗτος δὲ πάντων ἐστὶ χρειωδέστατος.
κήτη μεγάλα καὶ πολλὰ καὶ καρποὺς φέρων
τοὺς φυομένους νομάς τε τοῖς βοσκήμασιν
vv 813–815, ed Muller

The huge fish are doubtless sturgeon, which still abound in the Dnieper.

[7] See Note D, p. 211

regions;[8] so that little would be known concerning it. His erroneous view of its direction would however tend materially to vitiate all his ideas of the geography of this part of Scythia, and must be carefully borne in mind in attempting to arrange and explain his other statements on the subject.

§ 11. The last of the great rivers of Scythia which he mentions is the Tanais, with which he was well acquainted, by name at least: this he describes as flowing in the first place (like the Hypanis and Tyras) from *a great lake*, and discharging itself into *a still greater*, the Mæotis, which formed the boundary between the Scythians and Sarmatians. He adds also that it received a tributary river called the Hyrgis.[9] In point of fact the Don *does* rise in a lake, while the Bug and the Dniester *do not*, but it is one of such very small dimensions, as not even to figure on any ordinary map of Russia,[1] and it is wholly inconceivable that the informants of the historian had sufficiently accurate knowledge of these remote regions of the interior to be aware of this minute fact, while their general notions were so vague and incoherent. It is much more probable that in all three cases the lake was invented, or assumed by the persons from whom Herodotus derived his information, as the readiest means of accounting for the origin of a great river. At the same time the extensive marshes in the interior of Russia would favour the idea, and may perhaps have really contained accumulations of stagnant water of greater extent than they do now. In one respect indeed the knowledge obtained by Herodotus was superior to that possessed by many later writers. Both Hippocrates and Aristotle believed in the existence of a great chain of mountains "in the extreme north, beyond the limits of Scythia," in which all the greatest of these rivers took their rise, and to which they gave the name of the Rhipæan Mountains.[2] Herodotus on the contrary

---

[8] Herodot iv 53
[9] The Hyrgis is generally identified with the Donetz, but merely on the ground that that river is the most considerable affluent of the Don

[1] It is called Lake Ivan Ozero, and is situated in about 34° N latitude, but is described as a mere pool
[2] Aristot *Meteorol* 1 13 Hippocrates even accepts the popular notion that it

(as has been already mentioned), not only makes no mention of the existence of any such range, but his account of the great rivers just described, altogether excludes the supposition that they derived their waters from such a source.

§ 12. On the whole, the knowledge possessed by Herodotus of the five principal rivers of Scythia is very much what might have been expected. Their mouths and the lower portion of their courses would be well known to the Greek settlers on the northern shores of the Euxine, while vague and often erroneous rumours would be all that reached them concerning the sources of the same rivers, or the part of their course during which they flowed through wild and thinly peopled regions. In every instance indeed these great streams took their rise beyond the limits of Scythia proper, as defined by Herodotus, among the barbarous nations that are described as surrounding the Scythians, with whom the Greeks themselves had little, if any, intercourse.

§ 13. But if the account given by Herodotus of the five great rivers in question is tolerably clear and distinct, and their identification admits of no reasonable doubt, the case is altogether otherwise with regard to three other streams, all of which he distinctly places *between the Borysthenes and the Tanais*, and to which he gives the name of Panticapes, Hypacyris, and Gerrhus. Of these it may fairly be said that they have defied all the efforts of successive geographers to identify them with any known rivers, or to propose any plausible solution of the difficulty. The Panticapes is described as rising in a lake, having a course from north to south, therefore parallel with the Borysthenes, into which river it ultimately fell, apparently not far from its mouth. The intermediate space (which was a distance of three days' journey from west to east [3]) was occupied by the Husbandmen (Georgi) or agricultural Scythians, while the river in the lower part of its

---

was from thence the north wind blew. κέεται γὰρ (ἡ Σκυθικὴ χώρη) ὑπ' αὐτῇσι τῇσι ἄρκτοισι, καὶ τοῖσι οὔρεσι, τοῖσι Ρι-

παίοισι, ὅθεν ὁ βορέης πνέει (De Aeris, Aquis, &c. c. 95)
[3] iv 18.

course traversed the land which he calls Hylæa, or the Forest Region.[4] Next comes the Hypacyris, rising also in a lake, traversing the country of the Nomad Scythians, leaving the Hylæa on the right, and falling into the Gulf of Carcine, opposite the town of that name.[5] There is no river that at the present day at all corresponds with either of these; in fact, there is no stream of any magnitude between the Dnieper and the Don, except the Donetz, which is a tributary of the latter river, and does not approach the Palus Mæotis. The account is further perplexed by the statement that the Hypacyris, the most easterly of the two rivers, discharged its waters into the Carcinitic Gulf, which is unquestionably the Gulf of Perekop, *west* of the isthmus of that name.

Still more enigmatical is the description of the third river, the Gerrhus, which, according to Herodotus, was a branch of the Borysthenes, separating from that river at the place called Gerrhus, which (as we have already seen) was the farthest point to which the Borysthenes was navigable, and was distant forty days' voyage from the sea. In the lower part of its course the river Gerrhus separated the Nomad Scythians from the Royal tribe, and was in one part not less than seventeen days' journey distant from the Borysthenes. Yet it ultimately, instead of falling into the Palus Mæotis, joined the Hypacyris (!).

The whole account is utterly unintelligible, and is not only at variance with the actual geography of these regions, but may fairly be said to involve physical impossibilities.[6] It can only be explained on the supposition that Herodotus, who apparently never himself crossed the Borysthenes, was misled by the confused accounts of different travellers, of which, from his own imperfect ideas of physical geography, he was unable to see the contradiction.

---

[4] Her.' iv 54 It is remarkable that Ephorus, the next writer from whom we have any details concerning the land of the Scythians, describes in like manner a river Panticapes, *E* of the Borysthenes, and forming the boundary between the Georgi, or agricultural Scythians and the nomad tribes beyond (Ephorus, Fr 78, ed C Muller, Scymn Ch vv 843–852) [5] iv 55 [6] See Note E, p 212

§ 14. It is almost equally difficult to identify the rivers alluded to in another passage, where he tells us that there were four great rivers, which had their sources in the land of the Thyssagetæ, beyond the desert that bounded the Budini on the north, and after flowing through the territory of the Mæetæ, fell into the Palus Mæotis.[7] These he enumerates in the following order: the Lycus, the Oarus, the Tanais, and the Syrgis. Of these the Tanais is of course well known, and the Syrgis is probably the same that he elsewhere calls the Hyrgis, though he there describes it as a tributary of the Tanais, not as falling into the Palus Mæotis. The Oarus has been supposed by some modern writers to be the Volga, though that river in fact flows into the Caspian Sea, but there is really no clue to its identification.[8] Of the Lycus nothing whatever is known.

Even of the Tanais itself it may be observed, that though it was certainly identical with the Don, it may be questioned whether the Greeks were sufficiently acquainted with the upper part of its course to distinguish the main stream from its tributary the Donetz, which is itself a large river, and has the more direct course from north to south, while the Don itself makes so great a bend to the east, that it might readily be mistaken for a different river.[9]

§ 15. With regard indeed to all these streams it must be borne in mind that the geographical statements of Herodotus as to their sources, their course and their outflow, could be derived only from the reports of travellers, who had crossed them in their commercial journeys with caravans into the interior. The Greeks certainly had navigated the Borysthenes, the Hypanis and the Danube for a considerable distance from their mouths: but it is uncertain whether they had done so in the case of the Tanais, at least as early as the time of Herodotus,[1] and the

---

[7] iv. 123.
[8] See Note F, p 213
[9] Rennell's *Geography of Herodotus*, p. 57

[1] The Greek colony of Tanais, at the mouth of the river of that name, was certainly not founded till long after the time of Herodotus.

traffic from the Borysthenes eastward was in all probability carried on almost wholly (as it has been in modern times) by caravans of waggons across the steppes. A traveller accompanying such a caravan would readily observe and remember the number of considerable streams that he crossed, and might report correctly their general direction, and their names, at least those by which they were known at the point where he crossed them; for it must be remembered that it is not uncommon for a river to bear different appellations in different parts of its course—but he would have to rely upon vague hearsay as to the points from which they came or to which they ultimately tended. Purely geographical questions of this sort have little interest for a semi-barbarous people, or even for a half-educated traveller, and the statement that all the four rivers last referred to ran into the Palus Mæotis may very probably have been a mere conjecture hastily adopted by those who, like Herodotus himself, believed that sea to be nearly as large as the Euxine.

§ 16. Far more interesting and valuable than these professed geographical data, are the notices that Herodotus has preserved to us of the various tribes and nations that inhabited the wide tracts on the north of the Euxine and in the adjoining districts of Asia. This was precisely the kind of information that he was likely to obtain most correctly from the class of travellers to whom alone he could have recourse. Traders, travelling solely for commercial purposes, would be likely to trouble themselves little about purely geographical questions, but their attention would necessarily be directed to the manners and customs of the tribes that they visited, as well as to the natural productions of their countries, and the uses to which they were applied. Nor could they fail to notice the diversity or identity of race among neighbouring populations, as attested by the use of different languages, requiring in consequence a succession of different interpreters.

In one respect Herodotus is favourably distinguished from almost all his successors. With many ancient geographers the term Scythians was applied in as wide and vague a sense as that of Tartars has been in modern times. Just as under the latter appellation have been included tribes of Mongolian, of Turkish, and even of Finnish extraction, so did the later writers on ancient geography frequently extend the name of Scythians to all the nomad nations that inhabited the northern regions of Europe and Asia. Herodotus, on the contrary, uses the term in a strictly ethnographical sense.[2] With him the Scythians are a distinct people, differing from those that adjoined them on the east, north, and west,[3] and Scythia is a definite area, of the extent and configuration of which he seems to have formed to himself a distinct idea, though it is very difficult for us to represent to ourselves his conception of it.

§ 17. One point, however, is certain. He tells us distinctly that Scythia was bounded on two sides, the south and east, by the sea.[4] Hence it is clear that he regarded the Palus Mæotis —as was done by all subsequent geographers, including even Ptolemy—as extending *from south to north*, and thus forming the eastern boundary of Scythia. The Tanais, which prolonged the frontier between Europe and Asia and separated the Scythians from the Sarmatians, was also supposed to flow from north to south. These two sides he considered to be about equal, and supposed Scythia on the whole to be (of course speaking approximately) of a square form, extending inland about the same distance as the length of its sea-front, which he reckoned at twenty days' journey, or about 400 G.

---

[2] This remark, however, must be confined to the portion of his work (the fourth book) in which he is treating specially of the Scythians In another passage (vii. 64) he applies the name of Scythians to the Sacæ or Asiatic Scythians, in the same manner as is usual with later geographers

[3] He tells us that they called themselves Scoloti (Σκόλοτοι), and that it was the Greeks who gave them the name of Scythians (iv 6) No trace is found elsewhere of this native appellation, nor does it tend to throw any light upon the ethnic affinities or descent of the people designated by Herodotus under the name of the Scythians Few questions in ethnology have been more disputed than this. See Note H, p 215

[4] ἔστι γὰρ τῆς Σκυθικῆς τὰ δύο μέρεα τῶν οὔρων ἐς θάλασσαν φέροντα, τήν τε πρὸς μεσαμβρίην καὶ τὴν πρὸς ἠῶ (iv. 99)

miles.[5] It is evident that this idea of the conformation of the country is so widely different from its real position and figure, that it would be a mere waste of time to attempt to discuss it in minute detail, or attempt to reconcile it with the natural boundaries The important result is, that he considered the country inhabited by the Scythians (properly so called) to extend only about 400 G. miles inland, whether measured from the Euxine or the Palus Mæotis.[6] They therefore may be considered as occupying the whole of Southern Russia, including the Ukraine, Podolia, and the country of the Don Cossacks, together with Bessarabia and Moldavia to the banks of the Danube. But their limits towards the interior cannot be defined with any approach to accuracy.[7]

§ 18. The Scythian people, as conceived by the historian, was divided into several tribes, characterized by some difference in their modes of life and habits, as the Georgi or agricultural Scythians, the Royal, and the Nomad Scythians: to each of which he assigns a definite geographical position. But unfortunately he has described these positions and their respective limits, with reference to the rivers between the Borysthenes and the Tanais, in a manner which involves them in the same hopeless confusion that attends the determination

---

[5] ἔστι ὦν τῆς Σκυθικῆς ὡς ἐούσης τετραγώνου, τῶν δύο μερέων κατηκόντων ἐς θάλασσαν, πάντῃ ἴσον τό τε ἐς τὴν μεσόγαιαν φέρον καὶ τὸ παρὰ τὴν θάλασσαν (iv 101)
It seems difficult to understand how, in the face of these two passages, Mr Rawlinson can say "The truth seems to be that Herodotus regarded Scythia as having only one of its sides washed by the sea" (*Herodotus*, vol. iii p. 209), when he distinctly states, twice over, that it was bounded by the sea on two sides His whole conception of the geographical views entertained by Herodotus on the subject appears to me fundamentally erroneous · to which his mistranslation of the statement concerning the mouth of the Danube materially contributes

[6] He reckons (iv. 101) from the Ister to the Borysthenes ten days' journey, and ten more from the Borysthenes to the Palus Mæotis, calculating, as he himself tells us, 200 stadia to the day's journey This would give for the southern, or sea, front, 20 days' journey, equal to 4000 stadia (400 G miles) and he adds that the distance from the sea to the Melanchlæni, who adjoined the Scythians on the north, was also 20 days' journey Thus the extent of the boundary lines drawn towards the interior (τὰ ὄρθια τὰ ἐς τὴν μεσόγαιαν φέροντα) was the same as that of the boundaries on the other side (τὰ ἐπικάρσια), i e. the two sides washed by the Euxine and the Palus Mæotis.

[7] See Note G, p. 214.

of those rivers. All that can be affirmed with certainty is that he placed in the western part of Scythia a tribe whom he characterizes as the Ploughmen (Aroteres) because they cultivated the land in order to raise corn *for export*, without using it for their own subsistence: while the Georgi (or Agriculturists), east of the Borysthenes, subsisted on the produce of their own tillage, like all other nations. Beyond them towards the east were the Nomad Scythians, inhabiting an open steppe country; and again beyond them, extending to the Palus Mæotis and the Tanais, was the tribe of the Royal Scythians, who looked upon all the others as their slaves or vassals. The whole tract occupied by these successive tribes was an open treeless plain, with the exception of a district (apparently of small extent) near the mouth of the Borysthenes, which was called in consequence Hylæa, or "the Forest country"[8]

§ 19. Beyond the limits thus assigned by Herodotus to the Scythians that people, as he tells us, was encircled by a series of different nations, extending from west to east, in the following order: the Agathyrsi, the Neuri, the Androphagi, the Melanchlæni, the Geloni, the Budini and the Sauromatæ. All these tribes had their own separate rulers and were in the opinion of the historian distinct from the Scythians, though in some instances resembling them in their manners, and occasionally presenting a similarity of language. The Tauri also, who inhabited the peninsula that derived its name from them, were regarded by him as a distinct people from the Scythians.[9]

The first of these surrounding tribes was the Agathyrsi: a people who are distinguished by Herodotus as the most refined

---

[8] The limits and position of this tract cannot be determined, for the reason already stated, that they are inseparably connected with the enigmatical rivers Panticapes and Hypacyras But it appears to have been situated to the east of the Borysthenes and adjoining the sea No extensive forest tract exists in this part of Russia at the present day but the tradition still remained in the last century of some portions having been formerly covered with forests. (See Rennell's *Geography of Herodotus*, p 63, 4to ed) Portions of the valley of the Borysthenes, where the river spreads into a variety of channels, are indeed, even at present, overgrown with trees, and the same thing is the case with the other rivers, though in a less degree

[9] iv. 99.

among them, and who were remarkable also for the abundance of their gold ornaments. They may be considered on plausible, though hardly conclusive grounds, as occupying the region now called Transylvania, the gold mines of which may probably have been worked from the earliest ages.[1] Next to them came the Neuri, who resembled the Scythians in manners: but were said to have the peculiar power of transforming themselves for a few days every year into wolves.[2] This story, of which Herodotus frankly expresses his disbelief, is curious as the earliest allusion to the superstition of the "were-wolf," so generally prevalent among the northern nations of Europe. Another circumstance mentioned by Herodotus that the Neuri, about a generation before the expedition of Darius, had been compelled to quit their homes for a time, on account of the multitude of serpents, has at first sight a very fabulous air; but is in fact by no means improbable. A modern traveller,[3] who visited the German colonies in the south of Russia, found them still full of recollections of the difficulties with which they had to cope, when they first settled there about 30 years before, from the multitude of serpents with which the whole country swarmed; and which only gradually gave way before the increase of tillage and population. The Neuri are supposed by Schafarik, but on very slender grounds, to have been a Slavonian tribe: they apparently occupied the country near the sources of the Dniester, the modern Volhynia.

§ 20. Beyond the Neuri were the Androphagi, who, as their name imports, were cannibals, in which respect they stood alone among all the nations in this part of the world. Herodotus tells us that their manners were in all respects the most rude and savage with which he was acquainted: and that they spoke

---

[1] In other respects (says *Herodotus*, iv 104) their customs are like those of the Thracians. It is not improbable that they were in fact a race of Thracian origin [2] iv 105.
[3] Kohl, *Reisen in Sud-Russland*, vol ii pp. 153-156. The serpents in question, a species of viper (*Coluber trabalis*), are said to grow sometimes to a very large size But some of the stories related to Kohl bear the stamp of exaggeration, and remind one of similar legends in the early ages of Greece

a peculiar language, distinct from the Scythian.[4] All these particulars tend to support the conjecture of Neumann that they were a Finnish race: several of the tribes of that family being known to have retained the habit of cannibalism even in the middle ages.[5] They were separated from the country of the Scythians by a desert tract of considerable extent, and seem to have been situated nearly due north of the Greek settlements on the Borysthenes: but how far inland we have no means of determining.

Next to them—proceeding still from west to east—came the Melanchlæni, or "Black-cloaks," of whom we learn nothing, except that they were distinguished from the Scythians, whom they resembled in their other customs, by the constant use of the black dress, from which they derived their name.[6] But though their manners were like those of the Scythians, Herodotus expressly tells us that they were a distinct and non-Scythian race.

§ 21. The next nation to the Melanchlæni were the Budini, a people concerning whom we have more interesting information. They were (Herodotus tells us) a large and powerful nation, and were all of them distinguished by light blue eyes and red hair.[7] They were nomads like their neighbours on both sides, but their country was no longer the mere open

---

[4] Herodot iv 106.
[5] Neumann, *Die Hellenen im Skythenlande*, p. 212.
[6] iv 107. The Melanchlæni were already mentioned by Hecatæus They are noticed at a later period by Dion Chrysostomus (*Orat* xxxvi p 78) who says that the Olbiopolites had derived from them the fashion of wearing short black cloaks, which prevailed among them in his day
[7] There appears to me no doubt that this is the sense of the words of Herodotus. Βουδῖνοι δὲ ἔθνος ἐὸν μέγα καὶ πολλὸν γλαυκόν τε πᾶν ἰσχυρῶς ἐστι καὶ πυρρόν (iv. 108) The combination of πυρρός in the sense of "red-haired" with γλαυκός or γλαυκόμματος is one of

frequent occurrence (see Plut *Cat Maj* 1), and exactly corresponds to the "cœrulei oculi, rutilæ comæ" of Tacitus in speaking of the Germans (*Germania*) But it by no means follows that we are therefore to suppose the Budini to be of Germanic race, as has been suggested by Mannert, and partially adopted by Rawlinson The Russians are spoken of by an Arabic author as having 'red hair and blue eyes,' and the Thracians are also described as having the same characteristic. According to Humboldt (*Asie Centrale*, vol 1 p. 393), tribes with red beards and blue eyes are mentioned in the Chinese annals as living in the interior of Central Asia or Mongolia.

steppe or plain: it contained extensive forests, as well as lakes and marshes which abounded with beavers and otters. In the midst of these dwelt a tribe called the Geloni, who were often confounded with them, so that the name of Geloni was frequently applied by the Greeks to the whole nation of the Budini[8]—but incorrectly, as Herodotus assures us. According to him, the Geloni differed from the Budini in personal characters and in language, as well as in the habits of life. They were not nomads, but settled agriculturists, having gardens or orchards, and raising corn for their own consumption: they even possessed a city of large extent, surrounded by walls, built of timber, and containing houses and temples, also of wood. These temples, according to the informants of Herodotus, were dedicated to Greek divinities and adorned with altars and statues in the Greek fashion. In fact, he tells us, the Geloni were originally Greeks, who had quitted the trading-places on the coast and settled among the Budini; and their language was a mixture of Greek and Scythian.[9]

It is very difficult to give credence to this last statement. It would be an unprecedented thing for Greek settlers to have established themselves at such a distance in the interior, without keeping up any communication or intercourse with their countrymen on the Euxine; and the explanation suggested by Heeren that it was merely a Greek factory established thus far inland, for the purposes of trade, is wholly at variance with Herodotus, who evidently meant to describe these Geloni as a barbarian tribe, though more cultivated and civilized than their neighbours; and retaining traces of their Greek origin in their religion and language. Very little value can be attached to the former ground of identification; and if the Geloni were a Slavonian tribe (as has been suggested with some plausibility by Schafarik)[1] there would really be sufficient

---

[8] Herodot. iv. 109. Both names are found in the later geographers, but with no additional particulars, and apparently only derived from Herodotus.

[9] iv. 108.
[1] Schafarik, *Slavische Alterthumer*, vol. i. pp. 184-190.

resemblance between the deities of the two systems to lead readily to the belief. The wooden city, with its walls of wood, resembles very much the accounts we find of the old Slavonian cities: that of Saratov, on the Volga, is said to have retained its ancient wooden walls and towers down to a late period.[2] In the neighbourhood of that city, within the province to which it gives name, and between the Don and the Volga we may fix with reasonable assurance the position of the Geloni, and the surrounding nomad tribes of the Budini. This is an important point for the determination of the geographical position of other tribes, to be hereafter mentioned.

§ 22. East of the Tanais, but south of the Budini, dwelt the Sauromatæ, a nomad race inhabiting a region of open steppes, wholly destitute of trees, like the greater part of Scythia proper.[3] They occupied a tract fifteen days' journey in length, from the mouth of the Tanais towards the north. Most modern writers are agreed in identifying the Sauromatæ of Herodotus with the Sarmatæ or Sarmatians of later authors, who at a subsequent period crossed the Tanais, drove out the Scythians from the steppes north of the Euxine, and ultimately extended themselves into the plains of Hungary and Poland, where, under the name of Slavs, they still form the bulk of the population. The legend related by Herodotus which ascribes their origin to a casual mixture of certain Scythians with a body of Amazons,[4] is doubtless a mere myth, invented to account for the masculine and warlike habits of the women among them: and no dependence can be placed upon it, as evidence of any real connection of race between the Scythians and Sarmatians. But the case is otherwise with his statement of the resemblance between the two languages:[5] this is a point upon which the Greek traders were likely to be able to judge, and is certainly a circumstance of importance in attempting to determine the ethnographical character of the Scythians themselves.[6]

---

[2] Gobel, *Reise im Sud-Russland*, cited by Neumann, p 91. See also Schafarik, *l c* p 191.

[3] Herodot iv 21.
[4] iv 110–116
[5] Ib 117
[6] See Note H, p 215

Such was, according to Herodotus, the series of nations or tribes by which the Scythians were immediately surrounded. In most directions these tribes formed the limit of his knowledge and of the supposed habitable world. We hear nothing of any people beyond the Agathyrsi to the west: and he expressly tells us that the country to the north of the Neuri was, so far as he could learn, uninhabited. The Androphagi were themselves separated from the northern limit of Scythia by a desert tract of considerable extent; and beyond them again was an absolute desert, where no people were known to dwell. North of the Melanchlæni again nothing was known but uninhabited deserts. It is evident therefore that in these directions neither the Greek traders nor their Scythian informants had penetrated any farther.[7]

§ 23. But it was otherwise towards the north-east. Beyond the Budini, who, as we have seen, were situated in the neighbourhood of Saratov, between the Don and the Volga, there was also a desert tract, but only of seven days' journey in extent; and beyond this, in a somewhat easterly direction, dwelt the Thyssagetæ, a numerous and peculiar people.[8] They, as well as the Iurcæ,[9] who were contiguous to them in the same

---

[7] iv 17, 18, 20

[8] ἔθνος πολλὸν καὶ ἴδιον Herodot iv 22 He doubtless means by this expression to intimate his own conviction that the Thyssagetæ were a distinct people from their neighbours, Scythians and others But of course this does not exclude the probability of ethnographical relations between them The name has been regarded, naturally enough, as indicating a connection with the Massagetæ, who were not far distant towards the south-east, and both have been supposed to be related to the Getæ of the Gieeks, the supposed ancestors of the Goths (Donaldson, *Varronianus*, p 41, 2nd edit) Professor Rawlinson even goes so far as to assume boldly that the Thyssagetæ were the "lessei Goths" as distinguished from the Massagetæ or "greater Goths" (vol iii. p. 19, note). But there is no etymological support for this and all such inferences from mere names, the original forms of which we have no means of discovering, appear to me in the highest degree hazardous and uncertain See some judicious remarks of Niebuhr (*Researches*, p 82) Humboldt, however (*Kosmos*, vol ii p 176), adopts the Gothic hypothesis with regard to the Massagetæ without hesitation.

[9] The name of these Iurcæ has been transformed by Pliny (vi 7, § 19) and Mela (i c 19, § 116), both of whom are obviously copying Herodotus, into Turcæ, and they have in consequence frequently been supposed to be identical with the Turks But there is no reason to suppose the name of Turks to be anything like so ancient as this; and the coincidence is probably mere accident, having apparently originated

regions, were hunters, and subsisted by the chase: their whole country being overspread with forests. Beyond them again still bearing towards the east, dwelt a Scythian tribe, who were believed to have formerly emigrated from the land of the Royal Scythians, on the Euxine, and established themselves in these remote regions. Thus far, we are told, the country was level and fertile: but after this it became stony and rugged. After traversing a considerable extent of this rugged tract there occurred a people called the Argippæi, dwelling at the foot of a range of lofty mountains, who resembled the Scythians in dress, but spoke a peculiar language. They had flat noses and projecting chins, or jaw-bones, and were always bald from their birth upwards.[1] Their principal subsistence was derived from a kind of fruit, which they dried in solid masses, after straining off the juice, which they drank mixed with milk. This is precisely the same process used by the Calmucks of the present day in preparing the fruit of the bird-cherry (Prunus Padus), which with them also forms an important article of diet. The description of the physical characters of the Argippæi also resembles that of the Kalmucks, and other Mongolian tribes, as these would present themselves to an unscientific observer. The baldness indeed is not really common to the whole race, but peculiar to the sacerdotal caste: and must have been erroneously transferred to the whole people. It was doubtless the same confusion that gave rise to the notion preserved by Herodotus that the Argippæi were a sacred race, who never made use of arms and had no occasion for them, as no one ever attacked them: but the neighbouring tribes referred their disputes to them as arbiters.[2]

The mountains, at the foot of which the Argippæans were settled, can hardly be any other than the Ural:[3] and if we

---

only in a false reading of Herodotus On the other hand, it is certainly tempting to connect the name of the Iurcæ with that of the Yuruks, a wandering race of herdsmen akin to the Turcomans, who roam over the plains of Asia Minor But the similarity of name may well be in this case also merely casual
[1] iv 23 [2] Ibid.
[3] They are indeed supposed by Heeren (*Asiatic Nations*, vol. ii p 272) to

place them on the western or south-western slopes of that chain, there will remain abundance of room for the different tribes enumerated by Herodotus between them and the Budini. It is indeed impossible to assign to each of these tribes its precise geographical limits or position, but we trace distinctly, as we follow the course indicated by Herodotus, the transition from the open steppes to the forest-covered regions,—which were certainly far more extensive in ancient times than they are at the present day,[4]—and from thence to the rugged hilly tract immediately adjoining the mountains.

§ 24. The Argippæans were the last nation towards the north, with which the Greek settlers on the Euxine or their Scythian neighbours, had any direct communication. They were cut off on the north by an impassable barrier of lofty mountains; beyond which no one had ever penetrated : but the Argippæans reported them to be inhabited by men with feet like goats;— and beyond these again were a people who slept for six months in the year.[5] In these traditions—naturally treated by Herodotus himself as mere fables—it is not difficult to discern a germ of truth. The one is no more than a natural hyperbole to express the habits of an active race of mountaineers; the other is obviously founded on the well-known facts of the prolonged winter night of the Arctic Regions :[6] though, like most similar traditions, it was exaggerated far beyond the truth.

---

be the Altai, and the same view is adopted by Humboldt (*Asie Centrale*, vol 1 pp 389-407) But, notwithstanding these high authorities, it appears to me far more probable that the Ural Mountains are those really meant The course followed by Herodotus is clearly towards the N E (according to his own conception it was nearly N but verging somewhat towards the E), and this direction must inevitably lead to the chain of the Ural These mountains could not have been overlooked or ignored by the informants of Herodotus, and would constitute a natural barrier to all further communication in this direction It is true that the chain of the Ural in reality extends from S to N and not from W to E as Herodotus apparently conceived the mountains in question to do, but there are few points upon which the information of ancient writers was so often inaccurate or erroneous, as this of the direction of mountain ranges

[4] See this point fully examined and discussed by Neumann, pp 85-98.

[5] iv 25

[6] It is, however, justly observed by a recent traveller (cited by Mr Rawlinson) that the statement as reported to Herodotus was not that there was *a night* of six months' duration, which of course is only true at the pole itself,

But while the country north of the Argippæans was thus unknown to the Greeks, it was otherwise with the tract that lay to the east of them. Here dwelt the Issedones, a people who are represented as just and humane in other respects, but having the custom of eating the bodies of their deceased fathers, whose skulls they afterwards gilt and preserved as objects of reverence.[7] The name of the Issedones was certainly familiar to the Greeks long before the time of Herodotus. It was mentioned by Hecatæus of Miletus, as well as by Aristeas, who professed to have visited them himself.[8] Whether or not this was true, it may be taken as showing with certainty that they were already known to the Greeks on the Euxine in his time. They are placed by Herodotus, as we have just seen, east of the Argippæi: in another passage he tells us that they were situated "opposite to" the Massagetæ, whom he regarded as occupying an extensive tract to the east of the Caspian Sea.[9] The Issedones would in this case be due north of them,—a meaning which would suit very well with the passage in question—and may be placed in the broad steppes to the south-east of the Ural Mountains—now inhabited by the hordes of the Kirghiz.

§ 25. The regions north of the Issedones were equally unknown with those to the north of the Argippæans. But it was here that *they* placed the fabulous Arimaspians, and the equally fabulous Griffins. Herodotus is distinct in his assertion that this story was told by the Issedones, from whom the Scythians

---

but that the inhabitants slept for that period, which may be understood as arising from their keeping closely within doors through the long and dreary winter nights

A similar tradition as to the "land of darkness" in the far north was current among Oriental nations (see a note by Sir H Rawlinson on Herodotus, iv 25), and is mentioned by Ibn Batuta, who was informed that it was distant forty days' journey from the city of Bulgar, which he visited (*Travels of Ibn Batuta*, translated by Lee, p 78)

How easily such a statement might arise from exaggeration of a true fact is shown by Pliny in his account of Thule, where, after stating that there was no night there at the summer solstice, and no day at the winter solstice, he adds, "Hoc quidam senis mensibus continuis fieri arbitrantur" (iv c 16, § 104)

[7] iv 26
[8] iv 13 See above, Chap IV
[9] i 201 The conclusions to be drawn from this passage will be discussed in the next chapter

learnt it, and that it passed from them to the Greeks.[1] If any reliance can be placed on this statement, it would appear probable that the fable was connected with the fact of the abundance of gold on the flanks of the Ural and Altai mountains, the streams of which may have been worked by people in a very primitive state of civilization.[2] Herodotus himself, while rejecting as altogether fabulous the story of the griffins and the one-eyed Arimaspians, admits as a certain fact that by far the greatest quantity of gold came from the north of Europe (under which appellation he includes the tracts in question), "though how produced (he adds) I know not."[3] The abundance of gold among the Scythians on the Euxine, and its extensive use by them, is sufficiently attested by the contents of their tombs, which have been opened in modern times. Whatever therefore may have been the origin of the fable, the fact that large quantities of gold were brought from the interior of Northern Asia to the coasts of the Euxine is one that admits of no doubt.

To this fact we are probably indebted for the great extension of the geographical knowledge of the Greeks in this direction. The extent and accuracy of the information collected by Herodotus concerning the regions which lay to the north-east of Scythia, as compared with those which bounded it on the north-west and north, is very remarkable, and points, as was long ago remarked by Heeren,[4] to the existence of a well-established caravan route in that direction. But the commodities that can be carried long distances by caravans must necessarily be light, and readily portable. Gold was exactly a production of this kind, adapted for ready transport; and the gold-bearing regions of Northern Asia would naturally exercise a strong power of attraction upon the Greek settlers on the Euxine, as well as on the more civilized Scythian

---

[1] iv 27 · He adds that the *name* of Arimaspians was Scythian for that in the Scythian language "arima" meant *one*, and "spou," an eye

[2] See the remarks of Humboldt on this subject (*Asie Centrale*, vol 1. pp 330–408) [3] iii 116
[4] *Asiatic Nations*, vol ii p 285

tribes, who adjoined that sea. The only other production of these northern regions that was likely to be sought after by visitors from the south was their furs, which would be an indispensable article to the Greek colonists in Scythia, however little they were used to require them at home.

§ 26. It is a remarkable instance how little such sources of information as were open to Herodotus could be relied on for correct geographical knowledge, that, while he obtained these interesting and valuable particulars concerning the various nations and tribes that were successively met with in proceeding towards the north-east, no mention is found of the great river Volga, which must have been necessarily crossed on the way, and which was in fact a larger stream than either the Tanais or the Borysthenes. The supposition that the Oarus, mentioned by him in another passage among the rivers flowing from the land of the Thyssagetæ, was really the Volga, would not mend the matter, as there is no indication that he regarded that river as of any greater importance than the other streams with which he associated it.[5]

§ 27. On the other hand, the knowledge which Herodotus had acquired of these countries would naturally lead him to the inference, even if he possessed no specific information on the subject, that the Caspian Sea must be an inland sea, surrounded on all sides by land. This, indeed, results of necessity from the data with which he himself furnishes us. For he distinctly places the Massagetæ on the eastern side of the Caspian:[6] these adjoined the Issedones on the north, and the Issedones again were connected through the Argippæi and an unbroken chain of nations towards the west, with the Budini and the Scythians. But apart from this train of reasoning, it is probable that Herodotus had derived from some other

---

[5] It seems not improbable that the Volga was in fact confounded with the Tanais the two streams approach near one another in the part of their course where they would naturally be crossed by a traveller proceeding through the land of the Budini, and might be supposed by him to be only two branches of one great stream But in any case the omission is a remarkable one.

[6] i 201

source more definite information concerning the Caspian Sea, as he not only states distinctly,[7] as a fact, that it is a separate sea, not communicating with any other, but he gives an estimate of its length and breadth, which implies that it was habitually navigated.[8] In this respect it is remarkable that Herodotus was in advance of almost all his successors, who, from Eratosthenes to Pliny, agreed in describing the Caspian as an inlet from the outer Ocean. It is not till the time of Ptolemy that we find the correct view again prevailing.

SECT. 3.—*Expedition of Darius into Scythia.*

§ 1. The expedition of Darius against the Scythians is undoubtedly entitled to be regarded as an historical fact, however difficult it may be to admit many of its details as historically accurate. But we have here only to consider it from a geographical point of view; and in this respect we shall find that the narrative of it, as related by Herodotus, accords extremely well with the geographical account of Scythia and the adjoining lands given by the same author. So close, indeed, is the coincidence that, when we bear in mind how much vagueness and uncertainty still hung about the regions in question, it is impossible to avoid the inference that the two have been adapted to each other. Either the narrative of the campaign has been fitted into the geographical views obtained from other sources, or those views have been themselves derived from the information obtained during the expedition. The latter alternative is that adopted by Major Rennell, who supposes that Hero-

---

[7] 1 203

[8] Herodotus gives the length of the Caspian as fifteen days' voyage *for a rowing vessel* (εἰρεσίῃ χρεωμένῳ, Ib.), and the greatest breadth as eight days These proportions are very nearly correct, and I agree with Mr Rawlinson that there is no reason to suppose (as has been suggested by some critics, including Niebuhr) that he misconceived the position of the Caspian, and reckoned its greatest length from E to W instead of from N. to S This was certainly done by later geographers, but from whatever source Herodotus derived his information concerning this sea he certainly appears to have had a more accurate idea of its extent and configuration than any of his successors before Ptolemy

dotus " drew his materials for the inland part of the geography [of Scythia], scanty as they may be, from the history of this expedition." [9] But the historical details of the narrative are such as in themselves to present insurmountable difficulties to our receiving it as an accurate account of the operations of the Persian army; and the particulars previously given by Herodotus of the different nations that were successively visited by the invader, resemble much more the impressions that might have been gathered from the Scythians themselves, than such as would be derived from a rapid hostile incursion, traversing the lands in a hasty manner, and almost without seeing an enemy.

§ 2. The substance of the narrative of Herodotus is briefly this.[1] Darius having determined to take vengeance upon the Scythians for their inroad into Media (about 130 years before), assembled a great army, amounting to 700,000 men, with which he crossed the Bosphorus by a bridge of boats, and advanced through the land of the Thracians and the Getæ to the Danube, where another bridge of boats had been already prepared by the Ionian and other Asiatic Greeks, who furnished the greatest part of his fleet. From thence he plunged at once into the wilds of Scythia, leaving the Ionians to guard the bridge, and thus, in case of necessity, secure his retreat. But they were only ordered to remain at this post for sixty days. According to a preconcerted scheme, the Scythians offered no opposition to the advance of the Persians, but continually retreated before them, laying waste the country as they went, and directing their line of march eastward towards the Tanais. This course they continued till they came to that river, which they crossed, and the Persians after them, still continuing the pursuit. In this manner both armies traversed the land of the Sauromatæ, and entered that of the Budini. Here the Persians found the wooden fortress, already mentioned, which they burnt to the ground, and continued to

---

[9] Rennell's *Geography of Herodotus*, p 107, 4to ed.   [1] Herodot iv. 120-142

pursue the Scythians through the land of the Budini to the confines of the desert beyond.. Here Darius at length made a halt, on the river Oarus, where he erected eight large forts, at an interval of about 60 stadia apart, the remains of which were said to be still visible in the days of Herodotus.[2] From hence he turned westward, and having fallen in with other bodies of the Scythians, which retreated before him in like manner, was thus led on, first into the land of the Melanchlæni, afterwards into that of the Androphagi, and then of the Neuri. The Scythians intentionally led the Persians by this great circuit through the territories of those different nations, because they had previously refused to make common cause with the Scythians and unite in repelling the Persian arms. When they now found themselves threatened by this double invasion, they broke up in terror and confusion, and fled into the deserts towards the north. The Agathyrsi alone took up arms in their own defence, and, posting themselves on their frontier, forbade the entrance of the Scythians, who thereupon turned aside and re-entered their own land. Various attempts at negotiation now took place, but without effect; and at length Darius, finding his troops continually harassed by the Scythians, without any opportunity of striking a decisive blow, determined to retreat to the Danube, which he re-crossed in safety. The Scythians had indeed made two attempts to persuade the Ionians to destroy the bridge; and the term of sixty days had already expired, but the Ionian leaders judged it for their own advantage to secure the retreat of Darius, and consequently maintained the bridge in such a state that it was restored without difficulty.

§ 3. It is scarcely necessary to point out the difficulties and objections that present themselves at every step, if we attempt to consider this relation as an authentic historical narrative,

---

[2] iv 124 τῶν ἔτι καὶ ἐς ἐμὲ τὰ ἐρείπια σῶα ἦν Of course this was mere hearsay, though the expression would certainly lead one to suppose that Herodotus had himself seen them. If any remains of earthworks really existed on the banks of the Oarus, these would be naturally connected by the native tradition with the name of Darius.

like that of the campaigns of Alexander the Great, or the expedition of the younger Cyrus. As Mr. Grote remarks, Herodotus conducts the immense host of Darius from the Danube to the Tanais "as it were through fairy land," heedless of the distance, of the great intervening rivers (of which he himself elsewhere speaks as one of the great marvels of Scythia), and of the difficulty of obtaining supplies for a vast army, in a country almost devoid of natural resources, and in which whatever was to be found had been studiously destroyed.[3] The distance from the Danube to the Tanais was, according to Herodotus's own conception, forty days' journey for an ordinary traveller;[4] it could hardly, therefore, have been less than sixty days' march for an army; and yet Darius is represented as traversing the whole of this distance, apparently without a halt, and without a mention of any obstacle; then proceeding through the country of the Sauromatæ and the Budini to the river Oarus; halting there long enough to erect important works of fortification (the object of which is utterly unintelligible), and then making a vast circuit through the nations to the north of the Scythians, till he returned once more into their country, apparently at no great distance from the point at which he started. It was not till *after* the Scythians had led him this wild-goose chase through the desert regions of the north, that we are told they despatched messengers to the Danube to try the fidelity of the Ionians, but failed in the first instance *because the appointed sixty days had not yet elapsed!* But such a march as he is represented as having made could hardly have been accomplished, even supposing it feasible at all, in less than an hundred and fifty days, or five months.[5]

---

[3] Grote's *History of Greece*, vol. IV. p. 355

[4] He computes the sea front of Scythia from the Danube to the Mæotis at 20 days' journey (iv. 101), and the side perpendicular to it, parallel with the Mæotis (according to his conception) was of equal length Of course if Darius marched direct to the Tanais he would take the diagonal of the square, and thus cut off a portion of the supposed distance · but this it was impossible for him to do in reality.

[5] This is Major Rennell's calculation (vol 1 p 150), who therefore assumes that there must have been some error, when we are told that the 60 days had not elapsed But the question of

Now the duration of the expedition is precisely the point upon which Herodotus was most likely to be well informed, for this was the circumstance that must necessarily impress itself the most strongly upon the minds of the Ionians and other Greeks who kept watch at the bridge. His account of their proceedings has every appearance of being derived from good information; while that of the operations of the Persian army could only be derived either from the vague reports of those who returned after wandering in the unknown regions of Scythia, or (more probably) from the exaggerated accounts current among the Scythians themselves, and picked up from them by the Greek colonists on the Euxine. We may safely pronounce that narrative, as transmitted to us by Herodotus, to be impossible and unintelligible;[6] but this does not affect the geographical account of the regions in question, which is both intelligible, and consistent with the statements he has previously made concerning the order and relative positions of the different nations through whose territories Darius was supposed to have been led.

---

time is an essential element in the story, as told by Herodotus. Mr. Rawlinson indeed says (vol iii p. 118, note) that we do not know the *whole* time employed on the expedition But the narrative certainly excludes the supposition that any *long* interval elapsed between the first visit of the Scythians to the bridge (when the 60 days had not yet elapsed) and the second; and the whole of the great circuitous march, by which Darius returned into Scythia, is distinctly represented as having taken place before the *first* message was sent.

[6] See Note I, p 217

NOTE A, p. 161.

THE ACTÆ OF HERODOTUS.

We have unfortunately no English word which conveys the exact meaning of the Greek 'Ακτὴ, a clear comprehension of which is essential to the understanding of this passage, as well as of some others in the Greek geographers. It does not correspond either to a mere promontory (though used as such in poetical Greek), or to a peninsula strictly so called, but is something intermediate between the two. The term peninsula is indeed at the present day often vaguely applied to large tracts of land connected with the continent by a broad belt, not a mere isthmus. Thus we speak of the Spanish peninsula, the Scandinavian peninsula, &c.; and as thus employed, the word approaches closely to the meaning of the Greek 'Ακτὴ. But the latter term was applied also—and perhaps more properly—to a more advanced tract of land, projecting somewhat in the manner of a wedge from the mainland, and ending in a promontory. The two most characteristic instances of this meaning of the word are the ἀκτὴ of Attica—from which, according to some writers, that country derived its name—and the Argolic Actè, the tract of land projecting between the Saronic Gulf and the Gulf of Argos, and including the cities of Epidaurus, Trœzen, and Hermione.

On a large scale the country which we now term Asia Minor answers exactly to the first sense of the term; more especially as Herodotus supposed the neck connecting it with the rest of Asia to be much narrower than it really is. Hence there is no difficulty in understanding this, his first Actè. But it is more difficult to comprehend its application in the second instance. Herodotus, however, appears to have conceived Arabia, together with Syria and Assyria, as forming one great ἀκτὴ, of which, strange as it appears, he regarded Egypt and Libya (or the whole continent of Africa) as a mere appendage, attached to it by the Isthmus of Suez. This is much as if the whole of Greece (including Thessaly and Epirus) were considered as one great Actè, of which the Peloponnesus was only a subordinate part, attached to it by the Isthmus of

Corinth. But the disproportionate size of Africa, even according to the conception of Herodotus, renders such a view still more extraordinary.

NOTE B, p. 173.

THE CIMMERIANS.

It would be a very interesting ethnographical point to determine who these Cimmerians were, and it is obviously very tempting to identify them with the Cimbri and Kymry that appear at a later period in the west and north of Europe. But such inferences from mere resemblance of name are very apt to be misleading, and our materials are too scanty to enable us to attain to any satisfactory conclusion on this subject. While the general facts of the Cimmerian invasion of Asia, and their ultimate expulsion from their abodes on the north of the Euxine, may be regarded as well attested, it must be admitted that the details furnished by Herodotus appear in several respects to be untrustworthy. The main body of the Cimmerians, according to his account, fleeing from the Scythians, held their route along the *eastern* shore of the Euxine, between the Caucasus and the sea, a rugged and difficult tract, almost impassable for an army, and still more so for a migratory tribe like that of the Cimmerians. The pursuing Scythians, on the contrary (he tells us), missed their way, and kept the Caucasus on their right hand, so that they fell into Media, and thus became *by accident* the destroyers of the Median monarchy. Admitting the destruction of the Median monarchy by a Scythian invasion to be historically true, it seems impossible to believe the story thus told to connect it with the Cimmerian invasion of Lower Asia, though, as Mr. Grote observes (*History of Greece*, vol. iii. p. 332), it is not improbable that both movements were connected with some sudden development of the Scythian power or propulsion by other tribes behind them.

It is remarkable that the existence of such a simultaneous movement is affirmed in all the traditions connected with the Cimmerian invasion. Thus Aristeas of Proconnesus, in whose time (about B.C. 550) there were Cimmerians still remaining to the north of the Euxine, stated that the nations of the interior were all pressing upon one another, each urging the other onwards from north to south; the Issedones in the far north were being gradually driven out by the Arimaspians, and in consequence were in their turn pressing on the Scythians, and these again on the Cimmerians, who, being bounded by the sea on the south, could not transmit the pressure in their turn, and were compelled to leave the country (Herodot. iv. 13).

Herodotus himself, indeed, gives a different account of the origin of the movement. According to this, the first shock came, not from the north, but from the east, where the Massagetæ, an Asiatic nomad tribe, pressed so severely upon the Scythians,—who at that time dwelt wholly in Asia,—that the latter gave way before them, and, crossing the river Araxes, invaded the land of the Cimmerians, who felt themselves unable to resist so formidable a host, and abandoned their country without a contest (Id. iv. 11).

But whatever may have been the cause of the movement, the emigration of the Cimmerians appears to have been complete in the time of Herodotus, who no longer found any Cimmerians settled to the north of the Euxine, though, as he himself points out, there still remained manifest traces of their previous occupation of the country in the term "Cimmerian," attached by tradition to earthworks and other relics of the past, as well as in the names of localities, especially that of the Cimmerian Bosporus, as the strait between the Crimea and the mainland of Asia was universally called, to distinguish it from the Thracian strait of the same name (Id. iv. 12).

NOTE C, p. 177.

THE GREEK STADIUM.

As this is the first occasion on which I have had occasion to refer to the Greek mode of computation by stadia or stades, I may take this opportunity of stating that throughout the present work I shall uniformly assume that the Greeks employed but one measure under that designation, which was, as stated in the text, a hundred fathoms, or 600 Greek feet (Herodotus, ii. 149). This has been proved, in my opinion, beyond a doubt, by Col. Leake in his paper *On the Stade as a Linear Measure*, first published in 1839 in the Journal of the Geographical Society, vol. ix., and republished in his treatise *On some disputed Questions of Ancient Geography*, 8vo.

Lond. 1857.[7] But, in fact, the circumstance that neither Strabo nor any other ancient geographer adverts to the existence of any doubt on the subject, or to the use of any other than the ordinary Greek stadium, is conclusive in regard to the question. The incongruities and inaccuracies of different ancient writers in regard to distances have led many modern inquirers to the idea that they must have employed different scales of measurement, and therefore stadia of different lengths. Any one who has looked into the writings of D'Anville or Gosselin will be familiar with the confusion and difficulties arising from this source; and even Major Rennell fell into the same error, and thought it necessary to suppose the existence of an *itinerary* stade, distinct from the true one,[8] rather than admit the fact, confirmed by general experience both in ancient and modern times, that distances which are only estimated, and not measured, are almost always overrated. At the present day the controversy may be considered as settled. Dr. C. Muller, in his valuable edition of the Geographi Græci Minores, takes for granted that in all cases a stadium of 600 Greek feet is meant; and M. Vivien de Saint-Martin, in his most recent work (*Histoire de la Géographie et des Découvertes Géographiques*, 8vo, Paris, 1873), admits that the Olympic stadium of 600 feet was the only one in general use among the Greeks, and is therefore always to be understood when distances are given in stadia.

Another source of error was introduced at a later period by the conflicting results of the attempts of mathematical geographers to determine the circumference of the earth. Eratosthenes was thus led to the conclusion that a degree of the circumference was equal to 700 stades, while Posidonius, who was unfortunately followed by Ptolemy, calculated only 500 stades to the degree. But here, as we shall see more fully hereafter, it was the computation of the degree that was erroneous, not that there was any difference in the scale of measurement. A stade of 600 Greek feet was in reality very nearly the 600th part of a degree; ten stades are consequently just about equal to a nautical or geographical mile of 60 to a degree

---

[7] It had indeed been already clearly established by Ukert (in his *Geographie der Griechen und Romer*, vol 1 pt 11 pp 51–72), but his work was unknown to Leake A good summary of his arguments will be found in the article Stadium in Dr Smith's *Dictionary of Greek and Roman Antiquities*, p 893

[8] See his *Dissertation on the Itinerary Stade of the Greeks*, inserted in his *Geography of Herodotus*, Chap II

—a circumstance that materially facilitates the reduction of the measures given by ancient geographers into such as are familiar to the modern reader.

NOTE D, p. 183.

NAVIGATION OF THE BORYSTHENES.

This statement has given rise to much discussion. Several of the editors of Herodotus have suggested that the number should be *fourteen*, and this is strenuously maintained by Neumann (*Die Hellenen im Skythenlande*, p. 205). But it appears to me certain that Herodotus *wrote* forty, as, independently of the agreement of all existing MSS. of our author, the statement is repeated by Scymnus Chius (v. 816), as well as by Pomponius Mela, both of whom clearly derived it, directly or indirectly, from Herodotus. We are not entitled to alter the reading of an ancient author merely because it apparently involves an error in fact. Nor is there any reason to assume that fourteen days would be a more correct statement. Herodotus is clearly speaking of the voyage *up* the stream (μέχρι μέν νυν Γέρρου χώρου ἐς τὸν τεσσεράκοντα ἡμερέων πλόος ἐστί, γινώσκεται ῥέων ἀπὸ βορέω ἀνέμου, iv. 53), and the duration of this we have no means of measuring; but there is certainly no improbability in its taking *double* the time, allowing for the windings of the river, that would be occupied by a direct journey to the same point by land. There is therefore no real discrepancy, as has been assumed, between this statement and the assertion that the Scythian territory extended inland only twenty days' journey.

A more serious difficulty arises from the fact alluded to in the text, that the navigation of the Dnieper is obstructed, at a distance of about 260 miles from its mouth, by a succession of cataracts or rapids, "which limit the passage to the time of high water during the spring, and even then attended with some difficulty, and only of a fortnight or three weeks' duration" (Clarke's *Travels*, vol. ii., Appendix, p. 465, 8vo. ed.). As, however, the river is ascended by barges in the spring through its whole course, it is easy to suppose that the Scythians may have had *a knowledge* of it above the cataracts, whatever may have been the difficulty of its navigation.

It is curious—and inexplicable—that Strabo (vii. c. 3, § 17, p. 306) speaks of the Borysthenes as navigable only for 600 stadia from its mouth, though below the cataracts there can never have been any obstacle to the navigation, which is indeed particularly easy. (See Clarke's *Travels, l.c.*)

NOTE E, p. 186.

RIVERS OF SCYTHIA.

Professor Rawlinson justly observes that "there is the utmost uncertainty with respect to all identifications east of the isthmus of Perekop," the Tanais alone forming the exception. It is simply impossible to accept the statements of Herodotus as they stand, and even the favourite resource of modern commentators—to suppose that great physical changes may have taken place in the countries in question—will do little to remove the difficulty. The main point of all is the Gerrhus, which is clearly described as branching off from the Borysthenes, at the place of the same name, which was the farthest point of that river that was known to the Greeks (iv. 56). An ancient geographer would see no improbability in this, as such bifurcations were supposed to exist in other cases, as that of the Ister, which was believed by geographers much more advanced than Herodotus to send off an arm to the head of the Adriatic, while the main stream flowed into the Euxine. But there is in fact no such case known in physical geography.

The supposition of Professor Malden (cited by Sir R. Murchison, *Russia and the Ural Mountains*, vol. i. p. 574) that the Borysthenes may have originally formed a delta, and reached the sea by two separate mouths, is not destitute of plausibility; but it would offer a very inadequate solution of the difficulty. For the formation of such a delta is only possible at a short distance from the mouth of a great river, or where (as in the case of the Euphrates and Ganges) it flows for a long distance through marshy and alluvial lands. But the region where Herodotus places the river in question is the steppe country, which is throughout considerably elevated above the beds of the streams that traverse it. The formation of a gigantic delta in such a country may be safely pronounced to be physically impossible. And whatever may be thought of the distance assigned by Herodotus from Gerrhus to the sea (see Note D), the bifurcation must have taken place, according to his view, *a long way* up the course of the Borysthenes, as he supposes the two riveis Panticapes and Hypacyris, both of them considerable streams (ποταμοὶ οὐνομαστοί, c. 47 and 58), and taking their rise in two sepaiate lakes, to have their sources and their whole couise between the other two iivers, or rather arms of the same river! And he tells us, moreover, that the country of the agricultuial Scythians (the Georgi), which was situated between the Panticapes and the Borysthenes, was three days' journey in width, and extended up the Borysthenes for eleven days' vojage (iv. 18), while that of the nomad Scythians extended fourteen days' journey between the Panticapes and the Gerrhus (Ib. 19).

Even if we abandon the attempt to explain or reconcile these strange statements conceining the course and connection of the three rivers, the difficulty remains that nothing corresponding to them can be found between the prescribed limits. No streams of any considerable impoitance are found between the Dnieper and the Don (except the Donetz, a tributary of the latter); and those which exist all flow into the Sea of Azov, not into the Euxine.

Nor do the statements of latei wiiteis throw any light on the subject. Both Pliny and Mela mention the name of the Panticapes, but their accounts of these Scythian rivers are a mass of confusion, and Dionysius, who describes it as flowing from the Rhipæan Mountains (*Periegesis*, v. 315), is in direct contradiction with Herodotus.

NOTE F, p. 187.

THE RIVER OARUS.

The identification of the Oarus of Herodotus with the Volga was adopted by Major Rennell (*Geogr. of Herodotus*, p. 90, 4to. ed.), and has been accepted by most recent commentators. But it certainly rests on no adequate authority. If, indeed, the details of the expedition of Darius against the Scythians could be regarded as trustworthy, the supposition that the river Oarus, which was the limit of his progress towards the east, was the same with the Volga, would not be devoid of plausibility; but, as we shall hereaftei see, those details are so clearly unworthy of credit, that no dependence can be placed upon this argument, and there is really no other. The supposed iesemblance of the name Oarus to the Rha of Ptolemy, which is certainly the Volga, is so slight as to have no weight at all. On the other hand, in the passage under discussion in the text he enumerates the rivers in an order which would *seem* to place the Oarus to the west of the Tanais; while in the account of the expedition he clearly represents Darius as *crossing* the Tanais, and advancing *eastward* to the Oarus. But he there does not mention the Lycus at all, though on this supposition Darius must have crossed it *before* coming to the Tanais, and we should thus have a *fourth* river to account for between the Tanais and the Borysthenes, without anything really corresponding to it.

This discrepancy in regard to the rivers would tend to show that Herodotus derived his account of the expedition of Darius from a different quarter from that which furnished him with the account previously given of Scythia and the adjoining countries, notwithstanding the close agreement already pointed out in the arrangement of the surrounding nations.

NOTE G, p. 190.

LIMITS OF SCYTHIA.

The limits here assigned are materially less than those adopted by Mr. Rawlinson, who appears to me to extend the Scythia of Herodotus much too far to the north. He seems to have been in part led to this conclusion by assuming that it comprised the "two great basins of the Don and Dnieper," as well as the "two minor basins" of the Dniester and Boug (*Herodotus*, vol. iii. p. 210). But we know from Herodotus himself that both the two great rivers had their sources *far beyond* the Scythian territory; the one rising in the land of the Thyssagetæ, separated by a broad desert from that of the Budini, who themselves lay to the north-east of Scythia proper; while the sources of the Borysthenes were unknown to him; but they were clearly situated beyond the farthest limits of Scythia, with the whole of which he considered himself as well acquainted.

On the other hand, M. Neumann, whose general views on the subject appear to me to be sound and judicious, carries them, I think, to an extreme, and is disposed to restrict the Scythians of Herodotus within narrower limits than is reasonable or necessary. Whatever value we may attach to his statement of their extending 4000 stadia, or 20 days' journey, inland, it is certain that he regarded the Scythians as extending nearly, if not quite, to the sources of the Hypanis and the Tyras, as well as up the Borysthenes as far as Gerrhus. The hypothesis of M. Neumann, who would bring down Gerrhus *below* the cataracts of the Borysthenes, within a few days' journey of the sea, appears to me utterly at variance with the conception of Herodotus, who distinctly tells us (iv. 71) that the Gerrhi were the remotest tribe that was subject to the royal Scythians.

NOTE H, p. 195.

ETHNOGRAPHICAL RELATIONS OF THE SCYTHIANS OF HERODOTUS.

There are few questions in ethnography that have been the subject of more discussion and controversy in modern times than the origin and ethnical affinities of the people described by Herodotus under the name of Scythians. The prevailing opinion is that they were a Mongolian race, like the Kalmucks in modern days; and this view has been adopted by Niebuhr (*Kleine Schriften*, p. 362; *Vortrage uber alte Geschichte*, vol. i. p. 179), by Schafarik (*Slavische Alterthumer*, vol. i. p. 279), and by Neumann (*Die Hellenen im Skythenlande*, pp. 198, 199), as well as by our own historians, Thirlwall and Grote. On the other hand, several eminent philologers have contended that they were a people of Aryan or Indo-European race. Dr. Donaldson (*Varronianus*, 2nd edit pp. 40–45) attempts to prove that they were a Slavonian race, like their neighbours the Sauromatæ, and Jacob Grimm (*Gesch. der Deutschen Sprache*, vol. i. p. 219) maintains that there is sufficient evidence to assign them to the Indo-European family, without venturing to determine the particular branch to which they belong. The same hypothesis is adopted by Alexander Humboldt (*Kosmos*, vol. i. p. 491), Professor Rawlinson (*Herodotus*, vol. iii. pp. 192–205); and by Zeuss (*Die Deutschen und die Nachbarstamme*, pp. 285–299)

It may well be doubted whether we possess the means of arriving at a satisfactory solution of the question. On the one hand the elaborate account of the manners and customs, as well as the religious rites, of the Scythians, transmitted to us by Herodotus, presents so many points in common with those of existing Mongolian races, that it appears at first sight to be decisive of the subject : and the description of their physical characters by Hippocrates, who wrote but little after Herodotus, and undoubtedly refers to the same people (*De Aere, Aqua, et Locis*, c. 6, p. 558), tends to confirm this conclusion. But it must be admitted that there is so strong a general resemblance in the habits and manners of all the nomad races that have inhabited in successive ages the vast plains of Asia and Eastern Europe as to detract materially from the force of this argument. (See the judicious remarks on this subject of Humboldt, *Kosmos*, vol. i. p. 492.) On the other hand the linguistic grounds, which are principally appealed to by the advocates of the other theory, are scarcely sufficient to carry conviction to a mind not predisposed in their favour. The few words of the Scythian language quoted by Herodotus—who was himself wholly unacquainted with it—would naturally be liable to much distortion, and the same thing would apply to their proper names, which we possess only in the form into which they were altered by the Greeks. Philological conclusions based upon such slender materials are very far from possessing the conclusive authority which they justly claim when they rest upon a sufficient knowledge of the language.

The Scythians appear to have continued to occupy the regions north of the Euxine for some centuries after the time of Herodotus, but they gradually gave way before the advancing tide of the Sarmatian or Slavonian races from the east. Whether they were driven westward, or were gradually absorbed by the successive waves of nomad population that swept over their country, we have no means of determining, but at a later period they disappear both from history and geography, and Pliny's statement that in his time the (European) Scythians had become merged in the Sarmatians and Germans is probably well founded. (Scytharum nomen usquequaque transiit in Sarmatas atque Germanos, *H.N.* iv. 12, § 81.)

It is remarkable that the Alani, who were found in the fourth century after the Christian era in possession of the same tract, and whose manners, as described by Ammianus Marcellinus (xxxi. 2), present much resemblance to those of the Scythians of Herodotus, disappear in like manner from history, and their ethnical relations are almost equally uncertain.

NOTE I, p. 206.

EXPEDITION OF DARIUS.

This is the conclusion of Mr. Grote (*Hist. of Greece*, vol. iv. p. 354–360), as well as of Dr. Thirlwall (*Hist of Greece*, c. xiv. pp. 200–202), of Niebuhr (*Vortrage uber alte Geschichte*, vol. i. pp. 189–192), and, though in a modified form, of Heeren also (*Asiatic Nations*, vol. ii. p. 255). M. Duncker also, in his recent work (*Gesch. des Alterthums*, vol. ii. pp. 855-872), after subjecting the whole narrative to an elaborate discussion, rejects it as altogether unworthy of credit. Mr. Rawlinson has endeavoured, but, as it appears to me, with little success, to combat their arguments and diminish the improbabilities of the case. See his note on the subject in his *Herodotus*, vol. iii. p. 115.

In addition to the inherent difficulties of the story, it may be remarked that Ctesias, writing obviously from different materials, says simply that Darius marched *for fifteen days* into the Scythian territory, and then retreated to the Danube, which he recrossed, with the loss of a tenth part of his army (Ctesias, *Persica*, c. 17). Strabo's account is that the Persian army never even reached the Dniester, but suffered heavy loss from want of water in the desert between that river and the Danube, and that Darius, discovering his error, returned to the Danube (Strab. vii. 3, p. 305). This is treated by Niebuhr (*Kleine Schriften*, p. 372) as a mere suggestion, suited to the probabilities of the case; but on whatever authority it may rest, it at least shows that the narrative of Herodotus did not obtain credence in ancient times, any more than with modern critics.

It would be a mere waste of time to discuss the various theories of modern writers, who have attempted to explain away the narrative of Herodotus, while admitting its untenable character as it stands. To all such attempts we may reply in the words of Niebuhr: "As Herodotus tells us what is impossible, we know nothing at all historically respecting the expedition."

CHAPTER VII.

GEOGRAPHY OF HERODOTUS. ASIA.

SECTION 1.—*General Views.*

§ 1. WE have already briefly adverted to the extent and limits of the knowledge possessed by Herodotus of the continent of Asia. In general terms it may be said that the portion of that vast continent with which he was acquainted did not amount to one-third of the whole. But within these limits his information, though of course very imperfect, was more definite, and on the whole more accurate, than might have been expected. The reason is obvious enough. The fact is that his knowledge of Asia was almost entirely confined to the Persian Empire, which, as it then existed, comprised the whole of Western Asia (with the exception of the Arabian peninsula) from the Erythræan Sea to the Caucasus and the Caspian, and from the shores of the Mediterranean and the Euxine to the valley of the Indus. Within these limits he possessed definite, and as he himself considered, trustworthy, information, as to the provinces into which this vast empire was divided, and the various tribes and populations by which they were inhabited. Beyond them he had nothing but the vaguest hearsay accounts.

§ 2. Of the great peninsula of Arabia, which remained always independent of the Persian monarchy, he knew only in a vague and general manner that it was of great extent, and stretched farther to the south than any other part of Asia. As it is clear that the Red Sea was habitually navigated in his time, by the Egyptians and Phœnicians, throughout its whole extent, he must have thus obtained a notion of the length of Arabia on that side; but he appears to have considered it as extending much farther to the south, beyond the Straits of Bab-el-Mandeb; as he distinctly terms it the most southerly of all inhabited countries,[1] not excepting Ethiopia, which according to his idea trended away at once towards the west, from the point where it most nearly approached to the coast of Arabia. There can be little doubt that Herodotus applied the name of Arabia to the *west* coast of the Arabian Gulf or Red Sea, as well as the east coast; and it may therefore be doubted which of these portions he regarded as extending farthest to the south. But we must not hastily assume that he was aware of the much greater extension of the African coast in that direction. The spices of Arabia were already celebrated, and fabulous tales were current in the days of Herodotus concerning the difficulties encountered by the natives in gathering them.[2] The trade in these articles was almost certainly at this period exclusively in the hands of the Phœnicians, who would readily circulate such stories with a view to enhance the price of their commodities. It is worthy of notice that among the spices of Arabia Herodotus enumerates not only frankincense and myrrh, which are really produced in that country, but cinnamon and cassia also, which are at the present day not found nearer than Ceylon and the coasts of Malabar; but according to the uniform testimony of ancient authors were the production of the north-eastern angle of Africa, opposite to Arabia, to which they in consequence gave the name of "the Cinnamon region," or "Regio Cinnamomifera."[3]

§ 3. Herodotus repeatedly alludes to the Erythræan Sea, as situated to the south of Asia and extending from the entrance of the Arabian Gulf (or what we now term the Red Sea) as far as

---

[1] Herodot. iii. 107 He is here distinctly speaking of the whole inhabited world (τῆς οἰκευμένης), and places the Indians in the farthest east. the Arabians to the south and the Ethiopians to the *west*, or rather perhaps southwest; for this appears to be the sense in which he uses the phrase ἀποκλινο- μένης μεσαμβρίης παρήκει πρὸς δύνοντα ἥλιον, c. 114.

[2] Herodot iii. 107–112.

[3] This district would be probably included by Herodotus in Arabia, according to his acceptation of the term, but at all events its productions would be imported through Arabia, and therefore naturally regarded by him as the growth of that country.

the mouth of the Indus. The continuity of the ocean around the southern shores of Asia he considered to be established by the voyage of Scylax of Caryanda, who, by order of Darius Hystaspes, had descended the Indus to its mouth, and from thence sailed round to the head of the Arabian Gulf.[4] But he appears to have possessed no detailed information concerning this voyage, to which he distinctly attributes the *discovery* of these parts of Asia. And it is a curious proof of the imperfect state of his knowledge, that he would seem to have been ignorant of the existence of the Persian Gulf, as a deep inlet running far inland on the east of Arabia, as the Arabian Gulf did on the west. No indication at least of this remarkable feature in the geography of Western Asia is to be found in any part of his work; and he speaks of the Euphrates and Tigris as falling *into the Erythræan Sea*, without distinguishing the Persian Gulf from the open ocean. The name of Erythræan, or Red, Sea, is applied by him to the whole of this sea from India to the Straits of Bab-el-Mandeb; the long, narrow gulf, to which the name of the Red Sea is now exclusively appropriated, being uniformly termed by him the Arabian Gulf, and distinctly described as an inlet extending into the land of the Arabians *from* the Erythræan Sea.[5] He describes it as in length a voyage of forty days from the inmost recess (where Suez now stands) to the open sea, for a vessel using oars only; while it was so narrow that it could be crossed in its widest part in half a day. This is an obvious exaggeration, and is only applicable to the narrow arm of the sea which runs up to Suez, but such a transference to the whole, of what is really true of a part only, is one of the commonest errors in all popular descriptions, whether geographical, or of other kinds.

Unfortunately we have no clue to the actual distance, which Herodotus meant to designate by a day's voyage of a rowing-vessel;[6] the real length of the Red Sea (from Suez to the

---

[4] Herodot iv 44   [5] ii 11.
[6] The only other occasion on which he makes use of the same phrase is in regard to the Caspian, which he tells us was, in length, fifteen days' voyage for a rowing-vessel, and eight days in its

island of Perim) is about 1400 English, or rather more than 1200 geographical miles: if we suppose this divided into forty days' voyages, it would give somewhat more than 30 geographical miles per day, a distance not unlikely to be a fair average under the circumstances. It is evident from the manner in which Herodotus speaks of it that the voyage to the entrance of the gulf, where it expands into the open sea, was one not unfrequently made in his time, and hence its duration was probably well known. On another point also we find him possessed of correct information; namely, the occurrence of regular tides in the Arabian Gulf;[7] a phenomenon which always attracted the attention of the Greeks, to whom it was unfamiliar, from their absence in the Mediterranean. It is clear therefore that he had obtained, probably from Egyptian informants, accurate general notions concerning the Red Sea, but of the open ocean beyond, to which he applies the name of the Erythræan Sea, it is evident that he had nothing but the vaguest idea; though he was clearly aware of the existence of this great southern ocean, and tells us distinctly that it was continuous with the Atlantic Ocean beyond the Columns of Hercules, with which that familiar to the Greeks was also connected.[8]

§ 4. Of the countries beyond the limits of the Persian Empire towards the north, the information possessed by the historian was likewise of a very imperfect character. The nature of

---

greatest breadth (i. 203). But his information in this case was likely to be far more vague and inaccurate than in the case of the Red Sea, as the Caspian was little likely to be navigated in his day; and the passage therefore furnishes us with no trustworthy base of comparison. The Caspian is in fact not less than 750 miles in length, and 430 in its greatest breadth; but Herodotus had doubtless no idea of its real dimensions.

[7] Herodot. ii 11.

[8] τὴν μὲν γὰρ Ἕλληνες ναυτίλλονται πᾶσαν, καὶ ἡ ἔξω στηλέων θάλασσα, ἡ Ἀτλαντὶς καλεομένη, καὶ ἡ Ἐρυθρὴ μία

τυγχάνει ἐοῦσα. i. 102.

It is remarkable that this is the only passage in Herodotus where the name of the Atlantic for the western sea is found; but it is clear, from the incidental way in which it is here introduced, that it was one well known in his day. On the other hand, we may notice the want of any distinctive name by which to designate the Mediterranean "the sea which was navigated by the Greeks." The same want will be found in the geographers of a much later period.

those vast countries that are commonly comprehended under the popular appellation of Tartary—their physical peculiarities, and the nomad habits and shifting character of the population, resulting from those peculiarities, have in all ages rendered them difficult of access to strangers, and have thrown a haze of uncertainty around their geography that has not been cleared up until quite recently. It was not indeed till the publication of Humboldt's great work on Central Asia that the physical geography of those regions can be considered as having been established on a satisfactory basis. We cannot therefore wonder to find that in the time of Herodotus great misconceptions existed with regard to it. In one respect indeed (as we have already seen) he was in advance of all succeeding geographers for a period of some centuries—that he knew the Caspian Sea to be a distinct basin of water, having no connection with any other sea, but surrounded on all sides by nomad nations, with whose names and relative positions he was, in a general way, acquainted. He had also a correct general idea of the Caucasus, which in his day formed the northern boundary of the Persian Empire,[9] and which he correctly describes as the greatest and most lofty of all mountain ranges of which he had any knowledge,[1] and he notices the fact of its containing a population consisting of many different tribes and races of men. He justly contrasts the mountainous character of the region west of the Caspian with the boundless plains that formed its eastern shores. But with the real geography of the vast tracts to the east of that sea he was almost wholly unacquainted; the very imperfect information that he had obtained concerning them having led him into errors of the grossest kind.

§ 5. It is evident indeed that he had heard vaguely of the existence of a great river in that part of Asia, which formed the northern limit of the Persian Empire, beyond which dwelt

---

[9] Herodot. iii. 97
[1] i. 203 ὁ Καύκασος παρατείνει, ἐὼν οὐρέων καὶ πλήθει μέγιστον καὶ μεγάθει ὑψηλότατον.

a nomad people called the Massagetæ, whom Cyrus had in vain endeavoured to reduce to subjection, and who had continued ever after to defy the arms of the Great King. This river was called, either by his Greek informants or by the Persians themselves, the Araxes. Herodotus, who had already heard of a river of that name which rose in the mountains of the Matieni, on the borders of Armenia, and flowed into the Caspian Sea, seems (not unnaturally) to have confounded the two and thus involved himself in inextricable confusion.

Thus he describes the Araxes, which was crossed by Cyrus in his war against the Massagetæ, as a river, little, if at all, inferior to the Danube in magnitude, and containing numerous islands, some of them as large as Lesbos. It flowed through the broad plains, which extended to an unlimited distance on the east of the Caspian Sea.[2] All these particulars would suit tolerably well (allowing for some exaggeration) with the Iaxartes,[3] which was in all probability the stream really meant by the persons from whom Herodotus derived his information. But the historian confused them with what he had heard of the *true* Araxes, which he correctly describes as rising in the country of the Matieni, and flowing into the Caspian Sea.[4] This stream moreover really flowed from west to east, and he was thus led to regard the eastern Araxes also as following the same direction, and as flowing *from* the Caspian Sea instead of

---

[2] Herodot 1 202, 204

[3] The reasons for preferring the Iaxartes to the Oxus, which is the more important stream of the two, and is on this hypothesis unnoticed by Herodotus, are, besides some resemblance in the names that the former river undoubtedly became the frontier of the Persian Empire, to which Sogdiana was subject, as early as the reign of Darius, and in the time of Alexander there still existed a town called Cyropolis, near the left bank of the Iaxartes, which, according to tradition, had been founded by Cyrus himself The Massagetæ reappear in the account of Alexander's expedition, during his wars in Sogdiana (Arrian,

Anab iv. 16, 17), and were apparently at that time still independent, but their exact geographical position is not clearly indicated

[4] 1. 202 It is evidently the same confusion that led him to the strange statement that the Araxes had not less than forty mouths, one of which afforded a clear channel (διὰ καθαροῦ) into the Caspian, while all the others ended in marshes and swamps The first evidently refers to the true Araxes. the other supposed mouths must have had reference to the marshy tracts at the mouths of the Oxus and Iaxartes, in which those rivers might well be supposed to lose themselves.

towards it.⁵ Hence we find him in another passage describing the Araxes as flowing "towards the rising sun," and forming together with the Caspian Sea, the northern limit of Asia.⁶

§ 6. The Massagetæ were apparently the only people whom Herodotus knew even by name as dwelling in this part of Asia; he tells us that they were situated *opposite to* the Issedones,⁷ whom, as we have already seen,⁸ he placed in Europe, apparently to the south-east of the Ural mountains. Some accounts, he adds, represented them as a Scythian tribe, and he himself says that their manners and dress were similar to those of the Scythians. This was indeed probably the case with almost all the nomad races that have at successive periods occupied the vast steppes in this part of Asia; and this similarity of habits renders it almost impossible to judge of the true ethnical relations of any of these tribes mentioned by ancient writers. Herodotus himself appears to have regarded the Massagetæ as a distinct people from the Scythians, whom, according to the tradition which he adopts as the most plausible, they had themselves driven out of this part of Asia.⁹ But, as if on purpose

---

⁵ It is hardly necessary to remark that the Iaxartes does not in fact flow into the Caspian Sea at all, but into the Sea of Aral But as the existence of this last inland sea was unknown to *all* ancient geographers before the time of Ptolemy, and even after the Oxus and Iaxartes were well known as separate streams, *both* were regarded as falling into the Caspian—it is hardly worth while to notice this additional source of confusion

⁶ iv. 40

⁷ πέρην τοῦ 'Αράξεω ποταμοῦ, ἀντίον δὲ 'Ισσηδόνων ἀνδρῶν, i 201 The exact sense of this last expression is not easy to determine · but he probably means that they were to the south of them, facing them on the north It is in this sense that he employs the word ἀντίον in the passage already examined, where he compares the Nile and the Danube.

⁸ See Chapter VI p 199.

⁹ Herodot iv. 11. The ethnical relations of the Massagetæ are as uncertain as those of most of the other nomad nations of Asia and Northern Europe. Dr Donaldson considers them to be a Gothic race, arguing that the termination of the name is identical with that of the Getæ, and the same view is taken by Mr Rawlinson, who even attempts to explain Massagetæ as "the greater Goths," in contradistinction to the Thyssagetæ, or "lesser Goths" (*Herodotus*, note to iv 22) But all such conclusions from mere names are worth very little Niebuhr, on the other hand, Heeren (*Asiatic Nations*, vol ii p 279), and Schafarik (*Slavische Alterthumer*, vol. i. p. 279), concur in regarding them as a Mongolian race Humboldt was of opinion that they belonged to the Indo-European family, without attempting to assign them to any particular branch of it In the absence of all trace of their language the point must always remain uncertain

to increase the confusion, he adds that the Scythians were driven *across the Araxes*, and thereupon occupied the land of the Cimmerians. Here it has been supposed that the river meant by the Araxes was the Volga,[1] which would indeed render the geography in this particular case (comparatively) intelligible. But the fact really seems to be that the ideas of Herodotus—and doubtless of his informants too—upon the whole subject were so utterly vague, that it is impossible to extract anything with clearness out of the confusion. It must be remembered,—as some excuse for our historian—or rather as showing how extremely uncertain were the ideas of his countrymen on these geographical questions, that when the army of Alexander found itself actually on the banks of the Iaxartes, it was generally believed that that river was the same with the Tanais.[2]

The most remarkable circumstance mentioned by Herodotus concerning the Massagetæ undoubtedly is the great abundance of gold which they possessed, and with which they lavishly ornamented both themselves and the trappings of their horses.[3] Copper was also found in their country in great quantities, and was used for their arms and armour, while iron was unknown, as well as silver. They are described as ex-

---

[1] It is probable, as has been repeatedly suggested, that the name *Aras* or *Ras*, out of which the Greeks made Araxes, was in fact applied to all the great streams of this part of Asia it is probably the same root as we find in Rha, the name applied by Ptolemy to the Volga. According to Sir H Rawlinson, in "primitive Scythian," Aras signifies "great"

[2] Arrian, *Anabasis*, III 30, § 7 Arrian himself seems disposed to accept as a fact that the Tanais was the name of the river, but adds that it must be a *different* Tanais from the one that flows into the Palus Mæotis But there can be no doubt that the Macedonians in the first instance took it for *the* Tanais, and writers of the succeeding period, as Strabo has justly pointed out (XI. p. 509), *intentionally* confirmed the error. Aristotle also confused the Araxes with the Iaxartes, and regarded the Tanais as a branch of it (*Meteorologica*, I. 13, § 16)

It may be added that the views of Herodotus concerning the course of the Araxes are not more widely erroneous than those entertained in the last century with regard to the great rivers of Central Africa, and the supposed relations of the Niger with the Nile

[3] I. 215. Both gold and copper are found in large quantities in the Ural Mountains, but it is difficult to suppose the Massagetæ of Herodotus to have extended so far to the west It is probable, however, that some of the ranges of the Altai (still little known) may also contain these metals in equal abundance.

tending far to the east; but of their limits in this direction Herodotus had doubtless no knowledge; he seems however to have regarded the extreme east of Asia, beyond the Massagetæ, as well as beyond the Indians, as a vast tract of uninhabited deserts.

§ 7. The account given of India and its inhabitants by the historian is in many respects interesting and instructive. He appears to have heard vague reports of its great extent and population, as well as of the vast wealth of its inhabitants: he tells us indeed that the Indians were by far the most numerous people with which he was acquainted;[4] and that the tribute which they paid to Darius much exceeded in amount that of any other province of his vast empire.[5] But it appears certain that the Persian kings never extended their dominion beyond the Punjaub and the valley of the Indus, nor is it likely that they possessed even the lower part of that river, though its course had been fully explored by order of Darius. It may indeed be questioned whether they ever possessed any real sovereignty to the east of the Indus, which certainly formed the limit of the Persian dominions in this direction in the time of Alexander. But it is not improbable that Darius may for a time have levied tribute from the neighbouring princes beyond this limit; the amount of the tribute derived from India being greater than can well be supposed to have been drawn from the provinces west of the Indus only: and this is a point upon which Herodotus was more likely to have obtained correct information, than as to geographical details. Of the extensive and fertile regions of Hindostan proper he had unquestionably no knowledge: to him, as to all his Greek contemporaries, India was the land of the Indus, which he regarded as flowing "towards the east and the rising sun."[6] The Indians themselves dwelt the farthest towards the east of any

---

[4] iii 94 'Ινδῶι ἐ πλῆθός τε πολλῷ πλεῖστόν ἐστι πάντων τῶν ἡμεῖς ἴδμεν ἀνθρώπων, καὶ φόρον ἀπαγίνεον πρὸς πάντας τοὺς ἄλλους Again, in v 3, he speaks of the Thracians as the greatest and most numerous people *next to the Indians*

[5] Note A, p 255   [6] iv 40

people with which he was acquainted : beyond them in this direction there was nothing but sandy deserts, uninhabited and unknown.[7] What lay beyond these deserts no one (he tells us) was able to say : the extreme east of Asia, like the north and north-west of Europe, was wholly unknown, and there was no certainty whether it was bounded by the sea or not.[8]

§ 8. From the mouth of the Indus to the Arabian Gulf the voyage of Scylax of Caryanda (which has been already referred to) was regarded by Herodotus as establishing beyond a doubt that there was continuous sea. Unfortunately the historian has given us no particulars concerning this interesting voyage, and he seems to have possessed no detailed information with regard to it, notwithstanding the fact of its being commanded by a countryman of his own.[9] All that he tells us is, that Darius, wishing to know where the Indus had its outlet into the sea, sent out some ships, on board of which were Scylax of Caryanda, and other persons in whom the king had the greatest confidence. These set out from the city of Caspatyrus in the Pactyan land, and sailed "down the river towards the east and the rising sun" till they came to the sea; then turning to the west they sailed along by sea till they ultimately arrived, in the thirtieth month of their voyage, at the head of the Arabian Gulf, from whence the Egyptian king Necho had sent out his exploring expedition.[1] Herodotus, moreover, adds that, after this, Darius, having reduced the Indians to subjection, "made use of this sea." It would therefore appear that in this instance at least the voyage of discovery did not remain a wholly isolated occurrence. Yet we have seen how very imperfect was our author's knowledge of the Erythræan Sea; and we shall hereafter see that when Alexander sent out the expedition of Nearchus to explore the course of the Indus, all memory of this voyage of Scylax would seem to have disappeared.

Herodotus had heard of the existence of crocodiles in the

---

[7] iii 98, iv 40   [8] iv 44   [9] Note B, p 256   [1] iv 44

Indus, which was, in his opinion, the only river, except the Nile, in which they were found.² He had also heard that the Indians were clothed in cotton, which he describes as a kind of wool, the spontaneous produce of certain trees, but of a finer and better quality than that of sheep.³ They had also a large kind of reeds (doubtless meaning bamboos), of which they made their bows. But these are the only natural productions of the country (except gold) to which he alludes. His account of the manners and customs of the inhabitants contains some particulars that were probably never correct, certainly not as applied to the Indians properly so-called; while he notices few, if any, of those peculiarities, which have distinguished the true Hindoo races in all ages, and which attracted the attention of the Greeks as soon as they came in contact with them. But the Indian tribes which Herodotus directly describes, and whom he represents as living in a state of revolting barbarism,⁴ appear to have been situated on the borders, rather than within the bounds, of India proper, and may probably have been some remnants of the earlier races, who gradually disappeared before the advancing civilization of the Hindoos.⁵

§ 9. The only city which he mentions by name within the confines of India, according to his acceptation of the term, is Caspatyrus, placed by him in the Pactyan land, from whence, as we have seen, Scylax and his companions set out on their exploring voyage, but there are no means of identifying either the city or the district with any certainty.⁶ All that we know is that the Pactyans were situated to the north of the other Indians, apparently bordering on the Bactrians, whom they resembled in their habits of life, and in their warlike disposition. It is in connection with this tribe of Indians

---

² iv 44 ³ iii 106
⁴ iii 98–101.
⁵ One of the most revolting of these customs—that of killing and eating the aged and feeble members of their families—ascribed by Herodotus to a tribe whom he names Padæans (iii 99), is still said to prevail among the aboriginal races who inhabit the upper valley of the Nerbudda, among the recesses of the Vindhya mountains. (Duncker, *Gesch des Alterthums*, vol ii. p 268)
⁶ Note C, p. 256

that Herodotus tells us the strange story (copied by many succeeding writers) of the manner in which they procured the gold, with which they paid the Persian tribute. Gold indeed, he says, was produced in vast abundance in India, some of it washed down by the streams, and some dug out of the earth, but the greater part of it was procured in the following manner.[7]

Beyond the confines of the Pactyan land lay an extensive sandy desert in which there dwelt a kind of ants, not so large as dogs, but larger than foxes, which burrowed in the sandy soil, and threw up large heaps, like ordinary ant-hills, at the mouth of their burrows. This sand abounded in gold; and the Indians, traversing the desert upon very fleet camels, filled their sacks with sand from these heaps, and then retreated in all haste, pursued by the ants with such speed that, if they did not succeed in obtaining a considerable start, they had no hope of escaping from them.

§ 10. The locality from whence this gold was derived, is very obscurely indicated, though Herodotus appears to have conceived it as situated to the north or north-east of the Indian tribes to which he refers.[8] Heeren identifies it without hesitation with the desert of Cobi, on the north side of the mountains of Little Thibet, but there is really no foundation for this assumption. Herodotus never mentions the existence of any mountains in this part of Asia at all,[9] and hence it is evident that he had no real notion of its physical geography. The vague idea, that all to the east of the Indians was a sandy desert, probably arose in the first instance from the real fact of

---

[7] Herodot iii 105, 106

[8] Megasthenes (ap Strab xv. p. 706), in repeating the same story, places the scene of it among the Derdæ, "a people among the mountains towards the east of India," and describes the locality as a high table-land (ὀροπέδιον) of about 3000 stadia in circumference. Pliny, who probably derived the story from Megasthenes, writes the name Dardæ, and places them "in regione septemtrionalium Indorum" (*H. N.* xi. 30, § 111). They are in all probability the same people who are still known as Durds or Dards, and inhabit the lofty mountain tracts on the borders of Kafiristan and Thibet

[9] In this respect, as we shall see, Ctesias was far in advance of him, as he was aware that many of the tribes in this part of India inhabited rugged, mountainous districts.

the occurrence of a broad desert tract to the east of the fertile lands of the Indus, and would be confirmed by vague reports that similar deserts were found also to the east of Bactria and the adjoining countries. Almost all the mountain chains in this part of Asia appear to be highly auriferous, and there is no reason to doubt that very large quantities of gold may have been derived by the Indian tribes from the plains at their foot, where it would naturally be found in the shape of gold-dust, or gold-sand. That the Indian tribute was actually paid in this form into the treasury of the Persian king was a fact concerning which Herodotus would have been likely to have obtained correct information.

The story of the *ants* on the other hand is one of which it is very difficult to divine the origin; and of the various explanations that have been proposed, none can be said to be altogether satisfactory.[1] It appears certain however that the fable is a genuine Indian tradition,[2] though embellished by the informants of the historian; it is not only repeated by later Greek writers on India, such as Megasthenes and Nearchus, but reappears in the middle ages, and is found in the Arabian geographers.[3] One of the most curious points in the matter is that the animal, whatever it was, to which this strange misnomer was applied, was certainly a real creature, as not only does Herodotus tell us that specimens of them were preserved in the menageries of the Persian king,[4] but Nearchus—one of the most careful and accurate writers of his time—asserts that he had himself seen their skins.[5] And so persistent are such fables, when once propagated, that even in the sixteenth century one of these "Indian ants" was said to have been sent as a present by the Shah of Persia to Sultan Soliman[6] at Constantinople.

---

[1] Note D, p 257
[2] See a passage from the Mahábhárata, cited by Professor Wilson (*Ariana* p 135), where mention is found of "that gold which is dug up by Pippilikas (ants), and is therefore called Pippilíka (ant-gold)"
[3] See the passages collected by Larcher and Bahr in their notes upon Herodotus [4] iii 102
[5] Nearchus ap Arrian *Indica*, c 15.
[6] It is described by Busbequius

§ 11. With this exception it is remarkable that Herodotus tells us none of the fables which were current in later times about India, and which are found in such abundance in Ctesias and other subsequent writers. It is however not improbable that this was due rather to the scantiness of his information than to its authenticity. It is curious that he never even mentions the elephants of India, which naturally figure in so prominent a manner in the writings of all subsequent authors; nor does he notice its ivory or precious stones; even where he cites India in confirmation of his view that the extreme regions of the earth possessed the most valuable productions, he dwells only upon its abundance of gold and cotton; adding however, in a general way, that all the animals there,—both quadrupeds and birds—grew to a larger size than elsewhere.[7]

Section 2.—*Persian Empire: Satrapies.*

§ 1. Of the countries that formed part of the Persian Empire in his time, Herodotus had undoubtedly a general knowledge. He knew not only the provinces into which that empire was divided, but was acquainted at least with the names of the principal tribes and nations by which they were inhabited; and has preserved to us a catalogue of them, which is a document of the highest interest. Unfortunately he has not told us from what source he derived the account of the satrapies which he has inserted in his third book; but there can be no doubt that it was based upon authentic information, and was in all probability derived originally from some official record.[8]

But we must not hastily conclude that he possessed anything

(*Epist* iv p 343 ed Elzevii), *but only from hearsay*, as "formica Indica, mediocris canis magnitudine, mordax admodum et sæva." What the animal may really have been it is impossible to conjecture.
[7] iii 106

[8] The discovery and interpretation in modern days of the lists of subject tribes and races that are found on the Persian monuments, have supplied us with materials of the greatest value for comparison with those furnished by Herodotus

like a complete *geographical* knowledge of the countries in question. We have already seen how extremely vague were his ideas concerning the Erythræan Sea and the lands that adjoined it. It must be remembered also that he regarded the Euxine as far exceeding in length its real dimensions,[9] and as he had an approximately correct idea of the true position of its western extremity (near Byzantium), he necessarily extended it at the other end a great deal too far to the east. One effect of this error was to bring it nearly to the same meridian with that of the Persian Gulf; and there can be little doubt that in the passage already cited, where he describes four nations—the Persians, Medes, Saspirians and Colchians, as filling up the whole breadth of Asia from the Erythræan Sea to the Euxine, he considered them as lying nearly on the same line from north to south, so that the Colchians on the northern sea, would be (to use the phrase which he himself elsewhere employs) *opposite* to the Persians on the south; or as we should say, on the same meridian with them.[1] The Caspian Sea would be in consequence placed several degrees too far to the eastward, and the whole of the adjoining regions thrown into confusion, but as we have no details concerning these countries—Herodotus himself having evidently no clear idea of their position—we cannot trace any farther the results of this error.

§ 2. Even in regard to the great peninsula of Anatolia or Asia Minor—as it was called by later geographers[2]—with which Herodotus was comparatively familiar, as its coasts were surrounded by a girdle of Greek colonies, many of which the historian had himself visited,—his geographical knowledge, in the strict sense of the term, was very inaccurate. While

---

[9] See preceding Chapter
[1] It is in this sense (as we have seen) that he himself speaks of the mouths of the Nile as lying *opposite* to those of the Danube.
[2] It may be as well to mention here (once for all) that the name of Asia Minor, so familiar to the student of ancient geography, was not in use either among Greek or Roman writers until a very late period. Orosius, who wrote in the fifth century after the Christian era, is the first extant writer who employs the term in its modern sense.

the excessive length assigned by him to the Euxine necessarily led him to prolong the northern shores of the peninsula to nearly the same extent, he considered its breadth to be much less than it really is. For he tells us that from the mountainous district of Cilicia, the direct route across to Sinope on the Euxine, was not more than five days' journey "for an active man."[3] But the real breadth of the peninsula is in this part more than five degrees of latitude, thus giving about 60 G. miles *in a direct line* for each day's journey—a distance far exceeding what can be supposed to be intended by that expression:[4] and even the narrowest neck or isthmus (between the gulf of Scanderoon and Samsun, the ancient Amisus) is very nearly four degrees and a half.

§ 3. Farther to the east again he was not only familiar with the two great streams of the Euphrates and the Tigris, and knew that they both flowed from the mountains of Armenia: but he correctly describes several of the principal affluents of the latter stream; as well as the Choaspes, on which the Persian capital of Susa was situated. He had indeed special means of information in regard to this part of Asia, for there can be no doubt that Herodotus had himself visited Babylon, and perhaps even Susa itself.[5] It is at least highly probable that his

---

[3] i 72, ii 34
[4] Scylax (about a century later) gives the same estimate of five days' journey (*Periplus*, § 102), without adding the important qualification of Herodotus "for an active man" εὐζώνῳ ἀνδρί) It has been suggested that this expression points to the case of a courier; and that these may have accomplished in ancient times as long journeys as the Persian couriers at the present day, who not unfrequently travel on foot at the rate of 50 miles a day But there is nothing to indicate that Herodotus referred to any such exceptional rate of travelling, and the mountainous character of the country to be traversed is such as to add greatly to the difficulty of the journey (See Rennell's *Geography of Herodotus*, p. 190, 4to edit and Rawlinson's note on the passage in his *Herodotus*, vol 1 p 210) It seems more probable that Herodotus relied upon erroneous information Eratosthenes, at a later period, assigned 3000 stadia as the breadth of the isthmus, which (at 600 stadia to the degree) would be pretty nearly correct (ap Strab 11 1, p 68) Yet Pliny gives it as only 200 Roman miles, reducing it again even below the estimate of Herodotus, while Ptolemy on the other hand extends it to 6½ degrees of latitude, considerably beyond the real breadth

[5] I cannot at all concur with Mr. Rawlinson and Colonel Mure in regarding the passage in vi 119 concerning the Eretrians who were established at Ardericca as conclusive with regard to Herodotus having visited Susa. The

detailed account of the royal road from Sardis to Susa was derived in great part from personal observation. But of Upper Asia, as it was commonly called by later Greek writers [6]—the great table-land of Iran, which occupies the whole extent from the mountains that bound the valley of the Tigris to those on the west of the Indus, Herodotus cannot be said to have had any correct geographical knowledge whatever, though he knew the names and some other particulars concerning the nations which occupied it. The great mountain chains, which in fact determine the physical geography of all this part of Asia, naturally occupy a prominent part in the description of later geographers, and—though their real direction and relations were very imperfectly understood, yet we at least find that Eratosthenes and Strabo were fully alive to their importance. But no trace of such an idea is found in Herodotus. With the exception of the chain of Mount Caucasus, which (as we have seen) had at an early period attracted the attention of the Greek voyagers to the Euxine, and which is described by the historian as the loftiest of all mountains with which he was acquainted [7]—he does not notice any of the mountain ranges of Asia. Even in the description of the route from Sardis to Susa—already adverted to—he briefly notices the existence of a narrow pass or *gate* (Pylæ) at a

---

statement that they continued there down to his own time (οἳ καὶ μέχρι ἐμέο εἶχον τὴν χώρην ταύτην, φυλάσσοντες τὴν ἀρχαίην γλῶσσαν) is surely one that he might easily learn at secondhand, and the very same phrase is used by him in speaking of the Barcæans, who were transferred to a village in Bactria (ἥπερ ἔτι καὶ ἐς ἐμὲ ἦν οἰκευμένη ἐν τῇ γῇ τῇ Βακτρίῃ, iv 204), where we certainly cannot suppose Herodotus to have visited them in person,

At the same time if it be admitted that he actually went to Babylon—and this is agreed on all hands—there is certainly no improbability in his having continued his journey to the court of the Great King But the absence of any description or detailed notice of Susa itself appears to me conclusive against the idea of his having been there Few subjects could be more interesting to the Greeks than the court and capital of the Persian king, and Herodotus would have had abundant opportunities of introducing a description of them into his history, had he been able to do so from personal observation

[6] The expression ἡ ἄνω 'Ασίη is used by Herodotus himself in one passage (i 95, 'Ασσυρίων ἀρχόντων τῆς ἄνω 'Ασίης), but apparently in a wider sense than that in which it was employed by later geographers The Assyrian Empire extended to the Halys, and probably this was the limit which the historian had in his mind.

[7] i 203

particular point of the Cilician mountains,[8] as one of the difficulties which an army would have to encounter, but there is no other allusion to the great chain of Mount Taurus as one of the leading features of this part of Asia. While the systematic geographers of later times attached even an exaggerated importance to this mountain range, the very name of the Taurus is not found in Herodotus, though we can hardly doubt that he was familiar with it in its original and proper signification as applied to the mountains of Lycia and Cilicia. As a general rule it may be observed that there are few subjects upon which the ideas of an unscientific observer are apt to be so vague and uncertain as that of the conformation and character of mountain chains. Isolated peaks, like Ætna or Ararat, attract at once his attention and wonder: but it· is only the scientific traveller or geographer who will group into their natural order and connection the more complicated ramifications of extensive mountain ranges. At the same time it is but fair to Herodotus to observe that he has nowhere professed to give us any regular geographical sketch of Asia, with the exception of the brief outline already discussed, and he may not unreasonably have regarded the *ethnography* of the Persian Empire (to use the modern phrase) as having a more immediate bearing upon his historical subject than its physical geography.

§ 4. The most important passage in Herodotus for the geography of the Persian Empire—that in which he describes its division into satrapies by Darius[9]—is indeed primarily of an ethnographical character, though combined with information of a purely statistical nature, which has every appearance of being derived—though perhaps not directly—from an official record. But interesting as this enumeration of the provinces and nations subject to the Great King is in itself, it derives great

---

[8] This, as we shall see, was not the celebrated pass commonly known as the Cilician Gates, which was traversed by the younger Cyrus and by Alexander, but one farther east, on the frontiers of Cappadocia and Melitene
[9] iii. 89–97.

additional value from a comparison with the catalogue of the different tribes that sent their contingents to the vast army of Xerxes:[1] a statement evidently proceeding from a different and independent source, and remarkable at once for its general agreement, and for its occasional discrepancies with the list of the satrapies. We have now also the opportunity of comparing the two with the less copious and detailed—but undoubtedly authentic—lists of the different nations subject to the Persian king, found in the inscriptions of Darius himself at Behistun and Persepolis.[2] In the following brief review of the nations in question, the order adopted by Herodotus in the enumeration of the satrapies will be followed, as the most convenient for reference, notwithstanding its occasional deviations from geographical sequence.

§ 5. Beginning with Asia Minor (as was natural for the historian to do), we find that great country divided into four satrapies or provinces. The first of these comprised the Ionians, Æolians, Carians, Lycians, and Pamphylians: that is to say the inhabitants of the coast regions from the borders of the Troad to those of Cilicia (including all the Greek colonies with which the coasts were studded), together with the inland tribes of the Milyans, whom Herodotus regarded as a distinct people from the Lycians, and the Magnesians, whom he here separates from the other Ionians, with whom they were usually associated.[3]

The second satrapy contained the two well-known nations

---

[1] vii. 61–88.

[2] These lists are given by Mr Rawlinson in a note to his Herodotus (iii 94, note 6) The original inscriptions will be found in Sir H Rawlinson's *Memoir on Persian Cuneiform Inscriptions* (published by the Royal Asiatic Society in 1846), at pp xxvii 280 and 294.

[3] The omission of the Pisidians is remarkable, as they could hardly have been included among the Pamphylians Nor do they figure in the army of Xerxes Probably these wild mountaineers were not reduced to any real subjection, but continued to enjoy a state of virtual independence, as was the case with the Isaurians down to a much later period In the time of the younger Cyrus the Pisidians appear as a race of lawless freebooters, whom that prince proposed utterly to extirpate as the only means of effectually protecting the neighbouring nations against their incursions. (Xenoph. *Anab.* I. 1 § 11, 2, § 1)

of the Mysians and Lydians, together with three obscure tribes—the Lasonians, Cabalians, and Hygennians. Of these the two former names appear again in the catalogue of the troops of Xerxes, where they are associated with the Milyans:[4] and are apparently regarded by our author as the same people, originally of Mæonian race: the Hygennians are otherwise unknown.

In the third satrapy were comprised the Hellespontians on the right bank of the Straits (including probably the whole district subsequently known as the Troad), the Phrygians, the Asiatic Thracians (that is, as he elsewhere explains,[5] the Bithynians), the Paphlagonians, the Mariandynians, and the Syrians, by which term he here means the Cappadocians, who were generally known to the Greeks of his day by the name of Syrians or White Syrians.[6] This powerful people, whose native name of Cappadocians—under which they figure in the inscriptions of Darius—was well known to the historian, occupied in his time the whole of the interior of Asia Minor, from the river Halys on the west to the mountains of Armenia on the east, and from the Cilicians on the south to the shores of the Euxine. The Mariandynians (who here occur somewhat out of their place) though a comparatively insignificant tribe, were familiar to the Greeks from their occupying the shores of the Pontus in the neighbourhood of the flourishing Greek colony of Heraclea. The Chalybes or Chalybians, whose name is here omitted, but who are mentioned among the nations subdued by Crœsus,[7] occupied a district on the shores of the Euxine east of the Halys, which must also have been included within the limits of the third satrapy.

---

[4] vii 77. The names here appear under the slightly altered forms, Cabalians and Lysinians The discrepance of our existing manuscripts in regard to such obscure names is not to be wondered at

[5] vii 75   [6] 1. 72.

[7] 1 28 Mr Rawlinson suggests the insertion of their name in the catalogue of the army of Xerxes (vii 76), where the name of one of the nations described has undoubtedly fallen out of our MSS. The same conjecture was previously made by Wesseling (ad loc), but all such restitutions must be extremely uncertain, and the very rude style of equipment of the people in question appears unsuitable to a race so celebrated as the Chalybes for their skill as workers in metal

§ 6. The whole of the fourth province was occupied, according to Herodotus, by a single people—the Cilicians, to whom he assigns a far greater extent of territory than the later geographers, comprising not only the maritime province subsequently known by their name, but the whole chain of Mount Taurus, and the districts on each side of it, as far as the confines of Armenia and the Matienians. They were evidently a numerous and powerful people; and are distinguished as furnishing, in addition to an annual tribute of five hundred talents, three hundred and sixty white horses every year for the service of the Persian monarch.

The fifth province consisted of Syria (in the modern acceptation of the term) including Phœnicia and Palestine, with the island of Cyprus, and the sea-coast as far as the frontiers of Egypt, though the intervening strip of desert between these and the last outposts of Syria seems to have been always held by the Arabian tribes of the interior, who, though on friendly terms with the Persians, were never subject to the dominion of the Great King.

The sixth district consisted of Egypt, together with the Cyrenaica and the adjoining Libyan tribes. The Ethiopian tribes above Egypt, like the Arabians, were not subject to regular tribute, but presented an annual contribution in another form, consisting of gold-dust, ebony and ivory.

§ 7. Thus far the satrapies are enumerated by Herodotus in their natural geographical sequence; but he now—for what reason we know not—departs suddenly from that order, and enumerates as the seventh district one of the remotest provinces of the empire towards the east. The four nations of which it was composed are indeed all imperfectly known to us: and their geographical position has been a subject of doubt. But the Gandarians at least may be placed with reasonable certainty on the frontiers of India, in the modern Afghanistan,[8] and the

---

[8] We have seen that the Gandarians were already known, by name at least, to Hecatæus, who places the city of Caspapyrus in their territory (Hecatæus, Fr 178, 179) There can be no doubt that they are the same people who

other three tribes probably occupied parts of the same mountain-tract intervening between Bactria, Aria, and India. The Gandarians and the Dadicæ are again mentioned among the tribes that sent their contingents to the army of Xerxes; they were armed and equipped in the same manner as the Bactrians, but had a separate commander of their own. The Sattagydians and Aparytæ are not elsewhere mentioned, nor are the names found in any other ancient author: but the former have been identified with some plausibility with a people called in the Persian inscriptions Thatagush,—who there figure on the borders of Arachosia and India. It is to be observed that the name of the Arachosians does not appear in Herodotus; though it is found in the inscriptions of Darius, as well as in all the later Greek geographers: it is therefore not improbable that the district subsequently known as Arachosia formed a part of his seventh province, for which there would thus be ample room between Aria, Drangiana, and the frontiers of India.

§ 8. The eighth province consisted only of Susiana, or the land of the Cissians; corresponding nearly to the modern Khuzistan. It naturally derived its chief importance from the circumstance of Susa itself having become from the time of Darius the capital of the Persian monarchy, and for the same reason the name of the Cissians, which is hardly found in later geographers,[9] was familiar to the Greeks as early as the time of Æschylus.[1]

---

figure as the Gandharas in the legends and traditions of the Hindoos, and who appear to have been situated to the south of the Paropamisus or Hindoo Koosh (see Wilson's *Ariana*, pp 125, 131) The name is thought by many to be preserved in the modern Kandahar

The name of the Gandarii is not mentioned at the time of Alexander's expedition, but that of Gandaritis is applied by Strabo to a district west of the Indus in the valley of the Cabul river (xv p 697); and he also tells us that some gave the name of Gandaris to the territory beyond the Hydraotes, which was subject to the second Porus (Ib p 699) There can be little doubt however that the Gandarians of Herodotus and Hecatæus were a people to the west of the Indus

[9] Strabo only mentions it in passing as a name by which the Susians were *also* known (xv p 728) The modern name of Khuzistan is in some measure intermediate between the two.

[1] Æschyl *Persæ*, v 27

The ninth satrapy comprised all Babylonia and *the rest of Assyria*—a phrase of which it is not very easy to define the meaning. Herodotus generally makes no distinction between the Assyrians and Babylonians, and in his first book distinctly describes Babylon as *the capital of Assyria* after the fall of Nineveh. But we not only know that the two monarchies were in reality quite distinct; but the names of Assyria and Babylonia were retained in later times as characterizing separate districts; the former appellation, as thus employed, being confined to the great province *east* of the Tigris, of which Nineveh was the capital. Yet Herodotus, as we shall presently see, in describing the royal road from Sardis to Susa, appears to assign the whole tract on the left bank of the Tigris either to Armenia or Matiene, thus leaving no room on that side for Assyria at all. On the other hand he never uses the term Mesopotamia, which indeed could obviously never have been an ethnic appellation, and was probably only a term invented, or adopted, at a later period by Greek geographers.[2] It is therefore probable that the region which Herodotus meant to comprise in the ninth satrapy included all Mesopotamia as well as Babylonia, but did not extend to the east of the Tigris.

§ 9. The tenth government contained the important and well-known province of Media, of which Ecbatana was the capital,[3] together with two other tribes—the Paricanians and the Orthocorybantes—whose names are wholly unknown to us, though that of the Paricanians may perhaps be an altered form for Parætæcanians or Parætacenians, who are elsewhere mentioned by Herodotus as a Median tribe.

The eleventh district comprised four nations or tribes—none

---

[2] The name of Mesopotamia probably came into use among the Greeks after the conquests of Alexander It is in fact merely a translation of the name Aram-Naharaim, "Syria of the two rivers," by which the district was known to the Jews, and doubtless to the other Semitic nations. Arrian expressly tells us (*Anab.* vii 7, § 3) that it was a native appellation Among *extant* Greek authors it is first found in Polybius (v 44, 48)

[3] See Note E, p 258

of them apparently of much importance—the Caspians, the Pausicæ, the Pantimathi, and the Daritæ. The first of these was doubtless the same people that are found in the later geographers settled on the south-western shores of the sea to which they gave their name; they occupied the tract from the mouth of the river Cyrus or Kur to the S.W. angle of the Caspian Sea, known in modern times as Ghilan. The other three tribes, whose names are utterly unknown, may probably be placed on the southern shores of the same basin, in the modern province of Mazanderan, or the lofty mountains that bound it to the south. The greater part of this tract was included by later geographers in Hyrcania: but though the Hyrcanians figure in the array of the army of Xerxes, their name is not mentioned in the list of the satrapies.

§ 10. The twelfth satrapy included the Bactrians, "as far as the Ægli"—a tribe who have been supposed, but upon very slight grounds, to have been located upon the Iaxartes: this view, however, is difficult to reconcile with the fact that the Sogdians, of whose locality there is no doubt, and who intervened between the Bactrians and the Iaxartes, belonged to a different government. The twelfth satrapy was in fact probably confined to the Bactrians proper, who were doubtless in the time of Herodotus still a powerful and flourishing people.

The thirteenth province contained the Armenians, with the Pactyans, and other adjacent tribes extending to the shores of the Euxine. It must be observed that the Armenia of Herodotus was much less extensive than the country known by that name in later times, as he obviously assigned to the Saspeires or Saspirians, a considerable portion of the region known in later times as Eastern Armenia. The name of the Pactyans is not found elsewhere.[4]

---

[4] It is hardly necessary to observe that they were certainly distinct from the Pactyans, who adjoined the Indus, and in whose territory the city of Caspatyrus was situated (See above, p 227) But this case of the unquestionable occurrence of two distinct tribes of the same name in distant provinces, may act as a warning against the too hasty identification of different tribes, in other cases, merely on account of the similarity of name

The Pactyans who appear in the army of Xerxes (Herodot vii 67) were

§ 11. The fourteenth satrapy was an extensive one, and comprised some tribes known to be numerous and powerful, but whose limits are not easily defined. It included the Sagartians, Sarangeans, Thamanæans, Utians, and Mycians: "together with the islands in the Erythræan Sea." This last addition leads us to suppose that the southern limit of the province in question extended to the shores of the Indian Ocean.[5] and it is a plausible conjecture (though it must be admitted to be nothing more) that the Mycians occupied the district still called Mekran, on the southern border of the great table-land of Persia.[6] The Sarangeans may be confidently identified with the Zarangians or Drangians of later writers, who occupied the district now known as Seistan. On the other hand the Utians,—who appear in the army of Xerxes associated with the Mycians and Paricanians (evidently the people of that name assigned to the seventeenth satrapy), are otherwise unknown,[7] and can only be conjecturally placed in the southern portion of the empire, where they probably adjoined the Mycians. The Sagartians,—who were clearly a nomad race, and appear in the army of Xerxes as furnishing 8000 horsemen armed only with *lassoes*,—probably inhabited, or rather roamed over, the central districts adjoining the Great Desert of Iran. The Thamanæans are wholly unknown: but as Herodotus elsewhere[8] associates them with the Sarangians, Parthians, Hyrcanians, and Chorasmians, they evidently inhabited some part of the same great *plateau*.

§ 12. The fifteenth satrapy was composed of two nations only

---

clearly the *eastern* people of the name, from the borders of India.

[5] The islands in question can hardly be any other than those in the Persian Gulf, which (as already mentioned) Herodotus does not distinguish from the Erythræan Sea or Indian Ocean

[6] The name of the Mycians is cited also from Hecatæus *ap* Steph Byz s v Μυκοί, and the few words ἐκ Μυκῶν εἰς Ἀράξην ποταμόν may perhaps be regarded as affording an additional argument in favour of their being situated on the southern sea

[7] Major Rennell identifies the Utians with the Uxians of later writers, who inhabited the Bakhtiyari mountains, near Ispahan and between Susiana and Persepolis, but this is a mere conjecture The resemblance of name is by no means conclusive, and the mode in which they are associated with the Mycians, Paricanians, and Sarangeans would certainly lead us to a different conclusion

[8] iii 117

—the Sacæ and the Caspians. As the latter name has already occurred in the eleventh satrapy, and it is impossible to find a place for them here, in any connection with the Caspian Sea, it has been generally considered that the reading is corrupt, but none of the emendations proposed can be regarded as satisfactory. On the other hand the name of the Sacæ conveys little information, from the vague manner in which we know it to be employed. Herodotus himself tells us that the Persians gave the name of Sacæ or Sacans to all the Scythians; and this is confirmed by the evidence of the Persian inscriptions.[9] In the review of the army of Xerxes however we find the Sacæ in question associated under one commander with the Bactrians, though their arms and accoutrements were different. Hence it is probable that they were in reality the Scythian tribes bordering on the Bactrians and Sogdians to the east, a part of whom had submitted to pay tribute to the Persian king, and send their contingent to his armies. Their relations with the more civilized nations to which they adjoined were doubtless very similar to those of the Turcomans of the present day; nominally subject to the Persian Empire, when the government was strong, and lapsing into more complete independence whenever the pressure was removed.

§ 13. The sixteenth satrapy presents no geographical difficulties; all the four nations of which it was composed—the Parthians, Chorasmians, Sogdians and Arians—being well known. The Parthians, afterwards so celebrated a name, were at this time a comparatively unimportant people, inhabiting the slopes of the mountains on the north of the great plateau of Iran and the northern portion of the province now known as Khorasan. The Chorasmians, on the other side of the same mountain

---

[9] Herodot vIII 64 · The word used throughout the Persian inscriptions is "Saka." It is remarkable that Herodotus says the Sacæ in the army of Xerxes were in reality a Scythian tribe named Amyrgians ('Aμύργιοι), and in the inscription on the tomb of Darius at Naksh-i-Rustam one tribe of the Sacæ is distinguished as " Saka Humavarga " obviously the name which Herodotus has converted into Amyrgians (See Rawlinson's *Herodotus*, vol iv. p 65, notes 5, 6)

range, occupied the broad level tract east of the Caspian, known even at the present day by the name of Kharesm. The Sogdians held the fertile district eastward of the Chorasmians and north of the Bactrians, which was known to subsequent geographers by the name of Sogdiana, and has retained the appellation of Soghd down to our own times. Its position is most clearly marked by that of its capital, Maracanda or Samarcand. The Arians again occupied the tract on the southern slopes of the same chain of mountains, east of the Parthians, and within the limits of the modern Afghanistan, where their name is still preserved in that of Herat.

§ 14. The seventeenth satrapy consisted of two nations only; the Paricanians, whose name is otherwise unknown,[1] and the Ethiopians, whom Herodotus, for the sake of distinction, expressly terms the *Asiatic* Ethiopians. There is no doubt that these last,—who were associated in the army of Xerxes with the Indians,—were the inhabitants of the south coast of Beloochistan, extending along the Erythræan Sea from the mouths of the Indus to the entrance of the Persian Gulf; where to this day a people is found that are almost black, and as backward in civilization as they could have been in the days of Herodotus.[2] The Paricanians were probably the people of the interior of the same district, who may have been as superior to the inhabitants of the coast, as the Belooches are at the present time to the miserable race still found along the seaboard. The Ethiopians of Herodotus are doubtless the same people as were called by later Greek geographers the Ichthyophagi; the name of Gedrosia applied by them to Beloochistan in general is not found in Herodotus.

Nor does the far more flourishing and important province of Carmania (Kerman), appear in the list of the satrapies; but as Herodotus elsewhere includes the Germanians[3]—evidently

---

[1] They are certainly distinct from the people of the same name already mentioned in the tenth satrapy.
[2] vii. 78.

[3] i 125. This remarkable form of the name leads Mr Rawlinson to observe that it "may teach us caution in basing theories of ethnic affinity on a

the same people—among the agricultural Persian tribes, there can be little doubt that they were in his time included in Persia proper, which paid no tribute, and consequently do not figure in the list of provinces.

§ 15. We now return again to the north-west of the empire, where the Matienians, Saspirians and Alarodians composed the eighteenth satrapy. Of these the Matienians are well known as occupying a part of the high mountain tract on the borders of Armenia and Media, though it is difficult to fix their precise limits or situation;[4] the Saspirians or Saspeires have been already mentioned, as one of the four nations which, according to Herodotus, filled up the whole space from the southern to the northern sea. They are there placed between the Medians and the Colchians,[5] and must therefore have occupied the eastern portion of Armenia, on the confines of the modern Georgia.[6] The Alarodians are otherwise unknown,[7] though they figure again, in company with the Saspeires, in the army of Xerxes.

The nineteenth satrapy, which must have adjoined the preceding, was made up of a number of small nations or tribes between the borders of Armenia and the Euxine. Of these

---

mere name" (Rawlinson's *Herodotus*, vol. 1 p 672, note 3) It would have been well if he had more constantly borne in mind his own warning.

[4] It is remarkable that the Carduchians, who were found in possession of this mountain tract by Xenophon, and who were doubtless the same people as the modern Kurds, who have possessed it ever since, are not mentioned by Herodotus It is probable indeed that these lawless mountaineers were very imperfectly subject to the Persian rule, but as Herodotus appears to assign a much more important and extensive territory to the Matieni than they are found occupying in later times, it is not unlikely that he included in this a considerable portion of the tract really held by the Carduchians The limits of these mountain tribes must have been in all ages very uncertain.

[5] iv 37 The same statement is found also in i 104

[6] The attempt made by Mr Rawlinson (*Herodotus*, vol. iv p 229) to identify these Saspeires, or Sapeires (as the name is written in some MSS. of Herodotus) with the Iberians of later geographers, on philological grounds, appears to me very far-fetched and unsatisfactory. The ethnography of this part of Asia was even in the time of Herodotus almost as complicated as it is at the present day.

[7] The conjecture that the name of the Alarodians is connected with that of Ararat is not without some plausibility but if Sir H Rawlinson is correct in applying the name of Ararat to Armenia in general, we are left in complete uncertainty as to the geographical position of the particular tribe.

the Moschi or Moschians appear to have been confined to the interior, adjoining the Colchians, and did not extend to the sea-coast. The Macrones, Mosynœci and Tibareni may be placed with certainty on the coast of the Euxine, where they were encountered not long afterwards by Xenophon and his army.[8] Of these the Tibarenians lay the farthest towards the west, while the Macrones were situated in the neighbourhood of Trebizond. Between them and the Colchians must apparently be placed the obscure tribe of the Mares, mentioned only by Herodotus and Hecatæus. The Colchians themselves enjoyed a state of semi-independence, not being included in any satrapy, nor subject to any regular tribute, but sending every fourth year *a present* of 100 youths and 100 maidens to the court of the Great King.[9] It is clear therefore that in this direction the Persian dominion extended nominally to the great mountain barrier of the Caucasus.

The twentieth and last satrapy was that of India. The extent and limits of the Persian dominions in this quarter have been already discussed.

§ 16. In reviewing the elaborate list thus given by Herodotus of the numerous and varied races that made up the population of the Persian Empire, it will be seen that it departs altogether from anything like geographical arrangement. It is equally clear that it has no pretence to an ethnographical character, in the modern sense of the term—kindred tribes being assigned to different provinces, while others which appear to have belonged to wholly distinct races are united under one head. Its arrangement and purpose can only be clearly understood by regarding it as really what it professes to be—an authentic *statistical* account of the provinces into which the Persian Empire was divided, for administrative, or at least for fiscal, purposes; and the addition to every district of the amount of tribute at which it was assessed, clearly indicates that the whole statement must have been derived

---

[8] Xenophon, *Anabasis*, iv 7, v 45   [9] Herodot iii. 97.

from some authentic, and in the first instance doubtless an official, source.¹ The reasons for the peculiar arrangement followed we cannot divine; nor is it of much importance. It would be more interesting to know why in some cases the names of obscure and unimportant tribes are separately enumerated; while in others they are all included under one general head. Some of the more important omissions from the catalogue are also difficult to account for. But, whatever its imperfections, the list remains as one of the most valuable and important contributions to our knowledge of Western Asia, and affords a remarkable proof of the acquaintance already possessed by the Greeks with the resources of their formidable neighbour.

§ 17. There is another passage in Herodotus, which may deserve consideration by the side of that in which he enumerates the satrapies, because it contains the names of several of the nations of Upper Asia which figure in the list referred to. It is worthy of notice also as one of the few instances in which he gives us any information concerning the physical geography of that part of the great continent. Unfortunately the passage is one that presents difficulties of which we are unable to give any satisfactory explanation.

He tells us :² "There is a plain in Asia which is shut in on all sides by a mountain range, and this range has five openings. This plain once belonged to the Chorasmians, and is situated on the confines of the Chorasmians themselves, the Hyrcanians, Parthians, Sarangians and Thamanæans. But since the establishment of the Persian Empire, it belongs to the Great King. Out of the mountains which enclose the plain there flows a great river called the Aces, which was formerly divided into

---

[1] The authenticity of this record is not in my opinion at all impaired by the circumstance that there is some error in the numbers of our existing text, which prevents the aggregate of the separate tributes from agreeing with the sum total as computed by Herodotus himself (iii 95) The error is one which it is impossible for us now to correct, but such mistakes in numbers are of such common occurrence in Greek MSS that they raise no presumption against the accuracy of the original statement   [2] iii 117.

five streams and irrigated the territories of the aforesaid nations, passing through the several openings in the mountains to the corresponding people." After the Persian conquest however, the king took possession of the plain, and closed up all the outlets, so that he could at pleasure convert the plain into a lake, or, by opening one of the passages at a time, allow the water to flow out and irrigate the lands of any one of the nations interested. But this concession was never granted without the payment of a heavy sum of money, in addition to the ordinary tribute levied upon the people.

It is hardly necessary to say that the statement here presented to us is obviously, in its actual form, a fiction. No such valley or stream as those described by Herodotus could ever have existed in nature: but, allowing for obvious exaggeration, there can be no doubt that the story had some foundation in fact, and that the Persian government actually availed itself of the possession of the mountain valleys and the streams that flowed from them to regulate the supply of water, upon which the inhabitants of the low country were mainly dependent for the cultivation of their lands. Even at the present day in many districts of Persia the distribution of the water supply is an important source of revenue to the government. But the particular locality intended by Herodotus cannot be determined with any approximation to certainty. The names of the Chorasmians, Hyrcanians and Parthians would lead us to seek it in the mountain district in the north of Khorasan, forming the prolongation of the Elburz range towards the Paropamisus or Hindoo Koosh. But no river can be found in this region which at all answers the description. The name of the Aces is not found in any of the later geographers, and it has been vainly sought to identify it with the Oxus, which flows from a totally different region, and even with the Acesines! A more plausible suggestion is that it is the same with the Ochus or Tedjend, which has its source in the mountains near Meshed.[3]

---

[3] This river is apparently identical with, or receives as a tributary, the Heri-rud, or river of Herat But the physical geography of this part of the Persian Empire is still but imperfectly known

But it is clear that no river can really answer the description of Herodotus, by irrigating five different regions, situated in different directions. The most probable explanation of the story is therefore that there were really five rivers—each of the nations designated having its particular stream; and that these, which really flowed from the same range of mountains, were erroneously supposed to have had their common origin in one central valley. The possession of such a stream, and the power of applying it to purposes of irrigation, is in fact the *condition of existence* for any people in this part of Asia, and in this respect the statement of Herodotus is well founded. But it would be idle to attempt to identify the particular streams to which the account of his informants may really have referred. Even in modern times the rivers of this part of Asia were until quite recently very imperfectly known; in some cases indeed it may be doubted whether we yet possess correct information concerning them.

SECTION 3.—*Royal Road to Susa.*

§ 1. Before quitting the subject of Asia, there is one other passage of Herodotus that demands our attention, as partaking to an unusual extent of a positive geographical character, in which the historian has given us full and detailed particulars concerning the line of route from Sardis to Susa. The account in question is introduced (like many other episodes in Herodotus) in so singular a manner, and on an occasion when it is apparently so uncalled for, that we can only suppose the historian to have been desirous to communicate to his readers the information which he himself possessed, and to have availed himself of any opportunity for the purpose. According to his narrative, Aristagoras, the tyrant of Miletus, being desirous of obtaining the assistance of the Spartans in his revolt against Persia, presented himself before Cleomenes, king of Sparta, bringing with him a tablet of bronze, on which was engraved a map of the whole earth, with all the seas and rivers,[4] on which he pointed out to him the position of all the different nations that were subject to the Persian yoke, and lay on the line of route from Sardis to the capital.

These were, according to his enumeration; first, the Lydians, who immediately bordered on the Ionians; next, beyond the Lydians towards the east, the Phrygians; then, the Cappadocians; after them, the Cilicians, whose territory extended to the sea in which Cyprus was situated. Beyond these came the Armenians, and after them the Matieni, who extended to the confines of the Cissians, in whose territory Susa itself was situated—the city that was the residence of the Great King, and where all his countless treasures were deposited.[5]

Aristagoras, being afterwards interrogated by Cleomenes as to the length of time that would be required for the march up the country to Susa, unguardedly replied that it would be a three months' march; upon which Cleomenes at once broke off the negotiation. Herodotus, while blaming him for his imprudence, proceeds to show that the statement of Aristagoras was substantially correct, and in so doing gives us a curious and detailed account of the route in question.[6]

§ 2. This road (he tells us) throughout its whole course traversed an inhabited and secure country, and was marked from distance to distance by royal stations, where there were excellent sleeping-places or—as they would now be called—caravanserais. The distances also from one of these stations to another appear to have been well known, and they are enumerated by Herodotus with as much confidence, though not in the same detail, as those given by Xenophon in describing the march of Cyrus. In traversing Lydia and Phrygia (from Sardis to the river Halys) there were 20 stations, the distance being 94½ para-

---

[4] v. 49 τῷ δὴ ἐς λόγους ἤιε, ὡς Λακεδαιμόνιοι λέγουσι, ἔχων χάλκεον πίνακα ἐν τῷ γῆς ἁπάσης περίοδος ἐνετέτμητο, καὶ θάλασσά τε πᾶσα, καὶ ποταμοὶ πάντες

It is probable, as has been already pointed out, that this map, which appears to have been the first ever seen at Sparta, was copied from that drawn by Anaximander of Miletus See Chap IV p 122

[5] Herodot v 49   [6] Ibid v 52, 53

sangs. Here it was necessary to cross the Halys, which was strongly guarded, and to pass through a fortified post, with gates on the river. Thence through Cappadocia to the frontiers of Cilicia were 28 stations and 104 parasangs. The frontier was here guarded by a double set of gates and fortresses. Thence across Cilicia were only three days' journey, comprising 15½ parasangs. The river Euphrates, which could only be crossed in boats, formed the boundary between Cilicia and Armenia. In Armenia there were 15 stations, and the distance was 56½ parasangs. But in this part of the march there were four rivers to be crossed, none of which could be passed otherwise than in boats. The first of these was the Tigris; the second and third bore the same name, though they were distinct rivers, and the one had its source in the Armenian mountains, the other in those of the Matienians; the fourth was the Gyndes, already mentioned by Herodotus on a former occasion.[7] From Armenia the road entered Matiene, where were four stations (the distance is omitted), and thence into the land of the Cissians, in which 11 days' journey, and a distance of 42½ parasangs, brought one to the river Choaspes, on which Susa was situated. Thus (concludes our author) there are in all a hundred and eleven stations on the way from Sardis to Susa, and "if (he adds) the distances are correctly measured in parasangs, and the parasang is equivalent to 30 stadia (as it really is), the whole distance from Sardis to the palace at Susa would be 450 parasangs, or 13,500 stadia, which, at the rate of 150 stadia for each day's journey, would take exactly 90 days; thus tallying precisely with the computation of Aristagoras."[8]

§ 3. The itinerary thus presented to us is not only interesting as the first of a long series of documents of the kind, from which we shall derive important assistance, but is in itself a valuable contribution to our geographical knowledge. The particularity

---

[7] i 189 It was this river which, according to the strange story told by Herodotus, the elder Cyrus caused to be divided into 360 channels, in vengeance for one of his sacred horses having been carried away by the violence of the current, and drowned

[8] v 53

with which it is described is such as to show clearly that it was originally derived from some authentic source; but when we come to examine it in detail we encounter considerable difficulties. In the first place, the numbers are certainly inaccurate, for the sum of the separate distances does not agree with the sum total as given by Herodotus himself. In this instance, however, there is no difficulty in determining on which side the error lies; for the numbers given in summing up the general result are not only perfectly consistent with one another, but they agree with the conclusion which Herodotus meant to establish, namely, that the estimate of Aristagoras of 90 days, or three months, for the march up the country, was a correct one. The error must therefore lie in the details, and here it is much more difficult to detect it. The line of route here described, though styled "the royal road," and evidently the one habitually followed in the time of Herodotus, appears to have subsequently fallen into comparative disuse, and is not given in detail by any later geographer.[9] Moreover the boundaries of the different nations through which it lay are given very differently from those found in other writers, and if we adhere to our existing text (supposing the numbers only to be corrupt), it is certain that Herodotus must have assigned both to Cilicia[1] and Armenia a much greater extent than that which is usually given to them. The latter country in particular is made to include the whole tract on the left bank of the Tigris, or

---

[9] The younger Cyrus, when advancing towards Babylon, took a wholly different line of route—as did Alexander after him—descending at once through the passes of the Taurus into Cilicia, and thence crossing into the plains of Syria and Mesopotamia This is undoubtedly the most direct line and that which has been followed by most modern travellers But it was probably avoided in the time of Herodotus on account of the insecurity of the line through the Syrian deserts—a consideration which would not affect a general marching at the head of an army

Major Rennell has erroneously supposed the "royal road" to have been the same with that followed by Cyrus and described by Xenophon hence his examination of its details is rendered wholly worthless.

[1] The portion of Cilicia traversed by this route could be no other than the district of Melitene, which is not included by any other geographer under the name of Cilicia The "gates" mentioned by Herodotus cannot therefore be the well-known pass of the Pylæ Ciliciæ, traversed both by Cyrus and Alexander

Assyria Proper, as far as the river Gyndes. Fortunately the four rivers mentioned by Herodotus in this part of the route can be clearly identified: the Gyndes, as shown by Major Rennell and Mr. Rawlinson, can be no other than the river now called Diyalah or Dialeh,[2] which falls into the Tigris a little below Bagdad; the other two, *which had the same name*, were clearly the Greater and Lesser Zab, both of which were known in ancient, as well as in modern times, by the same appellation of Zabatus.[3] But if the Gyndes be taken as the frontier between Armenia and Matiene, the enormous extension thus given to Armenia is altogether at variance with the distance assigned to this part of the route;[4] the march through Assyria, from the river Gyndes to the neighbourhood of Mosul—the lowest point at which the road could well have crossed the Tigris,—being alone fully equal to the 56 parasangs allowed to Armenia, thus leaving the whole intermediate space, from the Euphrates to the Tigris, unaccounted for.[5]

These discrepancies in the details are the more to be regretted, as the sum total of 13,500 stadia, or 1350 G. miles, would appear to be a very fair approximation to the truth, so far as it is possible to judge without knowing the exact line of route. This lends additional confirmation to the conclusion already stated that the particular description of this "royal road" was derived by Herodotus from authentic and trustworthy information; and that he was led in consequence to find a place for it in his history.

§ 4. But notwithstanding the difficulties attending the adjustment of the details, as well as the uncertainty arising from the want of any trustworthy mode of computing distances,[6] it

---

[2] See Rennell's *Geogr of Herodot* pp 201, 327, Rawlinson's *Herodotus*, vol 1 p. 325, note 5

[3] This passage has been strangely misconceived by the author of the article TIGRIS in Di Smith's *Dict of Ancient Geography*, who supposes that Herodotus meant to say that the two rivers had *the same name with the Tigris*, and that "there were three rivers bearing the name of Tigris," which has the effect of wholly marring the accuracy of the author's statement, and throwing the whole subject into confusion

[4] It must be added that it is equally at variance with the extent assigned to Armenia in the description of the Satrapies

[5] Note F, p 259   [6] Note G, p. 261.

will be found that the route indicated by Herodotus may be traced with approximate certainty, if we assume it to represent what may be called *the upper road* from Sardis to the valley of the Tigris. As has been pointed out by M. Kiepert,[7] this would coincide *in great measure* with one of the great lines of the Roman roads, established at a much later period, which led from Sardis through Synnada and Pessinus to Ancyra, and thence to the passage of the Halys; from whence it continued onwards through Cappadocia to Cabira or Sebaste. Here it must have turned southwards, through Melitene, a district which Herodotus appears to have assigned to Cilicia; and from thence crossed the Euphrates into Armenia, and traversed that country (passing near the modern Diarbekr) to the passage of the Tigris, probably at Djezireh or Bezabde. Hence it would follow the left bank of that river, more or less closely, crossing in succession the other three rivers already noticed—the Greater and Lesser Zab, and the Diyala or Gyndes—until it diverged to Susa.

The line of route thus indicated has the advantage of crossing the Halys, the Euphrates and the Tigris, at points well known and frequented in all ages for the passage of those rivers.[8] This must always have been one of the most important considerations either for an army or a mere caravan; and, as we shall see, was in fact the determining cause which decided the line of retreat of the Ten Thousand Greeks under Xenophon.

---

[7] His memoir is inserted in the *Monatsberichte der Berliner Akademie* for 1857, pp. 123-140.

[8] Mr. Rawlinson, who supposes (*Herodotus*, vol iii p 258, note) the route followed to be the more direct line through the heart of Asia Minor, by Ak Shehr (Philomelium) and Kaisariyeh (Cæsarea) to Malatiyeh, has overlooked the important consideration that this road *does not cross the Halys at all*, the passage of which river is one of the points strongly insisted on by Herodotus.

NOTE A, p. 226.

INDIAN TRIBUTE.

THE Indians, according to Herodotus, paid a tribute in gold dust (ψήγματος) amounting to 360 talents of gold, which he reckons as equal to 4680 Euboic talents of silver. But where he compares this with the tribute of the other provinces there is some corruption in the text, which we are unable to correct with certainty; his calculations not being consistent with themselves.[9] Upon every supposition however the sum derived from India was enormously large, amounting in any case to nearly a third of the whole Persian revenues.

It is difficult to determine the exact meaning of the phrase used by Herodotus in speaking of the Indians φόρον ἀπαγίνεον πρὸς πάντας τοὺς ἄλλους. It certainly does not mean, as it is translated by Gronovius and Larcher, that the amount they paid was equal to that of all the rest; for this is wholly at variance with the statement of Herodotus himself concerning those amounts.[1] A comparison with the other passages cited by Schweighæuser—especially with viii. 44, where the Athenians are described as παρεχόμενοι νέας πρὸς πάντας τοὺς ἄλλους—seems to show clearly that in both cases the author means to indicate that the amount furnished was so exceptionally large as to deserve to be reckoned separately, and to be thus worthy of comparison with the sum total. In the case of the Athenians at Salamis indeed the Athenian fleet was very nearly equal to that of the other allies—180 ships out of 378—but this was certainly not the case with the Indian tribute.

---

[9] According to our present text he computes the whole revenue (including the Indian tribute) at 14,560 Euboic talents but his own figures would give only 13,710 such talents It is impossible now to say where the error lies.

[1] Mr Rawlinson translates it "a tribute exceeding that of every other people," which is somewhat ambiguous, but the original can hardly mean that it was greater than that of any other people taken singly

NOTE B, p. 227.

SCYLAX OF CARYANDA.

Scylax was a native of Caryanda, a city of Caria, within a very short distance of Halicarnassus. It was doubtless owing to the circumstance of his having accompanied the expedition that Herodotus had heard of it at all, but he had evidently nothing but very vague information concerning it, probably merely such rumours as might reach his native city, without Scylax having himself returned thither.

It is hardly necessary to say that the Periplus extant under the name of Scylax of Caryanda belongs to a much later date, being composed at least a century after the time of Herodotus. (This question will be fully discussed in Chapter XI.)

Dr. Vincent, in his elaborate disquisition on the voyage of Nearchus, has argued strongly against the reality of this voyage of Scylax. (*Commerce and Navigation of the Ancients in the Indian Ocean*, vol. i. pp. 301-310.) His arguments are, as from the nature of the case they must be, merely of a general kind, and it must be admitted that where our information is so vague and indefinite, it is impossible to do more than arrive at a conclusion upon such general impressions. But the voyage was not one to be compared in point of difficulty with that of the Phœnicians round Africa. the regularity of the winds at certain seasons in these seas is such as greatly to facilitate its accomplishment. and above all, the circumstance of its being commanded by a Greek and a countryman of Herodotus gives an authenticity to his source of information which is wanting in the case of the enterprise of Necho.

NOTE C, p. 228.

CASPATYRUS.

The city called by Herodotus Caspatyrus (Κασπάτυρος) is evidently the same that was already known to Hecatæus under the name of Caspapyrus (Steph. Byz. v. Κασπάπυρος. Hecatæus, Fr. 179), but that author calls it a city of the Gandarians, who are not included by Herodotus among the *Indian* tribes. The Pactyans are not mentioned by any subsequent writer, and neither their name, nor that of Caspatyrus is found in the account of Alexander's campaigns in this part of India. Heeren identifies Caspatyrus with the modern Cabul, while several other writers, among them Lassen (*Indische Alterthumer*, ii. p. 630) and Humboldt (*Asie Centrale*) would transfer it to Cashmir. But it certainly seems to be implied by the expressions of Herodotus concerning the voyage of Scylax that he regarded it as situated *on* the Indus. Beyond this we have really no clue to its position. Prof. Wilson considers the name of Caspapyrus to be identical with that of Casyapa-pur, or the city of Casyapa, which according to Sanscrit writers was the original appellation of Cashmir (*Ariana*, p. 137): but he points out that the name of Cashmir in early times was much more extensive than at present, and comprehended great part of the Punjab. He justly maintains that the city, from whence Scylax embarked on his expedition, must have been situated *on* the Indus.

The name is not found in the later Greek writers on India.

NOTE D, p. 230.

INDIAN ANTS.

Perhaps the most plausible suggestion is that of Professor Wilson (*Ariana*, p. 135), that the whole story arose from the circumstance of the gold collected in the plains of Little Thibet being commonly known as "ant-gold"—Pippilika—in consequence of a belief that it was laid bare by the ants, in the process of constructing their nests.

But this story seems to have got mixed up with one,—which may well have been founded upon fact,—of gold-dust being really brought to light by some kind of quadrupeds in the excavation of their holes or burrows. It was to these animals—perhaps of the marmot tribe—that the *skins* seen by Nearchus must undoubtedly have belonged; and specimens of them may, as asserted by Herodotus, have been sent to the court of Persia.[2] It may be added that the skins of these marmots are among the commonest of all the furs now brought to India.

---

[2] See Cunningham's *Ladak*, p. 233 (Lond. 1854).

NOTE E, p. 240.

ECBATANA.

Neither here nor in any other passage does Herodotus indicate the least doubt as to the city designated by him as Ecbatana, or Agbatana as he writes the name, which was one familiar to all the Greeks, long before his time, as one of the most famous cities of Asia (see the 'Persæ' of Æschylus, v. 16, 530) Nor is there the slightest hint to be found in any other ancient author of the existence of any other city of the name than the far-famed capital of Media: the site of which, though it has been the subject of considerable discussion, may be considered as conclusively established at the modern Hamadan. It is true that the description given by Herodotus (i. 90) of the city of Deioces, with its royal palace surrounded by seven circuits of walls, having their battlements of seven different colours, is wholly at variance with the situation of Hamadan but this whole account is so fanciful that it is very probably of mythical origin, and no allusion to anything of the kind is found in ancient authors who described the capital of Media from more authentic information. Polybius, however (who is unquestionably speaking of the city well known in his time) describes it as possessing a citadel of great strength and a palace of such surpassing extent and magnificence, as may well have given rise to exaggerated and fabulous reports   (Polyb. x. 27.)

The hypothesis suggested by Sir H. Rawlinson (in an elaborate memoir inserted in the *Journal of the Geographical Society*, vol. x), that there were two cities of the name of Ecbatana, one of them on the site of Hamadan, the other in Media Atropatene, or Azerbijan, at a place called Takht-i-Suleiman, where extensive ruins are still visible, is not supported by any ancient authority. nor is there in fact any other foundation for it than a notice by Moses of Chorene (an Armenian writer of the fifth century) in which he tells us that Ganzaca or Gazaca (the site of which is identified by Sir H. Rawlinson with Takht-i-Suleiman) was called "the second Ecbatana or the seven-walled city." (Mos Choren. ii. 84.) On the other hand Strabo distinctly tells us (xi. 13, p. 522) that Media was divided into two provinces, "the one called Great Media, of which Ecbatana was the capital, a great city, and containing the royal residence of the Median monarchs, the other called the Atropatian Media" It would be difficult to indicate more clearly that there was only *one* Ecbatana, and that was the well-known city, still flourishing in the time of Strabo, and used by the Parthian monarchs as their summer residence.

But Sir H. Rawlinson regards this passage, as well as many others, as only proving the confusion of ideas prevalent among the Greek geographers with regard to the *two* Ecbatanas, and even believes that Polybius fell into the same error and "confounded distinct notices of two different cities" in the elaborate description that he has left us of the Median capital, which was taken and plundered by Antiochus the Great. It would certainly seem more natural to suppose that a late writer like Moses of Chorene should have made a blunder in the single passage cited from him, than that all the historians and geographers, who wrote upon the affairs of Asia from the days of Alexander downwards, were ignorant of so important a fact in its geography.

NOTE F, p. 253.

ROYAL ROAD TO SUSA.

The only satisfactory solution of this difficulty is that proposed by Kiepert, to transfer the whole of these stations in Assyria from Armenia to Matiene, which would be quite in accordance with the comparative importance elsewhere allowed by Herodotus to that people. On the other hand, the position in which Matiene now occurs, *after* passing the river Gyndes, and occupying only a short space before coming to the frontiers of Susiana, is wholly unintelligible. The omission of the number of parasangs in this instance only, must certainly be the fault of our MSS., and points therefore to the existence of some corruption in the text. Moreover the most cursory examination of the route will show that it is in this portion of it that the 30 stations wanting to complete the sum total must have fallen out For the whole distance, after crossing the Euphrates to the passage of the Diyalah is not less than 400 G. miles, as measured on the map, and could not therefore have been computed at less than 140 parasangs, allowing for the windings of the road. Yet our existing text allows it only 56½ parasangs. a distance that would just about suffice for the route from the Euphrates to the Tigris, if we suppose the latter river to have been crossed at Djezireh (Bezabde), in all ages one of the most customary places of passage. In this case there remain about 240 G. miles *through Matiene* to the Gyndes or Diyala, which would not be sufficient to allow of the introduction of the 30 additional stations. But it is by no means clear that the Gyndes was the frontier. the boundary of Susiana was usually placed considerably farther south —and the distance from the frontier, according to Herodotus, to the city of Susa, being only 42½ parasangs, imperatively requires that it should be so in this case also.

In accordance with this hypothesis M. Kiepert (in the memoir referred to in the text, p. 254), who has been followed by Stein, in his recent edition of Herodotus (Berlin, 1859) proposes to read the passage of Herodotus (v. 52) after the sentence ἐν δὲ τῇ Ἀρμενίῃ . . . καὶ φυλακτήριον ἐν αὐτοῖσι as follows. ἐκ δὲ ταύτης [τῆς Ἀρμενίης] ἐσβάλλοντι ἐς τὴν Ματιηνὴν γῆν σταθμοί εἰσι τέσσερες καὶ τριήκοντα, παρασάγγαι δὲ ἑπτὰ καὶ τριήκοντα καὶ ἑκατόν, ποταμοὶ δὲ νηυσιπέρητοι τέσσερες διὰ ταύτης ῥέουσι, κ.τ.λ.

It must be admitted that the violence done to the existing text by this alteration is such as cannot be readily justified. But the passage as it stands is certainly defective and therefore corrupt. the numbers are confessedly erroneous. and the proposed correction renders the geographical explanation so satisfactory as to raise a strong presumption in its favour. But without attaching too much importance to the proposed correction as far as the numbers are concerned, it appears to me that there can be no doubt that a confusion has arisen between Armenia and Matiene, and that the passage concerning the four rivers applies to the *latter*, and not to the *former*, country. If this be once admitted, the whole geography of the route becomes comparatively clear.

It has been already observed that Herodotus appears to have given an extension and importance to the name of the Matieni far beyond that assigned to them by any other writer, and apparently includes great part of Media under that appellation. Now it is to be remarked that Xenophon in describing the march of the Greeks up the left bank of the Tigris, assigns all this portion of route, which lay through the Assyria of later geographers, to *Media*—a misconception clearly analogous to that of Herodotus.

NOTE G, p. 253.

UNCERTAINTY OF MEASUREMENT.

It must always be borne in mind in discussing this route, as well as all similar cases, that the parasang of the ancient Persians (like the *farsang* or *farsakh* of their modern descendants) was doubtless a mere itinerary measure, computed in reality from the time occupied in performing each journey, and liable therefore to considerable fluctuation. Herodotus, as well as Xenophon, reckons it equal to 30 stadia, which was probably a fair *average* computation: but Strabo points out that it varied considerably in different districts. The modern Persian farsakh is said to vary from 3 to 4 English miles, or from about 26 to 36 stadia.

Mr. Grote, in a note on the distances given in parasangs by Xenophon (vol. ix. p. 19, note), has justly pointed out that these *must* in many instances have been the result of mere computation. and would be very often greatly in excess of the truth. But he regards the distances given by Herodotus along the "royal road" as having been the result of actual measurement—a conclusion in which I cannot at all concur. Notwithstanding the use of the *word* measured ($\mu\epsilon\mu\acute{\epsilon}\tau\rho\eta\tau\alpha\iota$) by Herodotus, there appears to me no doubt that he meant nothing more than that kind of popular measurement, by estimation, which naturally comes to be applied to any frequented route, especially where it is traversed by regular couriers or messengers. Thus we find Mr. Ussher, in his recent journey from London to Persepolis (Lond. 1865), giving the distances on the route from Teheran to Tabreez in Persian *farsakhs* (or parasangs) because along this part of the road *he was able to travel post*, and consequently the computed distances were well known. Everywhere else he gives merely the time actually employed in hours of travelling. But this most convenient mode of estimating distances was wanting to Herodotus and Xenophon, from the want of any portable instrument for the measurement of hours.

That Herodotus meant nothing more than this, appears to me clear from his phrase, εἰ δὲ ὀρθῶς μεμέτρηται ἡ ὁδὸς ἡ βασιληίη τοῖσι παρασάγγῃσι; had the distances been really "measured and marked" from station to station, it could scarcely have occurred to him to express any doubt upon the subject.

CHAPTER VIII.

GEOGRAPHY OF HERODOTUS: AFRICA.

SECTION 1.—*General Knowledge of the Continent.*

§ 1. THE amount of knowledge possessed by Herodotus concerning the continent of Africa appears at first sight to present a striking contrast with his ignorance of the remoter regions of Europe. But the contrast is more apparent than real; and will be found to arise rather from our own familiarity with the one, and our comparatively imperfect knowledge of the other, than from any real superiority in the information possessed by Herodotus. His knowledge of the southern shores of the Mediterranean was in fact much of the same character with that of his acquaintance with the opposite coasts. There seems no doubt that he had himself visited Cyrene,[1] which was at that time an important centre of Greek life and civilization, and he had there obtained a pretty correct general account of the coasts of Africa and the tribes that inhabited them as far as the Lesser Syrtis and the confines of the Carthaginian territory. Beyond this to the west he either possessed no information, or did not think fit to communicate it to his readers. He was indeed, as has been already stated, familiar in a general way with the greatness and power of Carthage and the extent of

---

[1] The only passage from which this can be *directly* inferred is in Book II c 181, where he mentions a statue consecrated by Ladice, the Greek wife of Amasis, which was still existing in his t me, outside the gates of Cyrene, in a manner that clearly implies that he had seen it But the whole account of Cyrene and the adjoining regions in the fourth book bears throughout the stamp of having been derived from personal inquiries on the spot Indeed it is probably to this visit to Cyrene that we are indebted for the whole of this valuable and curious episode (iv c 105-125), which is very remotely connected with the general subject of his work.

her dominions; and he more than once cites the information which he had received from Carthaginians—probably merchants whom he had met at Cyrene or elsewhere.[2] But it may be taken as certain that he had not visited Carthage itself; and much of the information which he had thus picked up was of a vague and desultory character.

With regard to the interior of the continent, what knowledge he possessed was derived from two sources—partly from the information he was able to obtain in Egypt, and partly from the accounts that he gathered from his countrymen at Cyrene. But the natural peculiarities of Africa must in all ages have presented an almost insuperable barrier to intercourse with the interior; and these difficulties must have been vastly increased in ancient times by the want of camels, which do not appear to have been introduced into Africa until a much later period.[3] Hence the great desert, which extends almost without interruption from the confines of Egypt and Nubia to the Atlantic Ocean, naturally formed the limit of the knowledge possessed by the Greeks towards the south; and with one remarkable exception—to which we shall hereafter have occasion to revert— Herodotus appears to have had no conception that beyond this desert tract, there existed habitable and even populous regions. The course of the Nile was then, as it remains at the present day, the only natural highway from the Mediterranean to the remoter regions of Africa.

§ 2. But with the upper part of that river Herodotus was very imperfectly acquainted. As far as the confines of Egypt it was of course well known; and the historian had himself ascended it as far as Elephantine, just below the First Cataracts.[4] But he had also obtained what he believed to be precise and authentic information concerning its course for a considerable distance higher up, which he has imparted to us in a very curious passage. "Above Elephantine (he tells us) the ground

---

[2] Herodot. iv. 43, 195, 196, vii. 167.
[3] See Note A, p. 299
[4] μέχρι μὲν 'Ελεφαντίνης πόλιος αὐ-

τόπτης ἐλθών, τὸ δ' ἀπὸ τούτου ἀκοῇ ἤδη ἱστορέων, ιι. 29. See Note B, p 299

has a considerable slope, so that it is necessary for the boats which ascend the river to be fastened with tow-ropes on each side, and thus dragged up the stream. If the ropes should break, the boat is carried away at once by the violence of the current. This kind of navigation continues for four days' voyage, during which the river winds very much, like the Mæander. The whole distance which it is requisite to traverse in this manner is twelve *schœni*. After that you come to a level plain, in which the Nile encloses an island named Tachompso. Of this one half is occupied by the Ethiopians, who inhabit all the country above it: the other half by the Egyptians. Adjoining this is a large lake, the shores of which are inhabited by nomad Ethiopian tribes: the Nile flows into it, and you re-enter the stream after traversing the lake. But here you are compelled to land, to travel along the banks of the river for forty days: the navigation being rendered impossible by the number of sharp rocks and ledges, which occur in this part of the stream. After traversing this tract in forty days, you embark in another vessel and sail up the river for twelve days, at the end of which you come to a great city called Meroe, which is considered as the metropolis of all the Ethiopians."[5]

§ 3. The situation of Meroe is now well known,—though it is only in recent times that it has been explored and ascertained[6]—and it may be admitted that the account of Herodotus thus far presents a tolerable approximation to the truth, considering that it of course rests only upon hearsay information. The ascent of the rapids above Elephantine, commonly known as the First Cataract, is well described, though its duration is greatly overrated—the actual passage only requiring about five hours;[7] the island of Tachompso may probably be identified with that of Derar, a short distance above

---

[5] Herodot. ii. 29
[6] As late as the time of D'Anville the position of Meroe could only be determined approximately from Ptolemy and the Arabian geographers. Its ruins were first visited and described in detail by Caillaud in 1820 (*Voyage à Meroe, au Fleuve Blanc, &c*, Paris, 1826), and have been since repeatedly described by Hoskins, Ruppell, and Lepsius
[7] See Note C, p. 301

Dakkeh (the Pselcis of ancient geographers); and though there is no such *lake* as that said to occur immediately above, the error may have readily arisen from the term being used merely to designate an open reach or unencumbered expanse of the river. The rocks and obstructions to the navigation higher up are evidently those which really occur between the second and fourth cataract, on account of which almost all travellers who have visited Meroe have taken the route across the desert which here cuts off a great bend of the river.[8] But in the time of Herodotus it appears to have been customary to follow the banks of the river itself, and the estimate of 40 days' journey may on this supposition have been not far from the truth; but it is not clear at what point the navigation was resumed.

The existence of a civilized city and people at Meroe, worshipping the same deities as the Egyptians, is first mentioned by Herodotus, but was undoubtedly a fact well known to the Egyptians. We learn from the monuments still existing on the site that the earlier kings of Egypt had not only carried their arms into these remote regions, but had left there permanent records of their dominion; and we can hardly therefore doubt that the Egyptians in the time of Herodotus continued to maintain commercial intercourse with the inhabitants of the upper valley of the Nile as far as Meroe. But there is no reason to presume that such trade was carried higher up the river. Hence we find the information of Herodotus *above* this point of a totally different character from that below it. He had apparently no knowledge of the great affluents or tributaries of the Nile, which bear so important a part in the geography of its upper regions, nor does he anywhere allude to "the island" of Meroe, the designation by which that tract was generally known to later geographers. The only people of whom he had heard as situated beyond Meroe were a race

---

[8] Mr Hoskins, however, on his return journey from Meroe, followed the banks of the river throughout (*Travels in Ethiopia*, 4to Lond 1835, chap xii.-xviii.).

whom he terms the Automoli or Deserters, but whose native name (he adds) was Asmach. These were originally, according to the Egyptian tradition, a body of Egyptian warriors, who had migrated into Ethiopia, in the reign of Psammetichus (about B.C. 650), to the number of two hundred and forty thousand men, and had been settled by the king of Ethiopia in the extreme south of his dominions.[9] Admitting the number to be a gross exaggeration, there is nothing improbable in the tradition itself, and the comparatively late period to which it was referred is undoubtedly in favour of its authenticity. But when the informants of Herodotus placed this Egyptian colony at a distance beyond Meroe, equal to that from Meroe to Elephantine, it is obvious that there must be either great exaggeration, or some misconception, to which we have no clue.[1]

The total distance from Elephantine to Meroe is estimated by Herodotus at 60 days', or two months' journey;[2] and as he reckoned the land of the Automoli the same distance beyond Meroe, he was thus led to assign to this people a position four months' journey from the Egyptian frontier. "Thus far then (he tells us) the course of the Nile is known beyond the confines of Egypt." "It flows (he adds) *from the west and the setting sun.*"[3]

§ 4. These last words are so strikingly at variance with the real state of the case, as rendered familiar to us by modern maps, that most of the editors and commentators of Herodotus have shrunk from accepting them in their obvious sense, as applying to the *whole* course of the Nile beyond the limits of Egypt, and supposed Herodotus to speak only of the course of the river at the farthest point to which it was known,[4] assuming, as a matter of course, that he knew its direction from Meroe, and even from the land of the Automoli to be from south to north. But there is nothing in the text of

---

[9] Herodot. ii. 80 [1] Note D, p. 302. [2] Note E, p. 302.
[3] Herodot ii 31. [4] Note F, p 303

Herodotus to show this; and the passage already cited in a former chapter in which he compares the course of the Nile with that of the Danube seems clearly to prove that he considered the *general* direction of the former river, as well as the latter, to be from west to east. It is not improbable that this erroneous idea arose in part from the great bend or elbow which the Nile does actually make between Meroe and the Egyptian frontier, and which may easily have given rise to a misconception of its true direction.[5] Had Herodotus placed the land of the Automoli so far to the south as would have been required on the contrary supposition, he would have had to assign to the continent of Africa a breadth far exceeding that which it occupied in his system, according to which, as we have already seen, it was not to be compared in breadth (i. e. from north to south) with the opposite continent of Europe.

§ 5. The same view will be found to be entirely in accordance with the account given by Herodotus of the expedition of Cambyses against the Macrobian Ethiopians, which is utterly unintelligible on any other supposition. These Macrobians, as he tells us, dwelt "on the sea to the south of Africa,"[6] and he elsewhere distinctly speaks of them as living "at the extremity of the world."[7] But when Cambyses sets out to invade them, instead of ascending the valley of the Nile to Meroe, and thus penetrating as far south as he could, with the advantage of the river at hand, he plunges at once into the desert, apparently almost directly after leaving Thebes, and continues his march "through the sands" till compelled to return by want of provisions. It seems clear from this account that Herodotus did not consider these Ethiopians as dwelling *to the south of* those of Meroe beyond the Automoli, but *in a different direction,* so

---

[5] For more than four degrees of latitude above Syene the Nile flows nearly from S W to N E. The great bend or loop which it forms between this part of its course and Meroe was, doubtless, imperfectly known to the informants of Herodotus, and the historian may well have misconceived it.

[6] οἰκημένους Λιβύης ἐπὶ τῇ νοτίῃ θαλάσσῃ (iii 17).

[7] ἐς τὰ ἔσχατα τῆς γῆς ἔμελλε στρατεύεσθαι (iii. 25).

that the king had to leave the valley of the Nile, and strike across the desert, in order to reach the southern sea, while the Nile trended away towards the south-west and west. Later writers, being unable to find any such people as those described by Herodotus, confounded these Macrobian Ethiopians with those of Meroe, but this is certainly inconsistent with the views of the historian. Whatever may have been the origin of the fable, it is certain that, *according to his conception*, the Macrobians dwelt on the shores of the southern ocean, and had no connection either with Meroe or the Nile.

§ 6. But though the Nile was thus known, according to Herodotus, for a distance of four months' voyage or journey above the frontiers of Egypt, its sources, as he tells us, were altogether unknown; no one that he had met with, whether Greek, Egyptian or Libyan, being able to tell him whence the great river came.[8] It is hardly necessary to add that all succeeding geographers, down to our own times, have had to repeat the same tale.[9] But Herodotus, like many of his successors, had formed a theory of his own upon the subject, and it was one which certainly does credit to his sagacity, while it incidentally affords a curious gleam of information concerning the interior of Africa. Starting from the belief, already referred to, that the Nile, in the upper part of its course, flowed from west to east, he connected this with a tale which he had heard from some Greeks of Cyrene, who had themselves learnt it from Etearchus, the king of the Ammonians, during a visit to the celebrated oracle of Ammon.[1] Etearchus himself derived it from the casual visit of some Nasamonians, a Libyan tribe who dwelt around the bight of the Greater Syrtis. It is important, in estimating the authenticity of the narrative, to bear in mind the successive steps by which it passed to the knowledge of Herodotus.

---

[8] Note G, p 304
[9] Ptolemy may indeed be justly regarded as an exception for his view of the Nile as taking its rise in two lakes south of the equator, though so long discredited in modern times, has been now proved to be substantially correct
[1] Herodot. ii 32

§ 7. According to the statement of these Nasamonians, five young men of their nation, enterprising youths of the highest rank, had set out with the express purpose of exploring the deserts to the south of Libya, to see what they could discover. After passing through the inhabited region and the tract to the south of it, frequented by wild beasts, they entered upon the actual desert and journeyed through it for many days in a westerly direction, until at length they came to a grove of trees, with fruit on them, of which they began to help themselves, when there came up a number of men of small stature, who seized them and led them away prisoners. They were thus conducted through very extensive marshes, after passing which they came to a city the inhabitants of which were of a black colour, and of the same small stature with their captors. Their language was wholly unintelligible to the Nasamonians, and they were all of them skilled in magic. A large river flowed by their city, having its course from west to east; and in it were seen crocodiles. The young men returned in safety to their homes; and from this report Herodotus concludes that the river they had seen, flowing from west to east, with crocodiles in it, could be no other than the Nile.[2] We now know with certainty that this hypothesis is wholly untenable; but it must be remembered that it continued to be a favourite theory with modern geographers down to a recent period; and long after the immense interval was known which separated the Joliba of Western Africa from the upper waters of the Nile, the two were still supposed to be connected, if not continuous.

There seems no reason whatever for rejecting the narrative as fabulous, and it is perfectly credible that young men accustomed to the climate, and well provided with food and water (as we are told they were), may have made a journey across the desert which would be impracticable for more civilized travellers. But the extreme vagueness of the state-

---

[2] Herodot. ii. 32, 33

ment renders it almost impossible to judge of the point really attained. We are not told either the point from which they set out, or entered on the deserts, or the number of days occupied in the journey, either before or after their capture. The only definite statement is that after entering on the desert they travelled *towards the west*; and it is precisely this statement which the nature of the case compels us to reject, or at least to admit only with considerable modification. The Nasamonians (we are told) traversed in the first instance the two zones or regions which were well known to the inhabitants of Northern Africa, but to which Herodotus assigns more definite limits than they really possess;[3] and their express object being to penetrate farther than any one had done before, they would naturally take advantage of those inhabited districts which were known to them, as far as they extended. Now it appears certain from another passage in Herodotus (which will be more fully considered hereafter) that the fertile district of Fezzan, the land of the Garamantes,—was known to, and frequented by, the Libyans, in his time; and of this, therefore, as being within reach of the Nasamonians, and extending far to the south into the desert, the travellers would naturally avail themselves. But if they here plunged into the deserts, and directed their course *due west*, they had nothing but the vast deserts of the Sahara before them, and could never have come upon any considerable river. If they struck to the *south-west*, on the contrary, they would exactly hit upon the celebrated Niger—the Joliba or Quorra of modern travellers; while, if we suppose them to have travelled due south, they would have reached at a somewhat shorter distance the Yeou, a considerable river flowing from west to east, and entering the lake Tchad.

It is difficult to decide between these two theories: both alike require that we should depart from the direction assigned by Herodotus, but we have abundant instances of the extreme

---

[3] See p 274

vagueness of ancient writers with regard to the points of the compass; and it must be added that in this case the statement in some measure disproves itself: for, had the explorers really held a course from east to west, they would, according to the view of Herodotus himself, have been moving *parallel* to the Nile, and could therefore never have hit upon that river. The really important parts of the story undoubtedly are, that the travellers after traversing a great extent of desert, came to an inhabited land with trees, marshes, a great river flowing from the west and containing crocodiles, and a city occupied by a race of black people. The combination of these circumstances seems to render it certain that they had really crossed the great desert tract and reached the Negroland of Central Africa. It is far more difficult to determine the particular region which they visited. But on the whole the probabilities in favour of their having actually reached the Niger may be held to predominate, notwithstanding its greater remoteness from the point whence they probably started.[4] But whatever may have been the region actually visited by these Nasamonian adventurers, their expedition appears to have remained a wholly isolated fact. It is clear from the terms in which it is related by Herodotus himself, that their example was not followed. No commercial relations were established with the tribes beyond the great desert, and it is evident that with the exception of this single vague notice, Herodotus had no idea of the existence of the vast regions known in later times as Soudan or Negroland.[5]

§ 8. The only other passage in Herodotus which appears to point to any knowledge of the more distant regions of Africa towards the south, is that already alluded to, in which he describes the Macrobian Ethiopians, a people who were evidently regarded by him as the remotest inhabitants of Africa, of whom he had any knowledge. His information concerning them was however very vague and strongly mixed with fable. They dwelt.

[4] Note H, p 305.   [5] Note I, p 307

according to the account which he had received of them—an account evidently derived from Egyptian authorities,—" upon the shores of the sea to the south of Africa : " they were the tallest and handsomest race of men in the world, and lived on the average to the age of 120 years : gold was so abundant in their country that it was used even for the chains and fetters of prisoners, while bronze was on the contrary extremely scarce : they enclosed the dead in pillars of transparent crystal instead of coffins : their food consisted solely of meat and milk ; bread and wine being alike unknown to them. In addition to the simplicity of their diet, a marvellous fountain in which they bathed, was supposed to be one of the chief sources of the extraordinary health and longevity that they enjoyed.[6]

It was against this people that Cambyses undertook an expedition, in which both he and his army were very near perishing utterly in the desert. But the circumstances of this expedition are so briefly related by the historian as to be almost wholly unintelligible, and can hardly be said to throw any light upon the geographical position of the people against whom it was directed. Previously to undertaking the enterprise Cambyses sent an embassy to the king of the Macrobians, and for this purpose sent for interpreters from the Ichthyophagi, a people who are not elsewhere mentioned by Herodotus, but who are noticed by later writers, as settled on the west coast of the Red Sea, extending as far as the straits at its mouth. These Ichthyophagi therefore, it may be presumed, were a people of the same race with the Macrobians, and probably situated near them : a supposition which would concur with the expression of Herodotus that the latter dwelt on the southern sea at the farthest extremity of the earth.[7]

But the route by which Cambyses attempted to arrive at this remote region is very obscurely indicated, or rather can hardly be said to be indicated at all. On arriving at Thebes, we are told by our author, he sent off a detachment of his army

---

[6] iii 17-24 [7] See above, p 267

to attack the Ammonians and destroy the temple of Ammon; with the rest of his forces he proceeded against the Ethiopians, but having neglected to make due provision of food for his troops, before they had completed the fifth part of the journey, their provisions utterly failed, and they were reduced to eating their beasts of burden. Cambyses nevertheless still persevered and it was not till they had entered upon the sandy desert, where for want of all other resources his soldiers began to eat one another, that he was persuaded to abandon the expedition and return to Thebes, having lost a large part of his army.[8]

§ 9. Strabo and other writers of subsequent times, when the geography of Africa was better known, regard the expedition of Cambyses as directed against the Ethiopians of Meroë:[9] and on this supposition there would be little doubt that the desert in which his army suffered so severely was that between Korosko and Abu Hamed (on the *direct* route from Syene to Meroë) the horrors of which have been described in forcible language by all travellers who have crossed it.[1] But it is clear that this view of the subject was *not* that of Herodotus. These Macrobian Ethiopians (whom he mentions only in connection with this expedition of Cambyses) are distinctly described by him as dwelling on the southern sea, in the remotest regions of the earth; while the Ethiopians of Meroe dwelt on the banks of the Nile, and the Automoli or Deserters lived far *beyond* them, but still on the same river. No mention occurs of the Macrobians in the description of the Nile and the people that occupied its banks: nor any hint that they adjoined the Ethiopians of this quarter.[2] The fact appears to be (as already

---

[8] iii 25
[9] Strabo, xvii 1, p. 790.
[1] See Hoskins' *Travels in Ethiopia,* pp 19-32, Lepsius, *Briefe aus Aegypten,* pp 125-136
[2] Mr Cooley's attempt to identify the Macrobians with the Automoli (*Claudius Ptolemy and the Nile,* pp. 20, 21) appears to me utterly untenable.

The fabulous and mythical notions concerning the former people could never have attached themselves to a race who had established themselves in Ethiopia within historical, and even comparatively recent, memory, and the very existence of the tradition concerning the Automoli proves that they must have borne a marked resemblance to

VOL I.

indicated) that Herodotus, misled by his erroneous notion that the Nile flowed *from the west*, conceived the Macrobians to be situated in quite another direction, that Cambyses had altogether left the course of the river, and struck across the deserts towards the south, with the view of reaching their country, when the want of supplies compelled him to return. What the *real* circumstances of the expedition may have been we are wholly unable to judge : it is not improbable that some fabulous tales of an El Dorado on the southern sea may have tempted Cambyses to undertake a march of the extent of which he knew nothing. That the expedition, whatever its purpose or destination, proved an entire failure, and occasioned the loss of great part of his army, is all that we know about it.[3]

§ 10. It may therefore be safely asserted that, westward of Egypt and the valley of the Nile, the knowledge of Herodotus was confined to the regions of Africa north of the great desert. But with this portion of the continent he shows a degree of acquaintance, and a general conception of its physical features exceeding what might reasonably have been expected, considering the imperfect nature of his sources of information. In more than one passage he dwells upon the marked division of the regions in question into three zones or tracts, clearly characterized by nature. The first of these, extending along the sea coast of the Mediterranean, all the way from the frontiers of Egypt to Cape Soloeis beyond the Pillars of Hercules, with the exception of the portions occupied by Greek and

---

the Egyptians : a resemblance of which some traces are said to be still found in the inhabitants of Sennaar. But the whole description of the Macrobians represents them as a people unlike any other. Their fabulous characteristics are the *essential* part of the tradition concerning them, as their position on the southern ocean distinctly separates them from the Ethiopian races in the valley of the Nile.

[3] It is clear that the view taken by Strabo was not founded upon any more accurate information: as he confuses the expedition of Cambyses himself with his main army, with that of the detachment sent against the Ammonians, and speaks of "the army of Cambyses" having been *buried in the sands on the way to Meroe* (Strab xvii. p 820) It is not impossible that the expedition was *in reality* directed against Meroe, but it is certain that this was not the view taken by Herodotus himself, or by the persons from whom he derived his information.

Phœnician settlers, was inhabited by Libyans and races of Libyan origin; and though the greater part of these were merely nomad tribes, the whole tract was regarded by Herodotus as "the inhabited region" of Libya. Beyond this was what he calls "the wild beast tract," which was apparently considered as too much infested by wild beasts to be susceptible of permanent habitation. South of that again was a mere desert of sand, destitute of water and producing nothing.[4]

Though this division is somewhat too strongly marked, and was evidently conceived by Herodotus—with that love of symmetry and generalisation congenial to the Greek mind—as more definitely characterized than it really is, it is not without a considerable foundation in truth, and has been adopted, with some modifications, by the most eminent modern geographers, as well as by the Arabic writers of the middle ages.[5]

It is singular that it is much more clearly marked in the western part of Africa, with which Herodotus was comparatively little acquainted, than in those portions concerning which he had more definite information: but, speaking in a general way, the three zones may be fairly regarded as extending across Africa from the Atlantic Ocean to the confines of Egypt. The principal interruption to its symmetry, arising from the projection of the Carthaginian territory to the north, was unknown to Herodotus, who undoubtedly shared the error of almost all his successors in regarding the coast line of northern Africa as

---

[4] ii 32; iv 181 Thus the young Nasamonians, on their exploring expedition into the interior, at first passed through the inhabited region, then through that of wild beasts, and afterwards through the sandy desert

[5] Heeren, *African Nations*, vol i. pp. 6-9; Humboldt, *Aspects of Nature*, vol 1 p. 58; Ritter, *Erdkunde*, vol. 1. p. 838.

The "wild-beast" zone of Herodotus (ἡ θηριώδης) corresponds in a general way with the Biledulgerid or "Land of Dates" of the Arabs, a tract which they regard as comprising the whole of the district south of Mount Atlas to the borders of the desert, known to the Roman writers under the name of Gætulia In the eastern half of the continent it is much less clearly marked, there being no such important mountain range as the Atlas to constitute a great physical division The Harudsch or Black Mountains (the Mons Ater of Pliny) are however regarded by systematic geographers as a kind of representative or continuation of the same chain to the south of the Cyrenaica, though of such inferior elevation as hardly to deserve the name.

comparatively straight,[6] so that the parallelism of the three zones would be much more nearly preserved than is really the case.

§ 11. Closely connected with this division of Africa into three zones, was another of its physical peculiarities, on which Herodotus lays great stress, and in respect to which we again see his love of symmetrical arrangement cropping out in a remarkable manner. Immediately on the borders of the "wild beast zone," before one came to the pure unmitigated sandy desert, was a brow or ridge of sand,[7] in which there occurred from distance to distance inhabited spots, each of which was marked by the presence of large masses of salt, heaped up into hillocks, out of the summit of which gushed forth streams of clear, fresh water. The spots thus characterized were found at the distance of about ten days' journey from one another, forming a continuous chain from the borders of Egypt to the Atlantic.[8] The existence of these detached fertile spots in the midst of the sandy desert is a fact that must in all ages have impressed itself upon the minds of travellers and geographers: but it is singular that Herodotus, or his informants, were less struck with the contrast presented by the fertility of these oases[9] with the arid waste around them, than with the occurrence of large masses, or, as he calls them, "hills" of salt, in immediate connection with springs of fresh water. The statement that these springs in all cases gush forth from the very

---

[6] Note K, p. 308.
[7] His expression of ὀφρύη ψάμμου, literally "a brow of sand," has been generally translated as *a ridge;* and considered as showing that he was acquainted with the true conformation of the tract in question—a broad tableland of considerable elevation, in which the so called Oases occupy depressions or hollows of limited extent But it seems more probable that Herodotus, in common with almost all writers down to a very recent period, thought of the desert only as a vast sandy plain, and that the peculiar expression of ὀφρύη was used by him merely to describe a broad strip or band stretching across the continent A recent traveller indeed remarks, "how admirably his expression of 'a ridge of sand,' rather than a plain, describes the edge of the northern Sahara" (Tristram's *Great Sahara,* p 75), yet Herodotus had certainly never seen any part of the regions visited by Mr. Tristram, and had nothing but the vaguest information concerning them.
[8] Herodot IV 181.
[9] Note L, p. 308

midst of the salt hills is indeed an exaggeration; but all the oases abound in salt—sometimes found in such masses as to be used by the inhabitants for building purposes: while springs rise out of the sand, and even on the top of hillocks of sand, in the midst of the salt-covered plains.[1]

Strabo has aptly compared the fertile patches thus scattered amidst the deserts of Libya to the spots on a leopard's skin;[2] and they are in fact dispersed over the interior of the continent with as little order or symmetry as the spots in question: but Herodotus on the contrary supposed them to follow one another at regular intervals, and in a general direction parallel to that of the sandy zone itself, *i.e.*, from east to west.[3] His information was probably derived from traders, who knew only the particular line of route which they had themselves followèd, and had doubtless paid little attention to the bearings of the track from one station to another. But the permanent character of these fertile patches—which must in all ages have been equally marked by nature, and have formed as it were the stepping-stones by which alone it was possible to carry on communication across the desert—enables us in many instances to identify with certainty the localities intended by Herodotus, though both the distances and the directions will often be found erroneous.

§ 12. A singular mistake at the very outset tends to vitiate his whole line of positions. The first point which he mentions is the Ammonium or Oasis of Ammon, rendered so celebrated at a later period by the visit of Alexander—the site of which is well ascertained to correspond with that now known as the Oasis of Siwah.[4] Here there can be no doubt as to the locality

---

[1] See the extract from General Minutoli's account of the Oasis of Siwah, cited by Heeren (*African Nations*, vol 1 p 207), and Tristram's *Great Sahara*, p. 75.
[2] Strabo, 11 5, p. 130 The comparison has been frequently repeated by later geographers.
[3] Note M, p. 309

[4] The Oasis of Siwah was first visited and described by Browne in 1792, and its identity with that of Ammon fully established by Major Rennell (*Geogr. of Herodot* pp. 577–591) It has been since frequently visited and fully described by Hornemann, Caillaud, Minutoli, Mr James Hamilton and others. The results of all their inves-

meant, and its distance from the nearest point of Egypt is correctly given: but Herodotus erroneously conceived it to be situated *west of Thebes*, while it really lies about due west of the Lake Mœris, or the district of the Fayoum, from which it is in fact distant about ten days' journey. The effect of this error is to bring down the whole line of stations more than three degrees and a half of latitude too far to the south. It is probable that in this instance Herodotus had confounded the Great Oasis, which is really situated due west of Thebes, and where there was also a temple of Ammon, with the Oasis of Ammon properly so called, from which it is more than four hundred miles distant.[5]

§ 13. His next station is Augila, a place which still preserves its name unaltered in its modern appellation of Aujileh—a rare instance in African geography—and is correctly placed about ten days' journey to the west of the Ammonians.[6] It is still visited by the Arabs from the nearest sea-coast, as it was by the Nasamonians in the days of Herodotus, on account of the excellence of its dates.[7] But beyond this again, at the same distance to the west, he places the Garamantes, whom he himself calls a very great nation, though he appears to have conceived them as dwelling around a mere oasis like the others.[8] Here there can be no doubt that the same people are meant as those designated by later geographers under the name of the Garamantes,—the inhabitants of the region now called Fezzan, a district which has indeed very much of the character of an oasis, though of far greater extent. This

---

tigations are well brought together by M Parthey (*Das Orakel u die Oase des Ammon*, 4to Berlin, 1862, reprinted from the *Transactions of the Berlin Academy*)
The site of the celebrated temple and oracle of Ammon was first discovered by Mr Hamilton in 1853
[5] Note N, p. 309
[6] Hornemann reached Aujileh from Siwah after nine *long* days' journey, but the caravan travelled two whole nights, and both men and beasts were quite exhausted (*Travels*, pp 45, 46). The Arab geographers give the distance at ten days' journey.
[7] Hornemann, p 48
[8] Γαράμαντες . . ἔθνος μέγα ἰσχυρῶς, iv. 183
The whole district of Fezzan is not less than 300 miles in length from N to S. by about 200 from E. to W., but only a small portion of this is capable of cultivation

identification is confirmed by his notice, that the land of the Garamantes was distant in a direct line thirty days' journey from that of the Lotophagi, on the northern coast. This is in fact just about the true distance from Fezzan to the sea-coast at Tripoli or Mesarata, with which it must always have had a direct communication.[9] But on the other hand the distance from Aujileh to the nearest point of Fezzan is not less than sixteen days' journey, and the direction instead of west is nearly *south-west*. The effect of this second error is in great part to correct the former one, as Mourzuk, the capital of Fezzan, is in fact almost exactly in the same latitude as Thebes.

§ 14. At the present day a frequented caravan route proceeds from Mourzuk through Aujileh and Siwah to Cairo,[1] and it is probable that this was already the case in the days of Herodotus, and that the stations thus far were derived by him from communications with persons who were really acquainted with the route. The notice of the direct distance between the Garamantes and the Lotophagi on the sea-coast also points to the existence of intercourse in this direction, which would probably be that followed by traders from Cyrene. But it is much more difficult to determine the positions of the succeeding stages. According to our author there was another oasis ten days' journey beyond the Garamantes, inhabited by a people called the Atarantes,[2] and another again at the same distance beyond that, at the foot of a lofty mountain called Atlas, from whence the inhabitants derived the name of

---

[9] Captain Lyon in 1820 took just thirty days (exclusive of stoppages) on his return journey from Mourzuk to the sea

[1] This was the route by which Hornemann travelled He took sixteen days of rapid travelling from Aujileh to Zuilah (the first town where caravans halt on their arriving in Fezzan), but the distance is commonly reckoned at twenty days' journey.

[2] It must be remarked that this name has been corrupted in *all* existing MSS of Herodotus into Ἀτλαντες The reading Ἀτάραντες is restored from Stephanus of Byzantium and Eustathius (ad Dionys Per v 66), who however both cite the distinction *between* the Atarantes and Atlantes from an author named Rhianus, *not* from Herodotus, and there seems no doubt that the corruption in the text of Herodotus is at least as old as the time of Eustathius Yet it seems impossible that he can have called *both* tribes Atlantes, without any further notice or explanation Both names are in all probability only forms of the same

Atlantes. Mount Atlas is described, in terms which certainly seem to be derived from the old Greek fables connected with the name, as a lofty mountain of a circular form and so high that its summit could never be seen, being covered with clouds both in winter and summer, on which account the natives called it "the pillar of heaven."[3]

Both the name and the description, however fanciful and distorted, seem to require us to seek this last station in the regions to the south of the great chain of Mount Atlas, and not far from the foot of that chain. In this case the line of route must have turned up towards the north-west, from Fezzan by way of Ghadamis to Wargla or Tuggurt; and the next oasis from the land of the Garamantes would be that of Ghadamis,—the Cydamus of Pliny and Ptolemy—a place that could hardly have been at any time unknown to the nations on the coast. It is about the same distance from the borders of Fezzan towards the north-west as Aujileh is towards the north-east. This may therefore be fairly presumed to be the spot where our author places the Atarantes. But the position of the Atlantes cannot be determined with anything like even plausibility; no part of the real chain of Mount Atlas approaches sufficiently near to the central zone of desert to agree even approximately with the account reported to Herodotus, and the whole description is so fanciful as to render it very unlikely that it was based upon any authentic information.[4]

§ 15. Thus far, however, Herodotus himself supposed that he possessed accurate information; but beyond this he himself tells us that he was not able to give the names of the tribes that inhabited the sandy belt which he is describing. But he assures us that this peculiar zone itself extended to the sea beyond the Pillars of Hercules; and contained mines of salt, with the masses of which the inhabitants built their houses.[5]

---

[3] Herodot. iv 184
[4] See Note O, p 310
[5] It is singular that Herodotus should notice this peculiarity only in regard to the most distant of these Oases, the practice being really found much nearer

SECT. 1.   HERODOTUS: AFRICA.   281

To the south of this tract, which, sandy and sterile as it was, was thus studded from distance to distance with inhabited spots, the regions towards the interior of Libya are described as utterly desert, without trees, without water, without rain, without even wild beasts, and as Herodotus expressively adds, without any trace of moisture.[6] As applied to the vast desert of the Sahara this description is scarcely exaggerated; of the fertile and well-watered regions to the south of it Herodotus had evidently no suspicion, and his ideas of physical geography were too vague to lead him to the conclusion that if these regions were really traversed, as he supposed them to be, by a great river like the Nile, they could not be condemned to unmitigated sterility.

§ 16. The only notice which appears to refer to a people to the south of the tract which we have been here considering, is where he speaks of the Garamantes as carrying on expeditions in pursuit of the Troglodyte Ethiopians, whom he describes as the swiftest of foot of any people he had heard of, on which account they were pursued by the Garamantes in chariots and four. These Troglodytes, he adds, fed on serpents, lizards and other reptiles, and their language was like the squeaking of bats.[7] At the present day the inhabitants of Fezzan carry on similar *razzie* or slave-hunts, against the Tibboos of the interior; many of whom, inhabiting the more rocky portions of the desert, are still "dwellers in caves;" their agility is proverbial, and their language is still compared by their more civilized neighbours to the whistling of birds.[8] In calling these Troglodytes (of whose position he had probably no clear

home   Thus it is mentioned by Mr. Hamilton (*Wanderings in North Africa*, p 294) as still prevailing at Siwah, and by Dr Oudney in the western parts of Fezzan (Denham and Clapperton's *Travels*, p. 46) Pliny also notices it as the practice of a tribe in the interior from the Syrtis (*H N* v c 5, § 34)
    Herodotus justly observes that it is a conclusive proof of the perfect dryness of the climate, wherever it is found "for if it rained, the walls built of salt could not stand" (iv 185)
    [6] iv 185   καὶ ἰκμάδος ἐστὶ ἐν αὐτῇ οὐδέν
    [7] Herodot iv 183
    [8] Hornemann's *Travels*, p 119; Lyon's *Travels in Northern Africa*, 4to. Lond. 1821

idea) Ethiopians, Herodotus doubtless uses the term merely in the sense of "black men." The Tibboos are in fact, as a race, almost black, though they have not the distinctive features of the negro. It may well be doubted whether Herodotus ever saw a true negro, the curly hair, of which he speaks as distinctive of the Ethiopians, being found more or less markedly in all the black races of Northern Africa.

§ 17. With the Libyan tribes that bordered on the coast of the Mediterranean, from the confines of Egypt to those of the Carthaginian dominions, the information possessed by Herodotus, as might be expected, was comparatively complete and satisfactory. His knowledge of them was evidently derived from the Greek settlers at Cyrene and the neighbouring colonies, which were at this period flourishing and civilized communities; and not only carried on trade with the neighbouring tribes, but exercised in some degree a civilizing influence over them, so that those who most nearly adjoined the Greek territories—the Asbystæ and the Auschisæ—to a great extent imitated the customs of the colonists.[9] These last tribes he describes as being particularly skilled in driving chariots with four horses,[1] a practice which they may have derived from the Cyrenæans—who were renowned throughout Greece as charioteers; though Herodotus himself, in another passage, asserts that the Greeks themselves first derived the practice of yoking four horses abreast from the Libyans—a statement which it is difficult to accept.[2] But there seems no doubt that the use of chariots was general in his days among the Libyan tribes, though now wholly unknown in Northern Africa.[3]

---

[9] Herodot. iv. 170
[1] τεθριπποβάται δὲ οὐκ ἥκιστα, ἀλλὰ μάλιστα Λιβύων εἰσί (l c)
[2] Ibid. 189 The Greeks of Cyrene were undoubtedly distinguished for their skill as charioteers. Pindar celebrates the victories of Arcesilas of Cyrene at the Pythian games (Pyth iv. v), and Sophocles speaks of two Libyan charioteers as contending with those of the Greeks in the race where Orestes was supposed to have perished (*Electra*, v 702) But we cannot suppose that the poet here alluded to *native* Libyans
[3] Thus our author, as just mentioned, represents even the Garamantes of the interior as pursuing the Troglodytes with chariots and four ' (iv 183)

The enumeration of the tribes along the shores of the Mediterranean presents few geographical difficulties, though, as is always the case with nomad races, both their names and boundaries are in some instances different from what we find in later geographers. Thus the Giligammæ who, according to Herodotus, occupied the coast-district eastward of the Cyrenaïca, nearly to the confines of Egypt,[4] are not mentioned by any later writer; while the name of the Marmaridæ, who appear in all the other geographers—even in Scylax, not more than a century afterwards—as the chief people in this region, is not to be found in Herodotus at all. In this case there is little doubt that the same people is meant, and the change is merely one of name, though it is one of which we can offer no explanation.

§ 18. The coast of the Cyrenaïca, from the neighbourhood of Derne to that of Euesperides (the modern Benghazi) was wholly occupied by Greek settlements; here, therefore, the Libyan tribes of the Asbystæ and the Auschisæ were confined to the interior.[5] But to the west of these again on the sea-coast adjoining the bight of the Great Syrtis, we find the Nasamonians, a people of Libyan race, who are mentioned by all succeeding writers down to the time of the Roman Empire. The Psylli, who had formerly been the neighbours of the Nasamonians, had according to Herodotus ceased to exist in his time, having undertaken an expedition into the interior, in which their whole nation perished, being overwhelmed with storms of sand.[6] The story that they had thus marched into the desert "to make war on the south wind" is obviously a

---

[4] iv. 169.
[5] This was the country which produced the famous *silphium*, which was one of the principal sources of the wealth of Cyrene It is singular that this peculiar and valuable plant is only mentioned *incidentally* by Herodotus (iv. 169, 192), though he enumerates all the wild *animals* of these parts of Libya
[6] Herodot. iv. 173 Some confirmation of this story is found in the fact that no mention appears of the Psylli in Scylax, a century after Herodotus, though they reappear in Strabo (xvii. p 838). No mention occurs in Herodotus of their skill as serpent charmers, an art for which they were so celebrated in later times. (Lucan, *Pharsal.* ix vv 890–940, Plutarch, *Cat. Min.* 56, Plin *H. N.* vii. 2, § 14)

mere fictitious embellishment, but curious as showing the same kind of feeling in regard to this wind—the bane of all these regions of Africa—as that which led the Atarantians to curse the sun as he rose in the heavens.[7]

The long strip of coast from the bight of the Greater to that of the Lesser Syrtis (the modern Pashalik of Tripoli) was occupied in the time of Herodotus by three tribes, the Macæ, the Gindanes and the Machlyans, who succeeded one another from east to west, though their exact limits cannot be defined. Besides these the Lotophagi—a name evidently of Greek origin and retained from its connection with the Homeric poems—are mentioned as occupying a promontory projecting into the sea, which can be no other than the peninsula of Zarzis, adjoining to the Lesser Syrtis, and opposite to the island of Meninx, which was regarded by most ancient writers as the island of the Lotophagi. But Herodotus himself tells us that the use of the lotus-fruit as an article of diet was not confined to these Lotophagi alone, but was common to the neighbouring tribe of the Machlyans; it was doubtless in fact in more or less general use along this part of the coast, as it continued to be in the days of Polybius.[8]

The Machlyans, according to Herodotus, occupied the eastern shore of the Lake Tritonis; on the opposite side of the same lake were situated the Auseans, who were still a mere nomad tribe, like the others just enumerated; but beyond them, towards the west, were agricultural races, differing in many respects in their manners and customs from those to the eastward. It is evident that we here come in contact with the more civilized tribes, occupying the fertile regions of the modern Regency of Tunis, which, both under the Carthaginians and the Romans, was one of the richest countries of the Mediterranean. But the knowledge of them which had reached the ears of Herodotus, was still very imperfect. It is evident that his Cyrenæan informants were very little

---

[7] Herodot iv 144. Strabo relates the same thing of the Ethiopians in the upper valley of the Nile (xvii p. 822)   [8] Note P, p. 311.

acquainted with any part of Africa west of the Lesser Syrtis; probably they were prevented, by the commercial jealousy so frequent among ancient nations, from trading directly with any of the tribes subject to the Carthaginian rule, or from touching at any seaports, except Carthage itself. The information which Herodotus had received concerning the tribes beyond Lake Tritonis was further confused in his mind by the erroneous notions which he entertained of the geographical conformation of this part of Africa.

He evidently conceived the tribes which he enumerates in succession—the Maxyes, the Zaueces, and the Gyzantes,[9] as occurring in that order from east to west; while they probably in reality trended more towards the north, and the neighbourhood of Carthage. But no notice is found in Herodotus of the proximity of that great city. Nor does he appear to have been aware of the great fertility of this part of Africa; as he distinctly tells us that the district on the banks of the little river Cinyps[1] was the only portion of Libya that could bear any comparison in point of fertility with the richer districts of Europe and Asia.[2]

The island Cyraunis, which Herodotus places opposite to the Gyzantes, and describes as long and narrow, is clearly the Cercina or Cercinna of later geographers—still called Karkineh; though it is strangely supposed by Niebuhr to be the same with the island of Cerne on the Atlantic coast of Africa. Herodotus, as is justly observed by Major Rennell, "unquestionably intended an island in the Mediterranean, and

---

[9] Two of these tribes—the Maxyes and the Gyzantes—are evidently the same that were already mentioned by Hecatæus under the names of the Mazyes and the Zygantes (Hecatæus, Fr. 304, 306), but they are otherwise unknown It has been, however, suggested with some probability that the name of the Gyzantes or Zygantes reappears in that of the Byzantes or Byzacians, who gave name to the district of Byzacene, forming the southern portion of the Roman province of Africa. The attempt to connect the name of the Zaueces with that of Zeugitana is much more questionable.

[1] Note Q, p. 312

[2] Herodot iv. 198 Even Timæus, nearly two centuries after Herodotus appears to have been ignorant of the great fertility of the Carthaginian territories in Africa, for which he is deservedly censured by Polybius

that near Carthage." [3] It is true that no gold is now found in the island of Karkineh; but the story of its being found at Cyraunis, "in a lake, out of which it was drawn up by young maidens, by means of feathers dipped in pitch" is an obvious fable, and is related by Herodotus himself with an expression of doubt.[4]

§ 19. In some respects, however, he had formed a correct general idea of this western portion of Libya, as altogether different from the flat and sandy tracts towards the east, being in great part mountainous, well wooded and abounding in wild beasts, especially lions, elephants and serpents of vast size.[5] It was here also, according to the stories told by the Libyans, that were found the fabulous beings who were placed by a vague tradition somewhere in the interior of Africa—the men with heads like dogs, and those who had no heads at all, but had eyes in the middle of their breasts. But of such tales as these Herodotus is careful to express his disbelief. The stories of the existence of wild men and wild women may perhaps have arisen from the occurrence of large apes or Pongos, like those met with by Hanno on the western coast, though none such are now found to the north of the Great Desert.

§ 20. Two other points of interest in the geography of Northern Africa remain to be noticed. Herodotus repeatedly mentions "the Syrtis:" but always without any distinguishing epithet:[6] and it is clear that he knew of only one gulf of the name—that called by subsequent geographers the Greater Syrtis, between Berenice (Benghazi) and Leptis Magna (Lebdeh). Nor does he make any mention of its peculiar dangers, of which such exaggerated notions prevailed at a later period.[7]

On the other hand he speaks of the Lake Tritonis, in a manner that may almost lead to the inference that he confounded the inland lake of that name with the deep gulf known

---

[3] Rennell, *Geogr of Herodot.* p 639, 4to ed.
[6] ii. 32, 150; iv. 169, 173.
[4] iv. 195.   [5] iv. 191.
[7] Note R, p. 313.

to later geographers as the Lesser Syrtis, and now called the Gulf of Cabes. It seems certain at least that he regarded the Lake Tritonis, which he supposed to be of very large extent, as communicating directly with the sea.[8] It is not improbable that considerable physical changes may have taken place in this part of Africa, during the historical period, and that the Lake Tritonis may in the time of Herodotus have been much more extensive than the shallow salt lake (called Sebkah-el Faraoun) that now represents it. It appears probable also that it then had a narrow outlet by which it communicated with the sea, from which it is still separated only by a narrow isthmus of sand: but the information of Herodotus concerning these countries is far too vague for us to rely upon it as proving the extent of the changes that have taken place since his time. It must be added that the Lesser Syrtis is correctly described by Scylax, who wrote only about a century after our historian.[9]

§ 21. We have seen that Herodotus evidently possessed very imperfect information concerning the portion of Africa extending from Carthage to the Pillars of Hercules, though it was the part of the continent which was best known to later geographers. But he has preserved to us one curious piece of information concerning the trade of the Carthaginians with the regions beyond the Straits, which he derived (as he himself tells us) directly from Carthaginian informants.[1] Outside the Columns of Hercules (he says) there was a district, inhabited by natives of Libyan race, which was frequented by Carthaginian merchants. These were accustomed, on arriving at the spot, to land their cargoes and set out their wares on the seashore: they then kindled a fire and retired to their ships. The natives were guided to the spot by the smoke, and after examining the goods offered, deposited by them a quantity of gold, and retired in their turn into the interior. If the Car-

---

[8] Thus he speaks in IV. 179 of Jason being driven *among the shoals of Lake Tritonis* before he saw the land.   [9] Note S, p. 314.   [1] Herodot. iv. 196.

thaginians on landing again were satisfied with the amount of gold offered, they took it and went away: if not, they again withdrew to their ships, till the natives had increased it to an amount that they deemed satisfactory. Thus was the traffic carried on, with mutual confidence, but without any direct communication between the two parties.

No indication is furnished by Herodotus of the locality where this "dumb commerce" was carried on: but the fact of gold being the object of the trade leads to the inference that it was at a considerable distance towards the south, there being very little gold found north of the Sahara. The practice itself is found by modern travellers to exist in several countries of Africa, where the Moorish merchants have to deal with Negro tribes, who are probably afraid to show themselves for fear of being kidnapped as slaves.[2]

The only point on the Atlantic coast of Africa which Herodotus mentions by name is Cape Soloeis, which he regarded as the most westerly point of the continent. Of this also he had doubtless heard from Carthaginian traders: but we must not assume that, because he was thus rendered familiar with the name, he had any definite idea of its true geographical position.[3] There is certainly no foundation for the supposition that he was acquainted with the island of Cerne, so well known to later writers, as one of the principal stations of the Carthaginian commerce on the shores of the Atlantic.[4]

§ 22. In order to complete this review of the knowledge of the African continent possessed by Herodotus, it remains only to consider the very curious and important narrative upon which he founds his belief that it was surrounded by the ocean on the south, so that, as he expresses it, the Erythræan Sea (the Indian Ocean) and the Atlantic were one and the same. We have already seen that this was the prevalent idea in his time:

---

[2] See the account given by Captain Lyon (*Travels in Northern Africa*, p 149), and by Shaw (*Travels*, p 239) Ca da Mosto also mentions a similar practice in his day on the west coast of Africa (p 100 in Ramusio, vol 1)
[3] See Chap VI p 163, note
[4] Note T, p. 316.

most, if not all, preceding geographers having *assumed* the notion of a circumfluent ocean, surrounding all the three continents. This view however Herodotus rejected as not warranted by any credible testimony; but while he expresses his doubts of the existence of an ocean to the north of Europe and Asia, with regard to Africa, he says, no doubt can exist that it is surrounded by the sea (with the exception of the narrow isthmus of Suez) inasmuch as it had been circumnavigated by order of the Egyptian king, Necho.[5]

SECTION 2.—*Circumnavigation of Africa by Necho.*

§ 1. According to the information collected by the historian—the source of which he has unfortunately not indicated—the Egyptian monarch, who appears to have been a man of an enterprising character, and had previously made an attempt to connect the Nile by a canal with the Red Sea, having been foiled in this undertaking, turned his attention to warlike expeditions both by sea and land, and fitted out two fleets of triremes, one on the Mediterranean, the other at the head of the Red Sea, where he constructed docks, the remains of which were still visible in the time of Herodotus.[6] At the same time he sent out a squadron of ships, manned by Phœnicians, with orders to sail round Africa, and return by way of the Pillars of Hercules into the Mediterranean. These Phœnicians, setting out from the Red Sea, sailed along the southern ocean. When the autumn came on, they landed at the point of Libya where they found themselves for the time being, and having sown a crop of corn, waited there till it was ripe, reaped it, and then

[5] Herodot iv. 42. Λιβύη μὲν γὰρ δηλοῖ ἑωυτὴν ἐοῦσα περίρρυτος, πλὴν ὅσον αὐτῆς πρὸς τὴν Ἀσίην οὐρίζει, Νεκῶ τοῦ Αἰγυπτίων βασιλέος πρῶτον τῶν ἡμεῖς ἴδμεν καταδέξαντος.
[6] Id. ii 158, 159. Necho, or Neco, was the son of Psammetichus, and reigned from B.C. 610 to B C. 594. He therefore belonged to a period concerning which Herodotus had good historical information.

proceeded on their voyage. In this manner two whole years elapsed, and in the course of the third year, having doubled the Pillars of Hercules they returned in safety to Egypt.[7]

Herodotus adds a circumstance, which, he says, "appears to him incredible, but others may perhaps believe"—that according to the report of the navigators, while sailing round Africa, they had the sun on their right hand. We now know that this must really have been the case, had the voyage been actually performed, however strange it appeared to Greek hearers, and there is no circumstance that has had so much weight in obtaining credence for the narrative in question as this very statement, which was regarded by Herodotus himself as unworthy of belief.

§ 2. There are few questions in ancient history or geography that have been the subject of more discussion than the reality of this supposed circumnavigation. No doubt can reasonably be entertained that Herodotus has reported correctly the information he had received: and it is certain that he himself believed in the truth of the narrative, and looked upon it as establishing beyond a doubt the peninsular character of Africa, and the connection between the eastern and western oceans. But it was far from obtaining general credence in ancient times. Its authenticity was doubted by Posidonius as not attested by sufficient evidence,[8] and in this judgment Strabo concurs. Both these authors however believed in the geographical fact that Africa was surrounded by the Ocean, though they doubted any one having ever actually sailed round it. Polybius on the other hand expresses doubts whether the sea was really continuous to the south of Africa,[9] and Ptolemy at a later period wholly disbelieved it: they must therefore have rejected as unworthy of credit the narrative reported by Herodotus.

---

[7] Herodot. iv. 42.
[8] Posidonius ap Strab ii p 98 It is worthy of notice as showing how carelessly the ancients often cited their authorities, that Posidonius (or Strabo) refers to the expedition as having been sent out *by Darius*
[9] iii. 37.

Among modern writers on the contrary there has existed the greatest diversity of opinion. We now know with certainty that Herodotus and those who agreed with him in considering Africa as surrounded by the sea were geographically correct, and the *possibility* of the voyage cannot therefore be denied. But this is a very different question from that of its actual accomplishment.

§ 3. Among those who have believed in the authenticity of the narrative, Major Rennell is undoubtedly the one who has done the most to support it. He has shown,[1] 1. That the time allotted for the expedition was amply sufficient for its accomplishment even according to the slow rate of ancient navigation —a point which it appears strange should ever have been contested ; 2. That from the time the voyagers passed Cape Guardafui (the north-eastern point of Africa) supposing them to have chosen the right season of the year, they would be favoured by the northern monsoon, as far as the southern tropic, and would also have a strong current in their favour the whole way round the Cape of Good Hope;[2] 3. That along the western coast of Africa, so long as they were within the southern hemisphere, they would for the most part have been able to reckon upon a favourable wind, as well as a current to the northward. The combination of these circumstances undoubtedly proves that the circumnavigation of the continent would be much more easily effected from the East than from the West ; and thus tends to dispose of the argument against its probability that might be derived from the failure of other attempts made in the contrary direction (such as those of Hanno [3] and Sataspes), and from the very slow progress of the Portuguese discoveries in the same quarter.

---

[1] *Geography of Herodotus*, pp. 672–714.
[2] It is remarkable, however, that the Arabian navigators in the middle ages, who undoubtedly visited the eastern coast of Africa as far south as Sofala, never passed beyond Cape Corrientes, which formed the extreme limit of their knowledge in this direction

[3] There is, however, no evidence that the voyage of Hanno was undertaken with any view to the circumnavigation of Africa. It is, indeed, frequently referred to by later writers as such an attempt, and is even described by Pliny as having accomplished

§ 4. At the same time it must be admitted that the enormous length of the voyage—so entirely out of proportion to all that we know of as accomplished in ancient times, either before or afterwards; the difficulty of carrying provisions for such long intervals as would be required, notwithstanding the supposed halts for the sowing and reaping of successive harvests:[4] and the very imperfect account that appears to have been preserved of so important and remarkable an achievement—all contribute to raise a *primâ facie* improbability against the whole story which it is difficult to surmount.

The absence of all geographical details prevents the possibility of testing the truth of the narrative (as in the case of Hanno) by an examination of such statements. But it must be confessed that this total absence is in itself a suspicious circumstance. We do not know from whom Herodotus derived his information, whether from Phœnician merchants at Tyre,[5] or from the Egyptian priests: the latter is the more probable: but in either case it is singular that no single fact concerning the wild tribes with which the navigators must necessarily have come in contact, no "traveller's tales" about the marvels of such distant lands and the perils of so long a navigation, should have been preserved to the time of Herodotus, or have been known to his informants.

---

it (¹), but the original narrative of the voyage represents it only as undertaken for the purpose of founding colonies along the west coast of Africa

[4] Herodotus undoubtedly conceived the Phœnicians as repeating this operation more than once, though Major Rennell appears to have supposed it to have taken place only once. This is evident from the form of his expressions (προσίσχοντες ἂν σπείρεσκον. θερίσαντες ἂν τὸν σῖτον) as well as from the duration of the voyage Such a mode of meeting the probable difficulty from want of provisions seems to have suggested itself naturally to ancient navigators, as we find Eudoxus, when preparing for the circumnavigation of Africa, making arrangements to employ the same expedient (Strab ii. p. 100) Hence it would naturally be *supplied*, as a necessary incident, by those who believed in and reported the story

[5] Herodotus certainly visited Tyre (see ii 44); but, whether from the shortness of his stay or from some other cause, appears to have collected but little information there At least we do not find him referring to the testimony of Tyrian or Phœnician informants with regard to any geographical questions The Carthaginians, whom he repeatedly cites, he may have met either at Tyre or at Cyrene.

§ 5. The one only exception to this total want of circumstantial evidence is the fact reported by the navigators that in sailing round Libya they had the sun *on their right hand*. Such would undoubtedly have been the case if they had really penetrated into the southern hemisphere; but as no Greek had ever done this, Herodotus—whose theoretical knowledge of astronomy was certainly of the vaguest description—was naturally led to reject the statement as incredible. In modern times on the contrary, it has been frequently regarded as the strongest proof in favour of the whole account. A recent translator of Herodotus even goes so far as to say that "few would have believed the Phœnician circumnavigation of Africa, had it not been for this discovery." [6]

Yet it may well be doubted whether we are warranted in hastily assuming that such a statement must necessarily have been derived from personal observation. The Egyptian priests were well aware that the sun was vertical at Syene at the time of the summer solstice: and it was an inference so natural as to be almost inevitable that any one proceeding further south would have the sun *to the north* of him. The frequent intercourse with Meroe would confirm this view. It is probable moreover that Phœnician navigators had already frequented the coasts of the Erythræan Sea, considerably to the south of the Tropic of Cancer: and even in the particular voyage in question—if we suppose that the narrative had *any* foundation in fact, and that an exploring expedition was really sent out by Necho, it would easily have attained to latitudes where the phenomenon in question might be observed during a part of the year. Nothing is more common than to have theoretical inferences converted into statements of fact; and if the informants of Herodotus supposed—as he himself undoubtedly did, in common with almost all the Greek geographers in later times—that the continent of Africa trended away rapidly *to the west*, from near the mouth of the Red Sea, the assumption

---

[6] Rawlinson's *Herodotus*, vol iii p 35, note

that navigators proceeding along its southern coast, from east to west, would have the tropical sun to the north of them (and therefore on their right hand) would certainly not require a greater amount of astronomical knowledge than was possessed at this period both by Egyptians and Phœnicians.[7]

On the other hand it is certainly remarkable that no notice is taken, or at least no mention preserved, of the change of seasons in the southern hemisphere—a circumstance which must have been the more strongly impressed upon the minds of the navigators from its intimate connection with the choice of times for halting, with the purpose of sowing and reaping corn for their own supply.[8] Nor is anything said of other changes in the celestial appearances, such as the disappearance of the Great Bear and the pole-star, by which the Phœnicians were accustomed to steer, and the loss of which must therefore have been a source of great perplexity to them in the southern hemisphere. It may be said indeed, that the extreme conciseness of the narrative, as reported by Herodotus, renders all such *negative* arguments of little value : but unfortunately it is that very brevity, which, by depriving us of all incidental corroboration, leaves us simply to choose between the bare statement of the fact on the one side, and its great intrinsic improbability on the other.

Of course the statement of Herodotus, that the fleet returned by way of the Pillars of Hercules, would be conclusive evidence that it had really sailed round Africa; if we could rely upon its accuracy. But if we suppose the story to have acquired general currency, it would be readily seen that this must have

---

[7] Mr Cooley's remarks on this subject (in his edition of Larcher's *Notes on Herodotus*, vol ii p 30) are certainly well-founded See also Mr Blakesley's note to the passage, iv 42

[8] It is perhaps stretching this argument too far to lay much stress (as has been done by M Gosselin) upon the mention of *autumn* (ὅκως δὲ γίνοιτο φθινόπωρον) as the season for sowing their corn such a phrase might naturally have been introduced by Herodotus himself in relating the story he had heard But the arrangements of the voyagers for this object must have been so materially influenced by the changes of the seasons, both in the southern hemisphere and in the tropics, that it is difficult to understand how they could accommodate themselves to these alterations, without any previous knowledge to guide them

been the case, and such a fact would naturally be added by one of the successive narrators of the tale.

§ 6. The argument derived from the total neglect of this voyage and the important discovery supposed to have been thus made, in subsequent times, till it came to be totally disbelieved by the most judicious ancient geographers—an argument on which great stress has been laid by some modern writers, is certainly far from conclusive. Similar instances may be cited in comparatively recent times. Major Rennell has pointed out that the discovery of the eastern coast of New Holland, generally attributed to Captain Cook, had really been made by a Dutch voyager near 150 years before; a circumstance wholly unknown to the great navigator, as well as to all his contemporaries.[9] A still more striking instance (probably unknown to Major Rennell himself) was that of the discovery of the continent of North America under the name of "Vinland" by the Northmen in the eleventh century—a discovery which had been entirely forgotten, until it was brought to light again in our own days.

The expedition sent out by Necho—if we are to believe that the narrative had any foundation at all—was intended solely for the purpose of settling the geographical question, and resembled in this respect the voyage of Scylax of Caryanda, who explored the Erythræan Sea by order of Darius. The great length of time employed would in itself be sufficient to deter future navigators from attempting to follow the example for commercial purposes; and the discovery, even if it were really made, would not have had the effect of opening out a new commercial route to other lands.

The circumnavigation of Africa by the Portuguese, in the fifteenth century, was accomplished *with a view to arriving in*

---

[9] Rennell's *Geography of Herodotus*, p 714. See also Major's *Prince Henry the Navigator*, p. 442. From the researches of this recent writer it appears clear that a considerable portion of the coasts of Australia had been actually discovered by the Portuguese at a still earlier period, though never recorded in an authentic form, or at least in such a form as to attract general attention.

India; and the result fully justified the importance attached to it on that account.[1] No such prize would reward the Phœnician voyagers, or lead other navigators to follow in their track. Yet it certainly seems strange that they should not have held sufficient intercourse with the natives to discover the great abundance of gold existing among them, either on the coasts of Mozambique or those of Guinea; and gold was undoubtedly, in ancient, even more than in modern, times, the attraction which none could resist.[2]

§ 7. On the whole it may be said that the alleged voyage of the Phœnicians under Necho is one of those statements that cannot be disproved, or pronounced to be absolutely impossible; but that the difficulties and improbabilities attending it are so great that they cannot reasonably be set aside without better evidence than the mere statement of Herodotus, upon the authority of unknown informants.[3] We have abundant evidence in later times how easily such reports were got up and believed—as in the case of Eudoxus of Cyzicus (which we shall have occasion to consider hereafter), and the Indians, who were reported by Cornelius Nepos to have circumnavigated the north of Asia and Europe from the Erythræan Sea to the Baltic (!); and we shall see that in the case of Hanno, an expedition which did not really advance as far south as the Equator was magnified into a complete circumnavigation of Africa.[4]

§ 8. Herodotus, however, did not rest his belief in the peninsular character of Africa solely upon the history of this expedition, conclusive as he deemed it. "Necho (he tells us) was *the first* to prove it; but besides this (he adds) the Carthaginians assert the same thing." Whether they based their

---

[1] Hence the name of Cape of Good Hope, which was given to the southern promontory of Africa by John II, king of Portugal, 'in anticipation "of the realization of the long-coveted passage to India." (Major's *Prince Henry*, p 345)

[2] Sofala, on the coast of Mozambique, was during the middle ages the tract from which the Arabian traders derived their principal supply of gold
[3] Note V, p 317
[4] See the next Chapter

belief upon any alleged discoveries of their own, he has unfortunately left uncertain, though it appears probable that they did so.[5] But the historian breaks off abruptly to tell us of another attempt to circumnavigate Africa, which did *not* prove successful, and leaves us in the dark as to what the Carthaginians may have really accomplished.[6]

§ 9. The unsuccessful attempt, just adverted to, is thus related by Herodotus.[7] Sataspes, a Persian nobleman of high rank, having incurred the displeasure of Xerxes, and been condemned to death by that monarch, was allowed, at the intercession of his mother, to obtain a respite of his sentence on condition of sailing round the African continent. For this purpose he went down to Egypt, and having there obtained a ship and a crew, he set sail for the Pillars of Hercules. After passing through the Straits, he doubled the Libyan headland of Cape Soloeis, and proceeded from thence towards the south for a long distance. But after a voyage of many months, having passed over a vast extent of sea, and finding it still stretch farther and farther before him, he made up his mind to return. According to his report, the coast, at the farthest point which he was able to reach was inhabited by a race of men of dwarfish stature, who were clad in dresses made of

---

[5] Mr Rawlinson indeed translates the passage of Herodotus (iv 43) as distinctly asserting that "the Carthaginians, according to their own account, *made the voyage*" and Mr. Blakesley also understands the words in the same sense. But it seems to me clear that the true meaning of the passage is οὕτω μὲν αὕτη (ἡ Λιβύη) ἐγνώσθη τὸ πρῶτον (sc περίρρυτος ἐοῦσα) μετὰ δὲ Καρχηδόνιοί εἰσι οἱ λέγοντες (sc περίρρυτον εἶναι). This is the proposition that he sets out with asserting (iv 42), and that all the other statements are intended to confirm. He would probably have proceeded to tell us the grounds on which the Carthaginians based their confidence, had he not unfortunately been led away (as in so many other passages in his history) by the love of digression to recount the voyage of Sataspes, who did *not* succeed in circumnavigating Africa This account he had probably heard at Samos, whither the eunuch of Sataspes had fled with his treasures. It is certainly a mistake to suppose, as Larcher and Ukert have done, that it was this history of Sataspes, which Herodotus had heard *from the Carthaginians* The words ἐπεὶ Σατάσπης γε ... οὐ περιέπλωσε Λιβύην, ἐπ' αὐτὸ τοῦτο πεμφθεὶς are conclusive on this point.

[6] This is the more to be regretted, as there is great probability that their views were founded on the voyage of Hanno, concerning which we have authentic information from another quarter

[7] iv. 43.

leaves of the palm-tree. They were a harmless race, dwelling in towns and possessing cattle, but fled to the mountains on the approach of the strangers. He further alleged, as a reason why he did not continue his voyage, that his ship stuck fast, and would not advance any farther.[8] But this account, which Herodotus himself appears to have considered a mere pretence, did not satisfy Xerxes, who ordered the unfortunate voyager to be executed, as having failed in his enterprise.

Whatever may have been the real cause of his return, it is clear that Sataspes, by attempting the circumnavigation *from the west* encountered difficulties and delays which would not have presented themselves had he taken the contrary direction; but there seems no reason to doubt that he had advanced far enough to the south to come in contact with the negro tribes, beyond the great desert, who were comparatively civilized, having fixed abodes and dwelling in towns. Beyond this it is impossible to form any safe conclusion from such a meagre narrative.

---

[8] This is a favourite excuse, or fancy, with timid voyagers in all ages. The same reason was alleged by the Arabian navigators in the middle ages, as preventing their continuing their voyages beyond Sofala around the Cape of Good Hope.

NOTE A, p. 263.

USE OF CAMELS.

Mr. Kenrick (*Ancient Egypt*, vol. i. p. 76) notices the "almost insurmountable" difficulty of traversing the Sahara before the introduction of the camel, " which never appears in the monuments of the Pharaonic times." and he adds in a note: "We have such ample representations of Egyptian life, that if the camel had been naturalized there as a beast of burden, it must have occurred in the paintings."

Herodotus tells us that the Arabians brought camels laden with water-skins to supply the army of Cambyses on its march through the desert from Syria into Egypt (iii. 9). But notwithstanding this, they do not appear to have ever come into use among the Egyptians. Quintus Curtius indeed mentions their employment by Alexander the Great during his march to the Oasis of Ammon (iv. 30, § 12), but this appears to have been quite an isolated instance: and strange as it appears to us, it seems to be a well-established fact that the use of camels was practically unknown in Africa until after the Mahomedan conquest. (See the dissertation by Ritter, in his *Erdkunde von Asien*, vol. viii. part ii. pp. 705–710.)

Hence the accounts given by Heeren [9] and by Mr. Hoskins [1] of the supposed extent of the commerce of Meroe in very ancient times, which are based throughout upon the supposition of its being a centre from which large caravans of camels traversed the deserts in all directions, are almost wholly illusory.

NOTE B, p. 263.

DISTANCES ON THE NILE.

Yet even in regard to this part of the Nile his notions of the distances are very inaccurate. So much time and ingenuity have

---

[9] *African Nations*, vol. 1 pp. 430–472. [1] *Travels in Ethiopia*, 4to, Lond. 1835.

been spent in endeavouring to reconcile or explain the statements of ancient writers with regard to distances, in countries which were very imperfectly known, that it is important to observe how widely the statements of Herodotus differ from the truth, even in a country so well known as Egypt, which he had himself visited, and where there is no possibility of error as to the localities. Herodotus tells us in one passage that the distance from Heliopolis to the sea is 1500 stadia exactly (ii. 7), which would be equal to 150 geographical miles, or about 173 English miles: while in another passage (ii. 9), though apparently referring to the same computation, he allows only 1260 stadia for the same interval. The actual distance to the old Sebennytic mouth of the Nile—the nearest of the three, and therefore certainly the one that we should naturally suppose to be meant—is, according to Sir G. Wilkinson, only about 110 English miles, following the course of the river. If on the other hand we suppose the distance to be reckoned from the Canopic mouth, which was that generally resorted to by the Greeks, the distance would be about 150 miles, a tolerable approach to the truth. but the necessity of having recourse to this supposition in itself shows the vagueness of such estimates, considered as geographical *data*.

Again, the distances above Heliopolis, where no such ambiguity can arise, are equally overstated. Thus Herodotus reckons the distance from Heliopolis up the river to Thebes at 81 Egyptian *schœni* or 4860 stadia, equal to about 552 English miles, and that from Thebes to Elephantine at 1800 stadia, or more than 206 English miles. But the former distance (according to Sir G. Wilkinson) is really only 421 English miles, and the latter does not exceed 124 miles.

The source of his error is in this instance not difficult to discover. The distances are doubtless given by him according to the estimates of the Egyptian boatmen, who would express them in *schœni* ($\sigma\chi o\hat{\iota}\nu o\iota$), as indeed Herodotus himself does in several passages: and these he reduced into stadia, at the rate of 60 stadia to the schœne (ii. 6). But this Egyptian measure was, as we learn from Strabo (who had himself made the voyage up the Nile), a very vague and unsettled one, varying, he assures us, from 30 to 120 stadia. (Strab. xvii. c. 1, § 24, p. 804). No doubt the distances were in fact merely *estimated*, not *measured* at all. and this glaring instance sufficiently shows us how little such estimates are to be relied on.

On the other hand it is remarkable that Herodotus reckons it only nine days' voyage up the river from Heliopolis to Thebes, probably speaking from his own experience. but such a passage is unusually rapid, and twenty days is not more than "a fair average passage" from Cairo to Thebes. (Wilkinson's *Handbook for Egypt*, p. 2.)

It may be added that his enormous exaggeration concerning the size of the Lake Mœris, which he describes as 3600 stadia (360 geographical miles) in circumference (ii. 149), while according to the recent careful investigations of M. Linant de Bellefonds, cited by Parthey (*Zur Erdkunde des Alten Aegyptens*, p. 511), it could never have exceeded 48 to 50 geographical miles in circuit, shows how little dependence can be placed on such estimates: even where, as in this instance, Herodotus had himself visited the locality.

NOTE C, p. 264.

THE DODECASCHŒNUS.

Herodotus tells us that this part of the navigation, requiring the boats to be dragged by main force up the rapids, continued for 12 *schœni* (equal to 720 stadia); this required four days on account of the rapidity of the current and the consequent slowness of progress. This distance of 12 schœni from Tachompso to Syene or Elephantine is confirmed by an inscription of the time of Tiberius, discovered at Philæ. it afterwards gave name to a district called the Dodecaschœnus (Δωδεκάσχοινος), which occupied precisely this portion of the valley of the Nile. (Ptolemy, *Geography*, iv. 5, § 74.) The error of Herodotus appears to have arisen from his confounding the interval thus designated with that of the rapids, and supposing the difficulties of navigation to extend equally through the whole distance.

In other respects his description of the rapids themselves, and the mode of passing them, is very correct, and presents a striking contrast to the absurd fables current on the subject in later times. The First Cataract, as it is commonly called, is in fact merely a succession of rapids: the entire descent in a space of five miles being only 80 feet. (Kenrick's *Egypt*, p. 31.)

The Tachompso of Herodotus appears in Ptolemy (*l. c.*) under the form of Metacompso, which he places opposite to Pselcis, a well-known locality, the ruins of which are still visible at Dakkeh. But Herodotus was misinformed as to the size of the island, there being nothing in this part of the Nile but mere islets.

NOTE D, p. 266.

THE AUTOMOLI.

There seems no doubt that these Automoli of Herodotus, whom he mentions only by this Greek form of their name, are the same people noticed by Eratosthenes and several later writers under the name of the Sembritæ or Sebritæ, to whom a similar origin is ascribed: and the data furnished by these writers enable us to place them with reasonable certainty in the region of the modern Sennaar, in 13° to 14° N. latitude: and about twenty days' journey above Meroe. (See this subject fully discussed by St. Martin, *Le Nord de l'Afrique dans l'Antiquité*, pp. 24–29), and by Mr. Cooley (*Ptolemy and the Nile*, pp. 20–23); a work with which the French author seems to have been unacquainted.) It is impossible to account for the enormous exaggeration of the distance by Herodotus, except from the tendency to vague overstatements common in speaking of all remote and imperfectly known regions. The contrast it presents with the accuracy of his information concerning Meroe is an instructive example of the difference in the value of his statements according to the nature of his materials—a distinction which cannot be too carefully borne in mind in discussing the statements of ancient writers on geography.

NOTE E, p. 266.

DISTANCES ON THE UPPER NILE.

This is a very fair approximation to the truth. Timosthenes, the admiral of Ptolemy Philadelphus, also estimated the distance from Syene to Meroe at 60 days' journey, but whether by land or by water is not stated (Plin. *H. N.* vi. c. 99, § 183). The distances given by Herodotus in detail give only 56 days, viz., 4 days for the ascent of the rapids, 40 days by land, and 12 more by water to Meroe . but the omission is obviously to be supplied by the supposed lake, and the navigation thence to the beginning of the upper rapids. This would correspond with the interval between Dakkeh and the second cataract at Wady Halfa, which must always have been the point at which voyagers up the Nile quitted their boats and took to travelling by land. The navigation in this part being unimpeded, the distance might probably be accomplished without difficulty in four days.

NOTE F, p. 266.

COURSE OF THE NILE FROM WEST TO EAST.

Niebuhr is almost the only wiiter upon the subject who has seen the necessity of applying the words of Herodotus (ῥέει δὲ ἀπ' ἑσπέρης τε καὶ ἡλίου δυσμέων, ii. 31) to the course of the river from the country of the Automoli to Elephantine.[2] But Valckenaer, in a note to Herodotus (ii. 84), understands and explains the words in the same sense : " *Supra Ægyptum* fluit ab Occidente." Unless we thus understand them, the comparison of the course of the Nile with that of the Ister becomes quite unintelligible : for there would be no reason to assign to it this long course from the west. Colonel Leake and Mr. Rawlinson both translate the passage as if Herodotus had meant to say that *at that point*—the farthest to which it was known with certainty, the river came from the west, though up to the land of the Automoli it had had a course from south to north. But Herodotus would surely have given some clearer intimation of such a marked change in its direction had such been his meaning. The passage as it stands at present (μέχρι μέν νυν τεσσέρων μηνῶν πλόου καὶ ὁδοῦ γινώσκεται ὁ Νεῖλος πάρεξ τοῦ ἐν Αἰγύπτῳ ῥεύματος . . . . ῥέει δὲ ἀπ' ἑσπέρης τε καὶ ἡλίου δυσμέων), certainly seems intended to convey the same idea as we find elsewhere moie distinctly expressed in the case of the Borysthenes, the sources of which were also unknown—a passage in all respects very parallel to the one now under consideration : μέχρι μέν νυν Γέρρου χώρου, ἐς τὸν τεσσεράκοντα ἡμερέων πλόος ἐστί, γινώσκεται ῥέων ἀπὸ βορέω ἀνέμου (iv. 53). In both cases the natural interpretation of the words seems to be that

---

[2] *Geogr. of Herodotus*, pp 15, 20.

the *general* direction of the course of the river is meant, not merely its direction at the farthest point indicated.

It is singular that almost all the commentators conceive Herodotus to have *assumed* this westerly origin of the Nile, in consequence of the story of the Nasamonians. It appears to me that the course of his reasoning was just the converse. He knew, or supposed he knew, that the Nile in the upper part of its course, as far as it was known, came from the west. Beyond that, he says, no one knew anything about it. But when he hears of these Nasamonians having discovered a great river, *with crocodiles in it, flowing from the west,* he immediately concludes that that river can be no other than the Nile; an inference natural enough from the *data* that he possessed.

NOTE G, p. 268.

SUPPOSED SOURCES OF THE NILE.

The only exception was a tale told him by a certain priest, who was registrar of the sacred property in the temple of Athena at Sais in Lower Egypt, which Herodotus justly rejects as utterly unworthy of credit (ii. 28). According to this fable the real source of the Nile was just on the frontiers of Egypt, between Syene and Elephantine, where there were two mountains with sharply-peaked summits, called Crophi and Mophi, and between the two was an unfathomable abyss, from which arose the waters that were the real sources of the Nile, one half of which flowed towards the north into Egypt, the other half towards the south into Ethiopia. He added, that the abyss had been found to be unfathomable by Psammetichus, who had in vain attempted to sound its depths with a rope many thousand fathoms in length; a circumstance which, Herodotus justly observes, *if the fact was true,* might be accounted for by the violence of the eddy at this point, occasioned by the passage of the river between the two mountains.

It is unnecessary to point out the absurdity of a story, which represents the Nile above Syene as flowing *towards* Ethiopia instead of *from* it; but it is certain that traces of the same idea—whether really of Egyptian origin, or in consequence of its being told by Herodotus—are found current at a later period. Thus when Germanicus visited Egypt in the reign of Tiberius, he was shown the unfathomable abyss in question; and Seneca alludes to it as regarded by the natives as the source of the Nile (*Tacit. Annal.* ii. 61; Seneca, *Quæst. Nat.* iv. 2). Herodotus, however, appears to have heard nothing of it, when he himself ascended the river as far as Elephantine, and it was doubtless *on his return* to Lower Egypt that he first heard the tale from the priest at Sais, so that he had no opportunity of making enquiries on the spot.

It is certainly hard upon Herodotus that he has been frequently censured, both in ancient and modern times (Strabo, xvii. p. 819; Mure's *History of Greek Literature*, vol. iv. p. 387), for his credulity in relating such a story as this, though he in fact cites it only to express his utter disbelief of it, and thought the priest was making game of him (ἔμοιγε παίζειν ἐδόκεε φάμενος εἰδέναι ἀτρεκέως). But, as often happens in similar cases, an idea once started, however absurd, found supporters who attempted to give it a rational interpretation, and it was doubtless the tale told by Herodotus, which gave rise to the theory, found in some of the Arabic writers, of two Niles taking their rise together, and the one flowing to the north, the other to the south. But they judiciously placed these sources beyond the limits of their own positive knowledge.

It was probably this last theory, combined with a very confused and imperfect recollection of the passage in Herodotus, that led an eminent traveller in our own time to look for " the fountains of Herodotus " in the interior of the continent, far south of the Equator; forgetting that the " fountains " as described to the historian were to be found between Syene and Elephantine, within the confines of Egypt itself! (Livingstone's *Last Journals*, vol. ii. pp. 50, 169.)

NOTE H, p. 271.

EXPEDITION OF THE NASAMONIANS.

This view is maintained by Colonel Leake, in a paper published in the *Journal of the Geographical Society*, vol. ii. p. 1-28,[3] as well as by Major Rennell (*Geogr. of Herodot.* p. 432, 4to edit.), in whose

---

[3] The substance of this paper has been reproduced by Mr E B James in the article NIGER in Dr Smith's *Dict of Ancient Geography*, vol. ii. p 428.

time, however, the geography of Central Africa was still very imperfectly known. It is strongly opposed by Mr. Cooley (in his edition of Larcher's *Notes on Herodotus*, vol. i. p. 241), who contends that the river could be no other than the Yeou, the main river of Bornou, and regards it as "in the highest degree improbable" that the Nasamonians should have reached the Quorra, or river of Timbuctoo. But, without insisting too closely upon the direction assigned by Herodotus, it must be admitted that we do less violence to his statement by supposing them to have travelled in a *south-westerly* direction, than *due south*, which they must have done in order to reach Bornou. And with regard to the distance to be traversed, supposing them to set out from Fezzan, which is admitted by both hypotheses, the distance to be traversed before reaching the river of Bornou is not less than 12 degrees of latitude or 720 G. miles, as measured in a direct line on the map, while that to the nearest point of the Quorra hardly exceeds 900 G. miles. Supposing the one journey to be possible, it is difficult to say that the difference is such as to render the other impossible.

The theory of M. de St. Martin, which agrees in substance with that of M. Walckenaer, that the Nasamonians never crossed the great Sahara at all, but that the river visited by them was only the river of Wargla, to the south of Mount Atlas,[4] appears to me to satisfy none of the conditions of the problem. There is no permanent river there, but a mere *wadi*, with a lake, which becomes a mere bed of salt in the summer; there could never have been crocodiles in such a stream, nor could the inhabitants have been materially different from the other Libyan races. The oasis of Wargla is indeed exactly one of those described by Herodotus as situated in the "belt of sand," the broad expanse of the desert stretches out from thence both to the south and west.[5] It was this desert that he conceived the Nasamonians to have *crossed;* and there appears no alternative, but either to believe that they had really done so, or to reject the whole story as a fiction. Even if we adopt the latter course, it seems difficult to account for it without supposing that some vague rumour of the existence of such a river in the interior of the continent had reached the tribes on the sea-coast.

---

[4] St Martin, *Le Nord de l'Afrique dans l'Antiquité*, pp 16-20, Walckenaer, *Recherches Géographiques sur l'Afrique Septentrionale*, p 353
[5] See the description of it in Mr. Tristram's *Great Sahara*, p 218

NOTE I, p. 271.

DIFFICULTY OF COMMUNICATION WITH INTERIOR.

It has indeed been assumed by several modern writers, more especially by Heeren, that the caravan trade of Central Africa must always have been substantially the same; and that as there are now, and have been ever since the middle ages, frequented caravan routes from Tripoli by Fezzan to Bornou, and again from Morocco to Timbuctoo and the regions on the Niger, similar communications must have existed in ancient times. But there seems no doubt that the existing system of caravan trade dates only from the introduction of Islamism into Africa. It was the Arabs who first introduced the camel into Northern Africa, and without camels any extensive intercourse with the interior was impossible. The Negro races have never shown any disposition to avail themselves of this mode of transport, and at the present day the commerce of the interior is carried on almost entirely by Moorish, that is, by Mohammedan, traders. The spread of Islamism has doubtless led to increased communication from another cause, the necessity for the Mohammedan inhabitants of the outlying and detached regions of the continent to make the pilgrimage to Mecca. Even in the most flourishing times of the Carthaginians they do not appear to have made any use of camels; and as late as the days of Strabo the communications with the tribes of Western Africa who dwelt beyond the Sahara were scanty and irregular.[6] In the time of Herodotus there is certainly no indication that either the Carthaginians or the Greeks of the Cyrenaïca had any commercial intercourse with the regions beyond the Great Desert.

Heeren indeed dwells more especially upon the traffic in *gold*, and gold dust, which he supposes to have attracted the merchants of antiquity, as it has done the Moorish traders in later times, to brave the perils of the desert, on the north side of which, as he justly observes, little or no gold is to be found.[7] But there is in fact no indication to be found in Herodotus, that gold was brought from

---

[6] Strabo, xvii p. 828. The Pharusians (as he tells us), whom he considered as dwelling beyond the great desert in Western Libya, held only rare and occasional intercourse with the inhabitants of Mauritania, "tying skins of water under the bellies of their horses" in order to cross the desert; a remarkable proof of the shifts by which they endeavoured to supply the want of camels.

[7] *African Nations*, vol. i. p. 183.

the interior of Libya at all. It was indeed supposed to be found in fabulous abundance among the Macrobian Ethiopians, who dwelt on the southern sea (iii. 17), but all that is related of them has an air of mere fable. The historian also describes in detail the trade in gold carried on by the Carthaginians with the tribes beyond the Pillars of Hercules on the shores of the western Ocean, but no trace is to be found of the existence of any such trade *by land* with the interior of the continent.

NOTE K, p. 276.

ERRONEOUS POSITION ASSIGNED TO CARTHAGE.

Strabo supposed the parallel of Carthage to be only 1000 stadia (100 G. miles) to the north of that of Alexandria, and the innermost bight of the Great Syrtis to be less than 2000 stadia south of Carthage. The real difference is not less than six degrees and three-quarters of latitude, or more than 400 G. miles. Even Ptolemy fell into a similar error, and placed Carthage less than two degrees to the north of Alexandria. The influence of this error upon their conception of the geography of the Mediterranean will have to be considered hereafter. but its effect upon that of the interior of Africa was to bring the land of the Garamantes (Fezzan) nearly on a parallel with that of the Gætulians, the Biledulgerid of the Arabs: a change which must be carefully borne in mind in discussing the views of Herodotus upon the subject.

NOTE L, p. 276.

THE OASES.

The name Oasis or Auasis, which is of Egyptian origin, is not, indeed, found in Herodotus in this sense: it was probably first introduced by the Alexandrian writers, and was already familiar to Strabo. Herodotus in one passage speaks of an expedition sent by Cambyses against a *city* Oasis, where the capital of the Great Oasis, west of Thebes, is undoubtedly meant (iii. 26), but he does not seem to have had any idea of the term otherwise than as a proper name. Even at the present day the spot thus designated is commonly known as " el Wah," " *the* Oasis," in contradistinction to all others.

NOTE M, p. 277.

SYMMETRICAL ARRANGEMENT OF OASES.

This tendency to symmetry and regularity is not peculiar to Herodotus. The Arabian geographers, and the Arabs of the present day, commonly reckon "ten days' journey" from one of these halting-places to another, with little reference to the exact distance. The journey from the Oasis of Ammon (Siwah) to that of Augila is, in fact, just about ten days' journey, and this was probably the one best known to Herodotus, from the proximity of these two stations to the Cyrenaica. Edrisi, in his geographical work, reckons ten days' journey from Aujilah to Zala, and again ten days more to Zawilah, which was in his time the capital of Fezzan.

It must be remarked also that no allowance is made for the extent of the Oases themselves, though these in several instances occupy a district of considerable size, and that of Fezzan spreads out into an extensive region. Herodotus, indeed, appears to have regarded the "hill of salt," which he supposed to exist in each case, as the centre of the habitable district around it, and took no account of the extent of the latter.

NOTE N, p. 278.

CONFUSION OF GREAT OASIS AND THAT OF AMMON.

This appears to me by far the simplest solution of the difficulty. But with their usual unwillingness to admit that Herodotus can have made a mistake, several writers have suggested that an intermediate station has fallen out of the text, and that the route he has traced lay through the Great and Little Oasis to that of Ammon. It is not impossible that this may have been the case with regard to his original information, but there is no room to doubt the accuracy of the text of Herodotus as it stands : and this must be taken therefore as correctly representing his view of the matter. In like manner Heeren has suggested that another station may have been.

omitted between Augila and the Garamantes, the real distance being nearly double that indicated by Herodotus. But, as Niebuhr justly observes, the soundness of the text in all these passages admits of no doubt. and we have only to deal with them as we find them. Whether the original error lay with Herodotus or his informants, it is impossible for us now to determine.

It is, however, not improbable that the confusion in this instance may have arisen from the circumstance that the same Egyptian deity, whom Herodotus calls the Theban Zeus, and who was generally known to the Greeks as Zeus Ammon, had a temple also in the Great Oasis. Herodotus may have obtained his information concerning this temple *at Thebes,* while his accounts of the true Ammonium—the Oasis of Siwah—were almost certainly collected at Cyrene. Under these circumstances it seems not unlikely that he may have confused the two.

It must be added that his account of the expedition sent by Cambyses against the Ammonians (iii. 25, 26) is based upon the same misconception, as he represents the king as first detaching the troops for that purpose *from Thebes:* though the Ammonians really lay much nearer to Memphis, and nearest of all to the Lake Mœris. In this narrative, however, he clearly separates the Oasis, where the *city* of that name was situated, from the Ammonium. It was in the sandy desert *between the two* that the army perished.

That Herodotus should have fallen into error as to the true geographical position of the Oasis of Ammon is not surprising. Even Ptolemy—as M. Parthey has pointed out—brought it down much too far south, so as to make it almost precisely equidistant from Memphis and from Thebes. (Parthey, *Die Oase des Ammon,* p. 148 and see his map.)

NOTE O, p. 280.

THE ATLANTES OF HERODOTUS.

Mr Tristram suggests that the description of Mount Atlas as given by Herodotus may have arisen, in part at least, from confused accounts of Mount Zaghouan, the only conspicuous isolated mountain in the Regency of Tunis. (*The Great Sahara,* p. 77.) But Mount Zaghouan is situated far to the north of the line of oases which we are following, in the "inhabited district" of Herodotus and among the agricultural Libyans. It is quite clear that, according to the conception of Herodotus, the belt of sand in which these oases were situated extended continuously in a straight line to the western ocean (iv. 181, 185), and had nothing to do with the caravan routes *to Carthage*. Such a chain of oases, with or without salt rocks and hills, might, in fact, be traced throughout the whole tract: but his information concerning it was evidently of the vaguest description. Still the name of Atlas and the Atlantes certainly seems to indicate a connection—however confused and imperfectly understood—with the far-famed Mount Atlas, of which the name at least was so familiar to the Greeks. At the same time the name, whether Greek or Phœnician, was certainly not of indigenous origin, and the question naturally suggests itself, whether the description of this semi-fabulous mountain was not transferred by the Greek traders to a mountain of the interior, with which it had no real connection, on account of the *name* Atlantes (or some native form resembling it), which they had met with in that part of the country.

It is certain at least that Herodotus did not himself conceive these Atlantes as being situated in the neighbourhood of the Ocean: as he distinctly tells us that the ridge or belt of sand was continued beyond them to the Pillars of Hercules, and the region outside of them (διήκει δ' ὦν ἡ ὀφρύη μέχρι Ἡρακλέων στηλέων, καὶ τὸ ἔξω τουτέων, iv. 185), but that he is not able to give the names of the stations; thus implying clearly that he supposed there was room for more than one of them.

NOTE P, p. 284.

THE LOTOPHAGI.

Scylax extends the name of the Lotophagi to the inhabitants of the whole coast, between the two Syrtes, from the river Cinyps to the commencement of the Lesser Syrtis (§ 110, ed. Muller). But he describes the island, to which he gives the name of Brachion, though it is certainly the same with the Meninx of later writers, as particularly abundant in the fruit. Polybius, who visited the region in person, has left us a particular account of the lotus-tree and its fruit, which evidently excited great interest among the

Greeks, on account of its connection with the Homeric fable. (Polyb. xii. 2.)

The tree in question (the Rhamnus Lotus, or Zizyphus Lotus of botanists) is still found in abundance on the island of Djerba, or Gerba (the Meninx of Strabo and Ptolemy), and its fruit is still used as an article of diet by the Arabs, though modern travellers are far from finding in it the attraction that operated so powerfully on the companions of Ulysses (Barth, *Wanderungen in Nord-Afrika*, p. 262; Guérin, *Voyage Archéologique dans la Régence de Tunis*, vol. i. p. 206). They, however, speak in the highest terms of the beauty and fertility of the island, which is called by Barth "a terrestrial paradise," a circumstance which may have contributed to its being selected by tradition as the abode of "the dreamy lotus-eaters."

NOTE Q, p. 286.

THE RIVER CINYPS.

The river Cinyps of Herodotus, which is mentioned also by Scylax and the later geographers, can be certainly identified with the little stream called Wadi Quaam (but known also by various other Arabic appellations), which flows into the sea a few miles to the east of Lebdeh (Leptis). The plain on both sides of it, extending from Lebdeh to Mesarata, though now uncultivated, is still remarkable for its natural fertility; forming a striking contrast to the barren tracts on each side of it. (Beechey's *Northern Africa*. p. 51; Barth, *Wanderungen*, pp. 317-319.) In ancient times it possessed an almost proverbial celebrity for its productiveness, which probably arose in great measure from this exceptional mention of it in Herodotus (See Mela, i. § 37, and Ovid, *Ex Ponto*, ii. 7, 25. Cinyphiæ segetis citius numerabis aristas). It was doubtless well known to the Greeks of Cyrene, from whom he derived his information; and at an earlier period the Spartan prince Dorieus had attempted to found a colony there, but was driven out by the Libyan tribes, supported by the Carthaginians, who naturally resisted this attempt to extend the chain of Greek colonies so much nearer to their own frontiers (Herodot. v. 42). Scylax, however, speaks of the existence of a town upon its banks (§ 109), though he says that it was no longer inhabited in his time. But within a few miles of it arose the city of Leptis—called for distinction's sake Leptis Magna—which became, first under the Carthaginians, and afterwards under the Romans, one of the most important cities of Northern Africa.

NOTE R, p. 286.

THE SYRTIS.

It is singular that Herodotus, though well acquainted with the name and extent of the Syrtis, should say nothing of its physical peculiarities or the dangers of its navigation, which were well known to Scylax (§ 110). These last, though greatly exaggerated by ancient writers, are not without a foundation in fact; and arise from the extremely flat and low character of the coast, together with a number of sunken rocks, as well as the violence of the north winds, which have here an uninterrupted sweep across the broadest part of the Mediterranean. The tides, which are represented by ancient writers as one of the great sources of danger in *both* Syrtes, are in fact almost imperceptible in the Greater Syrtis, though they attain to greater importance in the Lesser Syrtis than at any other point in the Mediterranean, except Venice (Smyth's *Mediterranean*, pp. 187, 188; Rennell, p. 651). In this respect, as in several others, the writers in question seem to have confounded the characteristics of the two gulfs.

The extensive quicksands, which gave rise to the notion that the coast was "neither land nor sea, but a kind of mixture of both," have now in great measure disappeared; and along the whole of this line of coast Captain Beechey is of opinion that the land has been gaining on the sea, for that we find "the ancient parts filled up, the lakes converted into marshes, and the quicksands to have become solid and firm" (Beechey's *Northern Africa*, p. 272). Hence it is by no means impossible that the peculiar characters of this region were more strongly developed in ancient times, and afforded somewhat more foundation for the fables that were built upon them. The silence of Herodotus cannot fairly be cited on the other side as proving that these peculiarities did not exist in his time, or even that they were unknown to the Cyrenæans in his day. It is quite unreasonable to commend Herodotus (as has been done by some modern writers) for his superior information and accuracy, merely because he *says nothing about* the dangers of the Syrtis, of which he never mentions the name except incidentally.

NOTE S, p. 287.

THE LAKE TRITONIS.

Major Rennell, in whose time the geography of this part of Africa was still very imperfectly known, was the first to suggest that the Lake Tritonis of Herodotus was in fact identical with the Lesser Syrtis of later writers, or rather comprised that and the inland lake of Lowdeah united (*Geogr. of Herodot.* p. 662): and this view is supported by Mr. Rawlinson, who speaks of the Lake Tritonis as " an inner sea" which stood to the Lesser Syrtis in the same relation as the Sea of Azof to the Euxine. (Rawlinson's *Herodotus*, vol. iii. p. 154, note 1.) But I confess I cannot see any necessity for its adoption. The terms in which Herodotus speaks of the Lake Tritonis (ἡ Τριτωνὶς λίμνη) and the tribes that dwelt *around* it are certainly such as to imply *primâ facie* that it was a lake or inland piece of water: he nowhere alludes to its saltness, but calls it " a large lake" ἐς λίμνην μεγάλην Τριτωνίδα, iv. 179) and represents it as the boundary between the nomad Libyans and the agricultural tribes. Even at the present day the salt lake known under the various names of Chott el Fejij, Chott el Melah, and Sebkah Faraoun (which is termed by Shaw Shibkah el Lowdeah), is not less than 110 miles in length: and there can be no doubt that at an earlier period it was much more extensive and was united with various other salt lakes in the same region, so as to cover an area of nearly double that extent. (See the description of the recent French travellers, M. Guérin in the *Voyage Archéologique dans la Régence de Tunis*, vol. i. pp. 247-250; and M. Charles Martins in the *Revue des Deux Mondes* for July, 1864.) It is at present separated from the sea only by a low sandy isthmus not more than ten miles in width, and there is every reason to believe that this is nothing more than a bar of sand gradually thrown up by the action of the winds and tides. It is therefore not improbable that in the time of Herodotus, as well as in that of Scylax, it communicated with the sea by a narrow channel, or opening, which has gradually silted up.

Thus far the views of Major Rennell may be admitted to be well-founded and to display his usual sagacity. But when he argues that because Herodotus describes Jason as driven by a storm "into the shoals of the Tritonian Lake" before he saw the land, he must therefore have supposed it to be a gulf of the sea, not an inland lake, and that that gulf could be no other than the Lesser Syrtis (p. 663); he certainly seems to be requiring an unreasonable amount of accuracy from a writer who is relating a mere poetical legend, and applying it to a country which he never visited. Supposing the name of the Lesser Syrtis to be still unknown to fame, " the shoals of the Tritonian Lake " would not be an unapt designation of the shallows which were in fact situated close to its mouth.

The mention by Herodotus (iv. 178) of "a large river," called the Triton, flowing *into* the Tritonian Lake, is a difficulty which admits of no satisfactory solution. No such river exists at the present day, nor could there ever have been any considerable perennial stream in that region of Africa. But Herodotus had evidently no idea of the real nature of the Tritonian Lake—a vast expanse of very shallow salt water, which was probably, even in his day, often dry in many places: he supposed it to be a lake like any other, and that a lake of such extent should have a large river as its feeder was but a natural assumption. The same idea was as usual retained by later geographers, who ought to have been better acquainted with this part of Africa: Pliny (v. 4, § 28) speaks of a vast lake receiving the river Triton, from which it derives its name. Mela gives a precisely similar account (i. 7, § 36), and Ptolemy describes the river Triton as rising in the mountain of Vasaleton, and constituting *three* lakes, to one of which he gives the name of Tritonitis. The three lakes in question are probably only distinct names for three portions of the large expanse, which is sometimes united into one sheet of water, more often separated into three by dry intervals of sand covered with salt. (See the descriptions above cited.)

Scylax, who wrote only about a century after Herodotus, has left us (§ 110, p. 88, ed. Muller) a much more particular account of the lake Tritonis, as well as of the Lesser Syrtis, which he designates by that name, and describes as 2000 stadia in circumference, and much more dangerous and difficult of navigation than the other Syrtis. He then speaks of an island called Tritonis, which he places (apparently by a corruption of the text) in the Syrtis, and a river Triton. The lake (he adds) has a narrow mouth, in which there is an island, so that sometimes at low water there is no appearance of an entrance at all. The lake is of large extent, being about 1000 stadia in circumference—a statement much *below* the truth. Here it is not quite clear whether the *river* Triton is the same with the narrow channel communicating with the sea, or not, though this is the most probable explanation. Ptolemy also distinctly speaks of the outflow of the river Triton into the sea, which he places ten miles to the west of Tacape, the modern Cabes (Ptol. iv. 3, § 11), and there can be no doubt that he here means the same river, which he elsewhere mentions as having its rise in the interior and flowing *into* the lake (Ib. 3, § 19). Pliny and Mela add nothing whatever to our information.

The question is an interesting one, because it appears probable from recent geological researches that a great part of the Northern Sahara was at no very remote period covered by an inland sea, communicating with the Mediterranean at the Lesser Syrtis, and that it has been gradually elevated to its present level. Could we therefore prove that this communication was still open to some extent in the time of Herodotus, we should be able to trace the last stage of this geological change by historical evidence. Unfortunately the testimony of Herodotus is very vague, and apparently derived from imperfect information; while that of Scylax, which is more complete and definite, is in some degree marred by a corruption of the text, which seems to arise from an accidental omission in our manuscripts. (See C. Muller *ad loc.*)

NOTE T, p. 288.

THE ISLAND OF CYRAUNIS.

Niebuhr (*Geogr. of Herodotus*, p. 20), as already mentioned, supposes the island Cyraunis of Herodotus to be the same with the Cerne of later authors, and there appears no doubt that Diodorus confounded the two: but this is certainly not consistent with the text of our author, who, after describing the peculiarities of the island of Cyraunis, which he places *opposite to the Gyzantes*, and therefore certainly in the Mediterranean, adds (after a short digression) this *other tale* told by the Carthaginians concerning a place in Libya, outside the Columns of Hercules. It is this introduction of the one narrative, just after the other, that has apparently led to the confusion of the two, but Herodotus, in fact, carefully distinguishes them. This Cyraunis is clearly, as Rennell has pointed out (*Geogr. of Herodot.* p. 638), the same as the Cercina or Cercinna of Strabo and later authors, which agrees both in position and extent with the description of Herodotus.

The account given by Scylax (§ 112) of the mode in which trade was carried on by the Carthaginian merchants *at Cerne* has undoubtedly some resemblance to that related by Herodotus concerning a place (not named) on the Atlantic coast of Libya, but the similarity may have been easily produced by the actual occurrence of similar conditions. Moreover, the two accounts differ in one important particular, that while Herodotus mentions *gold* as the principal, or sole, subject of barter on the part of the natives, it is not even included by Scylax among those obtained at Cerne.

NOTE V, p. 296.

THE CIRCUMNAVIGATION OF AFRICA: OPINIONS OF MODERN WRITERS.

The narrative of Herodotus has been believed, and its authenticity supported, among modern writers, by Major Rennell (*Geogr. of Herodot.* pp. 672–714), by Larcher (*Notes on Herodot.* vol. ii. pp. 26–30), by Heeren (*Researches*, vol. ii. pp. 76–81, Engl. transl.), and Prof. Rawlinson (*Herodotus*, vol. iii. p. 45). Mr. Grote in his history (vol. iii. pp. 377–385) accepted the narrative as a historical fact, but I have reason to believe that he subsequently changed his opinion.

On the other hand it is rejected by Gossellin (*Géogr. des Anciens*, tom. i. pp. 204–216), Mannert (*Geogr. der Gr. u. Romer*, vol. i. pp. 19–26), Mr. Cooley in his English translation of Larcher's notes, pp. 30–32), by Dr. Vincent (*Commerce and Navigation of the Ancients in the Indian Ocean*, vol. ii pp 195–204), and by Sir G. Lewis (*Hist. of Ancient Astronomy*, pp. 508–515').

Ukert justly observes (vol. i. p. 48) that the question is one upon which opinions will always continue to be divided. The arguments on both sides may well be considered as exhausted: and the absence of all details precludes the possibility of adding to them by farther investigation.

CHAPTER IX.

VOYAGE OF HANNO.

§ 1. IT is unfortunate that, while Herodotus has dwelt at some length on the unsuccessful voyage of Sataspes, which added very little to the information possessed concerning Africa, he seems to have had no knowledge of the far more important and interesting expedition of Hanno in the same direction.[1] The details of this voyage, which have been preserved to us by a singular chance, while almost all other records of Carthaginian and Phœnician enterprise have perished, are well worthy of a careful consideration, and will find an appropriate place here, as there is every probability that the voyage itself, though not mentioned by Herodotus, must have taken place before the time of that historian.

The narrative that has been transmitted to us purports to be that of the commander of the expedition himself, inscribed on a tablet dedicated by him on his return in the temple of Cronos or Saturn, a name undoubtedly meant to designate the Phœnician deity Moloch. Such a dedication has nothing in itself improbable, and the brevity and the somewhat official style of the narrative itself corresponds with its supposed origin. The document in its present form being in Greek, must probably be regarded as a translation of the original; for though we have numerous instances in later times of bilingual inscriptions in Punic and Greek,[2] it is scarcely

---

[1] It is indeed not improbable that the accounts on which the Carthaginians based their confident belief that Africa could be circumnavigated, were connected with this voyage; but it is impossible to believe that Herodotus had any knowledge of its details,

to the marvellous character of which he could hardly have failed to advert.

[2] Hannibal, indeed, as we know, before leaving Italy, set up a bilingual inscription in the temple of the Lacinian Juno, recording his exploits, *in Punic and Greek.* but there was an

likely that such a practice would be resorted to at so early a period.³

The primary object of the expedition—as we are told at the outset—was not so much discovery, as colonization; hence Hanno sailed with a mixed multitude of men and women, amounting, it is said, to not less than 30,000 (a number in all probability exaggerated), and a fleet of sixty ships, all penteconters.⁴ After sailing through the Straits of Hercules and continuing their voyage for two days, they established their first colony, to which they gave the name of Thymiaterium; it commanded a great plain. Thence standing on towards the west they came to the headland of Soloeis, the promontory of Libya, where they established a temple to Poseidon. From thence they turned to the east, and after half a day's voyage came to a large lake or marsh near the sea, in which many elephants were feeding. After passing this lake and proceeding another day's voyage, they founded five towns by the sea-coast, to which they gave the names of Caricon Teichos, Gytta, Acra, Melitta and Arambis. Setting out again from thence, they came to a large river called Lixus, flowing from the interior of Libya. Its banks were inhabited by nomad Libyan tribes, who had flocks with them, and entered into friendly intercourse with the navigators. But the interior of the country, according to the statement of these Lixitæ, was occupied by wild and inhospitable tribes of Ethiopians, inhabiting a region abounding in wild beasts, and intersected by high mountains, from which the Lixus took its rise. These Ethiopians were Troglodytes, dwelling in caves and

---

obvious reason for this, as the record was left in a country where Greek was spoken. No such reason could apply to an inscription set up *at Carthage*

³ Note A, p 332.

⁴ It is not to be supposed that the colonists were all conveyed in the penteconters, which would have been much too small for the purpose. They were doubtless embarked in merchant vessels (ὁλκάδες), the greater part of which would be left behind as the successive colonies were founded The penteconters would serve for escort, and to explore the coast in advance and from Cerne onwards they might probably have gone on alone.

holes in the mountains, of strange aspect, and swifter of foot than horses.[5]

Hanno remained some time with the Lixitæ, and took with him interpreters from among them to accompany him on his voyage. Proceeding onwards they coasted along the desert for two days, holding a southerly course; and then turning eastward for one day's voyage, they came to a small island (only five stadia in circumference) in the inmost recess of a gulf, where they established a settlement, and called its name Cerne. Reckoning up the length of their navigation they came to the conclusion that Cerne was *opposite* to Carthage;[6] for the distance from the Columns to Cerne was the same as that from Carthage to the Columns.[7]

§ 2. From Cerne the navigators made two separate voyages to the south. In the first of these they came (after what interval is not stated) to a lake, containing three islands, communicating with the sea by a large river, and of such extent that it took them a day's voyage to penetrate to its inner extremity, which was overhung by lofty mountains, inhabited by wild men, clothed in the skins of beasts, who prevented the voyagers from landing by throwing stones at them. Sailing from hence they came to another broad and large river full of crocodiles and hippopotami. Here (for what reason we are not told) they turned about and returned to Cerne.[8]

§ 3. Setting out a second time from thence they held a direct course towards the south for twelve days, at the end of which time they arrived at a headland formed by high mountains, covered with thick woods of trees of many kinds. After doubling this headland in two days' voyage, they came to a vast gap or opening of the sea, on the other side of which was

---

[5] *Periplus*, §§ 2–7, ed. Muller
[6] Note B, p 333.
[7] *Peripl* § 8.
[8] Ib §§ 9–10. It is singular that Mr. Major (*Prince Henry the Navigator*, p. 92) should treat this return to Cerne as if it were a part of M. de St. Martin's "able analysis" of the voyage of Hanno, and is at a loss to understand his having put back "without any assignable motive.' What his motive may have been we know not, but the fact is distinctly stated by himself

a plain; from whence many fires were seen at night. After laying in a stock of water, they continued to coast along the land for five days, till they came to a large bay, called by their interpreters the Western Horn. In this was an island, on which they landed, but found no signs of inhabitants, seeing nothing but the forest in the day-time; but in the night many fires were seen to be burning, accompanied with the sound of musical instruments, flutes and drums and cymbals. The Carthaginians were seized with a panic terror and immediately quitted the island.[9]

Sailing from thence in all haste they passed along a district which seemed all in a blaze of fire; streams of fire as from a volcano pouring down from thence into the sea. Terrified at this appearance they hastened on, and came in four days to another place where the land was again all blazing with fire; in the midst of which was one fire that rose much higher than any of the rest, and appeared to touch the stars. By daylight it was seen that this was a very lofty mountain, which was called the Chariot of the Gods (Theon Ochema). Three days' farther navigation (still passing by streams of fire) brought them to a gulf called the Southern Horn. Here there was an island, containing a lake, with another island in it, which was full of wild men and women, with hairy bodies, called by the interpreters Gorillas. The Carthaginians were unable to catch any of the men, but they caught three of the women, whom they killed and brought their skins back with them to Carthage. This was the farthest limit of their voyage, as they were compelled by want of provisions to return.[1]

§ 4. Such is in substance the brief narrative of this remarkable voyage, which in many respects stands alone among the records of ancient geography. Notwithstanding the apparently marvellous character of some of the incidents recorded, it bears the unquestionable impress of being an authentic record of a real voyage; and even the geographical data will be found, on

---

[9] *Peripl.* §§ 11-14.   [1] Id. §§ 14-18.

a careful examination, to be for the most part easily reconciled with existing facts. Their simplicity and clearness, when considered alone, will indeed be found to present a striking contrast to the confusion in which they are involved, in the hands of later geographers.

There has indeed been great discrepancy of opinion among modern writers with regard to the distance actually traversed, and the farthest point to which the navigators attained. Gossellin refused to believe that they advanced farther than Cape Noun (in 28° 40' N. lat.);[2] but this view, though adopted by Walckenaer,[3] may be safely rejected as utterly untenable. It does not indeed satisfactorily explain or agree with *any* of the principal facts recorded, and is in fact based solely on the assumption that the ancients could not make voyages of any considerable length.[4] Major Rennell on the contrary, in a very valuable and elaborate examination of the question,[5] came to the conclusion that the Southern Horn—the farthest point actually attained by the expedition—was identical with Sherboro' Sound, just beyond Sierra Leone (in N. lat. 7° 45'), and startling as it may at first appear that the voyagers should have penetrated so far to the south, the arguments in favour of this view may be regarded as almost, if not quite, conclusive. It has been adopted both by the most recent editor of the Periplus of Hanno (C. Muller), and by M. de St. Martin in his elaborate and valuable work on the ancient geography of Africa. Both of these writers have supplied important corrections and additions, arising in part from our improved acquaintance with the west coast of Africa, since the time of Major Rennell, but the merit of having first established the true view of the question undoubtedly rests with the great English hydrographer.[6]

---

[2] *Recherches sur la Géographie des Anciens*, vol 1 pp 70–106
[3] *Recherches sur la Géographe de l Afrique*, p 362
[4] Note C, p 334

[5] *Geography of Herodotus*, pp 719–745, 4to ed
[6] See Rennell's *Geography of Herodotus*, § 26, St Martin, *Le Nord de l'Afrique dans l'Antiquité*, pp 330–400,

§ 5. The main point upon which the geography of the whole voyage may be considered to rest is that of the position of Cerne, the place from which the Carthaginian commander set out on his two separate exploring voyages to the south; and where he founded a colony, which undoubtedly continued to exist for a long period of time, and carried on a considerable trade with the nations of the interior.[7] Now the data for determining the position of Cerne are given with unusual precision. It was a small island, situated in the bight of a deep bay; and it was, according to the computation of the Carthaginian navigators—derived from their *sea-reckoning*—the same distance from the Straits or Pillars of Hercules on the one side that Carthage was on the other.[8]

Major Rennell (concurring on this point with D'Anville and several other writers) identified the island of Cerne with that of Arguin, a short distance to the south of Cape Blanco,[9] which became at one time a considerable trading station in the hands of the Portuguese;[1] and the same view was adopted by Ukert and Movers. But in the first place the size and position of the island of Arguin corresponded but imperfectly with the description of Cerne, and what was a more important objection its distance from the entrance of the Straits *greatly* exceeded that of Carthage. Major Rennell indeed sought to avoid this difficulty by pointing out that in these latitudes there is a constant southerly current, setting along the coast of Africa, which would undoubtedly have carried the Carthaginian ships much farther to the south than they were aware of, reckoning

---

and the commentary of Dr C Muller in his *Geographi Græci Minores*, vol 1. pp 1–14
[7] Note D, p 334.
[8] *Peripl* § 8
[9] The first to make this identification was a Portuguese pilot, cited by Ramusio in his commentary on the voyage of Hanno, referred to in Note A
[1] Ca da Mosto (*Viaggio*, p 99, in Ramusio, tom. 1 , Major's *Prince Henry*, p 254) The existence of this trade, in many respects resembling that of Cerne in ancient times, was one of the reasons which led to the identification of the latter with Arguin, but there is no *natural* communication with the interior to determine it, the trade was in both cases merely the result of the establishment of a factory on the coast Arguin is now abandoned, just as Cerne was, when the Carthaginian commerce declined, and is a poor and desolate island

only by their rate of sailing. But the difference, amounting to not less than 320 G. miles, was one that could hardly be thus accounted for; and it was principally this difficulty that led several modern writers to place Cerne ten degrees farther north in the neighbourhood of Aghadir or Santa Cruz, though no such island is now to be found there, and this position is as much too far to the north, as Arguin is to the south. We are indebted to Dr. C. Muller for first pointing out the existence, at a point intermediate between the two, of a small island, still called on the French charts Herné, in the bight of a deep bay, at the mouth of the Rio do Ouro. The situation of this island thus exactly agrees with the description of Cerne, while its position on the coast, more than 200 G. miles to the north of Cape Blanco (in lat. 23° 50′) reduces the allowance to be made for the current within a very probable amount. It will be found also that the account of the subsequent proceedings of the voyage accords much better with the position thus assigned to Cerne than with that of Arguin; and on the whole it may fairly be said that the solution thus proposed of this long disputed question may be considered as established with reasonable certainty.[2]

§ 6. Starting then from the position of Cerne, as a fixed point of departure, it will be found that there is little difficulty in determining all the more important points visited farther to the south—the physical peculiarities of the localities being such as to render their identification almost certain, even if there were more difficulty than actually exists in reconciling them with the distances stated. It must be observed that from Cerne onwards the voyage appears to have been one of discovery merely, no trace being found of any attempt at colonization to the south of that island.

---

[2] The suggestion thus put forth by M. Muller (*Prolegomena*, p xxvi) is adopted by M Vivien de St Martin (*Géographie de l'Afrique*, pp 382-3), and confirmed with additional arguments The name of Herné appears for the first time on the French charts, but we are assured that it is used by the Moors of the continent The Rio do Ouro was already known to the Portuguese navigators of the 15th century, but there has been no settlement there in modern times.

In regard to the first expedition we have no statement of distances, or of the time employed, but we learn that its limit was the mouth of a large and broad river, full of crocodiles and hippopotami. This description leaves no doubt that the river attained could be no other than the Senegal, called by later Greek and Latin writers the Bambotus, and described by Polybius in almost the same terms as by Hanno.[3] There is no river of any considerable size to the north of this, after leaving the confines of Mauritania, and certainly none in which either crocodiles or hippopotami could ever have lived.[4]

§ 7. In like manner the first point indicated in the second voyage can admit of no doubt. The lofty headland covered with large trees of various kinds, can be no other than Cape Verde, the only point of elevated land that projects into the sea along the whole of this line of coast, and which derives its modern name from the rich verdure of the woods with which it is covered.[5] The distance of twelve days' voyage agrees much better with the supposition that Cerne was at the Rio do Ouro than at Arguin. Beyond the promontory of Cape Verde, the coast again becomes flat and low, and the mouth of the Gambia forms a broad estuary with flat shores, which is evidently the " chasm " or wide opening of the sea next mentioned by Hanno. It was here that they first saw the fires, which afterwards figure so prominently in their narrative. The distance from thence to the deep gulf called the Western Horn[6] leads us to identify the latter with the bay or gulf of

---

[3] " Flumen Bambotum, crocodilis et hippopotamis refertum." Polyb ap. Plin. V. 1 § 10 The statements of Polybius in this passage will be examined in a future chapter.

[4] Note E, p 335

[5] See Ca da Mosto (in Ramusio, *Viaggi*, tom 1. p 105 *b*), who calls it "molto bel capo, ed alto di terreno." The expression of the Carthaginian navigator of " high mountains ' is undoubtedly an exaggeration, but it was natural that they should over-estimate the importance of the only high land they had seen for hundreds of miles

[6] It is a striking instance of the confusion into which the statements of the Periplus were thrown by later writers, that they transformed the deep gulfs, or inlets of the sea, described by Hanno under the name of the Western and Southern Horn into *promontories*, and applied the names accordingly. The Hesperi Cornu of Ptolemy and Pliny is no other than Cape Verde, which is also called Hesperium Promontorium,

Bissago, in which there are many small islands; but the identification of these inlets must remain somewhat uncertain; the coast of Africa in this part being indented by many deep bays. It is otherwise with the Theon Ochema, which may be safely assumed to be the mountain called by the Portuguese Sagres (a name afterwards corrupted into Sangaree) but which figures in some modern maps as Mount Souzos, in others is called Mount Kakulima. It is described as a lofty conical mountain, forming a conspicuous landmark in the midst of a flat coast,[7] thus according well with the appearance of the mountain as described in the Periplus; and the occurrence of a striking isolated peak in such a position is too remarkable a coincidence to leave any doubt upon the subject. Three days' navigation from hence brought them to the limit of their voyage, the Southern Horn—a deep gulf or inlet of the sea, which may be probably identified with Sherboro' Sound, the next opening beyond that of Sierra Leone, more familiar to us at the present day from the establishment of an English colony.

The distances given along this part of the coast from Cerne to the Southern Horn agree remarkably well with the real positions: but the natural characteristics of certain important points, especially the Cape Verde and the Mount Sagres, as well as the river Senegal, afford much the most satisfactory means of identification, and leave no reasonable doubt of the voyagers having really advanced as far as the point indicated. It may be added that this was the farthest point reached by any ancient navigators. Even in the days of Ptolemy the Theon Ochema was still the limit of his knowledge of the west coast of Africa.

§ 8. The circumstance that seems to have tended most to discredit the narrative of Hanno in the eyes of subsequent writers was the marvellous account that he gave of the "streams

---

[7] Rennell, p. 734, Roussin, *Mémoire sur la Navigation aux Côtes Occidentales de l'Afrique.* p 95 (cited by St Martin, p 394) Its striking character is sufficiently shown by the circumstance that the companions of Pedro de Cintra, who first discovered the mountain in 1462, considered it to be the highest mountain they had ever seen (Rennell, *l. c*)

of fire" and "pillars of fire" that he saw after passing Cape Verde.[8] Nor can it be doubted that the terror which these appearances excited in the minds of the navigators, and which is very naively confessed in the journal, led them to considerable exaggeration of what they really saw. But the phenomenon is readily explained by the practice, generally adopted by the negroes in this part of Africa, of setting fire to the long dry grass in the autumn, by which conflagrations are kindled of such an extent as readily to give rise, in the excited imagination of the voyagers, to the description that they have left us.[9]

§ 9. Another statement that was treated as fabulous in ancient times was the account of the wild men and women covered with hair, that they found in the island of the Southern Horn. Yet the fact that they brought back the skins of two of them to Carthage might suffice to show that the assertion was not without some foundation in fact. Pliny indeed adds that the skins in question were dedicated by Hanno in the temple of Juno at Carthage, and continued to be visible there till the destruction of the city.[1] There can be no difficulty in supposing these "wild men and women" to have been really large apes of the family of the Chimpanzee or Pongo, several species of which are, in fact, found wild in Western Africa, and

---

[8] These statements were (as was so often the case) distorted by the exaggerations of subsequent writers Thus Mela says (iii 9, § 94) " Ultra hunc sinum mons altus, ut Græci vocant Theon, *perpetuis ignibus flagrat*," and Pliny has the same assertion (*H N* vi 30, § 197), "Imminens mari mons excelsus *æternis ardet ignibus*, Theon Ochema dictus Græcis "

[9] See the passages quoted from modern travellers by Major Rennell (p 720), and by C. Muller in his notes to the Periplus (p 12).

This explanation was long ago suggested by Ramusio in his Commentary on the Periplus (*Viaggi*, tom i p 113 b)

from the information of a Portuguese pilot, notwithstanding which, various other suggestions, one more absurd than another, have been put forward by modern writers The word ῥύαξ was undoubtedly most commonly applied to a stream of lava from a volcano, and hence it seems to have been generally assumed that *volcanic* appearances were those indicated (see the passages cited in preceding note). But, independent of the extent of the phenomena described, which in itself would exclude such a supposition, there are in fact no appearances of recent volcanic action on this part of the coast of Africa.

[1] Plin. *H. N.* vi 31, § 200

some of them, as is now well known, attain to a stature fully equal to that of man.²

§ 10. It is curious and instructive, after seeing how well the leading geographical facts related by Hanno accord with our present knowledge of the regions in question, to observe how confused and uncertain were the notions concerning his discoveries entertained by later writers in ancient times. Pliny even speaks of him in one passage as having circumnavigated Africa from Gades to the borders of Arabia!³ In another place he stigmatizes him as the original author of many fables, repeated after him both by Greek and Roman writers, of which he places in the front rank the statement of his having founded many cities, no trace of which was visible in the days of Pliny! That author here speaks of his "Commentarii," but it appears certain that he had not seen them himself:⁴ and his account of the western coast of Africa, though containing some facts undoubtedly derived from Hanno, is, for the most part, taken from other authorities. Mela, on the other hand, correctly describes Hanno as having sailed round *a great part* of the continent, and been compelled to return, not from any difficulties of navigation, but merely from want of provisions. He adds also many particulars which are certainly taken, either

---

² The species to which modern naturalists have appropriated the name of Gorilla (derived originally from this narrative of Hanno) does not seem to be now found north of the equator, but large anthropoid apes are still found in the forests of Senegal, and near Sierra Leone, and it is probable that these were more common in ancient times, and spread over a wider area.

It is reported by modern travellers, in accordance with the experience of the Carthaginian navigators, that the males are never taken alive. Even the females (as the Carthaginians found) bit and fought with such violence that they were forced to kill them in self-defence.

The accuracy of Hanno's report on this subject presents a curious contrast to the exaggerations of later writers. Thus Mela, though directly citing Hanno as his authority, tells us: "Grandis littoris flexus grandem insulam includit, in qua tantum feminas esse narrant, toto corpore hirsutas et sine coitu marium sua sponte fecundas!" (iii. 9, § 93).

³ Plin *H.N* ii 67, § 169 "Et Hanno Carthaginis potentia florente *circumvectus a Gadibus ad finem Arabiæ* navigationem eam prodidit scripto."

⁴ This is apparent even from his own expression "*Fuere* et Hannonis Carthaginiensium ducis commentarii Punicis rebus florentissimis explorare ambitum Africæ jussi." (v. 1, § 8.)

directly or indirectly, from the narrative of Hanno, but he jumbles them together without any regard to geographical order, and thus involves them in inextricable confusion.[5] Arrian again, who evidently quotes Hanno only at second hand, unaccountably describes him as having sailed (after issuing through the Straits into the Ocean) for thirty-five days *towards the rising sun*, and then turning to the south, where he met with great difficulties from want of water, as well as the burning heat, and streams of fire flowing into the sea, which compelled him to return.[6] We should, indeed, have known very little about the voyage of Hanno, had not a fortunate accident preserved to us the original narrative.

§ 11. It is singular that, while the geographical statements preserved by Hanno from the remoter regions of Western Africa are thus found to be easily reconciled with the truth, it is much more difficult to arrange with any certainty the details of the earlier part of the voyage, from the Straits of Hercules to the Island of Cerne. Fortunately these are of comparatively little importance. The promontory of Soloeis is undoubtedly Cape Cantin, which the ancient navigators seem to have regarded as occupying a much more important position than it really does:[7] and as the *extreme western* point of Africa.[8] Hence, probably, it was selected by Hanno as the site of a temple to Neptune. But beyond this the geographical data

---

[5] Mela, iii. 9.
[6] Arrian, *Indica*, c. 43
[7] The same thing was the case in the early voyages of the Portuguese in these parts with regard to Cape Noun and Cape Bojador. Ca da Mosto, however, a little later, speaks of Cape Cantin as the most considerable headland along this coast Its abrupt elevation, "rising precipitously 211 ft. above the sea" (see a paper by Lieut. Ailett in the *Geographical Journal*, vol vi p. 308), coincides with the description of it in Scylax (ἡ ἀνέχει μάλιστα ἐς τὸν πόντον, § 112), and explains the choice of so commanding a site for a temple to Neptune.

The Cape Soloeis of Hanno and Scylax certainly corresponds to the Solis Mons and Solis Promontorium of later geographers: the Soloentium of Ptolemy, on the contrary, is situated much farther to the south, and has no connection with the headland in question
[8] It is hardly necessary to point out the gross error involved in this assumption Cape Cantin is really situated in 9° 17′ W. longitude, while Cape Verde, the real westernmost point of Africa, is in W. long 17° 32′, or more than eight degrees of longitude farther west.

are either imperfect or erroneous. It is obvious that the Carthaginians would never have founded five towns in immediate proximity to one another, but no mention is made of the intervals between them, or of the distance from thence to the river Lixus. The latter is called " a large river," which would lead us to identify it with the Wady Draa, much the largest river in this part of Africa, which descends from the southern slopes of the Atlas chain and falls into the Atlantic a few miles south of Cape Noun. But the statement which follows, that the voyage from thence continued *for two days* by the side of the desert, is certainly erroneous; the distance from the mouth of the Draa to the gulf of Rio do Ouro being not less than 420 G. miles, throughout the whole of which space the voyagers would undoubtedly be coasting the barren sandy shore of the desert, without a break or opening of any kind. On the other hand, if we read *twelve* days for *two*—the most natural suggestion, and that adopted by the latest editor of the Periplus— the number appears greater than necessary, and does not correspond with the supposed relation to Carthage. But however this difficulty may be solved, the importance attached to the river Lixus, and to its communications with the interior, certainly raise a presumption in favour of its being the same stream which is now called the Draa. The river Lixus of later authors, at the mouth of which there was a city of the same name, was certainly distinct from the one here mentioned, being situated only at a short distance to the south of Cape Spartel.[9]

§ 12. No mention is found in any subsequent writers of the colonies founded by the Carthaginians to the south of Cape Soloeis; they probably never rose to any importance, and as the power of Carthage declined, the trade with the western coast of Africa seems to have been gradually given up, and these settlements would naturally be abandoned. Even the

---

[9] The site of the Roman town of Lixus undoubtedly corresponded with that of the modern Al Araish, or Laraiche, at the mouth of a small river called the Wadi al Khos.

trade at Cerne, which (as we have already seen) was still active in the days of Scylax, had ceased to exist before the fall of Carthage: and the very site of the island was a subject of doubt with later geographers.[1] How easily all trace might be lost of such a site, as soon as it ceased to be resorted to as a trading station, is shown by the parallel case of Arguin, which was for a considerable time under the Portuguese a commercial station of no little importance; but is now a barren and desolate island, inhabited only by a few Arab fishermen.[2]

---

[1] Eratosthenes, indeed, still admitted the existence of the island, for which he is undeservedly censured by Strabo (1 3, p 47), and was probably acquainted with its true position It is net unlikely that the other fabulous tales which he reported concerning the west coast of Africa (πεπίστευκε δὲ καὶ περὶ τῶν ἔξω στηλῶν Ἡρακλείων πολλοῖς μυθώδεσι, Κέρνην τε νῆσον καὶ ἄλλους τόπους ὀνομάζων τοὺς μηδαμοῦ νυνὶ δεικνυμένους: Strabo, l c) were taken in like manner from the voyage of Hanno, with which Strabo seems to have been wholly unacquainted

[2] See the description of it by Capt Grover in the *Journal of the Geogr Soc.* vol. xvi pp. 165-167.

For the determination of the other details of this first part of the voyage, the reader may consult St Martin (*Le Nord de l'Afrique*, pp 356-380) and the commentary of Dr C Muller in his edition of the Periplus

NOTE A, p. 319.

EDITIONS OF THE PERIPLUS.

THE narrative of Hanno was certainly extant in Greek at an early period. It is cited in the work ascribed to Aristotle on Marvellous Narratives (§ 37), which belongs to the third century B.C.; as well as by Mela, Pliny, and many later writers; and Pliny expressly speaks of it as the source from whence many Greek and Roman writers had derived their information, including, as he considered, many fables (Plin. *H. N.* v. 1, § 8).

The authenticity of the work now extant under the name of the Periplus of Hanno, may be fairly considered as unquestionable. Though assailed by Dodwell, in a dissertation (*De vero Peripli, qui Hannonis nomine circumfertur, tempore*) inserted in Hudson's *Geographi Minores*, vol. i. it was successfully defended by Falconer, in the preface to his edition (1797), and is admitted by all the later editors without a doubt. Indeed the internal evidence, when fairly examined, is conclusive upon that point. But there has been great diversity of opinion as to the period to which the expedition is to be referred; on this point the narrative itself gives us no information; and the name of Hanno was so common at Carthage as to afford us very little clue to his identity (see Smith's *Dict. of Biogr.* art. HANNO). But it has been generally agreed among recent writers that the most probable conclusion is, that he was either the father or the son of the Hamilcar who led the great Carthaginian expedition to Sicily in B.C. 480. In the former case the Periplus may be probably assigned to a date about B.C. 520, in the latter it must be brought down about 50 years later. This last view is that adopted by C. Muller in his edition of the Periplus (*Geographi Græci Minores*, vol. i. pp. xxi–xxiv), where the whole subject is fully discussed; but, as between him and his grandfather, the choice must be admitted to be little more than conjectural. M. Vivien de St. Martin, however, prefers the date of B.C. 570, which had been previously adopted by Bougainville (*Mémoires de l'Académie des Inscriptions*, tom. xxviii. p. 287).

The Periplus was first published at Basle in 1533 (as an appendix to the Periplus of Arrian), from a MS. in the Heidelberg library—the only one in which it is found: it has been since repeatedly

republished in a separate form, with copious commentaries and
illustrations. Of these separate editions those by Falconer, 8vo,
1797, and by Kluge, 8vo, Lips. 1829, are the most valuable. The
treatise is also included in the editions of the *Geographi Græci
Minores* by Hudson, Gail, and C. Muller. The valuable and elaborate commentary of the latest editor may be considered as in great
measure superseding all others. Besides all these editions, it has
been made the subject of elaborate investigations by Gossellin, Bougainville, Major Rennell, Heeren, Ukert, M. Vivien de St. Martin,
and other geographical writers. Indeed there are few ancient
writings that have been the subject of more copious commentary in
proportion to its very limited extent. The earliest of these commentaries, inserted by Ramusio in his collection of voyages, is
curious and interesting as being derived from Portuguese sources,
who were in modern times the earliest explorers of these coasts.
That by the Spanish writer Campomanes (*El Periplo de Hannon
ilustrado*, appended to his *Antiguedad Maritima de Cartago*, 4to,
Madrid, 1756) is, on the contrary, utterly worthless.

NOTE B, p. 320.

POSITION OF CERNE.

It is rather difficult to understand the exact meaning of the
expression here used, κατ' εὐθὺ κεῖσθαι Καρχηδόνος. It is fortunately explained in part by the subsequent addition that the
voyage to Cerne from the Straits was of the same length as that
from Carthage to the Straits: but still the sense of the phrase
remains obscure. The first impression would be that it is used in
the same sense as we should say, it was on the same meridian with
Carthage. just as Herodotus describes the mouths of the Nile and
the Danube as lying *opposite* to each other (ii. 33, 34). And it certainly appears that the passage was so understood by later writers,
who interpreted it as "*ex adverso* Carthaginis." Corn. Nep. ap. Plin.
vi. 31, § 199. But these geographers, from Eratosthenes onwards,
all conceived the west coast of Africa as trending away rapidly
towards the east, immediately after passing Cape Soloeis, so that
the island of Cerne would thus be brought approximately (though
not of course exactly) to the same meridian with Carthage.
Hanno, however, gives no countenance to such a view, which seems

to have been adopted solely on theoretical grounds. His statements of the bearings of his course, wherever given, are generally correct, and the inference certainly is that the *general* direction of their voyage lay, as it really must have done, towards the south.

The distances from the Straits to Cerne and to Carthage, being supposed equal to one another, would form the two sides of an isosceles triangle, the base of which would be formed by a straight line joining the two: but certainly if the phrase means nothing more than this, it appears a strange one to have employed.

NOTE C, p. 322.

VIEWS OF HEEREN.

The views of Gossellin have been satisfactorily disproved by Major Rennell (see particularly p. 438), and are justly rejected by Heeren (*African Nations*, vol. i. p. 492), who admits that the expedition advanced as far as the Gambia. But he appears to have overlooked the important identifications of Cape Verde and the mountain called the Theon Ochema (both of them already pointed out by Major Rennell), and dwells mainly on the distances It appears to me far safer, in such a case as this, to rely mainly upon the description of marked natural features, where these are really prominent and striking, than upon statements of distances, which are liable to so many causes of error. At the same time the distances given, on the voyage beyond Cerne, agree very well with the truth, as soon as the position of Cerne itself is rectified in accordance with the view stated in the text.

NOTE D, p. 323.

NOTICE OF CERNE IN SCYLAX.

The existence of this trade is distinctly attested by Scylax (§ 112), who appears to have derived it from some authentic source, though he was imperfectly acquainted with the geographical position of Cerne, as he places it only twelve days' voyage from the Straits, and seven from the promontory of Soloeis. He was evidently unacquainted with the voyage of Hanno, as he treats Cerne as the farthest point to which navigation was possible. an idea that was very probably intentionally circulated by the Carthaginian traders. Nor does he allude to the circumstance that this island was said to be equidistant with Carthage from the Straits. a statement which is repeated by several later writers, who undoubtedly derived it in the first instance from Hanno. The statement of Scylax has, indeed, been a great difficulty with many modern writers, who have sought to reconcile it with the narrative of Hanno's voyage, though the two are, in fact, wholly incompatible, unless we make considerable allowance, as suggested by Rennell, for the effect of a southerly current. The voyage from Carthage to the Straits is estimated by Scylax himself at seven days and seven nights' voyage (equivalent to fourteen days on the ordinary mode of computation) *under the most favourable circumstances* (τοῦ καλλίστου πλοῦ, § 111, ed. Mull.).

NOTE E, p. 325.

THE RIVER CHREMETES.

It is much more difficult to determine the intermediate point mentioned in this first voyage. There is nothing to indicate its distance from Cerne, or its relative position with regard to the river next mentioned. But the description of a great river flowing from a lake, of such extent as to take a day's voyage to penetrate to its inmost extremity, can only be explained by supposing (as suggested by M. de St. Martin) that this was another arm of the Senegal, which in fact forms a great expansion or lake previous to its outflow into the sea, and may very probably have in ancient times had an outlet more to the north than any now existing. Yet the difficulty still remains, that the head of the lake is described as " overhung by lofty mountains," a circumstance that can hardly apply to any such lake in the delta of the Senegal.

The river in question is called in our existing text of the Periplus the Chretes (Χρέτης), but it has been supposed that this is a corruption, and that the true reading is Chremetes (Χρεμέτης), a name which we find mentioned by Aristotle as that of a large river on the West Coast of Africa (Aristot. *Meteorol.* i. 13; the name is found also in Nonnus, *Dionys.* xiii. 374, xxxi. 103), but is unknown to the later geographers. If the river alluded to by Aristotle is really the Senegal, a vague tradition of its importance may perhaps have been derived from this voyage of Hanno.

CHAPTER X.

WRITERS AFTER HERODOTUS.

SECTION 1.—*Ctesias.*

§ 1. WE have very imperfect means of tracing the progress of geographical knowledge among the Greeks during the interval of at least a century, which elapsed between the publication of the History of Herodotus and the expedition of Alexander into Asia. This period was indeed one of the most eventful in the history of Greece, and was, in many respects, the epoch of the greatest prosperity that that country ever witnessed. It was also one during which the intellectual activity of the Greek world developed itself on all sides; and among other forms of scientific inquiry that which regarded the form and constitution of the world in which they lived could hardly fail to attract the attention of the speculative Greek philosophers. But while the first foundations of such a scientific knowledge of the earth in its general relations,—or of geography considered as a part of cosmography,—must be assigned to the period in question, it does not appear that any great progress was made in that more detailed knowledge of the countries and nations occupying the known portions of the earth's surface, which is commonly understood by the term geography.

Nor were the limits of these known portions materially enlarged. The Greek world, with all its numerous colonies was still limited to the lands that surround the Mediterranean Sea; no Greek navigator had yet explored the waters of the Atlantic, and the Persian Empire on the east still included within its confines all that was really known to them of the continent of Asia. Within these limits their knowledge was doubtless more complete and accurate in detail; and many of the more outlying nations were become more familiar to them than they had been to their predecessors. But any approach to scientific geography was rendered impossible, not only by the very imperfect nature of their cosmographical notions, but still more by the want of instruments with which to make those scientific observations upon which all accurate geography must be based.

Yet it cannot be doubted that, had the works of some of the writers who flourished during this period been preserved to us in their integrity, we should have been able to form a much more complete judgment of the real extent and limits of the geographical knowledge of the Greeks. Unfortunately all those authors who would have been most valuable to us in this respect, have perished; and we are condemned to glean from the scanty fragments preserved to us by later writers some idea of the nature and value of their contributions.

§ 2. The works of the two principal historians that flourished in the generation after Herodotus were not calculated to throw any additional light on geographical knowledge. From the nature of its subject the great work of THUCYDIDES was limited to a narrow area; and though the clearness of his geographical descriptions, in the few cases in which he has thought it necessary to give them—as in that of Sicily in the beginning of the sixth book, and that of Thrace and Macedonia in the second—corresponds with the definite and philosophical character of his mind, his narrative was generally concerned with countries, and even localities, so well known to his readers, that he had little opening for the display of his talent in this respect.

§ 3. His contemporary ANTIOCHUS of SYRACUSE would undoubtedly have added much more to our information had his works been preserved to us. These consisted of a history of Sicily, and one of Italy, in both of which, but especially in the latter, he appears to have introduced numerous notices of a geographical character. But the few extant fragments are not sufficient to enable us to judge how far he entered into

VOL. I.

any general geographical description, or to estimate the extent of his knowledge of those parts of the Italian peninsula which had not been occupied by Greek colonists. Almost the only notice of interest that has been preserved to us by the citations from his work is the fact that he was one of the first Greek authors who mentioned the name of Rome. It is observed also that he did not concur in the ordinary tradition of its foundation by Æneas, or one of his descendants, but supposed it to date from a much earlier period.[1]

§ 4. Among the writers who, in the period immediately following Herodotus, contributed to familiarize the minds of the Greeks with the more distant portions of Asia, a prominent place must undoubtedly be assigned to CTESIAS, a native of Cnidus in Caria, and a physician by profession, who in that capacity resided not less than seventeen years at the court of Persia.[2] Such an interval must naturally have given him opportunities of acquiring statistical and geographical information concerning the provinces of that empire superior to what had been possessed by any other Greek. Nor did he neglect to avail himself of the facilities thus presented to him. Among the works with the composition of which he occupied himself after his return to Greece (B.C. 398) we find mention of a treatise on the revenues of the Persian Empire,—which it would have been interesting to compare with the information furnished us by Herodotus upon the same subject—as well as of two professedly geographical treatises—the one on rivers, the other on mountains. Both of these are totally lost, and a meagre abstract by Photius is all that remains to us of his principal work, the Persian history. Of the historical merits of the "Persica" in general, it does not fall within our province to speak; had the work been preserved to us in its entirety it would unquestionably have afforded us many interesting

---

[1] Dionys Halic 1 73.
[2] Concerning the life and works of Ctesias, see the Prolegomena to the excellent edition of his extant remains published by Bachr (Ctesiæ Cnidii Operum Reliquiæ, 8vo, Francofurti, 1824), and Colonel Mure's *History of Greek Literature*, vol v pp 482-500.

notices and casual details of a geographical character. We are told also by Photius that the author had appended to it a detailed account of the routes from Ephesus to Bactria and India respectively, with the number of days' journeys and the distances in parasangs,—a document that could hardly have failed to be of the highest geographical interest.[3] Unfortunately none of these details have been preserved to us; and the extant abridgement of the Persica cannot be said to add anything to our geographical knowledge.

§ 5. His only other work of importance—of which we possess in like manner a mere abridgement by Photius[4]—treated specially of India and the Indians; and derives its chief interest from being the first professed account of that important region. Unfortunately it was in this short treatise—for the "Indica" occupied only a single book, serving apparently as a kind of appendix to his larger work—that the defects of Ctesias,—his want of critical judgment and love of the marvellous—were the most strongly developed. India was already in his day become the "land of marvels" to all the neighbouring Asiatic nations, which it has continued down almost to our own times; and Ctesias, while residing at the Persian court, appears to have accepted without hesitation all the marvellous tales that he could collect concerning the distant regions of the East. The consequence is that while he laid the foundation for a vast mass of fables and absurdities, which continued to be propagated by successive writers down to the latest period of Greek literature, he contributed almost nothing to the real knowledge of the land of which he wrote.

---

[3] At the same time it is remarkable that no reference is made by any later writer to this itinerary, whence we may perhaps infer that it was not considered as based upon any adequate authority

[4] The abridgement is, however, in this case much more copious than that of the Persica the abstract of the Indica occupying eleven pages (in Bahr's edition), though the original was only in one book, while the 23 books of the Persica in the epitome of Photius fill only eighteen pages of the same edition. Besides this we have copious extracts from Ctesias by Ælian in his *History of Animals* (iv 21, 26, 27, 36, 46, 52, v 3, xvi 31, xvii 29), some of which are probably copied almost literally from the original.

So far as we can judge from the imperfect form in which his work has descended to us, his geographical knowledge of India was little, if at all, in advance of that of Herodotus. The enormous extent that he assigned to it,—representing India alone as equal to the whole of the rest of Asia,[5] was evidently a mere vague assertion. No trace appears of his having been acquainted even with the name of the Ganges, or with anything beyond the Punjab and the valley of the Indus. Of the latter river he says, with his usual exaggeration, that it was forty stadia broad in its narrowest part, and 200 stadia (20 G. miles) in its greatest width.[6] But he not only does not notice the existence of crocodiles in it, as had been correctly reported by Herodotus, but expressly says that it produced no other animals than a gigantic worm, seven cubits in length, which could drag into the river, and devour, oxen, and even camels.[7] He was indeed familiar with the use of elephants in war by the natives, but here again he distorts the fact by enormous exaggeration, representing the Indian king as marching to battle with a hundred thousand elephants (!), besides 3000 of superior strength and stature, which were employed in destroying the walls and towers of hostile cities.[8] His account of the powerful Indian dogs is more reasonable, and his mention of the use by the natives of eagles, kites, ravens, and crows in the pursuit of small game is curious as the first notice of falconry, a practice prevalent in the East from the earliest ages, but wholly foreign to the Greeks.[9]

§ 6. It is unnecessary to dwell upon the fabulous tales which he relates, both of marvellous animals,—such as the Martichoras or man-eater, the Griffins, which he describes as guarding the gold in the mountains of the interior, and the Unicorn, or wild ass with a single horn on its forehead—and of still more marvellous races of mankind, among which we

---

[5] Ap Strab. xv. p 689.
[6] *Indica*, § 1. He was, however, aware that it flowed for a part of its course through a mountainous country.
[7] Ibid § 27   Fragm. 15
[8] Fragm. 2
[9] *Indica*, § 11.   Fragm 7.

find the Pygmies, the Sciapodes, and the Cynocephali, or men with dogs' heads, who were more commonly assigned to the interior of Africa. But it would appear as if Ctesias had collected from all quarters whatever could serve to swell his list of marvels, and excite the wonder of his more ignorant and uncritical countrymen. That such a tissue of fables, " among the most extravagant ever brought within the compass of a single compilation in the most credulous times" should have been presented to the Greek public shortly before the days of Aristotle is indeed, as Colonel Mure justly observes, a singular phenomenon.[1] But we must remember, in justice to Ctesias and his contemporaries, that these fables, absurd as they were, were deemed worthy of being repeated by successive writers, and still found readers, if not believers, in the days of Pliny and Ælian. At the same time Ctesias himself early obtained, with the more critical part of the public, the reputation which he deserved of a worthless compiler of fables.[2]

§ 7. Among the few grains of real fact to be gleaned out of this mass of absurdities, is the notice that onyxes, sards or sardonyxes, and other precious stones used for signet-rings, were brought from the mountains in the interior of India. On the other hand he speaks of a river that produced abundance of amber, a substance that was certainly never among the productions of India. No mention is found (at least in the remaining extracts) of any of the customs peculiar to the true Hindoos, which so strongly excited the attention and curiosity of the Greeks, when they visited India with Alexander; indeed it may safely be asserted that there is hardly a single state-

---

[1] Mure's *History of Greek Literature*, vol. v. p. 497 The reader, who is curious in such matters will find in the same passage a good summary of all these absurd fictions Their only interest arises from the persevering manner in which they are quoted by successive writers in later times.

[2] Thus Aristotle says of him ὥς φησι Κτησίας, οὐκ ὢν ἀξιόπιστος (*Hist Animal.* viii. 28), and again in citing his testimony, εἰ δεῖ πιστεῦσαι Κτησίᾳ (Ibid. ii 1). Arrian, quoting his statement concerning the Indus, adds εἰ δή τῳ ἱκανὸς καὶ Κτησίας ἐς τεκμηρίωσιν (*Anab.* v. 4, § 2). See also Ælian (*Hist. Anim.* iv. 21), Lucian (*Vera Historia*, i. 3; ii. 31), and Plutarch (*Artaxerx* c i.). Strabo refers to him among the writers on whose statements no reliance could be placed (i. 2, p. 43 ; xv. 1, p. 689).

ment to be found in Ctesias, concerning either the country or the people, which has the appearance of being derived from any direct or trustworthy information. Yet he had the audacity to assert, while stringing together this tissue of absurd fables, that all his statements were strictly true, and were derived either from personal observation, or from the testimony of trustworthy witnesses.[3]

SECTION 2.—*The Anabasis of Xenophon.*

§ 1. The next author whom we have to consider is one of a very different stamp. The expedition of the younger Cyrus from Ionia to the neighbourhood of Babylon (in B.C. 401), with a view to the overthrow of his brother Artaxerxes, has been rendered for ever memorable, not only by the courage and skill with which the body of Greek mercenaries, who had accompanied him up the country, made good their retreat from the field of Cunaxa to the shores of the Euxine, but still more from the narrative of their adventures having been transmitted to us by one of those who had himself shared in all the difficulties and dangers of the retreat, and had taken an active part in surmounting them. The Anabasis of XENOPHON is certainly one of the most authentic, as well as one of the most delightful, episodes of ancient history; and whatever defects its author may elsewhere display in some of the higher qualities of a historian, the narrative in question will always remain one of the most perfect specimens of historical composition—where the writer is relating events of which he is able to speak from his own knowledge.

Geographically considered, the Anabasis must certainly have been an important contribution to the knowledge possessed by the Greeks of the countries to which it related. None of these countries were indeed altogether unknown to them; but their

---

[3] *Indica*, § 33.

information concerning them was undoubtedly very vague and superficial; the mountainous regions traversed by the Greek troops on their retreat were of the wildest character, and had doubtless been as little visited by peaceful travellers in those days, as they had been, until very recently, in modern times. There can hardly be a stronger testimony to the courage and perseverance of the Ten Thousand and their leader, than the fact that the rugged and inhospitable tracts through which they forced their way in midwinter, had remained down to our own days almost unexplored, and unknown to modern travellers, on account of the difficulties by which they were beset.

§ 2. It was fortunate that Xenophon, who accompanied the march in the first instance as a volunteer, and without the least idea how far it was going to lead him, appears to have preserved from the first a regular record of the route, noting not merely the principal places through which the army passed, but the number of days' march, and the distance from one point to another.[4] These distances were computed in parasangs, according to the Persian custom; and so long as the Greeks accompanied the Persian army, and their march lay along a line of route well known to the Persian officers, as must have been the case throughout the advance up the country, there can be no reason to doubt that they were substantially accurate.[5] But the case was very different with the retreat, especially with that part of it which lay through the mountains and high table-land of Armenia, through which there were certainly no frequented high roads, and where the Greeks were repeatedly left to force their way without the assistance of local guides. Upon what principle Xenophon calculated the distances under these circumstances it is not easy to say. We can only feel sure that any approach to real measurement was impossible, and it is obvious that the natural mode of computation by the time occupied on the march,

---

[4] Note A, p 359 [5] Note B p 359

would be extremely difficult of application. It must always be borne in mind that the Greeks had no portable instruments for measuring time, and that even the division of the day into hours was unknown, or at least unfamiliar to them in the days of Xenophon.[6] Hence this ready mode of estimating distances, so familiar to the modern traveller, would be altogether wanting. Still, while the troops were marching at an ordinary rate through a level, or even undulating country, a tolerable comparative estimate might be formed of the length of each day's march, and it is probably this which Xenophon sought to express in parasangs; but when their route lay through a wild and rugged mountain country, harassed at every step by the hostile tribes which occupied it, or toiling through deep and newly-fallen snow, it is evident how impossible it would be to preserve any reasonable estimate of the distances actually traversed, and how little dependence can consequently be placed upon the statements of them given by Xenophon.[7]

Making allowance for the inevitable errors resulting from this cause, we are able to trace for the most part in a general way the line of route followed by the army of Cyrus on its advance, as well as that taken by the Greeks in their memorable retreat. It is not to be denied that there still remain considerable difficulties to be cleared up in regard to details, arising however in all probability as much from our own imperfect knowledge of the countries in question, as from any want of accuracy on the part of the historian. Some of the most important points have indeed only been established in a satisfactory manner within a very recent period.[8] A brief

---

[6] According to Ideler (*Handbuch der Chronologie*, vol 1. p 238) the use of the word ὥρα or hour for the twelfth part of a day was not in use among the Greeks till after the time of Alexander

[7] Note C, p 361.

[8] For a fuller and more detailed examination of the geography of the route in question the reader is referred to Major Rennell's *Illustrations of the History of Cyrus's Expedition*, (4to. Lond 1811), as well as to the more recent works of Mr Ainsworth (*Travels in the Track of the Ten Thousand Greeks*, 8vo, 1844), and Prof Koch (*Der Zug der Zehntausend*, 8vo, Leipzig, 1850) Much valuable information has been furnished by Mr Hamilton (*Travels in Asia Minor and Pontus*, 2 vols 8vo, Lond 1842), and by Colonel Chesney's *Survey of the Euphrates and Tigris*

outline of the general line of route is all that can be here attempted.

§ 3. Setting out from Sardis in the spring of B.C. 401, Cyrus advanced through the centre of Asia Minor by a well-known line of route as far as Celænæ, an important city of Phrygia, on the site subsequently occupied by Apamea, close to the sources of the Mæander. Here he halted thirty days, during which time he received fresh reinforcements of Greek troops. It must be observed that the pretext under which he had assembled these under his standard, was that of an expedition against the mountaineers of Pisidia, who were practically independent of the Persian king, and infested the neighbouring countries with their incursions. As far as Celænæ his route was consistent with this object, as well as with his real purpose of advancing through the passes of Cilicia and Syria into the valley of the Euphrates. But from Celænæ he made a sudden *détour*—for what reason is not explained to us—and after striking northwards for some distance, till he approached the frontiers of Mysia, then turned again to the east and proceeded by another frequented and well-known road from the neighbourhood of Synnada (near Afium Kara Hissar) by Thymbrium and Tyriæum to Iconium, the last city in this direction that was included in his own satrapy.[9] Entering now upon what might be termed hostile territory, though meeting with no opposition, he marched for five days through Lycaonia, and for four more through Cappadocia, until he arrived at Tyana (called by Xenophon Dana), already a large and opulent city, situated at the entrance of the pass into Cilicia. This celebrated pass, subsequently well known as the Pylæ Ciliciæ, is described by Xenophon as impossible for an army to force, if properly defended. It had at first been occupied by the Cilician king Syennesis, but was abandoned by him without striking a blow, on learning that a small Greek force, dispatched

---

(2 vols 8vo. Lond 1850) The whole subject has been discussed in the most elaborate manner by Mr. Grote in the notes to the 69th and 70th chapters of his *History of Greece*.

[9] Note D, p. 363.

by Cyrus from Lycaonia, under the guidance of the Cilician queen, had crossed the Taurus by another route, and that the fleet of Cyrus had also arrived upon the coast. Cyrus was thus enabled to traverse the formidable pass without opposition, and descended to Tarsus in the midst of the Cilician plains.[1]

§ 4. Here another halt was made, of not less than twenty days. It must have been long evident—at least to the leaders of the Greeks, that the march against the Pisidians had been a mere pretence; and that the expedition of Cyrus was really directed against the Great King himself. The soldiers now mutinied, and refused to follow him any farther, but were gradually persuaded to proceed, partly under the flimsy pretext that he only meant to advance as far as the Euphrates, where a Persian general named Abrocomas, a personal foe of Cyrus, was supposed to be posted. Having thus induced the Greeks to follow him, Cyrus advanced through the succession of difficult passes in the neighbourhood of Issus, which played so important a part during the march of Alexander, but which on this occasion were unaccountably neglected by the Persian generals.[2] At Myriandrus, a city on the Gulf of Scanderoon, which was at this time a place of considerable trade,[3] Cyrus halted for a week, before breaking off all communication with the sea, his fleet having here met him for the last time. From hence he struck at once into the interior, and continued his march without interruption to the Euphrates. The details of this part of the march present no considerable difficulty, though the line of route is not otherwise known. He appears

---

[1] *Anab* i 2, § 21–25. For a description of these Cilician gates (see Ainsworth's *Travels in the Track of the Ten Thousand*, pp. 44–46, Chesney's *Euphrates and Tigris*, vol. 1. p 353, Langlois, *Voyage en Cilicie*, pp 367–370 All these modern writers fully confirm the accounts of Xenophon and other ancient authors concerning the formidable character of the pass, which would afford an impregnable position, if properly defended

[2] Note E, p. 364

[3] The *exact* site of Myriandrus has not been determined, but it is of little importance, as its position is well known within a few miles. It is placed by Strabo between Rhosus and Alexandria (xiv 5, p. 676) The foundation of the latter city, which speedily rose to be the most important place on the Gulf of Issus, had naturally the effect of producing the decline of the neighbouring towns.

to have reached the river at a point considerably above Thapsacus, and to have followed its course for some distance down to that place, which was at this period the customary place of passage, and where Cyrus accordingly prepared to cross the Euphrates.[4] Here there was again some hesitation on the part of the Greek mercenaries; but most of them saw plainly that the die was cast, and it was too late to recede; they accordingly crossed the river, and prepared to meet the army of the Great King.

The position of Thapsacus, though a point of the highest importance, not only for the geography of the Anabasis, but for that of the campaigns of Alexander, and the subsequent geography of Asia, has only been definitely ascertained within a very recent period. It was situated just above the modern town of Rakka, at the only point in the central course of the Euphrates where that river is fordable (though even here only at certain seasons of the year), for which reason it continued to be used alike by the Persian, Greek and Roman armies during a long period. It was also a commercial route of importance in ancient times. At the present day the place of passage is known as the ford of the Anezeh or Bedouins; and is in fact resorted to only by the wandering Arabs of the desert.[5]

§ 5. From Thapsacus the line of march lay along the left bank of the Euphrates as far as a river termed by Xenophon the Araxes, which may be safely identified with the Khabur (the Chaboras of Ptolemy and Pliny), as this is the only considerable river, which falls into the Euphrates in this part of its course.[6] The march from henceforth lay through a desert

---

[4] Note F, p 365
[5] Note G, p. 365
[6] All writers who have examined the subject have agreed upon this point, but no explanation has been offered of the *name* of Araxes given by Xenophon to the river in question It is curious, however, as tending to show the frequent use of that name in Asia, and thus helping to explain the confusion into which Herodotus fell upon the subject

It may be observed that the difficulty found by Major Rennell on account of the distance from Thapsacus, of 9 days' march and 50 parasangs, disappears as soon as Thapsacus is placed in its true position, instead of at Deir, little more

tract—regarded by Xenophon as a part of Arabia, though on the left bank of the Euphrates—of which the historian has left us a graphic description, confirmed by the observation of recent travellers. The whole country for five days' march was a level plain, without trees or inhabitants, and frequented only by wild asses, gazelles, bustards and ostriches.[7] Five days' march through this desolate region brought them to an uninhabited city named Corsote, from whence they had again thirteen days' march, through an equally sterile and uncultivated tract, to a place called Pylæ, situated on the verge of Babylonia, a name which Xenophon apparently applies solely to the rich alluvial country, abounding in villages, and intersected by canals of irrigation, which extended from hence without interruption to beyond Babylon.[8]

§ 6. Cyrus now found himself rapidly approaching the great army of Artaxerxes: and he was met by the king himself on the sixth day's march after leaving Pylæ. Unfortunately the details of the military operations that preceded and followed the decisive battle at Cunaxa cannot be traced with any certainty. Even the scene of the battle itself can only be approximately determined: the name of Cunaxa (apparently a mere Babylonian village) is not mentioned by Xenophon, and is preserved only by Plutarch, who doubtless derived it, as well as other particulars of the battle, from Ctesias, who was himself present with the army of Artaxerxes [9] According to the same authority it was 500 stadia distant from Babylon, though Xenophon was told that the field of battle was only 360 stadia from that great city.[1] But as this was mere hearsay evidence, the statement of Plutarch is probably in this instance the more trustworthy: and if it be followed, the field of battle may be placed a few miles to the south of the modern castle and

than 20 G miles above the confluence of the Khabur
[7] *Anab*. 1 5, §§ 1-3 Xenophon's strong personal propensity for the chase shows itself in the details he has given concerning these wild animals, and the difficulty of their pursuit
[8] Note H, p 366
[9] Plut *Artax* c 8.
[1] *Anab*. 11. 2, § 6

village of Felujah.² But the subsequent movements of the Greeks are almost wholly unintelligible to us: even the site of Sittace, the place where they ultimately crossed the Tigris, and which is called by Xenophon "a great and populous city,"³ cannot be identified, though it must probably have been situated a short distance to the south of the modern city of Bagdad. On the other hand recent researches have thrown considerable light on one of the difficulties that had been a great stumbling-block to all previous inquirers—the existence of a great line of wall, called by Xenophon the Wall of Media, which he describes as not less than 20 feet in thickness and 100 feet in height. It was said to extend 20 parasangs in length, and was not far distant from Babylon.⁴ Through this mighty barrier the Greeks passed on their way from the field of battle to the Tigris, so that Xenophon could not have been misinformed or deceived upon the subject, except as to its extent. It seemed impossible that no trace should be left of such a gigantic work: yet until very lately no remains were discovered, which could by any ingenuity be made to correspond with the position required by the narrative of Xenophon. But in the recent survey of this part of Mesopotamia, Lieut. Bewsher discovered the ruins of a wall, running from N.W. to S.E., which he was able to trace for a distance of 10½ miles, and which may probably have been much more extensive.⁵ Such a wall would lie directly across the route of the Greeks in proceeding from Cunaxa to the Tigris: and this discovery has tended much to clear up the topography of this part of Babylonia, as well as to confirm the accuracy of Xenophon's narrative.⁶

§ 7. It was from the time that they crossed the Tigris near Sittace that the retreat of the Greeks may properly be said to have commenced: their march was at first conducted in a

---

² Note I, p. 369.
³ Note K, p. 370.
⁴ *Anab* ii 4, § 12.
⁵ *Journal of Geogr. Soc.* vol. xxxvii.

p. 169. These remains are now known as Hubl es Sukhr—"the line of stones or bricks"
⁶ Note L, p. 370. See the Map.

friendly manner, and under the convoy of Tissaphernes, through the open country on the left bank of the Tigris, till they came to the river Zapatas, which is unquestionably the stream now known as the Great Zab, the Zabatus of Strabo. This is the first point on this part of their route which can be identified with certainty: the intermediate halting-places being still undetermined,[7] though one of them, Opis, is described as a large city. To the Greeks the halt on the Zabatus was one of the most important points of their expedition for another reason—that it was while encamped here, previous to crossing the Zab, that Clearchus and the other generals were treacherously seized and put to death by Tissaphernes. Henceforth therefore the Greeks had to continue their retreat through a hostile country, and with only such occasional and local guides as they could procure for themselves.

§ 8. Thus far their line of retreat had followed apparently that of the high road, or "royal road" of Herodotus, through the plains of Assyria towards the mountains of Armenia,[8] and it was doubtless by that line of route that Tissaphernes intended, or professed his intention, to conduct the Greeks back to Ionia.[9] But when the latter, under the command of Xenophon and their other new generals, after crossing the Zab, had continued their march for 9 or 10 days more along the left bank of the Tigris,[1] they had to force their way with much difficulty through a hilly tract, occupied by the enemy's troops; and after surmounting these obstacles they found their

---

[7] Note M, p. 372
[8] It is remarkable that all this part of the march, from the time they crossed the Physcus, is described by Xenophon as lying through *Media* (ii 4, § 27) Herodotus, as we have seen, included the same district in the land of the Matieni It seems clear that the name of Assyria was not in use as a territorial designation at this period It had perhaps been intentionally suppressed after the fall of the Assyrian monarchy, and was only brought again into use by geographers in later days
[9] This was evidently the route indicated also by Aiæus, the commander of the Persian troops in the army of Cyrus, when, after the battle of Cunaxa, he pointed out the impossibility of returning by the same route they had followed on their advance, but proposed to take another line which would be longer, but along which there would be no difficulty in procuring supplies (*Anab* ii. 2, § 11)
[1] Note N, p 374

farther advance effectually barred by the mountains descending abruptly to the stream, so as to leave no passage along the bank. The customary line of route was to cross the Tigris at this point, and take a westerly direction towards the Euphrates:[2] but the Tigris was much too deep to be forded, and to cross it otherwise in face of the enemy's cavalry was impossible. Hence the only course that remained for the Greeks was to strike at once towards the north into the mountains of the Carduchians, with a view to reaching the high lands of Armenia, from whence they could descend to the Greek colonies on the Euxine. By following this course they hoped to pass the Tigris and the Euphrates near their sources, where they would of course be fordable.[3]

The Carduchians were a warlike race of mountaineers, who had maintained their independence in the fastnesses of a wild and rugged country against all the efforts of the Great King: and they opposed a fierce resistance to the passage of the Greeks.[4] Seven days of almost continual fighting—during which the Greeks suffered more than they had done from all the armies of the Persian monarch[5]—at length brought them through the mountains to the valley of the Centrites, which separated the land of the independent Carduchians from the Persian satrapy of Armenia. Two days' march, after crossing this river, enabled them to surmount the sources of the Tigris, and three days more brought them to the river

---

[2] This was distinctly stated by the captives who were consulted by the Greek generals "the road to the west, crossing the river, led to Lydia and Ionia" (iii 5, § 15) Hence the Greeks were well aware that at this point they quitted the line of route which they *ought* to have followed, and took a direction altogether different

[3] This is distinctly stated by Xenophon as the reason for their directing their march towards the north (iv 1 §§ 2, 3) No allusion is made to any intention of reaching the Euxine, which was probably altogether an after-thought But the captives told them that, when once arrived in Armenia, it would be easy to proceed from thence in whatever direction they chose (ἐν-τεῦθεν δὲ εὔπορον ἔφασαν εἶναι ὅποι τις ἐθέλοι πορεύεσθαι iii 5, § 17)

[4] There can be no doubt that these Carduchi were the ancestors of the modern Kurds, who still inhabit the same mountain tract, and until very recently maintained their virtual independence against the Turks and Persians alike

[5] *Anab.* iv. 3, § 2.

Teleboas. They were now on the elevated table-land of Armenia, where they suffered severely from the severity of the weather, and from deep falls of snow. Struggling on through these difficulties, they reached the Euphrates, in the upper part of its course, and, as they were told, not far from its sources.[6] The river was here easily fordable, and they continued their march over the open, upland country, without any hostile opposition, and meeting with a friendly reception from the Armenian villagers, but encountering great difficulties from the snow.

§ 9. Thus far the course pursued by the retreating army admits of being traced with tolerable certainty, notwithstanding many difficulties in detail. The researches of recent travellers have established several points beyond any reasonable doubt. One of the most important of these—the point where they quitted the Tigris, and began their march northwards towards the Euxine, may be clearly placed near the modern town of Djezireh ibn Omar—the Bezabde of the Romans. It is immediately above this that the mountains close in upon the Tigris so abruptly as to render all farther progress along its valley impracticable, on which account the modern road crosses by a bridge of boats, and proceeds westward by Nisibin to Diarbekr.[7] This the Greeks could not do, and were thus compelled to plunge into the mountain region to the north. The Centrites again may be clearly identified with the Buhtan Chai, one of the principal tributaries of the Tigris, flowing from east to west, and constituting (as Mr. Ainsworth remarks [8]) a kind of natural barrier between Kurdistan and Armenia. The Teleboas may likewise be assumed with much probability to be the Kara Su, a tributary of the Euphrates, flowing

---

[6] *Anab.* iv 5, § 2.
[7] Mr. Layard, who descended the Tigris from the upper part of its course, has given a striking account of the narrow gorge through which the river flows between the village of Tilleh, "where it receives the united waters of Bitlis, Sert, and the upper districts of Buhtan," and the town of Djezireh (*Nineveh and Babylon*, pp 50, 51) The difficulties of the passage are such as to compel even an ordinary traveller to cross the mountains between the two points
[8] *Travels,* p. 166.

through the fertile valley of Mush. Xenophon's statement that in passing from one of these rivers to the other the Greeks had passed beyond the sources of the Tigris, can be readily explained by supposing that he took the northern tributary of that river (now called the Bitlis Chaï, or river of Bitlis) for the main stream. The real source of the Tigris, or at least what is considered as such by modern geographers, was far away to the west.[9] The place where they forded the Euphrates cannot be exactly determined, but it was evidently the Murad Chai, or eastern branch of the river, that is here designated.[1] That stream flows through the elevated table-land of Armenia, which has here an average height of from five to six thousand feet above the sea-level, an elevation that at once accounts for the great cold and deep snows for which this region has been always noted. Across this dreary tract the Greeks had to plod their weary way in the middle of winter: a feat which has not been performed by any modern traveller, still less by any modern army.

§ 10. But from this point it becomes impossible to follow the line of their farther progress with any reasonable probability. Its steps, as detailed by Xenophon, may be briefly recounted. From the spot where they crossed the Euphrates four days' march brought them to some Armenian villages, in the immediate neighbourhood of a palace or castle, where they halted for a week, and then continued their march across the snow-covered plain for three days more, without meeting with any villages. Here their guide, having unfortunately been insulted by Cheirisophus, abruptly quitted them, and they were left to find their own way, during a march of seven days (estimated at 35 parasangs), following apparently—during a part at least of their course—the valley of a river to which

---

[9] See Note O (p. 374).
[1] Xenophon is the only Greek writer who gives the name of Euphrates to this branch of the river, Strabo and the other geographers mentioning only the western or northern branch, which is still known as Frat. But Armenian writers apply the name of Euphrates to both arms, and the same usage probably prevailed among the natives in the time of Xenophon.

Xenophon gives the name of Phasis² Quitting this valley, they crossed a high mountain pass, where they were encountered by the combined forces of three mountain tribes, the Chalybes,³ the Taochi, and the Phasiani. After surmounting this opposition they made five long days' marches (called by Xenophon 30 parasangs) through the land of the Taochians, suffering severely from want of provisions, until they came to a fort or stronghold of that people, which they took by storm, and thus obtained abundant supplies. Hence they again marched for seven days through the country of the Chalybes, till they came to the river Harpasus, an important stream: after crossing which they entered the territory of the Scythini, and proceeded through it for eight days to a place called Gymnias, which Xenophon describes as a large and wealthy city.⁴ It was the first place which they had met with deserving this name since leaving Opis. Here they were received in a friendly manner by the ruler of the country, who furnished them with a guide, promising to conduct them within five days to a spot within sight of the sea. The promise was duly kept, and on the fifth day the Greeks beheld the long-looked-for Euxine, from the summit of a ridge or mountain called Theches.⁵ There still remained for them however five days' march—three through the land of the Macrones and two

---

² The expression of Xenophon, μετὰ τοῦτο ἐπορεύθησαν ἑπτὰ σταθμοὺς ἀνὰ πέντε παρασάγγας τῆς ἡμέρας παρὰ τὸν Φᾶσιν ποταμόν (IV. 6, § 3), would undoubtedly seem to imply that the *whole* march lay along the valley of the Phasis, but it may well be doubted whether this is intended

³ The Chalybes here mentioned are obviously wholly distinct (geographically speaking) from the people of that name, whom Xenophon subsequently found settled on the shores of the Euxine (v 5, § 1), and who were a branch of the Chalybes so celebrated among the Greeks as workers in iron It is singular that Xenophon himself in another passage (v 5, § 17) refers to these mountain Chalybes under the name of Chaldæans, and, according to Strabo (xii 3, p. 549), this was the name by which the Chalybes *on the Pontus* were known in his time

⁴ πόλιν μεγάλην καὶ εὐδαίμονα καὶ οἰκουμένην, ἣ ἐκαλεῖτο Γυμνίας (IV 7, § 19). The name is written by Diodorus Γυμνασία (Diod xiv 29).

⁵ *Anab* IV 7, § 21 No mention is found in Xenophon of the title of "the Sacred Mountain," which is applied to Mount Theches by later writers. Diodorus, who often differs from Xenophon in the names he employs, while following him in the substance of his narrative, calls it Mt Chenium (τὸ Χήνιον ὄρος, xiv. 29) He erroneously places it *fifteen days' march* from Gymnesia, the Gymnias of Xenophon, instead of five.

through that of the Colchians—before they found themselves at the Greek colony of Trapezus, or Trebizond. Here their wanderings and dangers may be considered as having come to an end: their subsequent progress along the southern coast of the Euxine—from Trapezus to Cotyora by land, and from thence to Sinope and Heraclea by sea—presents comparatively little interest, though not without value for its geographical details, as well as for the light which it incidentally throws upon the relations of the Greek colonists on the Euxine with their barbarian neighbours.

§ 11. The details of the march of the Greeks, as above given from Xenophon appear so distinct, and in themselves are so clear and intelligible, that it is the more disappointing to find the extreme difficulty of explaining, or reconciling them with the existing geography of the regions in question. We are still indeed, notwithstanding the researches of recent travellers, but imperfectly acquainted with the countries that must have been traversed by the Greeks, between the high table-land of Armenia and the Black Sea; but enough is known of their physical geography to show that they constitute one of the most rugged and intricate mountain tracts in any part of the world. If we consider the position of the Greek leaders, having to force their way through such a country, in the midst of hostile tribes, without maps, without compass, with mere local guides, who probably knew nothing of the neighbouring countries, and having themselves but a very vague general notion of their situation with regard to any known points, it cannot surprise us to find that the geographical data are in reality wholly incomplete.

From the passage of the Euphrates till they arrived at Trebizond, it may be fairly said that not a single point can be identified with any approach to certainty. The river Phasis may indeed be reasonably supposed to be the branch of the Aras or Araxes, which flows through a district still called Pasin in the upper part of its course,[6] and the presence of the Phasiani

---

[6] Brant's *Journey in Armenia*, in the *Journal of Geogr. Soc.* vol. x. p. 341

in the same neighbourhood would tend to confirm this view. It is certain at all events that it had nothing to do with the celebrated Colchian river of the name, though it is not improbable, as has been suggested, that the Greeks supposed them to be identical, and followed the course of the river farther than necessary under this impression. But it seems impossible to believe (as supposed by some modern writers) that they wandered for many days' march from their true direction, and then made a sudden return in order to recover it. No trace of such an error is found in the narrative of Xenophon, who could not have omitted to mention a circumstance which would have exercised so important an influence on the fortunes of the army. It is indeed utterly impossible to explain the distances given, and even if we admit these to be greatly exaggerated, the number of days employed on the march remains to be accounted for.[7] The river Harpasus cannot be identified with certainty; nor can we fix upon the spot from whence the Greeks first caught sight of the sea. Even the situation of Gymnias is equally uncertain; though it might have been thought that a great and flourishing city (as Xenophon calls it) within a comparatively short distance of the sea, must have been well known to the Greeks in after times. But no mention of the name is found in any later geographer; nor even of the tribe of the Scythini, whose capital it was. The other nations mentioned by Xenophon in this part of his route, the Chalybes or Chaldæans, the Taochi, the Phasiani, the Macrones, and the Colchians, are all of them known to us from other writers; but both the names and the abodes of these wild mountain tribes were so fluctuating and uncertain that we derive from them little assist-

---

[7] Col Chesney says of the route he followed from the mountain which he calls Gaur Tagh, that the journey from thence to Trebizond occupied five days, "owing to the necessity of passing along what in reality is more a winding chasm than a mountain valley in the ordinary acceptation of the word," and he adds that the marches of the Greeks through the mountains of Kurdistan and Armenia must often have encountered difficulties and delays of a similar character (*Euphrates and Tigris*, vol II p 232).

ance in determining the exact geography of this part of the march.[8]

§ 12. It may be observed that all these tribes, from the Euphrates to the sea, seem to have been in fact wholly independent of the Persian Empire; from the time the army quitted Armenia no trace is found of Persian authority. Even the petty nations that bordered on the Euxine, from Trapezus to the frontiers of Paphlagonia, the Mosynœcians, the Chalybians, and the Tibarenians, appear to have enjoyed a state of virtual independence, and the governor or ruler of the important province of Paphlagonia conducted himself towards the Greeks with all the freedom of an independent sovereign, though doubtless owning a nominal allegiance to the Persian monarch. It was not till the army landed in Bithynia that we again find the Persian satrap Pharnabazus taking part in opposing their progress.

§ 13. The narrative of Xenophon, it must always be remembered, was composed with a historical, not a geographical object. Hence the geographical details are introduced almost entirely for the purpose of explaining and rendering intelligible the operations of the Greek forces. Circumstances had indeed placed the historian very much in the position of a geographical explorer, or at least of a traveller through almost unknown regions; but the description of those countries and their inhabitants formed no part of his main subject. Such notices as we find of them are introduced merely incidentally from their natural connection with the incidents of the march, and never assume, as in Herodotus, the character of collateral episodes. But in the few cases where he has entered into more detail than usual—as in the description of the desert of Mesopotamia, in that of the underground dwellings of the Armenians, and the semi-barbarous habits and manners of the Mosynœcians —we recognize at once the character of an intelligent and trustworthy observer, and find cause to regret that he has not

---

[8] Note P, p. 375.

more frequently dilated upon such subjects. One peculiar circumstance which he relates—the singular effects produced upon his soldiers by the poisonous honey found in the mountains of the Colchians—has been completely verified by the observations of modern travellers.[9]

The other works of Xenophon are of no importance in a geographical point of view. His *Hellenica*, like the great work of Thucydides, of which it is the continuation, is confined to the affairs of Greece, and the countries immediately adjacent; while the *Cyropædia*, which, had it been a real history of the reign of Cyrus, could not have failed to be a work of much interest to the geographer, is in fact a mere historical romance; and the incidental notices of a geographical character that are actually found in it, are not only very vague and indefinite, but in many cases utterly erroneous and calculated to mislead the reader.[1]

---

[9] *Anab* iv 8, § 20. According to Mr Hamilton the deleterious quality of the honey is produced by the bees feeding on the flowers of the beautiful Azalea Pontica, which clothes the hillsides above Trebizond, and ascends the slopes of the mountains next the coast for a height of 4000 or 5000 feet, but is not found on the south side of the same range (Hamilton's *Asia Minor*, vol 1. pp 160, 164, 166) This observation exactly agrees with the narrative of Xenophon

[1] See the remarks of Col Mure in his *History of Greek Literature*, vol v pp 384-386.

NOTE A, p. 343.

COMPOSITION OF THE ANABASIS.

IT seems absolutely necessary to suppose that some such notes were preserved by Xenophon, otherwise it would have been impossible for him to have given the details of the march with the care and accuracy which distinguish them in all those parts of the route where we are able to verify them with any certainty. We know that the Anabasis—at least in the form in which it is now preserved to us—was not composed till many years after Xenophon's return to Greece, when he was settled at Scillus in the neighbourhood of Olympia; as he not only gives us a particular description of the grove and temple which he dedicated to Diana at that place, but speaks of his sons as grown-up youths of sufficient age to take an active part in the pleasures of the chase (*Anab*. v. 3, § 10), though he elsewhere speaks of himself as *childless* at the time he was with the army in Thrace, after the close of the expedition. (Ib. vii. 6, § 34.)

It is however probable that the work may have been in great part composed long before, or at least that he may have committed to writing some brief commentaries concerning the events which he had witnessed, while they were still fresh in his memory. But the whole series of marches and distances traversed could hardly have been preserved otherwise than by being committed to writing at the time; and there is certainly nothing improbable in such a supposition.

NOTE B, p. 343.

COMPUTATION OF DISTANCES IN PARASANGS.

The Persian measure of the "parasang" appears to have been in use throughout the monarchy in the days of Xenophon, as well as those of Herodotus (see Chapter VII.); and the distances along the frequented highways were doubtless estimated in those days in parasangs, as they are at the present time along the post-roads in *farsangs* or *farsakhs*. The origin of the name, as well as of the measure itself, is uncertain; but both Xenophon and Herodotus regard it as equivalent to 30 Greek stadia. (Xenoph. *Anab.* ii. 1, § 6; vii. 26. Herodot. ii. 6; v. 53.) Strabo however tells us that there was considerable discrepancy upon this point; some writers estimating it at 30, some at 40, and others again at not less than 60 stadia (xi. p. 518). He himself regards it, like the Egyptian *schœnus*, as of variable length. It was doubtless in reality a mere estimate, or rough itinerary measure, as is still the case with the modern *farsakh*. Of the latter Colonel Chesney says. "The modern farsang or farsakh of Persia varies according to the nature of the ground from $3\frac{1}{2}$ to 4 English miles per hour, and being almost always calculated for mules or good horses, under favourable circumstances it frequently exceeds 4 miles. The ancient parasang appears to have been fixed at 30 stadia, or 3 geographical miles. But this being also a road measure, it no doubt varied as at present, and was regulated according to the nature of the country." (Chesney's *Euphrates and Tigris*, vol. ii. p. 207.)

From a comparison of the distances given by Xenophon on the march *up* the country from Sardis to Thapsacus—two fixed points known with certainty—Colonel Chesney deduces the *average* length of the parasang as equal to 2·6 G. miles, but several portions of the route would give only about 2·10 G miles. Major Rennell estimated the parasang at 2 25 G. miles. Mr. Hamilton, computing only from distances in Asia Minor, reckons the parasang as something less than $2\frac{1}{2}$ G. miles. It is clear that no exact result can be attained by any such method, as we neither know the precise line of the ancient routes, nor have we any exact measurements of the modern ones. But it seems clear that while the modern *farsakh* generally *exceeds* 3 G. miles, the ancient parasang *on the average* fell considerably short of that length. There is nothing in this to surprise us, or lead us to have recourse to any far-fetched hypothesis to explain it; the tendency to *over*-estimate distances in travelling being much more frequent than the contrary error. Even along the highways and great lines of route—such as the "royal road" described by Herodotus—there is no reason to suppose that the distances were "measured and marked" as they unquestionably were along the Roman roads; any more than we are to suppose the roads themselves to have had any resemblance to those of the

Romans. The distances were doubtless mere *estimates*, as they are at the present day along the so-called post-roads of Persia. Thus the route from Teheran to Tabreez—one of the most frequented in modern Persia—is divided into stages from one post-station to another, corresponding precisely with the σταθμοί of Herodotus and Xenophon, and of just the same average length, varying from four to five and six *farsakhs*, though occasionally extending to seven or even eight. (Ussher's *Journey from London to Persepolis*, pp. 647–662.)

Mr. Ainsworth *assumes* the parasang to have been in all cases really equivalent to 30 stadia or 3 geographical miles; a fundamental error, the effect of which may be frequently traced throughout the whole of his work.

Colonel Chesney, while justly regarding it as a mere "road measure" supposes it to be, like the modern Persian *farsakh*, the equivalent of "an hour of time;" an assumption which may well be doubted. But even if it were so in its origin, and that the Persians had derived from the Babylonians the division of the day into twelve hours, it is certain that neither they, nor the Greeks, possessed any portable instruments for the measurement of time, and hence any attempt to estimate distances by this process must have been of the vaguest possible character.

NOTE C, p. 344.

RATE OF MARCHING.

Mr. Grote is almost the only writer who has made (as it appears to me) sufficient allowance for the full operation of these causes. Several of the modern geographical inquirers have been misled by a strong desire to reconcile or explain the distances given by Xenophon, without inquiring what probable foundation there could be for his statement of those distances. This defect is especially prominent in Mr. Ainsworth, in whom it is the more remarkable as, having himself travelled over a large part of the ground traversed by the Greek army, he would be naturally the more familiar with the great difficulties which it presented. Yet he uniformly translates the parasangs into miles, at the rate of 3 G. miles to a parasang, as confidently as if he were dealing with distances given in the Roman Itineraries, which had been really *measured* along lines of high road. Hence he does not hesitate to describe the Greeks as marching forty-five (geographical) miles in three days, through deep snow—in some parts, according to Xenophon's own statement, not less than six feet in depth. Such a march may be safely pronounced impossible. and the same criticism may be applied, with scarcely less positiveness, to many other portions of the march through this mountainous district. In one passage indeed Xenophon himself describes the army as marching for seven days *at the rate of* five parasangs a day (μετὰ τοῦτο ἐπορεύθησον σταθμοὺς ἑπτὰ ἀνὰ πέντε παρασάγγας τῆς ἡμέρας, iv. 6, § 4). and this may serve to give some clue to the mode of his computation. It is probable that he reckoned an *average* day's march at five parasangs, and estimated the distances accordingly, without making sufficient allowance for disturbing causes. Such a mode of calculation is the more remarkable, as he himself gives five parasangs as the ordinary rate of daily march, while the army was ascending the valley of the Tigris, under the charge of Tissaphernes, so that they were proceeding through a friendly, as well as a naturally easy, country (*Anab.* ii. 4, §§ 25-28). The first instance, after quitting the Tigris, in which he describes them as marching *more* than five parasangs a day, was through the country of the Taochi, where they were hard pressed for subsistence, in consequence of the barbarians having carried off all supplies into their strongholds, and they probably therefore were induced to make forced marches in hopes of arriving at fresh villages. Hence they are here said to have marched 30 parasangs in five days, or 6 parasangs a day. Again, after obtaining fresh supplies by storming the fort of the Taochians, they are said to have accomplished not less than 50 parasangs in 7 days, though engaged in continual combats with the Chalybes, whom Xenophon describes as the most warlike people they met with (*Anab* iv. 7, § 15). On the other hand, from the Harpasus to Gymnias, though apparently unopposed, and travelling in part through a level country (διὰ πεδίου), they resumed their customary rate of 5 parasangs a day: and after they had come in sight of the sea, where we might have supposed that they would be in haste to arrive at Trebizond, they advanced but 10 parasangs in three days through the land of the Macronians, and 7 parasangs in two days through that of the Colchians.

If any confirmation were wanting of the extreme vagueness and uncertainty of all estimates of distance under such circumstances, it will be abundantly supplied by a reference to the recent experience of the English expedition into Abyssinia. Here the distances traversed by the army were afterwards actually measured with a chain, and it was found that a day's march, estimated by experienced officers at 16 or 18 miles, often did not exceed eight!

Both Major Rennell and Col. Chesney repeatedly advert to the difficulties encountered by the Greeks in this part of their retreat, and the impossibility of their having actually performed the distances which Xenophon supposed them to have accomplished. Col. Chesney indeed admits that they could not have advanced more than a mile per hour through the snows of Armenia (vol. ii. p. 230): but he is misled by supposing the parasang to represent an hour's march, forgetting that such a mode of computation was wholly unknown to Xenophon.

NOTE D, p. 345.

ROUTE OF CYRUS THROUGH PHRYGIA.

This part of the route of Cyrus has been a source of much perplexity to modern geographers, especially to the earlier writers on the subject. The researches of modern travellers have thrown considerable light upon it, but without altogether explaining the difficulty. (See Hamilton's *Asia Minor*, vol. ii. pp. 198-204. Ainsworth's *Travels in the Track*, pp. 24-35. Koch, *Zug der Zehntausend*, p. 19.) It is clear that Cyrus, when he quitted Celænæ, for some reason which is not explained to us, instead of continuing his march direct towards Iconium, made a wide circuit, passing round the mountain group of Sultan Dagh, to the north, instead of taking the line of road to the south of it. By so doing he struck into a well-known and natural line of route, from the neighbourhood of Synnada (Afium Kara Hissar) to Iconium, and there can be no doubt that the towns of Thymbrium and Tyriæum may be placed along this line, though their exact site is still subject to some doubt. The place called Caystri Pedion must therefore be sought in the neighbourhood of the small lake called Eber Ghiol: but the station before this, called by Xenophon Ceramon Agora, cannot be determined even approximately. The expression, however, that it was "the last city on the side of Mysia" ($\pi \acute{o}\lambda \iota \nu$ $o \dot{\iota} \kappa o \upsilon \mu \acute{\epsilon} \nu \eta \nu$, $\dot{\epsilon} \sigma \chi \acute{a} \tau \eta \nu$ $\pi \rho \grave{o} s$ $\tau \hat{\eta}$ $M \upsilon \sigma \acute{\iota} \dot{a}$ $\chi \acute{\omega} \rho \dot{a}$, i. 2, § 10), points clearly to a situation towards the northern frontier of Phrygia (probably in the neighbourhood of Ushak); and it seems certain, therefore, that Cyrus, in starting from Celænæ, took in the first instance a direction somewhat to the westward of north, with which the presumed position of Peltæ would coincide. The motive for this sudden deviation from the ordinary line of route is unknown to us. but it greatly exceeds what can be supposed to have been made without some special reason. He must also have made an equally sudden turn after visiting Ceramon Agora with the view of regaining his general direction towards the south-east.

I concur with Mr. Grote in believing in the accuracy of Xenophon's description of;this part of the route, which lay through an open country, easily traversed by an army, and where the roads must have been well known to the Persian officers. The difficulty is, that the two most important points—Ceramon Agora and Caystri Pedion—are not mentioned by any other writer. and though the *names* of Peltæ, Thymbrium, and Tyriæum are mentioned by later geographers, it is in a manner that affords little assistance in determining their site. We have thus five stations along a line of march undoubtedly very circuitous—for it occupied not less than 92 parasangs, while the direct route from Celænæ to Iconium could not have exceeded 150 G. miles (or about 60 parasangs)—no one of which can be fixed with certainty.

It may be added, that this sudden deviation towards the north had the effect of turning his back upon the Pisidians, and must therefore have at once betrayed the fact that his expedition against that people was a mere pretence.

NOTE E, p. 346.

PASSES BETWEEN CILICIA AND SYRIA.

The topography of these passes has been carefully investigated by several modern writers—and Col. Chesney's survey and map of the localities have thrown much light on the matter. The passes having been undefended, Xenophon does not seem to have given full attention to their difficulties. Thus, while he mentions the actual fortified gates between Issus and Myriandrus, to which he gives the name of the Cilician and Syrian gates, from their forming at this time the frontier of the two countries (i. 4, § 4), he does not notice either the pass through the western branch of Mount Amanus (the Amanian Gates of Strabo), by which Cyrus must have descended to the Gulf of Issus, or the narrow pass of Beilan, by which, after leaving Myriandrus, he must have crossed the main ridge of Mount Amanus to enter into Syria, strictly so called. Neither of these passes however presented difficulties comparable to those of the Pylæ Ciliciæ, of which Xenophon speaks in such strong terms.

NOTE F, p. 347.

ROUTE FROM THE GULF OF ISSUS TO THE EUPHRATES.

The stations and distances given, after leaving Myriandrus, are

To the river Chalus.. .. .. .. 4 days, 20 parasangs.
  „ sources of the river Daradax 5 „ 30 „
  „ river Euphrates at Thapsacus 3 „ 15 „

Of these, the Chalus is evidently the river of Aleppo (itself called in later times Chalybon, whence the modern Haleb), but we cannot determine at what point the army crossed it. and the sources of the Daradax—also described as a considerable river, 100 feet in width, and where the Persian kings had a park—have not been identified, though that stream must certainly have been situated in the neighbourhood of the modern Balis. The position of Thapsacus renders it almost certain that the army must have reached the Euphrates some time before halting at that city, and followed its course downwards. though the words of Xenophon (i. 4, § 11) would certainly in themselves have led us to suppose that this was the first point where they touched on the Euphrates. This is a circumstance worthy of note in its bearing on other disputed questions in regard to the line of march.

NOTE G, p. 347.

THAPSACUS.

Major Rennell in his *Illustrations of the Geography of Xenophon* (p. 60), fell into the error (in common with D'Anville) of placing Thapsacus at the modern Deir, more than 100 miles lower down the river than its true position, and thus threw the whole geography of this part of the march into confusion. The true site was first determined by the regular survey of the Euphrates under Colonel Chesney, when it was found that the Euphrates was fordable at this point only. The existence of large mounds in the immediate neighbourhood points to the site of a city of importance, such as Thapsacus is described by Xenophon, who calls it "a large and wealthy city" (πόλις μεγάλη καὶ εὐδαίμων, *Anab.* i. 4, § 11): and such it continued to be during the greater part of the Macedonian period, but before the time of Strabo it had declined, and given way to the establishment of the customary passage at Zeugma (the modern Bir), more than 120 miles higher up the river.

The Euphrates was only fordable at this point at certain seasons of the year: at other times it was crossed by a bridge of boats. It was in this manner that Alexander afterwards crossed it (Arrian, iii. 7): and under the Seleucidan kings there was a permanent bridge of boats (ζεῦγμα) established there (Strabo, xvi. 1, § 21, p. 746). When Cyrus crossed the river at this point the Thapsacenes asserted that the river had never been fordable before, and had only become so in honour of Cyrus (*Anab.* i. 4, § 18): but it is evident that this was a mere piece of flattery, based upon the fact that it was subject to great fluctuations, and often impassable on foot.

(See Ainsworth's *Travels in the Track*, pp. 70-72 ; Chesney's *Euphrates and Tigris*, vol. i. p. 416, vol. ii. p. 213.)

It may be added that the river has here exactly the width reported by Xenophon of 4 stades or 800 yards (Ainsworth, *l. c.*).

NOTE H, p. 366.

POSITION OF PYLÆ.

The position of Pylæ unfortunately cannot be determined with accuracy, though it is an essential point in order to arrange the details of the subsequent operations. Its name appears to point to some unexplained peculiarity of its situation, but all that we learn from Xenophon is that it was apparently situated at the point where the barren, undulating, slightly upland country of Mesopotamia gives way to the level and fertile alluvial plains of Babylonia. (Compare i. 5, § 5, and 7, § 1.) This transition is described by all travellers as very strongly marked, and according to Mr. Ainsworth the point where it takes place in following the

NOTE II.   THE ANABASIS OF XENOPHON.   367

course of the Euphrates is about 14 miles above the village of Felujah. (Ainsworth's *Travels*, p. 81.) It is a few miles below that point that at the present day the Saklawiyeh—originally a mere artificial canal, but which has gradually become a tortuous river—leaves the Euphrates, and traverses the low country to join the Tigris below Baghdad.

Here therefore Mr. Ainsworth fixes the site of Pylæ; but it is impossible to reconcile this with the statements of the march from thence to Cunaxa; it was not till the sixth day after leaving Pylæ that the army of Cyrus came in sight of that of Artaxerxes, and though these were probably short marches, as Cyrus was advancing cautiously, expecting at any moment to meet the enemy, they could hardly be estimated at less than 60 miles. Now the site of the battle was, according to Xenophon 360 stadia (36 G. miles) from Babylon, or according to another account 500 stadia (see the next note), and this would place it not more than 30 miles south of Felujah, or less than 20 miles, if we adopt the statement of Ctesias. Hence Colonel Chesney would place Pylæ considerably higher up the Euphrates; and Mr. Grote considers it to have been situated only a few miles below Hit, which is more than 50 G. miles above Felujah. This is confirmed by a statement of Captain Jones that there is at this point (9½ miles S.E. of Hit) a place called Bekaa, an Arabic word signifying the same as the Greek Pylæ, and that there is actually a narrow pass at that place (*Journal of Geogr. Soc.* vol. xxxvii. p. 167). But it does not appear that there is at this point any such marked change in the character of the country as would correspond to the supposed situation of Pylæ; and the distance from Felujah appears much too great. Hence the position assigned by Mr. Grote seems to me as much too high up the stream, as that of Mr. Ainsworth would bring it down too low.

The position of Pylæ and that of Cunaxa are indeed to a considerable extent mutually dependent upon each other; and neither the one nor the other can be fixed on fully satisfactory data; but if the probable site for the battle, which will be considered in the next note, be adopted, Pylæ can hardly be thrown so far back as it has been by Mr. Grote. Very little assistance can be derived from the statement of the distances in the other direction. From the mouth of the Araxes (the Khabour), which is the last fixed point that can be determined with certainty, the army of Cyrus advanced (according to Xenophon) (i. 5) five days' march, amounting to 35 parasangs, through a desert country, at the end of which time they arrived at a large deserted city called Corsote, situated on the river Maskas, which was a hundred feet in width. But no such river is now found flowing into the Euphrates, and the site of Corsote cannot be identified. After laying in a stock of provisions here, they again proceeded through a barren country, affording no sustenance for either man or beast, for thirteen days' march (reckoned at 90 parasangs) which brought them to Pylæ (i. 5, § 5). We have thus an estimated distance of 125 parasangs, or 375 G. miles, with only one halting-place, which cannot be determined. The difficulties and privations of the march are described in a lively manner by Xenophon, and he tells us that the difficulty of procuring provisions led Cyrus to press on his advance with all possible speed, and to make forced marches. Hence we find them accomplishing 7 parasangs a day in the first stage of the march, and very nearly as much in the second, notwithstanding its long protracted duration. It may well be doubted whether both estimates are not materially over-rated. But besides this, the actual distance marched by an army, following the course of such a river as the Euphrates, cannot be judged without knowing how nearly they kept to it, and to what extent they were able to cut off its numerous windings. From the mouth of the Khabour to the Saklawiyeh is about 250 English miles, without following the minor sinuosities of the river; but the distance may be increased to a great extent, if we suppose the army to have kept as close as possible to its banks In such a case therefore any attempt to fix the position of Pylæ by reference to its distance from the Khabour would be utterly futile.

The only other place mentioned *by name* in this part of the march is a city called by Xenophon Charmande, which he terms "a large and wealthy city" (πόλις εὐδαίμων καὶ μεγάλη, i. 5, § 10), but which was situated on the other side of the Euphrates, on which account the army passed it by without halting, though they procured provisions from thence. For the same reason probably Xenophon has not mentioned its distance, stating only that it was passed during the march through the desert (κατὰ τοὺς ἐρήμους σταθμούς). The name is not found in any other author, but it certainly seems probable (as suggested by Mr. Grote) that the city designated could be no other than the Is of Herodotus (i. 179), still called Hit, which on account of its bitumen springs, must always have been a place of some importance. But even if this identification be admitted, it throws no light on the other points in dispute connected with this part of the march, as we are left in doubt as to the distance of Charmande from either Corsote or Pylæ.

NOTE I, p. 349.

SITE OF CUNAXA.

This was the conclusion arrived at by Mr. Grote (vol. ix. p. 56, note 2), and appears preferable to the site fixed on by Colonel Chesney (followed by Mr. Ainsworth), who placed the field of battle near a spot marked on his map by the Mounds of Mohammed, at the mouth of a river or canal called the Kutha (Chesney, vol. ii. p. 217; Ainsworth's *Travels*, pp. 81, 87). This site is about 20 miles farther south than that adopted by Mr. Grote, and by so much nearer Babylon; thus agreeing with the statement of Xenophon, rather than with that of Ctesias. But, as observed in the text, the testimony of Ctesias is in this case probably the best authority.

Since Mr. Grote's note was written, Lieutenant Bewsher, who has made a regular survey of this part of Babylonia, discovered that one of the mounds, which in this country always mark the sites of ancient habitation, is called Tel Kuneeseh; a remarkable resemblance to the ancient name. He himself indeed remarks that, "in a country where names of mounds are frequently changed—except indeed the larger ones—it seems improbable, *and almost too good to be true*, that this one particular spot, the site of which has been so long sought for, should have kept its name intact for nearly 2300 years." (*Journal of Geogr. Soc* vol. xxxvii. p. 166.) It must be added that the circumstance which he mentions that Kuneeseh is the Arabic for "church," tends to weaken the force of the inference from the coincidence of name; but on the other hand the position of the mound in question, which is situated just to the south of the canal known as the Abu Gharraib, 17 miles from Felujah, and 51 in a direct line from Babel, the northernmost of the ruins of Babylon (Bewsher, *l. c.*), agrees so well with the requirements of our historical data, as to lend a strong confirmation to the evidence of the name, and to leave little doubt that the plain between Tel Kuneeseh and the Euphrates—which has a width varying from 3 to 4 miles—was really the scene of the far-famed battle of Cunaxa. (See the map.)

NOTE K, p. 349.

SITTACE.

The disappearance of cities that have attained to considerable prosperity and opulence is a remarkable fact, of which there are many instances in these countries. Thus the site of Kufah—the original seat of the Caliphs, until their capital was transferred to Baghdad in 763—is barely to be identified. some insignificant heaps of pebbles scattered over the plain alone serving to indicate the site of what was once a great city (Ussher, *Journey from London to Persepolis*, p 465). Even of the opulent Seleucia, which in the time of Strabo contained 600,000 inhabitants and doubtless abounded in splendid buildings, nothing remains but long lines of earthen ramparts, inclosing the mere vestiges of former habitation (Layard, *Nineveh and Babylon*, p. 571). We cannot therefore wonder at the disappearance of all trace of the Sittace of Xenophon, which must have been situated in the neighbourhood of Baghdad, probably between that city and the site of Seleucia. It was certainly *above* the point of confluence of the Diyala, otherwise the Greeks would have had to pass that river, after crossing the Tigris of which there is no mention. The distance of 20 parasangs from Opis affords us no assistance, as the site of Opis itself is still uncertain.

The name of Sittace as a city is not found in later writers, but it must undoubtedly have been the capital which gave name to the province of Sittacene, and this, as we learn distinctly from Strabo, was situated between Susiana and Babylonia, on the east of the Tigris (Strabo, xv. 3, p. 732, xvi. 1, p. 744) though Sittace itself, as is plain from the narrative of Xenophon, was on the western or Babylonian side of the river (*Anab.* ii. 4, §§ 13-24).

NOTE L, p. 349.

THE MEDIAN WALL.

Previous to this discovery by Lieut. Bewsher of the remains of the wall in question, which may be considered as completely corresponding with what is required by the narrative of Xenophon, it was supposed by many writers that the Median Wall must have been a barrier across from the Euphrates to the Tigris, such as we find certainly existing at a later period. But this wall or rampart, the remains of which are still visible, and are known to the Arabs as Khalu Nimrud, or Sidd Nimrud, leaves the Tigris more than 50 miles above Baghdad, extending in a S.W. direction towards the Euphrates, and would, if prolonged to that river, strike it about 3 miles above the Saklawiyeh canal, and at least 8 above Felujah. (See the description of it in the *Journal of Geographical Society*, vol. ix. pp. 445-6, 473-4.) It was evidently this wall, of which the remains, already in a half-ruined state ("semiruta murorum vestigia") are noticed during the advance of the Emperor Julian down the valley of the Tigris (Ammian. Marcell. xxiv. 2, § 6). The objections to such a theory were insuperable; for it was utterly unintelligible that the Greeks should have returned so far northward, *after* the battle; and if they had passed through this wall, instead of bringing them towards the Tigris, they would have emerged into the barren stony plains of Mesopotamia, the Sidd Nimrud marking exactly the limit between these and the rich alluvial tract of Babylonia. Moreover Xenophon describes the army as passing, on the third day *before* the battle, a vast trench dug by order of Artaxerxes in order to impede the advance of Cyrus, but which after all he left undefended · and this trench, he tells us, was carried through the plain for a distance of 12 parasangs *to the Median wall* (i. 7, § 15). Such a line of defence is unintelligible, if the wall was a rampart extending across from the one river to the other. but would be an obvious expedient, if the wall had a direction obliquely through the centre of Babylonia, like the rampart of which the ruined remains were discovered by Lieut. Bewsher.

On the other hand Strabo mentions a wall, which he calls " the Wall of Semiramis" (τὸ Σεμιράμιδος διατείχισμα), which appears to have extended from the Euphrates to the Tigris at the point where they approached the most closely to one another (Strabo, ii. p. 80, xi. p. 529); and this has been supposed by Major Rennell and Mr. Grote to be the Median Wall of Xenophon. But in the first place no trace remains of such a bulwark, which, if it really existed at the narrowest part between the two rivers, must have been situated near the modern city of Baghdad, between Cunaxa and Babylon. and moreover the account given by Strabo (from Eratosthenes) is by no means clear, but seems to place this narrowest point at Opis on the Tigris, which must certainly have been situated considerably farther to the north than the real neck of the isthmus. It may well be doubted therefore whether there is not a misconception on the subject, and whether the Wall of Semiramis (of Strabo and Eratosthenes) was not in reality the same of which the remains are still called Sidd Nimrud (the Wall of Nimrud). But even if there ever really existed such a line of wall as that mentioned by Strabo, at the point where the two rivers approach within less than 20 miles of each other, it would not have corresponded near so well with the narrative of Xenophon as the wall discovered by Lieut. Bewsher, which must have lain directly across the route of an army proceeding from the Euphrates near Cunaxa to Sittace on the Tigris, whether we place that city below or above Baghdad.

It may be added that the remains of the Hubl es Sukhr show that wall to have been built of bricks cemented with bitumen, in accordance with the description of the Median Wall in Xenophon (ii 4, § 12), while the Sidd Nimrud is built of "the small pebbles of the country imbedded in cement of lime." (*Journal of Geogr. Soc.* vol. ix. p. 446.)

It would be obviously idle to attempt to identify the great ditch dug by order of Artaxerxes, any more than the two canals that were crossed by the Greeks on their way from the Median Wall to the Tigris. Such canals have been in all ages cut for the purposes either of irrigation or internal communication and when neglected readily assume in the course of time the aspect of natural rivers. Such is at the present time the Saklawiyeh, which is still navigable for a small steamer, and such was in the middle ages the Nahr Malcha, or Royal River, which is now dry in the main part of its course. A glance at the map given by Lieut. Bewsher (*Journal of Geogr. Soc.* vol. xxvii.) will sufficiently show by what a complicated network of canals and artificial streams all this part of Babylonia is intersected the greater part of which date from the period of the Caliphs of Baghdad—and have consequently tended to destroy all possibility of tracing its condition in ancient times.

NOTE M, p. 350.

MARCH ALONG THE TIGRIS.

The stages and distances given by Xenophon (ii. 4, § 25) after crossing the Tigris are as follows:

From the passage of the Tigris near Sittace,
to the river Physcus and the city of Opis   4 days, 20 parasangs.
thence through Media to the villages of
  Parysatis   6   „   30   „
along the left bank of the Tigris to the
  river Zapatas   4   „   20   „

The last ten days' march lay through an uninhabited country (σταθμοὺς ἐρήμους), with the exception of the villages of Parysatis, where they halted, but on the first day's march from these villages there was a large and wealthy city named Cænæ (Καιναί) on the other side of the river, from which the Greeks received abundant supplies. Unfortunately neither Cænæ nor Opis can be fixed with any certainty. Captain Lynch indeed considered some ruins that he had discovered near the junction of the Adhem with the Tigris to be those of Opis, in which case the river Adhem would represent the Physcus of Xenophon (*Geogr. Journal*, vol. ix. p. 472), and this view is adopted by Col. Chesney (*Euphrates and Tigris*, vol. i. p. 30) but the identification is far from certain. Opis is again mentioned during the campaigns of Alexander, in whose time it was still a large and important city, as it is described by Xenophon, though Strabo speaks of it as a mere village (II. 1, p. 80). But we have no other clue to its position, except that Eratosthenes (*ap. Strab. l. c.*) apparently designates it as marking one extremity of the Wall of Semiramis, a statement which can hardly be reconciled with the position assigned to it by Captain Lynch. Cænæ, of which the name is not found in any other writer, has been generally identified with the modern town of Senn, but the resemblance of name, as pointed out by Mr. Grote (vol. ix. p. 93, note), is really a delusion, and the situation of Senn, just opposite to the mouth of the Greater Zab, is certainly at variance with that assigned by Xenophon to Cænæ, which he places distinctly on the *first* day's march after leaving the villages of Parysatis. It would seem much more probable that Cænæ occupied the site now marked by the ruins at Kalah Shergat, which have been recently explored by Mr. Layard (*Nineveh and its Remains*, vol. i. p. 5, vol. ii. pp. 45-60). It is true that the existing remains appear all to belong to the ancient Assyrian city, but it is not at all improbable that it may have continued to be inhabited at a later period. At all events the Cænæ of Xenophon must have been situated somewhere in its immediate neighbourhood.

Another difficulty arises, in regard to this part of the march, from the omission of all mention of the Lesser Zab, an important stream, which the Greeks must necessarily have crossed. Herodotus distinctly mentions the two rivers of the same name, both of which had to be crossed in following the line of the "royal road," and the passage of such rivers is one of the points in general most studiously noted by Xenophon. It is impossible not to suspect that in this instance Xenophon's memory had played him false, and that he had forgotten the circumstance that there were *two* rivers of the name of Zabatus or Zapatas, *both* of which had been crossed by the army. In this case the villages of Parysatis were probably situated near the mouth of the Lesser Zab; the distance between the two rivers being 57 miles, which would just correspond with the 20 parasangs of Xenophon.

NOTE N, p. 350.

RUINED CITIES OF ASSYRIA.

It was on this part of their march, while the Greeks were advancing through the open country on the left bank of the Tigris, that they passed the two deserted cities named by Xenophon Larissa and Mespila, the gigantic ruins of which seem to have forcibly attracted his attention (*Anab.* iii. 4, § 7–12). These may be safely identified with the sites of Nimroud and Kouyunjik, which have been rendered so familiar to modern readers by the recent researches of Mr. Layard. But no plausible explanation can be given of the names by which they are here designated, and which are unknown to any other ancient writer. The curious legends which Xenophon relates concerning them, and which he obviously heard on the spot, show how entirely all trace of their true history and origin had already been lost in his time.

NOTE O, p. 353.

SOURCES OF THE TIGRIS.

The Tigris may be considered, like the Euphrates, as formed by the junction of two principal streams; of which the western branch is the more considerable, and is regarded by modern geographers as the true Tigris. This takes its rise in the mountains of Armenia, about 40 miles N.W. of Diarbekr, and within a very few miles of the nearest point on the Euphrates. But the stream which joins the river of Diarbekr about 80 miles (in a direct line) below that town is so important a tributary, that it is considered by many geographers as constituting what may be called the Eastern Tigris. This arm is itself formed by the junction of two others: the Buhtan Chai, sometimes also called the river of Sert—which is clearly the Centrites of Xenophon. and the Bitlis Chai, or river of Bitlis, which he appears to have regarded as the true Tigris. This flows from N. to S. and has its sources within a few miles of the Lake of Van: while the Buhtan Chai which flows from the E. rises in the mountains of Kurdistan, in a tract that has only recently been visited by any modern traveller.

NOTE P, p. 375.

DESCENT THROUGH ARMENIA TO TREBIZOND.

It may be worth while to add a few remarks on the geography of this part of the route, though there seems little hope that the difficulties with which it is perplexed will ever be wholly explained. Yet it may not be impossible at least to clear some of them away.

Major Rennell was, I believe, the first to identify the Harpasus of Xenophon (which he describes as a large river 400 feet in width) with the stream now called Arpa-su, or Arpa-chai, a northern tributary of the Araxes, and this view has been adopted by Mr. Ainsworth, as well as by most modern geographers. But the suggestion of Colonel Chesney and of Dr. Koch (which has been followed by Mr. Grote) that the Harpasus was in reality the Tchoruk Su, a large stream flowing through a deep valley which separates the mountains of Armenia from the ranges adjoining the Euxine (Koch, p. 201), is in reality much more plausible, as that river lay directly in the course of the Greeks towards the sea, while in order to reach the Arpa-chai we must suppose them to have made a great *détour* towards the N E., for which there was really no occasion. Mr. Ainsworth indeed carries them still farther to the north, into the heart of Georgia, a distance of 90 miles (!), and then brings them back again no less than 150 miles (!) through the country of the Chalybes to the frontier of the Scythini (*Travels*, p. 183), the whole of this enormous *détour* being required (as he himself confesses) only in order to explain the distances given by Xenophon in parasangs of three miles each. Dr. Koch on the other hand, while justly rejecting the theory of Mr. Ainsworth, supposes the Greeks, after reaching the Harpasus (Tchoruk Su) somewhere in the neighbourhood of the modern Ispir, to have wandered away to the eastward as far as Ardahan, and then returned to the same river in the neighbourhood of Ardvin, a supposition equally improbable and uncalled for.

The position of Gymnias would be the key to the whole question, if it could be ascertained; but unfortunately it is wholly uncertain; and the different sites that have been suggested are merely suited to the different views of modern writers as to the route of the army. It has thus been placed by Major Rennell at Comasour, by Mr. Ainsworth at Erzeroum, by Dr. Koch in the S.W. of Georgia; while Mr. Grote inclines to identify it with Gumisch Khana, a place on the high road from Trebizond to Erzeroum. But Gumisch Khana is only two or three days' journey from Trebizond, and less than 40 G. miles in a straight line; and it seems impossible to account for the ten days employed on the march between this point and the sea. Gumisch Khana is at the present day a place of importance on account of its silver mines, which, according to Mr. Hamilton, are "the richest and most important in the Ottoman dominion" (Hamilton's *Asia Minor*, vol. i. p. 234), and Mr. Grote considers these mines as affording a plausible explanation of the existence of a "great and flourishing city" in the midst of surrounding barbarians (vol. ix. p. 161). But there is no evidence that these mines were worked in ancient times, and had they been so, within so short a distance of the Greek colonies on the Euxine, it seems difficult to believe that some notice of the fact would not have been found in some subsequent writer, especially Strabo, who was himself a native of the neighbouring province of Pontus. Yet no mention either of Gymnias or of its silver mines is found in any later writer, excepting Diodorus, who evidently copied Xenophon, though he writes the name *Gymnasia* (Diod. xiv. 29).

The determination of the mountain of Theches, from whence the Greeks first caught sight of the sea, must obviously depend upon that of the route by which they were approaching the Euxine. In a country traversed by numerous ranges of high mountains—for the most part, as will be seen by a reference to Kiepert's map, running in a direction *parallel* with the coast—there must be many points from which a distant view of the sea would suddenly burst upon the eyes of a traveller, and wherever this first took place, under the peculiar circumstances of the Greek army, the sight would be almost equally impressive. On the modern road from Erzeroum to Trebizond, the sea is first seen from a place called Karakaban, about 25 miles from the sea, and at an elevation of between 5000 and 6000 feet; and is described by all travellers as extremely striking. But it seems impossible to account for the time employed by the Greeks on the descent to Trebizond, as well as for the details of their march thither, if we suppose this to be the point whence they first descried the Euxine. (See Mr. Hamilton's remarks, *Asia Minor*, vol. i. p. 166; and those of Mr. Grote, vol. ix. p. 162.) Mr. Ainsworth and Colonel Chesney transfer the scene much farther inland, to the mountains known as Kop Dagh and Gaur (or Gjaur) Dagh, forming part of the second, and more inland, chain, south of the valley of the Tchoruk, and the testimony of Colonel Chesney that he himself saw the sea in 1831 from the summit of Gaur Dagh, which is distant from it nearly 60 G. miles in a direct line (vol. ii. p. 232), shows at least that these inner ranges cannot be excluded from consideration. But either of these points seems as much too far inland, as Karakaban is too near the sea.

Mr. Hamilton is inclined to suggest that they first came in sight of the sea from some point in the range of mountains extending from Ispir to Baiburt, considerably to the east of the modern line of road to Trebizond (*l. c.* p. 167), and the same view has been adopted by M. Kiepert in his remarks on a paper by M Strecker. He supposes the Greeks to have crossed the mountains from Gymnias,—which he places in the neighbourhood of Baiburt, though not actually on the site of the modern city—by a pass leading into the valley of the Surmeneh, and to have descended that valley to the sea, which they would thus reach some distance east of Trebizond. This suggestion appears highly plausible; but the route in question has not yet been followed by any modern traveller, and we cannot therefore determine fully how far it answers the required conditions.

On the other hand the theory of a recent inquirer who believes that he has found the remains of the cairn of stones thrown up by the Greeks to mark the spot, on the summit of a mountain just to the south of the pass called Vavough Dagh, which is crossed by the road from Baiburt to Gumiseh Khana (*Journal of Geogr. Soc.* vol. xl. p. 463) may be almost certainly dismissed as untenable. Xenophon's account clearly implies that the place from which the sea was first descried lay on the line of march—not that they climbed a peak for the purpose. No general in his senses would have led his whole army up a mountain, for the mere purpose of seeing the sea, when he could himself have ascertained the fact of its proximity by ascending the summit with a reconnoitring party. The same objection applies still more strongly to the suggestion of M. Strecker that the Greeks ascended the Kolat Dagh, and after gazing on the sea from thence, descended again *on the south side* and made a great *détour* to the west before resuming the direct road to Trebizond.

The memoir of M. Strecker just cited (*Beitrage zur Geographischen Erklarung des Ruckzuges der Zehntausend durch das Armenische Hochland*, Berlin, 1870), together with the counter remarks of M. Kiepert, was unknown to me when the greater part of the above note was written. It was with great satisfaction that I found myself in accord with the eminent geographer of Berlin in respect to several of the leading points in dispute; especially the identification of the Phasis with the upper course of the Araxes, and of the Harpasus with the Tchoruk Su. If these points can be considered as sufficiently established, the only points of real interest that remain to be determined are, the site of Gymnias, and the spot from whence the Greeks first caught sight of the sea.

CHAPTER XI.

WRITERS AFTER XENOPHON.

SECTION 1.—*Ephorus. The Periplus of Scylax.*

§ 1. AMONG the historical writers who flourished in the period between the expedition of Cyrus and that of Alexander (B.C. 399–334) the one who would have contributed the most to our geographical knowledge, had his writings been preserved to us, is undoubtedly EPHORUS. A native of Cyme in Æolis, he composed a great historical work, in thirty books, which may fairly be regarded as the first attempt at a general history.[1] In this he endeavoured to comprehend the history of the barbarian nations, as well as that of the Greeks, though the latter of course constituted his main subject; and was related by him in detail from the return of the Heraclidæ to the siege of Perinthus by Philip of Macedon in B.C. 340.[2] His merits as an historian it hardly falls within our province to consider; but it may be observed that as in relating the earliest periods of Greek history he seems to have given particular attention to the origin and foundation of the several cities, he bestowed equal pains upon those of the later Greek colonies.[3] Hence we find him frequently cited as an authority upon these subjects by Strabo and other writers, and there is no doubt that many other statements are derived from the same source, although his name is not quoted. His work would therefore have supplied us, had it been preserved, with the most important contributions to that interesting subject,

---

[1] Polyb v 33 See Mure's *Hist. of Greek Literature*, vol v p 531.
[2] Diodor iv 1; xvi. 76.   [3] Polyb ix 1, xxxiv 1

a history of the Greek colonies.⁴ But besides such incidental notices of geographical facts, it appears that two whole books of his voluminous work were devoted to a general and systematic review of geography: on which account the fourth book is frequently quoted under the title of "Europe" or the Description of Europe: the fifth in like manner as that of Asia and Africa. Unfortunately our extant remains of these books are so imperfect that they afford us hardly any means of judging how far his geographical knowledge was in advance of that of Herodotus. By far the longest extracts that have been preserved to us, relate exclusively to the cities and institutions of Greece itself, and hence, however valuable in themselves, they have no geographical interest.⁵

§ 2. Of his general views of geography we learn only that he regarded the four most distant regions of the earth as occupied respectively by the Indians to the east, the Æthiopians to the south, the Scythians to the north, and the Kelts to the west.⁶ The latter people he considered as occupying all Spain as well as Gaul, and extending to the Pillars of Hercules, and even to Gadeira.⁷ For his ignorance in this respect he is sharply censured by later writers: and it is indeed a curious proof how vague and imperfect were the notions still entertained by the Greeks of the western regions of Europe. At the same time he seems to have been aware that the tracts occupied by the four nations were not of equal extent, but that the Æthiopians and the Scythians extended the farthest in space, so that he already regarded the inhabited world as an ob-

---

⁴ See especially Strabo, ix p 422, and Scymn Chius, v 115

The latter author (or rather the anonymous writer of the geographical fragment commonly bearing his name) appears to have in great measure followed the authority of Ephorus, and his statements concerning the foundation of the Greek colonies derived from that author, are among the most valuable parts of his work

⁵ The fragments of Ephorus were first collected by Marx, they have been more recently published by C Muller in his *Fragmenta Historicorum Græcorum*, tom 1 (Paris, Didot, 1841) They are here cited according to this last edition

⁶ Fragm 38, M ap Strabon 1 p 34 The same statement is evidently copied from him by Scymnus Chius, vv 170–177, but without citing him by name

⁷ Fr 43, ap. Strab iv 4, p 199.

long parallelogram, having its greatest length from east to west.

§ 3. Of the real extent of his knowledge towards the north we have no clear evidence, but he seems to have described the Scythian tribes in considerable detail, and the following summary of his information concerning them is extracted by a later writer: "Next beyond the Ister came the tribe of the Carpidæ, beyond them the Aroteres (evidently an agricultural tribe), and farther north the Neuri, extending to the limits where the land was rendered uninhabitable by frost. Towards the east again, crossing the Borysthenes, came the Scythians who inhabited the land of Hybla (probably the Hylæa or forest country of Herodotus). Beyond these inland were the Georgi (or agricultural Scythians) and beyond them an extensive tract of desert country: after passing which came the Androphagi (or man-eating Scythians), and beyond them again a vast desert. Crossing the Panticapes (*i. e.* proceeding *eastward* again, as he had done in the first instance from the Borysthenes) came the tribe of the Limnæans (or Lake-dwellers), and many other tribes not distinguished by separate names, but known by the general appellation of Nomades, very righteous people, so that they would not injure any living thing, but living in waggons, and subsisting on milk the produce of their mares.[8] Other Scythian tribes had crossed over into Asia, where they were known by the name of Sacæ. The most distinguished of the Scythian races were the Sauromatæ, the Geloni, and the Agathyrsi. The Mæoti gave name to the Lake Mæotis, into which the Tanais flowed. That river had its source in a lake, the limit of which was unknown, and flowed by two mouths into the Lake Mæotis."[9] In another passage, preserved to us by Strabo,[1] he pointed out that the manners both of the Scythians and Sarmatians varied greatly in the different tribes: some of them being savage to

---

[8] This description is evidently derived from Homer, whose expressions are almost literally *copied*

[9] Ephori Fragm 78, ed Muller; Scymn Ch v. 841-873, ed Muller.
[1] vii. 3, p. 302

such a degree as to feed on human flesh, others on the contrary refraining from all animal food, and subsisting entirely on the milk of their mares, leading a life of such simplicity and innocence as to deserve the epithet of Homer, that they were "the justest of mankind." If we compare this account with that of Herodotus, it is evident that the knowledge of the interior of Scythia had made little or no progress in the interval, while the arrangement and description of the tribes by Ephorus (at least in the form that it is transmitted to us) is much less clear and intelligible than that of the earlier historian. It must however be admitted that it is preserved to us only at second hand, and in a somewhat fragmentary form.

§ 4. The numerous quotations from Ephorus concerning the geography of Asia relate almost exclusively to the cities and inhabitants of Asia Minor, with which the Greeks were already familiar in his day, and cannot be said to add anything to our geographical knowledge. He described the peninsula of Asia Minor as inhabited by sixteen different nations: three of them of Greek origin, the Æolians, Ionians, and Dorians, and the remaining thirteen barbarians: the Cilicians, Pamphylians, Lycians, Carians, Bithynians, Paphlagonians, Maryandini, and Trojans on the coast, and the Pisidians, Mysians, Chalybes, Phrygians, and Milyans in the interior.[2] In this enumeration the omission of the Lydians is unaccountable, and perhaps merely accidental; but it deserves notice as an attempt to deal with the complicated question of the ethnography of the peninsula. In this respect it is curious to compare it with the similar enumerations in Herodotus.

§ 5. With regard to Africa on the contrary it is interesting to observe that he appears certainly to have known, and made use of, the voyage of Hanno: as he was not only familiar with the name of Cerne, but mentioned also that of a town called Caricon Teichos,[3] which is known only as one of the colonies

---

[2] Fr 80, ap Strab xiv 5, p 678
[3] Ephori Fragm 96, Steph Byz v Καρικὸν Τεῖχος. C Muller even considers that the voyage of Hanno was known to Pliny only through the work of Ephorus

founded by Hanno on the west coast of Africa. He evidently considered Africa as surrounded by the ocean, but stated that it was impossible to navigate from the Erythræan Sea to Cerne on account of the excessive heat.[4] He must therefore have rejected the story of the circumnavigation under Necho.

§ 6. The only specimen that has been preserved to us of the speculations of Ephorus on physical geography is very unfavourable. In regard to the much disputed question of the cause of the inundation of the Nile, he rejected the hypothesis that it was the result either of melting snow or rains in the upper part of its course, and considered it as owing to the spongy and porous nature of the soil of Egypt, which gave forth in summer, under the influence of the great heat, the moisture it had previously imbibed, and thus filled the river.[5] Of all the solutions of the question that had been propounded, as Diodorus observes, this was the farthest from the truth, and showed the most complete ignorance of the country.

§ 7. The important historical work of THEOPOMPUS, a contemporary and fellow-pupil of Ephorus,[6] would apparently have been of comparatively little geographical interest. It is however deserving of notice that he was, according to Pliny, the first Greek writer who mentioned the name of Rome, having recorded the capture of that city by the Gauls.[7] He appears also to have supplied additional information con-

---

[4] Plin vi 36, § 199 "Propter ardores." These words, as they stand in Pliny, can hardly be understood in any other sense, but I cannot help suspecting that Pliny has made some confusion with respect to the great fires and streams of fire of which the Carthaginian voyagers had related so much, on the western coast of Africa

[5] Ephori Fragm. 108; Diodor i 37, § 4, 39, § 7-13

[6] According to Suidas they were both born in the same year, but his date is probably erroneous It is certain, however, that they were fellow-pupils under Isocrates, and both of them survived the death of Philip, B C 336 Theopompus indeed appears to have been still living as late as B C 305. (See Clinton, *F. H* vol II p 374)

[7] Plin. *H N* III 5, § 57 (nam Theopompus, *ante quem nemo mentionem habuit*, Urbem dumtaxat a Gallis captam dixit) He had apparently overlooked the obscure notices of the name of Rome by Antiochus of Syracuse and Damastes already cited But Theopompus appears to have been really the first writer who mentioned any historical fact in connection with the city

cerning the nations of Italy in general, especially the Venetians, the Umbrians, and other nations who bordered on the Adriatic. The foundation of Greek colonies at Ancona, and in the islands of Issa and Pharos, during the reign of the elder Dionysius at Syracuse, must have naturally led to increased knowledge of the countries surrounding that sea. Theopompus also is cited as authority for various details concerning the manners of the Tyrrhenians (Etruscans),[8] which undoubtedly present a very exaggerated picture of the luxury and profligacy of their habits: but may nevertheless be taken as showing increased familiarity with that people. But the imperfect character of his purely geographical knowledge is sufficiently shown by his maintaining that the Danube communicated by one of its mouths directly with the Adriatic.[9] It is singular that this erroneous notion, which is not found in any earlier writer, had at this time become a fixed idea among the Greeks, of which, as we shall see, they were very slow to divest themselves.

§ 8. To the same period belongs the Periplus still extant under the name of SCYLAX, which is of interest as the first professed geographical treatise that has been preserved to us. It is a specimen of a class of works that seems to have been common in antiquity, professing to describe in regular order the coasts of the countries known to the Greeks, without any general geographical survey of the countries themselves, but merely giving very succinctly the names of the maritime cities and towns, the headlands and rivers, in the order of their occurrence, as they would present themselves to any one sailing along the coast, with the addition, in more or less detail, of the distances from point to point. The deficiencies of such a work, as compared with a regular treatise on geography, would be much less glaring, in the case of Greece and the adjoining lands than in any other instance, and as the Greek colonies were, almost without exception, situated on the sea-coast, all

---

[8] Fragm. 222 M ; ap Athenæum, xii p 517
[9] Theopomp ap. Strab. vii 5, p 317, Fragm 140 M

that was most interesting to the ordinary Greek mind would find its place in a Periplus such as we are describing. Towns and tribes in the interior were occasionally noticed, as it were in passing; in connexion with those of each district on the sea-coast. But this is rarely done except in the case of Greek cities.

§ 9. The date of the Periplus now extant has been a matter of much controversy. It is ascribed in the extant MSS. to Scylax of Caryanda, and was on that account supposed by the earlier editors to be the work of the navigator of that name, whose voyage down the Indus and from thence to the Arabian Gulf is recorded by Herodotus.[1] But the internal evidence of its belonging to a period long after the reign of Darius Hystaspis is conclusive: and Niebuhr was the first to show that it could not have been written before the time of Philip of Macedon. Recent editors have attempted to fix its date within more precise limits: but at all events it may fairly be considered as contemporary with the histories of Theopompus and Ephorus.[2]

§ 10. From its plan and arrangement it is not calculated to throw much light upon the extent or limits of geographical knowledge among the Greeks, being confined for the most part to the regions best known to them—those bordering on the Mediterranean Sea. The author begins from the Pillars of Hercules, and follows the northern coast of the Mediterranean from thence (including the Adriatic and the Euxine) as far as the mouth of the Tanais, which he regards as the boundary between Europe and Asia: and from thence he returns along the coasts of Asia and Africa to the point from which he started: adding however a brief notice of the western or Atlantic coast of Africa, as far as the island of Cerne. Of the western shores of Europe, on the contrary, he seems to have known almost nothing. After briefly mentioning Gadeira (Gades) he adds that, outside the Pillars of Hercules, there

---

[1] Herodot. iv 44. See above, Chap VII. p 227.   [2] Note A, p 404

are "many trading stations of the Carthaginians, and much mud, and high tides and open seas."[3] It is evident that these seas were never at this time visited by Greek traders, while the confused notions of the obstacles to their navigation, purposely diffused by the Carthaginians, were all that had reached our author's ears.

Even of the eastern coast of Spain his information is extremely imperfect, though this defect perhaps arises from the fault of our manuscripts. In its present form the Periplus only begins a regular description from the mouth of the Iberus (Ebro), though the author distinctly tells us that the whole extent of the coast of Spain (Iberia) was a voyage of seven days and seven nights: a very fair approximation to the truth.[4] His account of the other nations that bordered on this part of the Mediterranean is very brief and summary, nor is it easy to reconcile with what we know from other sources of the real history of the nations mentioned. Thus he describes the tract from the confines of Iberia proper[5] to the mouth of the Rhone as occupied by mixed races of Iberians and Ligurians; and the Ligurians alone as inhabiting the region from the mouth of the Rhone as far as Antipolis (Antibes); in which were the Greek cities of Massilia and its colonies; while he assigns the whole coast from thence to the confines of

---

[3] Ἀπὸ Ἡρακλείων στηλῶν τῶν ἐν τῇ Εὐρώπῃ ἐμπόρια πολλὰ Καρχηδονίων καὶ πηλὸς καὶ πλημμυρίδες καὶ πελάγη Peripl § 1.

His imperfect acquaintance with these regions is further shown by his statement (l c) that the strait separating the Pillars of Hercules was a day's voyage across an error which appears to result from his confounding the actual straits with the entrance to them between Gades and the opposite point of Africa—a distance which is estimated by several writers at a day's voyage

[4] He reckons (as we shall presently see) a day's voyage as equal to 500 stadia (50 G miles), and a night as equal to a day Hence his estimate of the *paraplus* of the coast of Spain would give 700 G miles, it really amounts to about 660, as far as Emporiæ, or near 680, if measured to the Pyrenæan Promontory (Capo di Creus)

[5] He nowhere defines exactly the point which he considers as the boundary of Iberia, but he evidently seems to regard Emporiæ (Ampurias) as the *last* Greek city in Spain and there can therefore be no doubt of his adopting the natural boundary, recognized by all subsequent geographers, in the headland where the Pyrenees descend to the sea But his omission of all mention of the Greek colony of Rhoda (Rosas) is singular.

Latium to the Tyrrhenians. The Latins held the sea-coast from the borders of Tyrrhenia to the Circeian promontory: then came the Olsi (Volscians) for a short distance: next in order, the Campanians, Samnites and Lucanians, the last people extending as far as Rhegium and the Sicilian Straits.[6] It is remarkable that he does not notice either the Arno or the Tiber: nor does he give the name of a single city, till he comes to Campania, with the exception of Massilia and its colonies, and the *incidental* mention of Rome:[7] the first passage in any *extant* author in which the name of the rising city is found. On the other hand he enumerates in detail the Greek colonies on the coast of Lucania, including even such comparatively unimportant towns as Pandosia, Hipponium and Mesma. In like manner his knowledge of Sicily, as might be expected, is detailed and accurate, while of Sardinia and Corsica he tells us nothing more than their names and their geographical position, with regard to which he was well informed.[8]

§ 11. He is also the first writer who has left us a detailed account of the shores of the Adriatic: and here his mention of the Greek cities of Ancona, Pharus, and Issa, which were not founded till the reign of the elder Dionysius, affords a clear proof that the Periplus could not have been written earlier than B.C. 380. His enumeration of the nations along the western shore of the Adriatic is clear, and consistent with all we know of their history from other sources. He assigns the coast as far as the mountain Orion (a name not found elsewhere, but which must clearly designate the mountain promontory of Garganus) to the Iapygians: next to whom came the Samnites: then the Umbrians, in whose territory was the Greek city of Ancona: next to these the Tyrrhenians, whose dominion

---

[6] Periplus, § 12 No mention is found of the Bruttians, as a people distinct from the Lucanians
[7] Ἀπὸ δὲ Ἀντίου (Antipolis) Τυρρηνοὶ ἔθνος μέχρι Ῥώμης πόλεως § 5.
[8] Thus he describes Sardinia as distant from Africa a day and a night's voyage, and two days and a night from the nearest point of Sicily. Both are very close approximations to the truth, reckoning the day's voyage at 50 G. miles. From the Tyrrhenian coast to Corsica he calls it a day and a half, which considerably exceeds the truth, the distance between the nearest points of the island and the mainland being less than 50 G miles

extended from sea to sea. After them came the Celts or Gauls, "who were left behind on the expedition of their brethren"—a remarkable passage, as the first mention of Gauls in this part of Italy—and then the Veneti, who adjoined the Istrians on the other side of the Adriatic.[9] On the other hand, that of the tribes, as well as of the islands and headlands on the opposite shore, is confused, and often unintelligible: a circumstance which may be owing in some measure to the peculiarly complicated and intricate character of the coast in question, as well as to the shifting and unsettled nature of the semi-barbarous Illyrian tribes by which it was peopled. But the detail in which he gives the nomenclature of these tribes, as well as the minuteness with which he describes the configuration of the coast, proves how much it was frequented, and how well its details were known to the navigators from the Greek colonies of Corcyra, Apollonia and Epidamnus.[1]

At the same time it is a remarkable instance of the persistence of a popular error once established, that in describing the coast of Istria, at the head of the Adriatic, he places there a river Istrus, and adds that it has another mouth by which it discharges itself into the Euxine.[2] This error—of which no trace is found in Herodotus—appears to have originated merely in the circumstance of the Greeks having found at the head of the Adriatic a people bearing the name of Istri or Istrians, which they at once connected with the celebrated river Ister. The confusion is the more singular as there is in fact no river

---

[9] §§ 14-19 Our author, however, fell into the error—shared by many subsequent writers—of supposing the innermost recess or head of the Adriatic (ὁ μυχὸς τοῦ Ἀδρίου κόλπου) to have been situated in the territory of the Celts, near the city of Atria, instead of in that of the Veneti (See on this point the remarks of Letronne, p 196)

[1] There is, however, according to our present text, one enormous error, where he speaks of the Hylli, an Illyrian tribe, as occupying a peninsula "a little smaller than the Peloponnese" (!)

(κατοικοῦσι δὲ χερρόνησον ὀλίγῳ ἐλάσσω τῆς Πελοποννήσου, § 22) Such a statement is not only absurd in itself, but utterly at variance with our author's own account of the distances along this part of the coast, yet we strangely find the very same error repeated in the geographical treatise ascribed to Scymnus Chius (vv 405, 406), more than two centuries after our author

[2] Μετὰ δὲ Ἐνέτους εἰσὶν Ἴστροι ἔθνος καὶ ποταμὸς Ἴστρος. οὗτος ὁ ποταμὸς καὶ εἰς τὸν Πόντον ἐκβάλλει (§ 20.)

of any considerable size or importance flowing through the land of the Istrians, or indeed into the upper part of the Adriatic at all. But the fable, once admitted, was seized upon by the poets and logographers with a view to explaining the supposed passage of the Argonauts by this route: hence geographers were determined to find a river that would answer their purpose, and gave the name of Ister or Istrus to the first stream that they could pitch upon.[3]

Scylax is also the first extant author who distinctly applies the name of Eridanus to the Padus or Po, the great river of northern Italy. But he has no mention of *amber* in connection with it: and he places the islands called Electrides, on the opposite or Liburnian coast of the Adriatic, apparently giving the name to some of the numerous islands in the Gulf of Quarnero.[4]

With the geography of Greece itself, as well as the northern and eastern shores of the Ægean, our author was naturally well acquainted: but these were of course familiar to all, and while his account of them is valuable to the student of ancient geography for its accuracy in detail, it cannot be regarded as having contributed anything to the enlargement of geographical knowledge.

§ 12. Of the Euxine also his account is very full and detailed, giving the names of many of the numerous petty tribes which occupied its eastern shores, from the entrance of the Palus Mæotis to the neighbourhood of Trebizond,[5] as well as of all the Greek settlements which studded its southern shore, many of these being inconsiderable places, which disappeared

---

[3] The river Quieto, which is supposed by Mannert and C Muller to represent the *Adriatic* Istrus of the ancients, is in reality a very trifling stream, that could never have been seriously supposed to be one of the outlets of a great river.

[4] § 21 The name of these Electrides or Amber Islands, as has been already pointed out (p. 14), was a mere fiction

[5] Among these tribes, however, we are surprised to meet with the names of the Melanchlæni and the Gelones, both of which are placed by Herodotus far in the interior of Scythia and on the European side of the Tanais (Herodot iv 20, 101, 107, 108). There is probably some error here, but the ethnography of the various tribes inhabiting the Caucasus has been in all ages so obscure that it is impossible to pronounce with certainty

in later times, and whose names are consequently not found in other geographers. The most easterly of these colonies were Dioscurias and Phasis, of which the latter was situated at the mouth of the river of that name, and may thus have commanded an important trade with the interior.[6] On the other hand the Greek settlement of Tanais, at the mouth of the river of that name, which became in later times an important emporium of commerce, is not mentioned by Scylax, and probably was not founded till after his time.[7] His account of the northern shores of the Euxine is indeed much less precise and full than that of the southern:[8] and he shared in the very exaggerated notion prevalent in his day as to the size of the Palus Mæotis, which he regarded as about *half* the size of the Euxine.[9]

§ 13. The description of the coasts of Asia Minor, from the Bosphorus to the Gulf of Issus, though copious and accurate,

---

[6] Xenophon, when he found himself at Cotyora, at the head of the Ten Thousand Greeks, entertained for a time the project of proceeding with his whole force *to Phasis* to found a colony there (*Anab* v 6, §§ 15, 36) Mr Grote justly points out that this means the town of that name, and not the river (*Hist of Greece*, vol ix p 185, note), but he considers Phasis to have been at this time "a native city," and not a Greek colony (Ib p 180) As however we find it recognised as such by Scylax, it is probable that it was already such in the time of Xenophon That leader may, however, well have thought that there was room for a larger and more important colony in so favourable a situation

[7] Strabo, who describes it as having been a flourishing place of trade, calls it a colony of the Greeks of the Bosporus (xi p 493), meaning probably from Panticapæum It was likely to be one of the latest, as it was one of the most remote, of their settlements, and may very well not have been founded till after the date of our Periplus It was just about this time that the Greek kings of the Bosporus were at the height of their power, and we know from Demosthenes (Or. adv. Leptinem, § 33) that the emporium of Theodosia, on the southern shore of the Tauric peninsula, had at that time only been *lately* established by Leucon, king of Bosporus Hence the mention of this place in the Periplus (§ 68) may be added to the numerous proofs of its late period which have been collected by the diligence of its editors

[8] It can hardly be otherwise than a mere accident that he omits all mention of the Borysthenes, as well as of the Hypanis and the city of Olbia, passing across the northern gulf of the Euxine direct to the Tauric Chersonese But it is more inexcusable that where he is enumerating the greatest rivers of Europe (§ 69), while he mentions the Tanais in conjunction with the Ister and the Rhodanus, he omits altogether the far more important Borysthenes.

[9] τοῦ ἡμίσεος τοῦ Πόντου ὄντος ἴσου τῆς Μαιώτιδος λίμνης Peripl § 69 See Chapter VI p 178

The statement here refers indeed (strictly speaking) only to the *length* of the Palus Mæotis, but even this is in reality less than a fourth part of the *paraplus* of the Euxine with which our author compares it.

presents nothing of any special interest. That of Phœnicia and Syria, on the contrary, as well as a part of that of Egypt, are in so corrupt and mutilated a condition as to be almost worthless. But the account of the African coast from the frontiers of Egypt to Carthage is one of the most complete and satisfactory portions of the Periplus, and its details are in general extremely accurate. The clear information that the author possessed concerning the two Syrtes, the island of the Lotophagi, and the Tritonian Lake,¹ contrasts in a striking manner with the vague and confused notions of these regions transmitted by Herodotus. Beyond Carthage on the contrary, his knowledge appears to have been comparatively meagre: but few names are mentioned, and the distances are not given in detail. The author contents himself with the general estimate that from Carthage to the Columns of Hercules was a voyage of seven days and seven nights under the most favourable circumstances.²

§ 14. While our author's knowledge of Gades and the coast of Spain beyond the Pillars of Hercules was, as we have seen, extremely imperfect, he gives us a brief but interesting account of the west coast of Africa as far as the island of Cerne, which he describes as situated twelve days' voyage from the Straits, and seven days beyond Cape Soloeis, with which he was evidently well acquainted, as he describes it as a promontory standing out boldly into the sea, and having an altar sacred to Poseidon on its summit.³ Intermediate between Cape Soloeis and Cerne he places a river called Xion, which can evidently be no other than the Lixus of Hanno.⁴ Cerne was the seat of a considerable trade, carried on by the Phœnician

---

¹ §§ 109, 110   ² § 111.
³ It is clear that the headland to which he gives the name is the same with the Soloeis of Hanno and his mention of the altar on the summit is probably derived from the voyage of that commander. At all events this part of his Periplus is evidently taken from Carthaginian sources.

⁴ The Lixus of our author on the contrary, at the mouth of which he places a Phœnician (*i.e.* Punic) city of the same name, with a Libyan town on the other side of the river (Peripl § 112), can certainly be no other than the river of Laraiche, to which the name was given by Pliny and later geographers

merchants with the Ethiopian natives of the opposite coast, from whom they obtained ivory and the skins of lions, panthers, &c., in exchange for pottery, ornaments of stone, sweet ointments, and other wares.[5] Beyond Cerne (says our author) the sea was no longer navigable on account of shoals and mud and sea-weed. But it was vaguely reported that there was continuous sea all along the southern coast of the Ethiopians, round to the shores of Egypt, so that Africa was in fact a great peninsula.[6]

§ 15. Of the Indian Ocean, or even the Red Sea, no mention is found in the Periplus, a circumstance which would appear the more remarkable in the supposed work of an author, who had himself navigated those seas, and been indeed their first explorer. But it seems to have been assumed by the earlier editors that he had described these portions of the world in another work, specially devoted to that object: a supposition in itself not improbable, but unsupported by any evidence.

§ 16. Of the general configuration, or geographical relations, of the countries and seas that he describes, our author gives us very little information. He in one passage indeed repeats the statement of Herodotus that the width of Asia Minor from sea to sea (measured from Sinope across to Soli in Cilicia) was five days' journey:[7] and in another states the breadth of Italy from the city of Spina on the Adriatic across to Pisa on the Tyrrhenian shore at three days' journey:[8] but these vague estimates are almost the only statements of the kind which he has furnished us.[9] His distances by sea are almost uniformly

---

[5] § 112 The notice in such a connection as this of *Attic* pottery (κέραμον Ἀττικὸν) is a curious proof of the established reputation of that manufacture

[6] Τῆς Κέρνης δὲ νήσου τὰ ἐπέκεινα οὐκέτι ἐστὶ πλωτὰ διὰ βραχύτητα θαλάττης καὶ πηλὸν καὶ φῦκος Λέγουσι δέ τινες τούτους τοὺς Αἰθίοπας (those on the mainland adjoining Cerne) παρήκειν συνεχῶς οἰκοῦντας ἐντεῦθεν εἰς Αἴγυπτον, καὶ εἶναι ταύτην τὴν θάλατταν συνεχῆ, ἀκτὴν δὲ εἶναι τὴν Λιβύην, § 112 He here uses the term ἀκτὴ precisely in the same sense that it is employed by Herodotus (See above, p. 161)

[7] § 102 He has, however, omitted to add the important words εὐζώνῳ ἀνδρὶ annexed to his statement by Herodotus (ii 34)

[8] § 17

[9] The two statements are indeed widely discordant if compared with the reality The actual distance from the

given in days' voyages:[1] but he tells us in one place that he
reckons a day's voyage as corresponding to 500 stadia, and a
night's voyage (where he mentions nights and days consecu-
tively) as equal to that of a day.[2] Of course this can only be
taken as an average computation : but it shows clearly what
was his mode of estimating distances : he ascertained as best
he could the length of the voyage by the number of days
or nights actually occupied, without any attempt to compute
the distance as a matter of measurement, or even estimate,
except by the rough process of rendering the number of days'
voyage into stadia on the general average thus assumed.

It is to be remarked that while the author, in more than one
passage, sums up the whole amount of the distances, so as to
give the total length of the *paraplus* or voyage along the coast,
with all its windings in detail, from the Pillars of Hercules to
the Tanais, and again from thence to the Nile, and back again
to the Straits, we find no attempt to estimate the length of the
Mediterranean, or even of the Euxine, as deduced from the
number of days' voyages in the most direct line. Probably
our author did not conceive such a calculation to fall properly within the province of his little work. But it is scarcely
conceivable that some such estimate should not have been
made even before his time by more systematic geographers.

His other statements of the more considerable distances will
be found on the whole very accurate, according to his own

Euxine to the Mediterranean, on the line indicated, exceeds 300 G miles in a straight line, while that across Italy from sea to sea is less than 100 G miles, without allowing for the distance inland of the two cities named

[1] Of course this applies only to the longer distances The shorter distances (of a few miles only) are naturally given in stades, and for this reason this mode of measurement is frequently employed in describing the coasts of Greece, where the subdivisions are given in detail But the same mode of computation is applied also to the coasts of Syria, Phœnicia, and Egypt,

which in this respect differ from all the rest of the work Probably this part of the Periplus was derived from a different authority

It is worth notice that this practice of giving the distances only in days' voyages, and not in stades, is mentioned as one of the peculiarities of the Peri-plus of Scylax of Caryanda by Marci-anus of Heraclea (*Epit Artemidor* § 2, p. 63). It is therefore probable that the Periplus known to that author (in the fourth century A D) under the name of Scylax was the same which we now possess.

[2] § 69

mode of computation. Thus as we have seen his estimates of the distances from Sardinia to Africa, and from Sardinia to Sicily, both of which must have been measured in a direct line,[3] are very close approximations to the truth, at the rate of 50 G. miles for a day's voyage. On the other hand he calls it a voyage of seven days and seven nights *under the most favourable circumstances*[4] from Carthage to the Pillars of Hercules, where we must therefore suppose him to mean a rate *above* the average; and accordingly we find that the distance is not less than 800 G. miles, or 8000 stadia, by the shortest course that a ship could follow.

§ 17. At the end of the extant Periplus is found an enumeration of the principal islands known to the author in the order of magnitude, beginning with 1. Sardinia as the largest of all: then 2. Sicily. 3. Crete. 4. Cyprus. 5. Eubœa. 6. Cyrnus (Corsica). 7. Lesbos. 8. Rhodes. 9. Chios. 10. Samos. 11. Corcyra. 12. Casos. 13. Cephallenia. 14. Naxos. 15. Cos. 16. Zacynthus. 17. Lemnos. 18. Ægina. 19. Imbros. 20. Thasos. The most remarkable point in this list is the superiority given to Sardinia over Sicily, in which respect the author is at variance with almost all other ancient writers on geography, as well as with the received opinion of his own time.[5] It is not worth while to discuss the correctness of the order of the smaller islands: but the total omission of the Balearic Islands, the largest of which is so superior to the greater part of those mentioned, shows how imperfect was the author's acquaintance with the western parts of the Mediterranean.

---

[3] Peripl § 7

[4] τοῦ καλλίστου πλοῦ, § 111 This is confirmed by the fact that he elsewhere calls it seven days and seven nights' voyage from the Columns to the limit of Spain (§ 2), a distance which, if measured along the coast, without following all its sinuosities, but little exceeds 620 G miles But here it was impossible to hold a direct course, and his estimate of the whole was merely made by adding together the separate distances from point to point.

[5] See Note B, p 406

Section 2.—*Aristotle.*

§ 1. It is much to be regretted that among the multifarious works of the great philosopher ARISTOTLE, there is none specially devoted to geography. The loss is the greater, as such a treatise would have afforded us a clear general view of the knowledge possessed by the Greeks upon this subject, before the great and sudden extension of their geographical horizon, arising from the conquests of Alexander. It is true that two of his extant works, the Meteorologica and the treatise On the Heavens,[6] contain numerous notices connected with physical geography, as well as with those general views of the cosmical relations of the earth to the other heavenly bodies, and its figure and position in the system, which must always form the basis of scientific geography. But he has nowhere attempted to connect these with the descriptive geography of the earth's surface, or to give any details with regard to that habitable world which was throughout the sole object of investigation with the Greek geographers.

After passing in review the opinions entertained by earlier philosophers, from Thales to Anaxagoras,—which we have already briefly examined—he establishes the position that the earth is a sphere, and that it is situated in the centre of the universe, where it remains at rest, while all the other celestial bodies, including the fixed stars, revolve around it.[7] The spherical form of the earth had become, in the time of Aristotle, a generally received tenet among philosophers. But he demonstrates it in two different methods; first, because this is the form which matter gravitating to a centre must necessarily assume, and it is a fact that all things do gravitate

---

[6] Περὶ Οὐρανοῦ There is no doubt of the genuineness of this work The treatise "On the Universe" περὶ κόσμου (*De Mundo*) on the contrary, which is found in our collections of Aristotle's works, appended to the *Meteorologica*, is undoubtedly spurious, and belongs to a much later age (See the Dissertation prefixed to Barthélemy de St Hilaire's translation of the *Meteorologica* (8vo, Paris, 1863); and Sir G Lewis's *History of Ancient Astronomy* p 218.)

[7] *De Cælo*, ii. 13, 14

from all sides to the centre of the earth; secondly, by the circular appearance of the shadow of the earth during eclipses of the moon, which he rightly considered to be produced by the interposition of the earth between the sun and moon.[8] Both these luminaries he considered to be spheres—an obvious conclusion; but he proceeded to infer that the planets and fixed stars[9] were also spherical bodies, which of course in his day there was no means of proving. It is more remarkable that he arrived at the conclusion that the earth itself was of small dimensions, as compared with the vast distance of the stars.[1] This he inferred from the changes which took place in the fixed stars, as viewed from different points, so that even a moderate change of place, as for instance from Greece to Egypt, was sufficient to produce a notable change in the aspect of the heavens. With regard to its positive magnitude he was content to acquiesce in the conclusion of certain mathematicians, to whom he refers without naming them, that it was calculated to be 400,000 stadia in circumference.[2]

§ 2. In the above views of the cosmical relations of the earth, Aristotle may be regarded as following, or rather concurring with, those of Eudoxus of Cnidus, which had been already put forth nearly a generation before; but he was not content with adopting them as already established, but considered himself bound to demonstrate them afresh. Hence he is not only the first extant writer to whom we are indebted for their statement, but is entitled to be considered as in great measure the original author of the system thus presented to us. The works of Eudoxus were for the most part of so distinctly astronomical a character that they scarcely claim

---

[8] Ibid ii 14, § 13.
[9] Ibid ii 11
[1] Ibid ii 14, § 14 The same thing is still more strongly asserted in the *Meteorologica*, i 14, § 19, where he says that the bulk of the earth is "nothing," in comparison with the heavens that surround it.
[2] Ibid ii. 14, § 16 καὶ τῶν μαθημα- τικῶν ὅσοι τὸ μέγεθος ἀναλογίζεσθαι πειρῶνται τῆς περιφερείας, εἰς τετταράκοντα λέγουσιν εἶναι μυριάδας σταδίων It is singular that this reference to certain unknown mathematicians, has been cited by many modern writers, as if it were a statement made by Aristotle himself, and entitled to implicit reverence as such.

any place in a review of the historical progress of geography.³

§ 3. Aristotle regarded the whole "habitable world," as it was always termed by Greek geographers, as confined to the temperate zone between the tropics and the arctic regions. All beyond the tropic to the south he asserts to be uninhabitable from heat, while the portions of the earth beneath the Great Bear were equally uninhabitable from cold. Hence the habitable world had natural limits in breadth, or latitude; while it had none such in length, or longitude; the tract between the Columns of Hercules and India enjoying a temperature which would allow of its being inhabited or visited, had not the extreme points been separated by so great an extent of sea.⁴ He adds moreover that there must certainly be in the southern hemisphere a temperate tract, corresponding to that in the northern; though he refrains from making any suggestion as to whether or not it was inhabited.⁵ The length of the known world, from India to the Columns of Hercules, he considers to be in the proportion of five to three to its breadth, from Ethiopia to the extreme parts of Scythia.⁶ Hence he justly treats with ridicule those who represented the *inhabited* world as *circular*; an idea which seems to have been still prevalent in his day, as it had been in that of Herodotus.⁷

§ 4. The Meteorologica of Aristotle contain numerous specu-

---

³ It appears, however, that Eudoxus left a work of a distinctly geographical character, called Γῆς περίοδος, to which Strabo frequently refers, though he gives us very little information concerning it But it would seem to have included a detailed description of Greece (Strabo, viii. p. 379, ix p. 390; x p 465)

⁴ *Meteorologica*, ii 5, §§ 13, 15

⁵ Ibid § 16 He points out, however, that for this region there would be a set of winds corresponding to those in the northern hemisphere, but with relation to *their* pole, the south wind answering to the north wind in our portion of the world, &c

⁶ Ibid § 14

⁷ Ibid § 13 It is a curious instance of the persistence of once-established errors, that this idea should have still maintained its ground But Aristotle's expression certainly points to it as the *customary* mode of drawing maps in his day Διὸ καὶ γελοίως γράφουσι νῦν τὰς περιόδους τῆς γῆς Perhaps the notion that the earth was spherical, which had become established among philosophers, tended by a confusion of ideas to fortify the supposition that the world in the popular sense (ἡ οἰκουμένη) was also round

lations upon subjects closely connected with physical geography, such as the winds, the changes of weather, with their accompanying phenomena of rain, hail, &c., earthquakes and their causes; and the more slow and gradual changes in the conformation of lands and seas. Among these last he correctly points out the process of alluvial deposition by which in so many places the land is gaining on the sea, and especially in the Palus Mæotis, which, as he affirms, was continually becoming shallower, and would no doubt be one day entirely filled up, and converted into dry land.[8] He adverts also to the currents by which that sea *flowed* into the Pontus, and that again into the Ægean; but erroneously considers them as connected with the difference in depth of the several seas, supposing, or rather assuming, that the Palus Mæotis was shallower[9] than the Euxine, that again than the Ægean, and the Ægean than the Sicilian Sea, which with the Tyrrhenian, was the deepest of all. The sea outside the Columns on the contrary he supposed, in accordance with a notion generally prevalent among the Greeks, to be muddy and shallow, and little agitated by winds.[1] It is remarkable that no other notice of the external Ocean, or its tides, a phenomenon so striking to the Greeks in general, is found in this treatise. Indeed the very name of the Ocean occurs only in one passage, in reference to the notions of "the ancients" concerning it.[2]

§ 5. Almost the only passage in the Meteorologica in which Aristotle has entered into any detailed statements of a strictly

---

[8] *Meteorologica*, 1. 14, § 29 The same speculation, as we shall see, was revived by Polybius
[9] Ibid. ii 1, §§ 12, 13.
[1] Ibid. § 14 The notion that this outer sea was undisturbed by winds (ἄπνοα) shows how little it was known to Greek mariners
[2] Ibid 1 9, § 6. In the spurious treatise *De Mundo* on the contrary the Ocean is distinctly described as surrounding the whole earth, and as identical with "the Atlantic Sea" (Πέλαγος δὲ τὸ μὲν ἔξω τῆς οἰκουμένης Ἀτλαντικὸν καλεῖται καὶ ὁ Ὠκεανὸς, περιρρέων ἡμᾶς c 3, § 8) The whole of this section, in which the author notices "the two very large islands called the Britannic, Albion and Ierne" (ἐν τούτῳ γε μὴν νῆσοι μέγισταί τε τυγχάνουσιν οὖσαι δύο, Βρετανικαὶ λεγόμεναι, Ἀλβιον καὶ Ἰέρνη, τῶν προϊστορημένων μείζους, ὑπὲρ τοὺς Κελτοὺς κείμεναι, § 13) bears the unquestionable stamp of a much more advanced stage of geographical knowledge than that of the age of Aristotle.

geographical character is that in which, after pointing out that almost all great rivers took their rise in great mountain ranges, he proceeds to add examples in proof of his assertion. "It is thus that in Asia most of the rivers and those of largest size descend from the mountain which is called Parnasos; and this is generally considered to be the largest of all the mountains that are situated towards the winter sunrise" (the south-east).[3] "For directly after you have crossed this, you come in sight of the outer sea, the limit of which is not known with any certainty to the inhabitants of these parts. Now from this there flow, among other rivers, the Bactrus, the Choaspes and the Araxes; of which last the Tanais is a branch, which parts off and flows into the Palus Mæotis. The Indus also takes its rise in the same chain, which has the largest stream of all rivers. From the Caucasus in like manner there flow many rivers, of great size, as well as surpassing numbers, among which is the Phasis. Now the Caucasus is the largest mountain towards the summer rising (the north-east), both in extent and height. .... Again it is from the Pyrene, which is a mountain towards the equinoctial setting (*i.e.* due west) in Celtica, that both the Istrus and the Tartessus flow: the latter towards the sea beyond the Columns, while the Istrus, after having traversed the whole of Europe, discharges itself into the Euxine. Of the other rivers towards the north, most take their rise in the Arkynian mountains, which are both in extent and height the largest in this part of the world. But under the Great Bear itself (in the extreme north) beyond the farthest limit of Scythia, are the mountains called Rhipæan, concerning the magnitude of which many tales are told that are clearly fabulous."[4]

It would be difficult to conceive a more utterly confused notion than this passage presents of the geographical relations of the mountain chains and rivers both of the east and the

---

[3] The phrase of the winter sunrise and sunset, and conversely, the summer rising and setting, are here used, as they always are by Strabo, to designate the *intermediate* quarters of the heavens (the N.E, S.E., &c), though of course not corresponding to them correctly.

[4] *Meteorologica*, 1. 13, §§ 15-22

west. Mount Parnasus is in all probability the same as was called by the Greeks in later times Paropamisus or Paropanisus: the name being wilfully assimilated to the familiar form of Parnassus: and it may be fairly supposed that the Araxes is confused with the Iaxartes, the connection of which with the Tanais long continued to be one of the prevailing errors of Greek geography. But the mention of the Choaspes in connection with this system is strangely erroneous, if the river of that name so familiar to the Greeks be intended.[5] Nor is it true that the Caucasus gives rise to many great rivers. Aristotle himself indeed was only able to mention the Phasis, which notwithstanding its mythical celebrity is but an unimportant stream, as compared with the great rivers of Asia, such as the Euphrates and the Tigris.[6] The whole passage indeed clearly shows how little progress had been made from the days of Herodotus to those of Aristotle in any definite knowledge of the geography of Asia.

§ 6. In regard to the west and north it will be seen at a glance that his notions were still more vague and erroneous. He had indeed heard the name of the Pyrenees, as a mountain chain in the west of Gaul;[7] but preposterously makes them the source of the Ister or Danube, while he ignores altogether the far greater chain of the Alps. His Arkynian mountains in the north are evidently an exaggerated notion of the Herkynian forest in Germany, a name which we shall find again appearing in a vague manner among the Greek geographers before they had any definite knowledge concerning it. But

---

[5] It is however more probable that the Choaspes here mentioned may be intended for the river of Cabul, which is called by the Greeks in general Cophen, but according to Strabo received a tributary named the Choaspes (Strab xv. 1, p 697) But even in this case Aristotle would seem to have confounded it with the far more celebrated river of the same name

[6] He tells us also that the Caucasus was said to have many lakes on its flanks; an entirely erroneous idea—the absence of lakes being, in fact, one of the leading peculiarities of that great mountain chain

[7] At the same time the name of the river Tartessus would show some idea of the connection of the Pyrenees with Spain It is impossible to determine what river is here intended, but the *name* was always connected with the southern regions of the peninsula

at the same time he could not divest his mind from the fiction of the Rhipæan mountains in the far north, "from which (he adds) most of the other rivers of the largest size, next to the Ister, are said to derive their sources."[8]

In regard to Africa it is not surprising that his information should be still more imperfect: but it is unintelligible that, while mentioning the Nile as rising in the Silver Mountains (Argyrus Mons), the only other names that he notices are those of the Ægon, and the Nyses—both of them otherwise wholly unknown, but which he describes as rising in the Æthiopian mountains—and the Chremetes, which flowed into the outer sea, a name equally unknown to later geographers.[9]

§ 7. We see therefore that, while Aristotle's views of the physical and meteorological conditions connected with geography, were decidedly in advance of those of earlier writers, his knowledge of the positive geography of the inhabited world was still very imperfect, as well as limited. His Meteorologica were certainly published before the expedition of Alexander into Asia had given a sudden extension to the horizon of Greek knowledge in this direction.[1]

In one respect indeed his adherence to the old ideas, generally received in his time, preserved him from an error, which obtained general acceptance among the Greek geographers for the next three centuries. He states distinctly that the Caspian Sea is entirely isolated, and is inhabited all round.[2] We have already seen that this fact was known to Herodotus; but as we shall presently see, a contrary view pre-

---

[8] ῥέουσι δ' οὖν οἱ πλεῖστοι καὶ μέγιστοι μετὰ τὸν Ἴστρον τῶν ἄλλων ποταμῶν ἐντεῦθεν, ὥς φασιν Ibid § 20

These words doubtless refer to the Borysthenes, and the other great rivers of Scythia, which are not otherwise mentioned

[9] The suggestion of some modern writers, who would identify the Chremetes with the Senegal, is certainly very far-fetched, but M Dureau de la Malle goes still farther, and supposes it to be the Zaire or Congo! (See Forbiger, *Géographie*, vol ii p 881, note)

[1] We have no positive evidence concerning the date of the *Meteorologica*, but it may safely be assigned to about B C 341–330

[2] ii 1, § 10 At the same time he commits the mistake of supposing the Caspian and Hyrcanian to be two distinct seas, instead of two names for the same (ἡ δ' Ὑρκανία καὶ Κασπία κεχωρισμέναι τε ταύτης καὶ περιοικούμεναι κύκλῳ) To suppose that he had any knowledge of the Sea of Aral is most improbable

vailed from the time of Alexander onwards, supposed to be founded upon actual observation: and this error was strangely perpetuated down to the time of Ptolemy.[3]

§ 8. In connection with the view above referred to, of the shallow and muddy character of the outer sea, beyond the Columns of Hercules, it may be worth while just to advert to the mythical tale of the supposed island of Atlantis, so fully developed by Plato in his two well-known dialogues, the Timæus and the Critias.[4] That the account there given of this vast island—larger than Libya and Asia united, which filled up the greater part of the Ocean west of the Columns—is a mere fiction for the purpose of affording a framework to his philosophical speculations, and is no more intended to be taken seriously as having any basis in historical fact, than the tale of Er the Pamphylian in the tenth book of the Republic, appears to me unquestionable. The great exaggerations as to numbers, and especially the carrying back of the supposed events to a period nine thousand years before, seem purposely designed to impart to the whole story an obviously mythical character, with which it would be a natural trait of artistic invention to connect the acknowledged fact of the shallow and muddy nature of the Western Ocean, by supposing it to result from the subsidence of this imaginary island.[5] Whether this mode of accounting for what was supposed by the Greeks in the days of Plato to be an undoubted fact, was first invented by the philosopher himself, or was an inference already drawn by earlier speculators from the obscure reports of Phœnician navigators, we have no means of judging. But in either case it appears to be clearly nothing more than a geological myth—an attempt to account for (supposed) existing phenomena by the operation of natural causes, concerning which there was no real information.[6]

---

[3] The spurious treatise *De Mundo* follows this later view, and describes, though not very clearly, the outer sea as communicating, "through a long and narrow channel," with the Hyrcanian and Caspian (c 3, § 12).

[4] Plato, *Timæus*, c 5, 6, *Critias*, c 3, 8

[5] Plato, *Timæus* and Scholia

[6] As the purely imaginary character

The only connection with our present subject of the Platonic myth, consists in the testimony it affords to this generally received belief in the unnavigable character of the outer sea; a belief which would be naturally encouraged, if not originally propagated, by the Phœnician and Carthaginian navigators, who sought to deter those of other nations from extending their voyages in this direction. But if Pliny is correct in representing the voyage of the Carthaginian Himilco into these parts of the Atlantic as contemporaneous with that of Hanno,[7] which we have already examined, these notions might reasonably be taken as resting upon positive observation. For it appears certain that Himilco represented his progress as having been checked by the difficulties of navigation, owing to the want of force in the winds, the heavy and sluggish nature of the sea, and the quantities of sea-weed which obstructed the motion of the ship.[8] It is very probably on this report that the ideas so long current among the Greeks were originally based.

of the Atlantis of Plato has been disputed by many writers, both in ancient and modern times, I rejoice to find my view upon the subject confirmed by the high authority of Professor Jowett. The author of the article ATLANTIS in Dr Smith's *Dictionary of Ancient Geography*, appears to me disposed to attach too much value to the myth in question, and especially to its *oriental* origin, of which I see no evidence, except the statement of Plato himself, that it was derived from the priests of Sais in Egypt For the divergent views of modern writers—some of whom have even imagined the supposed tradition to have reference to America (!)—I must refer my readers to the article just cited.

[7] Plin *H. N.* ii 67, § 169
[8] Fest. Avien *Ora Maritima*, vv. 115–130, 406–415. The subject of this voyage of Himilco will be more fully investigated in a future chapter, in connection with the geographical work of Rufus Festus Avienus, to whom we are indebted for what little information we possess concerning it.

NOTE A, p. 385.

AGE OF SCYLAX.

THE data afforded by the internal evidence of the Periplus itself for determining its age, which have been collected by Niebuhr (*Kleine Schriften*, vol. i. pp. 105-130 ; translated in the Philological Museum, vol. i. pp. 245-279), Ukert (*Geogr. der Griechen u Romer*, vol. i. pt. ii. pp. 285-297), Letronne (*Fragmens des Poemes Géographiques*, pp. 165-262), and other writers are well summed up by C. Muller in his edition of the Geographi Græci Minores (*Prolegomena*, p. xliii.). It may suffice here to mention the more important and conclusive of them. The mention of Thurii in Italy (not founded till B.C. 444), of Heraclea in the same country, founded in B.C. 433, of Tauromenium in Sicily (about B C. 394), of the *city* of Rhodes, which did not exist before B C. 408, and of Amphipolis, which was first settled by the Athenians in B.C 437—are alone sufficient to prove beyond a doubt that the work in question cannot have been composed till after the close of the fifth century B C. On the other hand, the absence of all notice of Alexandria in Egypt, or of any of the numerous cities founded by Alexander and his successors, is equally conclusive evidence that it belongs to a period antecedent to the reign of that monarch.

It is more difficult to determine it within narrower limits. but the following points may be regarded as establishing the fact that it could hardly have beeen composed before the accession of Philip of Macedon. 1. We find mention in the Periplus of the cities of Ancona, Issa, and Pharus in the Adriatic, all three of which were founded either wholly or in part by the elder Dionysius, about B.C. 385. 2. The Gauls are found at the mouth of the Po, " having been left there after the expedition " (§ 18), evidently that in which they took Rome B.C. 390. 3 The foundation of the Athenian colony at Neapolis, near Datum on the Thracian coast, which took place in B.C. 360, is particularly mentioned (§ 67). 4. Theodosia, on the coast of the Tauric Chersonese, appears among the Greek cities of that region this was first established by Leucon, king of Bosporus, between B.C. 393 and 355. 5. Messenia is separately described as an independent country, thus indicating a period subsequent to B.C. 370. 6. The towns of the Epicnemidian Locrians are assigned to the Phocians, to whose territory they were first annexed in B.C. 353.

It is difficult, if not impossible, to fix the date more closely than this on the one hand the mention of Olynthus, which was destroyed in B.C. 347, as a city still existing—would seem to place it before that year: on the other hand it is inferred by C. Muller from the mention of Echinus in Thessaly as a city of the Malians and from that of Naupactus as an Ætolian city (§ 62) that it must be brought down to the last years of Philip's reign. But the arguments from these two last points are not conclusive, as we do not know with certainty the date of the transactions alluded to: and it appears safer to acquiesce in the conclusion of Niebuhr, who assigns it to the period between B.C. 360 and 348.

The determination of the *exact* period of the composition of this little treatise is however of comparatively little importance. It would be far more valuable if we were able to determine how far it really represents the state of geographical knowledge at the time of its compilation, and how far it may be based upon previously existing materials, belonging to an earlier period. There are certainly indications that our Periplus was derived from different authorities, of very different degrees of value (see on this point Letronne, *l.c.* pp. 168-174): indeed it could hardly, in the nature of things, be otherwise: and we know from abundant evidence in later times, and in the case of far superior writers, how little pains was often taken to distinguish the materials thus employed. Unfortunately the means of discriminating are, in the present case, almost wholly wanting: and we must be content to take the work as we find it. The text, which is derived only from a single MS., is notoriously corrupt, and occasionally without doubt interpolated: though the absence of all notices relating to a time later than that of Alexander fortunately excludes the supposition of any extensive interpolation. But even after making full allowance for the operation of these causes, and for the barbarisms of later copyists, the style remains such as it is difficult to believe belonging to the age of Philip. Hence C. Muller (*Prolegomena*, p xlix.) has gone so far as to maintain that the work actually preserved to us is only a meagre compendium of the original—the work of a grammarian of the third or fourth century after the Christian era. It is, however, difficult to understand what could have been the object of such an abridgement at so late a period and it seems impossible to believe that any late writer, desiring to make use of the work for his own purposes, would have refrained altogether from any allusion to the great cities that had sprung up around the shores of the Mediterranean in the time of Alexander and his successors. It is this which gives the chief value to the Periplus. Mutilated and corrupt as it unfortunately is, we may yet rely upon its information, wherever it still remains intelligible, as belonging to an earlier period than any other extant geographical treatise, and giving us a picture of the Greek world, as it existed before the time of the Macedonian conquests.

NOTE B, p. 394.

ORDER OF ISLANDS IN THE MEDITERRANEAN.

A passage has been preserved to us from Alexis, a comic writer contemporary with Alexander the Great (Fr. 30, ed. Meineke), in which he enumerates the seven largest islands in order of magnitude, and this statement may naturally be taken as representing the received tradition on the subject. He gives them in the following order: 1. Sicily. 2. Sardinia. 3. Corsica. 4. Crete. 5. Euboea. 6. Cyprus. 7. Lesbos. That these seven were the largest islands in the Mediterranean came indeed to be an admitted fact, but there was some discrepancy with regard to their order, especially in respect to Corsica Timaeus alone took the same view with Scylax in placing Sardinia before Sicily; and he added that the largest of the Balearic Islands was the next largest "after the seven": for which he is taken to task by Strabo, who asserts that he is quite mistaken; "for that there are many others larger." But in point of fact the island of Majorca is not only entitled to rank next after Lesbos, but is considerably larger than that island. The order given by Timaeus is: 1. Sardinia. 2. Sicily. 3. Cyprus. 4. Crete. 5. Euboea. 6. Corsica. 7. Lesbos (ap. Strab. *l. c.*). Diodorus gives them in the same order (V. 17) except that he places Sicily first, adding that Sardinia was nearly the same size. The priority of Sicily was generally recognised in modern as well as ancient times, until Admiral Smyth ascertained by actual survey that Sardinia was slightly the larger of the two. (Smyth's *Mediterranean*, p. 28.)

CHAPTER XII.

EXPEDITION OF ALEXANDER.

SECTION 1.—*Campaigns in Central and Western Asia.*

§ 1. THE expedition of Alexander the Great into Asia marks an era of scarcely less importance in the progress of geography, than in the political history of the ancient world. It was not merely, or even principally, by its immediate results that it produced so great a change, but by the opening it afforded for subsequent exploration, and especially for the more careful examination of countries already known to the Greeks in a general way, but with which they were still very imperfectly acquainted. We have seen that Herodotus already possessed a general knowledge of the whole Persian Empire, of the satrapies into which it was divided, and the tribes and nations by which they were inhabited. But we have seen also how far he was from possessing an accurate or complete geographical idea of the countries in question. Nor is it probable that the Greeks knew more than this a hundred years later. The expedition of the younger Cyrus, the residence of Greek physicians and others at the Persian court, and the continually increasing intercourse of the Greeks with the neighbouring provinces of the Empire, had doubtless led to a fuller and more accurate knowledge of the provinces of Lower Asia; but with the remoter regions of the continent—known in later days as Upper Asia—they had still very little acquaintance. The vast tracts of the plateau of Iran—constituting the greater part of the modern Persian monarchy, as well as the still more remote provinces of Bactria and India, were still known to them almost in name only. Even after the conquests of Alexander, the limits of their geographical knowledge were extended but very little way beyond the confines of the former Empire of Persia, but within these limits their information had attained a vastly increased degree of clearness and certainty—exceeding indeed in some instances that possessed at any subsequent period down to quite modern times.

So imperfect was the knowledge of the interior of Asia possessed by the Greeks, when Alexander crossed the Hellespont and prepared to lead his armies into the heart of the dominions of the Great King, that his campaigns—especially after the death of Darius,—may be said to partake of the nature of an exploring expedition; and for this reason, as well as because they were generally taken by subsequent geographers as the basis of their description of the countries in question, it will be necessary briefly to follow the footsteps of the conqueror, and trace the course of his triumphant march from the Hellespont to the Sutledge.

§ 2. His campaigns in Europe, previous to crossing over into Asia, may be passed over with but slight notice, as being in themselves of comparatively little interest; besides which the information we possess concerning them is so imperfect that it is impossible to follow their geographical details. In his first campaign against the Triballians (B.C. 335), he crossed the ridge of Mount Hæmus (the Balkan), carrying by force of arms a mountain pass which is described as steep and difficult; then descending into the plains he defeated the Triballians in a decisive action, and afterwards advanced as far as the southern bank of the Danube. A considerable number of the Triballians and other Thracians had taken refuge in an island of the river called Peuce, where Alexander was unable to attack them; but he made a demonstration of force by crossing the river with a portion of his army in the face of the Getæ, who were assembled to oppose his passage, but who fled into the interior as soon as he succeeded in landing his troops. Alexander was too wary to follow them, and after burning one of their towns, situated but a short distance from the river, he recrossed the Danube without loss.[1]

This exploit was chiefly remarkable as being the first instance, after the ill-fated expedition of Darius, in which an invader had crossed the great river Ister, and for this reason it appears to have struck terror into the neighbouring tribes, many of which hastened to send embassies to the young conqueror. But neither the place where he effected this passage, nor that where he crossed the range of the Balkan can be determined. The island of Peuce, where the fugitive Thracians took refuge, is indeed usually identified with the large island to which that name was given by Strabo and later writers, formed by the separation of the different arms of the Danube near its mouth. But it is impossible to suppose the march of Alexander to have extended to this part of the river,[2] and the island here meant was doubtless one of the many small islands that occur in the Danube, throughout the lower part of its course. The Triballi, against whom the expedition seems to have been specially directed—perhaps out of revenge for the defeat sustained at their hands by his father Philip[3]—appear, so far as we are able to judge, to have occupied the region now known as Servia, extending from the Danube as far as the foot of the Balkan; but we have no means of determining by which of the passes Alexander forced his way across that mountain barrier. The whole account of the campaign as given by Arrian, though derived from the high authority of Ptolemy the son of Lagus, is very meagre and unsatisfactory—at least in a geographical point of view.

Two points of interest may however be noticed. We learn in the first place that the Getæ, who in the time of Herodotus

---

[1] Arrian, *Anabasis*, 1 c 1-4
[2] This is the conclusion of Mr Grote (*History of Greece*, vol xii p 33, note) in which I entirely concur Strabo indeed, who evidently wrote (as well as Arrian) with the narrative of Ptolemy before him, seems to have had no doubt that the island of Peuce here mentioned was the same with that which he elsewhere describes (from other authorities) as situated at the mouth of the Danube (Strab. vii pp 301, 305) But this is by no means conclusive   [3] Justin ix 3

dwelt in the plains of Bulgaria, *south* of the Danube,[4] were now to be found only to the north of that river, and had already occupied the same position which they continued to maintain for centuries afterwards.[5] Another circumstance worthy of notice is that among the different nations and tribes that sent embassies to Alexander at this period, in consequence of the sensation created by his daring passage of the Danube, we find mention of one from the Celts or Gauls "who dwelt upon the Ionian Gulf" (*i. e.* at the head of the Adriatic) ;[6] the first occasion probably on which the Greeks had any direct intercourse with a people who were before long to inflict upon them such severe disasters. They are described by Arrian (evidently copying Ptolemy) as "men of tall stature, and who had a high opinion of themselves." Their only apprehension, as they proudly answered to the young monarch, was "lest the sky should fall upon their heads."

§ 3. Alexander next turned his arms against the Illyrians, where he reduced a strong fortress named Pelion (situated somewhere near the Lake Lychnidus), and defeated a large force of the Taulantians,—a tribe who occupied the western parts of Illyria, in the neighbourhood of the Greek colonies of Epidamnus and Apollonia, but who had on this occasion come to the support of their eastern neighbours. He was still with his army in the heart of the mountainous region of Illyricum, when news reached him of the defection of the Thebans; and with that promptitude of decision and celerity of movement which were among his leading characteristics, he marched at once, through the passes of Mount Pindus to Pelinna in Thessaly,[7] and from thence without a moment's

---

[4] Herodot. iv 93, v. 3. See Chapter VI p 166

[5] It appears that these Getæ were not mere roaming tribes, but practised agriculture and must therefore have had settled abodes When Alexander crossed the river with one division of his army he advanced under cover of a heavy crop of corn (λήιον σίτου βαθύ,

Arrian, i 4, § 1).

[6] Arrian, *Anab* i 4, §§ 6-8 See also Strabo, viii p 301.

[7] In regard to the topography of this campaign. see Leake's *Northern Greece*, vol iii pp 323, 324 But the account given by Arrian is so meagre, that it is impossible to follow his movements in detail

delay into Bœotia. So rapid were his movements that he had descended into the plains of Bœotia and occupied the town of Onchestus within a short distance of Thebes, before the Thebans and their allies had any information of his march.[8] The brilliancy of this decisive exploit was a fitting prelude to his subsequent operations in countries even more remote and unknown than the Illyrian highlands.

§ 4. It was in the spring of the year B.C. 334 that Alexander crossed the Hellespont; and his decisive victory at the Granicus,[9] almost immediately afterwards, opened the way for him at once into the interior of Asia Minor. He was however by no means in haste to avail himself of the opening thus presented to him, and before attempting to advance against the Great King, he was careful to secure his communications with the sea, and to establish his base of operations along the coast of the Ægean. Hence, after possessing himself of the important position of Sardis—a fortress reputed to be impregnable, but which was yielded by the Persian governor without striking a blow—he directed his arms against the cities of Ionia and Caria, where the long sieges of Miletus and Halicarnassus occupied him throughout the remainder of that year. It was not till the middle of the winter that he was able to advance into Lycia, the cities of which submitted to him without resistance; and he from thence continued his march along the sea-coast of Pamphylia by Phaselis, Perga and Aspendus, as far as Side. His object in following this line of route was, by obtaining the submission of all these maritime cities, to secure possession of the sea-coast, and guard against the operations of the Persian fleet, which was at this time under the command of the able and enterprising Greek general Memnon.

Having accomplished this purpose he directed his course

---

[8] Arrian, *Anab.* 1 7, § 5
[9] This celebrated stream, rendered so famous in history by the victory of Alexander, is one of the many small rivers that descend from the slopes of Mount Ida to the Propontis It is now called the Khodja Su, and flows into the Sea of Marmora a few miles east of the site of the ancient town of Priapus

northwards into the interior of Asia Minor, advancing by Termessus and Sagalassus to Celænæ in Phrygia. On this line of march he had to force his way through the rugged and mountainous country of the Pisidians, a barbarian and warlike people, who had always maintained their independence against the Persian Empire,[1] and who now appeared in arms to dispute the passage of the Macedonian conqueror. Alexander himself though he defeated them in more than one engagement, and succeeded in effecting his passage through their country, was content with a little more than nominal submission, and left them still in possession of their mountain fastnesses. The Pisidians indeed seem to have retained a state of virtual independence in the wild ranges of Mount Taurus until they were finally subdued by the Romans.[2]

§ 5. Phrygia on the contrary was at once reduced to the condition of a regular province; a Macedonian governor being substituted for the Persian satrap. From Celænæ Alexander marched northwards as far as Gordium, on the river Sangarius, which he reached early in the year B.C. 333; here he halted for some time, and was rejoined by Parmenio, who had been detached with a part of his army to proceed from Sardis through Lydia into Phrygia; as well as by considerable reinforcements from Europe. It is not clear what induced him to move so far to the north;[3] but he appears to have been detained at Gordium, not only by the necessity of reposing his troops after their winter campaign, but by apprehensions of the plans of Memnon, who was carrying on successful operations in the Ægean with the Persian fleet, where he had already reduced the islands of Chios and Lesbos, and was meditating a descent in Greece itself. The untimely death of Memnon just at this juncture delivered Alexander from all apprehensions in this quarter; and he now at once prepared to advance into the heart of Asia, and seek an encounter with the Great King. It was from this time that his expedition assumed the character

---

[1] See Chapter X. p 345. [2] Strab xii p 571.
[3] Note A, p 466.

of an Anabasis, or march up the country, and resembles in some degree that of Cyrus against Artaxerxes, which we have already had occasion to follow.

§ 6. From Gordium Alexander advanced to Ancyra, where he received the submission of the Paphlagonians, who were allowed to continue in the enjoyment of the same virtual independence as they had always maintained under the Persians, being nominally subjected to the authority of the governor of Phrygia, but exempted even from the payment of tribute.[4] We have no details as to his subsequent march from Ancyra through Cappadocia to the foot of Mount Taurus[5] where he encamped on the same spot which had been occupied seventy years before by the younger Cyrus, at the entrance of the Cilician Gates.[6] This formidable pass—the strength of which appears to have excited the astonishment of Alexander himself as much as it had done that of Xenophon[7]—was abandoned without resistance by the Persian troops who occupied it; and the king descended without opposition into the plain of Cilicia, and took possession of the important city of Tarsus. Here he was detained for a considerable time by a severe attack of illness; when convalescent from this, instead of advancing at once into Syria, he turned his arms to the south-west, reduced the cities of Soli and Anchialus, and compelled the neighbouring mountain tribes to submission.

Meanwhile he had already dispatched Parmenio with a considerable force to occupy the strong passes which afforded the only communication between Cilicia and Syria, the military importance of which had been fully recognized at the time of the expedition of Cyrus. He now learned, while still in

---

[4] Arrian, ii 4, § 2, Curt iii. 1, § 22.
[5] The paucity of details concerning the marches of Alexander in this part of Asia contrasts strongly with the fulness of the information furnished by Xenophon
[6] This is distinctly stated by Arrian (ἀφικόμενος ἐπὶ τὸ Κύρου τοῦ ξὺν Ξενοφῶντι στρατόπεδον, l c § 3), and is without doubt correct Q Curtius erroneously supposes the locality to have been named after the *elder* Cyrus ("regionem quæ Castra Cyri appellatur, pervenerat Stativa illic habuerat Cyrus, cum adversus Crœsum in Lydiam duceret" iii 4, § 1)
[7] Note B, p 467

Cilicia, that Darius with an immense army had advanced to meet him, and was encamped at a place called Sochi, two days' march from the entrance of the passes. On receiving this intelligence Alexander hastened on by forced marches, and arrived without opposition at Myriandrus, at that time, as we have seen, a frequented sea-port at the foot of the pass leading directly into Syria.[8] But while he was thus pushing on by the direct road, Darius on his part had broken up his camp at Sochi, and crossed the ridge of Mount Amanus by another pass, apparently unknown to the Greeks, which brought him down to the Mediterranean near Issus, in the rear of Alexander's army, so as to cut off the communications of the Macedonian king, and thus compel him to an immediate action.[9]

§ 7. The disastrous result of the great battle which ensued (Nov. B.C. 333) had the effect of leaving all the maritime provinces of the Persian Empire open to the arms of Alexander: and while Darius fled to Babylon, where he occupied himself in collecting a still more formidable army, Alexander was able to devote himself without fear of interruption to the conquest of the important regions of Syria and Egypt. His operations during this time were in a military point of view among the most remarkable of his whole career: the sieges of Tyre and Gaza—which between them occupied not less than nine months—were calculated to call forth all the resources of his unrivalled genius, and it was here (as Mr. Grote justly observes) that he encountered the hardest fighting that he met with during his whole life.[1] But in a geographical point of view his campaigns in Syria and Egypt have comparatively little interest: he appears to have met with no difficulty in traversing the desert from Gaza to Pelusium,[2] and he did not attempt to ascend the Nile above Memphis.

---

[8] See Xenophon, *Anab* 1 4, § 6, and above, Chapter X p. 346
[9] Note C, p 467
[1] Grote's *History of Greece*, vol xii p 197

[2] This occupied him seven days, which, as the distance is certainly not less than 120 English miles, implies a rapid rate of marching But no notice of this is taken by the historians, as

His celebrated expedition to the oracle of Ammon alone calls for more particular notice. We have seen that the Oasis consecrated to the Egyptian divinity, to whom the Greeks gave the name of Zeus Ammon, was already known to them in the time of Herodotus:[3] its famous oracle was frequently visited by Greeks from Cyrene, as well as from other parts of the Hellenic world, and it vied in reputation with those of Delphi and Dodona.[4] But to traverse the desert which surrounded it, with an army, was an enterprise of difficulty, and requiring at once foresight and resolution. Still it cannot be doubted that the difficulties of the march were greatly exaggerated by the historians of Alexander, with the view of imparting something of a mythical character to an expedition which resulted in a declaration of the divine origin of the conqueror.[5] Alexander followed the line of the coast from the Lake Mareotis as far as Paraetonium—the frontier city of Egypt: and from thence he struck due south into the heart of the desert—eight days' journey across which brought him in safety to the Oasis and temple of Ammon. The circumstantial descriptions of this singular region, which are found in the historians of Alexander, are doubtless derived from the observation of eye-witnesses who accompanied the king; and agree perfectly with the accounts of modern travellers, who in recent times have repeatedly visited this outlying spot.[6]

Another remarkable circumstance by which Alexander's visit to Egypt was distinguished, and one that exercised a far more permanent influence, was his foundation of the city of Alexandria, on the shores of the Lake Mareotis: a short distance to the westward of the Canopic mouth of the Nile. This was the first, as it was destined to be by far the most important,

---

the route was one well known and frequently traversed. It appears from Herodotus (III 9) that under the Persian government arrangements were made for a permanent supply of water on this line

[3] Herodotus, II 32, III. 25 See Chapter VIII. p 277

[4] See especially the two passages in which Aristophanes alludes to the oracle of Ammon, as one familiar to all his hearers (Aristoph. *Aves*, vv. 619, 716)

[5] Note D, p 469.

[6] Note E, p. 470

of the numerous cities to which the great conqueror gave his own name

§ 8. With the commencement of spring (B.C. 331) Alexander repaired from Egypt into Phœnicia, and from thence, after a halt of considerable duration, he directed his march into the interior. He arrived at Thapsacus on the Euphrates in the month of July: but though the river might be expected to be fordable at this season of the year, he had had the foresight to send forward a Macedonian force to construct two bridges of boats, by means of which he effected the passage without difficulty or opposition.[7] From this point he had a choice of two routes; either to follow the left bank of the Euphrates directly towards Babylon (as Cyrus had done), or to traverse the northern part of Mesopotamia to the Tigris, and crossing that river, advance through the plains of Assyria, through which the Greeks under Xenophon had effected their retreat. But he appears to have been deterred from adopting the former line of march by the arid and burning character of the country, and the consequent difficulty of supplying his army with provisions and forage.[8] Hence he directed his march at first in a northerly direction, but afterwards turning to the east, and leaving the mountains of Armenia on his left, he followed apparently the direct route which led towards the upper course of the Tigris. He was led at first to believe that Darius—who had now assembled another army, still larger than that with which he fought at Issus—would here meet him, to dispute the passage of the Tigris, but on reaching that river Alexander found it undefended, and crossed it by a ford without opposition.[9] It was not till the fourth day's march through the plains of Assyria that he found himself in presence of the vast army of Darius. That monarch, warned by his disaster

---

[7] Note F, p 471
[8] Arrian, *Anab* III 7, § 3
[9] Arrian, *Anab* III 7, § 5, Q Curt iv 37, 38 The only difficulty encountered by Alexander at this point arose from the rapidity and strength of the river Concerning the point at which the passage took place, see Note G, p 472

at Issus, where he had imprudently engaged his vast host in the midst of narrow defiles and mountain passes, had this time selected for his battle-field an open plain, between the Tigris and the Lycus or Greater Zab,[1] near a village called Gaugamela, about 600 stadia (60 G. miles) from the city of Arbela, from which it was separated by the Lycus, the passage of which was, however, secured by a bridge. But the disciplined valour of the Macedonian troops asserted its superiority over the vast undisciplined hosts of the Persian monarch as decisively in the plains of Assyria as it had done in the defiles of Issus : and the battle of Arbela—as it was commonly named, notwithstanding the remoteness of the city from the actual field of battle[2]—was the death-blow of the Persian monarchy.[3] Darius fled in the first instance to Arbela, and from thence without a halt across the passes of Mt. Zagros to Ecbatana, leaving the direct route to Babylon and Susa open to the conqueror.[4]

§ 9. Alexander did not attempt to pursue the fugitive, and directed his march at once to the great cities, which now lay before him as the prizes of victory. Babylon and Susa successively opened their gates to the conqueror, who found in them vast treasures, the accumulated hoards of the Persian monarchs during a period of two centuries. From Susa he directed his march into Persia proper, with a view to occupy the important cities of Persepolis and Pasargada. The former

---

[1] There can be no doubt that the river called by Arrian, as well as by Strabo (xvi 1 p 737) and Polybius (v 51) the Lycus, is the same as that called by Xenophon by the native name of Zapatas, and which is still known as the Zab, or Greater Zab It is probable that the Greek names of Lycus and Caprus were given to the two rivers which in ancient as well as modern times bore the same appellation (now the Zab Ala and Zab Azful) for the sake of distinction, under the Macedonian monarchy.
[2] Note G, p 472
[3] The battle of Arbela was fought on the 25th or 26th of September, B C 331 (see Clinton, F H vol ii p 342) We are enabled to fix the exact date from the occurrence of an eclipse of the moon, immediately after the passage of the Tigris and eleven days before the battle (Arrian, Anab iii 7, § 6, Plut Alex 31) This eclipse attracted much attention in later times from the circumstance of its being observed also at Carthage : a fact of which Hipparchus made use in order to indicate the mode of determining the difference of longitude between two places
[4] Note H, p 475

VOL I.

of these, it would appear, still ranked as the second city of the empire in wealth and magnificence.⁵ But between the two capitals lay a rugged mountain district, inhabited by a people named the Uxii, a race of hardy and warlike mountaineers, who had always maintained their independence against the Persian monarchy, and compelled the Great King himself to pay them a sum of money as a tribute whenever he passed through their territory. Alexander, however, resented this demand as a humiliation, and succeeded not only in forcing his passage through their country, notwithstanding the formidable character of the passes it presented; but took their chief town, and compelled the whole people to a nominal submission. There still, however, remained other passes, of a still more formidable character—termed by the Greeks the Pylæ Persicæ, or Pylæ Susianæ—between the territory of the Uxians, and the plain of Persepolis, and these were occupied by a Persian force under Ariobarzanes. But all obstacles were overcome by the skill and courage of Alexander, who forced the passes, and made himself master without further opposition of the ancient capital of Persia.⁶

§ 10. Here he remained some time (it was now mid-winter); and before he continued his advance into the interior, he made several expeditions against the wild tribes of the neighbouring mountains, among whom we find the often recurring name of the Mardi. It was not till the spring of B.C. 330 that he moved northwards into Media, where Darius, who had remained stationary at Ecbatana, had been in vain endeavouring to organize a fresh army to oppose him. Disappointed of his expected reinforcements, the Persian king quitted Ecbatana, on the advance of the conqueror, with a very small force, and hastened to the pass called the Pylæ Caspiæ,⁷ with a view of taking refuge in the remote provinces of Parthia and Bactria. Alexander immediately pursued him, with a light detachment of troops, but having advanced as far as Rhagæ,

---

⁵ Strabo. xv. 3, § 6, p 729.   ⁶ Note I, p 475.   ⁷ Note K, p. 477.

within a day's march of the Caspian Gates, he found that Darius had already passed through that defile, and in consequence he halted for five days, to recruit and repose his troops. He then advanced through the pass, which was left undefended, and had reached the open country on the other side, when the news that Darius was a prisoner in the hands of his own officers, who were carrying him away captive, led Alexander to push on with the utmost speed in his pursuit, and by extraordinary forced marches, he succeeded in overtaking the fugitives on the fourth day, though not in time to save the life of the unfortunate Darius, who was mortally wounded by the conspirators, and expired before he fell into the hands of the conqueror.[8]

§ 11. Alexander now halted at Hecatompylus, which appears to have been at this time the chief place of the satrapy of Parthia, as it afterwards became the capital of the Parthian kings.[9] Here he waited for the arrival of the rest of his forces; and took measures for the organization of the government in the province thus newly acquired. We hear nothing of any resistance offered by the Parthians—a people destined hereafter to assume so formidable a character, but who were at this time but an inconsiderable tribe, and submitted without opposition to the Macedonian arms. The same was the case with the Tapuri, a mountain tribe who occupied the defiles and forests of Mount Elburz, through which lay the route from Hecatompylus to the Caspian, but who offered but little opposition to the passage of Alexander; and their satrap Autophradates hastened to tender his submission to the king, as soon as he arrived at Zadracarta in the plain of Hyrcania. It was otherwise with the Mardi, who occupied the mountain tracts to the west of them;[1] and confiding in the rugged and inac-

---

[8] Arrian, *Anab* iii. 20, 21.
[9] Note L, p 479
[1] The name of the Mardi, or Amardi, as it is written by Strabo (xi 8, p. 514) is one of those which we find recurring in different and distant parts of Asia, always as that of a warlike mountain tribe. Whether there was really any ethnic connection between the tribes thus designated, is a point on which it is now impossible to arrive at any conclusion

cessible nature of their country, at first defied the arms of Alexander, and compelled him to lead an expedition in person into their mountain fastnesses. Of the Hyrcanians properly so called we hear little; the Persian satrap Phrataphernes, who was governor of the province, submitted without resistance.[2]

§ 12. Alexander had now penetrated into regions that had hitherto been known only by name among the Greeks; his subsequent campaigns carried him farther and farther beyond the domain of their geographical knowledge. It is true that he did not, until he crossed the Indus, actually pass beyond the limits of what had been comprised within the Persian Empire; but though the *names* of the Bactrians, the Sogdians, and the Arians, had been familiar to the Greeks from the days of Herodotus,[3] their information concerning the regions inhabited by these nations was doubtless of the vaguest description; and the victorious progress of the Macedonian king from the shores of the Caspian to the banks of the Indus partook almost as much of the character of geographical discovery as of military enterprise. This portion of his career, indeed, became in the eyes of subsequent writers, the basis of all their geographical knowledge of the countries in question; and though on this occasion he established in the heart of Asia a nucleus of Greek civilization, which continued to maintain itself during a long period, and even acquired extensive developement, we shall find that very little information was derived from this source, and little was known of Central Asia in the days of Strabo, beyond what could be learnt from the historians of Alexander.

These campaigns have a further interest in the eyes of modern inquirers from the fact that as Alexander was the first, he was also the last, who ever led an European army through the regions in question. It is only in quite recent times that

---

[2] Note M, p 480.
[3] The Bactrians at least were already well known *by name* in the time of Æschylus, as they are repeatedly mentioned in the *Persæ* (vv 306, 318, 732).

even exploring travellers have been able to visit the remote provinces of Bactria and Sogdiana, and in attempting to trace the route of Alexander through these wild countries we shall find that our difficulties arise almost as much from our own imperfect knowledge of the localities, as from the deficiency of our ancient informants.[4] The task would indeed be a hopeless one, were it not for the physical peculiarities of the country, which must in all ages have determined the limited areas to which settled population was restricted, as well as the lines of route which communicated between them. The fertile valleys of Central Asia are almost as clearly marked by nature as the Oases of Africa; and the sandy deserts which separate them, as well as the Great Salt Desert that occupies so large a portion of the table-land of Iran, must in ancient, as in modern times, have always presented an impassable barrier to the extension of civilization.

§ 13. The marches of Alexander were therefore undertaken under conditions very similar to those which would be encountered by a modern caravan. "The great roads from Persia to India and Bactria (observes Professor Wilson) have always of necessity followed the direction to which the natural features of the country have confined them; and as these have undergone little material alteration since the Greeks marched to Bactria, there should be no great difference in the routes which are open to travellers in the present day. Passes through mountains, and paths across deserts, afforded access, no doubt, in various situations; but the roads available for commerce or for war, for caravans or armies, are in all probability much the same now that they always were. The general bearings and stages cannot be very dissimilar."[5] The same writer adds a warning—too often neglected by

---

[4] Great progress has indeed been made of late years in this respect, beginning with the travels of Sir Alexander Burnes in 1834, and the extension of the Russian power in this part of Asia will doubtless soon lead to a much more accurate knowledge of its geography, but no explorations have as yet been made with a view to connecting our increased information with the accounts of ancient writers

[5] Wilson's *Ariana*, p 170

modern inquirers into ancient geography,—against placing too much reliance on the distances transmitted to us; and observes that "ample allowance must be made for the inexactness of both ancient and modern measurements." The lines of route have, even in modern times, for the most part, not been fixed by survey; but merely calculated from the number of hours occupied in traversing them on a horse or a camel.[6] There can be no doubt that the same was the case with the distances recorded by ancient authors, with this great additional element of uncertainty, that as they had no portable instruments for measuring time, they could not have calculated the distances even in *hours*, but must have been reduced to the still rougher estimate of days' journeys. This is still the only method in use along the less frequented routes of the Persian Empire.[7]

Imperfect as an itinerary based upon such a mode of estimate must necessarily be, it is unfortunately a great deal more than we actually possess. In following the campaigns of Alexander we are perpetually reminded, by painful contrast, of the record which Xenophon has preserved to us of the march of the younger Cyrus to Cunaxa, and although we have seen how far this was from being free from geographical difficulties, and how little pretension it had to be based on anything like correct measurement, it is certain that such an itinerary of the marches of Alexander would be an invaluable addition to our knowledge. It has been indeed contended by some modern writers that not only was such an itinerary extant in ancient times, but that *it was based on actual measurement*, by officers specially appointed for the purpose. Unfortunately, such an assumption rests upon very slender authority, and it is certain

---

[6] There are however some important exceptions The route from Herat to Candahar, and that from Candahar to Cabul, have been actually measured by perambulator, and the results which are cited by Wilson tend to show how little reliance can be placed on the ordinary mode of computation The latter distance was found by this measurement to be three hundred and nine miles, though previously estimated at only two hundred and twenty-eight miles (Wilson's *Ariana*, pp 173, 175)

[7] Note N, p 481

that if any such record ever existed, the statements derived from it by extant authors are too few and too imperfect to be of much use to us in tracing the route of the great conqueror.[8]

Still, the leading outlines of his extraordinary progress from the Caspian to the Iaxartes, and from that river again to the Indus, can be distinctly followed. It will even be found, that in many instances, the distances given by ancient writers present a degree of approximation to those of modern travellers, exceeding what could reasonably be expected under the circumstances.

§ 14. From Zadracarta Alexander directed his march eastwards towards Bactria, where Bessus, the murderer of Darius, had assumed the tiara of the Persian kings, and was evidently preparing to set up an independent sovereignty. After traversing the northern portion of Parthia, he reached the confines of Aria, where he was met, at a place called Susia, by the satrap of the province, Satibarzanes, who hastened to make his submission to the conqueror, and was in consequence confirmed in the possession of his satrapy. But when Alexander was pushing on towards Bactria, and before he had yet quitted the confines of Aria, he suddenly learned that Satibarzanes was playing him false, and preparing to join Bessus, as soon as he saw his own province clear of the Macedonian army. Hereupon he suddenly turned upon the rebel satrap with his accustomed rapidity, and by a forced march of 600 stadia (60 G. miles) in two days, surprised him in his capital city of Artacoana, and crushed the insurrection at once. But being thus diverted from his original line of march towards Bactria, he did not resume it, and he appears to have thought it prudent to secure the neighbouring provinces of Drangiana and Arachosia before adventuring himself in the remote regions beyond the Paropamisus.

With this view he marched from Artacoana (which must have

---

[8] Note O, p 481.

been situated either on the site, or at all events somewhere in the neighbourhood of the modern Herat) in a southerly direction to Prophthasia, the capital city of the Drangians or Zarangians, who inhabited the country now known as Seistan. His halt in this remote and obscure locality was rendered memorable by the discovery of the conspiracy of Philotas, and the executions that followed, which have left one of the darkest stains upon the character of Alexander.[9] When he again moved forward, he followed the valley of the Helmund, and one of its tributaries, which constitute the natural highway in this part of Asia, as far as Candahar, and thence turning to the north-east, advanced through Arachosia, by the site of the modern Ghizni and Cabul, to the foot of the Hindoo Koosh, or Caucasus, as it was named by the Greeks.[1] Here he made a long halt: the winter was too far advanced for him to think of passing the mountains at that season: and his army had already suffered severely from the cold in traversing the inclement regions of the Paropamisadæ through which they had lately passed. He took advantage of the delay to found here a permanent monument of his power, while he at the same time secured his future communications, by establishing a city, to which he gave his own name: it was subsequently known, for the sake of distinction from the numerous other cities that bore the same appellation, as Alexandria ad Caucasum. Here he settled a body of 7000 Macedonians, veteran soldiers and others.

§ 15. It is not difficult, for the reason already stated, to follow the line of Alexander's march, during the above campaign, so far as its main outline and direction are concerned, though there is often much uncertainty in determining the precise localities indicated. There are in fact, at the present day, two roads leading from the Caspian Gates, or the neighbourhood of Teheran, to Meshed and Herat, one above the mountains, keeping throughout along the elevated table-land;

---

[9] Note P, p. 483.   [1] Note Q, p 484

the other descending (as we know Alexander to have done) into the plains of Hyrcania near the Caspian, and thence through the northern part of Parthia proper, to the frontier of the Arians near Meshed.[2] The latter of these, which is the one most frequented at the present day, is unquestionably that which was followed by Alexander. Of the two cities whose names are mentioned, the one, Susia—apparently the first place he came to within the limits of Aria—cannot be determined with any certainty, though it was probably situated not far from Meshed: the second, Artacoana, is generally placed at Herat. On this supposition it must be the same place that was subsequently known as Alexandria in Ariis.[3]

The direct road from Herat to Bactria would have lain through the mountain ranges now occupied by the Hazara tribes to the foot of the Bamian pass across the Hindoo Koosh: but it is probable that this road was in ancient, as it is in modern times, but little frequented, if not impassable for an army;[4] and the longer route, which was followed by Alexander, had the advantage of enabling him to reduce to subjection on his passage the districts of Drangiana, Arachosia, and the Paropamisus. By this means he would have secured the submission of all the nations to the south of the great mountain chain, before he crossed it into Bactria and Sogdiana. Of the tribes that lay along this line of march, the Drangians or Zarangians may be identified beyond a doubt as occupying the district now known as Seistan, on the banks of the Helmund, and the lake formed by its waters. Their capital city of Prophthasia may be in all probability identified with the modern Furrah, which is still the northern capital of Seistan, and a place of considerable traffic.[5]

From Drangiana onwards his course lay of necessity along the valley of the Etymander (Helmund) which presents a narrow strip of cultivated land, bordered on each side by arid

---

[2] See Wilson's *Ariana*, p 171.
[3] Note R, p 485.
[4] Note S, p 486
[5] Note T, p 488

deserts.⁶ Here he encountered a tribe called by the Greeks Euergetæ, but whose true name seems to have been Ariaspæ. Proceeding from thence to the northwards, and quitting the valley of the Helmund for that of one of its tributaries, he entered the province of Arachosia, and doubtless followed the line of route, in use at the present day, from Candahar to Ghizni: a road which (as Professor Wilson observes) is "recommended," or rather prescribed, by the character of the country, "being confined on either hand by lofty mountains of considerable elevation and arduous access."⁷ From thence still advancing onwards, in spite of the late season of the year, he crossed the mountain tract between Ghizni and Cabul, where his army suffered much from cold, as well as from the deep snows.⁸ It was doubtless the experience of the difficulties and privations here encountered that determined him to halt for the winter in the valley of Cabul, before attempting the passage of the still more formidable range of the Hindoo Koosh.

§ 16. One of the most important points in the geography of these campaigns is the determination of the exact site of the city founded by Alexander at the foot of the Caucasus, which continued for a long time to be a place of importance and one of the principal centres of Greek civilization in these remote regions. Its position may now be looked upon as clearly determined, at all events within very narrow limits. It was situated, as we learn from Pliny (who is here certainly following the geographers of Alexander),⁹ at the very foot of the

---

⁶ Elphinstone's *Caubul*, vol 1 p 153. Wilson's *Ariana*, p 177, note
Where it was crossed by Captain Christie the valley of the Helmund extended only about half a mile on each side of the river, beyond that the desert rose at once in perpendicular cliffs (See Appendix to Pottinger's *Beloochistan*, p 406)
There is indeed a more direct route from Furrah by Ghirishk to Candahar; but this lies through a poor and desert country: and M. Ferrier observes that any general proceeding with an army to Candahar would descend the valley of the Furrah-rud in the first instance, and afterwards ascend that of the Helmund. It had moreover the advantage of enabling Alexander to subdue the southern part of Seistan on his way.
⁷ Wilson's *Ariana*, p. 178 See Note U, p 488
⁸ Note V p 489
⁹ Plin *H N* vi 17, § 62. "Hanc urbem sub ipso Caucaso esse positam"

Sect 1   EXPEDITION OF ALEXANDER.   427

mountains (that is to say, of the lofty range of the Hindoo Koosh), and 50 Roman miles (40 G. miles) from Ortospana, which may be placed on satisfactory grounds on the site of the modern Cabul.[1] These indications point clearly to a position in the fertile region known as the Koh Daman, to the north of Cabul, at the foot of the Hindoo Koosh, and at the point of junction of the different passes leading across that mountain range into Bactria. Near this point of junction is situated the modern town of Charikar, in the neighbourhood of which are considerable ruins, indicating the site of a city of importance. Here therefore we may in all probability place the city of Alexander, which became, during a considerable period, the capital of the whole surrounding country, much as Cabul is at the present day. An additional confirmation of this conclusion is found in the name of Opiane given by some Greek writers to the district around Alexandria, and which is thought to be retained in that of the modern village of Opian, or Hupian, a few miles to the north-west of Charikar.[2]

§ 17. As soon as the spring was sufficiently far advanced for the passes of the Hindoo Koosh to be practicable, Alexander quitted his winter quarters (B.C. 329) and traversed the mountains, the passage of which, however, still presented great difficulties, and occupied him no less than seventeen days— reckoning apparently from the newly-founded city of Alexandria to Adrapsa or Drapsaca, the first city in Bactria.[3] It is a question of much interest to determine the pass by which he

---

[1] The name of Ortospana is not found in any of the extant historians of Alexander; but it is mentioned by Strabo, and his description of its position among the Paropamisadæ at the junction of three roads, one of which led directly into Bactria (εἰς Ὀρτόσπανα ἐπὶ τὴν ἐκ Βάκτρων τρίοδον ἥτις ἐστὶν ἐν τοῖς Παροπαμισάδαις, xv 2, § 8, p. 723), leaves little doubt that it must have occupied the site of Cabul, the importance of which is derived from that very circumstance.

[2] Note X, p 490

[3] The name is written by Arrian (iii. 29, § 1), the only one of the historians of Alexander who mentions it, Drapsaca (Δράψακα), but Strabo writes it in one passage Adrapsa (xv. 2, p. 725), in another Darapsa (xi. 11, p 516) The Drepsa of Ptolemy, though doubtless the same *name*, cannot be the same place, as that author places it in Sogdiana, considerably to the north of Maracanda (Ptol vi 12, § 6).

crossed the great mountain range; an inquiry intimately connected with that already touched upon, of the position of Alexandria. If that city be correctly placed in the neighbourhood of Charikar, it is unlikely that Alexander should have taken the pass of Bamian, as supposed by most modern writers, from its being the easiest and best known of the passes leading from *Cabul* into Bactria. But it appears that there are three other passes leading from the Koh Daman directly across the mountains, among which, at the present day, " the caravans make their selection, according to the season of the year, and the more or less peaceable state of the country which borders them."[4] It is far more probable that Alexander should have taken one of these passes, which led directly into Bactria, than the more circuitous route by Bamian: but it is more difficult to choose among them, and there is nothing to determine with any degree of certainty the position of the Bactrian city of Adrapsa or Drapsaca, which formed the termination of the pass on the other side. At the same time the probabilities seem in favour of his having followed the route which ascends the valley of the Panchshir, and crosses the mountains at its head by the pass known as the Khawak pass: from whence it turns to the left and descends to Anderab, a place which has been identified by several modern writers, though on very slender grounds, with the Drapsaca of Arrian.[5]

§ 18. Once across the great mountain barrier of the Hindoo Koosh, the progress of Alexander's arms was rapid and decisive. From Drapsaca he advanced at once to the capital city of Bactria—Zariaspa, or Bactra, as it was more commonly called by the Greeks—which was taken almost without resistance, Bessus having already retreated across the Oxus into Sogdiana. Thither Alexander at once prepared to follow him: and though the broad and rapid stream of the Oxus presented a natural obstacle of the most formidable kind, he effected the passage of that river with his whole army, without any opposition from

---

[4] Wood's *Journey to the Source of the Oxus*, p. 118.   [5] Note Y, p 492.

a hostile force.⁶ From thence he pushed on to Nautaca, a city of Sogdiana where Bessus had previously halted, and thence again to Maracanda, which is called by Arrian the capital of Sogdiana. The fugitive satrap had already fallen into his hands, and it was apparently the mere love of enterprise or discovery that led him to advance as far as the river Iaxartes, which had long formed in this direction the boundary of the Persian Empire, separating it from the wild and independent Scythian tribes beyond. Here he was preparing to found another city that should immortalize his name, and bear testimony to his victorious progress into these remote regions, when his project was interrupted for a time by a general revolt of the Sogdians and Bactrians, while the Scythians on the northern side of the river gathered in swarms on its banks, to be ready to take part, should the insurrection prove successful.

§ 19. Alexander now learned from experience that it was more easy to traverse these wild regions as a conqueror, than to reduce the warlike and lawless inhabitants to a condition of permanent subjection. The greater part of three campaigns (B.C. 329-327) was occupied by him in this task, in which he displayed his wonted energy and activity, especially in the reduction of the hill forts, which were believed by the natives to be impregnable, as they undoubtedly appeared on a first aspect. But we are wholly unable to follow in detail his movements in these countries, of which our own knowledge is still very vague and imperfect,⁷ while the ancient

---

⁶ On this occasion, Bessus having withdrawn and destroyed all the boats, Alexander crossed his whole army over, by means of skins or hides sewn together, *and stuffed with straw* (Arrian, *Anab.* iii 29, § 4) At a later period he crossed the Iaxartes in the same manner (Id iv 4, §§ 2, 4) It is singular that the custom, now universal in the East, from the Euphrates to the Indus, of using *inflated* skins for crossing, and even to a certain extent for navigating, rivers, seems to have been unknown in the days of Alexander, as it had been in those of Herodotus, whose description of the boats or rafts in use on the Euphrates excludes the idea of its employment. (Herodot i 194 See Mr Rawlinson's note on the passage.) It appears, however, that even at the present day the practice of stuffing the skins with straw is occasionally resorted to See a note to Ferrier's *Caravan Journeys*, p 429

⁷ Mr Grote justly remarks that in fact "these countries at the present

accounts are generally meagre, and wanting in geographical precision.

A few points only can be considered as satisfactorily determined. The site of Bactra, or Zariaspa, is still occupied by the modern Balkh, the chief town of the surrounding district. Maracanda also still survives in the well-known Samarcand, which attained to such great celebrity in the middle ages as the capital of Timour; and the river that flows by it, the Kohik, is unquestionably the Polytimetus of the Greeks.[8] The place where Alexander first reached the banks of the Iaxartes, and where he afterwards founded the town that was called by later geographers Alexandria Ultima, was probably in the neighbourhood of Khojend. But this last identification rests on no positive evidence,[9] and beyond this we have nothing to guide us. The sites of the two celebrated rock-fortresses called by the Greek historians the Sogdian Rock and the

---

moment are known only superficially as to their general scenery. for purposes of measurement and geography they are almost unknown" (vol xii p 273, note). Very little has been added to our knowledge since this was written The later travels of M Vambéry in 1863, while they threw much light upon the state of the country and its inhabitants, contributed but very little to our positive geographical knowledge.

The rugged mountain country in particular which occupies the eastern part of the Khanat of Bokhara, called by Arrian Paraetacene, and in which we must look for the hill-fortresses taken by Alexander, is still almost entirely unknown The recent occupation of so large a part of these regions of Central Asia by the Russians will doubtless lead before long to an improved knowledge of their geography, but I am not aware that any researches have yet been made which tend to throw light upon the proceedings of Alexander in this quarter

[8] The statement of Arrian (iv. 6, § 6) and Strabo (xi p 518, in both cases derived from Aristobulus), that this river, though a copious stream, is lost in the sands, and does not flow into the Oxus, has been verified by recent travellers (Burnes's *Travels*, vol iii p 139), and serves to show the accuracy of the information acquired by the Macedonians at this time

The same remark is applied, with equal justice, to the Arius (the Heriud, or river of Herat) and to the Etymandrus (Helmund), which flows through Drangiana (Arrian, *ibid*) The Epardus, associated with them in the same passage, as flowing through the land of the Mardi, is probably the Margus, or Murghaub (the river of Margiana) of which the same thing is true (See Burnes's *Travels*, vol. iii p 30)

[9] It is indeed probable from the configuration of the country that one customary place of passage of the Iaxartes must always have been somewhere in the neighbourhood of Khojend, but the nearest point on that river to Samarcand is at Chinaz, on the direct road to Tashkend, and there is no reason that Alexander should not have taken that route

Rock of Chorienes are wholly unknown; as well as that of the seven towns on the left bank of the Iaxartes, including the most important of them, which bore the name of Cyra or Cyropolis, and was reputed to have been founded by the elder Cyrus. Even Nautaca, which appears to have been a place of considerable importance, as it was selected by Alexander for his winter-quarters (in the winter of B.C. 328–327), cannot be determined otherwise than by conjecture; but as we know that it was situated between Samarcand and the Oxus, it is not improbable that it may have occupied the site of Kurshee, a town which is situated in one of those fertile oases that must always in this country have been a centre of habitation.[1]

It may be observed that no record of distances, or supposed geographical measurements, has been preserved to us in regard to these countries, except the very vague and general estimate of Eratosthenes that it was *about* 5000 stadia from Bactra to the river Iaxartes.[2] Such an omission, in regard to countries of so much interest in a geographical point of view, goes far to negative the supposition that any real *measurements* of the marches of Alexander had been made or preserved.

§ 20. The operations of Alexander, during the long time that he spent in these remote provinces were, however, by no means solely of a military character. While he destroyed, or at least dismantled, many of the previously existing towns and fortresses,[3] he is said to have founded not less than eight

---

[1] Burnes's *Travels*, vol ii pp. 221, 225 There appears, however, to be another line of route, somewhat more direct, from Balkh to Samarcand, passing by Shehr Sebz, or Kesh (the birthplace of Timour), and this may have been the route followed by Alexander, in which case Kesh may represent Nautaca

[2] Eratosth ap. Strab xi. p. 514 εἶτ' ἐπὶ τὸν Ἰαξάρτην ποταμόν, ἐφ' ὃν Ἀλέξανδρος ἧκεν ὡς πεντακισχιλίους. The estimate greatly exceeds the truth, if measured from Balkh to Khojend

[3] Among these Strabo mentions Maracanda, but it is certain that he did not destroy that city, though he may have dismantled its fortifications. Mr Vaux in Dr Smith's dictionary (art MARACANDA) erroneously represents Strabo as stating that Alexander *built* Maracanda, which is wholly incorrect It is called by Arrian (III. 30, § 6) the capital of Sogdiana (τὰ βασίλεια τῆς Σογδιανῶν χώρας) at the time when Alexander first invaded the country; and it is described by Q. Curtius as a great city, the walls of which were 70 stadia in circuit (Curt vii 6, § 10)

cities in the two provinces of Bactria and Sogdiana;[4] but unfortunately neither their sites nor their names have been transmitted to us. We know only that besides the city on the Iaxartes, there were at a later period two others, which bore the name of Alexandria—one in Bactria, another in Sogdiana near the Oxus. But it is by no means certain that either of these was actually founded by Alexander. A fourth city of the name (according to Pliny) was founded in Margiana,[5] a district which Alexander does not appear to have ever visited in person,[6] though it was in all probability reduced to subjection, or voluntarily tendered its submission, while he was subduing these provinces.

While the geographical information concerning these distant provinces furnished by the historians of Alexander is thus indefinite and incomplete, their account of the physical aspect of the regions now for the first time laid open to the Greeks is strikingly correct and characteristic. One of the first modern travellers who visited these countries, Sir A. Burnes, was struck with the accuracy with which their general character—

[4] Strab. xi. p. 518.
[5] Plin. vi. 16, § 46. It was afterwards destroyed by the neighbouring barbarians, but restored by Antiochus Soter, who gave it the name of Antiochia, under which it long continued to be the capital of Margiana. It probably occupied the site of the modern Merv, or Merve, on the Murghaub, which was formerly one of the principal cities of Khorassan, though now in a state of great decay (Kinneir's *Memoir of Persia*, p. 179, Burnes's *Travels*, vol. iii p. 218).
[6] Droysen alone supposes Alexander to have visited Margiana, on his march from Hyrcania towards Bactria, before he was recalled into Aria by the revolt of Satibarzanes. But this appears extremely improbable.
Q. Curtius indeed represents Alexander as having proceeded "ad urbem Marginiam" in his second campaign in Sogdiana (vii 10, § 15) for which the editors have substituted "Margianam," but this statement is not only inconsistent with the narrative of Arrian, but unintelligible in itself, and the words 'superatis deinde amnibus Ocho et Oxo" are in any case erroneous. The foundation of *six cities*, all situated "in editis collibus,' is wholly inapplicable to the oasis of Merv, and undoubtedly referred to the proceedings of Alexander *in Sogdiana*, as does the account which follows of the capture of the celebrated hill-forts Mutzell (*ad loc.*) has in vain attempted to explain and defend the confused geography of Curtius It is more probable that Marginia was really a town in Sogdiana. Dr. Müller in his map of Alexander's campaigns (in Dr. Smith's *Atlas of Ancient Geography*) identifies it with a place called Murginan or Margilan, on a river of the same name, which is plausible enough but all such conclusions must be regarded as merely conjectural

in which tracts of the richest and most productive soil alternate with barren wastes of sand—was described by Q. Curtius.[7] Strabo dwells more especially upon the great wealth and fertility of Bactria, which enabled its Greek rulers to found a powerful dominion there, and extend their rule over the neighbouring parts of Ariana and India.[8] The same phenomenon was repeated at a much later period when these secluded provinces of Central Asia became for a time the seat of the powerful empire of Timour and his successors.

§ 21. But undoubtedly the most important addition to the geographical knowledge of the Greeks, was that of introducing for the first time clear ideas concerning the two great rivers of Central Asia, the Oxus and the Iaxartes. We have seen how completely vague and confused were the views of Herodotus upon this subject, who knew only of one river to the east of the Caspian, to which he gave the name of Araxes, and regarded it as flowing eastward *from* the Caspian, instead of *towards* it. At a later period the passage in the Meteorologics of Aristotle, already noticed,[9] which could have been written but a few years before the expedition of Alexander,[1] while it shows that somewhat more definite ideas had already been attained by the more cultivated and inquiring minds among the Greeks, still presents them in a very confused condition. He here represents a mountain called Parnasus (evidently a corruption of Paropamisus) as the source of all the principal rivers in this part of Asia, from which flowed, besides other rivers, the Bactrus, the Choaspes, and the Araxes. Of this last (he adds) the Tanais is a branch, which parts off and flows into the Lake Mæotis. The Indus also (he says) takes

---

[7] Q. Curt vii 18, § 26; Burnes's *Travels to Bokhara*, vol ii p. 211.
[8] Strab xi p 516.
[9] See Chapter XI. p 399
[1] The *Meteorologica* could not have been written earlier than B C. 341, as an event is mentioned as occurring in the archonship of that year; while the passage before us, as well as the absence of all allusion to the newly-discovered regions of India, shows that they must have been composed before the arms of Alexander had made those countries known to the Greeks.

its rise in the same mountain, which has the largest stream of all rivers.²

Here there can be little doubt that the Araxes, though its name is given in the same form as that known to Herodotus, is meant to designate the Iaxartes; the Bactrus is probably "the river of Bactria"—that is, the Oxus; and the Choaspes may be meant to designate the river of Cabul, the Cophen of Arrian and Strabo, of which, according to these writers, the Choes or Choaspes was a tributary.³ So far therefore as regards the rivers having their rise in the same mountain chain the statement is founded in fact; but the name of the Oxus, so familiar in all subsequent ages, appears to have been still unknown; while the strange confusion which led to the belief that the Araxes or Iaxartes and the Tanais were only arms of one and the same river, would seem to have been already established. So fixed was that idea in the popular belief, that when the Macedonian army at length found itself on the banks of the Iaxartes, they universally regarded it as the Tanais, and conceived themselves to have reached the limit between Europe and Asia⁴ Even the well-informed Aristobulus appears to have uniformly designated the river by that name, adding however that it was called by the natives the Iaxartes.⁵

§ 22. But notwithstanding this confusion, which appears to have maintained its ground as a popular error until long afterwards, though rejected by the maturer judgment of geographers,⁶ the Greeks henceforth became clearly aware of the

---

² Aristot. *Meteorol.* 1 13, § 15
³ Arrian, *Anab* iv 23, Strabo, xv
⁴ It is singular that one of the proofs alleged as having convinced the Macedonians that the river in question could be no other than the Tanais, was the fact that there were fir woods in the territory beyond it, which must therefore be a part of Europe and not of Asia! (Strabo, xi 7, p 510)
⁵ Arrian, iii 30, § 11
⁶ Arrian, though he follows Aristobulus in describing the Iaxartes under the name of Tanais, adds, "It must

be another Tanais which is described by Herodotus as flowing into the Palus Mæotis" (*Anab* iii 30, § 8)
Strabo considers the notion to have been maintained with a view of representing that Alexander had conquered the whole of Asia it being generally admitted that the Tanais was the boundary between Europe and Asia, whereas in reality (as he remarks) a considerable part of Asia, from the Caspian Sea to the Tanais was not subjected by the Macedonians (Strab xi. p. 509).

existence of these two great rivers in Central Asia, both of them, as they conceived, rising in the Caucasus or Hindoo Koosh, and both ultimately flowing into the Caspian Sea. The Oxus especially appears to have attracted their attention in a remarkable degree. Aristobulus described it as six stadia in breadth, of great depth, and flowing with a strong current; and regarded it as the greatest of all the rivers of Asia, except those of India, with which, as he observed, no others could be compared.[7] The Iaxartes, though a stream of inferior dimensions,[8] derived great importance from its position, as it still continued to be the limit of their geographical knowledge towards the north-east; beyond that they had only vague ideas of wandering Scythian tribes, or uninhabitable deserts. At the same time it must be remembered, with regard to their information concerning both these rivers, that the accounts alike of their sources and their outflow rested upon mere hearsay. Alexander himself did not do more than cross them, several hundred miles above their mouths, and his information concerning their outlet was doubtless derived from the Chorasmians and other barbarians who dwelt on the east of the Caspian Sea, or occupied the steppes between its shores and the Iaxartes.[9]

§ 23. But though Alexander himself did not carry his arms beyond the Iaxartes—except for a very brief and fruitless

---

[7] According to Sir A. Burnes the Oxus, where he crossed it on his way from Balkh to Kharjee was 800 yards wide, and 20 feet deep, with a very rapid and turbid stream (*Travels*, vol. ii p 214) At a point considerably lower down, between Bokhara and Meiv, it was only 650 yards wide, but from 25 to 29 feet deep (Ib vol iii p 5)

[8] Burnes, vol iii, p 139

[9] I can find no authority for the statement of Sir H Rawlinson (*Proceedings of Geographical Society*, 1867, p 115), that Alexander "*sent his troops on an expedition along the shores of the Caspian*, while he himself crossed the Oxus and reached the banks of the Iaxartes, and that he must therefore have possessed accurate information as to those localities, and yet the account which his officers brought back to Greece was that both rivers fell into the Caspian." It seems clear that this was the general impression brought away by the followers of Alexander, and adopted by Aristobulus and other historians; but there is not a particle of evidence to prove that it was the result of positive exploration The only exploring expedition we hear of was that of Patrocles, the general of Seleucus, more than twenty years afterwards, to which we shall have occasion to revert hereafter

reconnaissance—he received during his stay in Sogdiana embassies from several of the neighbouring barbarian tribes, to tender their submission, or avert the apprehended invasion. Among these we find mentioned Pharasmanes, king of the Chorasmians, a people already mentioned by Herodotus, and who undoubtedly inhabited the tract now known as the Khanate of Khiva, which continued throughout the middle ages to bear the name of Kharezm. According to Arrian Pharasmanes assured Alexander that his dominions bordered on those of *the Colchians* and *the Amazons* (!), and offered to accompany the king on his march, if he were disposed to proceed from thence towards the shores of the Euxine.[1]

It was doubtless this idle boast, which only serves to show still further the utter vagueness of the ideas then current concerning the geography of this part of Asia, that gave rise to the fable repeated by later historians, of the visit of the queen of the Amazons herself to the conqueror—a story, as we are told by Plutarch, expressly contradicted as a fiction by Aristobulus, Ptolemy, and all the more judicious historians, but which still maintained its ground, and found favour with the rhetorical writers of a later period.[2]

Another tribe, with whose name we are familiar from other sources, the Dahae, are mentioned repeatedly among the races with which Alexander here came in contact, but there is nothing to assign them a definite locality.[3] Probably indeed they were a nomad race of warriors, like the Turcomans at the present day.

§ 24. Of the Scythians that occupied the country beyond the Iaxartes, we learn no particulars: they appear to have been

---

[1] Arrian, iv 15, § 4
[2] See Plutarch, *Alex* c 46, Strab xi p 505 The story is told in full detail by Q Curtius, vi 5, § 24–32, Diodorus, xvii 77, and Justin xii 3 It was already related, even within the lifetime of Alexander s contemporaries, by Onesicritus (Plut *l c*) and Chitarchus (ap Strab. *l c*), who was probably the authority followed by Curtius and Diodorus
[3] We only learn from Arrian that the Dahæ (Δάαι) were one of the tribes subject to Bessus, and that they dwelt south of the Tanais, *i e* the Iaxartes (iii 28, § 8). Strabo places them east of the Caspian, apparently between the Chorasmians and the Hyrcanians

regarded by the Macedonians, and by Alexander himself, as connected with the European Scythians, who occupied the steppes to the north of the Euxine and the Palus Mæotis: but this is no proof that they really were so. On the other hand the Massagetæ, who appear in Herodotus as a great nation occupying the whole country north of the Araxes (Iaxartes), here figure only as a subordinate Scythian tribe, apparently situated on the south of that river, within the limits of Sogdiana.

The Sacæ again are mentioned by Strabo, among the nations with whom Alexander at this time came into collision. But according to Arrian they had not been subject to the Persian Empire, but only served in the army of Darius as *allies*. In the time of Herodotus, however, they had clearly been included in the empire, and were comprised in the fifteenth satrapy. Strabo certainly places them among the nations on the southern side of the Iaxartes, as opposed to the nomad Scythians beyond that river.

How far the position of these tribes had really been shifted by those changes which were perpetually going on among the wandering populations of Central Asia, or how far the apparent changes result merely from differences of nomenclature we are unable to determine. But when we consider how vaguely the name of Scythians was employed in ancient times, just as that of Tartars has been in modern days, and how slowly our ethnographical information concerning the races of Central Asia has attained to anything like a clear and definite form, we cannot wonder to find the statements transmitted to us by the historians of Alexander, and by subsequent geographers, at once perplexed and bewildering.[4]

---

[4] Note Z, p 493

We are told indeed that Alexander, soon after his arrival on the Iaxartes, received an embassy from the king of "the European Scythians," and that he sent back with the envoys some of his own emissaries, with a view of exploring the nature and resources of the country (Arrian, iv 1, §§ 1, 2) These returned, after an interval of some months (Id iv 15), accompanied by a fresh embassy, with the most friendly offers and professions but there is nothing to intimate what was the country which they had really visited No subsequent reference is made to

One point, however, is clear; that the great mountain chain which bounded the provinces of Bactria and Sogdiana on the east, and so long formed the limit between Independent Tartary and Chinese Turkestan, remained at this time, and continued till long afterwards to oppose an absolute barrier to all intercourse towards the east: and it does not appear that even the vaguest rumours concerning the nations beyond that limit—who occupied the vast tracts of Mongolia or Chinese Tartary—had reached the ears of the Greek historians and geographers.

SECTION II.—*Military Operations in India.*

§ 1. IT was not till late in the spring of B.C. 327 that Alexander, after a halt of some duration at Bactra, recrossed the Hindoo Koosh with his army, with the view of directing his arms against India. The passage of the mountains appears to have been made with comparative facility, probably on account of the more advanced season of the year: but we are told that on this occasion he took a *different* and a *shorter* pass from that which he had followed on his advance into Bactria,[5] and only ten days were occupied in the passage of the Caucasus by this new route.[6] He halted for some time at his rising city of Alexandria, which he strengthened by the addition of new settlers, and thence proceeded to Nicæa,[7] and the river

---

any geographical information obtained by these emissaries.

It is curious also, that we find mention (Arrian, iv 1, § 1, Curt vii 6, § 11) of a tribe whom the Greeks called Abii ("Ἄβιοι), evidently with direct reference to the well-known passage of Homer, but whether there was any foundation for the name, or it was merely given to some Scythian tribe, on account of the resemblance of their manners to those described by the poet we are unable to determine. The latter supposition is, however, the most probable (See some judicious remarks by Major Rennell, *Geogr of Herodotus*, p 226)

[5] Strabo, xv 1, § 26
[6] Arrian, *Anab.* iv 22, § 4 See Note Y, p 492
The historians of Alexander all mention the great abundance of *silphium* which was found in the mountains of the Paropamisus There can be no doubt that the plant, which they here designated by this name was *assafoetida*, which still grows abundantly in these mountain regions, and is largely used by the inhabitants (Burnes, vol ii p 166)

[7] Arrian, *Anab* iv 22, § 6 This is the only mention found of a city of Nicæa in these regions, and Arrian gives us no information concerning it

Cophen.[8] Here he was met by Taxiles, an Indian king, whose dominions lay on the opposite side of the Indus, as well as by sundry chiefs of the tribes to the west of that river. Hence he dispatched Hephæstion and Perdiccas with a large portion of his forces down the valley of the Cophen to the territory of Peucelaotis on the western side of the Indus, with orders to secure the passage of that river and construct a bridge across it.[9] Meanwhile Alexander himself undertook the reduction of the mountain tribes north of the valley of the Cophen—wild mountaineers inhabiting a very rugged and difficult country, which is still so imperfectly known to Europeans, that there is hardly any part of the campaigns of Alexander, where we are so much at a loss to follow his movements. The difficulties which he encountered in these operations, both from the inaccessible

---

But there is no reason to question the fact of its existence. The suggestion of Ritter, followed by Droysen (*Gesch Alexanders*, p 363), that Nicæa was only a new name given to Ortospana the modern Cabul is wholly without authority, and seems at variance with the expressions of Arrian

The same view is however adopted by General Cunningham, who refers to Nonnus (xvi v 403) as showing that Nicæa was situated near a small lake But the authority of such a poet as Nonnus—who represents Nicæa as founded by Bacchus, and called after a nymph of that name (¹)—is utterly worthless on such a point, and it appears impossible that a city so well known as Ortospana could have been thus designated, without our finding any mention of it The suggestion that Nicæa occupied the site of Beghram appears to me much more probable (See Note X, p 491)

[8] There seems no doubt that the river Cophen (Κωφὴν) is the same that is now known as the river of Cabul, the main stream that flows through what may be considered as the central valley of all this mountainous region But the ancient writers appear to have had an erroneous idea of its course, the general direction of which they supposed to be from N to S or parallel with the Indus and the rivers of the Punjab (Strab xv 1, p 697) while its course below Cabul is in reality nearly from W to E Strabo distinctly describes the Choaspes as another river, falling into the Cophen at a city which he calls Plemyrium This is probably the same river that is named by Arrian Choes (*Anab* iv 23), and may perhaps be identified with the Kunar or Khonar, which descends from the valley of Chittral Wilson however supposes it to be the Alishung (*Ariana*, p 186), and all such conclusions are in truth little more than conjectural

[9] We have no details of the operations of this part of the army, who must have descended the valley of the Cabul river and traversed the formidable Khyber Pass , but, as they were accompanied by Taxiles and the chiefs of the tribes west of the Indus (Arrian, *Anab* iv 22, §§ 6. 8). they would probably experience no opposition in this part of their route Astes, the ruler of Peucelaotis, in vain opposed them in arms, but was defeated and his city taken

nature of the country, and the warlike character of its inhabitants, appear to have formed one of the chief inducements which led him to devote so much time and pains to the reduction of these obscure mountaineers; but to this was added a fresh stimulus from the notion which had gained ground among the Greeks—how or when we know not—that they had formed the scene of the exploits of Dionysus and Hercules, who had penetrated thus far into India, but no farther.[1] It was even reported, and believed, that the formidable rock fortress of Aornus, which was captured by Alexander, though reputed impregnable among the native tribes, could boast of having repulsed the arms of Hercules himself.[2] Neither the position of this fortress, nor that of any of the numerous "cities" said to have been reduced in the course of these operations, can be determined in a satisfactory manner. There, is, however, no doubt that the *district* of Peucelaotis was that immediately adjoining the Indus at its confluence with the Cophen, or river of Cabul, and its capital may probably be placed on the site of Hashtnagar, about 18 miles N. of Peshawer.[3] It is also generally admitted that the point where Alexander crossed the Indus, was the same which has in all ages formed the chief place of passage, adjoining the modern Attock.[4] Here the river is so much contracted that the construction of a bridge of boats presents no serious difficulty.[5]

§ 2. But with the exception of these two points there is scarcely a single name or site mentioned in the course of Alexander's campaign, from the time that he left Alexandria

---

[1] Note A a, p 496.
[2] Note B b, p 496
[3] Note C c, p 498
[4] General Cunningham indeed supposes him to have crossed the Indus at Ohind, which he identifies with Embolima But his reasons are very unsatisfactory
[5] A bridge of boats was yearly constructed at this point by Runjeet Sing, when he held possession of Peshawer as well as of the Punjab. The actual width of the river is estimated by Mr. Vigne at only 80 yards at one period of the year and 120 yards at another, "but the current was deep and rapid, and looked as if it would sweep away any obstacle" (Vigne's *Visit to Kabul*, &c , p. 241). Lieutenant Wood, who *measured* the width of the stream *at the fortress* of Attock, found it to be 286 yards, but he adds that "a little lower down where its channel is usually spanned by the bridge of boats, it is much more contracted" (Wood's *Journey to the Oxus*, p. 121)

at the foot of the Caucasus, till he crossed the Indus, which can be identified with any approach to certainty. So far as we are able to trace his movements, with the very imperfect information at our command, he appears to have pursued in general a course somewhat parallel to the river of Cabul, but instead of following the only route which would be practicable to a modern army—down the valley of that river and across the Khyber pass—he struggled on through the mountain country to the north of it, crossing in succession the rugged ridges that descend like gigantic spurs from the great central range of the Hindoo Koosh, and subduing tribe after tribe of the wild mountaineers that occupied the districts now known as Kafiristan, Chittral, and Swat The difficulties that he encountered during these operations—continued as they were throughout the winter—must have been such as could hardly have been exaggerated, and we cannot wonder at the especial admiration with which they seem to have been regarded by his contemporaries and historians. But even if we possessed far more accurate information than we can really pretend to, respecting these wild and secluded regions, we should still, in all probability, find ourselves wholly unable to trace his marches, or identify with any certainty the mountain strongholds that he reduced. The account of these campaigns that has been preserved to us is utterly vague and meagre. The historians that have transmitted it to us had assuredly no clear geographical conception in their own minds of the country in which they took place: and the same may be asserted with almost equal confidence of the writers whom they followed. A glance at the labyrinth of mountains and valleys, which occupy the whole space in question in the best modern maps,[6] will

---

[6] See for instance the excellent map of these regions published by Colonel Walker in 1868 No part of these wild mountain tracts *west* of the Indus has as yet been regularly surveyed.
Even in the latest number of the *Proceedings of the Geographical Society* (January, 1879) the editor can do no more than express a hope that before long "surveyors may proceed to map out the almost unknown regions of Kafiristan and the adjoining parts." (p. 64.)

sufficiently show how utterly bewildering they must have been to persons like the officers of Alexander, unaccustomed to the use of maps, ignorant of the use of the compass, and incapable of the simplest geographical observations. The capture of apparently impregnable rock-fortresses, the names of places which they dignified with the title of cities, and the passage of rivers that opposed difficulties to an advancing army—were the things that naturally impressed themselves on the memory of those who had taken part in these operations: and such are the records that have been preserved to us, with a very faint thread of geographical connection.[7]

§ 3. Equally impossible is it to determine, with anything like accuracy, the position of the different tribes against whom in succession Alexander turned his arms. Of these Arrian enumerates the Aspasians, the Guræans, and the Assaceni, which appear to have followed one another in this order [8] he mentions also cities called Ora, Massaga, Bazira, and one of the name of Nysa, to which the Macedonians attached especial importance on account of its supposed connection with Bacchus.

---

[7] It might have been thought that the rivers would have afforded us some clue through these difficulties. But this will be found on examination altogether defective. In the *Indica* (where he is probably following Nearchus) Arrian describes the Cophen as flowing through the Peucelaotis, and bringing with it the waters of the Malantus, Soastus and Garræus, to its outflow into the Indus (*Indica*, c 4) Of these the Soastus is in all probability the Swat, which flows through the district of that name, but unfortunately no mention of it occurs in the narrative of Alexander's campaign, where we find only the names of the Choes, Euaspla, and Guræus The last is probably the same as Arrian himself calls the Garræus but in this case the geographical order must be wrong It is easy to take existing rivers, and apply to them the ancient names in an arbitrary manner, but this is really all that can be done

[8] *Anab* iv 23, § 1. Strabo on the contrary (who undoubtedly wrote from good sources of information, and probably followed Aristobulus) enumerates the tribes between the Cophen and the Indus in the following order the Astaceni, the Masiani, the Nysæi, and the Hypasii then the kingdom of Assacanus, in which is Massaga, the capital of the whole country after that comes Peucelaotis, on the Indus (xv 1, § 27, p 698) Here he appears in the first instance to enumerate the tribes in the inverse order, as his Hypasii are probably the Aspasii of Arrian, and his Astaceni almost certainly the same with the Assaceni of that author, whose capital city was Massaga (Arrian, *Anab* iv 26, § 1) But Strabo supposed the two to be distinct, and separates them as widely as possible The confusion in our extant authorities is hopeless . whether it originated with them or with the contemporary writers whom they followed, we are unable to determine

But no one of these names can be associated with any of the localities known in modern times, upon any other than conjectural grounds. Even if we could follow the narrative of Arrian much more clearly than is really possible, it must be remembered that the details given by other writers are in many instances wholly at variance with it; and though the authority of Arrian is in general preferable to that of the other historians, it by no means follows that he is entitled to blind deference in regard to operations, the geography of which he certainly did not himself understand.

§ 4. From the time that Alexander crossed the Indus, his movements may be more clearly followed. His line of advance lay in the first instance through the territories of Taxiles (with whom he had already concluded a treaty) whose dominions extended as far as the river Hydaspes. His capital city of Taxila, which is described as one of the largest and wealthiest cities in India, was situated about 40 miles from the Indus, at a place called Shah Dheri, in the neighbourhood of Hassan Abdul, where very extensive ruins are still visible.[9] Alexander thence proceeded without delay to the Hydaspes (Jhelum), on the banks of which he was met by the Indian king Porus, his victory over whom was one of the most brilliant exploits of his whole career. To commemorate this great success he founded two cities: the one on the further side of the Hydaspes to which he gave the name of Nicæa; the other on the western bank of the river, which he named after his favourite charger, Bucephala.[1] But neither the site of these cities, nor the precise spot at which he crossed the Hydaspes, has as yet been determined on conclusive evidence, though it seems probable that the passage took place in the neighbourhood of Jelalpoor, about 25 miles below the modern town of Jhelum.[2]

Very much the same remark applies to the whole of the

---

[9] Note D d, p. 499.
[1] Arrian, v. 19, § 4, Strabo, xv. p 698. Diodorus (xvii 89) erroneously supposes them both to have been situated on the same side of the river.
[2] Note E c, p 499.

subsequent march through the plains of the Punjab to the banks of the Hyphasis. Its general direction is known, and we can identify without difficulty the rivers that he successively crossed—the Acesines or Chenab, and the Hydraotes or Ravee—as well as the Hyphasis, on whose banks he finally halted. This last is undoubtedly the modern Beias, Beas, or Beiah, a tributary of the Sutledge, though generally regarded by the Greeks as the main stream.[3]

§ 5. Unfortunately the point where Alexander reached the banks of this river—and where he erected twelve altars to commemorate the limit of his victorious career — cannot be regarded as determined within even approximate limits : though it appears probable that it was situated at some distance above the confluence of the two rivers, and not very far from the point where the Beas emerges from the mountain ranges that here form the underfalls of the Himalaya.[4] We learn indeed that throughout his advance Alexander kept as near as he could to the mountains; partly from the idea that he would thus find the great rivers more easily passable, as being nearer their sources; partly from an exaggerated impression of the sterile and desert character of the plains further south.[5]

§ 6. But when we endeavour to follow in detail the military operations of Alexander, we find ourselves almost entirely at a loss. It cannot be said that any of the tribes or cities mentioned by his historians in the northern part of the Punjab have as yet been identified with anything like certainty. While the general course of his march must have followed approximately the same line of route that has been frequented in all ages from the banks of the Indus to those of the Beas,

---

[3] Note F f, p 500
[4] Note G g, p. 503.
[5] Strabo, xv 1, pp 697, 700 The Dooabs, as the intermediate spaces between the rivers of the Punjab are called, really comprise a considerable extent of barren and desert country, as well as extensive tracts of dense jungle, which even at the present day are wholly uninhabited Any army moving across the direction of the great rivers must therefore in all ages have followed much the same course as that taken by Alexander

his expeditions against the various warlike tribes that refused submission to his arms led him into frequent excursions to the right and left of his main direction: and with regard to these localities we have in general no clue to guide us. The most important of these sites to determine would be that of Sangala, the capital of the Cathæans, which, according to the narrative of Arrian, was situated between the Hydraotes and the Hyphasis.[6] Hence it was placed by Burnes at Lahore, and by others at Umritsir. But on the other hand there are not wanting strong reasons for identifying Sangala with the Sakala of Indian writers, and this was certainly situated to the west of the Hydraotes, between that river and the Acesines.[7]

Equally uncertain with the position of the Cathæi is that of the kingdom of Sopeithes or Sophytes. In both cases we have indeed two different accounts which it is impossible to reconcile with one another. According to Curtius and Diodorus—who in this instance, as in so many others, are apparently following the same authority—the kingdom of Sopeithes was the last kingdom subdued by Alexander, before advancing to the banks of the Hyphasis.[8] Arrian on the contrary has no mention of Sopeithes or his kingdom during the advance of Alexander through the Punjab: but he describes the king as sending Hephæstion and Craterus with the land forces to the capital of Sopeithes, in the first instance, when he himself began the descent of the Hydaspes. Again, Strabo tells us that some writers placed the kingdom of Sopeithes, as well as the land of the Cathæi, between the Hydaspes and the Acesines, while others transferred them beyond both the Acesines and the Hydraotes.[9] It was evidently these last authorities that were followed by Curtius and Diodorus.[1] In this case it

---

[6] Arrian, *Anab.* v 22, 24 His statement is precise that it was only three days' march from the Hydraotes.
[7] Note H h, p 505
[8] Curtius, ix 5, § 24 ; Diodor. xvii. 91.
[9] Strabo, xv. 1, § 30, p. 699.

[1] The name of Sopeithes was remembered chiefly in connection with the formidable dogs that he exhibited before Alexander (Strabo, *l c.* § 31 ; Curt ix 1, § 31 ; Diodor. xvii. 92), and the district between the upper Ravee and the Beas is to this day

is difficult to avoid suspecting that there were two kings or chiefs who bore the same name, and were in consequence confounded with one another.

§ 7. When compelled by the discontent of his troops to return, instead of pushing on to the Ganges, and the populous and fertile regions on its banks—rumours of which had already reached his ears[2]—he appears to have retraced his steps by the same route as he had previously followed, as far as his newly-founded cities on the Hydaspes. Here he made a prolonged halt, while he was engaged in constructing a fleet on the river, with the view of descending, first the Hydaspes itself, and afterwards the Indus, to its mouth in the Erythræan Sea. Timber for this purpose was cut in the mountains of the Himalaya, which furnished it in abundance, and floated down the river to the spot where it was required.[3] Not less than eighty triaconters (vessels with thirty oars) were thus constructed, besides nearly two thousand boats and small vessels to serve as transports.[4] Alexander himself embarked on board the fleet, but a large portion of his army continued their march by land, one body under Craterus following the right bank of the river, another, under Hephæstion, the left.

His progress was however very slow, on account of the necessity of frequent halts to enable his land forces to keep up with the fleet. Moreover though it was perhaps his first object to descend the Indus, with a view to explore its outlet, and have the glory of navigating the Erythræan Sea—hitherto known

---

still renowned for the size and ferocity of its dogs (St Martin, *Géographie de l'Inde*, pp 108, 109) But not only is there no allusion in Arrian to this well-known anecdote, but according to his narrative it would not appear that Alexander himself ever came in contact with Sopeithes at all

[2] See especially the tales reported by Plutarch (*Alex* 62)

[3] Strabo, xv p 698 The same thing is frequently done at the present day Sir A Burnes remarks "The timber of which the boats of the Punjab are constructed is chiefly floated down by

the *Hydaspes* from the Indian Caucasus, which most satisfactorily explains the selection of its banks as the site of a naval arsenal by Alexander, in preference to the other rivers, by any of which he might have reached the Indus" (*Travels*, vol 1 p 110) The navigation of the Indus itself for a considerable part of its course below Attock is so dangerous on account of rapids, as to render it wholly unsuitable for the descent of a flotilla such as that of Alexander (Wood's *Travels*, pp 75-82)

[4] Note I 1, p. 506

to the Greeks only by hearsay—he was not disposed to be satisfied without reducing to submission all the barbarian tribes that occupied the country on each side of the Indus: and where they opposed any resistance he was always ready to lead an expedition in person against their cities. Hence the time occupied in the descent of the river was altogether out of proportion to that which would have been required by a mere exploring expedition.[5] According to the express statement of Aristobulus, Alexander set out on his voyage down the river a few days before the setting of the Pleiades—late in the autumn of B.C. 326—and the remainder of the autumn together with the whole winter and the following spring and summer— a period of about nine months—was employed in the navigation of the Indus and the military operations connected with it.[6]

§ 8. In a geographical point of view, the actual descent of the river presents few difficulties. Alexander found, in accordance with the information he had already received from the Indians of the Punjab, that the Hydaspes received the waters of the Acesines at no great distance below the point from whence he set out:[7] they were afterwards joined in succession by the Hydraotes and the Hyphasis, and their waters thus united into one main stream ultimately fell into the still greater stream of the Indus.[8] This last he descended as far as a city called Pattala, where the river divided into two main branches, forming a Delta like that of the Nile, but of still greater extent. He himself sailed down both arms in succession to the sea, and enjoyed the satisfaction of navigating the Indian Ocean. Here the unwonted phenomena of the tides— so little familiar to Mediterranean sailors—not only forced themselves on his attention, but caused considerable damage to his flotilla.[9] He had already determined to send out an

---

[5] Note K k, p 507
[6] Aristobul ap Strab xv 1, p 692.
[7] Note L l, p 508.
[8] Note M m, p 509
[9] The phenomena of the tides at the mouth of the Indus are indeed of a character to attract the attention even of more experienced navigators than those who accompanied Alexander Burnes remarks "The tides rise in

exploring expedition to trace the coast of the Ocean from the mouth of the Indus to the Persian Gulf, but the command of this he reserved for Nearchus, and meanwhile he himself returned to Pattala.

§ 9. This descent of the Indus by Alexander may be considered as constituting a kind of era in the geographical knowledge of the Greeks.[1] It does not appear that it was ever repeated: and while subsequent researches added materially to the knowledge possessed by the Greeks of the valley of the Ganges and the more easterly provinces of India, their information concerning the great river Indus and the regions through which it flows, continued to be derived almost exclusively from the voyage of Alexander and the accounts transmitted by his contemporary historians.[2] The magnitude of the stream itself appears to have excited their wonder and admiration, and if their statements on the subject appear tinged with exaggeration, it must be remembered that their voyage down the lower part of its course took place during the season of the inundation, where the waters spread far and wide over the surrounding plains, at the same time that the current is most rapid and violent.[3] The statement that it was 100 stadia (10 G. miles) in width *at such a season* would not exceed the truth, though it was of course not so understood by the Greek writers.[4] But when they speak of it as 40 stadia in its *average* width, and not less than fifteen where it was narrowest,[5] this is of course a great exaggeration.[6] It must be

the mouths of the Indus about nine feet at full moon, and flow and ebb with great violence, particularly near the sea, where they flood and abandon the banks with equal and incredible velocity It is dangerous to drop the anchor unless at low water, as the channel is frequently obscured, and the vessel may be left dry" (*Travels*, vol 1. p 217, *Journal of Geographical Society*, vol iii p 120)

[1] Note N n, p 509
[2] Though it appears certain that some of the Greek sovereigns of Bactria and the Paropamisan regions extended their dominions for a time over the valley of the Indus, as well as the Punjab, no trace is to be found in any of the later Greek writers of additional information derived from this source.
[3] Wood's *Journey to the Oxus*, p 43
[4] Strabo, xv 1, § 32, p 700. Other writers however, as he observes, diminished this statement to 50 at the widest part, and only seven at the narrowest.
[5] Arrian, *Anab* v 20, § 9.
[6] Note O o, p. 510.

remembered, however, that the Greeks did not navigate the Indus itself in the upper part of its course from Attock to Kalabagh—where the river is confined between high banks and flows with a very deep and rapid stream, but is of comparatively little width.[7]

All writers agreed in placing the sources of the Indus in the mountains to which they gave the name of Emodus or Emodes —a native appellation by which they here designated the Himalayas, but they justly regarded these as being only a part, or rather a continuation, of the same range with the Paropamisus or Indian Caucasus. They appear to have supposed the sources to have been not very remote from the point where the Indus issued from the mountains, at the gorge of Derbend (about 60 miles above Attock) where it first became known to them. Of its real origin in the remote valleys of Thibet they had of course no idea. It is indeed only in comparatively recent times that the physical geography of these regions has become known to Europeans.[8]

§ 10. Of the general character of the Delta of the Indus they obtained an accurate knowledge : and their descriptions of this part of the country are sufficiently characteristic. But here we are met by a serious geographical difficulty, in attempting to determine the position of Pattala, which was situated (by the general consent of all geographers) just at the point where the two principal arms separated to enclose the Delta. No distances are given in the descent of the river, and the only further clue to its position is that afforded by the vague statement, that the Delta itself was not less than that of Egypt. Onesicritus alone—the least trustworthy of all writers on the subject—reported the two arms of the Delta to be each 2000 stadia in length, from Pattala to the sea.[9] At the present day the principal bifurcation of the river takes place at Tatta, which in consequence is a place of importance, and carries on

---

[7] Wood, p 75-82.   [8] Note P p, p 511
[9] Onesicrit. ap. Strab xv p 701

a considerable trade. This position, as well as a certain resemblance of name, naturally led to the identification of Tatta with Pattala, and this view was adopted by all the earlier writers—D'Anville, Robertson, Rennell, and Dr. Vincent—as well as by Sir A. Burnes, the first explorer of the Indus in modern times. But Tatta is only about 60 miles from the sea, and any comparison of the Delta here formed with that of Egypt would be utterly preposterous.[1] It is moreover certain that this part of the course of the river has in all ages been subject to frequent changes: fresh channels have been formed, and old ones dried up, and it therefore must not be hastily assumed that the apex of the Delta is now the same as in ancient times. On the other hand a marked bifurcation of the river takes place just above Hyderabad (50 miles above Tatta), where an eastern arm branches off, which at the present day flows into the Runn of Cutch, and enters the sea by the estuary of Koree between Cutch and the plains of Sinde. This branch of the river (known as the Fulaili) has even now a great volume of water during the inundation, though it is dry for the greater part of the year. It is not at all improbable that this eastern branch of the Indus may in the time of Alexander have been as important as the western one, and may therefore be the arm that was considered as constituting the Delta, which would on this supposition but slightly exceed that of Egypt, and might therefore be aptly compared with it. In this case Pattala must have been situated at, or in the immediate neighbourhood of Hyderabad.[2]

§ 11. But while the accounts transmitted to us by the Greeks of the Indus and its tributaries are found to coincide so well with the modern geography of these regions, we have nearly the same difficulty as in the more northern parts of the Punjab in identifying the various tribes and nations with which Alexander came in contact in his descent of the Hydaspes, the Acesines, and the Indus. The Malli, a powerful and warlike

---

[1] Note Q q, p. 512.   [2] Note R r, p 513

tribe, possessing several strong cities, which were successively reduced by Alexander, are generally considered to be the people of Mooltan, the name of which city was formerly written "Malli-than" or "Malli tharun," and it may be admitted as probable that the two names are really connected.

The Malli seem to have occupied the country near the junction of the Hydraotes and Acesines, extending also across to the southern bank of the former river; their territory therefore in all probability included the site of the modern city of Mooltan. This has been identified by several writers with the capital or chief city of the Malli in the time of Alexander: but it is difficult to reconcile this with the account of his campaign as given by Arrian.[3]

The next people with whom Alexander came in contact were the Oxydracæ, described as being also a warlike and numerous nation, who made common cause with the Malli, and submitted together with them to Alexander, when he halted at the confluence of the Hydraotes and Acesines. It has been thought that a trace of their name may be found in that of Ooch, a city situated just below the junction of the Sutledge with the Chenab. Very little reliance can be placed on this etymology; but the position thus suggested would accord well with the narrative of Arrian, and on the whole it seems not improbable that the Oxydracæ may have occupied the district of Ooch, together with the adjoining province of Bahawulpoor.[4]

In descending the Indus itself from the point where it receives the combined waters of "the five rivers" to Pattala, at the head of its Delta, Alexander encountered, first, a people called the Sogdi, then two nations in succession, who are distinguished only by the names of their kings, Musicanus and Oxycanus, and lastly, a chieftain named Sambus, who ruled over a tribe of mountaineers, which must have been situated to the west of the Indus. But the various attempts that have been made to fix with any precision the position or limits of

---

[3] Note S s, p 514 [4] Note T t, p. 515.

these different tribes cannot be said to have arrived at any satisfactory result.[5] We find indeed a strong confirmation of the accuracy of the information transmitted by the Greeks, in the circumstance that the names of all, or almost all, the tribes thus mentioned by them, can be recognized under their native forms in the Sanscrit literature still extant.[6] Unfortunately we derive from these sources the *names* only, which are not mentioned in a manner to throw any additional light upon their geographical relations.

§ 12. One thing is clear, that Alexander himself was so far from looking upon his voyage down the Indus as a mere transient expedition for the purpose of discovery, rather than of conquest, that he was on the contrary careful to fortify his newly acquired dominions, by the establishment, from distance to distance, of permanent camps or stations, termed by his historians " cities," which were intended to hold the neighbouring tribes in check, as well as doubtless to operate indirectly as centres of commerce and civilization. Thus we are distinctly told that he left Philip as satrap of the country from the Acesines to the Indus, with orders to found a city at the confluence of the two rivers, and to construct naval docks there, judging the site likely to become that of a flourishing and important place.[7] Similar establishments were founded also at Pattala, as well as on the eastern arm of the Indus, where it spread into a lake near its mouth.[8] Unfortunately all these attempts at colonization were destined to prove abortive, and all trace of Greek civilization soon disappeared from the banks of the Indus.

§ 13. The accounts transmitted by the Greek historians of the wealth and populousness of the provinces of India, which were traversed by Alexander and temporarily annexed to his

---

[5] Note U u, p 516
[6] See the discussion of these tribes by M de St Martin (*Géogr. de l'Inde*, pp 116-122) and by General Cunningham (*Ancient Geography of India*, pp 215-248).

[7] Arrian, *Anab* vi 15, § 2
A strong fortress was also erected by Craterus in the capital city of Musicanus. Ibid § 7
[8] Id 20, § 5

dominions, are very remarkable. With every allowance for exaggeration—and there can be no doubt that they were in most instances derived from native information, and deeply tinged with Oriental exaggeration—they are still calculated to give us a high opinion of the flourishing condition of the countries in question, at this early period, and of their comparative advance in civilization. The Punjab is indeed one of the richest provinces in India, and though the desert tracts border closely on the Indus in the lower part of its course, there is still found throughout a belt of rich and fertile character, abounding in villages and towns. But when the Greek writers tell us that the district between the Hydaspes and the Hyphasis alone contained five thousand cities (!), none of which was less than that of Cos;[9] and that the dominions of Porus, which were confined between the Hydaspes and the Acesines—a tract not more than forty miles in width—contained three hundred cities,[1] it is evident that they were misled by the exaggerated reports so common with all Orientals, and which were greedily swallowed by the historians of Alexander, with a view of magnifying the exploits of the great conqueror.[2]

It is remarkable that while the Greek writers descant so fully upon the material wealth and prosperity of the part of India that had thus become known to them, they all agreed in the admission that no considerable part of this wealth was derived from gold. We have seen that according to Herodotus, the tribute of India was in his time paid to Persia in gold, an exception which he himself explains on the ground that gold was the especial product of that country. Nor can it be doubted that this was the prevailing idea among the

---

[9] Strabo, xv p 686
[1] Id xv p. 698
[2] Similar exaggerations are commonly found in Oriental writers of all ages. Thus Ferishta, the Mahommedan historian of India, gravely states that a queen of Guzrat (a part of Orissa) had a territory of 300 miles in length by 100 in breadth, in which were 70,000 (!) towns and villages, all well inhabited This would give, as Dr. Vincent remarks, one town and a village (or at least two villages) *for every square mile*, with 10,000 to spare! Dow's *Hindoostan*, cited by Vincent, p 83, note

Greeks: and was probably one of the inducements which led Alexander to undertake its conquest. But the testimony of Arrian is precise, that so far as the Macedonians actually penetrated, they found no gold in India.[3] The statement is the more remarkable, as gold is really found, though in comparatively small quantities, both in the Indus and Cabul rivers, and more abundantly in some of the smaller streams. It is procured by the natives by washing the sand of the rivers, especially after the annual swell has subsided.[4]

SECTION III.—*Return to Babylon.*

§ 1. When Alexander at length set out on his return westward, he divided his forces into three portions, which were destined to pursue different routes. While he himself with the main body of his army followed the direct route by land through Gedrosia and Carmania into Persia, he detached a large force under Craterus, with orders to proceed through Arachosia and Drangiana into Carmania, where it was to rejoin the main army. Meanwhile Nearchus was to conduct the fleet along the coasts of Gedrosia and Carmania into the Persian Gulf, an enterprise which was looked upon as far more perilous and adventurous than either of the land marches, on account of the unknown dangers of the Indian Ocean.

But the difficulties with which Alexander had to contend were of no ordinary description. Starting from Pattala, his march lay in the first instance through the land of the Arabies or Arabitæ,[5] which was reduced to submission without diffi-

---

[3] *Anab* v 4, § 4.
[4] Burnes's *Travels*, vol ii p 69 In the Ayeen Akbaree also it is mentioned that several of the streams that form the head of the Indus yield gold dust (Rennell, *Geogr of Herodot* p 305)
[5] The account of Alexander's march is too concise to indicate precisely the route followed, but if Pattala be placed at Hyderabad, he would seem to have taken a course nearly due west from thence to the mouth of the Arabis at Somneanee The range of mountains which here separates the two valleys is of comparatively small altitude, and is at the present day crossed by a frequented line of route from the valley of the Indus to Somneanee.

culty. These Arabitæ were an Indian tribe, having no connection with the Arabians, of whom their name naturally reminds us: they extended as far as the river Arabis (now called the Poorally), which formed the limit between them and the Oritæ. Alexander next traversed the country of these last, and occupied their villages in succession: one of these, named by Arrian Rhambacia, was selected on account of its favourable situation to be the site of a new settlement, which was designed to be the capital of a satrapy. Leonnatus was left behind with a part of the forces to superintend this establishment, and to await the arrival of Nearchus: meanwhile Alexander himself, after forcing the mountain passes that separated the Oritæ from Gedrosia, entered on the latter province. It was here that a long and toilsome march awaited him: the barren and desolate nature of the country to be traversed presenting difficulties far more serious than any to be apprehended from active opposition. We hear indeed nothing of any annoyance from hostile attacks, but the route lay through a desert tract, almost wholly destitute of water, and furnishing neither food for man nor forage for cattle.

§ 2. We are told that Alexander was induced to take this route from a vain desire to show his superiority to former conquerors: it being reported by tradition that Semiramis and Cyrus had lost their whole armies in traversing these dreary regions.[6] It is impossible to believe that the king was actuated by any such idle vanity: a more rational motive was supplied by his desire to keep near enough to the sea-coast to lend a hand from time to time to Nearchus and the fleet, for the safety of which he seems to have been nervously anxious. With this view he never deviated into the interior more than about 60 miles (500 stadia) from the coast, and by so doing had to traverse a sterile and desert region for a space of not less than sixty days' march.[7] This maritime region of Beloo-

---

[6] Arrian, *Anab.* vi. 24, Strabo, xv. 2, p. 686, 722.

[7] Arrian, *l. c* ; Strabo, *ib.* p. 723. See Note V v, p. 518.

chistan, now called the Mekran, is still but imperfectly known, and has only been partially explored in very recent times: but the information obtained concerning it seems in great measure to confirm the accounts transmitted to us by the historians of Alexander.[8] The sufferings endured by his army on this occasion from heat, thirst, and hunger, notwithstanding the efforts made by the king to remedy these evils by digging wells, and collecting supplies from the neighbouring districts,—appear to have far exceeded those encountered on the march to the temple of Ammon, or in any other part of his Asiatic campaigns. Great part of the camels and beasts of burthen perished by the way, and the loss of men was unquestionably great, though no estimate of its amount has been recorded.[9] But Alexander succeeded, notwithstanding all disasters, in bringing the bulk of his army in safety to a city called Pura, which is styled the metropolis of the Gedrosians, and was situated in a comparatively fertile region. Here he halted some time to refresh his troops, and then continued his march into Carmania, where his progress was attended with no further difficulties.[1]

§ 3. That province is described by ancient writers as a region of great fertility,[2] and the march of Alexander through it is represented as assuming the character of a festive procession rather than the ordinary movement of a military force. The contrast with the hardships so lately encountered in traversing the dreary deserts of Gedrosia must doubtless have contributed much to this impression. Other circumstances combined to render the passage through Carmania a period of rejoicing both to the army and its leader. While he was encamped at a distance of five days' journey from the sea, Alexander was agreeably surprised by the appearance of Nearchus in person, with the tidings of the safe arrival of the

---

[8] Note X x, p. 519.
[9] Arrian has no statement of numbers The assertion of Plutarch (*Alex* c 66), that he lost more than three-fourths of his whole army is doubtless a mere rhetorical flourish
[1] Arrian, *Anab* vi 22–26; Strabo, xv. 2, §§ 5–7
[2] See Note X x, p. 521.

fleet at the entrance of the Persian Gulf. About the same time also Craterus made his appearance, bringing with him the important division of the army entrusted to his charge, which he had conducted in safety through the provinces of Arachosia and Drangiana, and from thence into Carmania. It is remarkable that we hear nothing of any difficulties encountered on this long and circuitous march, though in addition to hostilities with the wild mountain tribes, he must have traversed a considerable part of the desert tract between Drangiana (Seistan) and the central districts of Carmania, a region at least as formidable to an army as the wastes of Gedrosia.[3] But the perils and hardships which were encountered by the king in person naturally threw into the shade those that had been overcome by his lieutenant.

To the voyage of Nearchus we shall recur hereafter. He was now sent back to his ships, loaded with praises and honours, with orders to conduct the fleet up the Persian Gulf to the mouth of the Tigris. The main body of the army was placed under the command of Hephæstion, with orders to conduct it through the maritime districts of Carmania and Persia to Susa:[4] while Alexander himself, with a light detachment of horse and foot, proceeded direct through the mountains to Pasargada and Persepolis. From thence, after a brief halt, he descended to Susa, where he was soon after rejoined by Nearchus also.

§ 4. The return of Alexander to Susa (in February B.C. 324) may be considered as marking the termination of his great eastern expedition. The few remaining events of his life have comparatively little interest in a geographical point of view. He appears to have followed the example of the Persian kings, his predecessors : and after spending the remaining part of the winter and spring at Susa, to have removed to Ecbatana for the summer : the elevated position of that city rendering it an

---

[3] Note Y y, p 521.
[4] This route is clearly the same as that now known as the lower or Ghe-rmsir road. (See Abbott, in *Geographical Journal*, vol xxv. p. 57)

eligible residence during the summer heats. At the same time he took the opportunity to explore in person the rivers of Susiana, and while he sent the main body of his army by land under the command of Hephæstion, he himself embarked on board the fleet and descended the river Eulæus to the Persian Gulf,[5] which he navigated as far as the mouth of the Tigris, and then ascended that river to the city of Opis,[6] where he rejoined the army under Hephæstion. It was at Opis that a memorable mutiny broke out among his soldiers, which led to the determination to send home a large portion of his Greek and Macedonian veterans under the command of Craterus.

Alexander's stay at Ecbatana was marked by the death of his friend Hephæstion. When the first extravagant outbreak of grief for his loss had in some degree subsided, the king was led, apparently by the mere craving for excitement, to conduct in person an expedition against the Cossæans, a predatory tribe of mountaineers, who appear to have occupied the wild mountain region on the borders of Media and Susiana, where they adjoined the Uxians, a people of similar habits and probably of kindred race.[7] The broad belt of rugged mountains, collectively known to later geographers as Mt. Zagrus, which extends from the confines of Armenia to the shores of the Persian Gulf, and forms at the present day the boundary between the empires of Turkey and Persia, has indeed in all ages been occupied by a number of wild tribes, who have maintained a practical independence in their mountain fastnesses, though compelled from time to time to a nominal sub-

---

[5] The relations of the river Eulæus with the Pasitigris and the other rivers of Susiana will be considered in a subsequent chapter.

[6] We have already seen (Chapter X Note M, p. 373) that the position of Opis cannot be determined with certainty. Though it appears at this time, as well as during the Anabasis of Xenophon, to have been a place of importance, it had sunk in the time of Strabo into a mere village (Strab xvi. p. 739). The rapid decline of the cities in this part of Asia has been already adverted to See Chap X. Note K.

[7] The Cossæans had never been permanently subdued by the Persians. The Great King was contented to pay them a sum of money, whenever he had occasion to pass through their territory on his way from Ecbatana to Babylon (Strab xv p 524) This was doubtless one of the causes, as in the similar case of the Uxians, that led Alexander to undertake their subjugation.

mission. On the present occasion we are told that the whole nation of the Cossæans was put to the sword,[8] notwithstanding which their name reappears in history shortly afterwards, as occupying the same abodes and exercising the same predatory habits.[9]

§ 5. It was during his stay at Ecbatana also that Alexander sent down an officer of the name of Heraclides into Hyrcania (Mazanderan) with orders to cut timber and construct ships for the navigation of the Caspian Sea. It was his intention to send a fleet to explore the shores of the Caspian, in the same manner as Nearchus had done those of the Persian Gulf and the Erythræan Sea, with the view of determining (we are told) whether it communicated with the Euxine, or was only a Gulf of the Indian Ocean.[1] These are the expressions of Arrian, which are doubtless taken from his original authorities. The sound view, held long before by Herodotus, that the Caspian Sea was wholly unconnected with any other, appears at this time to have been generally abandoned.

§ 6. In the spring of B.C. 323 Alexander returned to Babylon, which he appears to have designed to make the capital of his vast empire. On his way thither he was met by a number of embassies from various nations, with some of whom he had previously had no communication. It is probable that not only had the fame of his great exploits and conquests in Asia spread itself throughout the inhabited world; but that some rumours of the vast projects he was supposed to entertain of future conquests towards the West, as extensive as those he had already achieved in the East, had reached the nations with whom he might thus be brought in contact. It is remarkable indeed that almost all the legations mentioned by Arrian, as presenting themselves on this occasion, may be supposed to have been actuated by this motive, and were no doubt designed, not merely to congratulate the conqueror of Asia, but to pro-

---

[8] Arrian, *Anab.* vii 15; Diodor. xvii. 111; Plut. *Alex.* 72.
[9] Diodor. xix. 19.
[1] Arrian, *Anab.* vii. 16, § 2.

pitiate or conciliate the intending conqueror of Africa and Europe. Thus we find enumerated: the Libyans, meaning doubtless the tribes who bordered on the Cyrenaica; the Ethiopians, from beyond the confines of Egypt to the south; and the Scythians, from beyond the Euxine to the north. Among the nations on the Mediterranean Sea, we find mention, not only of the Carthaginians, and of the nations of Southern Italy, the Bruttians and Lucanians, then rising to importance as the Greek cities in that quarter declined, but of the Tyrrhenians also, and even of the still more distant Gauls (Keltæ) and Iberians. In several cases, we are assured that it was for the first time that individuals of these strange races had been beheld either by Greeks or Macedonians.[2]

It would be still more interesting if we could believe the statement found in some of the historians of Alexander that among the deputations which presented themselves on this occasion was one from the rising republic of Rome. Unfortunately the authority for this fact is not such as we can rely on with confidence, though it cannot be dismissed without hesitation as the fiction of a later time. It is reported by Pliny, on the authority of Clitarchus, a contemporary of Alexander,[3] but undoubtedly one of those writers to whom we are indebted for many of the marvellous and exaggerated stories with which his history has been disfigured. In this instance, however, it is not easy to see what motive he could have had, at so early a period, for the interpolation of a circumstance of which he could hardly have foreseen the importance.[4]

§ 7. There can be little doubt that Alexander at this time really entertained projects, however vague, of extensive conquests towards the west, and of extending the confines of his empire both in Europe and Africa. But the design upon which he was more immediately bent, was the circumnavigation

---

[2] Arrian, vii. 15; Diodor xvii 113.   [3] *Hist. Nat* iii 5, § 57.
[4] Note Z z, p 522

and conquest of Arabia, a vast country, of which little, if anything, more was known than in the days of Herodotus. With a view to this great enterprise he had already, before his journey into Media, given orders for the construction in the ports of Phœnicia, of numerous vessels, some of them of large size, which were then to be taken to pieces, and transported overland to the Euphrates, down which river they were afterwards floated to Babylon.[5] No less than forty-seven ships were actually conveyed overland in this manner to Babylon: of these two were quinqueremes, or ships with five banks of oars, three of four banks, and twelve triremes, the remaining thirty being smaller vessels, of only thirty oars each.[6] On his return to Babylon Alexander found there all these ships in a state of readiness, in addition to the fleet that had been previously under the command of Nearchus. But not content with this, he set to work to construct additional vessels of cypress wood, the only timber to be found in Babylonia; and began the excavation of a gigantic dock, designed to be capable of containing a thousand ships of war.[7]

Meanwhile, with that providence which characterizes almost all his enterprises, notwithstanding the charge of hasty rashness so frequently brought against him, he had taken advantage of the interval of delay during the construction of his fleet, to send out several officers, with light vessels of thirty oars, to explore the western shores of the Persian Gulf, and prepare the way for the more important expedition. One of these, Archias, proceeded as far as the island of Tylos, which was described as large and tolerably fertile, circumstances which render it certain that it must have been the island now known as that of Bahrein.[8] A second explorer, of the name of An-

---

[5] When we consider the amount of time and labour that it cost Colonel Chesney to transport his two small steamers in the same manner from Seleucia to the Euphrates, we are struck with wonder at the magnitude of the task thus successfully accomplished by the officers of Alexander But the secret of its success no doubt lay mainly in the unlimited command of labour which he possessed
[6] Arrian, *Anab.* vii 19
[7] Id. *ibid.*
[8] The island of Bahrein is now the centre of the pearl fishery in the Persian Gulf It is remarkable that

drosthenes, a native of Thasos, advanced somewhat farther and traced for some extent the coast of the Arabian peninsula.⁹ A third, named Hieron, a native of Soli in Cilicia, proceeded the farthest of all ; yet it is doubtful whether he actually doubled the promontory of Maceta or Macæ, at the entrance of the Persian Gulf, which had been already seen by Nearchus in his voyage along the opposite coast. He had been expressly charged by Alexander to circumnavigate the whole peninsula, to Heroopolis at the head of the Red Sea : but was deterred by the length of the voyage, and the barrenness of the coasts as he advanced. How far he really proceeded, we do not know : but he reported to Alexander on his return that Arabia was not inferior in extent to India.¹

The reports of these navigators were certainly not of an encouraging kind. Yet there is no doubt that the king not only adhered to his determination to send Nearchus with the fleet to undertake the circumnavigation of Arabia, but was himself prepared to set out with the army by land : an enterprise that could hardly have ended in anything but disastrous failure. His preparations were indeed completed, the fare-

---

no mention is found of this in respect to the island in question, though the existence of pearls in large numbers and of great value was noticed by Nearchus, at an island near the entrance of the Persian Gulf. Pliny is the first writer that distinctly speaks of the pearl fishery at Tylos, which he terms "insula plurimis margaritis celeberrima" (*Hist. Nat* vi 28, § 148). At the present day the pearls of the east coast are considered very inferior to those of Bahrein.

⁹ This is all that we are told by Arrian concerning Androsthenes, but his voyage is mentioned also by Strabo (xvi 3, § 2), and some particulars concerning the west coast of the Persian Gulf are cited from him by Eratosthenes. He visited the city of Gerrha, which became at a later period the chief emporium of all the trade of Arabia on this side. He described the islands of Tylos (or, as he wrote the name, Tyros) and Aradus, as ten days' sail from Teredon at the mouth of the Euphrates, and only one from the promontory of Macæ This last is an entire mistake, and probably arose from a confusion between Cape Rekkan, a projecting headland near the islands, with the more distant and more important headland of Cape Mussendom On the other hand Archias erroneously reported Tylos to be only one day and night's voyage from the mouth of the Euphrates (Arrian, *l c* § 6), an equally great error in the opposite direction.

¹ Arrian, *Anab* vii 20, §§ 7–10. Arrian here gives us no distinct intimation of how far Hieron had been able to advance, but he elsewhere (*Indica*, c 43) tells us that none of these navigators were able to double the headland of Macæ

well banquet given to Nearchus and his officers, and orders actually issued for the days of departure both of the fleet and army, when Alexander was arrested by the fatal fever, which resulted in his death, after an illness of only ten days (June, B.C. 323).

§ 8. His last employment previous to his illness had been that of descending the Euphrates, in order to visit an artificial cut or canal, named Pallacopas, designed apparently to carry off the surplus waters of that river during the time of inundation. Alexander was deeply interested in everything connected with the navigation of the Euphrates and the Tigris, and he now, after carefully inspecting the localities, gave orders for the construction of a new cut in a more advantageous situation.[2] At the same time he selected a site, which, though in the midst of the marshes of Lower Babylonia, appeared to him a favourable position for a city, and gave orders for the establishment of a colony upon the spot.

Of the vague projects attributed to Alexander had he survived, it is unnecessary here to speak: and Arrian justly observes that it is impossible to say what those projects may have really been. But the design ascribed to him of following up the circumnavigation of Arabia by that of Ethiopia and Libya, so as to return by the straits of Gades into the Mediterranean Sea,[3] is interesting at least as showing how deeply rooted was the conviction that Africa *could* be circumnavigated, and was only, like Arabia, a vast peninsula.

§ 9. Before quitting the subject of the geographical questions connected with the proceedings of Alexander in the East, it is necessary briefly to advert to the numerous cities founded by him in different parts of his dominions, many of which continued through long centuries and under successive dynasties to bear testimony to the foresight which dictated the original choice of the sites. It is indeed not always possible

---

[2] Arrian, *Anab* vii 21 See Note A A, p 524.
[3] Id. *ib.* vii 1, Plut *Alex.* c 68.

to determine whether these cities were actually founded by the conqueror himself, or dedicated to his memory by his successors, as we know to have been the case in some instances. But it is probable that the great majority of them owed their existence to Alexander himself. Besides the famous city of Alexandria in Lower Egypt—one of the few cities in the world that have retained their prosperity almost unbroken for more than two thousand years—there are not less than seventeen other cities of the same name which are known to us from ancient writers. Of these the most important are: 1. Alexandria ad Issum, on the east coast of the Gulf of Issus, founded to commemorate the great victory of Alexander over Darius: it is still called Iskenderun or Scanderoon, but is also known by the Italian name of Alexandretta. 2. Alexandria Troas, situated, as its name implies, in the Troad, on the shore of the Hellespont, a foundation in the first instance of Antigonus, but to which the name of Alexandria was given by Lysimachus. It became a Roman colony, and rose to be a city of great importance under the Roman Empire. 3. In Aria, probably occupying the site of the ancient capital of Artacoana, and of the modern Herat. 4. In Arachosia, apparently on the site of the modern Candahar.[4] 5. Alexandria ad Caucasum, called also Alexandria Opiane, situated at the very foot of the Paropamisus or Hindoo Koosh, known to the Greeks by the name of the Indian Caucasus. This continued for more than two centuries to be the centre of Greek civilization in these remote and mountainous regions.[5] 6. Alexandria Eschate or Ultima, founded by Alexander himself on the banks of the Iaxartes, to mark the farthest limit of his conquests in that direction. It was probably in the neighbourhood of Khojend.[6] Two other cities of the same name are mentioned by Stephanus of Byzantium in the same part of Asia; one in

---

[4] Ammianus Marcellinus, XXIII 6, § 72
[5] Concerning its precise site, see Note X, p 490
[6] Arrian, *Anab* IV. 1, § 3, Ptol VI. 12, § 6, Curt. VII. 6, § 24 Its exact site has not been determined See above, p. 430

Bactria and one in Sogdiana: besides which there was an Alexandria in Margiana, subsequently called Antiochia.[7] He is moreover stated to have founded two cities of the same name in India, besides those of Bucephala and Nicæa on the Hydaspes: and it has been already noticed that on his return march he left Leonnatus among the Oritæ to establish a new settlement, the name of which is not mentioned.[8]

His example in this respect was speedily followed by his successors, the kings of Syria and Egypt: and we find at a later period not less than ten cities in different parts of Asia bearing the name of Antiochia, six that of Seleucia, six others that of Apamea, after the wife of Seleucus Nicator; and six that of Laodicea, from different Syrian princesses of the name of Laodice. In like manner under the rule of the Ptolemies, the eastern and northern coasts of Africa became studded with settlements of the name of Ptolemaïs, Arsinoe, and Berenice, to many of which we shall have occasion to advert hereafter.

---

[7] It is almost certain that Alexander did not himself visit Margiana (see above, p 432), but he may well have founded a city in that remarkable oasis, during his prolonged stay in the neighbouring Bactria. Strabo indeed represents it as first founded by Antiochus Soter (xi 10, p 516); but Pliny distinctly tells us that it was first founded by Alexander, and again a second time by Antiochus (Plin. *H N* vi 16). Dr C. Muller, in the map of Alexander's campaigns in Dr. Smith's Atlas, represents this Alexandria as situated in the valley of the Murghab, at the point from whence Alexander turned off abruptly to Herat But the expressions of Strabo seem to me clearly to point to a site in the oasis of Merv, the fertility of which he extols in the highest terms.

[8] It is probable that this speedily disappeared, as did those in India itself Of the other cities of the name mentioned by Stephanus of Byzantium (v. 'Αλεξάνδρεια) we know nothing, and his notices are too brief to be relied on alone There is certainly considerable confusion in the article in its present state, and we have greatly to regret in this instance, as in so many others, that we do not possess it in its original form, instead of the meagre epitome, which is all that remains to us. Ptolemy has the names of eight cities of the name of Alexandria as existing in his time, among which is one in Carmania, not mentioned by Stephanus, (vi. 8, § 14)

NOTE A, p. 412.

GORDIUM.

The position of Gordium, notwithstanding the celebrity it derived on this occasion from the well-known story of the Gordian knot, which is related by all the historians of Alexander, is not definitely ascertained. Though the tradition referred to shews that it was supposed to have been once the capital of Phrygia, and it was apparently still a place of some importance in the time of Alexander, as it was chosen by him for his head-quarters during a considerable period, it speedily declined under his successors. Polybius terms it a small town (πολισμάτιον, xxiv. 20); and in Strabo's time it had sunk into a mere village (Strab. xii. 5, p. 568). But Livy, who undoubtedly copies Polybius, says that it was a place of great trade and commercial intercourse, on account of its position, at about the same distance from the three seas, and on the frontiers of several great nations (Liv. xxxviii. 18). This would sufficiently account for its being selected by Alexander as the place where he waited for his junction with Parmenio.

Quintus Curtius also says (iii. 1, § 12) that it was equidistant from the two seas, the Euxine and the Cilician; and though this is in any case erroneous, it would certainly seem to indicate a central position, such as that described by Livy. Most modern geographers have notwithstanding identified Gordium with a place called Gordiu Come, which was afterwards named Juliopolis and became a town of importance under the Roman Empire (Plin. v. 32, § 143, *Itin. Hier.* p. 574). But Juliopolis unquestionably lay within the confines of Bithynia, on the river Scopas, a small stream flowing into the Sangarius, while both Arrian and Q. Curtius describe Gordium as situated *on* the Sangarius. Nor can Juliopolis be said to occupy in any sense a central position. Hence Dr. Mordtmann has supposed it to have been situated in the upper valley of the Sangarius, a few miles west of Sivri Hissar, and this view is adopted by M. Perrot in the *Exploration Archéologique en Galatie et Bithynie* (fol. Paris, 1872, p. 155). But its ruins have not yet been identified, and hence the point must be regarded as still uncertain.

NOTE B, p. 413.

THE PYLÆ CILICIÆ.

"Alexander fauces jugi, quæ Pylæ appellantur, intravit. Contemplatus locorum situm, non alias magis dicitur admiratus esse felicitatem suam obrui potuisse vel saxis confitebatur, si fuissent qui in subeuntes propellerent." (Quint. Curt. III. 4, § 11.) The natural difficulties and peculiarities of the pass are described by that author with unusual fulness and accuracy. Compare the remarks of Xenophon (*Anab.* i. 2, § 21). The observations of modern travellers fully confirm the accounts of ancient writers as to the difficulties of this celebrated pass (see the passages already referred to in Chap. X. p. 346 *note*; and especially the remarks of Mr. Kinneir, pp. 115–120); and it is impossible not to wonder at the supine stupidity of the Persian commanders, who on the one occasion left it undefended, on the other, abandoned it without striking a blow, on the first appearance of Alexander himself at the head of his light-armed troops. (Arrian, *Anab.* ii. 4, § 4; Quint. Curt. III. 4, §§ 11–13.)

NOTE C, p. 414.

MOUNTAIN PASSES NEAR ISSUS.

The topography of the passes leading from Cilicia into Syria, and the movements of the Greek and Persian armies in connexion with them, before the decisive battle of Issus, were imperfectly understood by earlier writers in modern times, from the want of accurate knowledge of the localities. Considerable confusion has been also caused by the expressions of ancient writers, who have sometimes used the term "pylæ" to denote narrow defiles of very small extent, which were really closed by gates, at others have applied the same term to mountain passes of considerable importance and strength, with no such artificial defences. Such were the Cilician gates described in the preceding note; and the Syrian Gates (Pylæ Syriæ), which led directly from Myriandrus into the interior towards the Euphrates, and which certainly correspond to the modern Pass of Beilan. Xenophon on the contrary, as we have seen, gives the name of Cilician and Syrian gates to two actual fortified gates between Issus and Myriandrus, which in his time formed the frontiers of the two countries. (Xenophon, *Anab*. i. 4, § 4. See Chapter X. Note E, p. 364.)

Another source of confusion arose from the circumstance that *both* the mountain chains which descend from the great range of Mount Taurus to the sea, on each side of the Gulf of Issus or Scanderoon, were known to ancient writers as Mount Amanus. Hence Strabo (xiv. 5, p. 676) gives the name of the Amanian Gates ('Ἀμανίδες πύλαι) to a pass on the *west* side of the Gulf of Issus, where there appears to have been a small fort and an actual gateway; while Arrian certainly applies the term (τὰς πύλας τὰς Ἀμανικὰς καλουμένας, ii. 7. 1) to a pass across the mountain ridge which formed the *eastern* branch of Mount Amanus.

Bearing in mind these considerations, and with the more accurate knowledge of the localities, resulting from the observations of Colonel Chesney and others, the account given by Arrian becomes clearly intelligible. Alexander advanced from Mallus, where he had halted, on hearing that Darius was encamped with his whole army at Sochi, a place which cannot be identified, but was clearly situated in the great Syrian plain east of the Amanus (Arrian, ii. 6, § 3). He passed through the narrow defiles along the coast without difficulty, having previously sent Parmenio to occupy them (ii. 5, § 1), and thus encountered no obstacle in passing the gates which separated Cilicia from Syria—obviously the same described by Xenophon. But when he had arrived at Myriandrus, at the foot of the Beilan Pass, he learned that Darius, instead of awaiting his attack in the plains of Syria, had crossed the mountain (the eastern ridge of Mount Amanus) and descended upon Issus, where he found himself unawares in the rear of the Macedonian army. Alexander immediately turned back to engage him, reoccupied the passage of the gates without opposition, and the battle was fought on the river Pinarus, a few miles to the south of the town of Issus, from which it derived its name (Arrian, ii. 8; Strabo, *l. c.*). The Pinarus may be safely identified with the stream now called the Deli-tchai; and the pass called by Arrian the Amanian Gates, by which Darius crossed the mountains, is one that leads directly across the range to the head-waters of this stream, and descends its valley to a place now called Bayas.

The difficulties that remain in regard to the topography of the Gulf of Issus have reference to the position of the various towns on its shores, a subject that has been much complicated by the foundation, in later times, of the two cities of Alexandria (the modern

Iskenderun or Scanderoon), and Nicopolis. Besides these there were (in addition to Issus itself and Myriandrus, the only cities mentioned by the historians of Alexander), Rhosus, noticed by Strabo (*l. c.*), and Baiæ, evidently a watering-place that grew up in Roman times, and the name of which is found only in the Itineraries (*Itin. Ant.* p. 146, *Itin. Hier.* p. 580). Hence it is almost impossible to identify the various ruins which are scattered around the shores of this beautiful bay. But their exact determination is of little importance in connection with our immediate subject.

NOTE D, p. 415.

MARCH TO THE ORACLE OF AMMON.

Strabo justly remarks that this was probably the origin of the tales which were related, of the army being guided by two serpents, or according to another account, by two ravens, when they became bewildered in the desert (Arrian, *Anab.* iii. 3, § 3, Q. Curt. iv. 7, § 15; Diodor. xvii. 49; Strabo, xvii. pp. 813, 814). The story that the army was only saved from destruction by the sudden and most unusual occurrence of a storm of rain, when their provision of water had entirely failed them, after only four days' march, is wholly at variance with the foresight and care uniformly displayed by Alexander in such matters; nor is rain a very unusual circumstance in this country in the winter. It appears indeed that there are no wells on the direct line from the sea-coast to the Oasis, but a sufficient supply of water for the whole journey is carried without difficulty at the present day, by caravans, and Alexander could unquestionably have done the same (Browne's *Travels*, p. 16, Rennell, *Geogr. of Herodot.* p. 580). Nor could there be any want of native guides to a locality which, as we have seen, was frequently visited by travellers from various parts of the world, though Alexander was the first who conducted an army thither. What amount of forces he led with him we are not informed, but it was probably not considerable. No resistance could be anticipated from the peaceful and feeble Ammonians and Alexander only took with him from Memphis the select corps of the Hypaspists or foot-guards, with the light-armed Agrianes and archers, and a single squadron of cavalry (Arrian, *Anab.* iii 1, § 4). But it is by no means certain that even this force accompanied him on the march to Ammonium. It may be added that the time of year was favourable. M. Parthey has indeed inferred from an expression of Appian (*B. Civ.* ii. 149) that the expedition took place during the hottest season (Parthey, p. 164). but this is evidently a mistake, or rather a mere rhetorical flourish. Alexander did not enter Egypt till the autumn of the year B.C. 332, and quitted Memphis on his return to Phœnicia *early* the following spring. (See Clinton's *Fasti Hellenici*, vol. ii. p. 154, Grote's *Greece*, vol. xii. pp. 197–203.) The march to the oracle of Ammon must therefore have taken place in the heart of the winter.

It is singular that there was a discrepancy between the contemporary accounts as to the route followed by Alexander *on his return*: Aristobulus describing him as returning by the same route by which he had come, and Ptolemy the son of Lagus asserting that he had followed a more direct route to Memphis. (Arrian, *Anab.* iii. 4, § 5.) Such a difference between two of the most authentic and best informed historians shows us that we must be careful in accepting without question geographical statements concerning the operations of Alexander, even where they can be safely assumed to rest on contemporary testimony.

It is worthy of notice that Q. Curtius (who, in this instance, as in many others, may probably have followed good authorities) distinctly speaks of *camels* accompanying the army to carry a provision of water, though this also, according to his account, failed them *after the fourth day*. This is the only instance in which we find mention of camels thus employed by the Greeks in Africa. (Q. Curt. iv. 30, § 12.) See Chapter VIII. Note A.

NOTE E, p. 415.

THE OASIS OF AMMON.

It is only in comparatively recent times that the site of the Oasis of Ammon has been discovered and visited by modern travellers. The Oasis of Siwah was first seen by Browne in 1792, who however appears himself to have doubted whether this was the locality of the celebrated temple, a conclusion that was first established upon incontrovertible grounds by Major Rennell in his *Geography of Herodotus* (first edition), published in 1799. Meanwhile the site had been again visited by Hornemann in 1798, and afterwards by Cailliaud in 1819. Since that time it has been carefully examined and repeatedly described. among others by Minutoli, Jomard, Bayle St. John, and Hamilton. All the information collected by these successive travellers has been brought together and carefully analysed by M. Parthey in his excellent memoir (*Das Orakel und die Oase des Ammon*) published in the Transactions of the Berlin Academy for 1862, and reprinted in a separate form, 4to, 1862.

The greater part of these modern travellers have followed the more direct route from Cairo by the Fayoum, the part where the cultivated region of Egypt approaches most nearly to the Oasis but Browne followed nearly the same line as that taken by Alexander, proceeding along the coast from Alexandria as far as a point about 20 miles short of Parætonium, from whence he struck into the interior. The caravan with which he travelled took thirteen days on the journey, seven of which lay along the sea-coast and six across the desert. The latter portion comprised sixty-five hours and a half of actual travelling, a space which could hardly be traversed by a force like that of Alexander in less than eight days.

The *direct* distance from Siwah to the sea at Parætonium (Marsa Berek) is about 140 G. miles. To accomplish this in eight days would require a rate of marching somewhat exceeding that of the seven days from Gaza to Pelusium, and the difficulties of the march to Ammonium were probably in reality greater. But in the one case Alexander had with him a comparatively small force : in the other he was at the head of his main army.

NOTE F, p. 416.

THAPSACUS.

We have already seen that Thapsacus was at this period the habitual place of passage of the Euphrates, a circumstance which rendered it a place of great importance (see above, Chapter X. p. 365). It was here that the younger Cyrus crossed the river (Xen. *Anab.* i. 4, §§ 11, 17); and here also Darius crossed it on his advance to Issus, as well as on his retreat after the battle (Arrian, *Anab.* ii. 13, § 1, Q. Curt. iii. 7, § 1). The Persian king had, however, taken the precaution (as was afterwards done by Alexander) to construct a bridge of boats across the river, notwithstanding which his army occupied not less than five days on the passage (Q. Curt. *l. c.*).

No indication is afforded us of the route by which Alexander directed his march from Phœnicia to Thapsacus, a point of some geographical interest. Curtius indeed tells us that he took eleven days on the march (undecimis castris ad Euphraten pervenit, iv. 37, § 12), but without indicating the point from which they were reckoned; which renders the notice wholly useless. Cyrus, as we have seen, took twelve days on the march from Myriandrus to Thapsacus; but there is no reason to suppose that Alexander returned so far north before striking into the interior. We last hear of him at Tyre, and it is probable that he moved from thence to Damascus, which was at this time the most important city in Syria, and had been already reduced by Parmenio after the battle of Issus; and from thence through Cœle-Syria by Emesa to the Euphrates, but the route by which he crossed the desert, and the point where he first struck on the Euphrates, cannot be determined.

Thapsacus continued during the early period of the Seleucidan monarchy to be the customary point at which the Euphrates was crossed, hence the importance attached to it by Eratosthenes. It appears also from the expressions of Strabo that at this period the river was traversed by a bridge (meaning of course a bridge of boats); but in the time of the geographer this had ceased to be the case (he uses the expression ἀπὸ Θαψάκου καθ' ὃ ἦν τὸ ζεῦγμα τοῦ Εὐφράτου τὸ παλαιόν, xvi. c. 1, § 21); and under the Roman Empire it sank into a place of no importance—the customary passage of the Euphrates having then been transferred to Zeugma, opposite to the modern town of Bir. Hence we find Dion Cassius (xl. c 17) falling into the error of supposing that this was the point where Alexander himself had crossed the river. The paved causeways, of which the remains are still visible, leading down to the river on each side, probably belong to the period when there was the bridge of boats at this point.

NOTE G, p. 417.

BATTLE OF ARBELA.

Arrian has himself pointed out the error, which appears to have been widely diffused in his time, of supposing the battle to have been fought at Arbela, while it really took place at a distance of

600 stadia (60 G. miles) from that city (Arrian, *Anab.* v. 11, § 5). Gaugamela, near which it was actually fought, was, as he remarks, not a city, but merely a large village, and the name being strange and unfamiliar to Greek ears, they had preferred to call the battle after the more celebrated city of Arbela (Id. ib § 6). Strabo confirms this statement, and tells us, moreover, that the name of Gaugamela signified "the house of a camel," the village having been assigned by Darius Hystaspes as the place of support for one of his camels that had done good service in his Scythian expedition (Strab. xvi. 1, § 3).

The exact site of Gaugamela has not been determined, nor can this be wondered at a large village in an open plain is not likely to have left any permanent vestiges, and no tradition remains to point it out. Arrian tells us that it was situated on a small river, which he names Bumodus or Bumadus (the reading is uncertain), at a distance of 600 stadia from Arbela, but he afterwards adds—"or 500 according to the lowest estimate"—thus showing how vague was his knowledge of the actual distance. From Arbela to the river Lycus (the Great Zab), which was interposed between that city and the field of battle, is less than 20 G. miles in a direct line; and a further distance of 25 G. miles would carry us as far as the ruins of Nineveh, opposite to the modern city of Mosul on the Tigris. Yet there seems no doubt that the battle was really fought in the extensive open plain between the Tigris, the river Lycus, and the mountains of Gordyene. The river Bumodus affords the only clue to the nearer identification of the site, for the only considerable stream which traverses the plain in question is the Ghazir, which falls into the Zab about 20 miles above its junction with the Tigris, and there is little doubt that this must represent the Bumodus. In this case, indeed, the statement of Arrian concerning the distance of the field of battle from Arbela must be regarded as considerably overrated. On the other hand the position of the Ghazir would accord well with the statement of Q. Curtius that the Bumodus (or Bumelus as he writes the name) was 80 stadia distant from the Lycus (Q. Curt. iv. 36, § 10).

Mr. Layard, who, as he himself remarks, must probably, in his ride from Nineveh to Bavian, have crossed the very spot where the battle was fought, adds "The whole of the country between the Makloub range and the Tigris is equally well suited to the operations of mighty armies, but from the scanty topographical details given by the historians of Alexander we are unable to identify the exact place of his victory. It is curious that hitherto no remains or relics have been turned up by the plough, which would serve to mark the precise site of so great a battle as that of Arbela " (Layard's *Nineveh and Babylon*, p. 208).

Since the above remarks were written, the ground has been accurately surveyed by an engineer, M. Cernik, but his observations (which are published in Petermann's *Mittheilungen, Erganzungsheft*, No. 45) do not throw much additional light upon the subject; for the reasons already stated. It is clear from his map that the open undulating *plateau* which extends from the river Ghazir westwards to the Tigris, and in the centre of which is situated the modern village of Kermelis, was the scene of the great battle, but beyond this we cannot go. The distances given by him from Arbela by the direct road to Mosul are . from Erbil to Senieh, where it crosses the Zab, 30 kilometres, thence to Kermelis, 18 kilometres, and from Kermelis to Mosul, 25. The actual distance from the scene of action to Arbela could not therefore have exceeded 48 kilometres, or about 30 English miles, instead of the 600 stadia (60 G. miles) stated by Arrian.

Another question of interest in connection with the battle, which has hitherto received but little attention, is that of the place where Alexander crossed the Tigris. On this point our ancient authorities give us no direct information; but we learn from Arrian that after crossing the river *by fording it*, he marched for four days through the plain of Aturia (Assyria) with the Gordyæan mountains on his left hand (Arrian, III. 7. § 7), and it was only on the fourth day that his scouts brought him word that he was approaching the great army of Darius. This statement seems utterly at variance with the view, adopted by Mr. Grote as well as by other writers, that he crossed the Tigris at Mosul, *almost directly opposite to* the field of battle, from which it could not have been more than 20 miles distant. On the other hand Droysen, who carries him up the river as far as Jezireh-ibn-Omar (Bezabde), appears to err at least as much in the opposite direction; that place being not less than 85 G. miles above Mosul, and more than 100 from the scene of action. Colonel Chesney supposes him to have crossed at a place called Eski Mosul, about 25 miles above the present town of that name; and this seems the most probable suggestion. It appears that the Tigris is fordable at many points above Mosul, though not without difficulty, and the description given by Quintus Curtius of the difficulties encountered by Alexander and his army in crossing the river, is probably but little exaggerated (Q. Curt. ix. 37, 38).

NOTE H, p. 417.

RETREAT OF DARIUS TO ECBATANA.

The route taken by Darius in his flight from the field of Arbela to Ecbatana was probably that which enters the mountain chain of Mount Zagros near Rowandiz, and crosses the pass of Keli-Shin to Sidek and Ushnei. This route, which was first explored by Major (now Sir Henry) Rawlinson, and is described by him in the *Journal of the Geographical Society* (vol. x. p. 20-24), appears to have been in all ages a frequented passage from the plains of Assyria to the high table-land of Media . and would be a natural line of retreat for Darius, in order to secure his own safety by placing the defiles of Mount Zagros between him and the victorious Alexander. It is indeed expressly mentioned by Arrian that it was a route not easily practicable for a large army (ἡ δὲ ἐπὶ Μηδίας μεγάλῳ στρατεύματι οὐκ εὔπορος. *Anab.* iii. 16. § 2). This object once attained, and having reached the highlands of Media, he could easily turn off to the right to Ecbatana. In doing so he would gain the additional advantage of securing the only remaining royal city which he could hope to preserve from the hands of the conqueror. The suggestion of Sir H. R. that by following this pass he retreated in the first instance to the (supposed) northern Ecbatana (at Takhti-Suleiman), and afterwards removed from thence to the well-known city of Media, where we distinctly find him stationed when Alexander resumed operations against him, is one of those gratuitous, though ingenious, conjectures by which that author has sought to prop up his theory of the existence of *two* Ecbatanas. (See Chapter VII. Note E.)

NOTE I, p. 418.

PASSES BETWEEN SUSA AND PERSEPOLIS.

The exact line of route followed by Alexander on the march from Susa to Persepolis is difficult to determine. The geography of these rugged mountain tracts is still but imperfectly known, and the natural difficulties of the country are such that almost every line of route presents narrow defiles and passes resembling those described by the historians of Alexander. It appears to result clearly from the account of Arrian, when compared with those of Q. Curtius and Diodorus, that there were two separate passes, the one leading into the territory of the Uxian mountaineers, the other from thence into the valley of the Araxes and the plain of Persepolis, and that between them there intervened a space of five days' march. It was the second of these to which Arrian gives the name of "the Persian Gates" (Pylæ Persidis), while they are termed by Curtius and Diodorus "the Susian Gates" (Pylæ Susianæ). Both names clearly indicate that the line of route was one of ordinary communication between Susa and Persis, and Arrian incidentally notices the existence of a road practicable for wheel carriages (ἁμαξιτός). But this road led at each point through a narrow gorge which was closed by artificial fortifications, and occupied by a hostile force. In both cases, Alexander succeeded in turning the defile, and sending round a light body of troops, which fell upon the defenders from the heights above. and thus made himself master of the passes, which he would have been unable to force by a direct attack. (Arrian, *Anab.* iii. 17, 18, Q. Curt. v. 3-5, Diodor. xvii. 67, 68.)

The passes in question have been but little explored in recent times, almost all modern travellers having proceeded from Bushire direct to Shiraz. But in 1810 Colonel Monteith and Macdonald Kinneir followed a route from the ruins of Susa to Shiraz, which must nearly, if not quite, coincide with that taken by Alexander. (See Kinneir's *Geographical Memoir of the Persian Empire*, 4to. 1813, pp. 72-74, and a Memoir by General Monteith in the *Journal of Geogr. Society*, vol. xxvii. pp. 108-119.) The most formidable passes which they traversed were one between the valley of Basht and a rock fortress called Kalah Sufid, which would seem to correspond well with the pass through the land of the Uxians, with which it is identified by Colonel Monteith. and one called the Kotul Sucreab, but a few miles above it. But it seems impossible to accept this last as representing the Persian Gates, which were separated from the other pass by a considerable interval, and would seem to have been situated at only a short distance from Persepolis. It was apparently immediately after passing through them that Alexander descended to the river called by Diodorus and Curtius the Araxes, which is certainly the same as the stream now called the Bundamir, which is crossed in proceeding from Shiraz to Persepolis, and is a rapid and formidable stream.

The narrative of Arrian is unfortunately very far from clear. probably from his having himself but an imperfect idea of the localities. while those of Q. Curtius and Diodorus are evidently derived from a different authority, and it appears impossible to reconcile the two. But in this instance, as in many others, we feel strongly the disadvantage of being unable to consult the original and contemporary authorities. Had we possessed the original narratives of Ptolemy and Aristobulus, there is little doubt that we should have found in them local details which would have enabled us to decide the question. But a careful examination of the localities, with especial reference to it, might still throw much light on the subject.

NOTE K, p. 418.

THE PYLÆ CASPIÆ.

The Caspian Gates, or Pylæ Caspiæ, obtained, partly in consequence of the prominent position which they assumed on this occasion, a great celebrity among Greek geographers, and hold an important place in the geographical discussions of Eratosthenes. Though little known or noticed in modern times, they really constitute a pass of considerable importance, through which must always have lain the line of direct communication from Hamadan and the western provinces of the Persian Empire with Parthia, Bactria, and Ariana. The pass in question lies, not through the main ridge of Mount Elburz, which here separates the plains of Persia from the basin of the Caspian Sea, but through a lateral range or spur of those mountains, which strikes off to the south, where it terminates in the great salt desert of Khorasan: and the importance of the passage arises from the difficulty of turning or rounding it by passing through the desert. Hence it is still traversed by the most frequented route from Teheran to Meshed and Herat. The identity of this pass with the one now known as the Sirdar Pass, between Veramin and Kishlak in Khowar, has been fully established by modern travellers, and thus one of the most important points in the geography of Central Asia clearly fixed. (See Morier's *Second Journey in Persia*, pp. 363; Fraser's *Khorasan*,

p. 291-293, where the whole subject is fully discussed. also Mutzell's *Notes to Q. Curtius,* v. 35, § 1.) Sir A. Burnes fell into the error of identifying the Pylæ Caspiæ with the pass now called that of Gadook, which is one of those leading across the chain of Elburz into Mazanderan (*Travels to Bokhara,* vol. ii. p. 130), and he has been followed in this mistake by Wilson (*Ariana,* p. 171). Its identity with the pass of Sirdar was clearly pointed out by Rennell (*Geography of Herodotus,* p. 174 note). The descriptions of modern travellers agree almost exactly with that given by Pliny (*Hist. Nat.* vi. c. 14, § 43), which he must have derived from the historians or geographers of Alexander. No details are given by Arrian.

The city of Rhagæ, where Alexander halted in pursuit of Darius, was situated (according to Arrian) at the distance of one day's march from the entrance of the Caspian Gates. The site is generally supposed to be represented by the ruins of a large and important city, at a spot still called Rhei or Rey, about 5 miles S.E. of Teheran. Sir H. Rawlinson indeed would transfer it to Veramin, much nearer the pass but though the distance of Rhagæ from the entrance of the passes, which is given by Morier at ten *farsangs* (about 30 miles) exceeds any ordinary rate of marching, Arrian himself expressly terms it a very long or forced march (ὁδὸν ἡμέρας μίας, ἐλαύνοντι ὡς Ἀλέξανδρος ἦγε, iii. 20, § 2): and Veramin is certainly too near the entrance. Moreover the ruins at Rhey are apparently too extensive and important to belong to any other city than Rhagæ, which is described as having been in ancient times the second city of Media.

It is worthy of remark that Alexander, while pursuing Darius *by forced marches* from Ecbatana, did not arrive at Rhagæ till the eleventh day. According to Sir H. Rawlinson (*Journ. Geogr. Soc.* vol. x. p. 138) it is reckoned at the present day only nine stages or days' journeys (Menzils) from Veramin to Hamadan, but as the distance, as measured on the map by the direct route, is nearly 180 G. miles, these cannot be taken as *ordinary* days' marches. From Rhagæ onwards his pursuit became exceptionally rapid, and cannot be measured by any ordinary rate.

Colonel Chesney estimates the distance from Hamadan to Rhagæ at 250 miles (vol. ii. p. 303), but this must probably refer to the more circuitous route by way of Kasbin, which is the one usually frequented; and would certainly have been the one followed by an army, except under the peculiar circumstances of the march of Alexander.

NOTE L, p. 419.

HECATOMPYLUS.

We are indebted to Quintus Curtius and Diodorus for indicating Hecatompylus as the place where Alexander made this prolonged halt (Curt. vi. 6, § 15; Diodor. xvii. 75). The name is not mentioned by Arrian. The site of the city, though undoubtedly one of considerable importance, has unfortunately not been determined; it was clearly situated south of the mountain chain which forms the prolongation of Mt. Elburz, on the line of road leading from the Caspian Gates towards Meshed and Herat, but the two statements which have been transmitted to us concerning its distance from the former pass are widely divergent. Strabo, on the authority of Eratosthenes, places Hecatompylus at 1960 stadia (196 G. miles) from the Gates; while Pliny, who cites the itinerary given by Diognetus and Bæton, makes the distance only 133 Roman, or about 106 geographical miles. Hence the site has been fixed by some modern writers in the neighbourhood of Damghan; by others, including Professor Wilson (*Ariana*, p. 171) in that of Jah Jerm. This last position however would seem to carry us too far from the passes of Mt. Elburz, through which Alexander subsequently descended into Hyrcania. We learn from Polybius (x. 28) that Hecatompylus was situated at the point of junction of several roads leading across passes in different directions, it was by one of these (probably the same taken by Alexander) that Antiochus III. descended from thence into the plains of Hyrcania. These conditions would lead us to place it in the neighbourhood of Damghan, from whence a frequented pass leads direct to Astrabad and the shores of the Caspian. Other passes however communicate directly with Shahrood and Bostan, and Hecatompylus might therefore with equal plausibility be placed in the neighbourhood of those cities. Indeed according to M. Ferrier the latter position agrees much better with the account of Polybius than that of Damghan (Ferrier's *Caravan Journeys*, p. 69). No ancient remains have been discovered in any of these localities to assist us in determining the site.

NOTE M, p. 420.

ZADRACARTA.

The position of Zadracarta, the chief city of Hyrcania, is as uncertain as that of Hecatompylus; and the topography of this part of Alexander's operations is altogether incapable of being determined in detail with any certainty. This part of the chain of Mt. Elburz is traversed by several passes, all of them presenting considerable difficulties, and all clothed (on their northern slopes towards the Caspian) with the dense forests, which are described by Q. Curtius as characteristic of the defile traversed by Alexander.

It is probable that Zadracarta is the same place that is called by Strabo Carta (Κάρτα, xi. 7, p. 508), but that author furnishes us no clue to its position. The supposition that it is identical with the Ὑρκανία μητρόπολις of Ptolemy (vi. 9, § 7) is a mere conjecture. Q. Curtius indeed uses the term "urbem Hyrcaniæ" to designate the city, which is evidently the same as Arrian calls Zadracarta: but the words are probably meant to convey only the same meaning as those of Arrian where he calls it τὴν μεγίστην πόλιν τῆς Ὑρκανίας. Strabo on the other hand calls the capital of Hyrcania (τὸ βασιλεῖον) Tape (xi. 7, p. 508); and Polybius, who must probably have had good materials at command, gives it the (Greek) name of Syrinx (Σύριγξ, Polyb. x. 31). There is certainly no reason to assume that these different appellations all refer to the same city.

It is to be observed that our existing MSS. of Arrian write the name in one place (iii. 23, § 6) Zadracarta, in another (iii. 25, § 1) Zeudracarta, but there seems no doubt that the same place is meant in both passages. (See the notes of Schmieder and Kruger on Arrian, ll. cc. and that of Mutzell on Q. Curtius, vi. 18, § 22.) Droysen on the contrary maintains the two to be distinct, and supposes Alexander to have followed a pass which descends upon Sari in Mazanderan, and to have thence continued his march (after the expedition against the Mardi) to the capital of Hyrcania. It seems probable at all events that the latter (where Alexander halted before resuming his march into Bactria) was situated in the neighbourhood of Astrabad, not far from the south-eastern angle of the Caspian, but the exact site cannot be determined.

NOTE N, p. 422.

ESTIMATED DISTANCES

Sir H. Rawlinson observes in his able memoir on the site of the Atropatenian Ecbatana. "In illustrating the geography of the ancients we must pay particular attention to the rough estimates of distance which are calculated in stages or days' journeys. These stages, which answer to the Menzil of the present day, cannot be verified by their assimilation to any uniform distance, either along the road or upon the map, local causes will arise to lengthen or shorten them according to the character of the country which they traverse; and the only means of illustration is thus to compare the ancient estimate with the Menzils of the present day." (*Journ. Geogr. Soc.* vol. x. p. 137.) In like manner the itineraries of Ibn Haukil (an Arabian geographer of the 10th century), which are a valuable assistance for comparison with Alexander's marches, are computed always in Menzils or Merhileh, terms which (as his translator observes) "are employed indifferently by Mohammedans, to signify the halting-place after a day's journey, and thence denote the distance travelled in a day, which is a somewhat indefinite scale." (Wilson's *Ariana*, p. 174.) They thus correspond exactly to the use of the σταθμοὶ by Xenophon in describing the march of Cyrus. But as Professor Wilson observes "the term Merhileh often alternates in Ibn Haukil with stages of three farsangs, or from 12 to 16 miles, and it probably intends something of the same space."

NOTE O, p. 423.

SUPPOSED MEASUREMENTS OF ALEXANDER'S ROUTE.

Pliny has indeed preserved to us an itinerary of the distances from the Caspian Gates to the frontiers of India, following on the track of Alexander, which he derived from two writers named Diognetus and Bæton, whom he calls "itinerum ejus (Alexandri) mensores" (*H. N.* vi. 17, § 61); and one of these authors Bæton, is also quoted by Athenæus (x. p. 442 b.), who terms him ὁ 'Αλεξάνδρου βηματιστής. From these expressions it has been inferred by many modern writers that Alexander was accompanied by regular surveyors, and that the distances cited were *actually measured*. But of this there is no kind of proof. The work of the writers in question was termed Σταθμοὶ τῆς Ἀλεξάνδρου πορείας; a title which would indeed seem to indicate that it was a regular itinerary like the Σταθμοὶ Παρθικοὶ of Isidorus; but that it was not a *mere* Itinerary—such as we are familiar with in Roman and later times —is clearly shown by the few fragments still extant, which (except that already cited from Pliny) contain statements relative to the natural productions or inhabitants of the countries visited, such as would be found in any ordinary geographical work. A similar treatise called Σταθμοὶ Ἀσίας was written by a certain Amyntas,— of whom nothing is known but his name—and is rather more frequently referred to, but the references are all to passages of a similar description. (See the fragments of the three writers collected by C. Muller in the *Fragmenta Scriptorum de Rebus Alexandri Magni*, ed. Didot, pp. 134–137.) Strabo probably refers to one or other of these writers under the title of οἱ Ἀσιατικοὶ σταθμοὶ (xv. p. 723); and it seems probable that the statements as to distances, which he quotes from Eratosthenes (xi. p. 514), were based on the same authority. But admitting that the works in question were distinct *geographical* treatises upon the campaigns of Alexander, as distinguished from the historical works of Aristobulus, Ptolemy, and others, and that as such the authors would naturally give more attention to the number of days' marches (σταθμοὶ) and to the estimate of distances from one halting-place to another, there is absolutely no reason to suppose that they possessed or employed any means of measurement beyond what were commonly used in the East in all ages, the character of which has been considered in the text. The vagueness in the use of the terms *schœni*, or parasangs, by the Orientals is repeatedly referred to both by Greek and Roman writers; and even had such estimates been preserved by the writers in question, they would have been very far removed from the results of actual measurement. Such an itinerary of the campaigns of Alexander as Xenophon has given us of the Anabasis and retreat of the Ten Thousand would be a most valuable addition to our knowledge; but we have seen abundant proof how imperfect even such a record must be.

It is true that Pliny, in quoting the statements of Diognetus and Bæton, gives the distances in Roman miles (into which he must have *translated* them from the Greek stadia of the original); but this proves nothing, for the Greek writers would naturally give

NOTE P.   EXPEDITION OF ALEXANDER.   483

the results in this more definite form, after resolving the days' marches, or parasangs, into stadia according to some mode of computation, which appeared to them the most plausible. This is exactly what is done by Xenophon in his summaries of the distances actually traversed (*Anab.* ii. 2, § 6; v. 5, § 4), as well as by Herodotus in regard to the "royal road" from Babylon to Sardis; yet it certainly adds nothing to our belief in the accuracy of their rougher estimates previously given.

The itinerary given by Pliny is in any case a valuable auxiliary to our knowledge of the geography of Upper Asia: but there is no reason to attach to it any exaggerated importance. The general agreement of its numbers with those cited by Strabo from Eratosthenes shows that they were probably both derived from the same source, but there is not the least hint given by the latter author that they had any official character, or special authority: and the discrepancies which he occasionally notices rather seem to imply the contrary. The very slight attention which the statements of these writers appear to have attracted in antiquity presents a curious contrast with the confident assertions of modern writers concerning them, and the admiration bestowed upon Alexander for the care he took to have "his marches measured," and his dominions "surveyed" as he advanced. There is in reality no evidence that he did anything of the kind.

But even if the record originally preserved was more trustworthy than we have reason to believe, we are told by Pliny himself that the numbers varied in different copies ("in quibusdam exemplaribus diversi numeri reperiuntur"), while the same thing occurs in this passage, even more glaringly than usual, in our own manuscripts of Pliny.

NOTE P, p. 424.

RATE OF TRAVELLING ON DROMEDARIES.

On this occasion we are told that the messengers sent with the death warrant of Parmenio, who was then at Ecbatana, took the direct road across the desert to that place, and being mounted on dromedaries (δρομάδες κάμηλοι) accomplished the distance in *eleven* days, though it required not less than 30 or 40 days by the ordinary route, and at the usual rate of travelling (Strabo, xv. 2, p. 724;

Q. Curt. vii. 2, § 18). Of course under these circumstances we should expect an extraordinary rate of speed: but still the time allowed is surprisingly small. At the present day, according to Major Pottinger (*Beloochistan*, p. 229) *couriers*—of course on dromedaries—take eighteen days to traverse the desert from Kerman to Herat though this distance is little more than 400 G. miles, as measured on the map, while that from Furrah to Hamadan considerably exceeds 700 miles.

On the other hand, the time allowed for ordinary travelling appears also very short. The only route more direct than the circuitous one followed by Alexander himself through Meshed and Herat, is that across the desert by Yezd: but, according to Pottinger, it is 40 days' journey for laden camels by this direct route, from Yezd to Furrah (see his map). But from Yezd to Ispahan is a distance of 185 G. miles in a direct line; and thence to Hamadan nearly 240 more.

It may here be remarked that no mention occurs in any ancient author of a city on the site of Yezd, though it would appear probable that that fertile oasis in the midst of surrounding deserts, must always have derived some importance from its position. It was not till the middle ages that we hear of its attaining to commercial prosperity and consideration.

NOTE Q, p. 424.

THE INDIAN CAUCASUS.

The name of Caucasus, given by the Greeks to these mountains, which has been perpetuated down to our own days—for the name of Hindoo Koosh, by which they are still known, is nothing more than a corruption of "the Indian Caucasus"—appears to have been originally a mere popular appellation, applied in the first instance by the Macedonian officers to the stupendous range of mountains north of the valley of Cabul. The real Caucasus was the most lofty range of mountains known to the Greeks before this time, and they were generally regarded as the highest mountains in the world (Herodot. i. 203; Æschyl. *Prom.* v. 719). Hence when the army of Alexander came in sight of the vast mountain barrier that rose before them, as they advanced northward from Arachosia, they seem to have at once concluded that this could be no other than the Caucasus, just as they assumed the Iaxartes to be the Tanais. The attempts of systematic geographers to connect the two, and show that they really formed a part of the same mountain system, were evidently an afterthought, similar to the theory more generally adopted, which regarded these eastern mountain chains as a prolongation of Mount Taurus.

The idea may have been further encouraged (as suggested by Strabo, xi. pp. 505, 506, xv. p. 688) out of flattery for Alexander, as wishing to represent him as having surmounted with his army the far-famed heights of the Caucasus.

The fable which fastened on a cavern near the pass, as that where Prometheus had been confined (Strabo, xv. p. 688) is a striking instance of the readiness of the popular mind to give a local habitation to such current mythological tales. It is repeated by Q. Curtius, Diodorus, and the later geographers.

Strabo expressly tells us that the Macedonians gave the name of Caucasus to the whole range of mountains extending onwards (*i. e.* eastwards) from the land of the Arians: but that they were known to the barbarians by various appellations, as Paropamisus, Emoda, Imaum, and others, applied to different portions of the chain (Strab. xi. p. 511; xv. p. 689). Of these the name of Paropamisus, which continued to be applied specially to the great chain north of the valley of Cabul (to which the name of Hindoo Koosh is more particularly confined by the most recent geographers), is considered by Lassen, Prof. Wilson, and others to be connected with the Sanscrit "Nishadha;" and that the form Paropanisus, preserved by Ptolemy, would therefore be the more correct.

The term Paropamisadæ, applied by the Greeks to all the tribes on the south side of the mountains, in the valley of the Cophen and its tributaries, was probably a collective geographical name adopted for the sake of convenience, rather than a true ethnic appellation.

NOTE R, p. 425.

ARTACOANA AND ALEXANDRIA IN ARIIS.

This point has been very fully discussed by Prof. Wilson (*Ariana*, p. 151-52), who arrives at the conclusion that Alexandria in Aria was the same place as was previously called Artacoana, and that it occupied the site of the modern Herat. There appears to me strong evidence in favour of placing Alexandria on the same spot with Herat, or at least in its immediate vicinity, but the arguments for identifying it with Artacoana (the capital of the province when Alexander invaded it) are much less conclusive. Strabo, Isidore of Charax, and Ptolemy all distinguish Artacoana from Alexandria, regarding the former as still existing, long after the establishment of the Greek city (Strabo, xi. 10, p. 516; Isidor. *Stathm. Parth.* § 15; Ptolem. *Geogr.* vi. 17, § 6). Whether the last was a new foundation, or only a new appellation given to a previously existing city, we have no information: nor do we know whether the name dated from Alexander's own time, or from one of his successors. No mention is made of it by any of his extant historians, and if, therefore, we suppose it to be distinct from Artacoana, there is no clue to the position of the latter city with respect to Herat.

Susia, on the frontiers of Aria, towards Parthia, where Alexander first met the satrap Satibarzanes, has been placed by Wilson at Zuzan, about 60 miles west of Herat: but this seems to have lain quite out of the line of march of Alexander; and as there seems no doubt that the province of Aria comprised the whole of the fertile tract extending from Herat to Mashed, it would more naturally be sought in the neighbourhood of the latter city. Arrian clearly represents Alexander as having advanced *some distance* from thence on his route towards Bactria, when he was suddenly recalled by the news of the defection of Satibarzanes, and turned at once upon Artacoana. Dr. Thirlwall suggests Tus or Tous, the ruins of which still remain about 17 miles N.W. of Meshed, as the site of Susia, and this (which is adopted also by M. Ferrier, *Caravan Journeys*, p. 166) seems the most probable supposition.

NOTE S, p. 425.

ROUTES FROM HERAT INTO BACTRIA.

At the present day there are three routes leading from Herat into Bactria: one, the direct line through the mountains forming the continuation of the Paropamisus and by Murghab and Maimana to Balkh (Bactra). another through the country of the Hazaras and the southern ranges of the Paropamisus to Cabul and the foot of the direct passes across the Hindoo Koosh. this appears to be the route indicated by Strabo (xv. 2, § 8. ἡ μὲν ἐπ' εὐθείας διὰ τῆς Βακτριανῆς καὶ τῆς ὑπερβάσεως τοῦ ὄρους εἰς 'Ορτόσπανα ἐπὶ τὴν ἐκ Βάκτρων τρίοδον, ἥτις ἐστὶν ἐν τοῖς Παροπαμισάδαις), but has not been described in detail or traversed by any modern traveller, though said to be practicable (see Wilson, *Ariana*, p. 173, and Macartney in Appendix to Elphinstone's *Caubul*, vol. ii. p. 393). According to M. Ferrier it is rendered impossible for Europeans at the present day on account of the lawless and dangerous character of the Hazara tribes who occupy this part of the mountains. otherwise it would afford a short and practicable route direct from Herat to Cabul (Ferrier's *Caravan Journeys*, p. 221). But according to the information obtained by Lieut. Conolly in 1830, this line of route is "very difficult, leading continually over high and steep mountains," and though passed occasionally by parties of horsemen, would be wholly impassable to a modern army (Conolly's *Journey*, vol. ii. p. 42). The third is that taken by Alexander, turning off to the south to Prophthasia, and thence through Candahar to Cabul, and the same passes. Before Alexander was called off by the reported treachery of Satibarzanes he was apparently intending to march *directly* into Bactria, and may therefore have been about to proceed by the first of these routes. Strabo, quoting from Eratosthenes (xi. § 48) gives the distance from Alexandria in Ariis to Bactra at 3870 stadia (387 G. miles), which can only refer to the direct route. This was therefore known and frequented in the days of Eratosthenes: as would naturally have been the case after the establishment of permanent Greek settlements in Bactria. But even in the days of Alexander it appears to have been a well-known and recognised line of route by which he was about to proceed from Susia (in the neighbourhood of Meshed) to Bactria. The natural difficulties presented by this route appear to be inconsiderable (see Ferrier's *Caravan Journeys*, chaps. 14, 15). The chief obstacles he encountered were from the jealousy and treacherous disposition of native chiefs. Alexander had probably advanced as far as the valley of the Murghab, when the news of the defection of Satibarzanes led him to turn abruptly south to the neighbourhood of Herat. But the supposition that the point which he had thus reached was the same as was afterwards marked by the foundation of a city, named after him Alexandria, is wholly without authority.

NOTE T, p. 425.

PROPHTHASIA.

This identification rests on tolerably satisfactory grounds. There can be no reasonable doubt that Phra, which is described by Isidore of Charax, as the largest town in the district immediately north of Drangiana, is the same name with the modern Furrah, and we are distinctly told by Stephanus of Byzantium, on the authority of the historian Charax, that Phrada was the name of the city which was called by Alexander Prophthasia. (Isidor. § 16; Steph. Byz. s. v. Φράδα.) It is true that the distance given by Eratosthenes (ap. Strab. xi. p. 514) of 1600 stadia from Alexandria in Aria to Prophthasia considerably exceeds the actual distance from Herat to Furrah: but he himself adds that others gave it as only 1500 stadia. Prof. Wilson was led by this discrepancy to identify Prophthasia with the ruins of a city called Peshawarun, near the shores of the shallow lake which occupies the north of Seistan, about 70 miles south of Furrah. These ruins were first discovered by Captain Christie, but it appears from the observations of recent travellers, that they are not of ancient date. (Bellew's *Journey*, p. 245.) Similar ruins are scattered through the whole of Seistan, which is a district of great fertility, though of limited extent, and appears to have at one time supported a large population. The capital at the time of the Arab conquest in A.D. 652 still retained the ancient name of Zaranj, which obviously represents the Drangiana of the Greeks, or Zarangiana as Isidore writes the word. It was situated between the Helmund and the lake, near the ruins of the later city of Jellalabad. But there is no evidence from ancient writers of the existence of a city on this site, to which the capital was removed according to Arab tradition shortly before the Mahometan conquest. Seistan has of late years been repeatedly visited by modern travellers, but it is still imperfectly known. The results of recent explorations have been brought together by Sir H Rawlinson in the *Journal of the Geographical Society*, vol. xliii. p. 272.

NOTE U, p. 426.

INDIAN TRIBES WEST OF THE INDUS.

It is a point of some ethnographical interest that Alexander is described as encountering in this part of his advance, from Candahar to Cabul, tribes who are designated as "Indians" (τῶν Ἰνδῶν τοὺς προσχώρους Ἀραχώτοις. Arrian, iii. 28.) This confirms the traditions of the Hindoos themselves, that at this period tribes of true Indian origin occupied the valleys of the Paropamisus, and a considerable extent of country west of the Indus, from which they were gradually driven out by the pressure of invading tribes from the north. (Wilson's *Ariana*, p. 125; Cunningham, pp. 125, 133.) The Gandarians also, who occupied a part of the territory to the west of the Indus (see note to Herodotus, chap. VII. p. 238), were clearly an Indian tribe. Their name is, however, not found in the historians of Alexander. It may not be useless to observe that the resemblance to that of Candahar is purely accidental, the latter, which is that of the *city*, not of a people, being probably a corruption of Alexandria.

NOTE V, p. 426.

CLIMATE OF ARACHOSIA.

The great hardships and sufferings endured by the army of Alexander in this part of their march became a favourite topic of exaggerated declamation with the rhetorical writers of later days, and sometimes led to the misconception that they must have occurred during the actual passage of the Hindoo Koosh. The route from Candahar by Ghizni to Cabul presents indeed no serious difficulty to the advance of an army during the greater part of the year. but in winter the cold is intense, and the snow is such as fully to justify the Greek historians in their accounts. According to Elphinstone: "In proceeding east from Candahar, the cold of the winter increases at every stage. . . . Even at Kelat-i-Ghilzi snow falls often and lies long, and the Turnuk is often frozen so as to bear a man. . . . Ascending the valley of the Turnuk, we at last reach the level of Ghizni, which is generally mentioned as the coldest part of the plain country in the Caubul dominions. The cold of Ghizni is spoken of as excessive, even by the inhabitants of the cold countries in its neighbourhood. For the greater part of the winter the inhabitants seldom quit their houses; and even in the city of Ghizni the snow has been known to lie deep for some time after the vernal equinox. Traditions prevail of the city having been twice destroyed by falls of snow, in which all the inhabitants were buried." Elphinstone's *Caubul*, vol. i. p. 182.

The city of Ghizni, in fact, is situated at a height of not less than 7730 feet above the level of the sea, while the pass between that and Cabul rises to 8700 feet

Lieut. Conolly also speaks of the road from Candahar to Cabul as practically closed to travellers in the winter, on account of the depth of the snow-drifts, and the severity of the cold. (Conolly's *Journey*, vol. ii. p. 44.)

NOTE X, p. 427.

SITE OF ALEXANDRIA AD CAUCASUM.

Professor Wilson, (writing in 1841) remarks that the exact site of Alexandria ad Caucasum is " exceedingly difficult to determine, though it is not possible now to stray so widely from the spot, as geographers of the first merit deviated some few years ago, in fixing it at Ghizni or Candahar." (*Ariana*, p. 179.) Other writers, including Sir A. Burnes, were disposed to place it at Bamian, but this is wholly irreconcilable with the statement of Pliny concerning the distance from Ortospana (assuming that to be rightly placed at Cabul), and is moreover at variance with the explicit statement of Arrian (confirmed as it is by the nature of the case) that Alexander halted *at the foot of the Hindoo Koosh*, waiting till spring before he undertook the passage of that great mountain-chain, Now Bamian is situated in the midst of the mountains, *after* crossing the main ridge of the Hindoo Koosh (Burnes's *Travels*, vol. ii p. 163), where there could be no reason for making any halt of long duration. The plain or broad valley of Koh Daman on the contrary is a very rich and fertile district, of the beauty of which travellers speak in terms of great admiration, and extending up to the very foot of the great mountain barrier of the Hindoo Koosh. Such a site would be admirably adapted for the foundation of a permanent settlement; and in this valley, near the modern village of Charikar, are found ruins indicating the former existence of an important city. These ruins, which were first discovered by Mr. Masson, are regarded by Prof. Wilson as those of Alexandria ad Caucasum, and the same view has been adopted by M. Vivien de St. Martin, who has since investigated the subject with much care, as well as by Gen. Cunningham. The choice must be considered as lying between this spot and Beghram, about seven miles to the east of it, where a multitude of coins and other ancient relics have also been found,

NOTE X.   EXPEDITION OF ALEXANDER.   491

indicating beyond a doubt the site of an ancient city. The distance between Charikar and Cabul is indeed considerably less than that indicated by Pliny; but its position on the direct route to the passes which lead by the valleys of Ghorbund across the central range is a strong argument in its favour. At the present day "the caravans that proceed from Cabul across the Hindoo Koosh to Khulm (in the valley of the Oxus), pass through Charikar, a long straggling village, near the foot of the Koosh." (Vigne's *Visit to Ghuzni, Kabul, &c.*, p. 215.)

The position of Beghram is decidedly less favourable, and the abundance of ancient remains there may be explained by supposing that locality to have been the site of Nicæa, a city which must have been founded by Alexander about the same time with Alexandria, as we find it mentioned as already in existence at the time of his return from Bactria. (Arrian, iv. 22, § 6.)[1]

The argument derived by Gen. Cunningham, as well as by M. Vivien de St. Martin, from the proximity of a village named Houpian or Opian, which they regard as directly derived from the ancient appellation of 'Ωπιανή, is undoubtedly entitled to some weight, though by no means so conclusive, as it is considered by the latter author. The name of 'Ωπιανή is found only in Stephanus of Byzantium, who in his enumeration of the different cities which bore the appellation of Alexandria, mentions one ἐν τῇ 'Ωπιανῇ κατὰ τὴν Ἰνδικήν. The name being otherwise unknown, several of the editors have proposed conjectural emendations thus Freinshemius would read 'Οξιανή and Salmasius 'Αριανή. But the correctness of the reading is confirmed by the mention of the 'Ωπίαι as an Indian tribe cited by Stephanus from Hecatæus (v. 'Ωπίαι), and the MSS. vary only between 'Ωπιανή and 'Οπιανή. On the other hand, the supposed mention of the same name in Pliny (vi. c. 21, § 62), on which Gen. Cunningham lays much stress, is certainly an error, the reading "Alexandriam Opianes" being a mere conjecture of Pintianus (derived from the passage in Stephanus), while that of "Alexandri oppidum," which is found in all the MSS. is quite unobjectionable, and is justly retained by the recent editors. (See Sillig's edition of Pliny, *l. c.*)

---

[1] General Cunningham, however, claims the site of Beghram for Cartana, a city not mentioned by the historians or geographers of Alexander, but whose name is found in Pliny and Ptolemy (*Ancient Geogr. of India*, pp 26-29)

Both passages of Stephanus, however, point to the name as that of a district or territory hence the evidence of the modern appellation has comparatively little weight in determining the exact position of the city.

(See Wilson's *Ariana,* pp. 179-182; Vivien de St. Martin, *Géographie Grecque et Latine de l'Inde,* 1858, pp. 23-26; Cunningham's *Ancient Geography of India,* pp. 20-24.)

NOTE Y, p. 428.

PASSES OF THE HINDOO KOOSH.

Our knowledge of these passes was derived in the first instance from Lieut. Wood, who states that all the three most direct passes from Cabul into Turkestan lead through the plain of the Koh-Daman, "where diverging as they enter among the mountains at its head, they wind up the course of the different streams, from which the several passes take the names of Ghorbund, Parwan, and Panchshir." (Wood's *Journey to the Source of the Oxus,* p. 118, 2nd edit. Lond. 1870) He himself attempted the passage of the Parwan Pass, but was driven back by snow storms, and compelled to take the more open road by Bamian. This was in the month of November. in the following April he recrossed the Hindoo Koosh by the Panchshir Pass with comparatively little difficulty. This last is the route which Alexander is supposed by M. de St. Martin to have followed (*Géogr. de l'Inde,* p. 23). but when he adds "Il n'y a pas deux routes possibles," this positive assertion is based upon the assumption that Adrapsa or Drapsaca is identical with Anderab or Inderab at the foot of the Panchshir Pass, on the northern side of the great mountain chain. But this identification rests mainly on the supposed resemblance of name, which is certainly not close enough to be conclusive. and it seems more probable that Drapsaca —where Alexander halted some time to recruit his troops after their fatigues—was situated quite in the plain or fertile valley of the Oxus, in the same manner as the modern town of Kunduz.

General Cunningham has adopted the same view with M. de St. Martin, which appears on the whole the most probable. We learn that Alexander on his return from Bactria took *a different and shorter* route, descending to the same point—his newly-founded city of Alexandria. And this is easily explained, if we suppose him to have followed the route by the Panchshir Pass in the first instance, and to have recrossed the mountains by the more direct route known as the Kushan Pass, which leads from Ghori to Kushan at the entrance of the Ghorbund valley. The latter route, which is evidently the same that is called by Lieut. Wood the Ghorbund Pass, is frequented by travellers and caravans, and was even successfully crossed in 1840 by a troop of horse artillery. It could therefore offer no extraordinary difficulties to an army such as that of Alexander. (Cunningham's *Ancient Geography of India*, pp. 24, 25.)

Mr. Grote inclines to the pass of Bamian, because " it seems the only one among the four passes open to an army in the winter" (vol. xii. p. 271, *note*). But it is clear that the supposition of Alexander's having crossed the mighty range of the Hindoo Koosh " towards the close of winter " (Ibid.) is not only uncalled for, but at variance with the distinct statements of ancient authors. Arrian indeed conveys no definite information upon the subject, and the narrative of Curtius is very confused, but Strabo, whose narrative of this part of Alexander's movements derived from Aristobulus is remarkably distinct and clear (xv. p. 725), says that he traversed the land of the Paropamisadæ (*i.e.* from Candahar to Cabul) at the time of the setting of the Pleiades (ὑπὸ Πλειάδος δύσιν) *i.e.* the beginning of the winter : and suffered much from snow and hardships. He was still at the foot of the mountains on the south side : but having wintered there and founded a city (διαχειμάσας δ' αὐτόθι, καὶ πόλιν κτίσας) he crossed the mountain range into Bactria (ὑπερήκρισεν εἰς τὴν Βακτριανήν). It was not therefore till the spring (of B.C. 329) that he crossed the Hindoo Koosh, at which time all the passes are open, though still covered with snow, so that an army would suffer severely in crossing them, as we know in fact that Alexander's army did. (See Lieut. Wood's account of his passage of the Panchshir Pass in April. *Journey to the Oxus*, chap. xxiv.) It is said however that the Pass of Kushan is open all the year through.

NOTE Z, p. 437.

COMPARATIVE VALUE OF THE HISTORIANS OF ALEXANDER.

In all geographical inquiries and discussions of the difficulties that occur in attempting to trace the campaigns of Alexander, it is especially important to bear in mind the different character and value of the authorities from which our information is derived. Of these Arrian, who occupies beyond all comparison the foremost place, though writing centuries after the events which he records, bases his narrative, as he himself tells us, mainly, if not exclusively, upon those of Aristobulus and Ptolemy the son of Lagus, both of whom were companions in arms of Alexander, and accompanied him throughout his expedition. So far therefore as his narrative represents these authorities, it may be received as thoroughly trustworthy, or at least incomparably superior in this respect to any other that we possess. But moreover Arrian was himself a man who had received a military training, who had commanded armies and governed provinces, and was therefore the better able to understand and appreciate the true merit of such authors as those mentioned. To this it must be added, that we learn from his report to the emperor Hadrian concerning the shores of the Euxine (commonly known as the Periplus of the Euxine Sea) as well as from his having prepared and published the elaborate abstract of the voyage of Nearchus, which will be examined in the next chapter, that Arrian had a special turn for geography, and was therefore disposed to pay as much attention to the geographical, as to the historical, statements of his original authorities.

It is entirely in accordance with this that we find the notices in Strabo connected with the campaigns of Alexander (which are very numerous) almost always in agreement with those of Arrian. Strabo indeed appears to have written these portions of his work with that of Aristobulus constantly before him, and there is little doubt that many of his statements are derived from that author, even where he is not quoted by name.

But the case is quite otherwise with regard to the three other extant historians of Alexander—Diodorus, Plutarch and Quintus Curtius. All three of these writers appear to have chiefly followed the authority of Clitarchus, who, though a contemporary of the great king, was certainly not a writer of judgment and discretion, and had in a great degree the turn, unfortunately so common with the Greeks, of converting history into a rhetorical exercise, and looking far more to the opportunities afforded him for the display of his oratorical powers than to the accuracy of his facts or the truth of his historical details. (See Geier, *Alexandri Magni Historianum Scriptores*, 8vo. Lips. 1844, pp. 154–159; Heyne, *de Fontibus Diodori*, p. 115.) Unfortunately the same defect is found in his

Roman follower Quintus Curtius. It is impossible to read his history through without being struck with the fact that his main object was evidently to imitate, and if possible rival, Livy; and that the style, and not truth or accuracy was what he regarded as the main end of history. Unfortunately his success in this respect was such as to secure for him in modern times a degree of popularity that has tended greatly to vitiate the prevailing notions concerning the history of Alexander.[2] At the same time he has written with that careless indifference to geography which was so common among Roman writers; and though he has sometimes preserved to us names and details which would otherwise have been wanting, his geographical statements must always be received with caution, and are by no means implicitly to be relied on, in the absence of other evidence.

The same remark applies with equal force to Diodorus. Though his dry and prosaic narrative presents the strongest contrast with the turgid eloquence of Quintus Curtius, it is almost equally unworthy of confidence in regard to any details whether military or geographical, while the close agreement between the two shows that they are unquestionably derived from the same source. But we have abundant evidences from other parts of the history of Diodorus, where we have the opportunity of comparing him with better authorities, of his carelessness and inaccuracy in regard to geographical matters.

Nor is the case otherwise with Plutarch. If that writer has been justly termed the prince of biographers, the very qualities which entitle him to that praise are unfavourable to his value as a historian. To him everything is subordinate to the representation of his hero. It is the *man* Alexander with whom alone he is concerned; not the conquest of Persia and India, still less the geographical details of his campaigns, that he is desirous to bring before his readers; and if we find at times an incidental notice of value in regard to these subjects, it is rather accidental than introduced with a set purpose.

[2] It is remarkable that a writer so popular and well known in modern times as Quintus Curtius should not be mentioned by any ancient author, and we are consequently left in the dark as to the period at which he flourished. It may, however, probably be inferred that he was subsequent to Quintilian, who could otherwise have hardly failed to notice a writer of such oratorical pretensions.

NOTE A a, p. 440.

LEGENDS CONCERNING BACCHUS AND HERCULES.

The Greeks found, as they fancied, a confirmation of these legends concerning Bacchus, not only in the occurrence of names such as Nysa and Meron,—the resemblance of which was doubtless purely accidental,—but in the presence of ivy, as well as of wild vines, and the festive habits and bacchanalian processions of the natives. This account of their manners is confirmed by recent researches. "Ivy as far as has yet been ascertained, does not grow in the Cabul valley, but the grape flourishes and abounds in all the valleys of the Hindoo Koosh. The Kafirs, or people who dwell on the north of the Afghans, make wine, and old and young of both sexes amongst them drink it. They are very fond of drinking-parties, and of music and dancing." (Wilson's *Ariana*, p. 193.) It is not improbable that these so-called Kafirs are the remains of the aboriginal tribes, which in the time of Alexander were more widely spread, and inhabited many of the valleys now occupied by the Afghans. Even Strabo treats all these fancied resemblances as pure fictions, invented for the purpose of flattering Alexander, and rejects the supposed expeditions of Hercules and Bacchus to India as wholly fabulous (xv. i. § 8, pp. 687, 688).

NOTE B b, p. 440.

THE ROCK AORNUS.

The position of the celebrated rock fortress of Aornus, which holds so prominent a place in the narratives of Alexander's historians, has especially exercised the ingenuity of modern writers, but it cannot yet be said to be determined on satisfactory grounds. In fact there are so many sites in this rugged tract which suit with the general description of this impregnable fortress, that mere local resemblance has little weight, and we are so little able to follow the movements of Alexander through these regions that they afford us almost no assistance in the matter. If we can trust the expressions of Quintus Curtius and Diodorus, it rose immediately above the Indus, so that that river actually washed its base (Q. Curt. viii. ii. § 7; Diodor. xvii. 85), and this is confirmed by

EXPEDITION OF ALEXANDER.

Strabo (xv. p. 688), though not mentioned by Arrian It appears also from Arrian's narrative to have been situated *near to* (ξύνεγγυς) a town called Embolima, which he describes as some distance *above* the city of Peucelaotis, in the upper valley of the Indus; a position which explains Strabo's expression that it was *near the sources of the Indus*, a term by which he undoubtedly meant to designate the place where that river first issues from the gorges of the Himalaya. (See p. 449.) It seems probable therefore that the site must be sought in the neighbourhood of Derbend (about 50 miles above Attock), where the river issues out from the deep mountain gorges, through which its course has been confined for some time past, and emerges into the plains.

According to Major Abbott, whose view has been adopted by M. Vivien de St. Martin, the rock Aornus is represented by a projecting rock on the right bank of the Indus, opposite to the village of Torbela, about twenty miles below the gorge of Derbend; while the site of Embolima is marked by the names of *Amb* and *Balimah*, still retained by two old castles in the neighbourhood of Derbend. But such resemblances of name are worth very little, and Arrian's narrative would certainly lead us to suppose that Embolima was situated *below* Aornus. The name also is certainly Greek (at least in the form transmitted to us), and was probably applied to a place situated at the confluence of some other river with the Indus.

The whole subject is ably discussed by Mr. Grote (*History of Greece*, vol. xii. p 304, note), by M. Vivien de St. Martin (*Géographie Grecque et Latine de l'Inde*, p. 40-44, and by Mr. Long in Smith's *Dict. of Ancient Geography*, art. *Aornus*).

It has been since investigated anew by General Cunningham, who had the great advantage of personal acquaintance with the localities. (See his *Ancient Geography of India*, pp. 58-78.) But the site on which he has fixed—an isolated mountain called Ranigat, 16 miles N. of the town of Ohind on the Indus—though answering in some respects well to the description of the fortress of Aornus (he himself admits that the resemblance is incomplete), is liable to the insuperable objection that it is so far from the Indus as to be wholly at variance with the statements of Curtius, Diodorus and Strabo, as to its proximity to that river. It is singular that General Cunningham does not even allude to this difficulty, which must be considered as conclusive against the site in question. The authority of either Curtius or Diodorus *alone* might well be rejected, especially if *opposed* to Arrian, but that is not the case in this instance, while their *joint* statement is confirmed by that of Strabo, who certainly derived his information concerning the campaigns of Alexander in these regions from very good sources.

In accordance with this view General Cunningham would identify Embolima with Ohind, a town on the right bank of the Indus, about 18 miles above Attock; but his reasons for so doing are quite inconclusive in themselves. The one conclusion must stand or fall with the other.

The name Aornus is doubtless a Hellenised form of some native appellation—distorted so as to suit the fanciful etymology from ἀ and ὄρνις, as inaccessible even to birds. It is suggested by Professor Wilson that this was merely the Sanscrit term Awara or Awarana, signifying "an enclosure" or "stockade," so that Aornus was in reality nothing more than a stockaded enclosure, situated on a detached hill or mountain of difficult approach. (Wilson's *Ariana*, p. 192.) In this case we cannot hope for any assistance in determining the site from resemblance of name.

NOTE C c, p. 440.

PEUCELAOTIS.

The position of Peucelaotis, which appears sometimes as the name of a city, sometimes as that of a district, is very imperfectly marked by the Greek and Roman historians, though they all agree in placing the latter in the lower valley of the Cophen or Cabul river, corresponding to the district of Peshawer. The expressions of Strabo (xv. 1, § 27) would indeed seem to imply that the city was *on* the Indus, and close to the point at which Alexander crossed the river; but Arrian repeatedly uses the expression that it was *not far* from the Indus, which is doubtless the more correct. The district of the name probably extended quite to that river, while the city was at some distance from its banks. The form Peucelaotis is so peculiarly Greek, as applied to a district (as in the case of Pelasgiotis, Histiæotis, &c.) as to lead to the suspicion that it was of purely Greek formation; but it appears probable that it was really a corruption of the Sanscrit name Pushkalavati, which occurs in the Mahabharata. The position of this is considered by oriental scholars to be fixed at a place called Hashtnagar, on the north bank of the Cabul river, near its junction with the river of Swat. (St. Martin, *Géographie de l'Inde*, p. 37; Cunningham's *Geography of Ancient India*, pp. 49, 50.) This situation is certainly well in accordance with the expressions of Arrian.

NOTE D d, p. 443.

TAXILA.

The situation of Taxila between the Indus and the Hydaspes is unquestionable, but its precise site was, until very lately, the subject of much doubt. It was placed by M. Court, by Sir A. Burnes, and by Professor Wilson at Manikyala, celebrated for its *tope*, and where there are many other ruins. But the distances given by Pliny (vi. 17, § 62), on the authority of Diognetus and Bæton (the so-called *mensores* of Alexander) certainly seemed to coincide better with the suggestion of Major Abbott, adopted by M. de St. Martin, that we should look for it in the neighbourhood of Hassan Abdul, about 25 miles to the N.W. of Rawul Pindee. (See Burnes's *Travels*, vol. ii. p. 58; Wilson's *Ariana*, p. 196; St. Martin, *Géographie de l'Inde*, pp. 92–98.)

General Cunningham was the first to point out the existence of very extensive ruins in the neighbourhood of a place called Shah Dheri, about 8 miles S.E. of Hassan Abdul, which from their character and extent there seems every reason to believe to be those of Taxila. That city, the Indian name of which was Takshasila, continued to be a flourishing and important place for many centuries, and was still in existence in the seventh century after Christ. (Cunningham's *Ancient Geography of India*, pp. 104–120.)

NOTE E e, p. 443.

PASSAGE OF THE HYDASPES.

Besides the interest which naturally attaches to the scene of the great battle between Alexander and Porus, the site in question is of importance as being the point from which the king afterwards set out on his memorable voyage down the rivers to the Indian Ocean. All ancient writers agree in stating that the two cities,

Bucephala and Nicæa, were founded in commemoration of his victory, and were situated in the immediate neighbourhood of the spot where he crossed the river. Hence we might naturally look for some remains by which to identify the locality. But the difficulty arises rather from the abundance than the absence of such indications. Numerous ruins are found on both banks of the river for a space of about 40 miles below the modern town of Jhelum, extending as far as Jelalpoor and Harriah. But the question may be considered practically to lie between Jhelum, at which point one line of high road has in all ages crossed the Hydaspes, and the neighbourhood of Jelalpoor, about 30 miles lower down the river. It was at this latter point, to which there is also a frequented high road, that Mr. Elphinstone and his suite, on their return from Caubul, crossed the Hydaspes, and the spot was thought by them to correspond precisely with the description given by Quintus Curtius of Alexander's battle with Porus. (Elphinstone's *Caubul*, vol. i. p. 109, 8vo. edit.) Sir A. Burnes however inclined in favour of the neighbourhood of Jhelum, and the same view was adopted by General Court, who had investigated the subject on the spot, as well as at a later period by General Abbot. The question has been examined again with great care by General Cunningham, and the result of his researches seems to show that there is a strong predominance of argument in favour of Jelalpoor. In this case the town of that name probably occupies the site of Bucephala, while Nicæa may be placed on the same site with the modern town of Mong—only about six miles distant from the recent battle-field of Chilianwalla. (Cunningham, *Anc. Geogr. of India*, pp. 159-178. See also Burnes's *Travels*, vol. ii. pp. 49-51 ; and St. Martin, *Géographie de l'Inde*, pp. 99-102.)

NOTE F f, p. 444.

GEOGRAPHY OF THE PUNJAB.

At the present day we are so familiar with the geography of the Punjab, that it appears strange to recall how lately it is that we have acquired anything like a competent acquaintance even with its leading features. While in ancient times it was the first portion of India with which the Greeks and Romans became acquainted —indeed it may be said to be the only part of which they ever obtained any true geographical notion—it has in modern days on the contrary been the last region that has come within the domain of European knowledge. As late as 1775 when D'Anville published his *Antiquité Géographique de l'Inde*, the information possessed by that eminent geographer concerning this part of India was so imperfect that he was led into the grossest errors, and this portion of his work is a mass of confusion. Major Rennell was the first who was able, in part by the assistance of Oriental materials, to rectify these errors, and introduce a clear and intelligible view of the subject. (*Memoir of a Map of Hindostan*, p. 94–103, 3rd ed. Lond. 1793.) He himself observes that, as his own researches advanced, he was continually confirmed in his opinion of the accuracy of the statements transmitted to us by the historians of Alexander. Indeed there is no portion of the campaigns of that monarch in which the leading geographical features are more clearly marked, and can more readily be identified. That the case should be otherwise with regard to the various tribes and nations he encountered, can excite no surprise, when we consider how fluctuating are both the boundaries and appellations of such tribes, and how many successive waves of conquest have swept over the land since the time of Alexander. Moreover the operations against these different nations are generally indicated in the vaguest and most general manner, affording us little clue to their geographical position. (See the remarks of Major Rennell, p. 124.) Arrian himself had doubtless a very imperfect idea of the geography of the countries in question, and even if the writers whom he followed had supplied him with fuller details—which may well be doubted—he did not think fit to preserve them. As for Curtius and Diodorus their narratives are characterized, throughout the Indian campaigns, by even greater carelessness and inattention to geographical accuracy than that which generally marks their works.

The Punjab is (as its name imports) the "Land of the five Rivers," and all these rivers can be recognized and identified without difficulty. Even their names, which at first appear so totally different in their modern and ancient forms, will be found to present more points of resemblance than would be at first suspected, or else the change can be otherwise accounted for.

1. The Hydaspes is unquestionably the river commonly called in modern times the Jhelum (from a city of that name on its banks) but by Sanscrit writers the Bitasthá or Vitasthá, of which

the modern name of Behut (by which it is also known) is a mere corruption. The name is written by Ptolemy Bidaspes, a form that approximates more nearly to the Sanscrit than that usually adopted by Greek and Latin writers.

2. The Acesines is the Chenab, a name derived from the more ancient Sanscrit form Chandrabhága, which is traceable in the name Sandabala by which the river is designated by Ptolemy. The more usual form Acesines is said to have been an arbitrary change introduced by the Greeks with a view of avoiding a name supposed to be of ill omen.

3. The Hydraotes is the modern Ravee, an undoubted corruption of the Sanscrit Iravati, in which we trace without difficulty the origin of the Greek appellation.

4. The Hyphasis or Hypasis is unquestionably the modern Beas or Beyah, a name which is derived from the Sanscrit Vipásá. Here also the form preserved by Ptolemy, Bibasis, is the more correct, while that of Hypanis, adopted by Strabo and Diodorus, is clearly erroneous.

5. The Sutledge, which at the present day is reckoned the last of the five rivers, is not mentioned by the historians of Alexander, that conqueror having stopped short at the Hyphasis—but it appears in Pliny under the name of Hesidrus, while it is termed by Ptolemy Zaradrus. The Sanscrit form is Satadrus.

But while the principal rivers of the Punjab can thus be idenfied with certainty, it must not be too hastily assumed that they followed in the time of Alexander exactly the same course as at present. Since the country has been better known, abundant evidence has been brought forward to show that great changes have taken place even in recent times. Thus we know that the junction of the Sutledge and Beas, which now takes place about 40 miles above Ferozepoor, was formerly in the immediate neighbourhood of that city, and it was not till the year 1796 that the Sutledge suddenly changed its course, and joined the Beas at their present point of confluence. (Cunningham, pp. 217, 222.) Almost exactly the same thing occurred with regard to the Ravee (Hydraotes), which formerly flowed under the walls of Mooltân, and fell into the Chenab (Acesines) about 15 miles lower down. At the present day the junction takes place near Diwana Sinand, more than 30 miles above Mooltân. (Id. p. 221.) It is probable also that the Beas had in former days a wholly distinct course of its own, parallel with that of the Sutledge, and General Cunningham supposes it to have held this independent channel until it ultimately fell into the Chenab, and did not join the Sutledge at all. (Id. p. 223.) Still more remarkable is the change in the junction of the Indus itself with the Chenab, which in the time of Timour and Akbar took place opposite Ooch, though their streams now unite at Mittunkote, 60 miles lower down. This change has taken place since the commencement of the present century. (Id. p. 220.) There is great reason, as we shall hereafter see, to suppose that still more extensive changes have taken place in the lower course of the Indus since the period of the Mahometan conquest of Sinde.

NOTE G g, p. 444.

ALTARS ON THE HYPHASIS.

When we read the description of the twelve altars erected by Alexander on the western bank of the Hyphasis, which appear to have been massive constructions, destined by him to remain as monuments of the point to which he had advanced, we are almost tempted to hope that some vestiges of them may still be discovered. This hope would be strongly confirmed if we could believe the statement of Philostratus, that Apollonius of Tyana on his journey into India (in the 2nd century after the Christian era) found the altars still subsisting, and even their inscriptions still legible. (Philostr. *Vit. Apollon.* ii. 43)[3] But it is certain that no reliance can be placed upon that fabulous narrative; and the researches of modern travellers have failed to discover any trace of such monuments. If indeed they are to be sought (as is held by many modern writers) *below* the present confluence of the Beas with the Sutledge, the shifting character of the stream and its frequent changes leave little probability that the site can ever be ascertained. (This character of the Sutledge is sufficiently marked by its original Sanscrit name of Satadrus—" the hundred-channeled river.") But if the point where Alexander came to the banks of the Beas was situated (as appears most probable) at some distance *above* the confluence of that river with the Sutledge, the right

---

[3] Plutarch also speaks of the altars as still subsisting *in his time* (*Alex.* 62), but this is doubtless mere vague hearsay

bank is throughout considerably more elevated than the left, and hence any considerable changes in the channel are much less likely. Yet it appears that even in this part of its course the river carries away villages and even towns, and it is said that ancient ruins have been thus destroyed in quite modern days. Very little hope can therefore be entertained of the discovery of any monumental remains calculated to throw light upon this interesting geographical question. (See the descriptions of the rivers Beas and Sutledge in Elphinstone's *Caubul*, vol. ii. p. 426, and Burnes's *Travels*, vol. i. pp. 153, 157, vol. ii. 4-7.)

The altars were undoubtedly situated on the right bank of the Hyphasis. Pliny alone places them on the opposite or eastern bank. He says of the Hyphasis " qui fuit Alexandri itinerum terminus, exsuperato tamen amne, arisque in adversa ripa dicatis." (*Hist. Nat.* vi. 17, § 62.) But this is opposed to the concurrent testimony of the historians of Alexander, as well as to the probabilities of the case. (Arrian, *Anab.* v. 29; Curt. Diodor. xvii. 95.)

It appears to be well ascertained (as has been already mentioned) that the Sutledge, at a comparatively recent period, did not join the Beas till near Ferozepore, about 40 miles below the present junction (Burnes, vol. ii. p. 4, 5; Cunningham, p. 222) and this, of course, greatly increases the probability that Alexander reached the banks of the latter river above the confluence.

Though the Sutledge is in many respects the more important stream and has much the longest course, it is little, if at all, the larger river at the point of junction, and the united streams are known for some distance below the confluence by the name of Beas, as they appear to have been in ancient times by that of Hyphasis. But the combined stream in the lower part of its course is now generally known as the Garra. (Elphinstone, *l. c.*)

General Cunningham, in his recent work, places the site in question *below* the *present* junction of the two streams, but *above* the ancient confluence near Ferozepoor. This is liable to the objection that the interval between the two rivers could in this case have been only a few miles, while the measurements given by Pliny assign a distance of not less than 168 Roman miles from the Hyphasis to the Hesidrus or Sutledge, and the same from thence to the Jumna. (Plin. *l. c.* § 63.) But General Cunningham supposes Pliny to have misunderstood his authorities, and that these really gave only one distance—the interval between the Hyphasis and Sutledge being disregarded as practically of no account (p. 217).

This is cutting the Gordian knot with a vengeance! and is the less excusable in this case, as, if we suppose Alexander to have followed a more northerly route, keeping nearer to the mountains, the interval between the Beas and the Sutledge really becomes almost exactly equal to that from the Sutledge to the Jumna.

NOTE H h, p. 445.

SANGALA AND THE CATHÆI.

These arguments have been very fully urged by Gen. Cunningham (*Ancient Geography of India*, pp. 179-190), who had himself visited the site which he would identify with Sangala. It is situated in the midst of the plain called the Rechna Dooab, between the Ravee (Hydraotes) and the Chenab (Acesines) about 60 miles west of Lahore, and the local circumstances certainly seem to correspond very well with the description of the siege by Alexander. But if this be really the position of Sangala, we must suppose that after crossing the Hydraotes (which he is distinctly stated to have done) he *recrossed* that river in order to attack the Cathæans, and capture their chief city. That he should have turned aside from his general line of march for this purpose would be quite in accordance with his practice on other occasions, and is not inconsistent with the expressions of Arrian in regard to this particular expedition (*Anab.* v. 22) but if he recrossed the Hydraotes and returned so far westward, without our finding any indication of it in our existing historians, it will certainly prove that their narrative is even more vague and untrustworthy in a geographical point of view than we had been accustomed to suppose. The successive passages of the great rivers of the Punjab appear to form the distinct steps that mark the conqueror's progress; and if we cannot rely even upon these, the whole subject is thrown into hopeless confusion.

It is remarkable however that Strabo tells us that the Cathæans were situated, according to some authorities, between the Acesines and the *Hydaspes*, while others placed them beyond (*i.e.* eastward of) both the Acesines and the Hydraotes (xv. c 1, § 30, p. 699). The name of Sagala, which is probably identical with the Sangala of Arrian, is found also in Ptolemy (vii. 1, § 46), who however places it in the neighbourhood of the *Hydaspes*, thus apparently following the anonymous authorities cited by Strabo.

The Cathæi are described by ancient authors as one of the most powerful nations of India, and Strabo has preserved to us some curious particulars concerning their manners and customs (*l. c.*). They appear to have been closely connected with the Oxydracæ and the Malli, with whom they were probably conterminous, as the three nations made common cause against Alexander. (Arrian, *l. c.*) But this affords us little assistance in determining their precise position; that of the Oxydracæ being almost equally obscure.

The resemblance of name might easily lead us to suppose that there existed some connection between these Cathæans and the well-known mediæval appellation of Cathay, as applied to a region of the far east. But it is certain that the similarity is purely fortuitous; an instructive warning against too hastily building any conclusions upon such resemblances.

Sir A. Burnes, on the other hand, has suggested, very plausibly, that the name is connected with that of the Kattia, a predatory and warlike race who are found scattered at intervals through the plains of the Punjab, and even across the deserts to Delhi. They now live an erratic life, but are supposed by Burnes to be the aborigines of the country. (*Travels*, vol. i. p. 112.)

NOTE I i, p. 446.

BOATS ON THE INDUS.

The statement in the text is that given by Arrian in his *Anabasis* (vi. 2, § 7), and rests on the authority of Ptolemy. In his *Indica* however (c. 19, § 7), where he is apparently following Nearchus, Arrian states the whole number of ships at only eight hundred, including both ships of war and transports. Schmieder and some other editors would correct this to eighteen hundred: but it seems more probable that the basis of the two calculations was different. Ptolemy distinctly includes the ordinary river-boats, which would doubtless have been collected in large numbers to assist in transporting so great an army and its supplies; while the terms of Nearchus would seem to imply only ships of war or regular transports.

At the present day the Indus is navigated by a large number of boats or vessels of the country, some of them of large size. Near its mouth indeed it is navigable only for large flat-bottomed boats, called "doondees," which, though large and unwieldy, never exceed fifty tons in burthen. (Burnes's *Travels*, vol. i. p. 219.) But from Bukkur upwards it is navigated by a different description of boat called "shruk," "which is admirably adapted to the transport of troops, both horse and foot, from being as roomy before as astern." (Ib. p. 261.) The Chenab or Acesines is also navigable for boats of a similar description. (Ib. p. 276.) There can be no doubt that numerous vessels of this character would be found in the Indus and its tributaries as early as the time of Alexander, and Ptolemy expressly mentions that they were turned to account as part of his fleet. But the transports for his cavalry appear to have been especially constructed for the purpose; such a sight as a body of horses on board ship had never been before seen in these parts. (Arrian, *Anab.* vi. 3, § 4.)

The Mahomedan historians, with their customary exaggeration, speak of forty thousand (!) vessels as employed in the navigation of the Indus under the Mogul dynasty. (Abúl Fazil, quoted by Vincent, *Voyage of Nearchus*, p. 88.)

Alexander had, on a former occasion, when he first came to the banks of the Hydaspes and found himself opposed by Porus, transported the vessels of which he had previously made use for the passage of the Indus *overland* to the Hydaspes. (Arrian, *Anab.* v. 8, § 4.) But there is certainly no reason to suppose, as Dr. Vincent has done, that this was the case with the fleet with which he descended the river. It was in fact much more easy to construct a fleet on the Hydaspes than on the Indus. (See note to p. 446.)

NOTE K k, p. 447.

DESCENT OF THE INDUS.

Sir A. Burnes, who in 1831 ascended the Indus and its tributaries the Chenab and Ravee, to Lahore, took exactly sixty days on the *ascending* voyage at the most favourable season, but he considers it possible for a boat to "drop down from Lahore to the sea in *fifteen* days" at the very quickest, six of which would be occupied in the descent to Mooltan, and nine from thence to the sea. (*Travels*, vol. 1. p. 196, 197, *Journal of Geographical Society*, vol. iii. p. 113.) He estimates the distance from Lahore to the sea, by the course of the river, at about 1000 British miles (Ib. p. 195). The distance traversed by the fleet of Alexander must have been considerably less, as although the point from which it set out was (probably) at least as near the mountains as Lahore, the course of the Jhelum and Chenab, above their junction with the Ravee, is much less tortuous than that of the latter river.

Pliny absurdly asserts that Alexander took five months and some days to descend the Indus, *though he never proceeded less than* 600 *stadia a day.* (Proditur Alexandrum nullo die minus stadia sexcenta navigasse in Indo, nec potuisse ante menses quinque enavigare, adjectis paucis diebus. Plin. *H.N.* vi. 17, § 60.) He would thus have navigated the river for more than 9000 G. miles! It would be curious to know from what source Pliny derived this extraordinary statement, which he repeats without in the least perceiving its absurdity. But a descent of sixty miles in a day, as an *occasional* rate of progress, is by no means improbable.

NOTE L 1, p. 447.

CONFLUENCE OF THE HYDASPES WITH THE ACESINES.

The confluence of the Hydaspes with the Acesines appears as a point of much importance in all the accounts of the voyage of Alexander. According to the historians the junction of the two streams gave rise to dangerous rapids, accompanied with violent eddies and tumultuous waves, which not only caused great alarm to the Macedonian sailors, but occasioned the loss of several ships. (Arrian, *Anab.* vi. 4, 5, Q. Curt. ix. 4, § 9-14; Diodor. xvii. 97.) It is a strong instance of the carelessness of Diodorus in geographical matters that he represents these rapids as occurring at the confluence of the two rivers *with the Indus.* The circumstances are as usual amplified by Quintus Curtius with much turgid eloquence, but even in the more sober narrative of Arrian the dangers appear sufficiently formidable. Cherefeddin also, the historian of Timour, says that "the waves dashing against each other, made it appear like a troubled ocean" (cited by Rennell, p. 118). But it appears from the description of Sir A. Burnes, the first European who visited the spot, that these accounts, though not without foundation, are greatly exaggerated. "The river (he says) joins the Acesines with a murmuring noise, but the velocity of the current is inconsiderable, and vessels pass it without danger, except in July and August. There are no eddies or rocks, nor is the channel confined, but the ancient character is supported by the noise of the confluence, which is greater than that of any of the other rivers." (*Travels*, vol. i. p. 109.) The boatmen of the river however still regard the passage as a perilous one, during the season when the river is swollen. (Ibid.)

NOTE M m, p. 447.

COURSE OF THE HYPHASIS.

Arrian expressly says that the Hyphasis (meaning undoubtedly the combined stream formed by the Beas and Sutledge, now known as the Garra) falls into the Acesines (*Anab.* vi. 14, § 5) below its junction with the Hydraotes. He adds that the Acesines continues to retain its name, notwithstanding its junction with so many important rivers, until it finally discharged their united waters into the Indus. This still continues to be the case with the Chenab. (Burnes, vol. i. p. 78.)

It is singular that notwithstanding this distinct statement of Arrian, both Major Rennell and Dr. Vincent doubted whether the Hyphasis really fell into the Acesines, and the former even goes so far as to say "*the truth is*, that the Hyphasis (or Beyah) does not join the Chenaub, but after uniting its waters with those of the Sutlege, falls into the Indus a great way further down" (p. 129), and his map is constructed in accordance with this assumption.

As has been already mentioned (Note F f) it is probable that the Indus and Acesines in the time of Alexander met in the neighbourhood of Ooch, considerably above their present point of junction, but in this case there is no reason to suppose that the Hyphasis or Sutledge pursued a separate course till it joined the Indus. The contrary is distinctly asserted by Arrian, and on this point it is difficult to believe that the companions of Alexander could have been in error.

NOTE N n, p. 448.

THE INDUS IDENTIFIED WITH THE NILE.

So imperfect were the geographical ideas commonly entertained previous to this voyage of Alexander, that the king himself when he first came to the river and saw crocodiles in it, was convinced that it was the same with the Nile, and wrote a letter to Olympias containing this statement, which appears to have been extant at a later period. (Arrian, *Anab.* vi. 1; Strab. xv. 1, p. 696.) It was only on his march through the Punjab that he obtained more accurate information from the natives, and became convinced that it ultimately flowed into the Southern Ocean. It is remarkable to see how in this respect the geographical information of the Greeks seems to have retrograded since the time of Herodotus. No allusion is found to the voyage of Scylax related by that historian, which must either have been disbelieved or forgotten, while the just conclusions derived from it by Herodotus had fallen into the same oblivion.

But absurd as was this identification, the general resemblance between the Indus and the Nile, which are constantly brought into comparison by the Greek geographers (Strabo, xv. p. 692, &c.), is certainly such as to justify their observations. The resemblance of the lower valley of the Indus, from the time it has received the waters of the Punjab, with Egypt, is dwelt upon by modern travellers. "One description (says Mr. Elphinstone) might indeed serve for both. A smooth and fertile plain is bounded on one side by mountains, and on the other by a desert. It is divided by a large river which forms a Delta as it approaches the sea, and annually inundates and enriches the country near its banks. The climate of both is hot and dry, and rain is of rare occurrence in either country." (Elphinstone's *Caubul*, vol. ii. p. 225.)

NOTE O o, p. 448.

WIDTH OF THE INDUS.

According to Sir A Burnes the Indus where it has been joined by the rivers of the Punjab "never shallows, even in the dry season, to less than fifteen feet and seldom preserves so great a breadth as half a mile." (*Travels*, vol. i. p. 195.) "Near Hydrabad it is but 830 yards, at Tatta less than 700, and below the village of Hilaya, 15 miles from that town, it does not exceed 600." (Ib. p. 242) But in one part of its course above Bukkur, and below Mittun Kote (at which place it receives the united waters of the Punjab), it is more widely spread, so that it "often exceeds a thousand yards in breadth, and at Mittun was found to be even double that width." (Ibid. p. 260.)

Similarly exaggerated statements were current among the ancients with regard to the principal tributaries of the Indus. but we meet with others of a much more authentic character. Ptolemy the son of Lagus, as cited by Arrian (v. 20, § 8) stated that the Acesines, at the point where Alexander crossed it, was fifteen stadia in width, with a strong and violent current. This was the only one of the rivers of the Punjab concerning the size of which that author had left any definite information. and his accuracy is confirmed by Mr. Elphinstone, who says that the Chenab at the Wuzeerabad Ghat, where he crossed it on the 31st of July, "*measured* one mile three furlongs and twenty perches, from edge to edge of the water. The soundings were the same as the Jelum, fourteen feet the greatest, but the current was more rapid by a knot and a half." (Elphinstone's *Caubul*, vol. ii. p. 423.) The Jhelum (Hydaspes) was found by the same authority to measure at Jelalpoor one mile one furlong and thirty-five perches, though it had not then attained its full height (Ib. p. 421).

NOTE Pp, p. 449.

SOURCE OF THE INDUS.

The Afghans, even at the present day, regard the place where the Indus first issues from the mountains as very near the *source* of the river. (St. Martin, *Géographie de l'Inde*, p. 44.) The part of its course above Derbend is indeed the most imperfectly known of its whole stream, and it is a remarkable fact that down to the present time no European traveller has ever followed the valley between Acho and Derbend. In the last century modern geographers only knew vaguely that it must rise at some distance from a point where it appeared as a large stream; but even Major Rennell, as late as 1793, supposed it to flow from the north, and that it must have its sources on the *western* side of the range that runs northward from the Hindoo Koosh, and in which the Oxus also takes its rise. He was thus led to place the sources of the Indus nearly due north from Attock, while he supposed the river that flowed by Ladak, of the existence of which he had heard, to be a branch *of the Ganges*, and that another branch of the same river took its rise in the Lake

Mansarowar. (See the map annexed to his Memoir, p. 201.) D'Anville, about twenty years earlier, took much the same view of the sources of the Indus and the Ganges, while he supposed the Brahmaputra, which he rightly conceived to have its origin in the same mountain group, to be the same with the Irawaddy, and to flow through Pegu on its way to the Gulf of Bengal. (See the map annexed to his *Antiquité Géographique de l'Inde*, published in 1775.) This last error was first corrected by Major Rennell, in 1781. In criticising ancient geographers it is important to bear in mind how imperfect was our knowledge of many countries of the old world down to a very recent period, and how readily even the ablest modern writers have been led into false geographical combinations by imperfect information.

NOTE Qq, p. 450.

DELTA OF THE INDUS.

The statements of ancient writers concerning the *width* of the Delta, or the extent comprised between its two arms, are equally irreconcilable with the supposition that the existing Delta was meant. Aristobulus estimated the *base* of the triangle, or the interval between the two mouths, at 1000 stadia, but Nearchus reckoned it not less than 1800 stadia (Strab. xv. p. 701) Now, according to Burnes, the land embraced by the two actual arms of the Indus extends, at the junction of the rivers with the sea, to about 70 British miles, "and this, correctly speaking, is the existing Delta of the river." (*Travels*, vol. i. p. 208 , *Journal of Geographical Society*, vol. iii. p. 115.) But he adds that "the Indus covers with its waters a wider space than is thus described, and has two other mouths to the eastward of these, the Seer and Koree;" and with the addition of these (now forsaken) branches, the river presents a face to the sea of about 125 British miles. (Ib.) But these two arms have nothing to do with Tattah, and it is difficult to understand how Sir A. Burnes reconciled the statement which he repeatedly makes, that the Koree was formerly the eastern branch of the Indus, with his adoption of the view (generally followed in his day) which identified Pattala with Tattah.

The two main arms of the Delta of Egypt are more than 90 G. miles in length (as measured on the map, without following their windings in detail), while the sea front of the Delta, from the Pelusian to the Canopic mouth, is not less than 140 G. miles, or 1400 stadia.

NOTE R r, p. 450.

SITE OF PATTALA.

This view, which appears to have been first suggested by Pottinger, and adopted by Droysen and Benfey, has been worked out very fully by M. de St. Martin, *Géographie de l'Inde*, pp. 169–172, and has certainly great probabilities in its favour. The suggestion first thrown out by Capt. McMurdo, and which Prof. Wilson was inclined to adopt, that the bifurcation in the time of Alexander took place at a point much farther up the river, above Bukkur, where a dry channel or river-bed may still be traced, parting off from the main stream, and holding a direction towards the estuary of Koree, is liable to the great objection that the extent of the two arms would in this case enormously exceed those of the Nile, the *excess* being in this case as great as the *deficiency* if we place Pattala at Tattah, and it would also render it impossible to find room for the different tribes and cities reduced by Alexander between the confluence of the Indus with the Acesines, and the head of its Delta at Pattala.

But the point which both these views have in common, that the eastern mouth of the Indus was in ancient times by the estuary of Koree, close to the peninsula of Cutch, has certainly much to recommend it; and appears to be in accordance with all that we know of the changes that have taken place in this part of the country. Sir A. Burnes, though he continued to identify Pattala with Tattah, speaks of the Koree as "the eastern, though forsaken branch of the Indus," and even terms it "the largest of all the mouths of the river, having become a branch of the sea as the fresh water has been turned from the channel." (*Travels*, vol. i. p. 7.) There appears, moreover, to be authentic evidence of the waters in this instance having been artificially diverted from their course and prevented from flowing in their former channel, with a view to injure the inhabitants of Cutch. (Ib. pp. 215, 309.) At the same time we know that all this neighbourhood has been visited by repeated earthquakes, and it is not unlikely that changes of level resulting from this cause may also have contributed to alter the geographical features of the country. (See Lyell's *Principles of Geology*, vol. ii. pp. 98-102, 10th edition; and the valuable paper of Sir Bartle Frere on the Runn of Cutch, in the *Journ. Geogr. Society*, vol. xl. p. 121.)

Gen. Cunningham, who has most recently investigated the subject, concurs in placing Pattala on the same site with Hyderabad, which occupies a long, flat-topped hill that must have in all ages been favourably adapted for the site of a city. The name indeed is modern, but it is still known to the people as Neeruncote, by which name it is mentioned in the Arab historians and geographers. (Cunningham's *Ancient Geography of India*, pp. 279-285.)

NOTE S s, p. 451.

CITIES OF THE MALLI.

It must be borne in mind in discussing this question that the Ravee or Hydraotes, which at present joins the Chenab more than 30 miles above Mooltan, formerly held a separate course much lower down, and passed under the walls of Mooltan, completely encircling that fortress, before it joined the Chenab. (Cunningham, p. 221.)

General Cunningham, who has himself explored this part of the country, has endeavoured to trace the successive marches of Alexander in his expedition against the Malli, and to identify the towns and strongholds that he reduced. He considers the first city taken by him (Arrian, vi. 6, § 2) to be represented by Kot Kamolia, "a small but ancient town," about 44 miles to the S.E. of the junction of the Hydaspes and Acesines (the point from which Alexander set out), and only a few miles from the west bank of the Ravee. Harapa, a place where there are extensive ruins on the opposite side of the Ravee, about 16 miles from Kot Kamalia, he supposes to be "the other city" against which Perdiccas was dispatched with the cavalry, while Alexander himself attacked the former town (Ibid. § 4). The next city, taken by Alexander after crossing the Hydraotes (Ibid. 7, § 2, 3), he identifies with Tulamba, "a remarkably strong fortress" on the left bank of the Ravee, about 52 miles to the N.E. of Mooltan: while the fourth city, called by Arrian "a certain city of the Brachmans" (Ibid. § 4) he considers to be represented by the old ruined fort and town of Atari, 20 miles from Tulamba on the road to Mooltan. All these sites are marked by the presence of mounds, which, together with the large size of the bricks employed in the ruins, are considered to afford unquestionable evidence of remote antiquity. (Cunningham, pp 208-229.)

The above identifications appear plausible enough. But there is great difficulty in adopting the supposition that the capital city of the Malli (ἡ μεγίστη τῶν Μαλλῶν πόλις, Arrian, vi. 8, § 4) occupied the site of the modern Mooltan, the strongest fortress in this part of the country, and the natural strength of which must have been still greater when it was surrounded by the waters of the Ravee. But the capital was *abandoned* by the Malli, without an attempt at resistance, when they heard of the approach of Alexander. they withdrew to the north bank of the Hydraotes and being there attacked again by the Macedonians, fled for refuge to a neighbouring city that was strongly fortified (Ibid § 7). It was in the attack of this last city that Alexander himself was severely wounded and narrowly escaped with his life. General Cunningham has confounded this city with the capital of the Malli, or combined the two together, which is certainly at variance with the narrative of Arrian. Moreover that author clearly represents the place where the king was wounded as at some distance from the Hydraotes : and his description of the voyage down that river to its confluence with the Acesines, where the main army was encamped, implies one of longer duration than the few miles from Mooltan to the Chenab. Q. Curtius indeed represents it as a four days' voyage (ix. 23, § 3), but as he is evidently following a different set of authorities from Arrian, no reliance can be placed upon this.

NOTE T t, p. 451.

THE OXYDRACÆ.

The position of the Oxydracæ is much more obscurely indicated than that of the Malli. They are mentioned on more than one occasion as having combined with the Malli, and also with the Cathæi, to oppose the progress of Alexander. After the reduction of the several cities of the Malli, the Oxydracæ joined with them in sending deputies to tender their submission. But we have no account in Arrian of any military operations against them, or of the capture of any of their cities and we cannot infer with certainty from the manner in which he speaks of Alexander's descending the river to attack the Malli and Oxydracæ (vi. 4, § 3), that he actually traversed the territories of the latter people. All that we learn concerning them is quite consistent with the supposition that they lay on the east or left bank of the Sutledge—the province of Bahawalpoor—though they may very well have extended as far as its junction with the Indus, and the neighbourhood of Ooch.

General Cunningham alone places the Oxydracæ to the *north* of the Malli, which is certainly contrary to the natural inference from the narrative of Arrian. His principal reason seems to be that Pliny speaks of the turning-point of Alexander's career (meaning probably the spot on the bank of the Hyphasis where he erected his altars) as in the territory of the Sydracæ, which is probably the same name with that of the Oxydracæ. But the passage in question (in Sydracis *Expeditionum Alexandri termino*, xii. 6, § 24) is merely one of those passing notices hastily thrown in by the author, and which are of very little value in a geographical point of view.

We learn from Arrian that there was considerable confusion among Greek authors with regard to the Oxydracæ and the Malli, many writers asserting that the fortress in the attack of which Alexander was so severely wounded lay in the country of the Oxydracæ (a statement which we find repeated by Q. Curtius, ix. 18, § 26), but this he unequivocally rejects as a mistake. He evidently is here writing on the authority of Aristobulus and Ptolemy.

The name of the Oxydracæ (Ὀξυδράκαι) which is found in this form both in Arrian and Q. Curtius, is written by Strabo Σιδράκαι, and by Pliny (*l. c.*) Sydraci. It is clearly identical with the Sanscrit Sudraka or Suräka, who are found in the Mahabharata associated with the Malâva (Malli), just as the Oxydracæ and Malli are by the Greek writers. (St. Martin, *Géographie de l'Inde*, p. 116.) The Hydracæ (Ὑδράκαι) of Strabo are doubtless the same people.

NOTE Uu, p. 452.

CHANGES IN THE COURSE OF THE INDUS.

The collocation of these various tribes on the Lower Indus depends in great measure upon the determination of a preliminary question—that of the course of the Indus itself. Captain McMurdo in an interesting memoir published in 1834 in the *Journal of the Royal Asiatic Society* (vol. i. p. 20–44) was the first to draw attention to the great changes that have taken place in the course of the Indus, and which, as he shows, were not confined to the Delta or lowest part of the river, but have extended even to the part of its course more than 200 miles higher up. He seems to have clearly established the fact that even so late as the seventh century after Christ, the main stream of the Indus did not follow its present channel, but pursued a more direct course towards the sea, at a distance in some parts of sixty or seventy miles farther east than it at present flows. The old channel of the river, which is still distinctly to be traced, and is known as the Purana Deria or "old river," leaves the present stream at some distance above Bukkur, passes under the ruins of Alore, which was a large and flourishing city when it was captured by the Mahometans, and then holds a direct course towards the south, nearly as far as a city called Brahmanabad, above which it divides into two channels, the one having a direction to the S S.W. till it rejoins the present course of the river just above Hyderabad: the other having a south-easterly course towards the Runn of Cutch. (McMurdo, *l. c.*; Wilson's *Ariana*, p. 202; Cunningham's *Ancient Geography of India*, pp. 251, 252.) If this now deserted bed were the *main channel* of the Indus in the time of Alexander, which there is certainly strong reason to suppose, it explains the circumstance that no mention is found in the historians of Alexander of so remarkable a site as that of Bukkur, which could hardly have failed to attract their attention.

This important discovery at once sets aside all the conclusions of the earlier writers on the subject (Rennell, Vincent, &c.) who naturally assumed the Indus to have always followed its present course. The latest researches would apparently lead us to the following arrangement.—

1. The Sogdi, who were the first people encountered by Alexander in descending the main stream of the Indus, must be placed between the point of its confluence with the combined waters of the Punjab (which was at that time near Ooch), and that where the old channel of the river separates from the actual one. There are no means of fixing the site of their chief city with any certainty.

2. The kingdom of Musicanus, which was said to be one of the richest in India, may be placed on the banks of the Purana Deria or old channel of the Indus, and may well have deserved that character when it was irrigated by the waters of the river. It is

probable therefore that the chief city occupied the site of Alore, now in ruins, but celebrated by Mahometan traditions and histories as a place of great wealth and the metropolis of the whole surrounding country. This conclusion is adopted both by Prof. Wilson and Gen. Cunningham.

3. The kingdom of Oxycanus (called by other writers Porticanus) is more difficult to determine. but it seems to have *not* been situated on the Indus, and that Alexander quitted that river in order to attack it. The most plausible conjecture is that which would place it to the west of the Indus, on the banks of the river Gharra, and its capital city at Mahorta, near Larkhana, about 45 miles from Alore (Cunningham, pp. 259, 261). But the attempt to connect it with the Oskana of Ptolemy, which he describes as a city of Gedrosia (Ptol. vi. 21, § 5), appears to me entirely untenable.

4. The kingdom of Sambus is clearly to be placed in the district west of the Indus, at the foot of the mountain range that borders the broad valley on the west. The name of his capital city of Sindomana leads at once to identify it with Sehwân, an undoubtedly ancient site. The objection that Sindomana was clearly not on the Indus is at once removed, if the Indus flowed in its old channel, the nearest point of which is not less than 65 miles from Sehwân (Wilson's *Ariana*, p. 205; Cunningham, pp. 263–266).

NOTE V v, p. 455.

MARCH THROUGH GEDROSIA.

The length of time occupied on this march is surprising, especially as we are told that the army was compelled to make marches of inordinate length, in order to arrive at halting-places where water was to be obtained, a fact probable in itself. (Arrian, *Anab.* vi. 24, § 1, Strab. xv. 2, § 7, p. 723. See the remarks of Vincent, vol. i. p. 235, on this subject) But the troops were probably obliged to make frequent halts at the few places where they could supply themselves with water; and the accounts of the ancient writers which represent the country as a continuous sandy desert are undoubtedly exaggerated. No army *could* have marched through such a desert for sixty days without interruption. And so far as the Mekran is known, though generally arid and sterile, it contains throughout patches of a comparatively fertile character, producing excellent dates, though little or no grain. Moreover, time would necessarily be lost in the repeated attempts made to communicate with the fleet under Nearchus. The statement of Strabo that the days' marches amounted to two hundred, four hundred, and even six hundred stadia (70 miles) a day, is manifestly a great exaggeration, but forced marches would no doubt be required in order to pass from one station of wells to another. Such forced marches would however necessitate corresponding intervals of repose.

NOTE X x, p. 456.
ROUTE THROUGH GEDROSIA AND CARMANIA.

The description given by Sir H. Pottinger (*Travels in Beloochistan*, p. 131-134) of the desert which he traversed between Sarawan and Kullugan so closely resembles those preserved by Arrian and Strabo from the historians of Alexander, that it might almost seem to be translated from them. But the desert in question is situated in the northern part of Beloochistan, to the north of the range of mountains (the Mushti or Washati) which traverses the country from east to west, and apparently formed the northern limit of Gedrosia, while the route of Alexander unquestionably lay to the south of the same range. Strabo's testimony to his continued proximity to the sea is precise: and Sir H. Pottinger remarks that "had the Greek historians been even less explicit, the nature of the country alone must have decided any question that might have arisen upon this point" (*Travels*, p. 264). The interior of the Mekran is indeed still very imperfectly known: though the coast has been of late years thoroughly examined, for the purpose of laying down the line of electric telegraph from Gwadur to Kurrachee, and several lines of route have been followed, *crossing* it towards the interior of Beloochistan. But no traveller has as yet traversed its length from one end to the other, in the direction followed by Alexander. So far as we can judge he appears to have kept along a kind of plain or valley, which is found to run nearly parallel to the coast, between the interior range of the Mushti hills and the lower rugged hills that bound the immediate neighbourhood of the sea-coast. This line of route has been followed in very recent times by Major Ross from Kedj to Bela, and seems to form a natural line of communication, keeping throughout about the required distance (60 to 70 miles) from the coast. (See *Proceedings of Geogr. Society*, vol. xvi. pp. 139-141 and 219.) The arid and impracticable character of the coast district itself, which deterred Alexander from following that route (Arrian, vi. 23) is fully confirmed by recent accounts, but the more inland line of march, so far as is yet known, does not appear to traverse any such frightful deserts *of sand* as those described by the historians of Alexander.

Nor can the site of Pura, the place which formed the terminus of his toilsome march through the desert, be determined with certainty. It has been generally identified with Bunpoor, the most important place in Western Beloochistan, or with Puhra, a village in the same neighbourhood, but the resemblance of name is in this case of little value—Poor signifying merely a town—while the remoteness of Bunpoor from the sea, and its position to the north of the central chain of mountains, which Alexander must therefore have traversed in order to reach it, present considerable difficulties in the way of this view.

Unfortunately the subsequent march of Alexander through Carmania is as obscure as that through Gedrosia. The country being comparatively fertile, and his passage being unopposed, there was little to attract the attention of historians, and we are briefly told that the king proceeded into Carmania; and after that into Persia, sending Hephæstion with the bulk of the army by the coast road, while he himself, with a light-armed force, both of horse and foot, took the direct road to Pasargada. (Arrian, *Anab.* vi. 27, §§ 2, 3, 28, § 7, 29, § 1.)

But it seems clear that, until this separation, his line of march was throughout not very remote from the sea. When Nearchus arrived at the river Anamis, he learned that Alexander was " not far off," an expression subsequently explained to mean that he was at a distance of " five days' journey." (*Indica*, c. 33.) This at once excludes the supposition that Alexander was anywhere in the neighbourhod of Kerman, or the fertile district of northern Carmania. For the city of Kerman is at a distance of eighteen " menzils " or days' marches from Bunder Abbas on the Persian Gulf. (Pottinger, p. 227.) The same distance is estimated by Kinneir (*Geography of Persia*, p. 200) on the authority of a native traveller, at 177 *fursungs*. It must be somewhat more from the mouth of the Anamis. If indeed he had struck up so far to the north as Bunpoor, his natural line of route from thence to Pasargada and Persepolis would have lain through the fertile district of Nurmansheer, and Kerman, which was probably then (as we know it to have been in the times of Ptolemy and Ammianus) the capital of the province. But if Alexander had been following this inland route, his detaching Hephæstion to the sea would be inexplicable. If, on the contrary, he was still, as we find him when Nearchus first rejoined him, within easy reach of the sea-coast, it would be natural for him to continue his march with the whole army through the maritime districts of Carmania and Persia to Susa. Instead of so doing, he left his army to follow this route under the command of Hephæstion, while he himself struck up into the mountains to Pasargada.

The ancient accounts of Carmania in general differ much from the impressions of modern travellers, from which it is clear that a large part of the province is very arid and mountainous. But in such cases it often happens that the character of a particular district is transferred to the whole region. In some portions of Carmania there are tracts of great fertility. The district near the sea-coast around the river Minab (the Anamis of Arrian) and that of Giroft, in the interior—supposed by Dr. Vincent to be the place of meeting of Alexander and Nearchus—are both of them fertile and well-peopled districts. The former especially is called by the natives the Paradise of Persia. (Kempthorne in *Geographical Journal*, vol. v. p. 274.) The district of Nurmansheer in the interior is also a fertile and productive region, but this, like Kerman, seems too remote from the sea to agree with the accounts of the meeting of Nearchus and Alexander. It took Sir F. Goldsmid 16 days travelling to reach Bumm, the capital of this district, from Bunder Abbas on the Persian Gulf. (*Journal of Geographical Society*, vol. xlii. p. 65.)

It is curious that a large part of the province of Carmania is still virtually unknown, and just in the direction where Alexander would proceed from Gedrosia to the frontiers of Persia proper, large tracts of country are still marked on the latest map (that of Captain St. John in 1877) as "unexplored."

NOTE Y y, p. 457.

MARCH OF CRATERUS.

Dr. Vincent justly observes that "by a view of the map and a reference to the geographers, we can hardly discover the means of his [Craterus] avoiding some part of that desert on the east of

Carmania, which the Nubian geographer says is the largest in the world" (p. 340). Yet he *assumes* that Craterus had experienced none of the difficulties which Alexander had encountered in Gedrosia. This statement is not warranted by the ancient authorities, who, indeed, *ignore* all difficulties encountered by Craterus, but do not say that he met with none. The great desert of Kerman, which occupies the northern part of that province, and extends from thence to the confines of Yezd, Khorasan, and Seistan, is a vast tract of the most unmitigated barrenness, and a considerable portion of this, interposed between the fertile districts of Nurmansheer, in northern Carmania, and the Lake Zuriah in Seistan, must of necessity have been traversed by Craterus with his army. According to Sir H. Pottinger an Afghan army, which invaded Persia in 1719, suffered the most dreadful hardships in this waste, and after one-third of the whole had perished, the remainder reached Nurmansheer with the loss of all their equipage and baggage. (Pottinger's *Travels*, p. 229. See also Abbott in *Geographical Journal*, vol. xxv. p. 34, 37.) It has been more recently traversed by Sir F. Goldsmid on his way from Bunder Abbas to Seistan (*Journal of the Geographical Society*, vol. xliii. pp. 65–74), who, however, did not encounter any serious difficulties for an ordinary traveller. The line of route he followed must probably be much the same as that of Craterus, though in an inverse direction.

NOTE Z z, p. 460.

EMBASSY OF THE ROMANS TO ALEXANDER.

Both Niebuhr (*Roman Hist.* vol. iii. p. 169) and Mr. Grote (vol. xii. p. 335) attach much weight, and undoubtedly with good reason, to this argument. Clitarchus appears to have published his history some time before the death of Ptolemy Soter (B C. 283), and therefore before the war of Pyrrhus in Italy. It is difficult to believe that, until after that event, the Romans could have attracted so much attention among the Macedonian Greeks as to lead to the introduction of such a fiction. On the other hand, the opinion expressed by Livy that the Romans had at this time not even heard of the name of Alexander, is evidently absurd: as there is no doubt of the fact (stated by Arrian from his best authorities) that embassies were sent by other nations of Italy—the Bruttians, Lucanians, and Tyrrhenians If these nations were familiar with the name of the great conqueror, and aware of the commanding position that he occupied, it is incredible that the Romans should not be so likewise. Equally futile is the argument of Arrian that it was not consistent with the republican spirit of the early Romans to have sent such an embassy to a foreign king. He must have forgotten that they had already—some six years before—sought the alliance of Alexander, king of Epirus, the uncle of the great conqueror, and actually concluded a treaty with him. This circumstance may have naturally led to a more familiar acquaintance with the affairs of Macedonia and the neighbouring nations, and adds much to the probability of their having subsequently sent an embassy to the nephew.

Could we feel certain that the statement cited by Pliny was really made by Clitarchus, the probabilities would, as it appears to me, be greatly in its favour: but it is remarkable that Arrian, who also notices the story (*Anab.* vii. 15, §§ 5, 6), speaks of it as mentioned only by Aristus and Asclepiades, two authors of very little note, and certainly of a later period, and though he discusses at some length the probability of the incident, never alludes to Clitarchus, though a contemporary, and one of the most popular of the historians of Alexander. Still more important is it that Diodorus, who undoubtedly wrote with Clitarchus before him, and followed him as one of his chief authorities (see the remarks of Geier, *Scriptores Alexandri Magni*, p. 155; and of C. Muller, *Fragmenta Scriptorum Alex. M.*, p. 75), while mentioning the names of many of the nations that sent embassies on this occasion to Alexander (xvii. 113), says not a word about the Romans, though he at least must have been fully aware of the interest of such an incident, had it really occurred. This portion of the history of Q. Curtius, who was also to a great extent a follower of Clitarchus, is unfortunately lost. The authority of Justin is not worth much, but his silence on such a point is not without its importance. (Justin. xii. 13.) The statement of Strabo (v. 3, p. 232), referred to by Niebuhr (*l. c.*) that Alexander sent back some pirates from Antium that he had captured to the Romans, may much more probably refer to Alexander of Epirus than to the great conqueror. but the whole story has a very doubtful aspect.

NOTE A A, p. 463.

THE PALLACOPAS.

It is impossible to identify the Pallacopas with any reasonable certainty. The same circumstances that had rendered it defective in the time of Alexander for the purposes it was intended to serve, would almost certainly operate again to render useless the new cut made by order of the king. and this would in its turn be superseded by some later canal. The name is not found in the other historians of Alexander, or in the geographers. All that can be said is that it was a cut on the right (or western) bank of the Euphrates for the purpose of diverting the surplus waters of the river, during times of inundation, into the sandy tracts of Arabia, just as is done at the present day by the canal called Hindiyeh, which quits the Euphrates about 15 miles *above* Babylon, and forms the extensive marshes and meres on the west and south-west of Hillah. But it is clearly a mistake to suppose, as Col. Chesney did, that the one cut represented the other. (The same view is taken by Mr. Loftus (*Chaldæa and Susiana*, p. 42) who mistranslates the passage of Arrian to suit it.) The Pallacopas, according to Arrian, quitted the Euphrates 800 stadia *below* Babylon (vii. 21): and though the distance may be overstated, it must certainly be sought between Babylon and the sea. The suggestion of Capt. Felix Jones that an ancient dry water-course, called the Shat al Roumayieh, from its passing by a town of that name, represents the Pallacopas, is more plausible, though the distance from Babylon is much less than that given by Arrian. but no great reliance can be placed on any such identification.

The mode in which the Pallacopas is represented on several recent maps, as a canal having a course nearly parallel with the Euphrates and extending all the way to the sea, appears to me wholly at variance with the account given by Arrian of its character and purpose. There is no other authority. but the mention of it by Appian (*B. Civ.* ii. 153) shows at least that he understood its object as above explained.

CHAPTER XIII.

VOYAGE OF NEARCHUS.

§ 1. WE must now return to examine somewhat more in detail the voyage of Nearchus, who, as we have already seen, had conducted the fleet of Alexander in safety from the mouth of the Indus to that of the Euphrates. Such an enterprise was undoubtedly in those days a task of difficulty and danger, requiring great energy as well as prudence on the part of the commander. It moreover derived, even in ancient times, great additional interest from the circumstance of its being the first—or at all events generally believed to be the first—navigation of the Indian Ocean. The much more arduous voyage of Scylax in the same seas was either forgotten or disbelieved; and it seems certain that no full or authentic record of it had been preserved.[1] But the voyage of Nearchus has attracted an increased, and in some degree a disproportionate amount of attention, in modern times, from its having been preserved to us in a form so much more complete and authentic than any other record that we possess of a similar character. A detailed narrative of his voyage was written by Nearchus himself, of which Arrian has transmitted to us an abstract so full that it may to a great extent—for geographical purposes at least,—stand in the place of the original work. And it is interesting to see how accurately this account is found to tally, both in the geographical details, and in the particulars transmitted concerning the country and its inhabitants, with the results of recent observations. In proportion as we have in modern times become better acquainted with

---

[1] See the observations in Chapter VII. p. 227, Note B.

the wild and barren shores explored on this occasion, do we find the agreement with the statements of Nearchus more complete.[2]

Much labour has been bestowed by several modern writers, especially by the learned Dr. Vincent,[3] upon the examination and verification of all the details transmitted to us by Arrian, who has given us, with very few exceptions, a complete journal of the voyage, day by day, recording both the stations at which they brought to for the night, and the distances traversed.[4] Of the mode in which these last were computed we have unfortunately no indication.[5] It would be wholly foreign to the plan of this work to follow these inquirers into the minute details of their investigations, especially as the greater part of the coasts which were thus explored are of singularly little interest in themselves.[6] The really important results of the voyage of Nearchus are comparatively few; and lie within small compass; it will be therefore sufficient to give enough of the details of his narrative to show their close agreement with the geographical conditions as they are now known to us.

---

[2] Note A, p 542.

[3] His elaborate dissertation on the voyage of Nearchus was originally published in a separate form in 1797, and subsequently republished, together with that on the Periplus of the Erythrean Sea, as the first volume of his *Commerce and Navigation of the Ancients in the Indian Ocean* (2 vols 4to, Lond 1807) It is from this later edition that my citations are made
Dr Vincent's investigations were based in some degree upon imperfect information as to the actual geographical details of the countries in question, and for this reason have in some instances been superseded by later and more accurate knowledge. These more recent sources of information have been well turned to account by Dr C Muller, in his valuable commentary on Arrian's Indica, in the first volume of his *Geographi Græci Minores* (Paris, ed Didot, 1855), which now constitutes the most complete and satisfactory authority upon the subject.
The earlier dissertations by D'Anville and Gosselin are now of little value

[4] Arrian, *Indica*, c 21, foll. The citations from this work in the present chapter all refer to the edition by C. Muller

[5] Note B, p 544

[6] Lieutenant Kempthorne in his *Notes on the Eastern Shores of the Persian Gulf* (published in the Journal of the Geographical Society, vol. v.), remarks that "the whole of this coast from the Indus to Bussora, a distance of more than twelve hundred miles, is, with few exceptions, 'one vast and sterile waste, with high mountains rising at the back, wholly destitute of both trees and vegetation,'" p 270
This memoir of Lieut Kempthorne contains much valuable information as to the coasts and localities he visited, but his attempts to connect these with the voyage of Nearchus are for the most part hasty and ill considered

§ 2. It is unfortunate that Arrian has not preserved to us any statement of the number or description of the ships employed on this occasion. They formed without doubt but a small proportion of the numerous fleet with which Alexander had himself descended the Indus; and it may safely be assumed that they would consist principally of ships of war, or "long ships," as the Greeks termed their galleys for distinction's sake. But they were undoubtedly accompanied also by transports, apparently vessels of no great size, which had already formed part of the fleet on the Indus.[7] But we have no means of forming any estimate of the number of these, or of the troops and seamen on board.

It is still more to be regretted that we have no distinct account of the point from which the fleet took its departure.[8] It is certain that this was considerably lower down than Pattala, as we learn from the journal of the voyage that it was only 150 stadia from the sea. Alexander had indeed constructed naval stations (Naustathmi) at several points in the Delta of the Indus, and it appears that the one at which the fleet of Nearchus was assembled, and the last preparations made for the voyage, was situated on the western arm of the river, probably on a large island called Killouta. But in a locality where the channels and mouths of the river are per-

---

[7] In the few passages in which they are mentioned these vessels are called κέρκουροι, a term usually applied to small vessels; and the same that is employed by Arrian (*Anab* vi. 2, § 7) in describing the fleet that was collected by Alexander for the descent of the Indus

[8] Pliny, following Onesicritus, says that the fleet took its departure from a place which he calls Xylenepolis, but he complains that his author does not more accurately describe its position. "Primumque Xylenepolis ab Alexandro condita, unde ceperunt exordium, juxta quod flumen, aut ubi fuerit, non satis explanatur" (*Nat. Hist* vi. 23, § 96). The words "juxta quod flumen" can only mean, "which of the branches of the Indus."

Nearchus, as reported by Arrian (*Indica*, c 21, § 2), says only that they took their departure *from the naval station* (ἀπὸ τοῦ ναυστάθμου), and Alexander had caused so many of these to be constructed in the delta of the Indus, that the expression conveys no information The suggestion of Dr C. Muller, that it was situated on the island of Killouta (Κιλλουτὰ), mentioned by Arrian in his other work (*Anab* vi 19) as the place where Alexander stationed his fleet in descending the Indus, is plausible enough, but rests on no definite foundation.

petually shifting, it is impossible to fix its position with any certainty. Three days were employed in dropping down the river, the bar at the entrance of which presented so formidable an obstacle as to induce the Greeks to cut a channel through a narrow bank of sand in order to reach the open sea.[9] Having thus entered the ocean they proceeded as far as a sandy island called Crocala, and the next day reached a large and convenient harbour, to which Nearchus gave the name of the Port of Alexander.

§ 3. Here they remained for some time. Nearchus had originally intended not to commence his voyage until a later period of the year, when the monsoon, concerning which the Greeks had obtained accurate information, should be fully past; but the attacks of the natives had become so troublesome, after the departure of Alexander, that he had set out earlier than he designed. The consequence was that he found the south-west monsoon still blowing with great violence, and having found a secure station in the Port of Alexander, he remained there twenty-four days until the wind abated. It is probable that the harbour which afforded him this opportune shelter was no other than the port of Kurrachee, now one of the most frequented sea-ports in this part of India.[1] During their stay here the troops subsisted to a great extent on shell-fish, the enormous size of which, as compared to those in the European seas, naturally struck them with astonishment.

When the fleet was able to put to sea again (about the beginning of November), it proceeded along the coast towards the west, and in five days reached the mouth of the river Arabis, having accomplished a distance (according to their reckoning) of a thousand stadia (100 G. miles) from the mouth of the Indus.[2] This distance is undoubtedly over-stated and the details of this part of the voyage cannot be made out with any distinctness; but the Arabis, at the entrance of which they found a commodious port, is undoubtedly the Poorally,

---

[9] Arrian, *Indica*, c 21, § 6.   [1] Note C, p. 546.   [2] Ibid. c. 25, § 3.

the only considerable stream on this part of the coast, near the mouth of which is a small town called Somneanee, that is a place of some trade.[3]

§ 4. The coast thus far had been held by the Arabies, whom Arrian calls the last of the Indian tribes. From hence the navigators proceeded along the coast of the Oritæ, and after three days' voyage—during which they encountered a severe gale, in which they lost three of their ships—arrived at a place called Cocala, where, though there was no harbour, but merely an open roadstead, Nearchus landed his crews in order to refresh them after the fatigues they had undergone. Here he was met by Leonnatus, who (as we have seen) had been left behind by Alexander for that purpose, and was able to take on board provisions for ten days, as well as to repair his ships, and recruit his crews out of the forces of Leonnatus.[4]

Sailing hence with a fair wind he made good a course of 500 stadia to the mouth of a river, or rather torrent, called the Tomerus, where his landing was opposed by the natives in arms, and had to be effected by force, under circumstances strongly resembling those to be found in many modern voyages of discovery. The victory was indeed an easy one: the natives appear to have been mere savages, unacquainted with the use of iron or any other metal, and using sharp stones for knives, and spears with the points hardened in the fire.[5] Here Nearchus again remained for six days, and then made a short day's voyage to a place called Malana, which is termed by Arrian the limit of the Oritæ.

This part of the voyage presents no geographical difficulties. The site of Cocala cannot indeed be identified, because there is nothing to mark it, the locality being a mere open beach, off which it was possible for the ships to anchor. But the river Tomerus corresponds with that now called the Muklow, or Hingul: and Malana may be clearly recognized in a head-

---

[3] Kempthorne, in *Geogr. Journal*, vol v. p 264. Pottinger's *Travels in Beloochistan*, p 11

[4] Arrian, *Indica*, c 23
[5] Ibid. c. 24.

land which still preserves the name of Cape Malan or Malin. The distances however, as usual, are greatly overstated, the whole length of the voyage along the coast of the Oritæ being estimated at 1600 stadia (160 G. miles), while the real distance does not exceed 900 stadia in a direct line, and the windings of the coast are very trifling.

§ 5. From this point began the navigation along the barren and desolate coast of the Ichthyophagi, the name given by the Greeks to the poor miserable savages who inhabited the seacoast of the Mekran, or Gedrosia. This sterile tract extends for a space of more than 400 G. miles from Cape Malan to Cape Jask, preserving throughout a very uniform direction from E. to W., and presenting but few prominent geographical features. It is well described by Nearchus, in much the same terms as have been repeated by modern voyagers, as a barren and inhospitable coast, though presenting from distance to distance spots where palm-trees grew, and water was to be procured. Even where the coast was apparently a mere tract of barren sand, water was generally to be obtained (though often of bad quality) by digging wells of moderate depth near the shore.[6] The difficulties of the fleet on this account were consequently not so great as had been encountered by the army under Alexander. The time of year also was favourable, the winds at this season blowing generally prettily steadily from the land, and we do not hear of their encountering any gales, or being detained by contrary winds, throughout this part of their passage. Both the dangers and the hardships of this part of the voyage appear indeed to have been greatly exaggerated. Nor can we wonder at this. They were proceeding along an unknown coast, with a vast and unknown ocean beside them: and such exploring expeditions were almost entirely new to the Greeks. It was doubtless the same feeling that led them vastly to overrate the distances

---

[6] *Indica*, c 26 The same thing is found to be the case at the present day (See Vincent, p 234, and the authorities quoted by him)

actually traversed. The voyage along the coast of the Ichthyophagi, which had occupied them twenty days,[7] was estimated by Nearchus at "a little more than 10,000 stadia" (1000 G. miles), which, after making reasonable allowance for the windings of their course, along a coast offering few considerable sinuosities, is nearly, if not quite, double the truth.[8]

The natives of these sterile shores subsisted, as they do at the present day, almost entirely upon fish, which they frequently devoured raw, at other times drying it in the sun, and pounding it into a sort of meal, of which they formed a kind of cakes. Even the few horses and cattle they possessed were compelled to subsist on the same food.[9] They had very few boats and relied principally upon the supply of fish left stranded on the beach, or caught in stake-nets set up near the shore. Even their huts were constructed in great part of fishes' bones: in those of a superior kind they employed the bones of whales by way of beams or door-posts. This description of the natives and their habits of life coincides precisely with the observations of modern voyagers.[1] So strongly marked are the natural conditions, by which those habits have been inexorably prescribed.[2]

---

[7] See the careful computation by Dr Vincent Pliny, however, says that it took them thirty days, and his authority on a point of this sort is not wholly worthless.

[8] It may be observed that 10,000 stadia in 20 days would give 500 stadia a day, which is just the average of a day's voyage, as estimated by Scylax. This gives rise to a suspicion that the statement of the distance as given by Nearchus was merely based upon this rough mode of computation.

[9] *Indica,* c 29, Strabo, xv. 2, § 2. The same thing takes place at the present day Lieut Kempthorne says · "The inhabitants still live entirely on fish, the cattle having much the same diet as their masters, for the country is wholly destitute and barren, and yields no sort of grass. Vast stores of oysters, crabs, and all kinds of shell-fish are found on the coast, of which Nearchus's description is generally very accurate. In many places, both here and in Arabia, the cattle are fed entirely on dried fish and dates, mixed together, on account of the great scarcity of grass in these sunburnt and sandy regions" (*Journal of Geog. Soc* vol. v. p 270)

The strange assertion of Pliny (*H N.* vi 23, § 95), that Alexander "forbade the Ichthyophagi to subsist on fish," would have been equivalent to condemning them all to starvation

[1] Kempthorne, *l c* pp 270-273 The authority of two earlier voyagers, Capt Blair and Lieut Porter, is quoted by Dr. Vincent to the same effect.

[2] The modern name for this country, the Mekran or Makian, is in all probability derived from Mahi-Khoran, "fish-eaters," and thus exactly corresponds

§ 6. The geographical details of this part of the Paraplus offer no special interest, but they may for the most part be identified without difficulty, after making due allowance for the exaggeration of the distances. The first day's voyage from Malana brought them to a place called Bagisara, where there was a commodious port, after which they had to round a lofty promontory standing far out into the sea. This is clearly the headland now called Cape Arabah, on the east side of which is a bay, forming a deep and commodious port. Two days' voyage from thence brought them to a place called Calama, where there was a village and a few palm-trees. This name is still retained by a small river called the Kalami: and the island mentioned by Nearchus as about 100 stadia distant from the mainland is readily recognized in that now called Ashtola, one of the few islands along this coast, from which it is really about twelve miles distant.[3] The next point of importance was a lofty headland called Mosarna, projecting 150 stadia into the sea, on the west side of which they found a well-sheltered port.[4] This can be no other than the promontory now called Passenee, or Pasni, with a town of the same name, but the town and port are on the *east* side of the headland, instead of the west.

Here they found only a small village of fishermen, but obtained an important assistance by taking on board a pilot who was acquainted with the coast from thence to the confines of Carmania, and under his guidance and direction the remainder of the voyage presented comparatively little difficulty. From this time we find them sailing much at night in order to take advantage of the land breeze. Meanwhile their provisions were beginning to fail them, especially corn, of which they do not appear to have been able to get any additional supply after leaving Cocala. But, on the sixth day after leaving Mosarna, having found a town on a hill, with

---

to the appellation of Ichthyophagi given them by the Greeks (See Hughes's *Baloochistan*, p 152)

[3] Kempthorne, p 266   See Note D, p 547
[4] *Indica*, c 26.

some signs of cultivation round it, Nearchus landed his troops, and by making a hostile demonstration, compelled the inhabitants to furnish him with such stores as they possessed. These were however for the most part limited to cakes of meal made from dried fish, in the manner already described, with a slight mixture only of wheat or barley-flour. This town, the name of which is not given by Arrian, appears to have been situated on the bay of Gwettur, but the exact site cannot be identified.[5]

§ 7. From this point their voyage was conducted with much greater expedition than before. They had evidently acquired greater confidence in their navigation, besides having the advantage of a native pilot; and the crews suffered so much from scarcity of provisions, especially from the total want of flour or grain of any kind, that Nearchus was obliged to press the voyage by every means in his power. They thus accomplished a distance according to their own computation of 3750 stadia in six days—a rate of progress far exceeding what they had performed in the earlier part of their voyage. In the last instance they sailed on through a whole night and day continuously, in order to reach a long low headland, which formed the boundary between the Ichthyophagi and Karmania, and the next day, after rounding this point, they found themselves at a place called Badis, in a land of comparative fertility, where they were able to procure both dates and grain in abundance. The site of Badis may be fixed at, or in the immediate neighbourhood of the modern town of Jask; and the low promontory is undoubtedly Cape Jask, which forms a prominent feature on this line of coast.[6]

---

[5] *Indica*, cc 27, 28

[6] There is considerable confusion (as Dr Vincent has pointed out) in the earlier descriptions of this coast, between Cape Jask and Cape Bombareek, the next headland towards the N W, which is also a long low point, though marked by a singular detached rock This is the Carpella of Ptolemy, but is not mentioned by Nearchus, while on the other hand no mention of any promontory answering to Cape Jask is found in the Alexandrian geographer. There can be no doubt as to the correctness of the identification of Cape Jask (Vincent, vol 1 pp 280, 285): the uncertainty of the modern names may serve as a warning in similar cases which occur so frequently in comparing the accounts of ancient geographers.

§ 8. Before we proceed to follow the fleet on its subsequent progress along the coasts of Carmania and Persia, we must advert to two other points connected with the earlier part of the voyage. The first of these is the curious account given by Nearchus of their battle—the expression is not exaggerated—with a swarm of whales, which took place off a town called Cyiza. The presence of these sea-monsters was first announced by the columns of water shot up into the air by their " blowing ;" a phenomenon which was at first taken for waterspouts, but when the sailors were told by their native guides that they were produced by whales, " they were so terrified that the oars fell from their hands." Nearchus, however, encouraged them, and having drawn up his ships " in order as if for battle," commanded them all on a given signal to row rapidly forward towards the animals, and as they drew near to raise loud shouts, while the trumpets sounded for the attack, and the rowers made as much noise as possible with their oars. The astonished whales naturally plunged into the depths of the sea, and though they afterwards reappeared in another spot, the apprehensions of the sailors were removed, and Nearchus was hailed with loud applause as the saviour of the fleet.[7] Such was the terror of the crews on this occasion that it appears to have produced as much effect on their minds as all their sufferings from hunger and other hardships. At the present day whales are still frequently met with in this part of the Indian Ocean, and it is not uncommon for a steamer bound from Aden to Bombay to encounter " a school " (as it is termed) of whales similar to that which caused such alarm to the fleet of Nearchus. They however rarely approach so near the coast.

§ 9. A much more startling assertion is, that while the navigators were following the coast of India (under which head Nearchus included the territory of the Arabies and Oritæ, but not that of the Ichthyophagi), they found the shadows not to follow the same rule as in other countries, but either the sun

---

[7] Arrian, *Indica*, c. 30   Strabo, xv 2, § 12, p. 725.

was vertical at noon, or the shadow was cast *to the south*. He added, that the constellations and stars, which had usually been high in the heavens, now rose only just above the horizon, and those that were elsewhere constantly visible, rose and set again after a short interval.[8] Both these phenomena would of course be really observed by navigators in the Indian Ocean who advanced far enough to the south to be well within the tropic: but it is certain that no such effect as that first stated could be witnessed by Nearchus and his comrades, who at no period of their voyage were in a lower latitude than 24° 70', or more than a degree north of the tropic. Moreover, the time of year (November) was one in which the sun would be far to the southward of the equator, and therefore no such appearance could be seen, even had the voyagers penetrated—which assuredly they did not—far within the tropic. The only solution of this difficulty that seems to present itself is, that Arrian, though in general reporting his authority with great clearness, has in this instance misunderstood his author, and represented Nearchus as stating, *as a matter of his own experience and observation*, that which he had only reported as a fact witnessed by those who continued the navigation of the Indian coasts farther to the south.[9]

§ 10. After having refreshed his crews at Badis, Nearchus continued his voyage along the coast of Carmania, which, as he correctly observed, had from this point a general direction towards the north-west, and after proceeding 800 stadia they came in sight of the lofty promontory, called by the natives Maceta, which stands on the opposite side of the strait at the entrance of the Persian Gulf, and being only about 30 G. miles distant would of course be readily seen from the Persian coast.[1] Here Onesicritus, who appears to have acted as second

---

[8] Arrian, *Indica*, c 25
[9] Note E, p 548
[1] Cape Maceta is undoubtedly the same with the conspicuous headland now called Cape Mussendom it is lofty and rugged, and forms in fact the termination of a craggy ridge of mountains running through the whole province of Oman in Arabia, and here abutting on the sea It is so high as to be visible, not only from the coast immediately opposite, but all the way

in command, urged Nearchus to cross the straits to this headland, and prosecute their exploration along the coast of Arabia. Fortunately for the fleet Nearchus opposed this suggestion, and determined to continue the voyage along the eastern coast. Here two days more brought them to the mouth of the river Anamis, in the midst of a fertile district called Harmozia, where Nearchus halted to repose his forces after all their toils. It was here that they unexpectedly fell in with a Greek, who had strayed from the army of Alexander, and learned to their great satisfaction that the king himself was encamped within a distance of only five days' journey in the interior. Nearchus himself, having provided for the safety of the ships by drawing them up on the shore, and defending them with a rampart and trench, hastened to report to Alexander the safe arrival of the fleet; an announcement that was received with every demonstration of joy.[2]

The river Anamis, which from this circumstance assumed so important a position in the narrative of Nearchus, is clearly the same with the Minah or Minab, a considerable stream that flows into the northern angle or bight of the bay formed by the Persian coast opposite to Cape Mussendom. It flows through a very fertile district;[3] and the name of Harmozia, mentioned by Nearchus, was perpetuated down to a recent period in that of Ormuz, which became in the middle ages the centre of a flourishing and opulent monarchy.[4] The position of the camp of Alexander, where that monarch was evidently making a prolonged halt, is too vaguely indicated to be determined with any certainty: Dr. Vincent would place it conjecturally in the district of Giroft or Jeruft, a fertile tract in the interior, about

---

from Carpella (Cape Bombareek) See Vincent, vol. 1. pp 318, 321, and Kempthorne, in *Geogr Journ* vol. v. p. 272.

[2] Arrian, *Indica*, cc 33-35.

[3] The country adjoining the Minab is one of the most fertile in Persia, and is termed by the natives ".the Paradise of Persia" (Kempthorne, p 274)

[4] The name of Ormuz was originally given to a town or district on the mainland, and was afterwards transferred to the island more generally known by that name, when that became the centre of trade, and consequently the capital of all the surrounding coasts

85 G. miles from the mouth of the Minab.⁵ The suggestion is at all events a plausible one, and would suit well with the statement that it was from this point that Hephæstion was appointed to lead the main body of the army by the lower road, through Laristan, to the sea.⁶

After a few days spent in rejoicings and festivities, Nearchus returned to the fleet and resumed his voyage along the coast of Carmania, with the view of conducting the fleet to Susa. But his progress from thence along the eastern shores of the Persian Gulf presents comparatively little interest. Though it still partook in some degree of the character of an exploring voyage, as these coasts had never been navigated by Greeks, and their details were doubtless imperfectly known, there was a certain amount of trade carried on along them by native vessels, and the general direction and character of the coast were undoubtedly known to the Persians. From this time therefore the voyage became rather what we should term in modern days a surveying voyage than one of actual discovery.

§ 11. Immediately after leaving the mouth of the Anamis Nearchus mentions their passing by a small island, barren and rugged, after which they came to a much larger one that was fertile and inhabited, which he calls Oaracta. This is clearly the large island of Kishm, at the entrance of the Persian Gulf, while the barren islet, to which he gives the name of Organa, was destined at a later period to become one of the most important centres of commerce in the East, and obtained a world-wide celebrity under its mediæval name of Ormuz.⁷

The succeeding points in the voyage have no particular interest. After touching at several other islands, as well as at a small town on the mainland called Sisidone (probably the modern Duan) they visited a small island, the name of which is not given, but which is noted by Nearchus for its pearl

---

⁵ Vincent, p 338. The district of Jeruft is described by Mr. Abbott in the *Journal of Geogr. Soc* vol. xxv p 46

⁶ Arrian, *Anab.* vi 28, § 7. See Chapter XII p 457.
⁷ Arrian, *Indica*, c. 37 See Note F, p 549.

fishery, which was carried on in the same manner as in the Indian Ocean.[8] It is remarkable that this is the only notice found of the pearl fisheries for which the Persian Gulf is now so celebrated.[9] As they proceeded up the sea-coast of Persia Proper, the navigation became more intricate and difficult, the coast being described as abounding in shoals, rocks, and reefs, a character fully confirmed by modern observations. On one occasion three of the ships got aground on a sand-bank at low water, but were got off in safety,[1] and Nearchus had the satisfaction of accomplishing this difficult part of the voyage without the loss of a single vessel. They were however compelled to halt at the mouth of a river named Sitacus (the modern Jayrah) for not less than twenty-one days to refit the ships: and here also they laid in a fresh supply of provisions. From hence to the head of the Gulf the rivers and headlands may be identified with little difficulty: but the only marked geographical point is a peninsular headland named Mesembria, which is clearly the same occupied by the modern town of Abu-Shehr, or Bushire, now the principal trading-place on the Gulf.

No towns of importance were met with; a circumstance readily accounted for by the barren character of the shores. Nearchus indeed well describes the whole province of Persia as divided into three natural zones or belts, of which that along the sea-coast is sandy and barren from the extreme heat: farther inland comes a tract of great fertility, which enjoys a temperate climate, and produces all kinds of fruit, vines, &c., in great abundance, while it contains also extensive pastures and forests, and is traversed by abundant streams. North of this again is a cold and snowy region of a rugged and mountainous character.[2] This description is in substance repeated

---

[8] Arrian, *Indica*, c. 38, § 3.
[9] See Chapter XII. p 461, note.
[1] It appears probable that the place where this accident occurred is a long shoal or sandbank near the western extremity of the island of Kishm, called the Bassadore Bank, where Lieut Kempthorne himself got aground with his surveying vessel, the 'Clive' (*Journal of Geogr. Soc.* vol v. p. 280).
[2] Arrian, *Indica*, c. 40.

by Strabo,³ and entirely agrees with the observations of modern travellers.

§ 12. The boundary between Persia Proper and Susiana was marked by a river called by Nearchus the Arosis (by Strabo and other writers the Oreatis), which, as he remarks, was the largest stream he had seen since leaving the Indus. This is clearly the modern Tab, sometimes also called the Endian, or Hindian (from a city of that name on its banks), which is decidedly the most important stream that flows into the Persian Gulf on its eastern side. From hence the shores became so shoal and muddy, that the ships could no longer approach the land at night, as they were accustomed to do; but held their course along the outskirts of the mud banks till they reached a place called Diridotis, at the mouth of the Euphrates, which, though a mere village, was a place of considerable trade in the aromatic productions of Arabia, which were brought thither by merchants from that country.⁴

It is singular that though we are distinctly told in the first instance that Nearchus had been commissioned by Alexander to bring the fleet on to *Susa*,⁵ he had thus carried it to the mouth of the Euphrates, as if with the object of ascending that river to Babylon. But having learnt at Diridotis that Alexander himself was on his way to Susa, he turned back, and after retracing his course for some distance, and passing the marshy lake which was formed by the waters of the Tigris, he entered the river Pasitigris, and ascended it with his whole fleet as far as the point where Alexander had thrown across it a bridge of boats, for the passage of his main army to Susa. Here the land and sea forces were once more united, and the voyage of Nearchus was at an end.⁶

§ 13. The voyage had occupied almost exactly five months⁷

---

³ Strab xv. p 727
⁴ Arrian, *Indica*, c. 41, § 7. See Note G, p. 550
⁵ Id *ib* c 36.
⁶ Id *ib* c. 42 Concerning the Pasitigris of Nearchus, see p. 458, note.

⁷ See the careful computation of Dr. Vincent, p 495 Pliny says that the actual voyage had lasted less than three months, but it was nearly seven since Alexander had left them at Pattala Neither statement is accurate.

from the time the fleet left the Indus: but of this period considerable intervals had been taken up by long halts; especially that at first starting of 24 days in the port of Alexander, and more recently of 21 days in the mouth of the Sitacus. But even allowing for all such deductions, their progress had been unusually slow, a circumstance which was owing in great part to the nature of the voyage, the object of which, as Nearchus distinctly urged, was not merely to accomplish the navigation from point to point, but to examine the coasts as they went along, observe the nature of the country, and ascertain what towns or harbours were to be found.[8] The fulfilment of these purposes necessitated a very different rate of progress from that of an ordinary voyage, while under any circumstances the progress of a large fleet will be much slower than that of a single well-appointed vessel. Hence it is altogether delusive to refer to the voyage of Nearchus as a specimen of the rate of sailing of ancient navigators, and the distances that they could accomplish in a given time.

The success with which Nearchus had completed this enterprise, was a source of additional satisfaction to Alexander, as giving him favourable prospects for the scheme which he undoubtedly entertained of following it up by a similar voyage along the coasts of Arabia from the Persian Gulf to the Red Sea; a much longer and more perilous navigation, yet one which would probably have presented no insuperable obstacles to so able and cautious a commander as Nearchus. Had Alexander lived to see the completion of this greater design, he would not only have made a most important addition to geographical knowledge, but would have opened up the way for direct trade between Egypt and India, and have thus laid the first foundation of that regular intercourse with the latter country which assumed so much importance at a later period. As it was, the voyage of Nearchus was destined to remain an isolated effort, attended with very little result that had any

---

[8] Arrian, *Indica*, c. 32.

immediate bearing upon the commerce or civilization of the ancient world. It was a link in a chain of which the others were still wanting. It is indeed of peculiar interest to us as the first voyage of discovery of which we have any detailed narrative;[9] and it is certain that the commander displayed no common amount of ability in its execution. But while doing justice to the really great qualities of which Nearchus gave proof—to his energetic perseverance and courage, combined with prudence and caution—it is idle to compare him, as has been done by Dr. Vincent, to such navigators as Columbus and Vasco de Gama, whose exploits have exercised an enduring influence upon all succeeding ages.

---

[9] That of Hanno is, as we have seen, so imperfectly known to us as to admit of no comparison in this respect.

NOTE A, p. 526.

COMPARISON WITH PLINY.

WE cannot better appreciate the value and importance of the unusually authentic form in which the voyage of Nearchus has been recorded to us by Arrian, than by comparing it with the account of the same voyage as given by Pliny. (*Nat. Hist.* vi. 23, § 96–100.) That writer appears to have followed exclusively the authority of Onesicritus, without comparing it with the more authentic narrative of Nearchus: but even that of Onesicritus he in reality quotes only at second hand, from the work of Juba the Mauritanian, who had doubtless given a mere compendium or abridgement of the original. (This appears to be clearly the meaning of the words "indicare convenit *quæ prodit Onesicritus*, classe Alexandri circumvectus in mediterranea Persidis ex India, *narrata proxime a Juba*," § 96.)[1] The words "Onesicriti et Nearchi navigatio" correctly describe the *voyage*, but certainly do not imply that he had consulted the *work* of Nearchus himself: while the statement that follows, that it contained no regular enumeration of the halting-places or distances (nec nomina habet mansionum, nec spatia) is glaringly false, if applied to the methodical and regular journal that we have before us. In the following extract he gives indeed a certain number of geographical names of rivers, headlands, &c.; but none that were mere halting-places (mansiones), so many of which occur in the work of Nearchus, nor has he in any instance given the distances from point to point (spatia). The information he has furnished us is in this respect perfectly in accordance with what he tells us of the authority from which he wrote. Such an enumeration however—though very meagre and

---

[1] This is denied by M. Urlichs in his *Vindiciæ Plinianæ* (p. 95); but his view that the words "narrata proxime a Juba" refer to the intermediate stages between the voyage of Onesicritus and that which Pliny describes as practised in his own day appears to me entirely untenable Nor can I at all concur with him in thinking that Pliny must have seen the original work of Nearchus, because he includes him in the list of his authorities in the first book It is abundantly evident that Pliny cites many of these authorities only at second hand.

NOTE A.   VOYAGE OF NEARCHUS.   543

unsatisfactory as compared with the narrative preserved to us by Arrian—would not be without its value if the selection were made with method and accuracy. But unfortunately, whether from the fault of his authorities or his own, the abstract given by Pliny is so utterly confused and inaccurate that it may be safely pronounced altogether worthless. It will be sufficient here to give that portion of it which relates to the voyage from the mouth of the Indus to the entrance of the Gulf of Persia. After having justly censured his author for omitting to indicate clearly the point from which the fleet took its departure, he proceeds:

"Hæc tamen digna memoratu prodentur. Arbis oppidum a Nearcho conditum in navigatione ea, flumen Nabrum navium capax, contra insula distans LXX stadia, Alexandria condita a Leonnato jussu Alexandri in finibus gentis, Argenus portu salubri, flumen Tomberon navigabile, circa quod Pasiræ; deinde Ichthyophagi tam longo tractu ut XXX dierum spatio prænavigaverint; insula quæ Solis appellatur et eadem Nympharum cubile, rubens, in qua nullum non animal absumitur, incertis causis. Ori gens, flumen Carmaniæ Hyctanis portuosum et auro fertile; ab eo primum septentriones apparuisse adnotavere. Arcturum neque omnibus cerni noctibus, nec totis unquam. Achæmenidas usque illo tenuisse. Aeris et ferri metalla et arsenici et minii exerceri. Inde promontorium Carmaniæ est, ex quo in adversa ora ad gentem Arabiæ Macas trajectus distat L M. p. Insulæ tres, quarum Oracla tantum habitatur aquosa, a continenti XXV M p. Insulæ quatuor jam in sinu ante Persida. Circa has hydri marini vicenum cubitorum adnatantes terruere classem." (§§ 97, 98, ed. Sillig, whose text has been followed.)

It is hardly worth while to examine this extract in detail. This has already been done by Dodwell in his Dissertation on the Voyage of Nearchus; by Dr. Vincent (vol. i. p. 70–76), and by Geier (*Alex. Magni Histor. Scriptores*, pp. 80, 81, 104). The slightest comparison with the authentic narrative as preserved to us by Arrian will be sufficient to show that while Pliny has retained some names correctly, or in a form that can be easily recognized, and has preserved some interesting detached facts, the whole has been jumbled together in so confused a form, that we should be unable to derive from it any geographical conclusions at all, if we were not provided with the means of doing so by the assistance of other and more authentic sources. Fortunate is it for us that we possess a journal, of which (as Dr. Vincent remarks, p. 76) "the accuracy is as conspicuous as the inaccuracy of Pliny is demonstrable."

It is remarkable that Pliny in two or three other passages (vi. 107, 109, 124) cites *Nearchus* as his authority for distances along the coast, though he appears to have found none in the narrative which he had before him, when he wrote the passage which we are now considering. But in these cases also there can be very little doubt that Pliny quotes him only at second-hand, and has taken the statement of distances from some intermediate compiler. The numbers given are in every instance erroneous, but this may arise merely from the coruption of the text.

NOTE B, p. 526.

ESTIMATE OF DISTANCES BY SEA—SUPPOSED DIFFERENCE OF STADIA.

No ancient writer (as far as I am aware) has preserved to us any account of the mode in which ancient navigators computed or estimated the distances traversed by them at sea. No allusion is found to any process analogous to that of the modern *log*: a simple device, but by no means so simple that we are entitled to assume it to have been in use in all ages.

In regard to the voyage of Nearchus it will be found that the distances are uniformly over-rated. in most cases very far exceeding the truth. To such an extent indeed is this the case that it induced Dr. Vincent to adopt the suggestion of M. D'Anville, and assume that Nearchus had throughout reckoned by a different stadium from that employed in estimating distances on land. This was indeed, in the time of D'Anville, the ordinary mode of solving such difficulties, and attempting to save the credit of ancient writers for accuracy. But even if we overlook the extreme improbability that Arrian should have continued reckoning the distances in this part of his work by stadia of fifteen to the Roman mile, while he elsewhere uniformly employs the ordinary stade of eight to a mile, or that there should have existed a *nautical* stadium, not much more than half the common itinerary stade, without any hint of such a difference being found in any of the ancient geographers—it will be found on examination that even this bold hypothesis is far from removing the difficulty.

Though Dr. Vincent considers himself compelled, by the wide divergence of the measures of Nearchus from the truth, to adopt the supposition that they are reckoned in these short stadia, he nevertheless admits that even with this resource "it is not possible to establish a [correct] proportion of part to part, or perhaps to measure five hundred stadia in any detached portion of the course with satisfaction" (p. 55). Moreover when he comes to the part of the voyage along the coast of the Ichthyophagi, where the fleet encountered the greatest hardships and difficulties, he finds that "the stadium of D'Anville *is less applicable* to this coast," which measures only 450 miles in a straight line, and 625 (according to his own calculation) by the course of the fleet (p. 229). A pretty notable difference, which he explains principally by supposing that "their distresses caused the distances to appear longer, at the same time that they engaged the mind too much to allow of accurate calculation" (p. 230). What means of *accurate calculation* they possessed in any case he has omitted to tell us. But when the fleet reached the coasts of Carmania and proceeded up the eastern shores of the Persian Gulf, where they were comparatively free from anxiety and encountered no serious difficulties, it is found that the error is in the contrary direction, "the measures upon this coast proving as erroneous from deficiency as those on the coast of the Ichthyophagi from excess". a fault for which (adds Dr. Vincent) "no better excuse can be given than the situation of Nearchus in both instances. If distress magnified the length of his former measures, ease and security appear to have diminished those on the coast of Karmania" (p. 365). But such an explanation at once excludes the supposition of any real *measures* or *calculation* whatsoever, and if we are compelled to fall back upon mere *vague estimates* (which is undoubtedly the truth) it is surely much more simple to admit those estimates to be for a part of the voyage more widely erroneous than Dr. Vincent would allow, rather than have recourse to the forced assumption of a different mode of reckoning, in stadia of a kind of which we have no other mention.

The mode in which M. D'Anville arrived at his conclusion is indeed sufficiently extraordinary, and is justly rejected by Dr. Vincent, though he adopted his result as applied to the voyage of Nearchus. In a passage of Aristotle (*De Cœlo*, ii. 14) already adverted to, that philosopher estimates the circumference of the earth at 400,000 stadia, while it is well known that the same circumference was calculated by Eratosthenes at 252,000 stadia. *Therefore*, concludes the French geographer, the stadium of Aristotle must have been to that of Eratosthenes as 252 to 400; and it is reasonable to suppose that this was the stadium in use among the Macedonians, and consequently that employed by Nearchus. But in fact the attempt of Eratosthenes to measure a portion of a great circle on the earth's surface was, so far as we know, the first *real attempt* made by any Greek to measure or calculate the circumference of the earth at all. All previous measurements, or rather estimates, including that of Aristotle, were merely conjectural. and the true inference from the passage in question is, not that Aristotle employed a different stadium, but that he supposed the world to be vastly larger than it really is. We find accordingly that his estimate of the earth's circumference was universally rejected by later Greek writers, after the more accurate investigations of Eratosthenes

Major Rennell also justly rejected the Aristotelian stade of M. D'Anville, of which no trace is found in any ancient author. Yet he himself fell into a somewhat similar error, and was induced by a comparison of numerous distances, as stated by ancient authors, to assume "an average of 718 to the degree," for the Olympic or common stadium of Greece, giving 505 English feet to the stade, instead of 606 feet, which correspond with the 600 Greek feet universally recognized by the ancients as the length of the ordinary stadium. (Rennell's *Geography of Herodotus*, p. 31.)

NOTE C, p. 528.

PORT OF ALEXANDER.

This suggestion was first made by Major Rennell (*Memoir of a Map of Hindostan*, p. 187), and has been adopted both by Gossellin and C. Muller. The importance of the port of Kurrachee is such as to leave little doubt of its correctness. Dr. Vincent, in whose days Kurrachee was little known, placed the Port of Alexander just beyond Cape Monze, a view that is open to the unanswerable objection that there is no port of the kind to be found there; and he has thus thrown his whole geography of this part of the coast into confusion.

It must be admitted that on any view the topography of this portion of the voyage (from the mouth of the Indus to that of the Arabis) remains very obscure. it is difficult to understand how Nearchus should have rounded such a headland as Cape Monze without making any mention of it and the harbour called Morontobara or the Port of Women, described by Arrian as large, roomy, deep, and well sheltered, though having but a narrow entrance, (λιμὴν μέγας καὶ εὔκυκλος καὶ βαθὺς καὶ ἄκλυστος, ὁ δ' ἔσπλους ἐς αὐτὸν στενός, *Indica*, c. 22, § 5) has not yet been identified. This point is the more important as the name is still found in Ptolemy (vi. 21, § 2), and it must therefore probably have continued to be a place frequented by navigators.

NOTE D, p. 532.

THE ISLAND OF ASHTOLA.

Ashtola being the only island of any size along this coast, there can be little doubt that it is the same which is referred to by Nearchus in another passage (Arrian, *Indica*, c. 31) though he there says it was called by the natives Nosala. It was regarded by them with superstitious dread, believing that whoever landed there immediately disappeared. One of the transports was indeed actually lost, but Nearchus touched at the island with his own ship, and compelled his sailors to go ashore, without any ill effect. It is singular that a similar superstition should still linger about the island in modern times; Captain Blair, who was one of the first to explore these coasts (in 1774) having been warned by the natives at Passenee, that it would be dangerous to approach the island of Ashtola, *as it was enchanted*, and that a ship had been turned into a rock. (Vincent, vol. i. p. 299.) It abounds in turtle of large size and excellent quality. but no mention is made of these by Nearchus, nor does it appear ever to have suggested itself to the minds of the Greek voyagers to avail themselves of this important resource, though suffering so severely from want of provisions. It is remarkable indeed that no indication of the use of turtle as an article of food is found in either Greek or Roman writers.

NOTE E, p. 535.

SUPPOSED ASTRONOMICAL CHANGES.

This suggestion, which agrees in substance with the views of Gossellin and Schmieder, appears to me much more plausible than that proposed by Dr. C. Muller, that the statement in question was interpolated from Onesicritus, and did not really proceed from Nearchus at all. Apart from the improbability that Arrian, who has throughout followed the narrative of Nearchus with the utmost faithfulness, should, in one or two instances only, introduce statements from other sources without any hint that they were so derived, the particular fact in question is expressly cited *as being stated by Nearchus* (παραπλωόντων δὲ τὴν Ἰνδῶν γῆν . . . λέγει Νέαρχος ὅτι αἱ σκίαι αὐτοῖσιν οὐ ταὐτὸ ἐποίεον, c. 25). It seems therefore impossible to doubt that it was found in his narrative. But two circumstances seem to me to concur in favour of the other hypothesis: the one, that this passage occurs at the point where Nearchus, according to his own view, had arrived at the western limit of India,—the Arabies and Oritæ being regarded by him as Indian tribes. where he therefore seems to have paused, as we find him doing on other occasions, (see c. 29, 38, 40) to make some general remarks on the Indian coasts and people. On such an occasion he might easily have introduced the mention of so remarkable a phenomenon (to the Greeks of those days) which he had learnt from Indian navigators, who were doubtless even at that period in the habit of descending the western coast of the peninsula as far as Malabar. Even the words παραπλωόντων τὴν Ἰνδῶν γῆν may *perhaps* have in fact referred to such navigators, though, as they are introduced by Arrian, they undoubtedly can have reference only to Nearchus and his comrades. But another circumstance that appears to me unintelligible on the supposition that the statement was really made by Nearchus as a matter of his own experience, is, that, as the passage stands in Arrian, these appearances were only visible *when they stood far out to sea, towards the south* (ὅκου μὲν ἐπὶ πολλὸν τοῦ πόντου ὡς πρὸς μεσημβρίην προχωρήσειαν). Now their voyage was throughout a coasting voyage in the strictest sense of the term; they were never driven out to sea by violent gales, in fact they anchored off shore every night. It is certain therefore that they could never have been on any occasion more than a few miles to the south of the coast line; and of course no appreciable difference in the appearance of the sun and stars could have been produced by such a deviation. On the other hand, the words just cited would naturally find a place, if Nearchus were recounting the observations of others, and the *general* experience of navigators in the Indian seas.

There seems indeed little doubt that such perverted statements as to the astronomical phenomena observed were really made by Onesicritus (cited by Pliny, vi. 23, § 98 ; see above, p. 543), and are quoted from him by other writers, but it is incredible that Nearchus, whom we find throughout a careful and trustworthy authority, should have been guilty of so flagrant a departure from the truth.

NOTE F, p. 537.

ISLAND OF ORMUZ.

The fate of Ormuz has indeed been a singular one. The island itself is not only, as it is termed by Nearchus, barren and rugged in a supreme degree, but wholly destitute of fresh water. Yet the advantages of its opportune situation at the entrance of the Persian Gulf, and of its secure harbour, rendered it in the middle ages under its Arabian rulers, and still more after it had fallen into the hands of the Portuguese, one of the greatest emporiums of trade and consequently one of the wealthiest cities of the East. Barbosa, who describes it as it existed before its conquest by the Portuguese in 1514, has left a curious account of the variety and extent of its commerce at this period, when it served as the chief *entrepôt* whence the spices, gems and other productions of India and the silk of China, were carried to Alexandria, Cairo, and the chief cities of the West. (Barbosa's *Description of the Coasts of East Africa and Malabar*, published by the Hakluyt Society in 1866, pp. 41–45.) At a later period "the wealth of Ormuz or of Ind" had become proverbial for the riches of the East. (Milton, *Paradise Lost*, book ii. v. 2.) The island continued in the hands of the Portuguese till 1622, when it was wrested from them by the Persian monarch Shah Abbas, who demolished the city and transferred the inhabitants, as well as what survived of the trade, to the town of Bunder Abbas or Gombroon, on the mainland, nearly opposite to Ormuz. The island itself is described as "a mere barren rock, formed of rock salt and sulphur, and entirely destitute of vegetation. Its appearance is thus altogether the most desolate that can be imagined." (Kempthorne in *Geogr. Journal*, vol. v. p. 274.) It is inhabited only by a few fishermen, but a small garrison is maintained there by the Imam of Muscat. (For a more recent account of Ormuz, as well as of the neighbouring island of Kishm, see a paper by Col. Pelly, in the *Journal of Geogr. Soc.* vol. xxxiv. pp. 251-258.) The Arabic name of the island, before it assumed that of Ormuz from the neighbouring mainland, was Jerun or Djerun, in which some resemblance may perhaps be traced to the ancient appellation, which is written Organa by Arrian, but appears under the form Ogyris in Strabo and Pliny.

NOTE G, p. 539.

DIRIDOTIS

The name of Diridotis is not found in any ancient author. But Strabo and other authors place a city called Teredon at the mouth of the Euphrates, which appears to have been a frequented port under the Macedonian kings. (Abydenus ap. Euseb. *Chron.* p. 21.) Hence the two have been generally identified. But this seems to me very doubtful. Teredon enjoyed the reputation of being an ancient city, founded by Nebuchadnezzar (Strabo, ii. p 80, xvi. 3, p. 765; Dionys. Perieg. v. 980), while Diridotis is described as a mere village, though resorted to by the merchants of Arabia. It was probably therefore a mere temporary mart, at the actual entrance of the Euphrates, while Teredon may be sought for a little higher up. If there was any foundation for the tale of its ancient origin, it could not have been situated really at the mouth of the river in the days of Nearchus, on account of the rapid advance of the coast line. The suggestion of Col. Chesney (vol. ii. p. 355) that the site of Teredon is marked by a gigantic mound called Jebel Sanam, near the (supposed) Pallacopas branch of the Euphrates, and about 23 miles S.S.W. of Bassorah, is plausible enough.

It is more interesting to observe that the manner in which Nearchus speaks of Diridotis as situated *at the mouth of the Euphrates,* which was navigable for 3300 stadia from thence to Babylon, appears to show conclusively that the Euphrates in his time still communicated with the sea by an independent channel of its own.

CHAPTER XIV.

Successors of Alexander.

Section 1.—*Megasthenes.—Increased knowledge of India.*

§ 1. The death of Alexander the Great, with the confusion which followed it, and the internecine struggles among his generals, gave a severe check to the progress of geographical discovery, as well as to the general advance of civilization in the East. It is true that, for a time, the death of the great conqueror did not seem likely to be followed by the dissolution of his empire. While the rival candidates for power were contending among themselves for supremacy, the provinces, even the remotest of them, continued to acquiesce in Macedonian rule, and to be governed by Macedonian satraps. When at last a new order of things began to emerge out of the chaos, and it was evident that the great Macedonian empire would be permanently divided into several separate and independent monarchies, still the whole, or almost the whole, of the Asiatic conquests of Alexander remained united under one head. From the time that Seleucus Nicator established himself at Babylon in B.C. 312, he became virtually the lord and master of all the vast regions of Upper Asia, to which, after the fall of Antigonus (in B.C. 301) were added also Syria and great part of Lower Asia, or what we now call Asia Minor. Ptolemy meanwhile had not only fortified himself in the undisputed possession of Egypt, but held also the important island of Cyprus, with the maritime cities of Phœnicia, still the seat of an extensive and flourishing commerce.

Of the steps by which Seleucus established and secured his authority over the extensive satrapies from the Euphrates to the Indus we have unfortunately no information; the meagre historians of this period confining their attention almost exclusively to the contests between the rival competitors for power. But there appears no doubt that he was called upon to make a series of successive campaigns into different provinces, the governors of which had probably taken advantage of the confusion at head-quarters to establish themselves in virtual independence, trusting for safety to the remoteness of their situation, and the difficulty of approaching them. The details of these operations, had they been preserved to us, would doubtless have thrown much light upon the geography of Upper Asia, but as it is, they are a mere blank. All that we learn is that by degrees Seleucus consolidated his dominion over the whole of the eastern provinces, which had been comprised in the empire of Alexander, including the remote regions of Bactriana, Sogdiana, and the Paropamisus; and that he transmitted this extensive empire undiminished to his son Antiochus. That prince had indeed been already established during the lifetime of his father (B.C. 293) in the government of all the provinces east of the Euphrates, with the title of king. The statement that no less than seventy-two satrapies were subject to the authority of Seleucus,[1] if it be indeed founded on fact, would prove that he must have instituted a new administrative partition of his dominions, subdividing the previously existing provinces into much smaller governments; a measure that would indeed be dictated by sound policy, as tending to diminish the excess of power confided to former satraps.[2] But of such a system we find no other indication.

§ 2. On one point only do we obtain any further information concerning the proceedings of Seleucus in the East, and although the statements preserved to us are even here imperfect and unsatisfactory, they possess nevertheless a great interest. It is certain that Seleucus not only renewed the relations with

---

[1] Appian, *Syriaca*, c 62.
[2] Droysen (*Hellenismus*, vol i p 606) assumes it as certain that such a measure was adopted by Seleucus, and with the view indicated in the text. But the authority of Appian on such a point is unfortunately worth very little.

India which Alexander had begun, but materially extended them, and acquired important additional information concerning parts of that country to which the Greek arms never penetrated.

So far as we are able to discern, the Greek satraps, who had been appointed by Alexander to the command of the provinces adjacent to India, maintained the Macedonian power in the regions west of the Indus; but having taken part with Antigonus in the contest for Upper Asia, they naturally found themselves on hostile terms with Seleucus, who was consequently obliged successively to reduce them under his authority. This he appears to have successfully accomplished; and there is no doubt that he had at one period reunited under his government all the provinces that lay west of the Indus.

Meantime an important revolution had taken place in the regions east of that river. A native chief, whom the Greeks name Sandracottus—the original Indian form of the name is Chandra-gupta—had overthrown in succession the petty native dynasties that were reigning in the Punjab and had thus become the founder of a powerful monarchy, which he had subsequently extended by his arms eastward, from the banks of the Sutledge to the Jumna and the Ganges, where he overthrew the powerful monarchy of the Prasians, and thus established his authority over the whole of the north of India.[3] As soon therefore as Seleucus had recovered possession of the countries west of the Indus, he found himself in the presence of a powerful and warlike monarch, commanding resources of a very different character from any that had been opposed to Alexander.[4] In such a state of things the occurrence of hostilities between the two was almost inevitable, but of the

---

[3] Justin, xv 4 For the history of Sandracottus and the revolution effected by him in the kingdom on the banks of the Ganges, founded nearly a century before by the Magadha dynasty, see Lassen's *Indische Alterthumer*, vol II, Duncker, *Gesch. des Alterthums*, vol II.

pp 356-361
[4] Of course the statements that Sandracottus was at the head of an army of 400,000, or, according to others, 600,000 men, are to be taken merely as instances of Oriental exaggeration (Strabo, xv p 709, Plut *Alex*. 62)

SECT 1. SUCCESSORS OF ALEXANDER. 555

circumstances and character of these we are almost wholly ignorant. It appears certain that Seleucus crossed the Indus and invaded the dominions of the Indian king, but it is probable that he did not advance far;[5] at all events it is clear that the final result of his operations was not successful, as by the treaty which he ultimately concluded with Sandracottus, he not only yielded all claims to the Punjab, but ceded a portion of the districts of the Paropamisus and Arachosia, which had been previously held by the Macedonians, so that both banks of the Indus were now united under the authority of the Indian king.[6] Seleucus however received in exchange not less than five hundred elephants—an addition to his forces which he may well have regarded as an ample equivalent for the precarious possession of a few remote and barbarous districts. He hastened to return to Babylon to take part in the coalition against Antigonus (B.C. 302).

Throughout the remainder of his reign Sandracottus continued to maintain the most friendly relations both with Seleucus and his son Antiochus. He sent repeated embassies to Babylon, while the Syrian king in return sent a Greek of the name of Megasthenes, who appears to have enjoyed a high place in his confidence and favour, as envoy to the court of Sandracottus. Megasthenes repaired to the capital of the Indian king, at Palibothra on the Ganges, where he resided for some time, and brought away an amount of information concerning India in general, which became for a long time

---

[5] The supposition that Seleucus himself had penetrated as far as the Ganges, though adopted by several early writers, some of whom even supposed him to have advanced to Palibothra, is wholly untenable, and is deservedly rejected by Robertson and others. Pliny's expression, "Reliqua inde Seleuco Nicatori peragrata sunt," would certainly seem to imply that the king had really advanced as far as the Jumna, but even this is at least very doubtful, and very little reliance can be placed upon the precise phraseology of such a writer as Pliny (compare his expressions concerning Patrocles). The subject is well discussed by Schwanbeck in his edition of the fragments of Megasthenes, pp 12-18

[6] Strabo, xv. 2, § 9, p 724, Appian, *Syriaca*, c. 55. The extent of the territory ceded is not clearly indicated. It probably comprised only the districts between the west bank of the Indus and the mountains

the foundation and principal authority for all that the Greeks knew in regard to that country.

§ 3. The work of MEGASTHENES has unfortunately perished; but large extracts from it have been preserved to us, especially by Arrian and Strabo, both of whom have taken it as the base of their descriptions of India, in regard as well to its natural features, as to its political institutions and to the manners and customs of its inhabitants.[7] A considerable amount of information had indeed been already collected by the companions and generals of Alexander, and given to the world by Nearchus, Onesicritus and others, and it is not always possible to separate distinctly the statements derived from these different sources. In taking a brief review of the real extent and value of the knowledge of India acquired at this time by the Greeks, it is of little consequence to observe this distinction; but in general it may be assumed that the statements of Strabo and Arrian, for which no other authority is expressly cited, are derived from Megasthenes.

§ 4. Already before Alexander had reached the banks of the Hyphasis he had received information of the existence of a great and powerful empire established on the banks of the Ganges, the resources of which were doubtless greatly exaggerated by the native reports that were transmitted to him. According to these statements, Xandrames, the king of the Prasians, who ruled over the whole of the territories east of the Jumna, commanded an army of not less than 200,000 infantry, 20,000 cavalry, 3000 elephants, and more than 2000 war-chariots.[8] But with every allowance for exaggeration, there seems no doubt that even at this period there really existed a powerful monarchy, combining under its sway the whole of the fertile regions from the Jumna to the mouths of the Ganges: while the overthrow of the then existing dynasty by Sandracottus seems to have im-

---

[7] The fragments of Megasthenes have been collected, and published, with an excellent introduction, containing a full inquiry into his life and writings, by Schwanbeck, 8vo, Bonn, 1846 They are contained also in the 2nd volume of the *Fragmenta Historicorum Græcorum*, edited by C. Muller.

[8] Diodor xvii 93. Compare Plut. *Alex* 62, whose numbers are still higher.

parted fresh life and vigour to the whole empire, at the same time that he so materially extended its confines towards the west. The seat of government had been already established at the city which the Greeks called Palibothra, a form under which we readily recognize the native appellation of Pataliputra; it was situated at the junction of the Ganges with the Sone, a few miles above the modern city of Patna.[9]

§ 5. On his journey to the capital Megasthenes followed what was termed "the royal road," and it is to him that we are indebted for the only definite geographical data that have been preserved to us by ancient writers concerning this part of India. Unfortunately his statements of distances have been transmitted to us only by Pliny,[1] and the numbers as they stand cannot be regarded as trustworthy. But the general line of route may be clearly followed. The principal points or stages are thus given:—"From the Hyphasis to the Hesydrus (Sutledge), 168 Roman miles; thence to the Iomanes (Jumna), the same distance; thence to the Ganges, 112 miles; to the Rhodapha, 119 miles (though others made this distance 325); to the city of Calinipaxa, 167 miles (or according to others 265); thence to the confluence of the Iomanes and Ganges, 620 miles; to the city of Palibothra, 425; to the mouth of the Ganges, 638 miles."[2]

Setting aside the distances, which are involved in hopeless confusion,[3] we find the most important points on this line of route correctly given; it proceeded across from the Sutledge to the Jumna, thence to the Ganges, and afterwards descended

---

[9] The true site of Palibothra was first pointed out by Major Rennell (*Memoir of a Map of India*, p 50). His view has been generally adopted by recent writers

[1] Eratosthenes appears to have availed himself of the same authority, when he reckoned 10,000 stadia from the Indus to Palibothra (ap. Strab. xv. 1, § 11). The startling discrepancy between this statement, and the numbers given by Pliny is an additional proof of the utter unworthiness of the latter.

[2] Plin. *Hist Nat* vi 17, § 63

[3] Pliny himself tells us that the numbers were variously given by his authorities, and the instances in which he adds the different statements show how wide was the divergence between them When we add to this cause the diversity of numbers found in our existing MSS of Pliny, we may well pronounce any attempt to reconcile or explain them to be wholly futile

the valley of that river as far as the junction with the Jumna at Allahabad. The site of Calinipaxa, which, from the way in which it is mentioned, would seem to have been a place of importance, is wholly unknown: nor can we identify the river Rhodapha among the numerous tributaries of the Ganges. Megasthenes, indeed appears himself to have enumerated nineteen tributaries of the great stream, of which the names have been preserved to us,[4] but in no correct geographical sequence, and without any statement of distances: hence their identification is very uncertain.[5] Among the names that can be most clearly recognized is that of the Sonus, mentioned both by Arrian and Pliny, and still called the Sone, which falls into the Indus at Palibothra.

§ 6. Megasthenes was probably the first Greek who ever reached the banks of the Ganges—certainly the first writer who transmitted any account of it from personal observation. That his account should be tinged with exaggeration is not to be wondered at. We have seen how greatly they magnified in their reports the real dimensions of the Indus and its tributary waters: and the sacred stream of the Ganges was still more calculated to impress the imaginations of those who gazed upon it for the first time. We are told that it was 100 stadia in width *at its narrowest point,* and that where its waters spread out freely, one bank could not be discerned from the other.[6] Of its sources he had of course no definite knowledge, but was

---

[4] They are given by Arrian (*Indica,* c 4), but in a very careless and perfunctory manner Pliny also states the whole number at nineteen, but gives the names of only four, "besides those already mentioned," *i e*, the Iomanes and Rhodapha, and apparently regards these as the only ones that were navigable (*H N* vi. 18, § 65), though this is directly at variance with the statement of Arrian

The omission in the former list (that of Arrian) of the Iomanes or Jumna, the most important of all tributaries of the Ganges, and which was unquestionably known to Megasthenes, as it is twice mentioned in the description of the "royal road," is unaccountable But it shows how little reliance can be placed on such enumerations, when reported at second hand

[5] It has been attempted to determine them by means of the Sanscrit names, but it must be confessed with very imperfect success

[6] Arrian, *Indica,* 4, § 7 The statements quoted by Pliny are somewhat more moderate, making it only eight Roman miles at the narrowest, and 100 stadia in *average* width (Plin *H. N.* vi 18, § 65).

correctly informed that it took its rise in the Indian Caucasus (the Himalaya), and after flowing at first to the south, then turned eastwards, and pursued an easterly course as far as Palibothra.[7] Of the great bend that it makes towards the south, after passing that city, he had no knowledge, but described it as holding on the same course to its mouth in the Eastern Ocean. It is remarkable that he particularly stated that it had but *one mouth*, as distinguished from the Indus, which formed a Delta.[8] So imperfect was his information concerning the course of the river below Palibothra, that he seems to have had no idea of the complicated network of rivers really formed by the Ganges and its numerous arms, before they enter the Gulf of Bengal.

Palibothra itself was described as a very large city, situated at the confluence of the Ganges with another river (the Sonus or Erannoboas),[9] and built in the form of a parallelogram, eighty stadia in length, and fifteen in breadth: it was surrounded only with a wooden wall or stockade, but pierced with loopholes, and flanked by numerous towers, besides an outer ditch of vast dimensions, which was filled with water from the neighbouring rivers.[1] But no details are preserved to us of architectural splendour, or of that magnificence in the decorations of the court and palace which we are accustomed to associate with the capitals of Oriental potentates.

§ 7. The other cities of India, we are assured, were so numerous that they could not be counted; but Megasthenes

---

[7] Strabo, xv 1, § 13, p 690.

[8] Strabo, *l c*

[9] Some confusion has arisen in consequence of the statement that the river at the confluence of which with the Ganges Palibothra was situated was the Erannoboas (Arrian, *Indica*, c 4 The name is accidentally omitted by Strabo, having evidently fallen out of our text See Kramer's note), while the ruins generally regarded as those of Pataliputra are placed near the junction of the Sone, a large river, the name of which, as already observed, is readily recognised in the Sonus of Arrian and Pliny But although these authors certainly regarded the two rivers as distinct, there can be little doubt that they were in fact only two names for the same stream, the name Erannoboas being only a Greek form of the Sanscrit Hyranyavahas (the golden armed), which is the *poetical* designation of the Sone (see Ritter, *Erdkunde*, vol iv. pt. 1, p 508)

[1] Strabo, xv 1, § 36; Arrian, *Indica*, c 10 According to Diodorus (ii 39), Palibothra was founded and fortified by Hercules (!)

estimated—of course from mere hearsay authority—the number of nations or tribes that inhabited it at not less than a hundred and eighteen.[2] Of these, the Prasians, in whose country Palibothra was situated, were accounted the chief. Their relation with the Gangaridæ,[3] whose name is also frequently mentioned by Greek authors, is not clearly indicated; but the latter appellation seems to have been applied in a general way to all the inhabitants of the valley of the Ganges, while that of Prasians is evidently only the Greek form of the Sanscrit Pratschia—the people of the East—and was thus not a true ethnic appellation. It had doubtless been used to designate the kingdom founded on the banks of the Ganges, in contradistinction to those of the Punjab.

All the information collected by Megasthenes points to the conclusion that at this period the Indian monarchy was a powerful and well-organized government: the king was surrounded by a number of counsellors, who assisted him in maintaining a strict superintendence over all branches of the administration: justice was well administered: care bestowed upon the maintenance of the highways: and the revenues diligently collected. Sandracottus is said to have kept up a standing army of 400,000 men, with 30,000 cavalry and 9000 elephants.[4] These numbers are doubtless exaggerated, but there seems no reason to doubt the fact that his forces were really very numerous and well organized. The king himself, except when he went out to war or the chase, or for the performance of some special sacrifices, was hardly ever seen. Within his palace he was attended only by women, some of whom even accompanied him on his hunting expeditions and in war, and were especially charged to watch over his personal safety.

---

[2] Arrian (*Indica*, c 7) justly remarks on the inadequate means of information possessed by Megasthenes for such a statement

[3] The name is written by Plutarch (*Alex* 62) Gandaridæ, but they had nothing to do with the Gandarii of Herodotus, who dwelt west of the Indus

[4] Strabo, xv 1, § 53, p 709 Pliny, as usual, adopts the still more exaggerated statement of 600,000 as the number of the infantry (*H N.* vi. 19, § 68)

§ 8. Of the peculiar institutions of the Hindoos, their division into castes could not fail to attract the attention of the Greeks, and the statements of Megasthenes upon this subject, though not free from error, are in themselves very curious and interesting. According to his account the Indians were in his time divided into seven classes, every one of which kept itself quite distinct from the others, and could neither intermarry nor pass from one class to another. The first of these was formed by the wise men or philosophers, by whose advice and direction everything was managed: the second consisted of the agriculturists or tillers of the soil: the third, of shepherds and hunters: the fourth, of artisans and traders: the fifth, of soldiers: the sixth, of inspectors, or official superintendents appointed to examine every detail of the lives of others: the seventh, of other officials and councillors to whom the administration of public affairs was entrusted.[4] Megasthenes was undoubtedly led into error by supposing these two last classes, which really formed very distinct bodies of men, to constitute separate *castes*. He was also misled in describing the shepherds and hunters as similarly separated from all others: but these errors are easily accounted for, from the great tendency which has in all ages prevailed in India to render all such occupations hereditary, and thus maintain subordinate lines of distinction within the broader limits of the castes properly so called. These, as is now well known, were really only four in number, namely; the Brahmins, answering to the philosophers of the Greeks, but comprising also the official inspectors and ministers, whom they regarded as constituting the sixth and seventh classes; the Kshatriyas or warriors: the Vaisyas, including herdsmen and hunters as well as agriculturists; and the Sudras, or menial class, comprising also artisans and handicraftsmen of all descriptions. Besides these however there exist what are called the mixed castes, several of which are,

---

[4] Arrian, *Indica*, c 11, 12, Strabo, xv 1, §§ 39–41, 46–49; Diodor ii 40, 41. The accounts of all three authors are taken from Megasthenes, and are almost exactly the same.

VOL. I.

according to law at least, confined to the practice of certain trades or occupations.⁵

One circumstance which naturally attracted the particular attention of the Greeks was the absence of slaves: slavery as an institution, in the form in which it was universal in the West, being unknown among the Indians: and though the condition of the Sudras was in reality little removed from that of a servile class, this appears to have been so far ameliorated in practice as to escape the observation of foreign visitors. Nor do we find any allusion to the still more degraded class, called Pariahs, which now forms an important element in the social constitution of India. In other respects too the Greeks were led to form too favourable an estimate of the state of society among the Indians, as well as of their moral character. But this tendency to find a kind of Utopian perfection in any form of society widely different from that with which the observer is familiar, is an error of frequent occurrence in all ages.⁶ Thus Megasthenes represented the warrior caste as leading a life of perfect ease and enjoyment, when not called upon to go out to war, while the agricultural peasantry pursued their occupations in undisturbed tranquillity, being never interfered with, even when their district became the theatre of hostilities.

§ 9. Much attention was bestowed, both by Megasthenes and other Greek writers, upon the Brahmins, or philosophers as they termed them, whose doctrines and tenets were regarded by them as having much resemblance with those of Pythagoras. For us on the contrary it is interesting to compare the notices that have been thus preserved to us, with the full knowledge that we now possess of the philosophical and religious systems of the Hindoos; and it must be admitted that considering the difficulties under which the Greeks must have

---

⁵ See Colebrooke's *Enumeration of Indian Classes* in his *Essays*, pp 270–279

⁶ The flattering picture of China by Voltaire (*Essai sur les Mœurs et l'Esprit des Nations*) is an instance that will readily present itself to the mind of the modern reader

laboured in obtaining such knowledge, their information is singularly correct.[7] They mention also that besides the Brachmanæ or Brahmins, there existed another sect of philosophers whom they term Garmanæ or Sarmanæ, who led a life of hardship and privation in the woods, but enjoyed a great reputation for sanctity. It is probable that we have here a notice of the Buddhists, who were at this time rising to eminence, though still inferior in importance and consideration to the Brahmins, as they are justly described by the Greek writers. The name Sarmanæ is probably a corruption of Sramana, the native appellation of the Buddhist priesthood.[8] Others again practised austerities similar to those of the modern Fakeers, remaining immoveable in the same position, standing or lying naked in the full heat of the sun, &c. The practice of self-immolation by voluntary burning was also regarded by the Greeks as one characteristic of the Brahmins; a belief naturally confirmed by the conspicuous instance of Calanus, who having accompanied Alexander on his return from India, put an end to his life in this manner.[9] On the other hand the custom of widows burning themselves on the funeral pile of their husbands—so general among the Hindoos in modern times—is noticed by the historians of Alexander only as one of the peculiar customs of a particular tribe—the Cathæans—in the northern part of the Punjab.[1]

§ 10. Of the natural productions of India the accounts given by Megasthenes were in general very accurate. Fore-

---

[7] It is mentioned in one passage that the communications of the Brahmins with the messengers sent to them by Alexander had to pass through three successive interpreters, all of them illiterate and ignorant men (Strabo, xv. 1, § 64, p. 716).

[8] The name is written Γαρμᾶνες and Γερμᾶνες in our MSS and editions of Strabo, but Clement of Alexandria, whose account is obviously derived from the same source, writes it Σαρμᾶναι, which is doubtless the more correct form, for the reason given in the text (Clem. Alexandr. *Stromata*, i. 15, § 71).

[9] He is expressly described as having done this in accordance with the custom of the country (καὶ ἀποθανεῖν τῷ πατρίῳ νόμῳ, τεθέντα ἐπὶ πυρκαιάν. Strab xv 1, § 64.) Megasthenes, however, denied that self-immolation was inculcated by the precepts of the philosophers Ibid § 68

[1] Aristobulus, ap Strab xv 1, § 62, p 714, Diodor. xvii. 91.

most among these may undoubtedly be reckoned the elephants, with which the Greeks had for the first time become acquainted during the expedition of Alexander. But not only has he preserved to us many curious particulars concerning their natural history, and some interesting anecdotes of their sagacity, but has given a full account of the mode of catching and taming them, which agrees in almost every particular with those recorded by modern travellers.[2] The size and ferocity of the tigers in the land of the Prasians is also mentioned with wonder; and the gigantic serpents—the Pythons of modern naturalists—were perhaps still more calculated to excite astonishment. Nor can we wonder if the accounts of these monstrous reptiles were considerably tinged with exaggeration.[3] Even the parrots and monkeys were strange to the eyes of the Greeks, and bore a prominent part in their narratives. The abundance of peacocks too had been early remarked by the companions of Alexander.[4] They could not fail also to be struck with the vast forests of trees wholly different from any they knew elsewhere; and the peculiar character and mode of growth of the Banian or Indian figtree is described with great accuracy. In this instance indeed even their dimensions are not exaggerated. The vast size of the reeds (bamboos) also attracted particular attention, and the circumstance of trees growing actually in the sea (evidently mangroves) is noticed with wonder.[5]

Among the quadrupeds characteristic of India we find mention also of the rhinoceros, the name of which first became

---

[2] Megasthenes, Fr 36, 37, ed. Schwanbeck. Arrian, *Indica*, c. 13, 14, Strabo, xv 1, § 42

[3] It was Onesicritus alone, who was notorious for the gross exaggerations in which he was wont to indulge, that spoke of two serpents kept in confinement by Abisares, king of a mountain tribe above Taxila, of which one was 80 cubits, the other 140 cubits long! (Onesicrit ap Strab xv. 1, § 28, p 698) This is one of the marvellous statements for which Onesicritus is justly called by Strabo τῶν παραδόξων ἀρχικυβερνήτην Aristobulus and Nearchus, as usual, were much more moderate. The latter mentioned a serpent of 16 cubits in length as the largest that was actually caught by the Macedonians, but added that the Indians asserted they were found of much larger size (Arrian, *Indica*, c. 15, § 10)

[4] Q Curtius, ix. 2, § 13.

[5] Megasth Fr 19

known to the Greeks at this period.⁶ We have already seen how much they were struck with finding crocodiles in the Indus, though subsequent observation showed them that they were neither so numerous nor so formidable as those of the Nile. The resemblance of the two rivers in this respect seems to have led them to expect to find hippopotami also in the Indus; as they thought it worth while to notice especially that these were *not* found.⁷

The great size and power of the Indian dogs—some of which were said to be a match for a lion, and to despise any meaner foe—are especially mentioned as having attracted the admiration of Alexander.⁸ The most remarkable specimens were those exhibited by Sopeithes, the king of a tract at the foot of the Himalaya, near the banks of the Hyphasis, and the dogs of these mountain regions are to this day described as the largest and most powerful in India.

Of the more useful productions of the country the sugar-cane is noticed,⁹ though in a manner that would hardly lead us to suppose it was in very extensive use; rice is well described, as well as the mode of its cultivation; and cotton, or tree-wool, as it was called, the general use of which by the natives in the place of linen and woollen textures is attested by all Greek writers. They had even noticed the fact of its stones or hard seeds, which had to be extracted before the cotton could be carded.¹ Silk also is mentioned, though obscurely, and was supposed to be procured from the bark of a tree.² Cinnamon and other spices were said to be produced in the south of India, from whence doubtless they were transmitted in the way of trade to the regions on the banks of the Ganges.³

---

⁶ Q. Curt. ix. 1, § 5
⁷ Onesicritus alone, with his usual maccuracy, maintained that there *were* hippopotami in the Indus (Strabo, xv 1, p 690, Arrian, *Indica*, c 6)
⁸ Strabo, xv 1, §§ 31, 37, Diodor. xvii. 92, Ælian, *Hist Nat* viii 1 The fame of these Indian dogs had indeed previously reached the ears of the Greeks, as they are mentioned both by Xenophon (*Cynegetica*, c 10) and by Aristotle (*Hist An* viii 28) They had probably been already imported into Persia.
⁹ Strabo, xv 1, § 20
¹ Aristobulus, ap Strab. xv 1, § 21, p 694
² Strab *l c.*   ³ Id. § 22, p 695

§ 11. It is strange that a writer who has preserved to us so many valuable and trustworthy notices should have allowed himself to be led astray so as to relate the most absurd and extravagant fables. But not only did Megasthenes repeat the story of the gold-digging ants, as large as foxes—a fable for which there was certainly some foundation, however strangely perverted,[4] and assert the existence of unicorns, which he describes as horses, with heads like deer, and a single horn —a belief that still prevails in some parts of India; but he described winged serpents, winged scorpions, and other creatures equally anomalous. Still more absurd were the fables that he repeated concerning races of men of pigmy stature—some only five spans in height, some only three— of others without nostrils, others without mouths, supporting themselves only by smells; of wild men who had their feet turned backwards, so that the heels were in front; of men with ears like dogs, and only a single eye in the middle of their forehead; and others again with ears reaching to their feet, on which they used to lie down to sleep.[5] Some of these marvellous tales were certainly Indian fables, which had been really told to the travellers,[6] but others are unquestionably fictions already familiar to the Greeks, which were transplanted at pleasure from one unknown region to another.

§ 12. The direct information obtained by Megasthenes was confined to the two great valleys, or plains, of the Indus and the Ganges; of the mountain ranges and table-lands of the interior he seems to have had no knowledge. Probably the

---

[4] See this subject discussed in Chapter VII p 229, Note D. Megasthenes added the curious statement that these gold-digging ants were found among the Derdæ, a nation dwelling in the mountains in the east of India, where there was a great tableland (ὀροπέδιον) in which the gold was found (Fr. 39, ap Strab. xv i p 706). This points clearly to the gold being derived from the valleys of the Himalaya. The name of the Derdæ is obviously the same with that of the Daradæ or Daradræ of Ptolemy, whom that author places near the sources of the Indus (Ptol vii 1, § 42), and it is still retained by the Derds or Dards, who dwell in the mountains on the frontiers of Thibet, near the upper valley of the Indus

[5] Megasthen Fr 29, ed Schwanbeck Strabo, xv 1, § 57, p 711. Compare Pliny, *Hist Nat* vii 2, §§ 25, 26

[6] See on this subject the remarks of Schwanbeck in his introduction to the fragments of Megasthenes, pp 61-71.

dominions of Sandracottus were limited towards the south by the Vindhya mountains. But of the general configuration and extent of India, as a whole, he obtained a more accurate idea than under the circumstances could well have been expected. Thus while Ctesias had asserted that India was equal in extent to the whole of the rest of Asia, and even Onesicritus had maintained that it was a third part of the inhabited world, Megasthenes greatly reduced its dimensions, stating that its extent from the mountains on the north to the Ocean on the south was about 20,000 stadia (2000 G. miles). He added the important observation that its greatest length was from north to south; its breadth from east to west—which almost all other writers had regarded as the direction of its greatest extent—being really only about 16,000 stadia.[7] Both statements are indeed considerably in excess of the truth—the real length of Hindustan being in round numbers about 1800 English miles, and its greatest breadth about 1500 miles; but considering the nature of the information to which alone Megasthenes could have access, and the vague ideas previously entertained by the Greeks of the geography of these countries, it must be admitted that his numbers present a marked approximation to the real distances.

§ 13. Another point upon which Megasthenes appears to have been the first to obtain any definite information was concerning the large and important island of Taprobane, or Ceylon. Its name indeed had already reached the ears of the companions of Alexander; and was mentioned by Onesicritus, who stated that it contained large numbers of elephants, of larger size than those of India, and added vaguely that it was 5000 stadia *in extent*, without specifying whether he meant length or breadth [8]—and was distant twenty days' voyage from the main land. Megasthenes reduced this last statement to

---

[7] Strabo, ii 1, §§ 4, 7, 12; xv 1 § 12, Arrian, *Indica*, 3, §§ 7, 8 According to the latter writer, Megasthenes gave the length at 22 300 stadia, a state- ment of singular *preciseness*, considering the nature of his information.
[8] Strabo, xv. 1, § 15, p 691.

seven days—still a great exaggeration—and added that the island produced abundance of gold and pearls.⁹ His information was doubtless derived from merchants who traded thither for this last article. But his geographical idea of the position of the island was evidently very vague.

§ 14. Of the subsequent intercourse of the Greek monarchs with India we have very little information. We learn indeed that after the death of Sandracottus, a Greek of the name of DAIMACHUS was sent by Seleucus as ambassador to his successor Allitrochades (Amitraghades) and that he wrote some account of his journey, but his authority is rarely cited, and he is treated by Strabo as worthy of very little credit.¹ Much more trustworthy, according to that author, was Patrocles, an officer who held important commands both under Seleucus Nicator and his son Antiochus, and was entrusted for some time with the chief government of the provinces on the frontiers of India. But it is not clear that he himself visited that country, or at least that he ever crossed the Indus. Nor have we any account of the title or character of the work in which he had collected the results of his researches; but his geographical data were considered by Eratosthenes as more trustworthy than those of Megasthenes, and were made by that great geographer the foundation of his own description of India.² Still less do we know concerning a writer of the name of Dionysius, mentioned only by Pliny, according to whom he was sent ambassador to one of the Indian kings by Ptolemy Philadelphus.³ But such a mission was natural enough, with a view to counteract the influence of the Syrian kings, at the time that the Egyptian monarchs were striving to open a direct trade with India.

---

⁹ Megasthen Fr 18, Plin. H. N. vi. 22, § 81
¹ Strabo, ii. 1, § 9, p 70
² Strabo, ib. pp 68, 69, 70
³ Plin Hist Nat. vi. 17, § 58.

Section 2.—*Bactrian Provinces.—Patrocles.*

§ 1. From India it seems natural to turn to another quarter, where we might have reasonably hoped to find that the long continued Macedonian dominion would have led to increased geographical knowledge. But in this case we are destined to complete disappointment. We have seen how Alexander had carried his arms as far as the Iaxartes, and had not only subdued the remote provinces of Bactria and Sogdiana, but had founded several cities there, and established colonies of Macedonian soldiers to form a nucleus of Hellenic civilization. Nor did these settlements prove abortive. So far as our information enables us to judge, the cities thus founded maintained themselves for a considerable period, while the provinces in question, after continuing for more than sixty years under the government of Greek satraps, appointed by the Syrian kings, threw off the yoke and declared themselves independent of the Seleucidan monarchy.[4] Their rulers however were still of Greek origin, and there can be no doubt that they continued to retain a strong tincture of Greek culture, notwithstanding their remote and secluded position. But the disadvantages resulting from this cause were greatly increased, when the Parthians—a purely oriental tribe, probably belonging to the same race with the Turks—who had revolted from the Syrian kings much about the same time as the Bactrians, extended their dominion over the whole table-land of Iran, and ultimately established their authority even in the valley of the Tigris.

---

[4] The date of the first declaration of independence by the Bactrian satrap, Theodotus or Diodotus, cannot be fixed with certainty, but it may be determined within approximate limits. We learn positively from Strabo (xi. 9, § 2) that it preceded the revolt of the Parthians under Arsaces, and this is assigned by the best authorities to the year 250 B C (Clinton, *Fast. Hellen* vol. iii p 18.) Hence the revolt of Bactriana has been fixed by Bayer in 255 B C, and by Visconti and others, including Professor Wilson, in 256 (Wilson's *Ariana*, p 216) General Cunningham would assign it to the year 246 B C, but the arguments in favour of the earlier date appear to me to preponderate.

§ 2. The effect of this was completely to isolate the Greek kings of Bactria, and the regions over which they had established their rule—including Ariana and the Paropamisus, as well as the provinces of Bactria and Sogdiana—from the rest of the Greek world: and though it is certain that the germs of Greek civilization, once planted in these remote regions, maintained their ground with singular pertinacity for a long period, we are almost wholly without information concerning their progress and diffusion. The Bactrian provinces, north of the Paropamisus, were the first to succumb under an invasion of Scythian tribes from the north-east;[5] while the Greek rulers who had established themselves at the foot of the Paropamisus, and on the borders of Ariana and India, maintained their independent position down to a later period, and were able at times to extend their arms over the Punjab, and even the lower part of the valley of the Indus. But almost all definite historical information is wanting in regard to these remote and petty kingdoms: we know nothing of their political institutions or relations with the native powers, while in a geographical point of view the result is absolutely null. We find indeed a vague statement that these monarchs had carried their arms farther into India than Alexander had done,

---

[5] The period of this, like almost all the dates and facts connected with these Bactrian kingdoms, is uncertain: but the final extinction of the Greek dynasties in this part of Asia is assigned to the year 126 B C. and it appears probable that the provinces north of the Hindoo Koosh fell into the hands of the barbarians some time before those on the western border of India Recent researches in connection with the coins which have been discovered of late years in large numbers in this part of Asia, have established the existence of not less than twenty-nine kings or princes bearing pure Greek names, and consequently in all probability of purely Greek extraction So great a number of rulers during a period of only 120 to 130 years appears clearly to show that some of them were contemporaneous, and reigned separately in Bactria proper, Ariana, or the Indian provinces But all attempts to arrange them in any definite chronological order, or determine their geographical relations, are based almost entirely upon mere conjecture. See Wilson's *Ariana*, pp 215–300, and an elaborate series of papers by Major-General Cunningham in the *Numismatic Chronicle*, vols 8, 9, 10 The whole subject has been still more recently submitted to a careful re-examination by Dr von Sallet in the *Zeitschrift fur Numismatik*, Berlin, 1878, but his researches have only led him to acknowledge, even more strongly than his predecessors, the hopelessness of the task (see p. 207).

SECT. 2   SUCCESSORS OF ALEXANDER.   571

and opened out a more extensive knowledge of that country: and two of the kings in question, Menander and Demetrius, are especially mentioned as having passed the Hyphasis, which had been the limit of Alexander's conquests to the east, and advanced as far as the Jumna: they also recovered possession of the delta of the Indus, or Pattalene, and extended their dominion over some adjoining districts of the sea-coast.[6] But it is probable that these conquests were short-lived. Strabo distinctly observes that they had added nothing to the information previously possessed: and it is certain that we do not find in our extant authorities the slightest trace of any increased acquaintance with India, derived from the establishment of this Greek kingdom on its immediate frontiers. One curious circumstance is however recorded, which proves the extent of the commercial relations maintained by these kings with the adjacent parts of India; that when the Greek and Roman merchants visited Barygaza and the ports of Guzerat, more than a century after the Christian era, they still found the silver coins of Apollodotus and Menander commonly current among the traders of that country.[7]

§ 3. Equally little do we learn during this period concerning the provinces beyond the line of the Indian Caucasus. There is reason to believe that the Greek rulers of these countries founded there several flourishing cities, in addition to those already established by Alexander, and that the country rose under their government to a very prosperous condition.[8] The manner in which the same result was pro-

---

[6] Apollodorus ap Strab xi. 11, § 1, p. 516, xv 1, § 3, p 686 This Apollodorus, who was a native of Artemita in Babylonia, wrote a history of the Parthians, which is repeatedly quoted by Strabo, and appears to have contained some interesting notices concerning the Bactrian kings His date is unknown, but he seems to have written after the time of Eucratides, and apparently after that of Menander also His work can therefore be hardly placed earlier than 120 B C The fragments are published by C Muller in his *Fragmenta Historicorum Græcorum*, vol iv p. 308

[7] *Periplus Maris Erythræi*, c 47.

[8] Eight new cities were founded by Alexander in Bactriana and Sogdiana (Strab xi. 11, § 4) We have no details concerning those founded by his successors, but the name of Eucratidia points distinctly to its having been founded or rebuilt by Eucratides [Antiochia

duced, at a much later period, under Timour and his successors, is sufficient to show how easily such a state of things may have arisen; and the scanty and passing notices found in the Greek writers of the wealth and power of such monarchs as Euthydemus and Eucratides have been abundantly confirmed in modern times by the discovery of their coins in such numbers as to bear the strongest testimony to the truth of these statements. But of any extension of their commercial relations beyond the frontiers of the empire of Alexander, or any increased geographical knowledge of Central Asia we hear nothing.[9] It is much to be regretted that the history given by Polybius of the campaigns of Antiochus the Great in Upper Asia, against the lately revolted Parthian and Bactrian kings, has not been preserved to us, but as that monarch did not penetrate beyond the frontiers of these provinces, it could scarcely have added anything very material to our geographical knowledge.

§ 4. There was indeed one author of earlier date, from whom Eratosthenes appears to have derived much valuable information. This was PATROCLES, whose name has been already mentioned in connection with India, and who held for a considerable time under Antiochus I., the chief command of all the provinces from the frontiers of India to the Caspian Sea. In this position he appears to have taken great pains to collect statistical and geographical information concerning the countries under his government, and there can be little doubt that we should have derived many valuable details from his work had it been preserved to us. He is praised by Strabo for the accuracy of his statements and the soundness of his judgment,

---

Antiochia in Margiana, and Sotena in Aria are also ascribed to Antiochus Soter.

Justin's phrase, where he calls Theodotus "mille urbium Bactrianarum praefectus" (xli. 4), is a mere rhetorical exaggeration

[9] We know not what value to attach to the vague expression quoted from Apollodorus by Strabo (xi 11, § 1) that the Bactrian kings "extended their dominion as far as the Seres and the Phrynes," but the passage is interesting as being the first geographical notice of a people of the name of Seres, so celebrated in after times.

as well as for his abstinence from the fables with which so many writers had disfigured their narratives. We are told moreover that he enjoyed the great advantage of a statistical account of the provinces under his rule, which had been drawn up by order of Alexander himself, and was afterwards given to Patrocles by one Xenocles, who had charge of the treasury.[1] Though it is probable that such a document was drawn up with statistical and financial rather than geographical objects, it must have been in any case a valuable contribution to the knowledge of the countries in question. But it is unfortunate that the most important geographical statement that is transmitted to us on the authority of Patrocles is one that we now know to be entirely erroneous.

In the speech which Alexander himself is represented as addressing to his army on the banks of the Hyphasis, he pointed out that it was a comparatively short distance from thence to the Ganges and the Eastern Sea, and added that this Eastern or Indian Sea was continuous with the Hyrcanian (Caspian) on the one side and with the Persian Gulf on the other, all of them, as well as that which bounded Libya, being in fact portions of the one great circumfluent ocean.[2] The voyage of Nearchus conclusively established the fact that this was true as regards the Persian Gulf. This discovery appears to have tended strongly, by a false but natural analogy, to strengthen the belief that a similar communication existed with the Hyrcanian Sea also. Alexander had, as we have seen, already taken measures for an exploring voyage on the Caspian, when all his schemes of this description were interrupted by his untimely death. Nor does it appear that any of his successors found leisure to resume the project. But from the

---

[1] Strabo, 11. 1, § 6, p. 69 Strabo calls it an ἀναγραφὴ, or "register," an expression which clearly points to an official document, not a mere literary description.
[2] Arrian, *Anab.* v 26. How far the speech, as preserved to us, may represent that actually delivered by Alexander we have no means of judging; but it is certainly not the composition of Arrian, and on such a point as this would, in all probability, correctly give us the views of the king himself, which were doubtless shared by the leading officers of his army.

position of Patrocles he would be naturally led to make inquiries into the point, and it is strange that the result of these inquiries was to confirm him in the received view, so that he even maintained expressly that it was possible to sail round from India to the Hyrcanian Sea.³ His authority on this point was unfortunately universally received, and was adopted as conclusive both by Eratosthenes and Strabo. Thus, as Humboldt has observed, the conquests of Alexander became in this instance the means of retarding, instead of promoting, the progress of geographical knowledge.⁴

His information concerning the dimensions of the Caspian was more correct, as he justly reported it to be about the same size as the Euxine,⁵ while in regard to the Oxus and the Iaxartes he stated that they both flowed into the Caspian on its eastern shore, the mouths of the two rivers being separated by an interval of eighty parasangs.⁶ It is clear therefore that he, in common with the other geographers of his day, had no knowledge of the Sea of Aral, as distinct from the Caspian. But we are certainly not entitled to assume in consequence, as some modern writers have done, that the former was not then in existence, and that the Iaxartes really pursued an unbroken course to the Caspian. It is much more probable to suppose that the Greek settlers on the banks of the Upper Iaxartes, when they were told by the native tribes that the river flowed into a great salt lake or sea, took for granted that this could be no other than the Caspian, with the northern end of which they

---

³ Strabo distinctly says that it was not an ascertained fact that any one *had actually sailed* round from India into the Hyrcanian Sea, but that Patrocles affirmed that it was possible to do so (xi 11, § 6. οὐκ ὁμολογοῦσι δὲ, ὅτι περιέπλευσάν τινες ἀπὸ τῆς Ἰνδικῆς ἐπὶ τὴν Ὑρκανίαν ὅτι δὲ δυνατόν, Πατροκλῆς εἴρηκε) This statement is strangely misinterpreted by Pliny, who says that Patrocles himself had actually performed the voyage, and in company with Seleucus and Antiochus! ("circumvectis etiam in Hyrcanium mare et Caspium Seleuco et Antiocho præfectoque classis eorum Patrocle," Plin. *H N.* vi 17, § 58).

⁴ Aristotle, writing just before the expedition of Alexander, appears to have held the same view as Herodotus, that the Caspian was a wholly separate basin, not communicating with any other (*Meteorologica*, i. 13, § 29; ii 1, § 10) But his information was evidently very imperfect. See Chap XI. p 401

⁵ Strab. xi 7. § 1.
⁶ Strab xi 11, § 5.

were wholly unacquainted; otherwise they could never have supposed it to communicate with the Northern Ocean. Nor could they have been ignorant of the great river Volga, which flows into it at its northern extremity; but of which no mention is found in any Greek author before the time of Ptolemy.[7]

[7] It has been already pointed out (Chapter VI. p 213) that the identification of the Oarus of Herodotus with the Volga rests upon very slender foundation, but, even if it be admitted, that author had no knowledge of its flowing into the Caspian: on the contrary he supposed it to fall into the Palus Mæotis, of the extent of which he had a very exaggerated idea.

CHAPTER XV.

THE PTOLEMIES IN EGYPT.

SECTION 1.—*The Ptolemies in Egypt.—The Red Sea.—The Nile.*

§ 1. MEANWHILE the geographical knowledge of the Greeks was receiving important accessions in another quarter. Among the different kingdoms constituted out of the empire of Alexander there was none which inherited a larger portion of Greek civilization than that of Egypt. Founded in the first instance by a statesman of great wisdom and enlarged intelligence, it continued under his son and grandson Ptolemy Philadelphus and Ptolemy Euergetes, to be not only the centre of literary cultivation and learning for the Hellenic world, but became at the same time the most important emporium of trade and centre of commercial enterprise. The position of Alexandria was admirably selected with a view to its being the commercial capital of the Eastern Mediterranean; its port was spacious and secure, and it was free from that tendency to fill up with sand, which is the inevitable disadvantage of all the ports along the coast of the Delta. But it was not to the Mediterranean alone that the Ptolemies directed their attention. Their new capital was situated in a convenient position for communicating with the Red Sea, and by that means with the spice and incense bearing tracts of Arabia and the opposite coasts of Africa, as well as for the more distant, but still more important, trade with India.

§ 2. It must be remembered that, throughout the reigns of these first Egyptian monarchs, the cities of Phœnicia, which had always continued to carry on a flourishing commerce, and had hitherto possessed the exclusive monopoly of the trade of the Red Sea,—the Egyptians themselves having never shown any aptitude for maritime commerce—were subject to the dominion of Egypt; and the Ptolemies could thus avail themselves both of the skill of the Phœnician navigators and of the relations which their merchants had already established in these quarters. It was only necessary to divert the line of traffic,—which had been previously carried across the isthmus of Suez to the Mediterranean, and thence direct to Tyre,—to the Egyptian capital. With this view Ptolemy Philadelphus began with founding at the extreme head of the Red Sea, nearly in the position of the modern town of Suez, a city to which he gave the name of Arsinoe; and he next proceeded to open a direct communication by canal between that city and Alexandria.¹ But notwithstanding the facilities thus obtained, it was found that the dangerous character of the navigation of the inner bight or gulf of the Red Sea—the Heroopolites Sinus or Gulf of Suez—was such as to outweigh the advantage of the proximity to Alexandria; and a port was in consequence established nearly five hundred miles lower down, on the Egyptian shore, which gradually became the chief emporium for all the trade of the Red Sea. To this city Philadelphus gave the name of his mother Berenice, as he had called the other after his wife Arsinoe. From thence the merchandise had to be carried over land, a distance of more than 200 miles, to Coptos on the Nile, from whence it descended that river to Alexandria.² Two other settlements were founded during the same reign on the coast between Arsinoe and Berenice, Philotera and Myos Hormus, the latter of which, at a later period,

---

¹ This canal was in fact only the completion or restoration of one, which had been begun long before by the Egyptian king Necho, and afterwards continued by Darius Hystaspes, but had apparently been neglected and fallen into disuse (Herodot 11. 158, and see the note of Sir G Wilkinson on the passage, in Rawlinson's *Herodotus*, vol. 11 p 243) It began from the Pelusiac branch of the Nile, above the city of Bubastis, and was carried from thence to the Bitter Lakes, where it turned to the south, and thence proceeded direct to Arsinoe (Herodot *l. c.*; Plin *H. N* vi 29, § 165) In this latter part of its course, therefore, it must have followed nearly the same line with the modern canal across the isthmus of Suez.

² Strabo, xvii p 815 The ruins of Berenice were first visited by Belzoni, and have been more fully described by Sir G Wilkinson and by Lieut Wellsted in the *Journal of Geogr Soc* vol vi p 96

obtained the preference over Berenice, and became the chief trading-place with India.³ Its greater proximity to Coptos was probably the chief cause that led to this change.⁴

§ 3. But these establishments were by no means adequate to fulfil the objects of Ptolemy, who aspired to nothing less than securing the complete command of the Red Sea. With this view he founded towns, or at least established permanent stations, from distance to distance, all along the Egyptian coast of that sea from Berenice to the straits of Bab-el-Mandeb. One of the most important of these—situated in latitude 18° 40', about 50 miles below the modern port of Suakim — was named Ptolemais Epitheras, and destined principally, as its name indicates, as a station from which to carry on expeditions into the interior, with a view to the capture of elephants. This had indeed become a great object with the Egyptian monarchs. Ever since the conquests of Alexander in India had brought the Greeks into familiarity with the use of elephants in war, they had been eagerly sought after by the rival monarchs, and when the present of five hundred of them to Seleucus by the Indian king Sandrocottus⁵ had for a time given to the Syrian kings a preponderance in this respect with which no others could compete, the Ptolemies turned their attention to the possibility of training African elephants in the same manner as the Indian ones, and thus deriving an inexhaustible supply from the regions within their own command.⁶ The position of Ptolemais Epitheras⁷ gave them direct and ready access to the tracts on the banks of the Atbara and its tributaries, the very

---

³ Strabo, ii. p. 118, xvii p. 815. Concerning the position of Myos Hormus, see Note A, p. 607

⁴ Thus we find the Roman General, Ælius Gallus (in the reign of Augustus), on his return from his expedition to Arabia, landing at Myos Hormus and marching with his army from thence to Coptos (Strabo, xvi 4, p. 782).

⁵ See Chapter XIV. p 555

⁶ See Note B. p 607.

⁷ The site of Ptolemais Epitheras may be fixed (approximately at least) in the neighbourhood of Cape Mugda or Mikdam, in latitude 18° 40' (see C. Muller's note to Agatharchides, p 172). It was correctly placed within a short distance of this position by D'Anville, but Dr. Vincent transferred it much farther south, being misled by the error of Ptolemy, who followed Eratosthenes in placing it in the same latitude with Meroe.

same districts which have recently formed the well-known hunting-grounds of Sir Samuel Baker; and which no doubt then, as now, abounded in elephants and all other kinds of "large game." [8]

§ 4. Beyond this again towards the south, the name of another city of Berenice (called for distinction's sake Berenice-ad-Sabas), within less than a degree of the straits of Bab-el-Mandeb, another Arsinoe immediately close to the actual straits, and a third Berenice just without them, adjoining the headland of Deiré (Ras Bir), sufficiently prove the zeal and energy with which the Ptolemies carried out their policy of occupying and securing the whole of these coasts. The barren and inhospitable nature of the adjoining regions would exclude the possibility of colonization in the higher sense of the word, and all these stations in the neighbourhood of the Straits appear to have been employed principally with a view to catching elephants in the interior. But immediately beyond Deiré began a long line of coast stretching out as far as Cape Guardafui—the Noti Keras or Southern Horn of Strabo—which was an object of considerable interest to the Greeks from its producing, not only myrrh and frankincense, like the opposite shores of Arabia, but cinnamon also in such quantities that the whole tract came to be known both to Greek and Latin geographers, as "the Land of Cinnamon." [9] No trace is found of any settlement in these parts being established by the Ptolemies, though successive Greek navigators set up *stelæ* as landmarks along the coast,—probably indicating in each case the farthest point attained,—which bore the names of those who had erected them. It was thus that the names of Pytholaus, Lichas, Pythangelus, Leon and Charimortus were perpetuated.[1]

---

[8] It was probably from the same quarter that they imported the various strange animals that figured in the festive processions at Alexandria, among which we find mention as early as the reign of Philadelphus of a camelopard and an Ethiopian rhinoceros, besides oryxes, bubali, &c (Athenæus, v 32, p 201).

[9] ἡ κινναμωμόφορος. This designation was clearly well established in the time of Eratosthenes, as we find it continually cited from his work by Strabo. Concerning the production of cinnamon in these countries, see Note C, p 608.

[1] Strabo, xvi. 4, § 15, p. 774

With this exception very little notice has been preserved to us of the enterprising commanders by whom the exploring expeditions of Ptolemy Philadelphus were conducted, or of the successive steps by which the chain of Egyptian outposts already described was established along a line of coast fifteen hundred miles in extent.[2] There is however no doubt that the stations near the Straits, which bore the names of Berenice and Arsinoe were erected either during the reign of the second Ptolemy, or at latest in that of his successor, Ptolemy Euergetes. This period, indeed, appears to have been that when the Egyptian commerce was at its height, as it was that in which the kingdom in general enjoyed the greatest prosperity, and it may be reasonably presumed that their trading voyages had already been extended to their utmost limits.

§ 5. Much the most interesting and important question in regard to the maritime commerce of the Ptolemies is that which relates to their trade with India. That the Egyptian Greeks under their rule carried on an extensive trade in Indian commodities, and that Alexandria became at an early period the chief emporium of this lucrative commerce is a point upon which all writers are agreed. But of the nature and character of this trade we have very imperfect information. It has been assumed by many modern writers that they traded direct with the Indian peninsula, although from their ignorance or imperfect knowledge of the monsoons, and probably also of the general configuration of the countries bordering on the Erythræan Sea, their ships were compelled to follow the circuitous course from the Straits of Bab-el-Mandeb along the coasts of Arabia, Carmania and Gedrosia to the mouths of the Indus.

But it will be found on examination that there is great

---

[2] The names of Satyrus and Eumedes have been, however, recorded among those who were thus employed by Ptolemy Philadelphus, the former as the founder of Philotera, the latter of Ptolemais Epitheras (Strabo, xvi 4,

§§ 5, 7) We learn also from Diodorus that one of the captains sent out by Ptolemy Euergetes, to explore the Troglodytic coast, was named Simmias. His account of those regions was cited by Agatharchides (Diodor iii. 18)

reason to doubt whether any direct trade with India ever existed under the Ptolemies. While we have abundant notices of their commerce with both shores of the Red Sea, and the countries on each side after passing out of the Straits of Bab-el-Mandeb, for a certain distance; we find all information suddenly come to an end at Cape Guardafui on the one side, and at the boundary of the land of the Sabæans on the other. Eratosthenes indeed was acquainted with the name of Hadramaut (Chatramotitæ), as one of the provinces or portions into which Arabia was divided; but the later writers, Agatharchides and Artemidorus, who describe the coasts in detail, give no names or stations along this part of Arabia or the adjacent district of Oman. The name of the headland of Syagrus (Cape Fartak) which assumes so important a part in the works of later geographers, is not found in Strabo, and was therefore probably unknown to Eratosthenes, as well as to his immediate successors. The same thing may be remarked of the island of Socotora, on the opposite shore of the narrow sea, which under the name of the island of Dioscorides became familiar to the Greeks in later times, when they carried on direct trade with India. On the other hand it is remarkable that they not only speak of the land of the Sabæans (the district now known as Yemen) as one of the richest and most flourishing countries in the world—a character which it certainly does not deserve on its own account, though a tract of considerable fertility as compared with the rest of Arabia—but they expressly state that this prosperity was owing in part to their extensive commerce, the Sabæans themselves having many ships, some of them of large size, while their ports were frequented by trading vessels from all the neighbouring nations, especially from the mouth of the Indus, where Alexander had established his naval emporium.[3] It thus becomes extremely probable (to say the least) that the Alexandrian merchants may have derived their Indian wares from the ports

---

[3] Agatharchides, § 102, ap. Diodor. iii. 47; Artemidorus ap. Strab. xvi. 4, § 19.

of Sabæa, whither they would be brought by native traders, whether Arabian or Indian; and they would thus avoid the necessity of the long and perilous voyage to the coasts of Hindustan.

§ 6. The account given by Agatharchides of the commercial character of the Sabæans is confirmed at a later period by the author of the Periplus of the Erythræan Sea, who speaks of the merchants of Muza (a port just within the straits) as carrying on an extensive commerce and sending *their own ships* to the east coast of Africa and to the well-known Indian port of Barygaza.[4] The same writer expressly tells us that the port of Arabia Felix, by which he unquestionably means Aden, was *in former days*, when navigators did not yet venture to proceed from Egypt direct to India, or from India to Egypt, the emporium at which they mutually exchanged their commodities.[5] Though he does not in terms apply this to the trade of Egypt *under the Ptolemies*, the comparison which he implies with the state of things in his own day (when the course of trade had totally altered) leaves little doubt that this was the period to which he alludes.[6] Had the Greek navigators under the Ptolemies been in the habit of trading directly with India, it is inconceivable but that they should have brought home some notices of the country, its sea-coasts and the ports they visited, but, as we shall hereafter see, neither Eratosthenes nor any other of the geographers consulted by Strabo—though writing for the most part at Alexandria—contain the slightest additional information from this source, their knowledge of the continent of India being derived exclusively from the writings of Megasthenes and the other contemporaries of Alexander. Even the name of Barygaza, so important an emporium of Indian com-

---

[4] *Peripl. Maris Erythr* § 21.
[5] Ibid. § 26. He expressly compares it in this respect with Alexandria, as a place that exported not only its own commodities, but those which had been brought thither from a distance
[6] It is, however, very remarkable, upon this supposition, that no notice is found in any of these earlier writers (Agatharchides, Artemidorus, or Eratosthenes) of the port and promontory of Aden, which is not only one of the most marked features on the line of coast, but must always have been the chief natural emporium for all this part of Arabia.

merce, and situated at so short a distance from the mouths of the Indus, is not mentioned by Strabo and was apparently unknown to the Alexandrian geographers.[7]

We can hardly therefore be mistaken in concluding that, at all events under the reigns of the earlier Ptolemies, the voyages of the Alexandrian traders did not extend farther than Cape Guardafui on the one side, and the neighbourhood of Aden on the other; and that the lucrative trade with India, of which they possessed to a great extent the monopoly, was of a kind similar to that of the Venetians in later times, who supplied the rest of Europe with Indian commodities, which they themselves purchased at Alexandria.

§ 7. We have much less information concerning the progress made by the Ptolemies in the exploration of the interior of Africa; but we know that on this side also they made great additions to the geographical knowledge previously possessed of the countries vaguely known by the designation of Ethiopia. It was indeed impossible that a civilized and powerful state should be established in Egypt, without attempting to push exploring expeditions up the valley of the Nile, both in the hope of solving the long controverted question of the origin of that river, and with the more practical object of making acquaintance with the nations and countries on its banks, which were known to produce ivory, ebony, and other articles eagerly sought for by the Greeks, and which were supposed, though with little foundation, to be equally abundant in gold. The Ethiopians of the neighbourhood of Meroe had at this period assumed something of the character of a civilized community, and under the government of a native ruler, called

---

[7] Strabo in describing the extensive trade carried on in his day from Myos Hormus with India direct, expressly contrasts it with the state of things when *very few* ventured to sail thither for commercial objects (πρότερον ἐπὶ τῶν Πτολεμαικῶν βασιλέων ὀλίγων παντάπασι θαρρούντων πλεῖν καὶ τὸν Ἰνδικὸν ἐμπορεύεσθαι φόρτον, ii. 5, § 12, p 118). The voyage of Eudoxus of Cyzicus (about 120 B C), who certainly *did* proceed to India, is distinctly spoken of as something altogether new and exceptional (Strabo, ii 3, § 4, p. 98). See Chapter XVIII sect. 5.

by the Greeks Ergamenes, appear to have maintained friendly relations with Ptolemy Philadelphus, which would materially assist in the prosecution of researches farther south.[8] At a somewhat later period Meroe itself appears to have become a dependency of, if not actually subject to the Egyptian monarchy. This circumstance readily accounts for the increased knowledge obtained by the Greeks at this period of the course of the Nile above the second cataract and of the several confluents or tributaries of that great stream.

Herodotus, as we have seen, knew nothing of any rivers flowing into the Nile, and justly regarded it as one of the great peculiarities of that river, that during so very long a course it had no tributaries. Moreover, while he was familiar with the name of Meroe, as the capital city of the Ethiopians, he has no mention of the "island," as the surrounding territory was called by later geographers, in consequence of its being nearly encircled by the Nile and one of its tributaries. Eratosthenes, on the contrary, correctly described the "island" of Meroe as formed by the junction of the Nile with the Astaboras,—the stream which is now called, in the upper part of its course, the Tacazze, but near its junction with the Nile still preserves the name of Atbara. Above this was another similar island, formed by two rivers called the Astapus and Astasobas, concerning which there seems to have been some confusion, some writers describing them as two separate affluents of the Nile, others more correctly asserting that the Astapus was in reality the main stream of the Nile itself.[9] It was said to flow from some lakes farther to the south; but no one pretended to have any accurate knowledge of its source. On the other hand, the correct view of the cause of its periodical inundations, that they were produced by the summer rains in these southern regions, appears to have been generally adopted, though

---

[8] See the article ERGAMENES in Dr. Smith's *Dict of Ancient Biography* vol ii

[9] Eratosthen. ap. Strab xvii. 1, p. 786

various other fanciful theories were from time to time promulgated by philosophers.[1]

§ 8. There is therefore no doubt, notwithstanding the confusion in regard to the names, that the Greeks were at this time well acquainted with the course of the Nile as far as Khartoum, at the junction of the two streams now known as the Blue and White Nile—the Bahr el Azrek and Bahr el Abiad; and for a certain distance up those rivers. It was above their junction, in the so-called island formed by the two, that dwelt a people termed by Eratosthenes and later writers the Sembritæ, who, according to the current tradition, were the descendants of a body of Egyptian exiles who had quitted their country in the reign of Psammetichus.[2] We here recognize at once the Automoli of Herodotus, though the reports which had reached that historian had greatly exaggerated the remoteness of their situation.[3] They evidently occupied in reality the region now known as Sennaar.[4]

It was the natural consequence of this intercourse with Meroe that the Greeks of Alexandria should acquire accurate information concerning the course of the Nile between that city and Syene, and from this period accordingly we find them well acquainted with the great bend formed by the river in this part of its course, as well as with the second, or as it was termed, "the great" cataract, concerning which such absurd fables were propagated in later times.[5] But the difficulties presented by this, as well as by the other obstacles to the navigation of the river in this part of its course, would naturally

---

[1] Strabo, xvii 1, p 789
[2] Eratosthen ap. Strab xvii. 1, p 786.
[3] Herodot ii 30 See Chapter VIII
[4] The name of Sennaar is given at the present day to the district between the Bahr el Azrek or Blue Nile and the Bahr el Abiad or White Nile, constituting a *quasi* island precisely analogous to the so-called "island" of Meroe The town of the name is situated on the Blue Nile, about 150 miles above Khartoum
[5] No distinct mention of the Second Cataract is found in Herodotus, though he was aware that the navigation of the Nile in this part presented great difficulties (see Chapter VIII) The first mention of "the Great Cataract" is found in Eratosthenes, but he does not appear to have countenanced the absurd exaggerations concerning it, which are found in Pliny and later writers

prevent any considerable traffic from being carried up or down the Nile; and there is reason to infer that the intercourse with Meroe was carried on principally by caravans across the desert, from the ports on the Red Sea. The direct distance by this line of communication is stated at only ten or twelve days' journey.[6] No allusion is found in any ancient writer to the route which has been generally followed by modern travellers, which quits the Nile at Korosko and strikes across the desert to Abu Hamed, thus cutting off the whole of the great bend of the river, as well as avoiding the cataracts.

§ 9. We are told by Diodorus that Ptolemy Philadelphus himself carried his arms into Ethiopia, and thus led to a more extensive knowledge of the regions of the interior:[7] but the expressions of the historian are vague, and it is very doubtful whether that monarch himself conducted any expedition of importance. Meroe also appears to have continued virtually independent, and we have no proof of any attempts being made to establish the authority of the Egyptian monarchs farther up in the interior. The supposition that Ptolemy Euergetes had made extensive conquests in Ethiopia, at the head of an army which he conducted in person, rests solely on a misconception of the celebrated monument of Adulis, which records the exploits of an Ethiopian king of much later date. That monument was undoubtedly erected in the first instance during the reign of Ptolemy Euergetes, but there is no reason to suppose that it was set up by that monarch in person or that he had himself visited this remote corner of his dominions.[8]

A considerable amount of information seems to have been collected by the explorers and traders of the Egyptian monarchs concerning the various wild tribes in the interior, with

---

[6] Eratosthenes ap. Strab xvii 1, p. 786. In another passage, where he is following Artemidorus, Strabo states the distance from Meroe to the Arabian Gulf at fifteen days' journey for an active traveller (εὐζώνῳ ὁδὸς xvi. 4, p 771)

At the present day, since the foundation of Khartoum, and the establishment of regular communications with the upper regions of the Nile, most travellers proceed by sea to Suakim, and thence across the desert to Khartoum.

[7] Diodor 1 37
[8] Note D, p. 609

whom they came in contact in their expeditions in pursuit of elephants and other game: but no notice is found of the rugged and lofty table-land of Abyssinia, which forms so important a feature in the physical geography of these regions: nor even of the great mountain barrier that bounds it on the east, and presents so conspicuous an object, when viewed from the Red Sea.

Nor do they appear to have obtained any knowledge of the countries lying to the west of the Upper Nile—now known as Kordofan and Dar Four; while below these the great Nubian desert opposed an impenetrable barrier to their explorations in this direction. The Egyptian kings had indeed early extended their dominion over the whole of the Cyrenaica, as far as the confines of the Carthaginians, and had founded a city of the name of Berenice on the very border of the Great Syrtis; but we hear nothing of their having instituted any exploring expeditions into the interior of Libya, or established any commercial relations with the native tribes of Central Africa. It is remarkable that the Greek monarchs of Egypt, like the native Egyptian kings, do not appear to have ever thought of introducing the use of camels into Africa: without which useful auxiliary it was almost impossible to carry on any extensive journeys or explorations into the interior of the continent.

§ 10. To the period of the earlier Ptolemies belongs a writer, who is frequently cited by extant geographical authors, and whose work appears to have exercised considerable influence upon the progress of geography in the times immediately succeeding him. TIMOSTHENES, a native of Rhodes, who held the important position of admiral of the Egyptian fleet under Ptolemy Philadelphus,[9] drew up a treatise "concerning Ports,"

---

[9] Strabo (ix 3, p. 421) terms him ὁ ναύαρχος τοῦ δευτέρου Πτολεμαίου, but Marcian of Heraclea calls him ἀρχικυβερνήτης, a term which would imply more scientific acquaintance with practical navigation (*Epit. Artemidor.* § 2). His work, which was in ten books (Strabo, *l. c*), would appear to have been still extant in the days of Marcian. It is also referred to by Agathemerus (*Geograph* 1. § 7), but it is always difficult to judge whether these cita-

which is repeatedly cited by Strabo, and appears to have been one of the chief authorities followed by Eratosthenes. It was evidently not confined to the mere description of the cities or harbours on the Mediterranean, but gave the distances from one to the other, with indications of their relative position and bearings.[1] Such a work was apparently designed as a practical guide to the navigator, but must have contributed also materially to the more definite geographical knowledge of the seas and coasts which it comprised: and it is not surprising to find that it became one of the principal authorities upon this particular branch of the subject. Eratosthenes indeed, whose work so long retained its position as the standard treatise on geography, is said to have made such extensive use of the work of Timosthenes, as to amount to direct plagiarism.[2] But from the total loss of his writings we are unable to judge of the real extent of the obligations of the great geographer of Cyrene to his predecessor. It appears certain however (so far as we can judge from the extant citations) that the treatise of Timosthenes was confined to the "Inner Sea" or the Mediterranean and its dependencies: it could therefore hardly have added much to the geographical knowledge of the Greeks in point of extent, however much it may have contributed to accuracy of details. Strabo indeed speaks of Timosthenes, as well as his successor Eratosthenes, as showing great ignorance of Gaul, Spain, and the western regions of Europe in general: a criticism that is probably well-founded, though Strabo himself (as we shall hereafter see) was far from possessing as correct ideas as he himself imagined, concerning the western half of the Mediterranean.[3]

---

tions by late authors are really taken from the original works, or copied at second hand.

[1] Thus he stated that Metagonium on the coast of Africa was *opposite to* Massilia, an error for which he is justly censured by Strabo (xvii. 3, p 827).

[2] Marcian of Heraclea goes so far as to assert that Eratosthenes transcribed the whole treatise into his own work, making only a few additions (*Epit.*

Artem. § 3) But this statement seems wholly at variance with the much more trustworthy authority of Strabo, that while Eratosthenes praised the work of his predecessor above all others, he differed from him upon many points (ὃν ἐπαινεῖ μὲν ἐκεῖνος μάλιστα τῶν ἄλλων, διαφωνῶν δ'ἐλέγχεται πρὸς αὐτὸν πλεῖστα Strabo, ii 1, § 40, p 92)

[3] Marcian also, in whose days of course all parts of the Mediterranean

In one respect, Timosthenes (we are told) made a step in advance of all his predecessors—that he was the first to point out the arrangement of different countries according to the winds that blew from the different quarters, or as we should say, the different points of the compass, and in so doing introduced a greater number of these divisions than had been before in use.[4] Thus he placed the Bactrians in the extreme east (Apeliotes), the Indians in the south-east (Eurus), the Ethiopians and the Red Sea in the south-south-east (Phœnix), the Ethiopians above Egypt in the south (Notus), the Garamantes above the Syrtis in the south-south-west (Leuconotus), the western Ethiopians above the Mauri in the south-west (Libs); the Columns of Hercules, and the confines of Africa and Europe in the west (Zephyrus), Iberia (Spain) in the north-west (Argestes), the Kelts in the north-north-west (Thrascias), the Scythians above Thrace in the north (Aparctias), the Pontus, Mæotis and Sarmatians towards the north-north-east (Boreas), and the Caspian Sea and the Sacæ towards the north-east (Cæcias).[5]

SECTION 2.—*Progress of Discovery in Western Europe.—Pytheas.—Timæus.*

§ 1. While the conquests of Alexander the Great and the kingdoms established by his successors were extending the geographical knowledge of the Greeks towards the east, other causes were producing the same effect in regard to the west and north-west of Europe. We have seen how imperfect was the information possessed by the Greek geographers as late as the time of Ephorus and the coast-describer Scylax, concerning everything beyond the Pillars of Hercules; and although we

---

were well known, censures Timosthenes for his ignorance of the counties around the Tyrrhenian Sea, and from thence to the Straits, as well as of the southern coast from Carthage to the Straits, and expresses his surprise that Eratosthenes should have followed him so implicitly (*Epit Artem* § 3)
[4] Note E, p 610.
[5] Agathemerus, c. 2, § 6.

know that the name of the Cassiterides—as islands in the western sea, from whence the Phœnicians brought large supplies of tin—was well known before the time of Herodotus, that historian had been unable to obtain any definite information concerning them,[6] and the Greek writers who followed him appear to have been equally ignorant in this respect.

But about the period at which we are now arrived—the generation following the death of Alexander—we find altogether new names and new geographical notions concerning the western regions of Europe, which, although still in a very vague and fluctuating form, had acquired a hold upon the popular belief, and undoubtedly indicate an increased acquaintance with this portion of the world. For these notions, and for the first introduction into the domain of geographical science of some leading facts, though confused and distorted by many errors and fables, the Greeks were indebted to a writer named PYTHEAS, a native of Massilia.

Though the discoveries, or alleged discoveries, of Pytheas, were a subject of much controversy among ancient writers, and were fully discussed by some authors still extant, no definite statement has been preserved to us as to the period at which he lived, or the date of the publication of his work. Even as to its form and character we are left almost wholly in the dark,[7] and with this additional disadvantage, that what little informa-

---

[6] Herodot. iii 115 See Chapter VI. p 164.

[7] The title of his work is uncertain. The ancient authors cite it under various names. Marcian of Heraclea classes him amongst the writers who had left Περίπλοι, but it is clear that he uses the word in a general sense, as he includes Eratosthenes in the same category. The Scholiast on Apollonius Rhodius (iv. 761) cites it as Γῆς περίοδος, but it is very doubtful whether he had himself seen the work. An astronomical writer of the first century B.C refers to his authority, ἐν τοῖς περὶ τοῦ Ὠκεανοῦ; but this is probably only a general expression So far as we can gather, it seems probable that Pytheas wrote a geographical work, in the course of which he gave an account of his own voyages and explorations, but described other countries also, from the information that he had collected

There is no reason to suppose that he left more than one treatise of the kind. The original work may probably have been lost at an early period. Strabo evidently knew it only through Eratosthenes and Polybius; and there can be little doubt that the citations of Pliny, and later Greek writers, are in like manner all made at second hand

tion we possess concerning it is derived principally from the controversial notices of hostile critics, who were disposed to decry the whole production as a tissue of fables. With regard to his date, it is certain that he wrote not only before Eratosthenes, who relied much upon his authority, but before Dicæarchus, who was a pupil of Aristotle, and died about B.C. 285.[8] He may therefore probably be regarded as about contemporary with Alexander the Great.

§ 2. According to Polybius, Pytheas had given an account of a voyage undertaken by himself, in which he had not only visited the island of Britain, but had travelled over a considerable part of it, and stated it to be more than 40,000 stadia (4000 G. miles) in circumference.[9] Beyond Britain to the north lay another island, to which he gave the name of Thule, and he stated that the sea in these parts assumed a thick and sluggish character, like neither land nor sea, but resembling in consistence the molluscous animal, or jelly-fish, called the *pulmo marinus*, or sea-lung. This substance he had himself seen, but the other phenomena he described only from hearsay. Returning from this expedition to Britain, he visited the whole of the coasts of Europe bordering on the ocean, from Gadeira (Gades) as far as the Tanais.[1] The whole of this account is rejected by Polybius in a summary manner, and he elsewhere asserts broadly that the whole of the north of Europe, from Narbo in Gaul to the Tanais was still wholly unknown, and that everything which was related concerning it was mere fiction.[2] Eratosthenes was more cautious, and while he appears to have doubted some of the statements of Pytheas, he gave credence to those which related to Britain as well as to the coast of Iberia (Spain) and Gadeira.[3] He also received as a

---

[8] According to Strabo, Polybius censured Eratosthenes for believing Pytheas, when Dicæarchus had not done so (Strab. ii p. 104) It appears also from Pliny (xxxvii 2, § 36) that Timæus, who wrote about 264 B C., had made use of the work of Pytheas

[9] Note F, p 612.

[1] Polyb ap. Strab ii. p 104

[2] Polyb iii. 38 If these expressions are to be taken literally, he must have treated the existence of *Britain* as equally fabulous with that of Thule But this is scarcely probable

[3] Eratosth ap Strab *l. c.*

fact the existence of Thule, as the most northern land known, a view which, though rejected both by Polybius and Strabo, came to be part of the generally received system of ancient geographers.

§ 3. In attempting to determine the degree of credit that can be attached to Pytheas, we labour under the very great disadvantage that the original work is lost to us, while the few notices that have been preserved relate almost exclusively to the most disputed points, and to those statements that were controverted by later authors. As we learn from Polybius that Eratosthenes relied mainly upon Pytheas for the account of Iberia, we must presume that the latter had given some account of his voyage along the Atlantic coast of Spain, and doubtless that of Gaul likewise. Had we possessed this account we should have been far better able to judge of the general trustworthiness of his information, and could hardly have been left in doubt as to whether he had really made the voyage or not. It is true that Strabo speaks in disparaging terms of the ignorance of Eratosthenes concerning Iberia and the west of Europe in general:[4] but his censures are not always well-founded; and it is remarkable that the only statement which has been preserved to us from the work of Pytheas concerning the western coasts of Gaul, is one in which he shows himself better informed than Strabo. He represented the land of the Ostimii—the Osismii of later authors[5]—who inhabited a part of Bretagne, as forming a great promontory, extending far out to sea.[6] Strabo, on the contrary, attached no importance to the projection of this part of the coast, and thus gave an entirely wrong configuration to the Gaulish coast adjoining the ocean, by neglecting one of its most essential features.

---

[4] Strabo, ıı. 1, p 93; 4, p 104

[5] The name is indeed found in our existing text of Strabo only in a corrupt form, the MSS. giving in one passage (ı p. 63) 'Ὠστιδέους or 'Ὠστιαίους, in another (p 64) 'Ὠστιδαμνίων, and in a third Τιμίους (ıv. p. 195). But a comparison of the three, which all unquestionably refer to the same people, leaves little doubt that the true reading is, as restored by Kramer, 'Ὠστιμίους (see Kramer's note to vol. i p 97 of his edition)

[6] Id. ı. 4, p. 64, ıv. 4, p. 195

Eratosthenes followed Pytheas, and his map of this part of Europe was in consequence far superior to that of Strabo.

Pytheas was indeed in error in supposing this headland to be the most westerly point of Europe, extending farther west than Cape Finisterre in Spain, but errors of longitude of this kind are of all others the most excusable. He was, moreover, correctly informed that there were several islands in the open sea, west of this promontory; one of which was named Uxisama, and lay three days' voyage from the mainland.[7] Though this distance is greatly overstated, as in many similar instances, there seems no doubt that we have here a distinct indication of the Isles of Ushant.

Another passage, which is unfortunately not very intelligible in its present form, proves at least that Pytheas spoke of the voyage along the north coast of Spain, and the course of navigation that it was desirable to pursue.[8]

§ 4. With regard to Britain again we are left in uncertainty to what extent Pytheas professed to have carried his personal explorations;[9] and his statement of its dimensions was undoubtedly exaggerated, though by no means to the extent supposed by some ancient writers. He was also in error (if he is correctly reported by Strabo) in stating that the promontory

---

[7] Id. i. 4, p. 64.

[8] It appears that Eratosthenes stated, on the authority of Pytheas, that the voyage along the northern shores of Spain was easier, in sailing towards Gaul, than by standing out towards the open Ocean (τὰ προσαρκτικὰ μέρη τῆς Ἰβηρίας εὐπαροδώτερα εἶναι πρὸς τὴν Κελτικὴν ἢ κατὰ τὸν Ὠκέανον πλέουσι), a fact which Artemidorus denied (Strab. iii 2, § 11). It is not easy to say what the exact sense of these words is, but it is probable that they are correctly translated by Groskurd to mean that the voyage from west to east, such as a navigator would make, starting from Gades and rounding Cape Finisterre, was more favourable than in the contrary direction At all events they certainly seem to indicate a practical acquaintance with the navigation along the northern coast of Spain.

[9] The expression of Polybius, as it appears in our existing text of Strabo (ii. p. 104), is ambiguous, but the emendation of ἐμβαδὸν introduced by the recent editors has the effect of rendering Pytheas chargeable with a monstrous exaggeration by saying that he had travelled *by land* through the whole of Britain, a statement which cannot fairly be forced upon him without better authority. Groskurd adheres to the old text, and translates ἐμβατὸν as equivalent to ὅσον ἐμβατὸι ἦν; which certainly gives the reasonable meaning of the passage. Schweighauser, in his edition of Polybius (xxxiv. 5), receives these words into the text, on the suggestion of Tyrwhitt.

of Cantium in Britain was several days' voyage from the coast of Gaul.[1] In respect to the island of Thule—a name which he was undoubtedly the first to introduce into ancient geography, where it ever after maintained its place—his account was evidently extremely vague. We learn only that he stated it to be situated six days' voyage to the north of Britain:[2] but according to Strabo he said nothing of whether it was habitable or not. It was *beyond* Thule that the navigation became impassable on account of the sea assuming a thick and gelatinous consistency. But there is no reason to assume, as has been done by some modern writers, that Pytheas himself professed to have visited Thule: indeed the expressions of our extant authorities would rather lead to an opposite conclusion.[3] But this is one of the points on which it is impossible to speak with confidence in the absence of the original work.

On the whole it is certain that the idea formed by Pytheas (and derived from him by Eratosthenes) of Britain as an island of vast extent, stretching far away to the north, but having another island called Thule still farther to the north,[4] was much more correct than that of Strabo, who conceived Britain as stretching lengthwise opposite to the coast of Gaul, as far as the mouth of the Rhine, with Ierne (Ireland) lying far away to the north of it. It must be observed, moreover,

---

[1] Strabo, i. 4, § 3, p 63 At the same time he was the first writer who mentioned the name, so familiar to all later geographers

[2] Id 4, § 2 p. 63, Plin. *H. N.* ii. 75, § 187

[3] The only ancient writer, who distinctly speaks of Pytheas as having *visited* Thule is the astronomer Cleomedes, in citing his statement concerning the astronomical phenomena witnessed there; and he introduces it with a vague "ἐν ᾗ γεγονέναι φασὶ Πυθέαν," and had evidently not consulted the original work (Cleomedes, i. 47, ed Bake)

[4] It appears to me impossible to identify the Thule of Pytheas with any approach to certainty; but he had probably heard vaguely of the existence of some considerable island, or group of islands, to the north of Britain, whether the Orkneys or the Shetlands it is impossible to say No reliance can be placed upon the alleged distance of six days' voyage from the mainland (see the case of Uxisama, just cited); and he seems to have regarded it as belonging to the group of the British Islands (Θούλην τὴν βορειοτάτην τῶν Βρετανvικῶν, Strab. ii. p. 114), an expression which would at once exclude the possibility of his referring to Iceland, even if the inherent improbability of the case were not decisive against this supposition.

that however vague or inaccurate may have been his description of Britain, he was, so far as we know, the first Greek writer who gave any account of the British Islands at all.[5] If its existence was previously known—and it does not appear that Pytheas claimed to be its *discoverer*—it could only have been through vague reports obtained by the Greeks of Massilia from the Gaulish traders, who possibly, even at this period, extended their communications from one sea to another.[6] But it seems certain that Pytheas was the first who imparted to his countrymen any definite information on the subject.

§ 5. Still more difficult is it to arrive at any conclusion with regard to the remaining portion of the alleged voyage of Pytheas.[7] The statement that he proceeded along the northern coasts of Europe *as far as the Tanais* is of course impossible in fact, though it would not appear so to the imperfect geographical ideas of the Greeks, and Pytheas might as readily have taken some important river flowing into the North Sea or the Baltic for the Tanais, as the companions of Alexander mistook the Iaxartes for the same river. Hence some modern writers have supposed that he actually proceeded as far as the Vistula: others, more reasonably, that he stopped short at the mouth of the Elbe.[8] On the other hand the expression used

---

[5] The Pseudo-Aristotelian treatise de Mundo (Περὶ Κόσμου), in which mention is found of "the two British Islands" (αἱ Βρεταννικαὶ νῆσοι), with the addition of their names, Albion and Ierne, is undoubtedly a spurious production, and belongs to a much later period than that of Aristotle, probably even subsequent to the Christian era. Yet it is cited both by Forbiger and by Dr Latham (in Dr. Smith's *Dict. of Geography*, art. BRITANNICÆ INSULÆ), as if Aristotle himself were acquainted with the names of Albion and Ierne.

[6] The voyage of the Carthaginian Himilco was undoubtedly made at a much earlier period, but no Greek author shows any acquaintance with his authority.

[7] The expressions of Polybius, as quoted by Strabo (II. p. 104), have been understood by some modern writers, as if Pytheas had made *two* distinct voyages, in the one of which he explored Britain, in the other he traced the northern coast of Europe from Gades to the Tanais. But this seems most improbable. He must have already visited the western and northern coasts of Spain and Gaul, in order to arrive at Britain; and if, after making an excursion to explore the coasts of Britain, he returned from thence to Gaul, and carried on his voyage towards the east, this would sufficiently coincide with the statement of Polybius.

[8] This is the view taken by Ukert (tom. 1. pt. 11 p. 307).

by Polybius that he followed the coast "as far as the Tanaïs" may be employed only in the same sense, as he himself immediately afterwards says that the north of Europe extending "from the Tanais to Narbo" was wholly unknown:[9] where he clearly refers to the northern coast opposite to each.

Here therefore we are entirely at fault. But we may probably connect with this part of his voyage the statement preserved to us by Pliny of the account he gave of the production of amber: "According to Pytheas (says that writer) the Guttones, a German nation, dwelt on an estuary of the Ocean, of the name of Mentonomus, extending for the distance of 6000 stadia. From this at the distance of a day's voyage was an island called Abalus, on which in the spring amber was cast up by the waves, and was a kind of scum produced by the coagulation of the sea (concreti maris purgamentum). The inhabitants used it instead of wood for their fires, and sold it to their neighbours the Teutoni. Timæus also (he adds) gave credence to this account, but called the island Basilia."[1]

This passage has been repeatedly cited as if it proved that Pytheas had himself visited the land where the amber was found: but it is certain not only that it asserts nothing of the kind, but that it points in reality to an opposite conclusion. Pytheas *may* have visited the land of the Guttones (though even this is not stated by Pliny), but he clearly seems to speak of the island of Abalus from hearsay only. Had he visited any of the regions along the coast of the Baltic, where amber was really found, he would hardly have been told that it came from a distant island. On the other hand, if he explored the coasts of Germany, eastward from Britain, he would doubtless have made diligent inquiry for the land where amber was produced, and might have been readily misled by some such information as that transmitted to us in his name.

It is certain also that in the passage of Pliny we are far

---

[9] Polyb. *l. c.*   [1] Plin *H. N.* xxxvii. 2, 11, § 35.

from possessing a correct report of the statement of Pytheas: we have seen in repeated instances how careless that author is in the citation of his authorities: and in the present case the words "Guttonibus *Germaniæ* genti" render it almost certain that Pliny is not quoting the expressions of Pytheas himself, the name of Germany in this general sense being certainly of later introduction, and first brought into use by the Romans.[2]

Supposing however, as is certainly probable, that the work of Pytheas did contain some such statement concerning the origin of amber as that cited by Pliny, we are left wholly in uncertainty as to the locality which he meant to designate. The assumption of many modern writers that amber is found only on the shores of the Baltic is certainly an error. We shall see that Roman writers at a later period speak distinctly of its being met with on the shores of the North Sea and in the adjacent islands: and at the present day it is found in sufficient quantities to be of considerable commercial importance on the west coast of Schleswig, and occasionally, though more sparingly, on that of Holstein also.[3]

§ 6. It must be added that Pytheas was the first—so far as we know—to report various particulars concerning the inhabitants of these northern regions, which were undoubtedly correct; such as the gradual disappearance of various kinds of grain, as one advanced towards the north, the use of fermented liquors made from corn and honey, and the habit of threshing out their corn in large barns—instead of the open threshing-

---

[2] The name of the Germani, as a tribe or nation, was indeed known to the Greeks not long after this; as we find it in the treatise *De Mirabilibus*, erroneously ascribed to Aristotle (§ 168), but belonging in reality to the succeeding century. Posidonius also appears to have been familiar with it (ap Athenæum, iv. 39, p. 153). But the extension of the name as a geographical term, as here used by Pliny, was, as we are expressly told by Tacitus, of recent introduction in his time (Tacit. *Germ.* c. 2).

[3] For this important fact, though already indicated by Ukert, we are indebted principally to the work of Dr. Redslob (*Thule: die Phonicischen Handelswegen nach dem Norden*, Leipzig, 1855, pp 26, 27). Sir G Lewis and most other modern writers on the subject have assumed that amber was found *only* on the shores of the Baltic. The existence of two amber regions will be found to explain many difficulties.

floors of the Greeks and Italians—on account of the want of sun and the frequency of rain.[4]

On the whole then, notwithstanding the extremely vague and defective character of our information, it appears that there is no reason to doubt the fact that Pytheas really made an exploring voyage along the north-western coasts of Europe —setting out from Gades, and proceeding perhaps as far as the mouth of the Elbe—from which he brought back much valuable information, though in part undoubtedly founded on mere hearsay, and partaking of the vague, and even semi-fabulous character, which such reports are liable to assume. The extravagant pretensions that have been put forward by some modern writers on his behalf, contending that he carried his personal explorations as far as the Vistula on the one hand, and the Shetland Islands, or even Iceland, on the other, have tended to increase the air of fable thrown around his voyage, and have led some critics in very recent times to follow the example of Polybius and Strabo, and reject the whole story as a fiction.[5]

§ 7. But whatever may be the conclusion at which we arrive with regard to the veracity of Pytheas, regarded as an exploring voyager and discoverer—a question upon which it is difficult to form an opinion, in the absence of the original narrative—there can be no doubt, as has been already pointed out, that he was the first to embody in his work a considerable amount of new information concerning the north-west of Europe. That portion of the map of Europe, which in the time of Herodotus had been a mere blank, had been now partially filled up, and had assumed much the same general aspect as it was destined to retain till after the time of Strabo.

In one respect the merit of Pytheas is generally acknowledged by ancient writers, even by those who otherwise reject

---

[1] Strabo, iv. 5, § 5   [5] Note G, p. 612

his testimony. He was a good astronomer, according to the ideas of his day, and bestowed much care upon the determination of the latitude, and observation of celestial phenomena, at the places he visited. Thus in the first place he determined the latitude of Massilia, his native city, with great care, and his observation, which was adopted by Hipparchus, was in reality a very close approximation to the truth; though rejected without reason by Strabo.[6] It appears also that he recorded several other observations of a similar kind, of which the one that is most frequently cited, and that gave rise to the most controversy, was that concerning Thule. In this instance there can be no doubt that he was reporting merely what he had heard, or perhaps only what he inferred from the gradual change that he had observed as he himself proceeded northwards.

Unfortunately in this instance the reports at second-hand in our existing authorities differ so widely that it is impossible for us now to determine with certainty what Pytheas really stated, but it appears probable that he conceived Thule as lying under what we now call the Arctic Circle, or parallel of $66\frac{1}{2}°$ N. latitude, where the day at the summer solstice is twenty-four hours in length, and that he reported this as a fact.[7] The phenomena of the long days and short nights, with continuous daylight, in the latitude of the Orkneys or Shetlands, would really be remarkable enough to give rise to much exaggeration, and it is certainly not unlikely that he had collected some hearsay statements of the kind: but it is most improbable that Pytheas had himself penetrated to these remote regions. Much less is it necessary to suppose that he

---

[6] We shall hereafter see that the ancient geographers in general fell into a grave error, which contributed greatly to distort their maps of Europe, by adopting the statement of Hipparchus that Byzantium and Massilia lay in the same parallel of latitude But it is remarkable that here it was the position of Byzantium that was erroneously given by Hipparchus, while that of Massilia, which he fixed on the authority of Pytheas (who had himself made observation with the gnomon), was almost exactly correct (Strab ii 5, p 115)

[7] Note H, p. 613.

had visited Iceland, where he could himself have really witnessed the phenomenon. But he was undoubtedly correct in asserting that Thule, which he placed six days' voyage north of Britain, lay far to the northward of the lands on the Borysthenes, in the interior of Scythia, which were regarded by many of the Greeks as the most northern region of Europe. In this conclusion he was followed both by Eratosthenes and Hipparchus, though Strabo rejected it with undeserved contempt. On another point also Pytheas was the first to communicate to the Greeks more definite and correct notions. This was with regard to the tides of the Ocean, concerning which he reported that they increased as the moon became full, and diminished as she waned.[8] Though of course this statement is not accurate, it not only shows a clear perception of the main fact that the tides were produced and regulated by the moon, but an acquaintance with their periodical fluctuations, in accordance with the phases of that luminary.[9]

§ 8. It is remarkable that no mention is found in connection with Pytheas and his voyage of the Cassiterides or Tin Islands, from which the Phœnicians continued to draw their principal supplies of that valuable metal—the discovery or exploration of which would seem to have naturally formed one of the principal objects of his voyage. This is the more remarkable as we find in the time of Posidonius that Massilia had opened a regular trade with these islands, and their tin was brought overland to that city from the western ports of Gaul.[1] There can be little doubt that at this period Massilia, which had long been a flourishing commercial city, was extending its trade in all directions through Gaul, and to the shores of the Ocean, both towards the west and the north. The prospect of competing with the Phœnicians in the lucrative trade in tin would naturally offer special attractions; as did that for

---

[8] Plutarch, *de Placit Philosoph* iii. 17

[9] Plutarch, however, appears to have misunderstood what he was reporting, and to have confounded these fluctuations with the *daily* variations of the tides

[1] Posidon. ap. Strab. iii. 2, p 147.

amber with the North Sea. In both cases it is probable that the Greeks of Massilia had very imperfect ideas of the position of the lands from which these valuable commodities were brought: but they had doubtless obtained vague information concerning them from the native traders, and these would stimulate them to further inquiries, and explorations on their own account. This would account for the extension of their geographical knowledge in this direction, and may have been the cause that induced Pytheas to undertake a voyage from Gades to Britain and the shores of the North Sea.

§ 9. Another writer, who appears to have contributed in a considerable degree to the extension of the geographical knowledge of the Greeks in regard to the west of Europe, was TIMÆUS, a native of Tauromenium in Sicily,[2] who wrote an elaborate historical work, in which he treated very fully of the foundation and history of the Greek colonies in Italy and Sicily; a subject that naturally led him to treat of the western parts of the Mediterranean, and the countries bordering upon them. Thus we find from existing fragments that he gave some account of the Tyrrhenians or Etruscans, the Romans,[3] and the Carthaginians, as well as of the principal islands in this part of the Mediterranean, Sardinia, Corsica, and the Gymnesian Islands, known to the Romans as the Balearic. He is severely censured by Polybius for the inaccuracy of his geographical statements, and especially for his ignorance of the natural productions of the different countries that he described;[4] but he himself boasted of the great pains and labour he had incurred in collecting information concerning the manners and

---

[2] The exact age of Timæus cannot be determined, neither the date of his birth nor that of his death being accurately known, but his great historical work (of which that of Polybius was in some sense a continuation) ended with the year B.C. 265 (Polyb 1. 5). As he lived to the age of 96 he probably survived its completion by many years; but the date of its publication is the most material.

[3] Timæus was the earliest author who assigned a date for the foundation of Rome, which he regarded as contemporary with that of Carthage, and placed it 38 years before the First Olympiad, or B C. 810 (Dionys Halic. *Ant Rom.* i 74)

[4] Polyb. xii 3, 4.

customs of the Ligurians, Celts, and Iberians;[5] and there is little doubt that had this part of his work been preserved, we should have found in it many curious and valuable notices. Of geographical observations, in the strict sense of the word, we find very few cited, and it is evident that Timæus paid much less attention to this branch of his subject than his predecessor Ephorus had done.[6] The only example that has been preserved to us of his attempts at the explanation of physical phenomena is singularly unfortunate. We are told that he accounted for the flux and reflux of the waters of the Ocean, by supposing the water to be driven back by the flooding of the great rivers that flowed from the mountains of Gaul, and to return as these subsided.[7] Such an explanation shows an entire want of comprehension of the nature of the phenomenon itself. It is curious only as showing that the Greeks were already familiar with the fact of great rivers (the Garonne and the Loire) flowing through Gaul into the Atlantic Ocean.

Timæus appears to have derived his information concerning the lands on the shores of the Ocean, to the west and north of Europe, chiefly from Pytheas: he followed that writer in regard to the land from whence amber was brought, though he called the island Basilia, which was named by Pytheas Abalus.[8] But the most curious notice that is preserved to

---

[5] Id. xii 28 a If, however, these researches were in any degree the result of personal observation, they must have been made at an early period of his life, as he himself stated in his history that he had resided at Athens nearly fifty years without once quitting it (Ibid. 25 d)

[6] His views on two points, however, which are regarded as erroneous by Strabo (xiv 2, p 654)—that Sardinia was larger than Sicily, and that the chief of the two Gymnesian or Balearic Islands (Majorca) was the largest island in the Mediterranean after Lesbos—were far from meriting the reprobation of the geographer Sardinia is in fact, according to the computation of Captain Smyth, slightly larger than Sicily, while Majorca is not only entitled to rank next after Lesbos, but is considerably larger than that island, though not usually comprised by ancient writers among the seven chief islands of the Mediterranean (see note on Scylax). In this respect, therefore, Timæus was certainly better informed than most of the Greeks

[7] Timæus, Fr 36. Plutarch *de Placit Philosoph* p 901

[8] Plin *H. N* xxxvii. 11, § 36. In another passage, however (iv. 27, § 94), Pliny cites Timæus as calling the island Raunonia, and placing it in the

us from this part of his work is the statement that tin was brought from an island named Mictis, which was distant six days' voyage from Britain, to which the Britons navigated in vessels of wicker-work covered with leather.[9] There can be little doubt that we have here the first mention of the Cornish tin-trade, in connection with Britain, and that the island of Mictis is the same as that called by Diodorus Ictis, which he describes as the chief emporium to which the British tin was brought for exportation.[1]

§ 10. Independently of any professed geographical treatises, it is evident that at this period the Greeks had acquired a general familiarity with the countries of Western Europe, Gaul, Spain, and Liguria, as well as with Italy and the Italian islands, wholly different from that which they possessed a century before. This is sufficiently attested by the incidental notices of the productions of those countries and of natural phenomena observed there, which we find in THEOPHRASTUS, who wrote about the commencement of the third century B.C., and still more in the treatise "On Wonders," ascribed to Aristotle, but really belonging to the middle of the same century. Thus we find in Theophrastus mention of several plants and trees as flourishing in Tyrrhenia, Latium, &c.: a special notice of the extensive forests of Corsica, the pine-trees in which were said to exceed all others in size:[2] a curious and accurate description of the promontory of Circæum or Monte Circello;[3] an account of certain kinds of sea-weed

---

Ocean to the north of Scythia, at a day's voyage from the mainland There can be little doubt that both statements refer to the same story, but whether the error rests with Timæus or with Pliny we are unable to decide.

[9] Unfortunately this notice is transmitted to us by Pliny in such a form as to be almost unintelligible. His words are. "Timæus historicus a Britannia *introrsus* sex dierum navigatione abesse dicit insulam Mictim in qua candidum plumbum proveniat Ad eam Britannos vitilibus navigiis corio circumsutis navigare" (Plin *H N* iv. 16, § 104) Here it is impossible to say what sense we are to attach to the word "introrsus," upon which the interpretation of the whole passage, in a geographical sense, depends But there seems little doubt that we have here the first obscure intimation of the story which we find developed in a more complete form in Diodorus.

[1] Diodor. v 22
[2] *Hist Plant.* v 8, §§ 1, 2.
[3] Ibid § 3.

which grew in the Ocean beyond the Pillars of Hercules;[4] and the fact that native cinnabar was found in the interior of Spain.[5]

The notices preserved by the unknown author of the treatise "De Mirabilibus" are unfortunately mixed up, as might naturally be expected from the character of the work, with much of fable; and its date is in some degree a matter of uncertainty, but it contains some notices of interest. Among these may be mentioned the statement that the Ister rose in the Hercynian forest—a name which here appears for the first time.[6] At the same time the author repeats the popular notion that one arm of that river flowed into the Adriatic and the other into the Euxine. He placed also the Electrides or Amber Islands, in the inmost bight of the Adriatic, but connected them with the Eridanus, which he undoubtedly supposed to be the Po.[7] He is also the first extant author who mentions the iron mines of Æthalia (Elba), though these had doubtless been worked by the Tyrrhenians long before;[8] and has a very curious notice of certain vaulted buildings or Tholi, in the island of Sardinia, which probably refers to the singular edifices called Nuraghe still found in that island.[9]

It is remarkable also that the name of the Rhenus or Rhine had reached his ears, and was mentioned by him in conjunction with the Ister, as one of the two great rivers of the north. Both of them, he adds, were navigable in summer, but in winter were frozen hard, so that you might ride across them. Equally interesting is it that he describes the Rhine as flowing by the land of the Germans (Γερμανοὺς), as the Danube did by that of the Pæonians.[1] This is the first mention that is found in any ancient author of the name of Germans.[2]

---

[4] Ibid. iv. 6, § 4; 7, § 1.
[5] *De Lapid.* c. 8, § 58.
[6] *Mirab Auscult.* § 105. Aristotle himself (*Meteorologica*, i 13, § 19) describes the Ister as rising in the Pyrenees.   [7] Ibid § 81.
[8] Ibid. § 93.   [9] Ibid. § 100.
[1] Ibid. § 168. The Pæonians here meant are clearly the same people with the Pannonians of later writers. The confusion between the two names is found in Greek authors of much later date.
[2] It is remarkable that this passage should have been overlooked by Ukert in his elaborate investigation of the origin and introduction of the name (*Geographie*, vol iii pt 1, p 71).

§ 11. We are indebted to this compiler also for two interesting notices concerning the little known regions beyond the Pillars of Hercules. The one relates that the Phœnicians who dwelt at Gadeira, having sailed for four days with an east wind, discovered some banks, dry at low water and covered with quantities of sea-weed, where they found vast quantities of tunny fish of such superior quality that, when salted or pickled, they were carried to Carthage and retained by the Carthaginians for their own exclusive use.³ The other refers to the discovery in the sea beyond the Pillars, at a distance of several days' voyage, of an island of considerable extent, uninhabited, but abounding in timber of all kinds, possessing navigable rivers, and admirably fertile in all kinds of fruits. It was repeatedly visited by the Carthaginians, and partially colonized, but subsequently abandoned by order of the government, and all intercourse with it prohibited, for fear that it should attract too great a number of colonists to the detriment of the mother country.⁴ This account agrees so closely with that of Diodorus⁵ as to leave no doubt that they are both taken from Timæus. It is worthy of notice that in this, the earliest notice that is preserved to us of the Fortunate Islands of the West—which we shall find reappear in so many forms—*one* island only is spoken of, and that is described in a manner that leads us at once to identify it with Madeira.⁶

§ 12. Various causes must have no doubt contributed at this period to awaken increased interest and curiosity concerning the nations of Western Europe. The sudden inroads of the Gauls, who had not only overrun the northern provinces

---

³ Ibid. § 136.
⁴ Ibid. § 84.
⁵ Lib v c. 19, 20. Diodorus, however, represents the island as inhabited and even abounding in splendid buildings! His whole account is indeed much more highly coloured and exaggerated than that of our author
⁶ The abundance of wood, presenting so striking a contrast to eyes accustomed to the barren shores of Spain and Africa, is characteristic of Madeira, the name of which is derived from this circumstance, *madera* being Portuguese for timber The existence of *navigable* rivers is of course an exaggeration, but with this exception there is nothing in the account given by our author that is not probable enough.

bordering upon Thrace and Macedonia, but had for a time overthrown the Macedonian monarchy itself, and then crossing over into Asia rendered themselves equally formidable to the Greek rulers of Asia Minor, would naturally direct the attention of the Greek writers to the original abodes, as well as to the national characteristics, of these formidable invaders. At the same time the extension of the Carthaginian power in Spain could not fail to lead to a more complete and accurate knowledge of that country, at all events of its eastern portions, and though this may have been but imperfectly transmitted to the Greeks, there are not wanting indications of increased freedom of intercourse among all the commercial nations of the Mediterranean. In addition to Alexandria, Rhodes had assumed a prominent place among the trading communities of Greece, and continued for a considerable period to enjoy the highest wealth and prosperity.[7] Byzantium also, from its position, commanded all the commerce of the Euxine. Syracuse was at the height of its prosperity, and under the mild and beneficent rule of Hieron enjoyed a long period of unwonted tranquillity, during which it rose to the greatest opulence. Carthage, though declining in power after the First Punic War, still retained a very extensive commerce, and appears to have held more communication with the Greeks than at an earlier period, though the latter were still jealously excluded from the trade beyond the Pillars of Hercules, which continued to be centred exclusively at Gades.

---

[7] Diodor. xx. 81; Polyb. iv. 47. In B C 219 the Rhodians were compelled to engage in war with the Byzantines, by the complaints of the other trading cities, διὰ τὸ δοκεῖν αὐτοὺς προεστάναι τῶν κατὰ θάλατταν. Polyb. l. c.

NOTE A, p. 578.

MYOS HORMUS.

THE position of Myos Hormus has been the subject of considerable doubt. It was placed by Wilkinson and Wellsted at Abu Schar, in latitude 27° 24′, nearly opposite the angle of the Sinaitic peninsula, where there are considerable remains of an ancient town. But Dr. C. Muller has shown that it was in all probability situated at Ras Abu Somer, about half a degree farther to the south, where there is a good port with three small islands, and in the immediate neighbourhood a remarkable mountain, conspicuous by its red colour, thus answering precisely to the Scarlet Mountain ($\H{o}\rho o\varsigma$ $\mu\iota\lambda\tau\hat{\omega}\delta\epsilon\varsigma$) placed by Agatharchides in the neighbourhood of Myos Hormus. (Agatharchid. § 81, ed. Muller.) In this case the ruins visible at Abu Schar probably mark the site of Philotera, which is placed by Artemidorus to the *north* of Myos Hormus, though Ptolemy places it farther south, having apparently transposed the two positions. (See C. Muller's elaborate note on Agatharchides, *l. c.*) The same view is adopted by M. de St. Martin (*Le Nord de l'Afrique*, pp. 255–258).

NOTE B, p. 578.

AFRICAN ELEPHANTS.

It is well known that at the present day the African elephant is generally reputed to be untameable, and nothing seems to have more excited the wonder of the Abyssinians, during the late war, than to see the manner in which the Indian elephants that accompanied the English army were trained to perfect obedience. Yet it is certain that not only were the Ptolemies able to train the elephants of Ethiopia for purposes both of war and parade, but their example was quickly followed by the Carthaginians, who employed elephants in Sicily as early as the First Punic War, before the death of Ptolemy Philadelphus. All the elephants used by them, including those carried by Hannibal into Italy, were undoubtedly of African origin. The elephants also which are represented on Roman coins and monuments belong in all cases to the African and not the Indian variety. the very large size of the ears constituting a criterion by which they are easily recognized.

The inscription on the monument of Adulis, erected in the reign of Ptolemy Euergetes, distinctly ascribes to his father Philadelphus the merit of being the first to procure Ethiopian elephants and train them to service in war. A large number of these accompanied the army of Euergetes when he carried his arms into Asia and overran the dominions of Seleucus II. (Mon. Adulit. ap. Clinton, *F. H.* vol. iii. p. 382.) The statement of Agatharchides that Ptolemy Philadelphus was the first to train elephants for war, which justly excited the surprise of Photius, was doubtless intended to apply only to African elephants, and as thus understood, was strictly correct. (Agatharchides ap. Phot. p. 717.)

NOTE C, p. 579.

LAND OF CINNAMON.

There is no doubt not only that the Regio Cinnamomifera (ἡ κινναμωμόφορος) of the ancients was the tract of Northern Africa extending to Cape Guardafui, but that it was from thence that both the Greeks and Romans actually derived their principal, if not their sole, supply of that valuable spice. The geographical term is first found in Eratosthenes (ap. Strab. ii. pp. 63, 72, &c.) who appears to have applied it to the whole coast extending from near the Straits of Bab-el-Mandeb to Cape Guardafui, and at a later period we find the Periplus of the Erythræan Sea enumerating *cassia*—a term which was usually applied to cinnamon— among the productions exported from all the ports along this line of coast, from Malao (Berbera) to Cape Guardafui, or the Promontory of Spices (Aromatum Promontorium), as it was called by all later writers, evidently from this very circumstance. (*Periplus Mar. Erythr.* §§ 8–12.)

But while no difficulty arises on the geographical point, there has been much question raised as to the ancients having really derived their cinnamon from thence. In modern times cinnamon is almost exclusively procured from Ceylon, or from regions still farther to the east and still more unknown to the ancient traders, China and Java. Nor is it now known to exist in the part of Africa from whence the Greeks and Romans procured it. though that region still abounds in myrrh and frankincense. Hence it has been supposed by some modern writers that it was only brought by sea to the ports in the neighbourhood of Cape Guardafui, and thence imported by the Arabian and Greek merchants, in the same manner as the Indian merchandise was from Aden and other ports on the coast of Sabæa.

The testimony of the ancient writers however is too distinct and precise to be thus set aside: and Mr. Cooley has moreover shown that its cultivation in Ceylon dates from a comparatively recent period. The same view is adopted and confirmed by Sir E. Tennent, who has investigated the subject with much care. It is certain that no ancient writer alludes to cinnamon being brought from thence or from the adjoining coasts of India, even after the direct trade was opened with those countries. It seems therefore impossible to doubt that the cinnamon used by the Greeks and Romans—which was probably of an inferior quality to that of Ceylon—was really brought from the north-east corner of Africa, the land of the Somáli, a tract still very imperfectly known, and where it is not improbable that the cinnamon may still be found wild.

(See Mr. Cooley's paper on the *Regio Cinnamomifera of the Ancients*, in the *Journal of Geogr. Soc.* vol. xix. and Sir E. Tennent's *Ceylon*, vol. i. p. 599-604.*)

NOTE D, p. 586.

MONUMENT OF ADULIS.

It is now well known that the celebrated Monument of Adulis, for our knowledge of which we are indebted to a monk of the sixth century, Cosmas Indicopleustes, consisted in fact of two separate portions, the inscriptions on which were copied by the traveller, as if they had formed part of the same record. The former part belonged to a stela or pyramid set up in the reign of Ptolemy Euergetes, and recounting the exploits of that monarch,

---

* The same view had been already urged by Dr Vincent, vol ii p. 512.

especially his invasion of the Syrian monarchy, in which he penetrated beyond the Euphrates, and conquered or at least reduced to submission the provinces of Babylonia, Susiana, Persis, Media, and the rest of Asia as far as Bactriana; but containing no allusion to any conquests in Ethiopia, beyond the incidental notice already alluded to, of his having made use of Ethiopian elephants. The second part, which is of much later date, recounts the exploits of an Ethiopian king of Axum in Abyssinia, who appears to have conquered all the neighbouring tribes in that part of Africa, and even carried his arms across the Red Sea into Arabia. The confusion resulting from the union of the two, which had misled even Dr. Vincent and Ukert, was first cleared up by the English traveller Mr. Salt. (A full account of the monument and its inscriptions will be found in Boeckh's *Corpus Inscript. Græcarum*, tom. iii. p. 508 and foll) See also St. Martin, *Le Nord de l'Afrique*, p. 224. Clinton (*F. H.* vol. iii. p. 382 *note*) has given the first part of the inscription relating to Ptolemy Euergetes, but has erroneously added as referring to the same monarch the conclusion which belongs to the Axumite king.

NOTE E, p. 589.

THE WINDS AS KNOWN TO THE GREEKS.

The number of divisions thus established by Timosthenes was twelve in all . and this appears to have been the number generally recognized among the later Greek geographers. No trace is found of a subdivision into sixteen parts, according to the custom of modern navigators and geographers. But the statement of Agathemerus that Timosthenes distinguished twelve winds, by inserting four additional ones between those previously known and admitted, is certainly not correct. Aristotle, in his *Meteorologica* (ii. 6), distinctly enumerates twelve winds, and the quarters from which they blow; and though his list differs slightly from that ascribed to Timosthenes, this arises only from the variations of names, many of which were of local attribution. His enumeration is as follows. The west wind, Zephyrus, blew from the equinoctial setting . and opposite to this was the east wind, Apeliotes, from the equinoctial rising. The north wind, called Boreas and Aparctias, blew from the north, the region of the Great Bear (Arctos). Opposite to this was the south wind, Notus. The Cæcias blew from the summer rising (north-east), and opposite to this was the Lips, from the winter setting. The Eurus blew from the winter rising (south-east), and opposite to this was the Argestes (north-west) known also as Olympias and Sciron. These therefore formed four pairs respectively opposed to each other, but besides these there were others which were not so precisely opposite: these were the Thrascias, intermediate between the Argestes and the Boreas: the Meses, intermediate between the Boreas and Cæcias; the Phœnix, between the Eurus and Notus; the Libonotus in the corresponding position, between the Lips and Notus, is not mentioned, the name being apparently not familiar to the Greeks in his day.

But though this amount of subdivision was recognized by the more scientific writers, there can be no doubt that eight winds only were popularly known. This is the number found on the monument at Athens, commonly called the Tower of the Winds, where their names are thus given: Boreas, Cæcias, Apeliotes, Eurus, Notus, Lips, Zephyrus, and Sciron.[8]

It is evident however that the ancients, even the geographers, made no attempt to divide the circle of the heavens into regular portions corresponding with our quarters (N.E., S.W., &c.), independent of the winds. The only mode in use to designate these points of the compass (as we call them) was by reference to the summer and winter changes in the place of the rising and setting of the sun: as is done by Aristotle in the passage just cited, and by Strabo throughout his work. Of course such a mode of expression was inaccurate, and had the further disadvantage that it ought in strictness to vary with the latitude of each place: as for instance between Athens and Alexandria. But no such accuracy was observed in practice: and the expressions of "the winter sunrise" or "the winter sunset" would be used generally as equivalent to south-east and south-west respectively. At the same time most scientific observers would be aware that there was a greater interval between these points and the four cardinal points, on the one side than the other; and hence arose the intercalation both by Timosthenes and Aristotle of four such points, without the four corresponding ones introduced in our modern division.

---

[8] This monument, more correctly termed the Horologium of Andronicus Cyrrhestes, belongs probably to the second century, B C.

It will be seen that where the whole circle is thus divided into twelve regions instead of sixteen, none of the points, except the four cardinal ones, can exactly correspond with those of our modern divisions. Hence the use of the terms North-north-East, South-south-West, &c., in the translation of the passage from Timosthenes is necessarily inaccurate, and has been adopted merely for the sake of convenience.

NOTE F, p. 591.

DIMENSIONS OF BRITAIN.

It is worthy of remark that Diodorus, writing after Cæsar had given so much more information concerning Britain, and an approximate estimate of its true dimensions, should return nearly to the statement of Pytheas, though with an affectation of accuracy, which was evidently founded on no real authority. He makes the whole circumference 42,500 stadia, the three sides being respectively 7500, 15,000 and 20,000 in extent. (Diodor. v. 21.) But he correctly calls the side opposite to Gaul, the *shortest* side of the triangle: while Strabo, who had a wholly erroneous idea of the position and extent of Britain, makes its side opposite to Gaul, which does not exceed (he says) 4400 stadia, the greatest length of the island. (Strabo, iv. 5, § 1, p. 199.)

It is not improbable that in this part of his work Diodorus followed Timæus.

NOTE G, p. 598.

SIR G. LEWIS ON CREDIBILITY OF PYTHEAS.

This has been especially the case with Sir G. Lewis, who in his dissertation on the Navigation of the Phœnicians (inserted in his *Historical Survey of Ancient Astronomy*, chap. viii.) has treated Pytheas with the same contempt as Polybius did, without adverting to the points in which our present full knowledge of the northern regions of Europe has shown that Pytheas was right, and Polybius and Strabo were wrong. That Pytheas did not really visit Thule may be readily admitted, and it is improbable that he really advanced along the northern shores of Germany farther than the Elbe. Even at a much later period we find the Roman fleet that first penetrated to the mouth of that river claiming to have reached the confines of the known world (*Mon. Ancyran.* p. 34.) But this is no reason for disbelieving altogether the fact of his having personally explored a considerable portion of the countries to the north of Europe that were previously unknown to the Greeks.

Besides the chapter of Sir G. Lewis just referred to, the credibility of the voyage of Pytheas and of his geographical information is fully discussed by Gossellin in his *Recherches sur la Géographie des Anciens* (vol. iv. p. 168–179), by Ukert (*Geographie der Griechen und Romer*, vol. i. pt. 2. p. 298–309, vol. iii. pt. 1. p. 5, § 6): and in the article PYTHEAS in Dr. Smith's Dictionary. References are given by Ukert to the earlier authorities on the subject. See also Redslob's *Thule*, cited in note to p. 597.

NOTE H, p. 599.

ASTRONOMICAL PHENOMENA AT THULE.

This is the distinct statement of Pliny in one passage (iv. 16, § 104), "Ultima omnium quæ memorantur [insularum] Thule, in qua *solstitio nullas esse noctes* indicavimus, cancri signum sole transeunte, nullosque contra per brumam dies." But he adds: "Hoc quidam senis mensibus continuis fieri arbitrantur": and in the previous passage to which he here refers (ii. 75, § 187) he himself cites Pytheas as having stated that this—the continuous day for six months, and continuous night for the other six—was what actually occurred at Thule. It is much more probable that Pytheas had made the more correct and rational statement, and had been misunderstood by those who did not see the absurdity of the other supposition.

In another passage Strabo refers to him as having placed Thule, which he calls "the most northern of the British Islands," in a latitude where the arctic circle coincided with that of the summer tropic—a distinct astronomical statement which would be equivalent, in the language of modern geographers, to saying that it was situated under the Arctic Circle. (Strabo, ii. 5, § 8, p. 114.) This is of course incorrect, if we suppose Thule to have any connection with the British Islands, so as to represent the Orkneys or Shetlands (even the latter group extending only to 60° 50′ N. lat.), but by no means so gross an exaggeration as it was supposed to be by Strabo and others, who were ignorant of the true position of these northern countries. It is one also to which Pytheas would have been easily led, if we suppose him to have picked up his information concerning Thule at second hand . the absence of any *apparent* night in these high northern latitudes being readily transformed into the assertion that the actual, or astronomical, day was of twenty-four hours' duration. Pytheas was doubtless astronomer enough to discern that this must be the case *somewhere*, as one advanced towards the north, and he might therefore readily accept the hearsay statement that it was the fact in the island to which he gave the name of Thule.

It may be observed that at a much later period we find Cæsar himself repeating the tale that there was continuous night for thirty days at the winter solstice, but which had been transferred to the islands between Britain and Ireland. (Cæs. *B. G.* v. 13.)

CHAPTER XVI.

ERATOSTHENES.

§ 1. WE are now arrived at the period when geography first began to assume something of a regular and systematic character; and to be based, however imperfectly, upon fixed scientific principles. It is to the Alexandrian school that we are indebted for the first steps in this direction: and ERATOS-THENES, who presided over that school during the space of more than forty years,[1] may be regarded as the parent of scientific geography, as he was also in great measure of systematic chronology. The way had been undoubtedly prepared for him by the astronomical researches of his immediate predecessors, and he was himself fully acquainted with all the astronomical science of his time: while the recent extension of geographical knowledge among the Greeks from the various causes which we have been just passing in review, had accumulated a mass of information greatly exceeding that at the disposal of earlier writers.

The position of Eratosthenes himself was peculiarly favourable. He was born at Cyrene in B.C. 276, and having early devoted himself to the study of philosophy and learning, passed a considerable time at Athens, from whence he was invited to Alexandria by Ptolemy Euergetes, and placed at the head of the Library, a position of the highest literary distinction, which gave him the command of the accumulated stores of learning that had been brought together by the enlightened monarchs of Egypt during three generations. Eratosthenes continued to

---

[1] According to Clinton (*F H.* vol. iii p 37), he succeeded Zenodotus as librarian at Alexandria, about B C. 240, and continued to hold this situation till his death in B.C. 196.

hold this important post till his death, about B.C. 196; and left behind him a number of works, some scientific, others purely literary. All these have unfortunately perished; and though enough has been preserved of his geographical treatise to enable us in great measure to judge of its character, and to form a tolerably clear idea of his system, yet we shall find, as we pursue our examination, abundant reason to regret the imperfect character of our materials.[2] In another respect also we are unable to estimate justly the amount of merit due to Eratosthenes, from our very deficient knowledge of the actual state of geographical science previous to the commencement of his labours.

§ 2. It is certain indeed that Eratosthenes was not the first among the writers of this period who attempted to bring together in one general view the results of recent discoveries and observations, and survey the progress that had been made in the knowledge of the different countries of the world. DICÆARCHUS, a pupil of Aristotle and a friend of Theophrastus, who flourished about a hundred years before Eratosthenes, B.C. 326-296,[3] had left several geographical works, one of which, termed Γῆς περίοδος, was apparently, from its title, a general geographical treatise: and would seem to have comprehended a summary view of the position and dimensions of the habitable world, as then known, not altogether dissimilar from that given by Eratosthenes. But the few citations that are preserved to us are not sufficient to enable us to judge fairly of the relation which it bore to the work of the later author. We learn however from Strabo,[4] that Polybius, while he passed by the earlier writers on geography as unworthy of serious consideration, entered into an elaborate criticism of Dicæarchus and Eratosthenes as representing an improved

---

[2] The fragments of the geographical work of Eratosthenes were first collected and edited by Seidel (*Eratosthenis Geographicorum Fragmenta*, 8vo, Gœttingæ, 1789), and more fully, together with the remains of his other works, by Bernhardy (*Eratosthenica*, 8vo, Berolin. 1822)

[3] Clinton, *F H* vol. III. p. 474; C Muller, *Fragm Hist Gr* vol. II. pp. 225, 226

[4] II. p. 104.

state of geographical knowledge. We may therefore infer that the former also had treated the subject in something like a scientific manner.

Dicæarchus had also written (besides many valuable works of a historical character) a complete geographical, or rather topographical, description of Greece—a treatise which would have been of the highest interest to us had it been preserved; and we learn incidentally that this was accompanied by maps, which were still extant in the days of Cicero, and were regarded by him as of high authority.[5] Three fragments of considerable length belonging to a work of this description have been preserved to us, and are published in all the editions of the minor Greek geographers, to which the name of Dicæarchus has been usually applied, but there is no authority for this attribution, though they probably belong to about the period of that author.[6]

§ 3. On another account also Dicæarchus deserves a place in reviewing the progress of geographical knowledge, that he was the first, so far as we know, to attempt a scientific measurement of the height of mountains; a task which he undertook, we are told, at the request of certain kings,[7] probably those of Macedonia. It was not likely that the results of such a first attempt should be satisfactory: but the few and scanty notices of them that have been preserved to us are so uncertain and inconsistent with one another, that we cannot safely judge of their character. Thus we are told on the one hand that he determined the height of Cyllene in Arcadia to be rather less than 15 stadia, or 9000 Greek feet, and that of Atabyrius in the

---

[5] "Peloponnesias civitates omnes maritimas esse hominis, non nequam, sed etiam tuo judicio probati Dicæarchi *tabulis* credidi" Cic *Epist ad Att* vi 2 Osann considers these *tabulæ* to have been attached to the Γῆς περίοδος, while C Muller doubts their having any reference to *maps* at all The passage is certainly not conclusive

[6] See this point fully discussed by C.

Muller in his edition of the *Fragmenta Historicorum Græcorum,* vol i. pp. 229 –232. The fragments themselves are published by the same author in his *Geographi Græci Minores,* tom. 1 pp 97–110. They are contained also in the second volume of Hudson's edition of the same writers

[7] *Requm cura* montes permensus. Plin. *H N* ii. 65, § 162.

island of Rhodes (a mountain of very inferior altitude) to be 14 stadia.[8] On the other hand Pliny asserts that he ascertained Pelion to be the highest of the Greek mountains, but that it did not exceed 1250 paces (6250 feet) in perpendicular height.[9] If he really came to the conclusion that Pelion exceeded in elevation the neighbouring mountains, Ossa and Olympus, his method of observation must have been singularly inaccurate; the former being in fact at least 1000 feet higher than Pelion, while Olympus exceeds it by 4700 feet, little less than half its total altitude.[1] Olympus is indeed by far the highest mountain in Greece, while Pelion is inferior to Parnassus, Cyllene, Taygetus, and several others. But Dicæarchus at least deserves credit for having attempted to determine the perpendicular altitude by a mathematical process.

§ 4. There can be no doubt that before the time of Eratosthenes the ideas of the learned world upon the subject of geography had assumed a more regular and systematic form. And it is certain also that these had been embodied in the form of maps, which, however imperfect, were unquestionably very superior to anything that had preceded them. We have seen that the first use of maps had been introduced at a very early period by Anaximander. and that maps of the world were not uncommon in the time of Herodotus, though based on the crude ideas of the period, and on hasty assumptions that excited the ridicule of the historian. Nor can it be doubted that the discoveries resulting from the conquests of Alexander, and the extension of geographical knowledge under his suc-

---

[8] Geminus, *Elem Astronom* c. 14. The actual height of Cyllene is 7788 feet, that of Atabyrius only 4560 The former was generally regarded as the highest mountain in the Peloponnesus. according to Strabo it was reckoned by some to be 20 stadia in perpendicular height; by others (probably referring to Dicæarchus) only fifteen. But another statement, cited from Apollodorus, made its height 80 feet less than nine stadia, or only 5320 Greek feet (Steph Byz. s v. Κυλλήνη; Eustath. ad *Hom Odyss*. p 1951)

[9] Plin. *H. N.* 11. c 65, § 162. "Dicæarchus, vir in primis eruditus, regum cura permensus montes, ex quibus altissimum prodidit Pelion MCCL passuum ratione perpendiculari."

[1] Admiral Smyth gives the height of Pelion at 5200 feet, Ossa at 6100, and Olympus at 9850 feet above the sea

cessors, would have gradually found their way into such maps; but we know from frequent experience, even in modern times, how slowly established errors are discarded, and how long they maintain their ground, even in the face of more accurate information. The same thing was still more the case in ancient times, and it is highly probable that if we could now recover the map of the world as it was generally received in the time of the first Ptolemies, we should find it still retaining many of the erroneous views of Herodotus and Hecatæus.

It appears indeed from repeated statements of Strabo that Eratosthenes made it the object of his special attention to "reform the map of the world," as it had existed down to his time,[2] and to reconstruct it upon more scientific principles. It is this enlarged and philosophical view of the subject which constitutes his especial merit, and entitles him to be justly called the father of systematic geography. The materials at his command were still very imperfect, and the means of scientific observation were wanting to a degree which we can, at the present day, scarcely figure to ourselves; but the methods which he pursued were of a strictly scientific character, and his judgment was so sound that he proved in many instances to be better informed and more judicious in his inferences than geographers of two centuries later.

§ 5. In regard to the fundamental idea of all geography—the position and figure of the earth—Eratosthenes adopted the views that were current among the astronomers of his day, which had been received almost without exception from the times of Aristotle and Euclid.[3] He regarded the earth as a sphere,[4] placed in the centre of the universe, around which the

---

[2] Διορθῶσαι τὸν ἀρχαῖον γεωγραφικὸν πίνακα was the problem that he had set before himself. Strab. ii. c. 1, § 2. These words point clearly to the previous existence of a generally recognized map of the inhabited world (τῆς οἰκουμένης), probably that of Dicæarchus.

[3] A convenient summary of these views will be found in Sir G. Lewis's *Historical Survey of Ancient Astronomy* (pp. 187, 188), extracted from the Phænomena of Euclid. The great geometer had preceded Eratosthenes by nearly a century.

[4] Strabo repeatedly censures Eratosthenes (i. pp 62, 65) for dwelling at unnecessary length upon the proofs of

celestial sphere revolved every twenty-four hours: besides which, the sun and moon had independent motions of their own. The obliquity of the sun's course to that of the celestial sphere, was of course well known: and hence the great circles of the equinoctial, and the ecliptic, or zodiacal circle, as well as the lesser circles, called the tropics, parallel with the equinoctial, were already familiar to the astronomers of Alexandria. Moreover it appears that these conceptions, originally applied to the celestial sphere, had been already transferred in theory to the terrestrial globe. Thus the idea of the globe of the earth, as it would present itself to the mind of Eratosthenes, or any of his more instructed contemporaries, did not differ materially from that of the modern geographer. For all geographical purposes, at least as the term was understood in his day, the difference between the geocentric and the heliocentric theories of the universe would be unimportant.

§ 6. But Eratosthenes had the merit of making one valuable addition to the previously existing ideas upon this subject, by a more careful and successful measurement than had ever been previously attempted, of the magnitude of the earth, or circumference of the terrestrial globe.

He was not indeed the first who had attempted the solution of this problem, which would naturally engage the attention of astronomers and geometers, as soon as it was agreed that the earth was of a spherical form. Aristotle refers to the calculation of "mathematicians" who had investigated the subject (without naming them) that the earth was 400,000 stadia in circumference.[5] At a later period Archimedes speaks of 300,000

---

the spherical character of the earth, a fact which he appears to have regarded as too well known to require demonstration. But though it was undoubtedly a received tenet *among philosophers* in the days of Eratosthenes, it had probably not yet acquired the same general acceptance as in the time of Strabo, two centuries afterwards.

⁵ *De Cœlo*, ii 14, § 16 It is a singular instance of that blind reverence for antiquity which has misled so many modern writers, that this passing notice of Aristotle, on which he himself evidently laid no stress, and had taken up (as he himself tells us) on the authority of others, should have been received as unquestionably correct Hence D'Anville and Gossellin, in order to explain its apparent inaccuracy,

stadia as the measurement usually received, a statement apparently founded on the calculations of Aristarchus of Samos, one of the earlier astronomers of the Alexandrian school.[6] But we have no information as to the data on which these first crude attempts were based, or the mode by which the authors arrived at their results.

The method pursued by Eratosthenes was theoretically sound, and was in fact identical in principle with that which has been adopted by astronomers in modern days. Assuming (in accordance with the general belief) that Syene in Upper Egypt was situated exactly under the Tropic of Cancer: assuming also that Alexandria and Syene were on the same meridian, and at the distance of 5000 stadia from one another, he measured the shadow of the gnomon at Alexandria in order to determine its latitude, and thus ascertained that the arc of the meridian intercepted between the two, was equal to one-fiftieth part of a great circle of the sphere. Hence he at once deduced the conclusion that such a great circle, or the circumference of the globe, would amount to 250,000 stadia.[7]

§ 7. The only theoretical error in this mode of calculation was in the assumption—which was inevitable in the days of Eratosthenes—that the earth was exactly spherical, instead of being as it really is, a slightly oblate spheroid, and that therefore a meridian great circle was equal to that of the equator. And the error proceeding from this cause, which would not exceed $\frac{1}{300}$th part of the whole, is wholly unimportant

---

have assumed that Aristotle must have been employing a smaller stade than that generally known to the Greeks, such as would really give 400,000 stades for the circumference of the earth, and have then proceeded to make use of this smaller or *Aristotelian* stade for the measurement of distances in the marches of Alexander and the voyage of Nearchus (see Chapter XIII. p 545). Yet it is evident that no value was attached to this statement by any ancient writer from the time when Eratosthenes and Hipparchus had instituted more accurate investigations of the same problem.

[6] Archimed *Arenarius*, p. 320, ed. Torelli.

[7] The method pursued by Eratosthenes is fully stated and explained by the astronomer Cleomedes, in his work on the Circular Motion of the Heavenly Bodies (Κυκλικὴ Θεωρία Μετεώρων, i. c 10, ed Bake), and will be found in Bernhardy's *Eratosthenica*, Fr. 42. The date of Cleomedes is uncertain, but he may probably be assigned to the first century before Christ.

as compared with the *practical* errors arising from the defective means of observation.

In the first place it was assumed that Syene lay directly under the tropic, it being a well-known fact that at the summer solstice the sun could be seen from the bottom of a deep well, and that at the same time the gnomon cast no perceptible shadow.[8] But though these facts were perfectly correct as matters of rough observation, such as could be made by general travellers, they were far from having the precise accuracy requisite as the basis of scientific calculations. Syene is in fact situated in latitude 24° 5′ 30″,[9] or nearly 37 G. miles to the north of the tropic. In the next place Alexandria, instead of being exactly on the same meridian with Syene, lay in fact not less than three degrees of longitude to the west of it: an error of no trifling moment when the distance between the two was assumed as the basis of calculation. But a much graver error than either of these two was that caused by the erroneous estimate of the actual distance between the two cities. What mode of measurement had been resorted to, or how Eratosthenes arrived at his conclusion upon this point, we are wholly without information: but it may well be doubted whether he had recourse to anything like actual mensuration.[1] Indeed the difficulty which modern experience has shown to attend this apparently simple operation, where scientific accuracy is required, renders it highly improbable that it was even attempted; and the round number of 5000 stades at once points to its being no more than a rough approximation. But even considered as such, it exceeds the truth to a degree that

---

[8] Strabo, xvii. p. 317. The same thing is told by Seneca, Pliny, and Lucan. It is remarkable that no mention of it occurs in Herodotus, though the fact must have been well known to the Egyptian priests, and was one likely to attract the attention of all travellers

[9] Wilkinson's *Egypt and Thebes*, p. 415.

[1] We are told indeed by Martianus Capella (cited by Bernhardy) that this distance was derived from actual measurement, but the authority of so late a compiler is altogether worthless; and there is no doubt that the Greeks in the time of Eratosthenes had no power of making a trigonometrical survey, without which any such measurement is impossible

one could hardly have expected, in a country so well known as Egypt, and in an age so civilized as that of the Ptolemies. Alexandria is in fact situated at a distance of about 530 geographical miles (5300 stadia) from Syene, as measured on the map *along the nearest road:* but the *direct* distance between the two, or the arc of the great circle intercepted between the two points, *which is what Eratosthenes intended to measure,* amounts to only 453 G. miles or 4530 stadia.[2] Eratosthenes therefore in fixing the length of this arc at 5000 stadia, was 470 beyond the truth. But this was not all. The difference in latitude between Alexandria and Syene really amounts to only 7° 5′, so that the direct distance between the two cities, supposing them to have been really situated on the same meridian (as Eratosthenes assumed them to be) would not have exceeded 425 G. miles, or 4250 stadia, instead of 5000. His arc was therefore in reality 750 stadia too long.

It is remarkable that while the terrestrial measurement was thus grossly inaccurate, the observation of latitude as deduced from the gnomon at Alexandria was a very fair approximation to the truth: a fiftieth part of a great circle being equivalent to an arc of 7° 12′, thus exceeding by about 7′ only the true interval between Alexandria and Syene,[3] while falling short of that between Alexandria and the real tropic by about 30′ or half a degree.

§ 8. It appears indeed almost certain that Eratosthenes himself was aware of the imperfection of his data, and regarded the result of his calculation only as an approximation to the truth. Hence he felt himself at liberty to add 2000 stadia to the 250,000 obtained by his process, in order to have a number that would be readily divisible into sixty parts, or into degrees of 360 to a great circle.[4] The result would of course be that

---

[2] Leake *On some disputed Questions of Ancient Geography*, p 101.

[3] The latitude of Alexandria is 31° 10′ 45″, that of Syene as already stated 24° 5′ 30″, the exact difference between the two is therefore 7° 5′ 15″

[4] It is by no means clear whether the division of the great circle into degrees was known to Eratosthenes, or at least was adopted by him. It would rather appear from a passage in Strabo (ii. p. 113) that he divided the equator

each degree would be equivalent (according to his calculation) to 700 stadia; though it in reality contained no more than 600 of the ordinary Greek stadia of 600 Greek feet in length. Hence it has been supposed by many modern writers that Eratosthenes really employed stadia of this length, or in other words that where he estimates distances in stadia, he is not using the term in the usual sense—the only one that would be understood by his contemporaries, or by subsequent Greek writers —but means everywhere stades of 700 to a degree, or rather more than 514 Greek feet each.[5] These writers in fact *assume* that Eratosthenes *must* have known the true length of a degree, and the real circumference of the globe, and that *therefore* his stade must have been a different measure from that in ordinary use. But the account of his operation, which is given us with great clearness, proves—as might indeed almost have been assumed without it—that he in reality followed the converse method. He started from what he believed to be a well-ascertained terrestrial measurement, and deduced from thence the circumference of the globe and the length of its aliquot parts. His conclusion was erroneous, because his data were inaccurate, and his observations defective. But none of the writers who have transmitted to us the details of his calculation, have given us the slightest hint, or evidently had any idea, that he was not employing the customary Greek stade, the length of which was familiar to them all.

After all it must be admitted that the calculation of Eratosthenes, considering the disadvantages under which he laboured, came surprisingly near the truth. His measurement of 250,000 stadia (the immediate result of his calculation) would be equivalent to 25,000 *geographical* miles, while

---

into *sixtieths*, without carrying the subdivision further But this would equally require the addition of 2000 stadia to allow of the division into whole numbers.

I have however continued to employ the familiar phrase of stades of 700 *to a degree*, rather than 4200 *to a sixtieth*, as involving no substantial error, though the term may be slightly inaccurate

[5] This was especially the case with Gosselin, whose calculations are in almost all cases based upon this assumption

the actual circumference of the earth at the equator falls very little short of 25,000 *English* miles.[6] The error in excess therefore amounted to less than one-seventh part of the whole.[7]

§ 9. Having thus laid the foundation of what has been called in modern times "geodesy"—the determination of the figure and dimensions of the earth, considered in its entirety, as a part of the system of the universe, Eratosthenes next proceeded to consider that portion of it which was in his time geographically known, or supposed to be inhabited. And here it must be observed that the relation between the habitable world, which was alone regarded as coming within the scope of the geographer (properly so called), and the terrestrial globe itself, was, in the days of Eratosthenes, and even long afterwards, a very different one from that which we now conceive as subsisting between them. Ever since the discoveries of the great Portuguese and Spanish navigators in the fifteenth and sixteenth centuries opened out to us new continents, and extensions of those already known, far beyond anything that had previously been suspected or imagined, men have been accustomed to regard the "map of the world" as comprising the whole surface of the globe, and including both the eastern and western hemispheres, while towards the north and south it is capable of indefinite extension, till it should reach the poles, and is in fact continually receiving fresh accessions. With the Greek geographers on the contrary, from Eratosthenes to Strabo, the known or habitable world (ἡ οἰκουμένη) was conceived as a definite and limited portion of the earth's surface, situated wholly within the northern hemisphere, and comprised within about a third of the extent of that section.

---

[6] The exact amount, according to the most recent calculations, is 24,899 English miles (Herschel's *Outlines of Astronomy*, p 136)

[7] Eratosthenes attempted also to determine the distances of the sun and moon from the earth. But here the entire want of any trustworthy basis of calculation led, as might be expected, to wholly erroneous results. He computed the distance of the moon at 780,000 stadia, and that of the sun at 4,000,000 stadia (see the passages cited by Clinton, *F. H* vol. III. p 515). No account is preserved of the process by which he arrived at these conclusions.

Towards the north and the south it was conceived that the excessive cold in the one case, and the intolerable heat in the other, rendered those regions uninhabitable, and even inaccessible to man. That there *might* be inhabitants of the southern hemisphere beyond the torrid zone, or that unknown lands *might* exist within the boundless and trackless ocean that was supposed to extend around two-thirds of the globe, from west to east, was admitted to be theoretically possible, but was treated as mere matter of idle speculation, much as we might at the present day regard the question of the inhabitants of the moon.[8]

§ 10. The first task of the geographer therefore, according to the notions then prevailing, was to determine the limits and dimensions of the map of the world which was to form the subject of his special investigations. This question, which was taken up by Eratosthenes at the beginning of his second book, had already been considered by several previous writers, who had arrived at very different results. On one point indeed they were all agreed, that the length of the habitable world, from west to east, greatly exceeded its breadth, from north to south.[9] Democritus, two centuries before Eratosthenes, had asserted that it was half as long again as it was broad, and this view was adopted by Dicæarchus, though recent discoveries had in his day materially extended the knowledge of its eastern portions.[1] The astronomer Eudoxus on the other hand maintained that the length was double the breadth; Eratosthenes went a step farther and determined the length to be *more* than double the breadth, a statement which continued to be received by subsequent geographers for more than three centuries as an established fact.[2] According to his calculation (the steps of which will hereafter be examined

---

[8] Strabo, ii 5, § 13, p 118.
[9] It is hardly necessary to observe that the traces of this primitive conception are still preserved in the terms *latitude* and *longitude*, as used by modern geographers. But the scientific use of those terms appears to have been first introduced by Ptolemy, or at least is not found in any earlier writer
[1] Agathemerus, i. c. 1.
[2] Strabo, 1. p 64.

more in detail) the length of the known world from the Atlantic to the Eastern Ocean amounted to 78,000 stadia, while its breadth from the parallel of the Cinnamon Land to that of Thule did not exceed 38,000 stadia.

As Eratosthenes had computed the equatorial circumference of the globe at 250,000 stadia, it was easy to derive from this, by mere geometrical calculation, the conclusion that in the parallel of Rhodes and the Pillars of Hercules, the circumference would amount to about 200,000 stadia. Hence he found that the length of the known or habitable world was rather more than a third of the whole circumference of the globe in this latitude.[3] The remaining interval he conceived to be filled up by sea, so that, as he observed, "if it were not that the vast extent of the Atlantic sea rendered it impossible, one might even sail from the coast of Spain to that of India along the same parallel."[4] A curious speculation, as the first suggestion, though of course merely as a matter of theory, of the circumnavigation of the globe!

§ 11. Having thus determined the area with which he had to deal, the next step was to divide this space at intervals by lines parallel to the equator, traversing the whole length of the area, or, as we should now call them, parallels of latitude, passing through given points. For this purpose Eratosthenes began by tracing one main line, which extended from the Sacred Promontory (the westernmost point of the Iberian peninsula) between the Pillars of Hercules, along the whole length of the Mediterranean to the island of Rhodes and thence to the Gulf of Issus. Hence it was prolonged along the southern foot of the chain of Mount Taurus, which he conceived as a continuous range of mountains, of great width, but preserving an uniform direction from west to east, and

---

[3] Strabo, i. p. 65. The passage is unfortunately mutilated, and cannot be restored with certainty, but the words τὸ λοιπὸν μέρος παρὰ τὸ λεχθὲν διάστημα ὑπὲρ τὸ τρίτον μέρος ὂν τοῦ ὅλου κύκλου can clearly have no other signification than that given in the text.

[4] Strabo, i. p. 64. ὥστε εἰ μὴ τὸ μέγεθος τοῦ Ἀτλαντικοῦ πελάγους ἐκώλυε, κἂν πλεῖν ἡμᾶς ἐκ τῆς Ἰβηρίας εἰς τὴν Ἰνδικὴν διὰ τοῦ αὐτοῦ παραλλήλου

continued under the name of Caucasus along the northern frontier of India, until it ended in the Eastern or Indian Ocean.[5]

A similar proceeding had been already resorted to by Dicæarchus, who had in like manner divided the known world by a longitudinal line, traversing its whole extent from the Columns of Hercules to the range of Imaus, which he took as the line of separation of the northern and southern portions, describing the different regions and countries with reference to this imaginary line, and not according to the customary division into three continents.[6] It does not appear that Eratosthenes attached any such special importance to this particular line, but it was evidently selected by him as traversing a number of points the position of which was known, or supposed to be known, and as being the only line which through its whole length passed through regions with which the Greeks were in some degree acquainted. It was also supposed to be the line which traversed the inhabited world in its greatest length, from the farthest extremity towards the west to the supposed extreme point to the east; and hence the distances measured along this line would give as their result the total length of the earth's surface, as known to geographers.

It is evident that the determination of any such line as this, with any approach to accuracy, required the possession of a number of correct observations of latitude for different points along its whole extent; but such observations were almost wholly wanting. It was not merely that in the age of Eratosthenes the only methods available for this purpose were of a rude and imperfect description, and could not be relied upon for accuracy, except within very wide limits, but it is certain that no such observations were in existence, unless in

---

[5] Strabo, ii 1, § 1.

[6] Agathemerus, *Geograph* i c. 1, § 5. It is remarkable that many modern writers, including the accurate Colonel Leake, should state that this line was termed by Dicæarchus the διάφραγμα τῆς οἰκουμένης, and refer to the above passage of Agathemerus as their authority. But no such statement is found in Agathemerus, nor have I met with the expression in any ancient author.

a very few and isolated cases. Hence we cannot wonder that the attempt thus made came out in some points very wide of the truth; the remarkable thing is rather that—for the western portion of its course especially—the line should have made as near an approximation to correctness, as proves to be the case.

§ 12. This fundamental parallel of latitude (as it may be called for want of a better distinctive term) was supposed to begin at the Sacred Promontory (Cape St. Vincent) which was generally (though erroneously) regarded as the westernmost point of Europe, whence it passed through the Strait of the Columns, or Straits of Gibraltar, the Sicilian Strait, and the southern extremities of the Peloponnese and Attica, to Rhodes and the Gulf of Issus. Of these points, if we take the parallel of 36°, which really passes through the Straits of Gibraltar, as representing that intended by Eratosthenes, we shall find that the Sacred Promontory is placed just about a degree too far south, while the Sicilian Strait, or Strait of Messina, is brought down more than two degrees to the south, into the position of the island of Gozo near Malta; on the other hand the same parallel passes within less than half a degree of Cape Malea (generally regarded by the ancients as the southernmost point of the Peloponnese); while it actually traverses the southern portion of the island of Rhodes, about 25 miles from the city of that name, and approaches within the same distance of the entrance to the Gulf of Issus or Iskenderun.

It is certain indeed that Eratosthenes himself was to a great extent aware of the imperfection of the means at his command, and did not regard his proposed line as a matter of scientific accuracy, but only as a rough approximation. This is evident from the manner in which he speaks of the Gulf of Issus without indicating any particular point of it, and of Rhodes, without stating whether the island or the city was meant; but still more from his repeatedly referring to the parallel in question as passing through *Athens* and

Rhodes,[7] though he elsewhere indicated distinctly that the parallels of the two cities were separated by an interval of 400 stadia (40 G. miles).[8] Such a difference he regarded as *immaterial* in considering such distances as the diameter of the known world.

After making due allowance for this admitted vagueness and laxity, it will be seen that the only instance in which any very serious error is involved in the line of the assumed parallel is in regard to the position of the Sicilian Strait, which is brought down nearly into the latitude of Malta. But so grave an error in regard to a place which must have been so familiar to the Greeks, sufficiently shows how little attempt could as yet be made to base these geographical conclusions upon trustworthy *data*. In the present instance the mistake made by Eratosthenes was continued by almost all subsequent geographers till the time of Ptolemy.[9]

Closely connected with this error was the false conception formed by all the earlier Greek geographers of the north coast of Africa, which they supposed to have a nearly uniform

---

[7] Hence we find him (as reported by Strabo) continually referring to this line, sometimes as the parallel *through Rhodes*, at others as that *through Athens*, without naming any other points. In one instance only does he designate it by the fuller description as ἡ διὰ Στηλῶν καὶ Ἀθηνῶν καὶ Ῥόδου γραμμή (ιι. 1, § 24, p. 79)

The strange false reading that had found its way into all our MSS. of Strabo, in several of the other passages, where ὁ δι' Ἀθηνῶν κύκλος had been corrupted into ὁ διὰ Οἰνῶν κύκλος or παράλληλος, and had remained uncorrected by all editors down to Kramer, had the effect not only of introducing into the geography of Eratosthenes a name first known to the writers of the Roman Empire, and of which no mention is found in the description of India and the far East, where it would have found its appropriate place, but of referring to this remote and unknown locality as a familiar designation for this important parallel The correction of these passages by Kramer (followed by the most recent editors) so as to accord with the correct reading found in others precisely similar, has had the effect of removing one of the greatest stumbling-blocks to the student of ancient geography. (See Kramer's note on Strabo, ιι. p 65)

[8] Strabo, ιι. 1, p. 87. The real difference is much greater; Athens being situated in 37° 58′ N latitude, while the city of Rhodes was in 36° 26′; but Eratosthenes, like all the other Greek geographers, brought down the promontory of Sunium, and with it the whole of Attica, and Athens itself, much too far to the south.

[9] Hipparchus was indeed an exception, who brought down the parallel passing through Rhodes (corresponding with that in question) considerably to the south of Syracuse (Strabo, ιι. p 134) Strabo, however, recurred to the erroneous view of Eratosthenes.

direction from east to west, with the exception of the two bays called the Syrtes, which they regarded as mere indentations, thus ignoring altogether the manner in which that coast projects to the northward in the neighbourhood of Carthage. Carthage itself was thus placed far to the south of its true position,[1] while the island of Sicily was brought down to meet it; it being well known that the interval between the two was not very considerable.

§ 13. Having thus drawn one main line through the whole length of the Mediterranean from the Strait of the Columns to the Gulf of Issus, Eratosthenes next proceeded to draw a meridian line at right angles to it, passing through Alexandria and Rhodes, which he considered to be on the same meridian. This assumption involved in the first instance an error of considerable amount, the city of Rhodes being really situated more than a degree and a half of longitude to the west of Alexandria, while Syene, which (as we have already seen) he also regarded as on the same meridian, lay in reality three degrees to the east of it. Producing this line in both directions, he conceived it as passing through Meroe to the south (which is really situated very nearly in the same longitude with Syene), and thence up the course of the Nile to the land of the Sembritæ, the remotest people in this direction of whom he had any knowledge. Northwards again from Rhodes it was supposed to pass through Byzantium (which lies in fact between the meridians of Alexandria and Rhodes) to the mouth of the Borysthenes, a very vague designation, as that river forms an extensive estuary, the whole of which however lies two or three degrees farther to the east than Byzantium.[2]

---

[1] Strabo supposed Carthage to be only 900 stadia or 90 G. miles to the north of the parallel of Alexandria, though there is in reality a difference of more than five degrees and a half of latitude between the two cities (Strabo, ii p 133)¹ It is remarkable that this erroneous position of a city so well known to navigators appears to have been founded on supposed astronomical observations with the gnomon (Strabo, *l. c*) See the passage cited in Note A, p. 661.

[2] If the Greek city of Olbia or Olbiopolis, situated near the mouth of the Borysthenes, was the point referred to

§ 14. At the same time this erroneous conception of the relative position of these points in longitude was combined with equally mistaken ideas of their distance in latitude, which had the effect of placing the mouth of the Borysthenes 9350 stadia to the north of Rhodes; while the real interval in latitude between the two, is only about 10½ degrees, or 630 G. miles. It is evident how defective a map must necessarily prove, which was based in the first instance on such *data* as these; but it cannot be denied that in his whole course of proceeding Eratosthenes showed a clear comprehension of the problem which presents itself to the scientific geographer, and the method he pursued was undoubtedly the best that was possible for him under the disadvantages in which he found himself. It was the want of trustworthy observations for latitude and longitude, and the extremely defective character of all calculations of distances, that opposed an insuperable barrier to the attainment of anything like scientific accuracy.

The Greeks were undoubtedly familiar at this period with the use of the gnomon in determining latitudes, and as we have seen in the case of Alexandria, such observations, when carefully made, were susceptible of a considerable degree of accuracy: but this was rarely the case, and in the majority of those instances—very few in number as they are—in which we know that such observations were actually made, the result is far from satisfactory.[3] More generally the latitude seems to have been inferred from the determination of the length of the day at the summer or winter solstice, a method which could give at best but a rough approximation, and which was greatly vitiated by the very imperfect means at the command of ancient astronomers for the measurement of time. But defective as these modes of observation were, they would still have offered a comparatively trustworthy basis, had there been a

---

—which is probable, as it was the only spot where any observations could have been made—the error in longitude would be just about three degrees.

[3] Note A, p 661.

sufficient number even of such rough observations available: but this was certainly not the case, and the whole course of the subsequent discussion of the positions assumed by Eratosthenes sufficiently proves how little reliance was placed on authorities of this kind by succeeding geographers.

§ 15. But if the means at the command of Eratosthenes for the determination of latitudes were thus imperfect, far more was this the case with regard to longitudes. Here indeed the want of any precise mode of observing diurnal time, or of comparing such observations with one another, was absolutely fatal. Hipparchus indeed had the sagacity to point out that the observation of eclipses might be applied to this object; but even if the idea had occurred to earlier astronomers, it is certain that no observations had been made with such a view; and the few general notices of such phenomena were wholly destitute of the accuracy requisite for scientific objects. Even in the time of Ptolemy, more than three centuries later, we shall find that scarcely any observations of this kind were available.[4]

The entire want of any accurate knowledge of longitudes, even in the case of well-known localities, is sufficiently proved by the circumstance that Eratosthenes placed Carthage and the Sicilian Strait on the same meridian with Rome, though the one lies more than two degrees to the west, the other more than three degrees to the east of that city![5] The effect of this error, combined with the one already noticed in regard to the latitude of the Sicilian Strait, was of course totally to distort the map of this part of the Mediterranean.

---

[4] See Ptol *Geogr* i, c 4 The most noted example of such observations, to which even Ptolemy refers as a typical instance, was that of the celebrated eclipse that occurred before the battle of Arbela (B C. 331), which was said to have been observed at Arbela *at the fifth hour,* and at Carthage *at the second hour* This would imply an interval of forty-five degrees of longitude between the two cities, the real difference being less than thirty-four degrees! So that the error amounts to just about one-fourth of the whole distance. The vagueness of the observation is in this case sufficiently attested by the form in which it is reported

[5] Strabo, ii. p. 93 Yet Strabo, while censuring Eratosthenes for his inaccuracy in this respect, himself falls into the grave error of placing Rome *far* to the west of Carthage.

§ 16. At the same time that the means of correcting a map by the only secure criterion—the determination of latitudes and longitudes—was thus in great measure wanting; even the measurement of ordinary distances was, as we have already had repeated occasion to observe, of the rudest description. And this was especially the case with regard to distances by sea. We have seen that the ancient navigators had no means of determining their progress analogous to the modern log, so that the computation of distances by sea was really nothing more than rendering the number of days or nights' voyage by a rough estimate into stadia. This was the method avowedly employed by Scylax, and doubtless also by Timosthenes, upon whose statements Eratosthenes appears to have in great measure relied for the geography of the Mediterranean.[6] Imperfect as such a process would be, it would still give something like an approximation to the truth, wherever the voyage was one that was frequently or habitually made: in other cases it would be altogether uncertain. When we compare the principal distances given by Eratosthenes in the Mediterranean with the results of modern observation, we shall find the fluctuations arising from these causes very much what might have been expected.

Thus the distance from the Straits of Gibraltar to Carthage is estimated at 8000 stadia, and that from Carthage to the Canopic mouth of the Nile, just beyond Alexandria, at 13,500 stadia. The former of these, which agrees with the computation of Scylax, is a very fair approximation to the truth, while the latter, though considerably in excess, if compared with the direct distance, according to the course which a modern vessel would pursue, is not materially so, if we allow for the principal sinuosities of the coast, of which the ancient navigators were in this instance unaware. The whole length of the Mediterranean was apparently computed by Eratosthenes at 26,500 stadia;[7] an estimate naturally in excess of the truth,

---

[6] See Chapter XV. p. 580.
[7] This number is indeed nowhere given *directly*, but results from the combination of the distance from

as it was arrived at by adding together distances from point to point, estimated according to the course of navigation, and then computing the whole, as if they formed one continuous and uniform line. Yet, notwithstanding this grave defect in the mode of calculation, the error in excess is by no means so great as might be expected.[8] The distance from the Straits to Issus comprises in reality about $41\frac{1}{2}$ degrees of longitude, which would give in round numbers a little more than 2,000 geographical miles, or 20,000 stadia, for the length of the Mediterranean, as measured along the same parallel of latitude. It would be indeed impossible in reality to sail in a direct course from the one extremity to the other, on account of the projection of the African coast to the north; but of this Eratosthenes was unaware. Hence one unavoidable source of error in his computation.

But erroneous as the result thus attained may appear, when compared with our improved modern methods of calculation, it is remarkable that it is not only much nearer the truth than that adopted by Ptolemy three centuries later, but it is actually a better approximation than was arrived at by modern geographers till about two centuries ago. While Eratosthenes made the length of the Mediterranean about 6000 stadia, or 600 geographical miles, too great—an error of rather more than one-fifth—it is a fact that the best modern maps in use, as late as the year 1668, assigned it a length of *fifteen degrees* in excess of the truth, or nearly *one-third* greater than the reality.[9]

§ 17. A few of the other more important distances given by Eratosthenes will tend to show how far he had arrived at a reasonably correct idea of the map of the Mediterranean.

Rhodes (which Eratosthenes looked on as on the same meridian with Alexandria) to Issus, with those already cited from the Straits to the Canopic mouth.

[8] Note B, p. 662.

[9] Gossellin, *Géographie des Grecs analysée*, p. 42. The maps published by M Sanson in 1668 placed the Gulf of Issus 60° of longitude from Cape St. Vincent. The real interval is just about 45°, Cape St Vincent being in 9° W. long, and the Gulf of Issus being intersected by the meridian of 36° E. longitude.

Thus we find that he reckoned 7000 stadia from the Pillars of Hercules to Massilia, and 6000 to the Pyrenees—that is to the point where these mountains abut on the Mediterranean. Both distances are below the truth, but present a very fair approximation, if they are measured on the map without following the minor sinuosities of the coast. On the other hand his estimate of the length of the Euxine from the Bosphorus to the mouth of the Phasis was 8000 stadia, though the distance is really less than 600 G. miles (6000 stadia):[1] but to this he added 600 stadia more for the distance from the Phasis to Dioscurias, which he, in common with all the other Greek geographers, regarded as the easternmost extremity of the Euxine.[2]

§ 18. But while Eratosthenes possessed pretty accurate knowledge of the shores of Spain and Gaul that border the Mediterranean, his information as to the rest of those countries was very imperfect. His knowledge of the western regions of Europe, and the shores of the Atlantic, was indeed derived almost exclusively from Pytheas, to whom, as we have seen, he was far from attaching unlimited credit; but he regarded his account as on the whole the most trustworthy that he possessed, and it is certain that in many respects his information was more correct than that of several later geographers.

He even followed Pytheas in regard to Thule, the existence of which he clearly admitted: and adopted the statement of the same author with respect to the length of the solstitial days and nights in that island.[3] Hence he was justly led to

---

[1] It is probable that an exaggerated idea of the length of the Euxine had become *traditional* among the Greeks, like so many similar errors. We have seen how greatly it was over-rated by Herodotus (see Chapter VI p. 177)

[2] The permanence of this error, in which even Strabo participated, serves to show how little care was bestowed by ancient navigators upon correct bearings, and, consequently, how little assistance they could derive from these in determining their longitudes.

Dioscurias, which was placed both by Eratosthenes and Strabo 600 stadia (60 G miles) *east* of the mouth of the Phasis, was really situated to the N.N W. from that point, and about 20 G. miles farther *west*

[3] It must also have been from Pytheas that Eratosthenes derived the statement that to the inhabitants of Thule the arctic circle (in the Greek sense of the term) coincided with the tropic (ap. Strab 11. 5, § 8, p. 114)

infer that the parallel of Thule was the most northerly with which he was acquainted, and placed it 11,500 stadia to the north of that passing through the mouth of the Borysthenes— a conclusion for which he is severely taken to task by Strabo,[4] though it in reality comes very near the truth.[5] At the same time he placed the northern part of Gaul on the same parallel with the Borysthenes; which last, as we have already seen, he erroneously placed considerably too far to the north.

But the error resulting from this cause was not very material: and though it had the effect of *elongating* the great island of Britain much beyond the truth, it is certain that the map of these western regions as conceived by Eratosthenes, had considerably more resemblance to the reality than that afterwards drawn by Strabo.[6] It is remarkable that no mention is found either in the extant notices of Eratosthenes, or of his guide and predecessor Pytheas, of the second of the two great British islands, Ierne.[7] But no negative inference can safely be drawn from this, on account of the fragmentary character of these notices.

Eratosthenes appears to have had no accurate knowledge of the regions north of the Euxine, so as to have any definite points in this part of the world to compare with those in the west of Europe. Observations would doubtless be here entirely

---

[4] i 4, p. 63.
[5] The real difference in latitude between the mouth of the Borysthenes and the Shetland Islands (supposing them to be the Thule of Pytheas) does not exceed $13\frac{1}{2}°$ of latitude, or about 810 G. miles. but if Thule be placed, as Eratosthenes supposed it to be, under the arctic circle, the difference would be about 20° or 12,000 stadia
[6] Yet Strabo confidently asserts that Timosthenes and Eratosthenes "were utterly ignorant" concerning Spain and Gaul, and still more so in regard to Germany and Britain (τελέως ἠγνόουν τά τε 'Ιβηρικὰ καὶ τὰ Κελτικὰ, κυρίῳ δὲ μᾶλλον τὰ Γερμανικὰ καὶ τὰ Βρεττανικά Strab. 11. 1, p. 93).

[7] The names of Albion and Ierne are found (as has been already mentioned, p 398) in the treatise *De Mundo* (περὶ Κόσμου), ascribed to Aristotle, but that work is unquestionably spurious, and belongs to a much later period The name of Ierne is first found *among extant authors* in Strabo, though there can be little doubt it was known long before. Polybius uses the expression "the British Islands" (αἱ Βρεταννικαὶ νῆσοι, 111 57), showing clearly that he was aware of the existence of more than one of them. Unfortunately the part of his work containing a fuller account of them is lost (see Chapter XVII.).

wanting: but it appears singular that the long continued intercourse of the Greek colonies with the Scythian tribes of the interior had not led to any increased geographical knowledge in this quarter. Eratosthenes must indeed probably have known, as well as Strabo, that the mouth of the Tanais lay considerably to the north of that of the Borysthenes, but we do not find that any notice was taken of this fact in arranging the distances for his map of the world.

He was equally unacquainted with the northern shores of Germany, and though he certainly supposed that there was continuous sea to the north of Europe, as well as Asia, this was either a mere hypothetical inference, or a conclusion from the erroneous idea that Pytheas had sailed along these northern shores as far as the Tanais. So far as we are able to judge, his knowledge of the extensive regions to the north of the Danube and the Alps was of the vaguest and most imperfect character. We learn only from an incidental notice that he mentioned the name of the Hercynian forest;[8] by which he probably meant the Black Forest, in which the Danube takes its rise. The same statement, as we have seen, is already found in the treatise *De Mirabilibus* ascribed to Aristotle.

§ 19. The parallel of Thule being thus taken for the most northern limit of the habitable world, that which passed through the land of the Sembritæ on the Upper Nile was assumed to be the southernmost. This parallel was placed by Eratosthenes 3400 stadia to the south of Meroë—which would bring it down to the south of Sennaar—and he correctly estimated that the same parallel, if produced eastwards, would pass through the Land of Cinnamon, and the easternmost promontory of Africa, which was also at that time the most southerly point of the continent known to navigators. He further assumed—for here he had unquestionably no real information—that Taprobane, the southernmost land of which he had heard in connection with Asia, lay on the same parallel

---

[8] Cæsar, *B. G* vi. 24.

with the Region of Cinnamon, so that this line passed through all the most remote regions towards the south, and might thus be fairly taken as the southern limit of the habitable world.[9]

It is unfortunate that we do not know with certainty at what distance from the Equator Eratosthenes conceived this line to be drawn, but it may be inferred from a comparison of other authorities that he fixed it at 8300 stadia from the equinoctial line:[1] a position very near the truth, if we suppose Eratosthenes to have here been calculating by his own estimate of 700 stadia to a degree, as in this case he would naturally do.[2]

§ 20. The other distances along his principal meridian line he estimated as follows: from Meroë to Syene 5000 stadia; from Syene to Alexandria 5000; from Alexandria to Rhodes 3750; from Rhodes to the Hellespont 4350; and from thence to the mouth of the Borysthenes 5000; thus giving as the sum total 26,500 stadia from his southernmost parallel to the Borysthenes, or, with the addition of the 11,500 stadia assumed from thence to the parallel of Thule, 38,000 stadia for the total width of the habitable world.

Of these distances that from Alexandria to Rhodes was the result of a gnomonic observation made by Eratosthenes himself[3] —the distance having previously been estimated *by navigators* at 4000, or according to others as much as 5000 stadia—a striking instance of the vagueness of their mode of reckoning.[4] The distance from Syene to Alexandria was *supposed* to have

---

[9] The information possessed by the Greeks in the time of Eratosthenes concerning the peninsula of India, and still more concerning Taprobane itself, was so utterly vague and erroneous that it is impossible to regard this assumption as more than a lucky guess, founded on the belief that Taprobane was the most southerly portion of Asia, and perhaps confirmed by the notion (utterly unfounded in itself) of that great island extending from east to west towards the Land of Cinnamon

[1] Note C, p 664

[2] A line drawn through the Land of Cinnamon and the south of Sennaar would about coincide with the parallel of 12° N. latitude Of course this would give 8400 stadia as the distance from the equator, reckoning 700 stadia to a degree. The result adopted by Eratosthenes therefore, whatever the process by which he arrived at it, differed from the truth only by 100 stadia, or 10 G. miles

[3] Note D, p. 665.

[4] Strabo, 11. 5, p. 125

been measured, though, as we have already seen, it was really wide of the truth; the position of Meroe also had been determined by astronomical observation; but all the others could only be the result of vague computation from the distances estimated by navigators.

The effect of such a mode of computation would be unquestionably to exaggerate the distance; but it seems incredible that such a geographer as Eratosthenes should have taken the actual distances traversed on such a circuitous voyage as that from Rhodes to the mouth of the Borysthenes, and added them together in order to obtain the direct distance, or interval of latitude between the two points. Yet even this hypothesis fails to explain the full amount of the discrepancy. The distance from Rhodes to the Hellespont, as measured on the map by the nearest course that would be possible for a vessel to pursue, on account of intervening headlands and islands, is (in round numbers) only about 300 G. miles, or 3000 stadia instead of 4350; that from the Hellespont to the Bosphorus, about 150 miles; and from the Bosphorus to the Borysthenes, where it was easy to pursue a direct course, about 390; thus giving a total result of 8400 stadia, instead of the 9350 assigned by Eratosthenes.

At the same time it must be observed that the effect of this excess in the computation of the distances was in great part neutralized, *as affecting the latitudes,* by his erroneous allowance of 700 stadia to a degree. Hence he placed the mouth of the Borysthenes in 48° N. latitude, which is only about 1½° to the north of its true position.

§ 21. In continuing the line which he had assumed as his main parallel of latitude, from the Gulf of Issus eastward across the continent of Asia, Eratosthenes encountered difficulties of another kind. Here, however, he derived important assistance from the conquests of Alexander, and the itineraries of those who had accompanied him, as well as from the statements of Patrocles, who (as we have seen) had himself held important governments in Upper Asia. He conceived the line in question to be carried from Issus to Thapsacus on the Euphrates, thence to the Pylæ Caspiæ, next, to the foot of the Indian Caucasus, and from thence in a straight line to the Indian Ocean. Throughout its whole length he regarded this line as nearly coinciding with the southern foot of Mount Taurus, which he considered as a vast range of mountains, occupying in parts a width of not less than 2000 stadia, and stretching in a direct line, nearly parallel with the equator, from the interior of Lycia and Cilicia, where they were familiar to the Greeks, north of the plains of Mesopotamia and Assyria, as well as of the table land of Persia, and the plains of India, till they ultimately ended in the unknown ocean that formed the eastern boundary of Asia.

Imperfect as was such a view, there can be no doubt that we trace in it some approach to a true conception of the leading facts in the geography of Asia, and to that systematic grouping of the subordinate ranges of mountains, without which it is impossible to form a clear idea of the physical geography of a great continent. It is perfectly true that the range of Mount Taurus, which occupies so prominent a position throughout the south of Asia Minor, is connected with the lofty mountain ranges of Armenia and Koordistan, and through them with the range of Elbourz to the south of the Caspian, which is again connected, though more irregularly, with the stupendous range that was known to the Greeks by the names of Caucasus and Imaus, and was justly regarded as forming a continuous mountain barrier to the north of India. The course of this vast mountain system is indeed very far removed from the regular and uniform direction which was ascribed to it by Eratosthenes, and it is connected with various other mountain chains, some of them of great height, that branch off to the north and south, of which comparatively little notice was taken by the Alexandrian geographer: but the great leading fact that Asia is traversed in about the latitude supposed, by a broad belt of mountains, was rightly conceived, and tended to throw much light upon its physical configuration.

Nor do the leading points through which Eratosthenes drew his assumed line deviate very widely from the required position. If we take as before the parallel of 36° to represent the line in question, we shall find that it passes a very few miles to the north of Thapsacus on the Euphrates, and after traversing the mountain regions of Koordistan and the plains of Media, passes within less than a degree north of the Pylæ Caspiæ, and about the same distance to the north of the Hindoo Koosh, where it was traversed by Alexander.[5] From this point indeed the great chain of the Himalayas trends away rapidly to the south-east—a fact of which Eratosthenes was wholly ignorant. He accordingly regarded the mountain chain as still preserving its direction from west to east, in accordance with the supposed course of the Ganges, which was believed by all the Greek geographers at this period to hold a due easterly course to its outflow in the eastern ocean.

§ 22. The distances as computed by Eratosthenes along this main parallel were: from Issus to the Euphrates 1300 stadia;[6] from the Euphrates to the Pylæ Caspiæ 10,000 stadia; thence to the foot of the Caucasus 14,000; and from thence to the mouth of the Ganges 16,000 stadia.[7] These distances were almost all based upon the itineraries of Alexander and his generals, or, in the case of India, upon those which had been furnished to Seleucus. They therefore inevitably laboured under the disadvantage of being *itinerary* distances, converted into rectilinear ones, and laid down on the map as such, without attempting to correct them either by observations of longitude, or by any trigonometrical measurements, neither of which were at the command of the Greek geo-

---

[5] The parallel of 36° actually passes about 50 miles south of the Caspian Sea, and the same distance south of Balkh, the ancient Bactra. It is just about a degree to the north of the city founded by Alexander at the foot of the Caucasus, which may very probably have been the point intended by Eratosthenes under the vague general designation of "the Indian Caucasus"

[6] No indication is here given of the point on the Euphrates intended; but it is probable that Thapsacus is meant as being the customary place of passage In that case the distance is almost precisely correct, as measured on the map in a direct line, without any allowance for itinerary excess.

[7] Ap Strab 1 4, § 5, p. 64

grapher. The consequence is, as might be expected, that the distances greatly exceed the truth, and we cannot be surprised to find that in this instance the error is far greater than in regard to the length of the Mediterranean.[8] But defective as were the materials at the command of Eratosthenes for all this part of Asia, they were nevertheless considered so valuable that two centuries later Strabo was still content implicitly to follow him, because he could obtain no better information.[9]

The whole sum of the distances thus computed by Eratosthenes for the length of the habitable world, from the Sacred Promontory to the eastern extremity of India gave a result of 70,800 stadia. To this he added 2000 stadia more to the west of the Sacred Promontory—apparently with the view of allowing for the supposed projection of the coast of Gaul beyond that of Spain[1]—and again 5000 more to the eastward, where he considered the extreme point of India to project to the south-east, so as to be 3000 stadia east of the extremity of his main parallel. By these additions he attained a total sum of 77,800 stadia; thus making the length slightly to exceed twice the assumed breadth.[2]

---

[8] In attempting, however, to compare these distances with the reality we labour under the great difficulty of not knowing the precise line of route along which they were measured; and any line of march likely to be followed by an army would of necessity be extremely circuitous. The *direct* distance, as measured on the map from Thapsacus to the Pylæ Caspiæ but little exceeds 620 G. miles or 6200 stadia: while that from the Pylæ to Alexandria at the foot of the Caucasus gives only about 970 G. miles or 9700 stadia. The excess of the itinerary distances employed by Eratosthenes amounts therefore in the one case to more than *two sevenths*, in the other to nearly *two fifths* of the whole. The whole interval *in longitude* between the Gulf of Issus and the foot of the Hindoo Koosh, which was what he in reality was attempting to estimate, is in fact only about 33°, which in lat 36° is equivalent to 1600 G. miles, or 16,000 stadia, instead of 25,300 stadia, which was the result of the computation of Eratosthenes.

[9] περὶ ὧν Ἐρατοσθένης οὕτως εἴρηκεν· οὐ γὰρ ἔχομέν τι λέγειν βέλτιον περὶ αὐτῶν Strabo, xv. 2, § 8, p 723.

[1] He conceived, in accordance with the erroneous view universally entertained in his time, that the Sacred Promontory (Cape St. Vincent) was the most westerly point of Spain : but he supposed, still more erroneously, that the promontory of Calbium, the westernmost point of Gaul—which evidently corresponds with one of the headlands of Finisterre in Brittany—extended still further to the west. This idea was apparently derived from Pytheas. (See Chapter XV. p 593.)

[2] It is curious that this assumption had come to be regarded so completely

§ 23. Eratosthenes undoubtedly conceived, in accordance with the prevalent belief in his day, that the Ocean was found immediately to the east of India, and that the Ganges flowed directly into it. Just to the north of the Ganges the great mountain chain of Imaus, which he regarded as the continuation of the Indian Caucasus and the Taurus, descended (according to his ideas) to the shores of the Eastern Ocean; and he appears to have given the name of Tamarus to the headland which formed the termination of this great range.[3] From that point he supposed the coast to trend away towards the north-west, so as to surround the great unknown tracts of Scythia on the north, but sending in a deep inlet to the south which formed the Caspian Sea.

Of the northern shores of Asia or Europe he had really no more knowledge than Herodotus, but, unlike that historian, he *assumed* the fact that both continents were bounded by the Ocean on the north; a fact which is undoubtedly true, but in a sense so widely different from that supposed by Eratosthenes that it can hardly be held as justifying his theory. In fact the conclusion of Eratosthenes was mainly based upon the erroneous belief that the Caspian communicated with the Ocean to the north in the same manner that the Persian Gulf did to the south; a view which was adopted by all geographers for a period of three centuries, on the authority of Patrocles.[4]

It was doubtless from the same authority that Eratosthenes derived his statement as to the dimensions of the Caspian Sea, as well as that concerning the outflow into it of the rivers Oxus and Iaxartes, which he asserts in a remarkably distinct and positive manner.[5] Yet the erroneous idea of its com-

as an admitted principle, that Strabo treats it as a matter of course that Eratosthenes, having fallen into error with regard to the breadth of the known world, *must necessarily* be wrong in respect to the length also: for that it was a fact agreed upon by all the best authorities that the length was more than double the breadth (1. 4, § 5, p. 64). Eratosthenes therefore having, as Strabo considered, exaggerated the breadth by carrying Thule to so high a latitude, was compelled to give an undue extension to the length also, in order to preserve the assumed proportion between the two.

[3] Note E, p 666
[4] See Chapter XIV p. 574.
[5] He stated that the part of the circumference of the Caspian "which

munication with the Ocean to the north sufficiently shows how far from trustworthy the information possessed by the Greeks really was.⁶

§ 24. His ideas of the geographical position and configuration of India were in great measure erroneous. He conceived it indeed to be of a rhomboidal form, which may be regarded as a rough approximation to the truth, and he even knew that the two sides which enclosed the southern extremity were longer than the other two. But as he supposed the range of Imaus that bounded the country to the north to have its direction from west to east, while the Indus flowed from north to south, he was obliged to shift round the position of his rhomb, so as to bring the other two sides approximately parallel to the two thus assumed. Hence he conceived the projecting angle of India to have a direction towards the south-east, instead of the south, and even (as we have already seen) supposed it to advance farther towards the east than the mouth of the Ganges. He appears in fact to have obtained—probably from the information collected by Patrocles—a correct general idea of the great projection of India in a southerly direction towards Cape Comorin, but was unable to reconcile this with his previously conceived notions as to its western and northern boundaries, and was thus constrained altogether to distort its position in order to make it agree with what he regarded as established conclusions. It was doubtless from the same source that he had learnt the name of the Coniaci, as the people inhabiting this southernmost point of India;⁷ a name which henceforward became generally received, with slight modifications, by ancient geographers.

He was familiar also with the name of Taprobane, which

---

was well known to the Greeks" (τὸν ὑπὸ τῶν Ἑλλήνων γνώριμον) was 5400 stadia in extent; that from thence along the coasts of the Anariaci (?), the Mardi, and Hyrcanians *as far as the mouth of the Oxus* was 4800 stadia, and *thence to the Iaxartes* 2400 (Strabo, xi 6, § 1, p. 507) Patrocles had stated the latter distance at 80 parasangs (Id xi 11, § 5), which exactly coincides with the distance given by Eratosthenes

⁶ To this may be added their ignorance of the great river Volga, the name of which is first found in Ptolemy.
⁷ Ap Strab xv. 1, p 689

had indeed been known to the Greeks since the days of Alexander, but his ideas of its position were extremely erroneous, as he placed it south of the headland of the Coniaci (Cape Comorin), at a distance of seven days' voyage from the main land, and extending for a space of 8000 stadia in length, *from east to west*, towards the extreme point of the Cinnamon Region on the coast of Africa.[8] At the same time he placed the two (as already noticed) in the same latitude, as the most southerly regions of the inhabited world.

§ 25. Imperfect as was the geographical knowledge of India possessed by Eratosthenes, it was not surpassed by any later geographer, until after the time of Strabo. He was also the first to bring together anything like definite information with regard to Arabia, a country which on account of its proximity to Egypt, could not fail to attract in a high degree the attention of the Greeks under the Ptolemies. We have seen that Alexander, at the time of his death, was preparing a voyage of discovery for the circumnavigation of the great peninsula of Arabia. The project thus interrupted was not resumed by any of his successors; but although we have no account of any regular expedition by which the coasts of Arabia, from the entrance of the Persian Gulf to the Straits of Bab-el-Mandeb, were examined and surveyed, in the manner that the coast from the mouth of the Indus to that of the Euphrates had been by Nearchus, there appears no doubt that the circumnavigation had been accomplished. It is probable indeed (as has been already shown) that the Greek traders from Alexandria did not usually extend their voyages beyond the southern coast of Arabia Felix; but this does not exclude the possibility of a few more adventurous spirits having continued them to the Persian Gulf, or even to India itself.[9] But even if this navigation were in practice confined to native

---

[8] Ap Strab xv 1, p 690.
[9] The voyage of Eudoxus, who undoubtedly visited India in person, did not take place till after the time of Eratosthenes

traders from the Sabæan ports, it would doubtless be easy for the Greeks to obtain from them sufficient information to ascertain in a general way the extent and character of the Arabian peninsula. The fact that it presented no very serious difficulties to the navigator was in any case sufficiently proved by the existence of this trade. Hence Eratosthenes had no difficulty in arriving at a general notion of Arabia so far as the sea-coasts were concerned.

The peculiar characteristics of the interior of that country presented the same obstacles to a more extensive acquaintance in ancient times that they have continued to do down to our own days. But the proximity of two such flourishing and civilized states as the Egyptian monarchy on the one hand, and the Syrian monarchy, with its seat at Babylon or Seleucia, on the other, could not fail to exercise considerable influence even on the wild tribes of Arabia. In consequence of this we find that a considerable commerce had developed itself, which was carried on by caravans across the deserts from one side of the peninsula to the other. Thus Gerrha, on the western coast of the Persian Gulf, had already become an important centre of trade; the spices and other productions of the southern districts of Arabia, as well as of the opposite coasts of Africa being brought thither by caravans, and afterwards sent on from thence to Babylon and Seleucia.[1] These caravans took forty days for the overland journey from Hadramaut.[2] Other similar caravans carried on the communication from Ælana, at the head of the eastern branch of the Red Sea (now called the Gulf of Akabah), through the western portions of Arabia, and reached the district of the Minæans in seventy days. Ælana was the port of Petra, which seems to have been already rising into importance as an emporium of trade : and from thence other caravans boldly struck across the desert direct to Babylon, a distance estimated by Eratosthenes at 5600 stadia.[3]

§ 26. His general description of the physical characters of

---

[1] Eratosthen. ap Strab xvi 3, p 766
[2] Ibid. 4, § 4, p. 768.
[3] Ibid. § 2, p. 767.

Arabia is very correct. The northern portions of the peninsula, bordering on Judæa and Cœle Syria, were barren and sandy, producing only a few palm-trees, thorny acacias and tamarisks, and devoid of running water, but having wells from distance to distance. The inhabitants were wandering tribes of Arabs, dwelling in tents and subsisting on their herds of camels. The more southern districts, on the other hand, which felt the influence of the ocean, and were subject to periodical rains in summer, were fertile and produced abundance both of grain and cattle.[4] This portion of Arabia was divided into four districts, inhabited by four principal tribes: the Minæans adjoining the Red Sea, whose chief city was Carna or Carnana; the Sabæans, whose capital was Mariaba; the Catabanians, extending to the Straits of Bab-el-Mandeb; and the Chatramotitæ, the furthest to the east, whose capital was Sabata.[5] The name of this last people is evidently still retained in that of Hadramaut; of the others, the Minæans were apparently the occupants of the Hedjaz: while the Sabæans unquestionably held the fertile district of Yemen, the chief city of which retained the name of Mareb till a late period. The site of the Cattabanians is clearly indicated, but their name is otherwise little known. According to Eratosthenes their territory produced frankincense, while myrrh was brought from that of the Chatramotitæ,[6] both of which were important articles of export; but it is probable that the greater part of these aromatic spices were in reality brought from the opposite coast of Africa, as well as the cinnamon for which it was famous.[7]

§ 27. No settlements had been formed by the Egyptian

---

[4] There was however one remarkable exception It is strange to find him stating that these more fertile regions of Arabia possessed abundance of cattle and beasts, except *horses*, mules, and swine (Strabo, xvi 4, § 2, βοσκημάτων τε ἀφθονιά, πλὴν ἵππων καὶ ἡμιόνων καὶ ὑῶν). Nor is there any allusion to horses being more frequent among the wandering tribes of the interior

[5] Eratosthen. ap. Strab. xvi. 4, § 2.

[6] Id. ibid 4, § 4.

[7] It may be observed that Nearchus, when he came in sight of the headland of Maceta—the easternmost promontory of Arabia—was told that it was *from thence* (i e from Arabia) that *cinnamon* and other similar productions (τὰ κινάμωμά τε καὶ ἄλλα τοιουτότροπα) were conveyed to Babylon and Assyria (Arrian, *Indica*, c. 32, § 7).

monarchs upon the Arabian coast of the Red Sea, but the African side had, as we have already seen, been lined by an almost continuous chain of trading stations, forming permanent settlements, though prevented by the barrenness of the adjoining tracts from ever rising into colonies of importance. Hence Eratosthenes was well acquainted with the extent and dimensions of the Red Sea, which he describes as extending 9000 stadia from the head of the gulf adjoining Heroopolis (the Gulf of Suez) to the station of Ptolemais Epitheras, and 4500 from thence to the Straits. Both statements are very fair approximations, the former, however, somewhat exceeding, while the latter rather falls short of, the truth.[8] He also estimated the distance from the Straits of Bab-el-Mandeb to the extremity of the Cinnamon Region (Cape Guardafui) at 5000 stadia—a very close approach to the truth. But he appears to have had no knowledge of the coast of Africa beyond that point, which indeed continued until long after to be the farthest limit of Greek navigation in that direction.[9]

§ 28. We have already seen how greatly the knowledge of the upper course of the Nile and its tributaries had advanced under the Ptolemies. This was in part the consequence of direct exploration from Egypt, but still more from the establishment of a comparatively civilized state at Meroe, which carried on considerable intercourse both up and down the river. It is evident also that Meroe maintained direct communication with the Red Sea, from which it was distant only ten or twelve days' journey:[1] and it was this communication that enabled Eratos-

---

[8] Ibid § 4, 768 He appears, however, in one respect to have formed an erroneous idea of the figure of the Red Sea, which he conceived to have a direction nearly due N. and S from Heroopolis to Ptolemais Epitheras, and thence to trend away to the S E The general direction of this vast inlet is in reality remarkably uniform throughout its whole length from N N W. to S S E But the notion entertained by Eratosthenes of its forming a considerable bend or elbow at the point mentioned, was received by all ancient geographers down even to the time of Ptolemy

[9] Thus Strabo writing on the authority of Artemidorus, a century later than Eratosthenes, speaks of the coast towards the south, after doubling the Southern Horn (Cape Guardafui), as wholly unknown (p 774)

[1] Eratosth ap Strab xvii. 1, p 786 At the present day there is a regular

thenes to connect his observations on the Upper Nile with those on the Red Sea, where he placed Ptolemais Epitheras on the same parallel with Meroe. At the same time he correctly placed Meroë itself at just about the same distance from Syene that the latter was from Alexandria.[2] With the intermediate part of the course of the Nile he was well acquainted, and described clearly the great bend made by the river between Meroe and the Second Cataract—an important feature in the geography of this part of Africa, which has only become known to modern geographers in quite recent times.[3]

The knowledge possessed by Eratosthenes of the relations between the Nile and its tributaries was not indeed, as has been already pointed out,[4] altogether free from confusion, arising principally from the different names given by the native tribes to the different branches of the river, and even to different portions of the main stream. But with due allowance for this source of error it must be admitted that the information of Eratosthenes was not only superior to that of any ancient writer down to the time of Ptolemy, but was much more correct than that possessed by modern geographers until a very recent period.[5] Thus he clearly understood that the so-called "island" of Meroe was formed by the junction of two streams, the easternmost of which was the Astaboras (still called the Atbara), and the westernmost the Astapus, though according to others its proper name was the Astasobas, while

---

caravan trade from Suakin to Berber on the right bank of the Nile, just below its confluence with the Atbara, and about 60 G. miles below Meroe.

[2] This was probably derived from the astronomical determination of its position already referred to (see Note A). But there must have been at this period a more direct caravan route in use, as is the case at the present day, without following the circuitous course of the Nile, and this would afford the means of direct measurement, or rather computation of the distance.

[3] Colonel Leake observes that "the remarkable bend of the Nile in Nubia here described by Eratosthenes was first verified in modern times by the information procured by Burckhardt" (*Journal of Geogr. Soc.* vol. ii. p. 24).

[4] Chapter XV. p 584.

[5] M. Gosselin, writing near the end of the last century, observes "Quant au Nil, Eratosthenes décrit la partie supérieure de son cours avec assez d'exactitude pour que, depuis son siècle, on n'ait rien eu d'important à y ajouter, ni à y corriger" (*Géographie des Grecs analysée*, p 21). This first volume of his work was published in 1790.

the name of Astapus properly belonged to another branch which flowed from certain lakes to the south, and formed in fact the main and direct stream of the Nile itself.[6] We have here a distinct indication of the White Nile, or Bahr-el-Abiad; and this is confirmed by the mention of another "island" formed by the confluence of two streams, higher up than that of Meroë, which was inhabited by the Sembritæ, the descendants of an Egyptian colony. This can clearly be no other than the district of Sennaar, comprised between the two main branches of the river, the Blue and White Nile.[7]

Of the highlands of Abyssinia on the contrary he appears to have had no knowledge; though he was certainly not ignorant of the existence of mountains in that direction, and correctly ascribed the periodical inundation of the Nile to the regular rains that fell in these elevated regions within the tropics.[8] This theory indeed appears to have been generally adopted in his time.

It is worthy of remark that everything points to the information of Eratosthenes having been derived from the inhabitants of the valley of the Nile itself, as would naturally be the case where a civilized community was once established so far up the river as Meroe: while Ptolemy on the contrary, at a much

---

[6] Eratosthen. ap Strab xvii i. p. 786. τὸν δὲ Ἀστάπουν ἄλλον εἶναι, ῥέοντα ἔκ τινων λιμνῶν ἀπὸ μεσημβρίας, καὶ σχεδὸν τὸ κατ' εὐθεῖαν σῶμα τοῦ Νείλου τοῦτον ποιεῖν This notice appears to me conclusive against the theory of Mr Cooley (*Claudius Ptolemy and the Nile*, 8vo Lond 1854), who maintains that the ancients were altogether unacquainted with the White Nile, and that all their accounts of its upper course refer exclusively to the Blue Nile or Abyssinian river.

Apart from the direct testimony of Eratosthenes, it is most improbable that the Greeks of the second century B.C., to whom Meroe was as familiar as Khartoum is to us at the present day, should not have known of the union of the two great streams, little more than 100 miles above it

The lakes (λίμναι) from which it was supposed to flow, probably referred to the vast marshes which it forms above lat. 10°. It is very unlikely that any rumour of the Victoria and Albert Nyanza had reached his ears

[7] The comparative civilization, and skill in the mechanical arts, possessed by the natives of Sennaar at the present day, as compared with the other native tribes by which they are surrounded, is supposed by some modern writers to be derived from their Egyptian descent See Cooley's work above cited (pp 22, 23) and the authorities there referred to

[8] τὴν δὲ πλήρωσιν αὐτοῦ τοὺς θερινοὺς ὄμβρους παρασκευάζειν Strabo, *l c* Proclus *ad Platonis Timæum*, p 37.

later period, seems to have derived his accounts as to the upper course of the river from the Red Sea. Hence arises in part the difficulty of reconciling the two authors. But the statements of Eratosthenes, taken by themselves, are perfectly clear and intelligible.

He was also the first to mention the name of the Nubians (Νοῦβαι), whom he describes as occupying the country on the west of the Nile, from the neighbourhood of Meroe to the bend of the river. They were a great nation, not subject to the Æthiopians of Meroe, but forming numerous petty sovereignties of their own.[9]

§ 29. Of the rest of Africa Eratosthenes probably knew little, if anything, more than was already known to Herodotus. But as no extracts have been preserved to us from this part of his work, we can only infer that he furnished no information beyond what was in the possession of all later geographers. In one respect however he was certainly better informed than many of his successors,—that he mentioned the island of Cerne, and many other Phœnician settlements beyond the Columns of Hercules, on the west coast of Africa. His knowledge of these was probably derived from Carthaginian sources[1]: but as the settlements themselves had disappeared at a later period, the fact of their existence was disbelieved, and the statements of Eratosthenes were summarily rejected by Artemidorus and Strabo.[2]

---

[9] Ap. Strab. xvii. p 786. According to Mr Cooley (*Claudius Ptolemy and the Nile*, p 41) the name of Nubians, which is not a native appellation, was at first applied only to the natives of Kordofan (immediately west of Sennaar), and it was not till a later period that that people occupied the lower districts between Meroe and the frontiers of Egypt This would be entirely in accordance with the statement of Eratosthenes, as cited by Strabo.

[1] The voyage of Hanno had unquestionably taken place long before the time of Eratosthenes, but we have no means of judging whether it was known to the Alexandrian geographer. No allusion to it is found in Strabo; unless it be assumed to be the authority referred to in the next note.

[2] Strabo, 1. p 47 (compare xvii. p 829). πεπίστευκε δὲ καὶ περὶ τῶν ἔξω στηλῶν Ἡρακλείων πολλοῖς μυθώδεσι, Κερνήν τε νῆσον καὶ ἄλλους τόπους ὀνομάζων, τοὺς μηδαμοῦ νυνὶ δεικνυμένους. The disappearance of such a settlement as Cerne is readily explained by the parallel case of Arguin, a barren island on the same line of coast, occupied by the Portuguese for a period of centuries, and which at one time carried on a

There can be no doubt that he conceived Africa to be surrounded by the sea to the south, in accordance with the notion prevalent in his time; and which, as we have seen, was already held by Alexander himself. This much might be clearly inferred from his frequent use of the term Atlantic, as applied to the Indian Ocean; but we are distinctly told that he regarded the whole surrounding ocean as continuous, so that the Western Ocean and the Erythræan were parts of the same sea.[3] But it does not appear that he attempted to support this theoretical conclusion by a reference to known facts, and we must therefore infer that he attached no value to the alleged circumnavigation of Africa by order of Necho.[4]

§ 30. In the absence of the original work it is impossible for us to judge how far Eratosthenes entered into a detailed geographical account of the various countries of which he spoke: but as his whole treatise on geography was comprised in only three books, and the third of these alone was devoted to what can be strictly called geographical details, it is evident that any such review must have been very brief and summary. As far as the fragments preserved enable us to form a conjecture, it would appear that he certainly gave a brief enumeration of the leading geographical features of the coasts,[5] as well as of the tribes of the interior; and he undoubtedly added some notices of the natural productions of the country, or the manners and character of the inhabitants, but it is probable that these were principally confined to the more remote and less known regions of the world. His object certainly appears to have been rather to present a general picture of the world as then known, than an elaborate geographical description of

---

considerable trade, but is now utterly desolate and inhabited only by a few Arab fishermen

[3] Strabo, 1, 3, § 13, p. 56. καὶ γὰρ κατ' αὐτὸν Ἐρατοσθένη τὴν ἐκτὸς θάλατταν ἅπασαν σύρρουν εἶναι, ὥστε καὶ τὴν Ἑσπέριον καὶ τὴν Ἐρυθρὰν θάλατταν μίαν εἶναι

[4] See Chapter VIII. sect. 2.

[5] It was evidently in this part of his work that he made so much use of that of his predecessor Timosthenes, that he is accused by Marcianus of Heraclea of having plundered it bodily (Marcian. Epit. Artemidor. § 3. Ἐρατοσθένης δὲ ὁ Κυρηναῖος, οὐκ οἶδα τί παθὼν, τὸ Τιμοσθένους μετέγραψε βιβλίον, βραχέα τινὰ προσθείς). See Chapter XV. p. 588.

the different countries of which it was composed. All such details could be easily filled in at a subsequent time, if the general outlines were correctly drawn. The object of Eratosthenes was to lay a secure foundation upon which succeeding geographers could build: and so successfully did he execute this task, considering the materials at his disposition, that the map of the world, as laid down by him, received scarcely any material improvement until the time of Ptolemy.

§ 31. Another part of the system of Eratosthenes, concerning which we have very imperfect information, is his division of the inhabited world into sections, to which he gave the strange designation of Sphragides ($\sigma\phi\rho\alpha\gamma\hat{\iota}\delta\epsilon\varsigma$), or "seals." The origin of this term is unknown, and it was not adopted by any other geographer. Nor is it easy to discern what was the purpose of its introduction, or the nature of the division intended. These sections indeed had so far a relation to the fundamental parallel of latitude drawn by Eratosthenes in the manner already described, that they were all placed to the north or south of that line, so that it should form (in part at least) one of their boundaries; but in other respects they were very irregular, being neither conterminous with countries, nor with any geometrical divisions of the earth's surface. The first section indeed comprised India only, and would therefore answer the first condition. The second also might be thought to fulfil the same purpose, though much less perfectly: it comprised Ariana, under which name Eratosthenes appears to have included (as was done by Strabo after him),[6] Aria, Parthia, Drangiana, Arachosia, Gedrosia and Carmania, or all the provinces from the Indus to the frontiers of Media and Persia Proper. This section was bounded on the west by an imaginary line drawn from the Pylæ Caspiæ to the frontier of Carmania on the Persian Gulf, which Eratosthenes conceived as situated on the

---

[6] Strabo, indeed, in the description of all these countries, their boundaries and extent, distinctly follows the authority of Eratosthenes, adding that he had no better information ($o\vec{v}$ $\gamma\grave{\alpha}\rho$ $\check{\epsilon}\chi o$-$\mu\acute{\epsilon}\nu$ $\tau\iota$ $\lambda\acute{\epsilon}\gamma\epsilon\iota\nu$ $\beta\acute{\epsilon}\lambda\tau\iota o\nu$ $\pi\epsilon\rho\grave{\iota}$ $a\vec{v}\tau\hat{\omega}\nu$, xv. 2, § 8, p. 723).

same meridian. Hence the eastern and western boundaries would be approximately parallel,[7] and the whole section presents the form, roughly taken, of a parallelogram. But the third section, which was conceived to be still bounded by the chain of the Taurus on the north (continued in a supposed straight line from the Caspian Gates), and by the imaginary line above described on the east, was limited on the west by a line drawn from the Armenian mountains (the prolongation of Mount Taurus) to Thapsacus on the Euphrates and then down that river to the Persian Gulf.

Here we find no apparent connection with any national divisions; while the approach to any regularity of figure is of the most imperfect description. But this is still more the case with the fourth section, which extended from the Euphrates to the Mediterranean, and to the Isthmus of Suez on the west, while it was bounded on the south by an imaginary line across the deserts of Arabia from the head of the Red Sea to the Euphrates near Babylon. It thus presented something like a triangular form, having its base on the Mediterranean, and its vertex on the Euphrates. Unfortunately, while Strabo goes into a long and tedious discussion of the boundaries and dimensions of this section, he has omitted to continue the enumeration of these divisions, so that we are left wholly in the dark as to the nature and extent of the sections into which Eratosthenes subdivided Africa and Europe, as well as Asia north of the Taurus.[8] In the absence of such information it is very difficult to see what geographical meaning Eratosthenes attached to the subdivisions in question, or what purpose they were intended to serve.

§ 32. On one subject, which occupied an important place in

---

[7] Eratosthenes, as we have already seen, supposed the Indus to flow from N to S., while the Ganges flowed from W. to E. For this he was censured by Hipparchus, who maintained that the Indus flowed towards the south-east (Strabo, ii 1, § 34, p 87) Its real course deviates considerably to the *westward* of south, so that its mouth, taking the centre of the Delta as such. is situated 4½° of longitude to the *west* of Attock.

[8] It seems probable that the peninsula of Arabia constituted the fifth Sphragis, but this is not stated by Strabo

the work of Eratosthenes, as well as in those of many of his successors, he certainly entertained sounder and more judicious views than most of the Greek geographers. The feeling of blind reverence for Homer and his works, which had grown up in Greece itself, but had attained to a still higher development in the schools of Alexandria, had led to a belief that his statements were to be received with deference as authorities not only in matters of history and mythology, but on questions of geography also. Nor was this confined to Greece itself and the lands immediately adjoining, where the accuracy of the long array of names exhibited in the Catalogue of the Ships, and the appropriateness of the descriptive epithets so often appended to them, were the subject of well-merited eulogy;[9] but the same confidence was reposed in the statements of the poet concerning the more remote localities described in the wanderings of Ulysses and Menelaüs, and even in his casual notices of the Ethiopians and Scythians.[1]

Eratosthenes on the contrary had the boldness to assert that while Homer was well acquainted with Greece and the regions near at hand, he was ignorant of those more remote:[2] and that his narrative of the adventures of Ulysses, interwoven as it was with obvious fables, that no one could dream of understanding in their literal signification, was no more amenable to the test of geographical, than of historical truth. He appears to have given especial offence by saying that people would never find out the real localities described in the Odyssey—the islands of Æolus, Circe, Calypso, &c., until they found out the cobbler who had sewn up the bag of Æolus.[3] All these localities had, long before the time of Eratosthenes, been identified with well-known spots: and the inhabitants of the places thus pitched upon naturally clung with tenacity to the supposed traditions

---

[9] See Chapter III p. 42.
[1] This tone, as has been already remarked, pervades all the discussions of Strabo in connection with this subject.
[2] Strabo, l. 2, § 7, p 18 'Αλλ' οὐδὲ τὰ σύνεγγυς μόνον, ὥσπερ 'Ερατοσθένης εἴρηκε, καὶ τὰ ἐν τοῖς "Ελλησιν, ἀλλὰ καὶ τῶν πόρρω πολλὰ λέγει καὶ δι' ἀκριβείας "Ομηρος
[3] Strabo, l. 2, § 15

that connected them with the works of the great poet. The grammarians and critics of Alexandria sought to support these pretensions by the most far-fetched interpretations, and had recourse to the most ingenious devices, rather than own that the object of their worship could have been ignorant of regions which in his day no Greek had ever visited; or could have given the reins to his poetic fancy, without troubling himself about geographical accuracy. Unfortunately we only know the views of Eratosthenes from the adverse criticisms of Strabo, who has undoubtedly in this, as in other instances, taken little pains to do justice to the arguments of his adversary : but it is clear that Eratosthenes maintained that the chief purpose of Homer, as of all other poets, was to delight and amuse, rather than to instruct, his hearers,[4] and that he purposely transferred the fables of Circe and Calypso, of Æolus and the gloomy land of the Cimmerians, to the boundaries of the Ocean and the unknown regions of the far west, that he might freely indulge his fancy, without the stern restraint of reality. In these general views Eratosthenes was much more in accordance with the judgement of most modern critics than were his contemporaries or successors, of whom Strabo in particular attacks him with a vehemence worthy of an orthodox divine assailing a heretical commentator. But such sceptical criticisms evidently made little impression on the Greeks in general: even the grave and sober-minded Polybius adhered to the popular application of the fables, and sought to explain the tales of Æolus and Scylla, as if it was certain that Ulysses had really visited the Lipari Islands and the Straits of Messina.[5] How far Eratosthenes carried his doubts we are unable to determine, in the absence of the original work: but it would appear that while doing full justice to the accuracy of Homer's geography, as far as related to Greece and the neighbouring islands, he had discarded altogether the wanderings of Ulysses, as unworthy of serious consideration in a geographical point of view.

---

[4] Strabo, 1. 2, § 3, p 15.   [5] Polyb. xxxiv. 2, 3, ap. Strab. i. pp. 23, 24.

He asserted also that the notices of Egypt in the Odyssey showed great ignorance of that country; and denied that Homer had any knowledge of the voyage of Jason and the Argonauts to the river Phasis.[6] For both these assertions he is severely taken to task by Strabo, but on both points the verdict of any impartial reader of the Homeric poems will be in favour of Eratosthenes.

§ 33. Physical geography, in the modern sense of the term, was still quite in its infancy in the days of Eratosthenes, and it cannot be said that he did much to impart to it a scientific character. We have already seen indeed that in treating the mountain chains of Asia as one continuous range, to which he applied the name of Taurus, he may be regarded as having made a first attempt, however rude, at that systematic description of mountain ranges to which we now give the name of orography. He had also, as already stated, arrived at a sound conclusion concerning the causes of the inundation of the Nile —a subject that must naturally have engaged the attention of a geographer resident in Egypt. On the other hand he started a strange hypothesis, that the surplus waters of the Euphrates were carried by subterranean channels to Cœle Syria, and thence again underground so as to feed the streams which broke out near Rhinocorura and Mount Casius.[7]

§ 34. Eratosthenes also adopted, and apparently developed at considerable length, an idea first suggested by the physical philosopher Strato,[8] that the Mediterranean and the Euxine Seas had originally no outlet, and stood in consequence at a much higher level, but that they had burst the barriers that

---

[6] In the last of these views he was followed by Demetrius of Scepsis (Strabo, i 2, p 45) The arguments of Strabo on the other side are confined to the repeated assertion that these were facts *universally admitted* (τῶν δὲ περὶ τὸν Ἰάσονα συμβάντων καὶ τὴν Ἀργὼ καὶ τοὺς Ἀργοναύτας τῶν ὁμολογουμένων παρὰ πᾶσιν, l c)

[7] Eratosth ap Strab. xvi 1, § 12, p. 741 Strabo only ventures to express a doubt concerning this extravagant suggestion (οὐκ οἶδα δὲ εἰ πιθανῶς εἴρηκεν)

[8] Strato of Lampsacus, an eminent Peripatetic philosopher, who had devoted his attention so particularly to the physical branches of philosophy as to be currently known by the surname of ὁ φυσικός. He succeeded Theophrastus as the head of the Peripatetic school in B C 287.

confined them, and thus given rise to the Straits of the Bosphorus, the Hellespont and that of the Columns. In proof of this theory he alleged the presence of marine shells far inland in Libya, especially near the temple of Jupiter Ammon, and on the road leading to it, as well as the deposits and springs of salt that were also found in the Libyan deserts.[9]

Such a speculation has been frequently revived in more modern times;[1] nor can it be said to be altogether without foundation, though it may safely be asserted that no such violent and sudden disruption as that supposed by Strato and Eratosthenes could have actually caused the formation of such straits as the Bosphorus and Dardanelles, or the Straits of Gibraltar. Nor can the occurrence of marine remains, regarded as a general phenomenon, be ascribed to the cause in question; but the most recent geological researches have all tended to establish the fact that the Libyan desert, as well as a great part of the still more extensive desert of the Sahara, was covered by the sea at a comparatively recent period.

It is remarkable that one of the arguments brought forward by Strato in support of this hypothesis was the existence of a submarine ridge or bank, extending across the Straits from Europe to Africa, by which, as he contended, the two had been originally united.[2] Such a bank really exists, though at so considerable a depth as to render it remarkable that its existence should have been discovered by ancient navigators.[3] At the same time both Strato and Eratosthenes were aware of the great depth of certain portions of the Mediterranean, especially the Sicilian and Sardinian seas—as compared with other parts of the same great basin.[4]

---

[9] Strabo, 1 3, pp. 49, 50
[1] See Admiral Smyth's *Mediterranean*, p 114–122 The same theory has been fully developed by M Dureau de la Malle in his work entitled *Géographie Physique de la Mer Noire, de l'Intérieur de l'Afrique, et de la Méditerranée*, 8vo, Paris, 1807.
[2] ὅτι καὶ νῦν ἔτι ταινία τις ὕφαλος διατέτακεν ἀπὸ τῆς Εὐρώπης ἐπὶ τὴν Λιβύην Strabo, 1. p 50.
[3] Smyth's *Mediterranean*, pp 159,160.
[4] Strabo, 1 3, p 50 Posidonius reported the Sardinian Sea to be the deepest of all, and to attain to a depth of 1000 fathoms Id p 54 Such a statement must, however, have been merely conjectural.

§ 35. We learn also from Strabo that Eratosthenes, in order to prove that the world, though spherical, was not *exactly* so, entered into a long enumeration of the changes of its surface produced by the action of water, of fire, of earthquakes, volcanic eruptions, and other similar causes.[5] Though Strabo is undoubtedly right in regarding the effect of all such operations as insignificant in relation to the figure of the whole earth, it would have been very interesting to have known in detail the facts cited by Eratosthenes, and the view which he took of their results. But here, as in so many other cases, we unfortunately know his arguments only through the criticisms of his adversaries. We learn however that he was of opinion that the highest mountains did not exceed ten stadia (6000 feet) in perpendicular altitude,[6] a conclusion probably based on the measurements of Dicæarchus already noticed.

---

[5] Strab. ib p. 49.
[6] See the fragments cited from Theon Alexandrinus (p. 23) and Simplicius (*ad Arist de Cœlo*, ii. p 136) by Bernhardy in his *Eratosthenica*, fr. 39, p 56.

NOTE A, p. 632.

OBSERVATIONS OF LATITUDE.

AMONG the few points of which we know with certainty that their latitudes had been determined by direct observation were Massilia and Byzantium: and from the time of Hipparchus onwards it became a received fact among geographers that they were in the same parallel of latitude, though there is really a difference of more than two degrees between them. Yet we are distinctly told by Strabo that Hipparchus himself repaired to Byzantium for the purpose of observing its latitude, and found his gnomonic observations to coincide with that of Pytheas at Massilia. (Strabo, i. 4, § 4. p. 63.) It is strange that in this instance it was the great astronomer that was in error, while the observation of the much-decried Pytheas was almost precisely correct. Hence Eratosthenes and his successors who accepted the conclusion of Pytheas placed Massilia very nearly in its true position, which rendered their map of the western Mediterranean much more correct than that of Strabo: while on the other hand Byzantium was pushed up far to the north of its true situation, and hence the map of the adjoining regions became distorted to correspond with it.

Again, we know that Eratosthenes himself made corresponding observations of latitude at Rhodes and Alexandria, (Strabo, ii. p. 126) and the *astronomical* result of these observations was very nearly correct, though he was led into error in computing the *distance* between the two by his erroneous estimate of 700 stadia to a degree. But at the same time he placed a point so well known as Athens only 400 stadia (40 minutes) to the north of Rhodes, while the difference between the two really exceeds a degree and a half. On the other hand Eratosthenes possessed a determination of unusual accuracy for the latitude of Meroe, which he placed within less than half a degree of its true position. For this observation he was indebted to a certain Philon, who had himself made a voyage up the Nile to Ethiopia, where he had observed both the proportion of the gnomon to its shadow, and the number of days (45) before the summer solstice, when the sun became vertical. (Strabo, ii. 1, § 29, p. 77.)

We have no account of the authority on which the Straits of Gibraltar were placed in the same latitude with Rhodes : but it was a fortunate circumstance that these two extreme points should have been so correctly assigned, while intermediate positions, such as Carthage and the Straits of Messina, were placed so wide of their true position.

In the case of Carthage, as already observed, the erroneous latitude assigned to it was based, or supposed to be based, upon direct observation. Thus Strabo assumes, or refers to it as a well-known fact, though without mentioning his authority, that the gnomon there was to its shadow as eleven to seven (ii. 5, § 38, p. 133), a proportion which would correspond with 32° 30′ N. latitude, about 4½ degrees south of its true position!

NOTE B, p. 635.

GOSSELLIN'S THEORY.

According to M. Gossellin indeed the result attained by Eratosthenes was one of surprising accuracy. Assuming that the latter was employing *stadia of* 700 *to a degree*, and allowing for the proper reduction of degrees of longitude along the parallel of 36° latitude, he arrives at the remarkable result that the length of the Mediterranean as given by him was within 1° 22′, or less than a degree and a half, of the truth. (*Géographie des Grecs analysée*, p. 40.) So striking is the exactness of this coincidence, that M. Gossellin himself observes it cannot be ascribed to Eratosthenes himself, as it proves an amount of mathematical skill and knowledge far exceeding that possessed by any Greek in his day. Hence he is driven to the very extraordinary hypothesis that Eratosthenes derived his information from materials which he found in the Alexandrian library, and which proceeded from an ancient people who possessed the skill and knowledge of astronomy and mathematical geography attested by such a result. These materials Eratosthenes made use of *without understanding them* (!): hence he fell into errors which require to be explained and rectified before we can do justice to the value of his authorities. (Ibid. pp. 43–50.)

This far-fetched hypothesis may justly be discarded without

further investigation, as resting upon no substantial basis whatever. It has however been adopted by M. Dureau de la Malle (*Géogr. Physique*, &c. p. 147). But it must be observed that almost all the remarkable instances of close conformity with the truth produced by M. Gossellin are obtained *by more or less altering the data* as given by Strabo, or by introducing arbitrary assumptions of his own. Thus when he proceeds to reckon the distance from the Gulf of Issus eastward to the mouth of the Ganges—a distance which we *know* Eratosthenes to have computed from the itinerary measures of the marches of Alexander, and other similar materials (Strabo), and which comes out in M. Gossellin's hands almost as exact as that from the Sacred Cape to the Gulf of Issus, this coincidence results in great part from his reducing the number of itinerary stades by one-tenth, and by his arbitrarily fixing on Chandernagore —which is more than 50 miles from the sea and not on the Ganges at all—as the point to compare with the supposed mouth of the Ganges, conceived by Eratosthenes as situated on the Eastern Ocean.

M. Gossellin himself remarks that *all* the intermediate distances given by Eratosthenes are inexact, though the great distances (the sums total) are, *or ought to be considered* as correct (p. 45). The first admission is no doubt true, but the second is only attained by a series of arbitrary changes and alterations of numbers, which are made with the express purpose of bringing about a correct result.

We have seen that Eratosthenes in computing 700 stades to a degree of a great circle was not, as supposed by M. Gossellin (as well as D'Anville and many other modern geographers) *employing a different stade* from that familiar to all the Greeks, but was *adopting an erroneous calculation of the length of a degree.* Hence the assumption that, in computing distances such as those along the line of the Mediterranean, or the prolongation of it across Asia, Eratosthenes was throughout reckoning by stades of 700 to a degree, is wholly without foundation. In regard to the first indeed it is most probable that he was following Timosthenes, from whom we know him to have borrowed largely [see Chapter XV. p. 588]; while the latter were undoubtedly taken either from Patrocles or from the authors of the itineraries of Alexander. Yet all these authors wrote before any one had heard of stades of 700 to a degree and were merely using the ordinary Greek stade as universally received. It must be added that though Strabo was well acquainted with the measurement of the earth's circumference by Eratosthenes, and with the resulting value of its subdivisions, he has nowhere given the slightest hint, or evidently entertained the least suspicion, that that author in his numerous statements of distances was employing any other stade than that in general use among all the Greeks.

NOTE C, p. 639.

SOUTHERN LIMIT OF THE HABITABLE WORLD.

The calculation by which this result is arrived at is as follows. We know from the astronomical writers, Ptolemy and his commentator Theon, that Eratosthenes fixed the interval between the tropics at 11/83ds of the whole meridian circle,[7] which would place the tropic of Cancer in N. latitude 23° 51′ 20″. This would give in round numbers 16,700 stadia between the tropic and the equator (at 700 stadia to the degree), and as Eratosthenes had reckoned 5000 stadia from Syene to Meroe, and 3400 from Meroe to the Land of Cinnamon, there remain 8300 between this limit of the habitable world and the equator.

This conclusion, which is adopted both by M. Gossellin and Dr. C. Muller, is confirmed by the fact that the distances given by Eratosthenes, on this calculation, result in placing Thule at a distance of 46,300 stadia from the Equator, or 16,700 from the pole: exactly the same distance as the tropic from the Equator: and this precisely accords with the statement of Eratosthenes himself (derived from Pytheas) that at Thule "the summer tropic coincides with the arctic circle" (παρ' οἷς ὁ αὐτός ἐστι τῷ ἀρκτικῷ ὁ θερινὸς τροπικὸς κύκλος. Strabo, ii. 5, § 8, p. 114), or according to the modern use of the expression, that it was situated under the Arctic Circle. The distances given thus make up exactly the 63,000 stadia required for the quadrant of a meridian great circle, in accordance with the 252,000 stadia adopted by Eratosthenes as the circumference of the globe.

---

[7] Ptolemæi *Magna Syntaxis*, 1 10, p 18. The statement is given somewhat more clearly by Theon in his commentary on the passage (p 60), καὶ οὗτος ὁ λόγος ὁ αὐτὸς σχεδὸν τῷ τοῦ Ἐρατοσθένους, ᾧ καὶ ὁ Ἵππαρχος ἐχρήσατο, ὡς ἀκριβῶς εἰλημμένῳ, καὶ γὰρ ὁ Ἐρατοσθένης διαιρήσας τὸν ὅλον κύκλον πγ εὕρισκε τὴν μεταξὺ τῶν τροπικῶν τῶν αὐτῶν ια καὶ ἔστιν ὡς τξ πρὸς μζ μβ′ μ″ οὕτως πγ πρὸς ια.

There remains indeed one difficulty which we have no means of solving, that Strabo, who in all that relates to mathematical geography generally follows the authority of Eratosthenes, and in this very passage distinctly refers to his calculations, has placed the parallel of the Region of Cinnamon (which he also assumes as the limit of the habitable world) at 8800 stadia from the Equator, without any indication of his difference from Eratosthenes, or of his reasons for the alteration. (Strabo, ii. 2, § 2, p. 95.) But as he at the same time reduces the distance from Meroe to this extreme limit to 3000 stadia, instead of the 3400 allowed by Eratosthenes, the resulting difference is in great measure neutralised. The grounds of both changes remain equally unexplained.

NOTE D, p. 639.

DISTANCE FROM ALEXANDRIA TO RHODES.

This we are distinctly told by Strabo (ii. p. 126) αὐτὸς δὲ διὰ τῶν σκιοθηρικῶν γνωμόνων ἀνευρεῖν τρισχιλίους ἑπτακοσίους πεντήκοντα. But it must be observed that Eratosthenes must here have been led into error by his own previous calculation that there were 700 stadia to a degree. For in this case he had no means of *measuring* the distance—having himself rejected the estimates of navigators—and therefore all he could do was to ascertain by his gnomon the difference of latitude, and *convert this into stades at the rate which he had obtained from his supposed measurement of the arc between Syene and Alexandria.* This is well explained by Col. Leake (*Disputed Questions of Ancient Geography,* p. 92), and is important to bear in mind, as we shall find that Posidonius was led to an erroneous computation of the earth's circumference by supposing this arc between Rhodes and Alexandria to have been actually *measured* by Eratosthenes.

The result of this error would naturally be that Eratosthenes (believing his gnomonic observations to be approximately correct, as was really the case) would overrate the distance, and this we find to be the case, for though his computation gave a material reduction upon the estimate of the navigators, it was still considerably in excess of the truth—the real distance between Rhodes and Alexandria being only about 330 G. miles, or 3300 Greek stadia instead of 3750 (Leake, *l. c.*). Yet we afterwards find Strabo and other later writers reverting to the original rough estimate of 4000 stadia; so little reliance did they place upon the mathematical calculations of scientific geographers like Eratosthenes!

NOTE E, p. 644.

PROMONTORY OF TAMARUS

Strabo, xi. 11, § 7, p. 519. This name of Tamarus is found only incidentally in this single passage. It is difficult to conceive whence Eratosthenes could have derived it, as the promontory in question had no real existence, but was a geographical fiction, or rather inference, that the chain of Imaus *must* end in some such headland.

The name is however again found under the form Tamus, in Pomponius Mela, who describes it as the eastern extremity of the chain of Mt. Taurus (iii. 7, § 68). The Tabis of Pliny, which he calls "jugum incubans mari quod vocant Tabin" (vi. 17, § 53) is evidently only a corruption of the same name: though it has been strangely identified by Mr. Clements Markham with the northern point of *Siberia*, a country of which the existence was as utterly unknown to Pliny as that of America.

It was here—if anywhere—that we should have expected to find mention of Thinæ, a name so strangely introduced into all our editions of Strabo down to a very recent period. (See note to p. 630 of this chapter.) Yet the name is wholly wanting where it would be appropriately found, as marking the termination of the principal parallel of latitude on the Indian Ocean, though it was introduced repeatedly, according to the old reading, to designate the very parallel in question.

END OF VOL. I.

www.ingramcontent.com/pod-product-compliance
Lightning Source LLC
Chambersburg PA
CBHW052108010526
44111CB00036B/1552